CONVERGENCES

THEMES, TEXTS, AND IMAGES FOR COMPOSITION

Christian Morris

CONVERGENCES

THEMES, TEXTS, AND IMAGES FOR COMPOSITION

ROBERT ATWAN

Director, The Blue Hills Writing Institute at Curry College

Series Editor, *The Best American Essays*

BEDFORD/ST. MARTIN'S

BOSTON ■ NEW YORK

For Bedford/St. Martin's

Senior Developmental Editor: Ellen Thibault
Senior Production Editors: Bridget Leahy and Anne Noonan
Assistant Production Manager: Joe Ford
Marketing Manager: Molly Parke
Associate Editor: Stephanie Naudin
Production Assistant: Lidia MacDonald-Carr
Copyeditor: Linda McLatchie
Text Design: Delgado and Company, Inc., and Judith Arisman, Arisman Design Studio
Cover Design: Billy Boardman
Cover Art: Boy on pogo stick. © Miguel Salmeron / Getty Images
Composition: Pre-Press PMG
Printing and Binding: R. R. Donnelley & Sons, Inc.

President: Joan E. Feinberg
Editorial Director: Denise B. Wydra
Editor in Chief: Karen S. Henry
Director of Marketing: Karen R. Soeltz
Director of Editing, Design, and Production: Marcia Cohen
Assistant Director of Editing, Design, and Production: Elise S. Kaiser
Managing Editor: Elizabeth M. Schaaf

Library of Congress Control Number: 2008925871

Manufactured in the United States of America.

3 2 1 0 9 8
f e d c b a

For information, write: Bedford/St. Martin's, 75 Arlington Street, Boston, MA 02116 (617-399-4000)

ISBN-10: 0–312–46734–6
ISBN-13: 978–0–312–46734–0

Acknowledgments

As series editor of *Best American Essays* and a longtime textbook author, I confess that the essay, as a form and a medium, is my first love. The idea for *Convergences* — a book that pairs the essay with compositions from other media — came from watching my children and my students connect the ideas they discovered in their textbooks to the ideas they saw in other kinds of texts. A TV show, a news report, a video, a cartoon, an ad: all these things are compositions, even if they are not traditionally part of the syllabus for a composition course. I found myself playing with this idea of *connections*, and wondering what a composition text might look like that was built around strong essays that were paired with pictures, ads, and Web sites. As I worked, I realized that convergences were suddenly everywhere — I could connect the dots between everything I saw, read, and watched — and the result is *Convergences*.

Convergences is built around clusters. Pairing a strong essay with other kinds of texts — a poster, a Web site, an essay, and a poem, for example — not only gives students more to think about critically but also gives those students more to write about. Take the issue of *diversity* as it is treated in this textbook. Rather than re-treading familiar ground in a single essay, *Convergences* includes a dynamic collection of texts in the cluster "Who Wants Diversity?": a controversial essay by David Brooks; images from *America 24/7*, a groundbreaking photographic project to "capture America"; and an ad from the *Islam in America* series. The essay provides a lens with which to read the photographs; the photographs and ad complicate the position Brooks takes in his essay. And as a whole, the cluster brings together a lot of smart people trying to persuade others to their way of thinking about an incredibly important issue using a variety of media. It's powerful stuff.

Students need a coherent methodology to read — and to make — increasingly complex rhetorical choices. As the first edition of *Convergences* came together, it became clear that reading texts in a cluster was, simply, a richer way to think about composition — about *what* people say, *how* they say it, and *why* it matters whether we see something on TV or read it in a book. And there was my methodology: message, method, medium. In these pages are texts that represent multiple media and genres — essays, advertisements, the web, news, comics, television, and film, to name just a few. The purpose of including visual texts in a composition reader is not to pander to students' "MTV" aesthetic; every composition represented in these pages is the result of careful choices made by a writer or a designer or an artist. Students who use *Convergences* will learn to ask certain questions about what the text is trying to say, how it goes about saying it, and what impact medium has on the message as they read (and compose). What's the best way to tell the story of your life — through words or pictures? How would the Gettysburg Address have been received if Lincoln had delivered it on PowerPoint? How does Adbusters design an advertisement to combat advertisements? My hope is that the students using this book will learn to ask these questions, among others.

Convergences is built around themes that vividly connect with the lives of today's students. Students will be invited to consider what makes a film a cult classic; they will meet a presumably ordinary guy who sold his entire life on eBay; they will think about fast food as a metaphor for American culture; they will be asked to imagine the inside of their cars as a sacred space; and they will experience what it might be like to live in the Mall of America. All six chapters mirror the traditional arrangement of the composition reader, starting with the personal and moving to the public. But in this reader, these familiar categories get a new dimension:

1. Depicting Identities outlines the way verbal and visual portraits and even eating habits reveal certain details while hiding others.

2. Telling Stories traces how narrative works across different media and genres — fairy tales and urban legends, mini- or "found" narratives, an iconic painting, movies, photo journalism, the traditional essay, and memoir.

3. Shaping Spaces focuses on what it means to think spatially — whether the space is a piece of paper, a room, a basketball court, the World Wide Web, or the human imagination.

4. Making History suggests that describing the past means interpreting it.

5. Dividing Lines shows how different groups of people draw and erase lines between "us" and "them."

6. Packaging Culture unwraps some of the things marketers and advertisers sell beyond products — environmentalism, health, ethics, celebrity, youth, "coolness," and shopping itself.

Convergences is a solid, traditional composition reader. An extraordinary collection of essays helps keep Convergences connected with the composition classroom. Though the thematic clusters include a unique array of media and genres, each cluster is solidly anchored to a strong model of writing. For example, this edition features a coming-of-age memoir by John Edgar Wideman in which the noted novelist recalls the first shot he made on a basketball court as a young child; a slow-motion analysis of why The Wizard of Oz manages to entertain us year after year by Salman Rushdie; a reflection on the aesthetic errors of cosmetic surgery by the controversial critic Camille Paglia; and an argument justifying the publication of horrific photographs by the essayist and screenwriter Nora Ephron. Such accomplished essays — and there are many more — will provide excellent models for teaching personal voice, narrative, and expository methods, as well as the skillful use of physical and illustrative detail.

Because Convergences is a composition reader, it provides multiple occasions for writing throughout the text.

- Consider before you read questions, new to this edition, prepare students to get the most out of each reading.
- Message, Method, and Medium questions ask what texts say, how they go about saying it, and what impact medium has on message.
- Questions for Writing prompt students to make connections within and outside the text as they write critical responses to what they've read.

New to This Edition

Thirteen new thematic clusters — on topics students care about — include "You Are What You Eat," with a photo essay and a brief argument by Michael Pollan;

"Mental Space: The Human Imagination," with an essay by Sims creator Will Wright and images from virtual communities; and "A New Ethics of Consumption," with a humorous commentary by Bill McKibben, a spoof on the over-the-top in-flight magazine *SkyMall*, and a treatise against bottled water.

All Kinds of New Texts — To Spruce Up Your Syllabus

- New verbal texts (more than 60) include essays by major writers such as Jhumpa Lahiri on dual identities; the *Freakonomics* authors on names and class; and Brent Staples on being a black man in public space — familiar works and themes that you expect to see in a composition reader. You'll also find a Greek myth, an urban legend, and a twentieth-century diatribe against science.

- New visual and multimedia texts (more than 200) include a graphic memoir by Alison Bechdel, an annotated painting by Edward Hopper, a bevy of found artifacts, documentary photos of the Civil War and civil rights era, and America's very first cartoon.

More help with reading and writing. The clusters include new pre-reading questions and discussion and writing prompts following the texts. More questions in the margins of the readings spark analytical thinking, and writing assignments at the end of each chapter are now labeled to make clear the many kinds of writing students are being asked to do (for example, analyze, compare, make a case). Handy new chapter and cluster menus make the book even easier to use.

A Revised Introduction That Teaches Reading, Analysis, and Writing

- A new section on the book's approach tracks a single message ("Will you marry me?") through a series of annotated images, showing students that there are many ways to convey a message, and many ways to unpack them in their writing.

- A new annotated student essay models the kind of writing done for the composition course. Northwest College (Wyoming) student Milos Kosic draws on three readings from the "What's in a Name?" cluster to make a case about identity, memorials, and history. The paper, documented in MLA style, has also been annotated to help students see the writing techniques at work.

- A new section on comics presents a work by the great Art Spiegelman and helps students approach graphic texts critically. Like the student essay mentioned above (and the essay, photo, and ad carried over from the first edition), this comic has been annotated with notes that point out ways of reading and thinking about the work.

Supplements

Instructor's Manual: *Resources for Teaching CONVERGENCES* gives instructors tips on teaching each selection and ideas for generating class discussion and in-class writing. It also explores additional connections between selections and gives suggestions for further reading, thinking, and writing. (ISBN-10: 0–312–47083–5 or ISBN-13: 978–0–312–47083–8)

A helpful web site: bedfordstmartins.com/convergences. This site includes Bedford/St. Martin's TopLinks — a topical links database accessible through the above site — which guides students to the links with the most useful information on the important authors and complex ideas presented in *Convergences*.

Re:Writing is a comprehensive web site designed to help students with their most common writing concerns. They'll find advice from experts, models they can rely on, and exercises that will tell them right away how they're doing. And it's all free. (See bedfordstmartins.com/rewriting.)

Packaging Options

Bedford/St. Martin's *ix visual exercises* CD-ROM allows your students to do things they can't do in a book—manipulate images, change type color or size, drag pictures around to make their own visual argument, or see a movie. This resource can be purchased standalone or packaged with *Convergences* at a discount, provides a space to play around with texts, to explore the impact of visual organization and composition, and to develop a vocabulary for working with all kinds of texts. (See bedfordstmartins.com/ix. To order *Convergences* with *ix*, use package ISBN-10: 0–312–47428–8 or ISBN-13: 978–0–312–47428–7.)

Re:Writing Plus. Because composition is getting redefined—when, where, and how we see it—Bedford/St. Martin's is committed to developing new kinds of tools for the changing classroom. The first-ever peer review game, the most innovative and interactive help with writing a paragraph, tutorials and practice with

writing that show how it works in your students' real-world experience, hundreds of models of writing across the disciplines, and hundreds of readings: these six collections meet composition where it happens, online, all the time. This resource, a $19 value, can be packaged at a discount with *Convergences* (See bedfordstmartins.com/rewritingplus. To order *Convergences* with *Re:Writing Plus*, use package ISBN-10: 0–312–53667–4 or ISBN-13: 978–0312–53667–1.)

Bedford/St. Martin's **Trade-up Program.** You can add more value and choice to your students' learning experiences by packaging *Convergences* with one of a thousand titles from our sister publishers such as Farrar, Straus and Giroux and St. Martin's Press — at a discount of 50% off the regular price. (See bedfordstmartins.com/tradeup.)

Acknowledgments

I thank those colleagues who offered thoughtful reviews of the first edition of *Convergences*: Kimberly D. Braddock, Idaho State University, English and Philosophy Department; Patricia Burdette, Ohio State University; Dion Cautrell, Ohio State University–Mansfield; Keith Comer, Idaho State University; Clark L. Draney, Idaho State University; Paul Fectueau, Washburn University; Lynda Feldman, Jefferson Community College; Jennifer Firestone, Fordham University; Melody Gough, University of Nevada, Reno; Katherine M. Gray, Lynchburg College; Jefferson Hancock, Cabrillo College; Abigail Martin, Florida International University; Elizabeth Caemasache McKenna, University of Central Florida; Ailish Hopper Meisner, Goucher College; Suzanne E. O'Hop, Northand Pioneer College; Jason A. Pierce, Mars Hill College; Gabe Popovich, Purdue University; Leandra Preston, University of Central Florida; John E. Ribar, Nova Southeastern University; Jeff Rice, University of Detroit; Patricia C. Roby, UW–Washington County; Shant Shahoian, Moorpark College; Kay J. Walter, Idaho State University; Susan Wellington, SUNY–Oswego; and Jennifer Locke Whetham, Bellevue Community College.

Several people helped me shape the revised introduction and offered in-depth comments on drafts of the early chapters, and I want to offer them special thanks: Heidi Wilkinson, California Polytechnic State University; Brock Dethier, Utah State University; Bruce Henderson, Fullerton College;

Linda Overman, California State University–Northridge; Deborah Coxwell-Teague, Florida State University; and Karen Felts, Orange Coast College.

I am also grateful to Deborah Coxwell-Teague for inviting me to Florida State University to speak with graduate students on using *Convergences* in the composition classroom. I'd like to thank those FSU graduate students for a number of practical suggestions that I was able to incorporate into the third edition.

Responding to sample chapters and an early outline for the first edition, several reviewers offered a number of useful suggestions and pointed out some encouraging directions. I remain grateful to Elizabeth Abrams, University of California, Santa Cruz; Angi Caster, Highline Community College; Jeff E. Cravello, California State Polytechnic University; Carrie Heimer, University of New Hampshire; Charles Hood, Antelope Valley College; Priscilla Kanet, Clemson University; David Norlin, Cloud Community College; and J. Wylene Rholetter, Auburn University. Sometimes enthusiastic and sometimes critical, these reviewers helped keep me focused on practical instructional goals. I tried to follow their advice as much as possible.

For their thoughtful reviews of the second edition, I thank Deborah Coxwell-Teague, Florida State University; Karen H. Gardiner, University of Alabama; Emily Hegarty, Nassau Community College; Jessica Ketcham, Louisiana State University; Janet Kirchner, Southeast Community College; Jan LaVille, Des Moines Area Community College; Andrew Levy, Queensborough Community College/CUNY; Stephen B. McNutt, University of Iowa; Erika Nanes, University of Southern California; Joey Nicoletti, Kent State University; Elizabeth Nygaard, Des Moines Area Community College–Boone Campus; Lorna L. Perez, University of Buffalo; Valerie A. Reimers, Southwestern Oklahoma State University; Michael Anthony Sohan, University of Louisville; Jennifer Walsingham, University of West Florida; Lynne B. Welch, Marshall University; and Stephanie Wells, Orange Coast College.

I am indebted to the staff of Bedford/St. Martin's for their magnificent support, starting with retired publisher Charles E. Christensen and the president, Joan E. Feinberg, who discovered the seeds of this project lying dormant in a proposal I had prepared for a different kind of book. Still, *Convergences* would not have taken root without the energetic support of the first and second editions' editor, Alanya Harter, whose flow of ideas and grasp of cultural and media studies, along with her remarkable sense of design, made it seem as though I had working behind me an entire editorial team. I'm also grateful to Associate Editor Stephanie Naudin, who attended to many tasks, including the development of the Instructor's Manual and web site.

I want to acknowledge the contributions of designer Anna Palchik, who helped us update the design of the book for greater impact and coherence. Given our extremely tight schedule, I appreciate the Herculean efforts of all those in production, especially Production Editors Bridget Leahy and Anne Noonan, who adroitly kept a complicated production process in motion, ensuring that everything flowed smoothly through often challenging channels. Joe Ford oversaw the composition process, and Elizabeth Schaaf managed production concerns. I'm grateful also to Editor in Chief Karen Henry and Editorial Director Denise Wydra for their ideas early on and their continuing support of the project.

Most especially, however, I want to thank my editor on this edition of *Convergences*, Ellen Thibault, who miraculously juggled more moving parts than seems humanly possible. I am indebted to her numerous revision ideas, editorial acumen, and always steady judgment.

I wish to acknowledge the assistance of several other individuals who work outside of the Bedford/St. Martin's home base. In clearing permissions and obtaining the images for the book, Arthur Johnson and Naomi Kornhauser expertly transformed a possible table of contents into an actual one. Linda McLatchie did a wonderful job copyediting the manuscript; I appreciate her insightful suggestions. Mabel Bilodeau and Jeannine Thibodeau handled the difficult task of proofreading such a wide diversity of material. I appreciate enormously the work that Stefanie Wortman of the University of Missouri put into the Instructor's Manual; as a comprehensive introduction to the ways of reading the convergences of media, messages, and methods, it can stand entirely on its own.

I'm also much indebted to Rodes Fishburne, Associate Editor of *Forbes ASAP,* for first calling my attention to the idea of convergence while I was consulting with him on potential contributors to the magazine. *The Big Issue IV:*

The Great Convergence (October 4, 1999), with essays by Kathleen Norris, James Burke, Stanley Crouch, Edward O. Wilson, Kurt Vonnegut, and Jan Morris, along with many other distinguished writers and thinkers, remains one of the best introductions to this important concept.

Finally, I appreciate the support I received from Helene Atwan and my children, Gregory and Emily. I dedicate this book to them.

—R. A.

CONTENTS

4 MAKING HISTORY 363

CONVERGENCES

THEMES, TEXTS, AND IMAGES FOR COMPOSITION

INTRODUCTION

INTRODUCTION

Every time you see a term boldfaced or highlighted on the page—in this introduction and throughout the book—it means that the term also appears in the glossary at the end of the book, along with page numbers to help you find examples of the term in action.

2

What is **convergence**? The word essentially means "coming together at a single point from different directions." We speak of several roads converging into a single road or opposing views converging into a unified position. In April 1912, the British luxury ship *Titanic* and a colossal iceberg converged in the North Atlantic in one of the twentieth century's most famous disasters. In this book you will find numerous examples of how the ongoing and large-scale convergence of technology, media, and culture is rapidly altering traditional patterns of communication and demanding new critical aptitudes and new perceptual skills. Reading, writing, and the capacity to decipher visual material will be more important than ever before.

We want you to look at every text and think about

1. *What* it is saying—its *message*.
2. *How* it goes about saying it—its *method*.
3. *Why* it is delivered to you in a particular way—its *medium*.

These three perspectives are so interdependent that it is difficult to detach one from the others. Your final response to any given work should take all three perspectives into account. But for instructional purposes, we focus on message, method, and medium as separate windows through which we can view a chosen text.

Convergences was designed to help you develop the critical tools necessary for understanding how a wide variety of verbal and visual texts are conceived, composed, targeted, interpreted, and evaluated. The book encourages you to examine every selection from three different, though interrelated, critical approaches: *message, method, medium.*

MESSAGE

We typically use the word **message** in three ways: as a discrete unit of communication ("You have an important message"); as a condensed moral or central idea ("What's the message of *The Wizard of Oz* ?"); and, informally, as a strong signal or gesture that drives home an unmistakable point ("Don't worry, he'll get the message"). In each sense, a message—whether verbal or nonverbal—has something to do with **content** and meaning, which is how we will consider it throughout this book.

When we make attempts to interpret any sort of written or visual material, we are usually asking ourselves a series of questions: What is this short story about? What does this painting mean? What is the point of this editorial? In some texts, the message or meaning may be fairly obvious. We are all familiar with reading comprehension tests in which we are asked to identify the main point of a short prose passage. Similarly, a letter to a newspaper, for example, may make a single, unambiguous point, and that's that. In some short essays, the central message may be spelled out in no uncertain terms.

In everyday communication, for convenience, we often boil the content down into its essential message. We reduce a ten-page proposal to its main point or points. We summarize a crime story in a few words. We outline the plot of an action film. But identifying the message or meaning of more complicated works can require more critical effort and even some creativity. The message may not stare us in the face or jump off the page. The main point or central idea may be impossible to state directly. There may even be more than one message. A writer or artist may do something unexpected, and you may need to supply missing information to understand the work. For example, the painting on the side of the building shown on page 4 looks at first glance like an enormous highway sign. It means more when we learn that San Francisco artist Rigo worked with the people who lived in the community—a newly built project—to come up with the message you see. Rigo had originally planned to paint an arrow pointing up with the message "Sky Here." What does it mean to use the iconography of road signs in public art, and to display the resulting work not in a gallery but in an urban landscape where the audience is composed of commuters in their cars? If you saw the picture here without the explanation provided by the caption, what would you think Rigo is suggesting about community, art, or life?

3

J. Howard Miller, *We Can Do It!* 1942. The now-iconic image of "Rosie the Riveter" is the centerpiece of this World War II poster aimed at persuading women to be patriotic and work hard for the war effort. During World War II, some six million American women went to work in shipyards and in factories that produced munitions, filling the spots left open by men who were fighting in Europe or the pacific. In doing so, women began to occupy a traditionally male realm and to experience new economic freedom. J. Howard Miller orignally created this poster for Westinghouse Electric Corporation. It is the best-known representation of Rosie, a character inspired by a woman named Rose Will Monroe (b. 1920, who moved from Kentucky to Michigan to work as a riveter in an aircraft factory) and modeled on another woman named Geraldine Doyle (also a factory worker in Michigan). Rosie's image, which in the 1940s appeared in film, magazines, and advertising, was emblematic of the new societal expectations of women and their role in the workplace during the war era. (National Archives photo no. NWDNS-179-WP-1563)

Rigo 08, *Innercity Home*.
San Francisco artist Rigo 08 (his name changes with the year) builds his art around the iconography of road signs. *Innercity Home*, a thirty-seven-foot-tall replica of an interstate sign, is painted on the side wall of a housing project in San Francisco. One tenant said of the piece, "On this street you are either on the way up or on the way down; we want to show which we are." (Photo courtesy of Gallery Paule Anglim)

4

In trying to identify a work's message or meaning, be careful not to merely note its subject or theme. To say, for example, that a particular essay is "about terrorism" is not the same as identifying its message. That requires another step: What exactly is the essay saying about terrorism? What attitude does the author have toward that subject? To take another example, saying that Shakespeare's *Hamlet* is a play "about revenge" does not in any way tell us what message Shakespeare wants to deliver on that complicated dramatic subject. Finding the message can at times require a deep penetration into the text.

We usually know that a work is complex when we cannot easily produce a brief summary or main point, a caption or callout that conveniently supplies us with the gist of the entire work. Many works of literature and art (as you will discover in the following chapters) are intricate and contain several levels of meaning with different and perhaps contradictory messages. In some fiction, we may not be able to find a moral center or a character whose judgments we can rely on. This is not necessarily the result of an artistic flaw or failure; it is more than likely intentional. In many creative works, the burden of discovering a message or formulating a meaning will seem to fall entirely on the reader or viewer. Many works of art and literature do not "contain" a message or meaning the way a can of vegetable soup contains its ingredients. The individual reader or viewer is responsible for the construction of meaning. It is good to be wary, of course, of reading more into a picture or an essay than what is there, making a text more complicated than it really is. Yet you also have to remember that "reading into" a work is the only way to establish its meaning, to get at any internal contradictions, and to expose hidden agendas.

Ron English, *Camel Jr's*.
Ron English is an artist who appropriates the methods and media of advertising. In this example, he uses colorful, inviting graphics on a billboard to make a statement about the way Camel brands and markets its products. English, who calls himself a landscape painter, began his career actually altering landscapes, painting over billboards and changing the focus of their messages from marketing to social awareness. (© Ron English)

As you look for meaning, also be careful of too quickly dismissing some works as simple, trivial, or inconsequential. Many of the texts in this book—essays, poems, photographs, ads—look simple and casual on the surface, yet their simplicity often masks an impressive complexity. Many great works can support an infinite amount of "reading into." Many artists strive for a surface simplicity, even an innocence that camouflages complicated ambitions. And this is true not only of literary and artistic works. In the following chapters, you are encouraged to probe deeply into works that may seem unremarkable—advertisements, web pages, maps, news photos, magazine covers, comic strips, posters, and so on. Your effort to find more than meets the eye should lead to insightful observation and productive discussion.

5

METHOD

The message is *what* a text is saying; the **method** is *how* it goes about saying it. Everything we see, read, or hear is expressed in a particular fashion, no matter how ordinary it seems. "Hello," "Hi," "Hey," "Dude!" "Good morning," "How's it going?" "How are you?" "Whassup?" "What's happening?" and "How you doing?" are all common greetings, but each one represents a different method for delivering a message, with varying levels of formality and tone. A Polaroid snapshot and a black-and-white studio photograph may each be taken of the same subject at the same time and in the same position, but the two pictures will suggest different moods and approaches. As you examine the selections in this book (or any text outside it), ask yourself, *Why did the author or artist choose this means of expression and not another?* Why does the advertising copywriter use just these words or the photographer shoot from just that angle? Why does the poet make just this comparison and not another one, or why does a fiction writer tell a story from one character's perspective instead of another's?

Indeed, there are countless ways to consider methods of expression. Each field—art, literature, photography, film, cartooning, television production, and so on—has developed over time its own professional vocabulary to describe specific procedures and techniques. For example, in Chapter 1 you will see how the nearly universal and mysterious appeal of Leonardo da Vinci's *Mona Lisa* was achieved by his use of a special artistic procedure that enabled him to blur out lines and create an ambiguous effect of shadows and blended colors. As you proceed through this book, you will be exposed to various methods used throughout the various media.

One of the most familiar tools used to study methods of expression is **rhetoric**. Developed in ancient Greece, rhetoric was first employed to teach orators the most effective ways to express themselves and persuade audiences. Its formulations were gradually systematized and applied to all kinds of written language, with particular emphasis on the methods of constructing arguments. Traditional rhetoric has lately been brought to bear on the visual arts. We now see the convergence of traditional rhetorical methods with the techniques of film, art, photography, and graphic design.

When we ask questions about method, we are basically asking about how a text has been composed. **Composition** is a term that can be applied to all sorts of expression. It is a key term in writing, music, art, architecture, photography, film, design, typography, and advertising. It essentially refers to the way something is made or made up (the word means "putting together"), particularly the way in which its parts are arranged and how they relate to the whole. Understanding composition requires an ability to discern the planning that went on behind the scenes. We can observe such internal elements as patterns, balance, harmony, intersecting shapes and lines, symmetry or asymmetry, repeated forms and their variations. In doing so, we are paying attention to how visual or verbal texts are built.

Look closely, say, at Weegee's photograph of two teenagers who just crashed a stolen car (p. 7), and you will see masterly composition. The street-wise photographer eloquently uses the contour of the vehicle's window to frame the incident and at the same time discovers a way to mirror the intimacy of the central image. The more closely you study the photograph, the more you will see. Though the photo may seem spontaneous and natural, that level of composition is no accident. It is artful. It involves seeing with a purpose.

Or consider a typical television news story. It can be composed in many different ways: it could be structured solely by the newscaster speaking directly into the studio cameras, or it could involve a split screen as the newscaster speaks with a

7

Weegee, *Car Crash Upper Fifth Ave., July 13, 1941*. This black-and-white photograph is a good example of photography as a medium that shows us an event as it actually happened—and as a text that has been carefully composed, framed, and focused on particular details. For more examples of Weegee's photography, see Photojournalism, pages 236–252. (Weegee [Arthur Fellig]/International Centre of Photography/Getty Images)

reporter on the scene, or it could simply show action accompanied by the newscaster's or reporter's voice-over. Producers are keenly aware of the many possible variations in structure and design, and their decisions determine how a story will generally be positioned and perceived. We experience these broadcasting methods so routinely that as viewers we usually pay no attention to the way someone in charge of production has purposefully decided to structure the news. But every now and then we become aware (sometimes alarmingly) that the same story, perhaps even with identical footage, has been covered differently by different networks. Change the compositional structure of a news story, and you change the viewers' perception of the event.

No matter what sort of text you are considering—whether a newspaper editorial, an automobile advertisement, a rap CD, or a web page—you can be sure that it will exhibit elements that reveal its main compositional characteristics. A single-page color ad for a luxury car that you flip past in *Time* magazine has been composed with the utmost care; the ad's creators paid attention to shading,

Eugene de Salignac, *Brooklyn Bridge Showing Painters in Suspenders,* 1914. This image provides another example of the use of framing in photography. It was taken by Eugene de Salignac (1861–1943), who worked as the photographer for the Department of Bridges/Plant and Structures from 1906 to 1934, an architectural boom time for New York City. De Salignac documented the creation of major buildings, roads, subways, and bridges, including the Brooklyn Bridge, which opened in 1883. According to de Salignac's notes, he took a photograph of a group of painters at work on the trusses of the Bridge on September 22, 1914. He returned two weeks later and posed the painters (dressed in suits and free of their gear) on the wires to resemble notes in a musical scale. (Courtesy NYC Municipal Archives)

8

balance, and textual design. A ten-word advertising headline may be the result of ten staff meetings in which a creative team worked at getting every syllable to sound just right.

In a wholly verbal text such as a novel, essay, poem, or short story, composition is largely a matter of arrangement, style, and built-in patterns of sound and imagery. It is through studying composition that we can imagine the writer at work, engaged in the verbal construction of a text and occupied with its development and design. For some creative writers, the art of composition is the central consideration and subsumes all other matters. A novelist may feel that creating interesting characters or devising a compelling plot is secondary to the overall compositional design. The artistic belief is that the composition reveals the writer's genius and originality. The great American novelist Henry James thought that his characters were essentially "compositional resources"; that is, they existed mainly to serve the structure and design that James was interested in most. This is an extreme position, yet it should remind us to consider in any work how the parts are related to the whole.

In visual texts, composition is often a matter of spatial relations: How has the artist, designer, film director, or photographer first framed a space and then arranged the various elements inside it? How are images grouped? How is your eye drawn to particular features? What do you tend to notice first? What is the connection between center and periphery, foreground and background? If the visual material incorporates or is aligned with print (as in most web pages), how do they share the space? Do they seem to be competing for attention? Are they in harmony? Space can also be a decisive factor in printed texts. On one level of reading, we usually visualize **perspective** or **point of view** as well as the actual spaces being described. On another, deeper level, we can visualize a work's architecture, its spatial form as opposed to its linear or narrative structure. In other words, to fully appreciate the composition of a work, especially a serious work of literature, we may need to go beyond its temporal movement and form a mental picture—a map or a diagram—of its interrelated themes and imagery. We need to picture its internal networks and circuitry.

An effective way to visualize a work's compositional method is by means of an outline. We tend to be more conscious of how to structure or arrange something when we ourselves need to produce it. Most of us, by our first year of college, have learned that essays and research papers often require an outline. The outline is essentially a planning document that reveals how the various parts of our paper will be arranged. The longer and more ambitious the project, the more complex and layered our outline will be. When we are outlining papers, we are confronting the issue of compositional structure: how our paper should be organized, which points should receive more prominence than others, how topics should be divided and subdivided, and so on. Although most students are taught to construct outlines for their own work, they don't often try outlining the already finished works they are reading. Yet going back over assigned reading texts as we prepare for discussion or writing and then trying to outline them is a very useful way of getting closer to the text (whether fiction or nonfiction) and of discovering the method behind it.

Our outlines needn't be overly detailed or comprehensive, and we can apply them to media other than print. For example, a movie is an incredibly structured visual and aural composition—so much so that one of America's top screenwriters, William Goldman, claims that structure is the single most important and most challenging element of any film script. Quite a few people, it was reported, tried outlining the sequence of Christopher Nolan's *Memento,* the intricately backward-plotted film about short-term memory loss that captured enormous critical attention in 2001, just to understand what was happening. Such outlines as this, known as plot outlines, can be extremely useful in helping reconstruct a narrative.

For other visual media such as painting and photography, outlining may seem irrelevant because there appear to be no divisible parts: the image is all there in front of us at once, unbroken and nonsequential. Yet the imagery of these texts—especially if they are the work of professional and talented artists—has also been carefully organized and arranged. Certain images

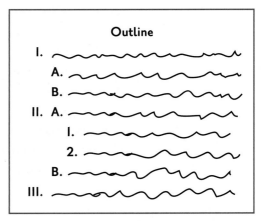

are foregrounded while others remain in the background, sometimes very faintly. Often the painting or photograph is composed so that a viewer will follow a particular angle of vision or a deliberate sequence of images that the artist calculated in the planning stage. As you examine, for example, Sally Mann's *Candy Cigarette* (p. 137), try keeping track of how your eyes take in the picture. What elements of the photo are you drawn to first? Which elements take more time to register? If you then record in your notes this sequence of movements, you will discover a good deal about the compositional methods of photography.

In understanding a text's method of expression, we should also be careful to observe **patterns**: regular or repetitive arrangements of elements within a text. For example, an artist may have composed a painting by arranging objects in various triangular sets (e.g., three tables, three floral vases, three windows); a piece of popular music will almost always contain regular rhythms and beats, sometimes persistently, so that they run without alteration for several minutes; a film director may show certain images over and over, perhaps using windows or glass to foreshadow ominous moments, as in Sam Mendes's *Road to Perdition* (2003). The use of such repetition may be so unobtrusively integrated into the film as a whole that we might not ever notice it unless it's pointed out to us. But the fact that we aren't conscious of such patterns while experiencing the film doesn't mean they are not exerting an effect on us. Usually, unless we are especially trained in a particular field, we need to experience a text multiple times to thoroughly understand its methods of composition. Once we detect its patterns, we can articulate how a painting, song, film, or photograph achieves its effects.

MEDIUM

Every expression of meaning we encounter reaches us in some particular way: a song on the radio, a poem on a greeting card, a reminder in an e-mail message,

---

COMMENT

"In a culture like ours, long accustomed to splitting and dividing all things as a means of control, it is sometimes a bit of a shock to be reminded that, in operational and practical fact, the medium is the message. This is merely to say that the personal and social consequences of any medium—that is, of any extension of ourselves—result from the new scale that is introduced into our affairs by each extension of ourselves, or by any new technology."

—Marshall McLuhan, from *Understanding Media* (1964)

a commercial on television, a speech at a conference, a painting on the wall of a museum. Messages and methods are often shaped for the medium that will convey them. Therefore, in order to understand the full significance of any form of expression, from a newspaper editorial to a web-page advertisement, we need to be attentive to the medium through which we experience it. Listening to a novel on tape is a different experience from reading the book, though every word is identical. Different again is seeing a movie version of the same novel. *Convergences* should help you understand those differences.

Medium is a complex term, with a wide range of connotations. For our critical purposes, you need to be aware of two key meanings, both of which are important as you consider and evaluate the selections in this book. First, the word "medium" refers to the physical material an artist uses in the creation or construction of a work: Michelangelo worked with marble; Mary Cassatt, with oils and pastels; Winslow Homer, with watercolors; Jasper Johns, with acrylics. A second, more familiar, use of the term "medium" refers to the various channels of communication by which expression is transmitted. We usually refer to these channels in the plural: "media" or "mass media." These include such print media as newspapers, books, and magazines; such electronic media as radio and television; and such interactive media as web sites and CD-ROMs. It is important to remember that media are normally defined by their processes or equipment, not by their content or methodology. Advertising, for example, is not in itself a medium, but it relies on various media—print, broadcasting, billboards,

11

Apple, Inc., *The iPhone.* Released in June 2007, the iPhone is an Internet-enabled mobile phone that allows users to browse the web, e-mail, play media (through its iPod capabilities), take pictures, and send visual voice mail. This multimedia piece of technology was named *Time* magazine's 2007 "Invention of the Year." (AP Images/Jason DeCrow)

the Internet—to get its messages delivered. Thus, ads prepared for a multimedia campaign will significantly differ according to whether they are intended for radio, television, magazines, or outdoor display—even though the advertised product remains the same.

Artists, writers, critics, and even entertainers expect us to be especially alert to the ways the medium will shape the message or influence the methods behind its creation. They are also attuned to how various media can be combined and refashioned to transform conventional patterns of expression. *Saturday Night Live* once featured an episode of a newscast in which the screen was gradually covered with so many message windows and information bars that viewers could no longer see the newsroom itself. The episode satirically reveals how television news now blatantly borrows from web-page design. Through its exaggerations, the comedy skit makes us notice—in case we had not before—the appropriation of one medium by another. The skit also forces us to ask some serious questions: Why has television news broadcasting adopted this web-page format? What purpose does it serve? What do television producers think they gain by imitating the Internet? And how does television's appropriation of web-page layout affect the way we receive and interpret the news?

These are the kinds of questions we hope you will ask of the selections in *Convergences.* They are not necessarily new questions—writers, artists, and critics have asked them for generations. But with the enormous growth of digital communications and the rapid convergence of media (along with the merger of mass-media industries), such questions have more urgency today than ever before. The boundary lines between advertising and information, news and entertainment, reality and representation, live action and animation grow fainter and fainter with each technological innovation. It has become increasingly harder to tell if a gesture or comment was scripted or spontaneous, whether an event was staged or impromptu. Through digitization, voices can be fabricated, photos can be doctored, and film can be altered. Readers and viewers need to be skeptical of claims, reports, and cited evidence; writers need to be especially cautious about the sources of their information.

It is easy to forget that media exist. We often look past the means of communication and think that what we are hearing and seeing is real. A photographic portrait may represent someone we know, but it is not that person—it is first and foremost a photograph. When we watch a breaking story on a news program, we are not witnessing the actual events—cameras and competitive news teams frame and select what we see and hear. A historical movie may be 5 percent fact and 95 percent entertainment. This may seem quite obvious, yet there is a strong tendency to confuse representation with reality. If we are to expand our ability to understand all kinds of verbal and visual texts—as this book encourages us to do—then we must develop an awareness of how media penetrate nearly everything we see and hear. We need to understand how one or another medium is always present, molding and filtering expression, even when it pretends to be invisible—even when it disguises itself as reality.

MESSAGE, METHOD, MEDIUM: WILL YOU MARRY ME?

To understand better how message, method, and medium converge to express an idea, let's examine the various ways that a common but highly significant question can be expressed and conveyed. Let's look at how someone might ask another person to get married. For many, the marriage proposal is one of life's milestones and has been portrayed often in novels, movies, songs, and pictures. The proposal has even developed its own iconography, such as the familiar image of a man kneeling down on one knee petitioning a woman to be his wife. But people also like to discover novel ways to—as we say—"pop the question." On pages 14–15, you will find several rather innovative ways to express a proposal of marriage.

These proposals involve the interrelation of message, method, and medium. In all of them, the message is essentially the same: a marriage proposal. This is so whether it is expressed in a conventional fashion—"Will you marry me?"—or as a plea, "Marry me," or without words, just an engagement ring hopefully offered. Even though the messages are the same and serve the same purpose, each is composed and delivered differently. One proposal is mowed into a field in such a way that it can be observed only from an elevation; another is composed of seven letter tiles on a Scrabble rack; another marriage proposal takes the form of an engagement ring in a glass slipper; yet another takes the form of letters on a billboard.

All of these proposals demonstrate how similar content can be differently composed and then differently conveyed. Take another example. According to a recent *New York Times* article by Kathryn Shattuck, men have been hiring their own photographers to secretly snap the moment they propose.[1] As Shattuck puts it: "Whether inspired by tenderhearted sentiments, the desire to record history in the making, or something more narcissistic, some marriage-minded men are remaking one of humanity's most private moments into one that can be instantly shared with family, friends and even, thanks to the Internet, virtual strangers. They are conspiring with photographers who, with all the stealth of covert operatives, lurk in crowds, behind bushes and in the darkened recesses of restaurants to capture the delighted, unposed reaction of the fiancée-in-the-making." (See page 16.)

Again, the message is the same: "Will you marry me?" But in this case, the message is presented orally as the man theatrically drops to bended knee, assuming the "staged" gesture for the purpose of being photographed. The medium in this case is a digital photograph that can be printed or delivered electronically

13

---

[1]From "Will You Marry Me? Say Cheese!" by Kathryn Shattuck, published in *The New York Times,* September 20, 2007.

Message	Method	Medium
Marriage proposal	Words and linked hearts mowed	A field

Brian Rueckl, *Stacy Will You Marry Me?* Brian Rueckl (age twenty-three) of Luxemburg, Wisconsin, asked his fiancée to marry him with the help of a field, some GPS software, and a small airplane. After a year's planning and forty hours of work to mow his 40,000-square-foot proposal, Rueckl, an employee of the USDA's Farm Service Agency, brought Stacy Martin up 1,000 feet over the field in a plane. At first, she didn't realize the message was for her. "I was in shock and forgot to say, 'yes,'" Martin said. (© Brian Rueckl)

14

Message	Method	Medium
Marriage proposal	Spelled out with Scrabble game letters	A Scrabble rack

Lew Robertson/Corbis, *Marry Me*. This photograph was taken by a Los Angeles–based photographer who specializes in food, beverage, and stock photography and is distributed by Corbis, a company that licenses all kinds of photography—fine art, historical, business, technology, celebrity, travel, and nature—for reproduction in print publications and online. The exact circumstances of the creation of this image are not known, but it was most likely staged by the photographer, perhaps in consultation with editors at Corbis. Its audience and purpose are very different, for example, from those of the photo that documents Brian Rueckl's proposal to his fiancée. (© Lew Robertson/Corbis)

Message	Method	Medium
Marriage proposal	Placement of ring in glass slipper	Slipper on a platter

Heather and Ed, *Engagement Ring in Glass Slipper.* A couple named Heather and Ed were engaged at Disney World on August 19, 2006. Ed had arranged for a weekend trip to Disney's Beach Club Resort and an engagement dinner at the Magic Kingdom. He worked it out with the restaurant manager that at the end of the meal, the waiter would bring, on a covered dish, Heather's engagement ring in a glass slipper on a bed of rose petals. Heather writes (on the couple's engagement blog, goofygall1975.com, where this photo was posted) that toward the end of the meal, "Ed looked so nervous. . . . The waiter came out a few times and asked if he was done." Ed writes: "I really was done. . . . I just wanted a few more minutes to gather my thoughts and get ready to ask 'the' question!" At last, the waiter brought the covered dish. Heather writes: "There was a glass slipper on rose petals. In the slipper was a rose, and MY RING around the rose!!!!! I was SO surprised. . . . Ed was down on one knee in front of me, a photographer was there, the manager was there, and I think the waiter too. . . . I don't even remember saying 'yes' but I know that I did. . . . Ed worked so hard to make this so special and it was . . . and so romantic!!!" (Reprinted by permission of Heather Paige-Webb)

15

Message	Method	Medium
Marriage proposal	Letters on a black background with background of hearts	A billboard

Larry, *Johnnie, Will You Marry Me?* This image of a billboard proposal appeared on November 20, 2006, in the Greenville Daily Photo blog, which is hosted by a couple named Denton and Connie Harryman, who are based in Greenville, South Carolina (greenvilledailyphoto.com). According to the post that accompanies the photo, the billboard was located in Greenville on Academy Street, near Washington Street. Some readers posted comments on the image. One blogger (Mandy) wrote: "I once saw a plane fly over with a tail message from this guy to a girl. I read in the paper later that she was so embarrassed she turned him down!" Another (Lisi) wrote: "This is so sweet and romantic. . . . In Vancouver, I was watching an ice hockey game in the stadium and a guy proposed on the big screen . . . very romantic!" There was also some debate about whether "Johnnie" is a man or a woman. One blogger (Isabella) wrote: "I tend to believe it's a gay couple making a political/social statement. But in any case, I hope Johnnie accepts and everyone lives happily-ever-after." Another (Denton) wrote: "Sadly if this is a gay couple they will not be allowed to legally marry in South Carolina." (© Denton Harryman)

on the Internet. The photograph is, of course, silent; the message—"Will you marry me?"—is expressed only by the conventional gesture. If the staged proposal had instead been filmed for video distribution, say for YouTube, the audience might hear the exact words, and the medium would be different.

As you examine the verbal and visual texts assembled in this book, it will be helpful to note the differences among the message, the method, and the medium or, to put it another way, to carefully distinguish among (1) the content of a work, (2) the particular way it is composed, and (3) how it is conveyed to you.

Jake Price, *Say Yes.* This photo appeared in the Fashion and Style section of *The New York Times* on September 20, 2007. It accompanied an essay by Kathryn Shattuck, "Will You Marry Me? Say Cheese," on the trend for couples to have photographers document their engagements. Pictured here is Guildry Santana proposing to Emily Cappella in New York City, on August 24, 2007, at the intersection of Eighth Street and Astor Place. Santana hired Jake Price, a photojournalist "known for covering wars and disasters," to capture the moment paparazzi style. Santana and Price planned where Santana would propose to Cappella, where they would stop in the street, how Santana would stand so that Price could get both of their faces, and what to do if the plan fell through. It went off without a hitch. According to Shattuck: "Neither Mr. Santana nor Ms. Cappella recall seeing more than a blur as Mr. Price circled them and snapped away." Cappella said of the photos that she planned "to email them to [her] whole family and all [her] co-workers." (© Jake Price)

Determining how something is conveyed or transmitted—the medium—can sometimes cause difficulties in our interpretations. For example, all of the paintings or photographs you see in this book are reproductions. Obviously, you are not observing Leonardo da Vinci's *Mona Lisa* on page 145 but rather a reproduction, which cannot provide you with a sense of the portrait's actual physical appearance in the Louvre Museum in Paris. If the *Mona Lisa* is one of the thousand things you want to see before you die, then you will need to visit the Louvre and join the crowd standing in front of it.

Let's take another example. On page 15, you are not looking at an actual glass slipper containing a ring but rather a photograph of that object reproduced in this book from another photograph. Therefore, you will frequently need to distinguish between the **primary medium** and other secondary means of delivery or conveyance. For example, the primary means by which the ring is conveyed is a glass slipper—that's literally where the ring first appeared (one assumes that the ring is no longer in the slipper). But you now see it only by means of a photograph that depicts the physical artifact of the ring in the slipper. As you proceed through this book, you will often need to make a careful distinction between how a work—especially a visual work—would appear if you were present to see it as opposed to how it appears in a reproduction. At times, the discrepancy will be enormous; for example, Brian Rueckl's "Stacy Will You Marry Me?" (p. 14) is approximately $2\frac{1}{2}" \times 1\frac{1}{4}"$ as reproduced here; in actuality, it covered 40,000 feet of farmland (an entire acre), a size that must have made a startling impact on a viewer. Throughout the book, captions will identify significant physical features of reproduced visual material.

Stefan Sagmeister, *Things I Have Learned in My Life So Far*. Unlike the marriage proposal examples on pages 14–16, this artwork features many different messages—but uses the same method (embossing of metal) and medium (metal key rings and tags) throughout. The sayings on these keys come from the diary of Stefan Sagmeister, an Austrian-born artist and graphic designer based in New York City (sagmeister.com). In other works, he has reproduced each saying in different forms, including on a billboard and on the cover of a business report. He is inspired by the art of his Austrian grandfather, who was trained in sign painting and traditional calligraphy applied in gold leaf and who created wooden panels featuring his own philosophies, such as, "This house is mine and it isn't mine. The second guy won't own it either. They will carry out the third one, too. So tell me my friend, whose house is it?" Sagmeister says, "I am following his tradition with these typographic works." This image was previously published in the fall 2006 issue of *Key, The New York Times Real Estate Magazine*. (Design by Sagmeister Inc. Photo by Tom Schierlitz)

UNDERSTANDING TEXTS: AUDIENCE, PURPOSE, AND CONTEXT

In *Convergences,* you will be asked to examine all kinds of written, oral, and visual expressions as though they are "texts" to read—and then you will be asked to write about them. The book invites you to take the concept of reading (and to some degree writing) beyond the printed word. You already read texts that are not written down on paper: you might talk about reading signs and signals, or reading someone's mind, or reading the future. You read music, maps, dials, charts, trails, and thermometers. To confirm reception, airline pilots say "I read you loud and clear." In a famous autobiographical passage, Mark Twain recalled how as a riverboat pilot he learned to "read" the Mississippi River.

To help you read and understand the many types of texts in *Convergences*, we provide pre-reading questions, call-out questions in the margins, and post-reading questions for discussion and writing. Message, method, and medium questions to help you read closely appear at the end of each cluster; and a variety of assignments at the end of each chapter help you bring it all together. In addition, we want you to also consider the familiar categories of questions for talking about all texts—audience, purpose, and context.

19

AUDIENCE

Who is the text written or composed for?

Nearly every type of expression, and certainly all published or displayed works, are designed for an **audience**. A conversation might have an audience of one; a television show, an audience of millions. It helps to think about the identity of an audience in two ways: first, as the actual audience that reads, hears, or views a work or performance; and second, as the hypothetical audience imagined by the creator of the work. Let's take a magazine article as an example. The actual readers would be found among the subscribers and others who happen to pick up the magazine at a newsstand or perhaps at a dentist's office. This could, of course, be a

> COMMENT
>
> "When a word starts to buzz, it vibrates everywhere—as soon as 'convergence' was in the air, the world seemed to be full of things that called out to be described by it. There were now interdisciplinary scientific fields like neurolinguistics and sociobiology; new musical styles like Afropop, jazz-funk, and just plain 'world'; new entertainment genres like infomercials and advertorials. The popularity of such portmanteau words is a sign of the current fascination with hybrids and convergences."
>
> —Geoffrey Nunberg, linguistics professor at Stanford University
> and usage editor of the *American Heritage Dictionary*

20

***Audience Wearing 3-D Glasses,* February 5, 1953.** An audience watches the screening of *Bwana Devil* in Hollywood. (© Bettmann/Corbis)

very mixed lot, with few characteristics in common. Publishers, however, do an enormous amount of costly research in an attempt to obtain at least some general characteristics of their readership. If the magazine article appeared in, say, *Rolling Stone* or *Spin,* there is an excellent chance that the actual audience consists of young males with an interest in rock music and countercultural values. The magazine *Essence* is written almost exclusively for African American women. Nearly all magazines (in fact, nearly all commercial media) today are designed around the interests of targeted audiences based on sex, age, race, ethnicity, political views, social and economic status, and so on.

Information about an audience can also be obtained by paying attention to the kinds of advertising or commercials that surround the material. Because advertisers pay dearly for space and time (aside from what it costs to prepare the messages themselves), they devote a great deal of research to making certain they reach precisely those audiences appropriate for their product. You will not see laxatives or luxury cars advertised on children's programs; you will see them featured on the nightly news. An observant survey of the ads in any given magazine will give you a pretty good indication of its anticipated audience.

A more interesting way to consider audience is to proceed inside out instead of outside in. That is, you infer the intended audience from the work itself. Sometimes a work will explicitly identify its audience; an essay might begin: "Are you an American parent who is fed up with the way liberals have taken over our schools?" But more often than not, you will need to consider what the writer's vocabulary level, formality or informality, and range of references tell you about the reader he or she imagines or expects. A scientific essay on the human brain written especially for neuroscientists will contain terms and references that would not appear in a similar essay targeted to a general audience. We can also look at the extent to which authors explain or qualify their references to infer the level of expertise they expect their readers to possess.

With visual works, inferring audiences may present a bit more difficulty. How can we tell from only a photograph itself the kind of audience the photographer wanted to reach? Here, clues can be found by considering the photo's subject and style. Are there elements of either that would turn off, offend, or shock some people? Do any features indicate that the photographer is saying something socially, politically, or artistically that he or she imagines a general public might not find acceptable? Does the photographer appear to identify with his or her subjects, or do you detect a satirical or hostile presence behind the camera? When photos of the homeless appear in upscale magazines, we know the photographer did not imagine other homeless people as an audience. Also, artworks sometimes contain references and allusions to other works that could indicate a desire on the part of the artist to separate insiders from outsiders—those who get the "quotations" and those who don't.

Another feature to look for—especially in prose fiction and film—is the inclusion of someone in the work who stands in for the intended audience. Movies frequently embody the audience in a particular character; a hero or heroine may represent the values, perspectives, or ideology of the people to whom the moviemakers want to appeal. People often "identify" or have the most sympathy with one particular character in a movie. Print ads and commercials almost always feature characters that represent a vast population of consumers. Whatever kind of text you are examining, always check to see if it contains representations of an audience.

PURPOSE

Why was this text written or composed?

A work's **purpose** is its overall goal or aim, the effect it hopes to achieve, the agenda or cause it promotes, the response it expects to receive from an audience. All expression is designed, consciously or unconsciously, to do something—to have some immediate or delayed effect. Someone puts up a sign to warn, draws a cartoon to amuse, writes an essay to explain, pens a letter to console. The famed dramatist and screenwriter David Mamet succinctly, though perhaps extremely, observes: "People only speak to get something."

Identifying a work's purpose will help us evaluate its success or achievement. It is generally unfair to judge a work by criteria that do not apply to it. We should not approach a news story with the same literary expectations that we do a lyric poem. Nor should we judge a lyric poem by the same standards as a news story.

The purposes behind the construction of each are not at all similar, even if the topic happens to be the same.

Some works may explicitly state their purpose. A newspaper editorial endorsing a political candidate may ask you directly to vote for that candidate. In some political posters, the message and the purpose are identical, as in the famous recruiting poster depicting Uncle Sam saying, "I Want You." But as you will note in many of the selections that follow, identifying a work's purpose may require some probing and careful consideration. This is especially true of literary and artistic expression that deliberately avoids the outright declaration of any purpose. A talented painter who produces a work of art in support of AIDS victims may not make that purpose crystal clear—many artists do not believe in editorializing and would prefer that their audiences be hesitant in reducing their work to a slogan. Many works of art do have a political purpose (antiwar, pro-choice, fascist), and it is important to recognize that purpose. Yet at the same time, we should make sure we have not oversimplified the work's message or its method.

Many works or performances may be said to contain multiple purposes. An entertaining comic strip may be driven by a hidden agenda; readers can be amused even without seeing the more subtle purpose. The jokes of some comedians penetrate more deeply than casual listeners may realize. Most TV infomercials appear to propagate useful information (and the hosts try to maintain this posture),

22

Vietnam Veterans Memorial. As she designed the Vietnam Veterans Memorial, the architectural designer Maya Lin knew her exact purpose, yet she never deviated from making sure the monument would reflect her personal vision of what a war memorial should be and do. For her, purpose and art are the same. For more on the Vietnam Veterans Memorial and issues of representation, see "What's in a Name?" in Chapter I (pp. 110–127). (© Todd Gipstein/Corbis)

but their primary purpose is to sell something. In fact, given the way commercial realities affect every medium, many published, displayed, or performed works will be enlisted for advertising duty. When someone drinks a Coors beer in a movie, it is not because the character is thirsty but because the brewery paid the film-makers for what's known in the marketing business as "product placement." Newspapers and magazines practice self-censorship by suppressing or altering stories and articles that might offend their major advertisers. Television shows try to avoid negative comments concerning their sponsors and may even include material that will reinforce the advertising messages. In your reading and viewing, it is a good idea to determine when information or entertainment has an unannounced commercial intent.

CONTEXT

Where has the text come from?

A book reviewer writes, "Can such trash ever be considered enlightening or entertaining?" The publishing company prints an ad with a quote from the review: "enlightening . . . entertaining." When this sort of distortion occurs, we usually say that something was "taken out of context." What is context? Every work or expression possesses one. The word has two primary meanings, both of which are crucial to understanding what we read, see, or hear. The first meaning pertains to whatever immediately surrounds a word, image, or passage. We often need to know an expression's context to understand it fully. The second meaning refers to a work or expression's surrounding environment or conditions—a text's historical, social, or economic context.

23

Understanding both meanings of context is essential to interpretation. There was (and to some extent still is) an influential set of art and literary critics who believed that a work can be understood only in and by itself—in other words, that text and context are identical. According to this school of thought, understanding *Hamlet* requires nothing more than reading the play itself (not that such a reading is nothing). Only the reading matters. No biography of its author, no knowledge of historical events that surrounded its performance, no awareness of class or economic conditions need enter into our criticism. Any references to issues or concerns outside the play might be interesting, but they contribute nothing to our understanding.

Most contemporary critics, however, prefer to work with the broader meaning of context. Thus, the physical characteristics of Shakespeare's stage, the social and economic features of the audience at the time, the acting techniques then in fashion, the political environment—all these factors should and would contribute to our understanding of *Hamlet,* just as they would any play from any era. In this sense, the context of a work can seem to expand infinitely. A front-page newspaper photograph can be read in the context of the surrounding stories on that page, the entire paper, the newspaper business in general, global politics, and so on. The context of a web page might be the sum of its links, perhaps the entire Internet.

www.cnn.com. The screen shot taken here is a web page, produced in the context of the news media; the context of CNN specifically; the terrorist attacks of 9/11; media coverage; possible agendas of the U.S. government; and how people use the web to access news. All these elements are part of the context of this page (CNN ImageSource)

In *Convergences,* we do consider context, but we try to make it a workable idea that stays grounded in the work at hand.

A textbook like *Convergences* has obviously drawn all of its material from other contexts: we found essays, short stories, and poems in magazines, newspapers, and books and on the web. One piece originally appeared in the literary magazine, *Tin House,* while others come from *Time* or *Newsweek;* the range is wide. We found paintings, art, photographs, and other visual texts in galleries, newspapers, books, and magazines and on the web. Still, you will see most of it retooled and formatted to this context: the textbook. We have tried to give you at least a little background and information about the context for each text, sometimes even showing you how we found it.

COMMENT

"Context is crucial in the theater, which only pretends to exist in a world of its own creation. Most mundanely and tangibly, though not insignificantly, a show cannot escape its physical environment. It generally takes place on some kind of stage in some kind of building, the properties of which (size, location, condition) have a palpable effect on the show's artistic strategies and intent, not to mention the expectations of an audience."

—Bruce Weber, theater critic

READING AND WRITING ABOUT TEXTS

We have seen how any selection in *Convergences* can be approached through a frame that focuses on what it says (**message**), how it is composed (**method**), and how it reaches us (**medium**). We have also seen that in addition to these three key concepts, every selection can be viewed in terms of its **audience** (for whom is the work intended?), its **purpose** (what motives inspired or required it?), and its **context** (what immediately or broadly surrounds it?). Throughout *Convergences,* you will find questions and assignments designed to reinforce these six critical concepts that apply to all written, artistic, and commercial works.

Because the selections in this book represent so many different types of written and visual texts, from comic strips and web pages to poems and short stories, it would be unwieldy to try to cover each one in a short introduction. You will, however, find relevant information on critical approaches to various kinds of texts in the introductory notes or the accompanying commentary to most of the selections. For now, we will examine in detail approaches to four types of material that will be featured throughout all the chapters in *Convergences:* essays, photographs, advertisements, and comics. This material makes up a large percentage of what we see and read every day. With an emphasis on verbal and visual elements—along with their many combinations—the following examples and lists of questions will be applicable to many other texts from different media that you will encounter in this book, in other courses, and in your daily life.

ESSAYS

Although essays appear in many shapes, sizes, and styles, there are today essentially three dominant types:

1. **Personal essays** in which authors write directly of their own experiences. The personal essay usually contains autobiographical details and usually is written in the first person. But personal essays can—and often do—take a reflective or meditative turn and express the writer's thoughts about certain topics or issues. The personal essay grows out of a long literary tradition and is likely to use more literary techniques than other types of essays. Personal essayists may experiment with structure, style, and compositional methods and frequently concentrate on mood, characterization, dramatic tension, figurative language, and narrative. In many ways, the personal essay can resemble fiction and even poetry. See Judith Ortiz Cofer's "Silent Dancing" on page 68 as an example of a personal essay.

25

2. **Informative essays** in which authors write about specific topics with the primary purpose of conveying information. Known generally as an "article," this is the most common type of essay published today; it is a staple of most magazines and newspapers, to which readers turn for news reports, advice, interviews, and other types of information, whether it's a background story on the latest presidential candidate or a short history of the T-shirt. Informative essays may contain some elements of first-person writing, but the main ingredient is information about a topic. Unless it's written by an expert who has all the necessary data at her fingertips or is intended to convey information based on someone's observations as an eyewitness (e.g., a war correspondent), the informative essay is largely research-driven, and therefore writers of informative essays need to be careful about sources. Although in popular periodicals footnotes are often avoided, the writers usually mention in their essays the sources of their information and quotations. (See Joseph A. Harriss's "Seeking Mona Lisa" on p. 146 as an example of an informative essay.)

3. **Opinion essays** in which authors present their own viewpoints on an issue, usually one that is socially, politically, or culturally controversial. Newspapers and magazines are fueled by opinion essayists who represent a spectrum of political perspectives and usually deliver their arguments in the space of a 750-word column (which is why they are called "columnists"). Nearly every major newspaper features an editorial page, on which it publishes— usually anonymously—the paper's position on a current issue, as well as an "op-ed"

QUESTIONS FOR READING AND WRITING ABOUT AN ESSAY

As with any text, reading an essay should be approached with a dual purpose: identifying the argument or message made in the essay as well as determining how that argument or message is structured. There are many essays and short stories in *Convergences*; the following questions will help you chart the development in a longer, often complicated piece of prose:

- What happens in the course of the essay? What stance is adopted at the beginning, and how does that stance change by the essay's end?

- What tone or voice does the author use? What do word choice and figurative language suggest about the essay's overall message?

- What relationship is assumed between writer and reader? Is the audience already in league with the author, or must readers be convinced to accept the author's position?

- What is the essay's purpose? To inform, persuade, or entertain? A combination of these purposes?

page (the page opposite the editorial page), which usually contains diverse opinions of regularly bylined columnists along with opinions submitted to the paper by outside writers. Like personal essayists, opinion essayists often write in the first person singular and rely on personal experiences, but their motives are generally far less literary and autobiographical and much more concerned with supporting or denouncing a policy or a position. Columns represent only one type of opinion essay. Many magazines, especially those that are closely aligned with a cause or political agenda, publish long opinion essays. Another common type of opinion essay includes reviews in all fields (e.g., literature, art, science, film) that depend on evaluative judgments supported by critical arguments. (See David Brooks's "People like Us" on p. 493 as an example of an opinion essay.)

The above examples refer mainly to essays we find in print, but it's important to remember that we often hear essays read on radio and experience them being delivered on television or via the Internet. Some of Martin Luther King Jr.'s now famous essays were spoken live to huge audiences. It's important to remember also that many essays contain elements of all three popular types outlined above. Like Stephen Jay Gould's essay on page 28, they blend personal experience, information, and opinion. Gould's 9/11 essay, it should be noted, first appeared as an "op-ed" item in *The Boston Globe,* and although he includes a personal episode and some information about ground zero, you will see that these elements are mainly in support of an opinion he holds about human life in general.

An annotated essay
Stephen Jay Gould, A TIME OF GIFTS

September 26, 2001

A TIME OF GIFTS
By Stephen Jay Gould

The patterns of human history mix decency and depravity in equal measure. We often assume, therefore, that such a fine balance of results must emerge from societies made of decent and depraved people in equal numbers. But we need to expose and celebrate the fallacy of this conclusion so that, in this moment of crisis, we may reaffirm an essential truth too easily forgotten, and regain some crucial comfort too readily forgone. Good and kind people out- number all others by thousands to one. The tragedy of human history lies in the enormous potential for destruction in rare acts of evil, not in the high fre quency of evil people. Complex systems can only be built step by step, whereas destruction requires but an instant. Thus, in what I like to call the Great Asymmetry, every spectacular incident of evil will be balanced by 10,000 acts of kindness, too often unnoted and invisible as the "ordinary" efforts of a vast majority.

We have a duty, almost a holy responsibility, to record and honor the vic- torious weight of these innumerable little kindnesses, when an unprece- dented act of evil so threatens to distort our perception of ordinary human behavior. I have stood at ground zero, stunned by the twisted ruins of the largest human structure ever destroyed in a catastrophic moment. (I will dis- count the claims of a few biblical literalists for the Tower of Babel.) And I have contemplated a single day of carnage that our nation has not suffered since battles that still evoke passions and tears, nearly 150 years later: Antietam, Gettysburg, Cold Harbor. The scene is insufferably sad, but not at all depress- ing. Rather, ground zero can only be described, in the lost meaning of a grand old word, as "sublime," in the sense of awe inspired by solemnity.

In human terms, ground zero is the focal point for a vast web of bustling goodness, channeling uncountable deeds of kindness from an entire planet— the acts that must be recorded to reaffirm the overwhelming weight of human decency. The rubble of ground zero stands mute, while a beehive of human activity churns within, and radiates outward, as everyone makes a selfless contribution, big or tiny according to means and skills, but each of equal worth. My wife and stepdaughter established a depot on Spring Street to col- lect and ferry needed items in short supply, including face masks and shoe inserts, to the workers at ground zero. Word spreads like a fire of goodness, and people stream in, bringing gifts from a pocketful of batteries to a $10,000 purchase of hard hats, made on the spot at a local supply house and deliv- ered right to us.

I will cite but one tiny story, among so many, to add to the count that will overwhelm the power of any terrorist's act. And by such tales, multiplied many millionfold, let those few depraved people finally understand why their vision of inspired fear cannot prevail over ordinary decency. As we left a local restaurant to make a delivery to ground zero late one evening, the cook gave us a shopping bag and said: "Here's a dozen apple brown bettys, our

28

① Gould uses these words early in the essay— they suggest an image of balancing scales.

② Many essays arise out of a specific occasion; Gould does not disclose the occasion until the middle of the second paragraph.

③ In writing the essay, Gould has accepted the responsibility to record the decency and kind- ness of most human beings. He then goes on to "cite but one tiny story" that encapsu- lates his central idea.

best dessert, still warm. Please give them to the rescue workers." How lovely, I thought, but how meaningless, except as an act of solidarity, connecting the cook to the cleanup. Still, we promised that we would make the distribution, and we put the bag of 12 apple brown bettys atop several thousand face masks and shoe pads.

Twelve apple brown bettys into the breach. Twelve apple brown bettys for thousands of workers. And then I learned something important that I should never have forgotten—and the joke turned on me. Those 12 apple brown bettys went like literal hot cakes. These trivial symbols in my initial judgment turned into little drops of gold within a rainstorm of similar offerings for the stomach and soul, from children's postcards to cheers by the roadside. We gave the last one to a firefighter, an older man in a young crowd, sitting alone in utter exhaustion as he inserted one of our shoe pads. And he said, with a twinkle and a smile restored to his face: "Thank you. This is the most lovely thing I've seen in four days—and still warm!"

4 *Note how many times in the final two paragraphs Gould repeats this relatively tiny number. He wants us to see how small the restaurant's gesture is in terms of the overwhelming number of rescue workers.*

5 *Note how Gould sets up a transformation by at first thinking the brown bettys were "meaningless" and "trivial."*

1 These words suggest the image of balancing scales. Gould wants us to understand that evil does not tip the scales. By the end of the opening paragraph, we know the main point, or central thesis, of the essay: the world contains many more good people than bad. Note that he makes the point but that he hasn't yet demonstrated it; he hasn't provided us with any evidence to believe what he says. When in the essay does he offer the evidence?

2 Gould begins his essay with broad generalities and abstractions about the proportion of good and evil in the world and concludes his essay with small concrete details. Why is this technique effective? Do you think his essay would be just as effective if the opening and conclusion were reversed?

3 This is one of several times Gould explicitly states his purpose in writing the essay—an explicitness that you won't find in most essays. Earlier he says that "we have a duty, almost a holy responsibility, to record and honor the victorious weight of these innumerable little kindnesses." Where else does Gould state his purpose? Does the repetition make his essay stronger?

4 Gould reinforces this discrepancy by letting us know that they placed the twelve apple brown bettys "atop several thousand face masks." At the same time that he contrasts the disproportion in numbers, he also makes us aware of the contrast between practical necessities and a few delicious treats.

5 Many essays end with a sudden revelation or illumination. The writer learns something new or recognizes something he or she should already have known. Yet Gould doesn't spell out that significance for his readers; instead he ends the essay with the appreciative remarks of one of the rescue workers. How are we supposed to interpret the final quotation?

PHOTOGRAPHS

Compared to literature and painting, photography is a fairly recent addition to human art and culture, dating back only to the middle of the nineteenth century, when the technology for taking pictures was initially developed. At first, the general public—though impressed by what photography could achieve—did not consider it an art form because it seemed overly dependent on equipment and mechanical know-how. After all, the photographer didn't "create" a picture the way a painter created one. But toward the end of the nineteenth century, as it grew increasingly associated with painting and was adopted and even promoted by famous painters, photography grew into an accepted art form with its own famous photographers and its own magazines, movements, and exhibitions. By 1928, Laszlo Moholy-Nagy, one of the world's leading photographers and critics, would claim that "the illiterate of the future will not be those who are ignorant of literature but those who neglect photography."

What does it mean to be "literate" in photography? Moholy-Nagy's claim about photographic literacy didn't mean that the public should learn the artistic skills required to be a professional photographer, although at the time he would have had little idea how many millions throughout the entire world would one day be equipped with cameras. He meant instead that the public should learn to "read" a photograph critically, the way a work of literature is customarily read, with an understanding of its design, patterns, purpose, meaning, and methods of composition. As we come to understand photography better, we will be able to discern its aesthetic effects and range of personal creativity as well as its manipulative effects—that is, the ways in which a photograph can be falsified or distorted for political, commercial, sensational, or censorial purposes.

30

QUESTIONS FOR READING AND WRITING ABOUT A PHOTOGRAPH

- Is the photograph meant for a particular context? Is it solely a work of art, or does it have a commercial purpose?

- How are color choice and linear composition used to convey emotion or symbolism? Remember that no choice is a given—even in photography, the choice of black and white versus color is a deliberate one. You might ask yourself, for example, what a black-and-white photograph suggests, both historically and figuratively. Is the photographer trying to convey a sense of truth, simplicity, or nostalgia?

- Is the subject matter abstract or representational? What does this choice tell us about the relationship between the subjects represented and the idea about the subjects?

- What is the scale of the work? What might this suggest about the photographer's perception of the subject's degree of importance?

Recent advances in digitization have led to new levels of artistry, as professional and even amateur photographers can experiment with pictorial effects as never before. But digitization has also led to an increase in pictorial manipulation that worries critics and journalists, who fear that such falsified or distorted images could be used to misinform the public. Just as a reporter may abuse his responsibility by fabricating quotations, so can a news photographer doctor photos to alter the public's perception of an event or a political figure. Such deliberate manipulation of photos is only an extreme strategy for shaping public sentiment. Many news photos convey a social or political "spin" without any doctoring at all. By choosing to frame an image to include one element and exclude another, to capture a political figure with a grim or puzzled expression instead of a pleased or happy smile, news photographers (and the editors who decide which pictures will be shown) can attempt to manipulate public response.

In *Convergences,* you will find many different types of photographs—some intended to be museum-quality works of art, some professionally snapped for the daily newspaper, some meant to document social conditions, and some designed to be commercially persuasive, to name just a few. How we critically consider and evaluate any photograph will depend on a number of factors, including its level of artistry, its particular purpose, and the context in which it appears. The more information we have about a photograph, the better equipped we are to analyze it. Despite the wide variety of photographs we experience daily, nearly every photograph we encounter invites us to distinguish certain elements and ask certain questions.

One thing we try to do consistently in *Convergences* is to present images with some information about their context. It helps to know, for example, that the photograph on pages 32–33, *Sara, 19,* was taken by photographer Lauren Greenfield as part of a larger exhibit and book, *Girl Culture* (2002). Greenfield's project grew out of her interest in "the element of performance and exhibitionism that seems to define the contemporary experience of being a girl." But *Sara, 19* can be read as a self-contained text without the context, as we show in the annotations that follow.

31

"Photography is an ideal medium with which to explore the role of image in our culture. The camera renders an illusion of objective representation, just like a mirror. But as every woman knows, a mirror provides data that, filtered through a mind and moods, is subject to wildly differing interpretations. This project has been my mirror and my attempt to deconstruct the illusions that make up our reality."

—Lauren Greenfield, from *Girl Culture*

1. Framing is one way that a photographer can focus in on a particular subject. The angle of this shot—with the photographer right behind the young woman— invites us not only to participate in the act of "checking out" this woman but also to identify with her as the subject of attention. The gaze of the men, which could be connected by three lines of a triangle to her body, is another frame for the subject.

2. Lighting is a technique that many photographers use to their advantage. The way the shadow falls further narrows the space that the young woman has to walk in down the street (it is narrowed even more by the bodies of the two men she's about to cross paths with), transforming a wide sidewalk into a narrow corridor. It's almost as if she's walking a gauntlet.

3. Color choice and linear composition help underscore the impact of this image. If the image were in black and white it might read as more "arty," but color adds a sense of urgency and reality, a sense that this photograph was taken recently, of real people. The trees, which in another context we might read

① *The subject of this image is the young woman walking away from the camera. Her body is literally framed by the bodies of three men, all looking at her, which suggests spectatorship.*

② *The wall on the left, the shadow it casts on the sidewalk, and the vertical line of the sidewalk all add another frame to the image—a narrow line that recedes into the distance.*

③ *We assume that there's a street cropped out of this shot—but the truck and trees on the right, which continue as far as we can see, obliterate our sense of any movement in this urban setting besides that of the people in the foreground.*

④ *This little bit of sky is the only "breathing space" in the picture.*

⑤ *Lauren Greenfield is known for her work documenting the lives of children "growing up too fast."*

Lauren Greenfield, *Sara, 19*
(© Lauren Greenfield 2002)

as a spot of color in an urban setting, are dark and constitute another wall facing the brick wall on the other side of the frame. The only spots of color are the band of exposed skin on the woman's back and the colored T-shirts and hats worn by the men—with the effect that our eye is drawn to that vulnerable exposed space between her shirt and her jeans.

④ The line that the woman is walking seems to recede directly into the space between the twin towers in the distance—the buildings underscoring a sense that this woman's walk will continue indefinitely, as she is hemmed in literally by buildings and figuratively by men looking at her. The only open space is the little patch of sky between buildings and trees.

⑤ If we did some research to find more about the context for this image, we would discover that Greenfield is well known for her work documenting children who grow up too fast; most of her photographs, like this one, are not posed. Knowing more about Greenfield's artistic projects would inform the way we see this single example.

ADVERTISEMENTS

Advertising represents one of the oldest forms of human communication. Traces of ads can be found throughout ancient civilizations and preliterate cultures, where images painted on walls and signboards served to alert people to trades and products. Later a steady growth of promotional writing accompanied the technological development of the printing press as countless pamphlets appeared throughout Europe trying to persuade people to colonize the New World. In fact, one of the earliest documents in American colonial history was Captain John Smith's 1631 promotional pamphlet *Advertisements for the Unexperienced Planters of New England.*

Advertising as we've come to know it, however, began in earnest around the middle of the nineteenth century with the onset of the Industrial Revolution as manufacturers sought consumers for their latest products. The pages of newspapers and popular magazines of the time were packed from top to bottom with advertisements for everything from corsets and buggies to cast-iron stoves and the latest cure for the common cold. The first four-color ads began appearing in the 1890s; since then, with one technological development after another, advertising has become an inseparable part of the human environment. It not only affects the larger economy, as consumer spending fuels production and growth in capitalist nations, but also plays a significant cultural role, as it daily generates new images, symbols, and desires that have an enormous impact on the lives of many millions.

Although the purpose of advertising is largely to persuade someone to buy something, its verbal and visual modes of persuasion have multiple psychological and social effects. For example, a society daily exposed to television commercials for so-called fast-food restaurants may find its dietary habits permanently altered within a generation. But that alteration, however momentous, is only one effect, for the

---

QUESTIONS FOR READING AND WRITING ABOUT AN ADVERTISEMENT

As you learn to read advertisements critically, it is important to extend your notion of an ad's purpose beyond that of bottom-line profit for the company. Pairing legitimate ads with the spoof advertisements shown in this book will help you deconstruct advertisers' strategies. The following questions are meant to help you read below the deceptively simple surface of most ads:

- What is actually being sold in the ad? The product itself, or an ideology or image that the advertisers want you to associate with the product?

- Does the ad appeal to your emotions, your sense of logic, or your respect for the company's reputation? Or does it use a combination of these appeals?

- What is the most important element of the ad? Text? Graphics? A catchy slogan or jingle? The company's logo? Where is your eye first drawn? What pieces of the ad pop out?

commercials also shape lifelong attitudes toward food and eating as well as establish in consumers' consciousness a data bank of logos, imagery, and psychological associations that can be tapped for other purposes, such as sports or patriotic causes. The persuasive effect of advertising, therefore, does not end with the purchase of a product but reaches deep throughout a society and becomes intricately entangled with other products, values, and sentiments. Every individual commercial for automobiles seen on television during a given evening may be trying to sell you a different car, but the cumulative cultural effect on you—and the general population—will be the prestige value of new-car ownership. After all, one central theme of American advertising has long been that the "new" is better than the "old."

The British cultural critic Raymond Williams once complained that the major problem with advertising wasn't that it promoted a materialistic view of the world but that its message was never materialistic enough. His point was that advertising traded mainly in promoting cultural values, images, and symbols and that it rarely provided useful, specific information about any product that would lead us to make rational decisions about purchasing it. One leading advertising adage is that you don't sell the steak; you sell the sizzle! Because they are so closely linked with social and cultural values, advertisements and commercials can be viewed as complex texts well worth analyzing and decoding. Much time, effort, and money go into the construction of advertisements and especially large-scale advertising campaigns. In every ad, there is usually more than meets the eye or ear—visual and verbal tactics designed explicitly or subliminally to influence our individual behavior, to direct our impulses, and to promote certain social and cultural values.

In reading ads, we almost always encounter highly compressed verbal and visual texts. Print ads have little space to capture our attention, and audio commercials must do so in the span of a few seconds. Thus, language and imagery need to be as selective as possible: one phrase may have multiple meanings; one image may contain several levels of suggestion. At first, the words and images may appear so casual or common that no analysis is required. But by taking a closer look at ads and commercials, we can usually see how deliberately they are crafted and how artfully they go about their business of persuasion.

In *Convergences,* you will find many different kinds of advertisements, some promoting consumer products and others advocating causes or positions on controversial issues. Although these may seem like entirely different cases, both kinds of advertisements employ identical techniques and similar persuasive strategies. Even though the advocacy ads may appear to be more ideologically oriented, it's important to remember that an ideology operates to a greater or lesser degree in all commercial texts. Whether the purpose of the ad is to promote a product or to advance a position—for example, to sell cigarettes or to discourage smoking—its underlying motive is persuasion.

Consider the following advertisement sponsored by a national organization founded in 1972 called Negative Population Growth (NPG). This print ad, which appeared in major magazines nationwide, addresses the issue of overcrowding and proposes a solution. The ad consists of both verbal and visual texts, with the visual text also cleverly containing a verbal text.

35

The Census Bureau projects that there will be 400 million people in the U.S. by 2050.

Remember when (this) was heavy traffic?

Ask any of (your) neighbors — things have changed over the past few years. Traffic has gotten worse and schools more crowded. Large developments, eight-lane highways and shopping centers have replaced open fields and wooded areas. (Our) suburban communities are overwhelmed by the demands of a larger population.

According to the Census Bureau, the U.S. population will grow from 284 million today to over 400 million within the next fifty years — with mass immigration accounting for over 60% of that growth. Every year, our outdated immigration policy brings over 1,000,000 people to the United States. If immigration and population growth continue at these unsustainable levels, a livable America will become a thing of the past.

Negative Population Growth
2861 Duke Street, Suite 36
Alexandria, VA 22314
(703) 370-9510

NPG
www.npg.org

1. *The headline pulls us into the ad by asking a question. "Remember when" suggests right off a feeling of nostalgia*

2. *The word "this" is intended to direct our attention to the photograph.*

3. *In the opening paragraph of ad copy, the pronouns switch from "your" to "our."*

4. *The visual content of the ad depicts a folksy homemade sign that reinforces nostalgia for a less crowded past.*

5. *The second paragraph introduces both statistical data and the ad's central message.*

36

(Courtesy of Negative Population Growth, 2861 Duke Street, Suite 36, Alexandria, VA 22314, www.npg.org)

1. Effective advertisements often use questions in their headlines. This strategy puts the reader directly into the ad by requiring a response. Although it doesn't look it at first, the headline is a direct address to the reader, but with the "you" implicit rather than explicit. Grammatically the question reads: "(Do you) remember when this was heavy traffic?" Note too that the headline consists of ten syllables; known as pentameter, this is one of the most common metrical constructions in poetry. The intended effect is to sound smooth and memorable.

2. Advertising often relies on the intentional use of ambiguous words or statements. Note that in the context of the headline we do not know exactly what "this" refers to. It is also somewhat unclear from the photograph, since cars or traffic are not depicted. The reader is asked to infer from the rustic sign and its natural setting that traffic at an earlier time on some unidentified road in some unidentified community was far less of a problem than it is at present. Note that "heavy traffic" in the headline is used ironically to suggest the opposite—that is, that what we might call "heavy traffic" at one time would be considered "light traffic" today.

3. Advertisements are always addressed to some particular audience. That audience is known in the advertising profession as the "target audience." It may be defined by sex, income bracket, age, educational level, hobbies, or other characteristics. Although anyone who saw this ad in a magazine could read it, not everyone who reads it would be part of its intended target audience. For example, the target audience of this ad is someone who very likely owns a home in the suburbs and has neighbors who are worried about overcrowding. The use of "your" targets an individual reader; the later "our" makes that individual a part of a larger group brought together by a common problem. When an ad addresses "you," it wants you to identify with its target audience. This strategy is helped enormously by the English-language convention in which the word "you" can be at the same time both singular and plural.

4. The visual element of the ad shows a handmade sign set in a rural landscape. We have no idea where this place is. We see no traffic or even a road. The sign uses different typefaces, presumably painted from a stencil. It is intended to look homemade and unofficial. It clearly has no legal authority. The sign lets us know that the area is a natural habitat for many creatures. Note that the word "SLOW" on the sign is the most prominent word in the entire ad and that it reinforces the central message of the text that America must slow down its population growth.

5. The ad's first paragraph is closely linked with the headline and picture; it helps establish the image of suburban neighborhoods afflicted with problems of overcrowding due to "the demands of a larger population." But the second paragraph introduces a new point, one that is only loosely connected to the first paragraph. Not only are we presented with statistics that support the sense we may have of overcrowding, but more important, we are informed that this rapid growth is due to outdated "mass immigration" policies. The ad's overall purpose, then, is to warn suburban communities that their way of life is being threatened by the nation's current immigration policies. The ad hopes to generate a negative attitude toward America's immigration policies and assumes that in the long run its message will affect voting and community activism. Some versions of the ad invited more immediate action, as they included cut-out coupons that could be sent with a donation to NPG.

COMICS

People enjoyed stories, poems, plays, art, and music long before critics tried to explain them. The same is true with today's comics, which can refer to many forms of sequential art—the traditional comic book (*Superman*), the familiar comic strip (*Peanuts*), the graphic novel (*Maus*), or the graphic memoir (*Persepolis*). Because storytelling—whether fictional or factual—is a central feature of today's artistically fashioned and literary comics, these works are often referred to in general as graphic novels and are featured in bookstores under that category. But the preferred term among practitioners seems to be "comics," with the term used as a singular. This is how Scott McCloud, one of America's most astute creators of comics, defines the medium:

> com-ics (kom'iks) **n.** plural in form, used with a singular verb. **1.** Juxtaposed pictorial and other images in deliberate sequence, intended to convey information and/or to produce an aesthetic response in the viewer.

Essentially, comics art relies on a combination of images, words, and graphic layout to tell a story. This is unlike the typical editorial or magazine cartoon, which makes a political point or cracks a joke within a single frame. Cartoons historically preceded the sequential comic strip, but the two forms developed alongside each other as they shared space in the popular periodicals of the day.

A relatively new art form, comics had their origins in the latter part of the nineteenth century, when they emerged in popular newspapers and magazines, a result of new technologies in printing and lithography. Though often exceptionally drawn, they were not considered to be an artistic endeavor but merely an ephemeral and low form of entertainment. This was true of the next stage of comics as well: the adventure, action, and horror comic books of the 1930s and 1940s were often condemned by parent and church groups as total trash that could lead young people down the road to delinquency (see "A Father's Guiding Hand" on p. 46).

With the rise of the underground comic books that grew out of the counter-cultural movements of the 1960s, comics began to be seen as an art form designed for an adult audience. Politically radical, explicitly sexual, and exploding with satire, comix (the *x* suggested an adult alternative to comics as well as X-rated) such as *Zap* pushed the edges of expression further than readers ever expected and—largely due to the pioneering methods of one artist, Robert Crumb—caused the medium finally to be taken seriously in the artistic and literary community. By the 1970s and 1980s, comic books had become hot collector's items, and fan shops were thriving.

The first American cartoon. *Join, or Die, The Pennsylvania Gazette,* **May 9, 1754.**
The first cartoon in America was printed alongside an editorial by *Pennsylvania Gazette* publisher Benjamin Franklin on the "disunited state of the British Colonies." The cartoon of the divided snake, symbolizing the eight individual colonial governments of the time, was also based on the popular legend that if you joined together the cut pieces of a snake before sunset, the snake would come back to life. (*The Pennsylvania Gazette* reprinted courtesy of The Library Company of Philadelphia. Cartoon from the Library of Congress)

40

OPENING OF THE HOGAN'S ALLEY ATHLETIC CLUB.

◀ **The first American comic strip. R. F. Outcault, *The Yellow Kid and Hogan's Alley*, 1894.**
Richard Felton Outcault (1863–1928), who came to be known as "the Father of the
American Comic Strip," created the first mass-produced comic strip in the United
States. His *Hogan's Alley* series portrayed nineteenth-century New York City with a
grittiness that would have been familiar to its residents at the time. The strip first
appeared in black and white in *Truth* magazine (1894) and later in color as a popular
feature in *The New York World* (late 1894–1898). In response to reader enthusiasm,
the strip began to center on the Yellow Kid, a bald waif in a yellow dress who speaks a
kind of immigrant and working-class street jargon conveyed through captions on his
frock or below the panels. Packed with social commentary as well as the ethnic stereotypes of its time, *Hogan's Alley* is a universe away from political correctness (as can be
seen in the example on p. 40 from an 1896 strip). However, the popularity of its superstar, the Yellow Kid, illustrates both the power of comics art and a character's potential to sell merchandise. In his brief four-year life, the Kid sold cookies, bubble gum,
soap—even whiskey and cigars—and his image appeared on lapel pins, key rings, stat-
uettes, dolls, bowling games, and many other toys. *MAD* magazine fans may also note
his more-than-passing resemblance to wunderkind Alfred E. Neuman, created in 1955.
(Reprinted courtesy of The Ohio State University Cartoon Research Library)

Detail from *The Yellow Kid and Hogan's Alley*

A milestone in comics history occurred in 1980, when Art Spiegelman founded the arty "graphix magazine" *Raw*, which featured cutting-edge new work by such artists as Robert Crumb, Charles Burns, Ben Katchor, and Lynda Barry. But the most important work to come out in *Raw* was Spiegelman's own—his serialized tale of the Holocaust, which portrays the Nazis as cats and Jews as mice. Released as a graphic novel in 1987, *Maus* proved to be an instant publishing phenomenon, and, though hardly the first of its kind, it can be said to have launched the era of the graphic novel (a term favored by book publishers but not always by the artists themselves). In 1992, Spiegelman received a Pulitzer Prize for Literature, the first comics artist ever to be so honored.

Since the 1990s, comics artists have experimented with different genres of graphic narratives: Ho Che Anderson began his three-part graphic biography of Martin Luther King Jr. in 1992; in 1993, Joe Sacco covered the Arab-Israeli conflict in *Palestine,* an outstanding example of "comics journalism"; and Iranian-born Marjane Satrapi published her award-winning graphic memoir *Persepolis: The Story of a Childhood* in 2000. Recently, Alison Bechdel's *Fun Home: A Family Tragicomic* (2006), a story that Bechdel describes as mainly about her father, has broken new ground for the graphic memoir. A clear indication that comics and graphic narratives now play a major role in mainstream publishing was shown recently with the release of *The Best American Comics 2006.* Many prestigious literary periodicals have also begun to feature graphic novels and nonfiction.

Even though graphic narratives and comics may now be mainstream, they still remain critically underappreciated. How should we read comics art? If comics art is a genuine art form practiced by artists with creative talents equal to poets, novelists, and dramatists, then how should it be experienced? Comics criticism has developed slowly, and much of it concentrates on content: greater attention is given to the social, cultural, political, and biographical dimensions of the works than to their formal or aesthetic characteristics. In other words, critics tend to focus more on the messages of the art than on the creator's compositional methods and the special characteristics of the medium.

In his important book *Comics, Comix, and Graphic Novels: A History of Comic Art* (1996), Roger Sabin describes the kind of study he believes comics art should receive: he approves of new studies "analyzing the mechanics of how the medium works." Such studies show

that comics are a language: they combine to constitute a weave of writing and art which has its own syntax, grammar and conventions, and which can communicate ideas in a totally unique fashion. They point, for example, to the way in which words and images can be juxtaposed to generate a mood; to how the amount of time that is allowed to elapse between images can be used for dramatic effect; to the way that cinematic cutting can be used for extra movement; and to the fact that, ultimately, there is no limit to what a comic can do other than that imposed by a creator's imagination.

Not surprisingly, some of the most illuminating criticism of comics art has come from the artists themselves, who are more likely to describe the techniques of their craft and discuss the medium they work in. Two of the earliest works of comics criticism and still among the most influential are Will Eisner's *Comics and Sequential Art* (1985) and Scott McCloud's "comic book about comics," *Understanding Comics* (1993). Both of these books are indispensable to anyone who wants to learn the compositional methods of comics and appreciate the overall artistry of the medium.

To fully appreciate comics, we need to understand the dynamic interrelationship of three essential elements: words, images, and layout. The reader should learn to see these in a unified fashion and not simply follow a verbal storyline while basically ignoring the way the images and overall graphic design contribute to the aesthetics of the whole. The images, then, are not merely intended to illustrate a verbal concept or narrative, and the graphic design is as much a part of the story as the verbal element. To read comics art appreciatively, we need to process words, images, and layout all at once, simultaneously as a unified entity.

43

QUESTIONS FOR READING AND WRITING ABOUT COMICS ART

- Is the creator's dominant style realistic or cartoonish? Do the figures appear to be caricatures, or do they have individual identities? Do the images appear abstract or concrete?
- How integrated are the images, words, and layout? Do they all appear to be part of a unified whole? Do you find yourself paying more attention to the words than to the pictures? Does one element seem much more significant than another?
- To what extent do the creator's methods rely on established conventions, such as icons, visual clichés, and familiar symbols? To what extent does the work appear challenging and innovative?
- How well does the comics art achieve its purpose? Does it seem appropriate to its subject matter, whether autobiography, adventure, biography, science fiction, or another genre?

◀ (Book cover, from *Maus I: A Survivor's Tale/ My Father Bleeds History* by Art Spiegelman, copyright © 1973, 1980, 1981, 1982, 1984, 1985, 1986 by Art Spiegelman. Used by permission of Pantheon Books, a division of Random House, Inc.)

(Front cover, from *Persepolis: The Story of a Childhood* by Marjane Satrapi, translated by ▶ Mattias Ripa & Blake Ferris, copyright © 2003 by L'Association, Paris, France. Used by permission of Pantheon Books, a division of Random House, Inc.)

Comics art consists only of ink on paper, either in color or in black and white. The artist needs to conjure up ways to make readers feel they are experiencing with all their senses a dynamic world full of movement, sound, action, events, moods, and emotions. How this is done will differ among various talented creators, each of whom will have developed a distinctive and recognizable style, but by and large they share a common vocabulary to describe their compositional methods.

One characteristic common to all comics is **closure**. Scott McCloud borrows the term from perceptual psychology to describe a key feature of comics art: the way it requires a reader's cooperation to convey its full meaning. As McCloud puts it, closure is the "phenomenon of observing the parts but perceiving the whole." For example, he says, "comics panels fracture both time and space, offering a jagged, staccato rhythm of unconnected moments. But closure allows us to connect these moments and mentally construct a continuous unified reality." In the psychology of visual perception, much study is devoted to the way in which the mind fills in gaps to form an image of a whole. Why should two dots and a line inside a circle look like a human face? Why do we "see" movement in a sequence of static pictures? It is important to keep in mind that especially in comics art the reader plays a very large role in what happens on the page.

In the analysis of Art Spiegelman's "A Father's Guiding Hand" that follows, you will find a convenient identification of the key elements that go into the construction of comics art, whether it takes the form of serialized newspaper strips or longer graphic narratives. This particular example is one of a series of graphic autobiographical essays that Spiegelman has been publishing over the past few years. The key terms are numbered for brief definitions and then linked to a fuller discussion of how they relate to comics composition in general. These explanations will offer you a starting point in approaching the many other comics creators who appear in *Convergences,* such as Marjane Satrapi, Lynda Barry, Chris Ware, Nathan Huang, Peter Bagge, and Alison Bechdel.

1. Panels are the basic structural units of comics art. The spaces between them are known as gutters. Extra-large variations of panel dimensions are called splash panels (see p. 48).

2. The verbal element of comics is technically known as its lettering. Lettering can be found inside word balloons to convey dialogue or as captions that speak directly to the reader.

3. Motion lines are one of the most familiar methods of depicting movement in comics. Also known by cartoonists as zip ribbons, such lines can indicate speed, spin, pace, direction, impact, or whatever movement the artist wants to convey.

(First published in *Virginia Quarterly Review*, Winter 2006v © 2006 by Ar Spiegelman, reprinted with permission of The Wylie Agency, Inc.)

Six years earlier, Dr. Fredric Wertham had been as shocked by these comics as I was.

SHOCK SuspenStories

Evidently they caused juvenile delinquency.

His crusade left only relatively insipid comics on the newsstands...

APPROVED BY THE COMICS CODE AUTHORITY

Relatively INSIPID Comics

the only ones I'd seen 'til my father intervened.

4 Comics often express emotions visually. The sweat beads flying off the character's forehead indicate intense emotion—in this case, shock.

My father knew a lot about bargains...

...but *nothing* about the comic book burnings and the Senate hearings that put many comics publishers out of business.

See page 50 for an explanation of the iconography used in this frame.

47

HEY, POPS- THOSE COMICS YOU GOT ME WEREN'T BAD! HERE'S A QUARTER FOR NEXT WEEK'S BATCH!

...BUT NEXT TIME TRY NOT TO BUY ANY WITH "LOVE" OR "ROMANCE" IN THE TITLE!

5 Spiegelman portrays his childhood self as a juvenile delinquent. He expects readers to instantly recognize this through the use of iconography.

1. **Panel.** The panel is the basic structural unit of comics. Also called a *box* or *frame,* it establishes the dominant verbal and visual sequence. Panel size can vary, but creators like Art Spiegelman usually maintain a fairly consistent size throughout the strip or graphic narrative. Every now and then an extra-large panel, known as a **splash panel**, is used for visual effect, an effect that would be lost if all panels varied in size. The space separating the panels is known as a **gutter**. Creators can alter the dimensions of panels or gutters to suggest changes in the passage of time. Note that Spiegelman's short graphic essay consists of ten equally sized panels, a half-page splash panel, and one panel drawn with no frame. Why do you think Spiegelman injected these two variations—the splash panel and the unframed panel?

2. **Lettering.** The verbal text of comics is usually entered by hand and will display various styles, from print to cursive. Lettering is most often used for

dialogue inside **word balloons**, with the tail of the balloon pointing to the speaker, or as wavy-edged **thought balloons** with a tail of bubbles to indicate who is thinking. Balloons can also be used for sound effects and can be jagged-shaped (called **splash balloons**) to emphasize dramatic tones (see below). The lettering outside balloons, called **captions**, is often directed to the reader (it is not dialogue) and either conveys the storyline or provides information. In this panel, Spiegelman indicates the narrative with a caption ("He kept forgetting, but eventually . . .") and the dialogue between father and son with word balloons.

3. **Movement.** Unlike animated films, comics is a static art. Creators therefore have discovered various effective ways to suggest motion. One common way they accomplish this is through panel sequence. Here's an example: in panel 1, we see a pitcher wind up; in panel 2, we see a batter poised to swing; in panel 3, we see only the baseball in the air; and in panel 4, we see a bat striking the ball. Rapid action has been conveyed here by the juxtaposition of four separate images, and the reader will instantly picture the entire

sequence as though it were a film. In such a sequence, the creator will also employ **motion lines**. These are various types of lines or streaking images—sometimes called **zip ribbons**—indicating direction, speed, spin, and impact. Spiegelman uses a bold spiral line to show himself falling "head over heels" into an adult world. Why do you think he changes his self-image in the unframed panel and uses the cartoonist's cliché of a banana peel to demonstrate the fall?

4. **Emotion.** Comics artists have developed numerous ways to display the emotion of a character or the mood of a situation. Some of these methods have become standard—sweat beads, tears, smiles, frowns, dark clouds, menacing shadows. Gestures (a raised fist) and postures (slumped shoulders) can also show at a glance a character's feelings. Moreover, color choice can indicate emotional states and mood tones. Note that Spiegelman shows his younger self

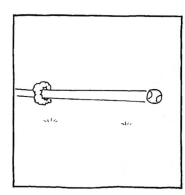 

(Courtesy of Billy Boardman)

49

sharing a similar shocked emotion with the character who earlier led the war against comic books, Dr. Fredric Wertham. The emotion is displayed visually through the use of sweat beads on the forehead and the wide-eyed look of shock that appears on both Spiegelman's and Wertham's faces (panels 6 and 8). Note, too, that Spiegelman verbalizes the emotion of being shocked by having the word appear as the name of the comic book.

5. **Iconography.** Images that are instantly recognizable as standing for something are known as **icons** (the sort you find on a computer screen). Icons are frequently used in comics and cartoons to stand for concepts, institutions, affiliations, character types, and so forth. For example, political cartoonists use a donkey to stand for Democrats and an elephant for Republicans, assured that every reader will recognize the meaning of the images. Spiegelman shows his character turning into a juvenile delinquent by picturing him in a black leather jacket and dark sunglasses, with a cigarette dangling from his mouth, and sporting a greasy, slicked-back pompadour haircut.

James Dean in *Rebel Without a Cause.* The image of the leather-jacket-wearing, cigarette-smoking, be-pompadoured tough guy was popularized in the famous 1955 film, *Rebel Without a Cause,* in which James Dean (left) plays a troubled teen in a new town. In "A Father's Guiding Hand," Art Spiegelman adapts this iconic image to make a comment about adolescence and self-image. (Warner Bros./The Kobal Collection)

THE STUDENT ESSAY: A SAMPLE RESPONSE TO THE WRITING ASSIGNMENTS FOUND IN *CONVERGENCES*

In this book, you will find many assignments asking you to write an essay in response to verbal and visual texts. For this edition, we asked Milos Kosic, a student at Northwest College—a two-year college in Powell, Wyoming—to write an essay responding to a writing assignment based on the cluster of materials in "What's in a Name?" (pp. 110–127). The purpose of Kosic's sample essay is to demonstrate how an actual student might tackle a particular writing assignment that asked him to combine a critical analysis of the readings with relevant personal experience. Naturally, every student will come up with a different response, but Kosic's example clearly shows an effective way to approach such assignments.

Following is the assignment that Kosic responds to in his essay.

Analyze. In just about every culture, people's names are significant. What about your name? What is its significance to you, your family, and your community? Consider the "What's in a Name?" cluster and write a brief critical essay (of 750 to 1,000 words) about the issues—personal and cultural—surrounding naming. In your essay, be sure to address at least two texts in the cluster. For example, you might choose to respond to Manuel Muñoz's "Leave Your Name at the Border" (p. 112), which addresses the question, What happens to non-English names in an English-centered culture? You might also respond to the analysis by Steven Levitt and Stephen Dubner ("Trading Up: Where Do Baby Names Come From?" p. 118) about the economic and social dynamics behind naming. How do our names impact how we think of ourselves—and how others think of us? What do the lists of the most popular names in the United States (p. 123) suggest about naming—and our collective attitudes toward names? Your essay should provide a solid critical analysis (what is the significance of the naming?), draw from materials in the cluster (what do others have to say about naming?), and incorporate relevant personal experience and insights (how do I relate to this topic personally?).

Milos Kosic   Kosic 1
February 1, 2008
Northwest College, WY

It's Not the Name That Matters

"Over 70,000 died," says Cody as we look at the black walls of Vietnam Veterans Memorial. It's raining so hard in Washington that even though we are under an open umbrella, our clothes are soaking wet. Our bodies shake from the cold, and our shoes squish with every step. But we are not concerned about whether we will get sick or not. Thinking about comfort here would be inappropriate.

"Did you get our shadows in it?" asks Cody, referring to our reflections in the wall.

"Yeah, I'm recording them," I answer.

"That's way cool, dude."

Whenever he can, Cody avoids calling me Milos. Sometimes I feel sorry for him, because no matter how hard he tries, he always mispronounces it. Either he says "s" at the end instead of "sh" or makes the "o" sound too long. I believe that every time he tries to say "Milos" (pronounced Mee'-lösh) and a different word comes out of his mouth, he curses both my name and the people who gave it to me.

There's nobody to blame. My parents are innocent. They wanted to call me Marko, naming me after the most popular hero of Serbian traditional songs. But in the hospital wing where I came into the world, it happened that all of the baby boys in the nursery had been named Marko. Confronted with the sad discovery that their name choice was not so original, my father and mother, who believed that their child had to be unique, decided to look for a back-up. Milos was the ad hoc second choice.

Luckily, Serbia has many heroes and historic figures. There was bound to be a famous Serbian Milos. I was determined to discover one and looked into the history books. I found out that the guy who killed a Turkish king a long time ago was also named Milos (Milos Obilic, to be exact). Naming someone after a great person is a tradition in Serbia. Now instead of having to tell others that I am not the namesake of anyone special, my parents can proudly say, "He is like the famous warrior."

As I grew up, I didn't show any signs of becoming a hero. One thing that was remarkable about me, though, was my inability to pronounce the sounds "sh" and "ch," which meant that pronouncing my own name was a serious problem. Thanks to my lovely cousin Lidija, my speech disability

1 The essay opens with a concrete scene.

2 Kosic introduces the main topic of his essay within a particular context.

did not pass unnoticed. Every time we had a big family gathering, Lidija would dedicate herself to drawing attention to what my "talent" was.

"Come on, tell us your name. Tell us what your parents called you!" she would insist.

Gullible kid as I was, I would answer, "My name is Miloff," and all around I would hear plenty of laughter.

At some point during my teenage years, as my voice changed, I over-came my speech disability. But if in my childhood I was the only one who couldn't pronounce Milos correctly, since I've come to the U.S., I'm now the only one who can.

When I came to the U.S. to attend college, I left my name at the border. Unlike Manuel Muñoz (author of "Leave Your Name at the Border"), however, I never thought that doing so was especially significant. It was something that made sense to me. Americans cannot say Serbian words and names correctly, and I sometimes mangle English with my strong Slavonic accent. If pronuncia-tion really matters, then for the sake of saving their language, Americans should immediately escort me back to the border. I would have no right to complain. Luckily this hasn't happened. Now it's time for me to show, as Muñoz says, the ability "to sustain more than one way of being" (114).

You can call me Milo. You can call me Miles or Meat-loaf, I'm fine. But I wonder what kind of person you see behind that name. Do you see a stranger? A good friend? Do you mispronounce my name because you simply cannot say it right, or you don't even want to try because for you, I'm unimportant, someone who doesn't deserve your respect?

In their essay "Trading Up: Where Do Baby Names Come From?" Steven D. Levitt and Stephen J. Dubner explain that parents choose their child's name believing that the right one can predict personal success (120). But when you meet someone named Donald, do think of someone like Donald Trump or Donald Rumsfeld—or Donald Duck?

At the Vietnam Veterans Memorial, among the 59,256 names, none of them seems better than another. As Maya Lin says in "Between Art and Architecture," "a sense of quiet, a reverence always surrounds those names" (126). The carved black stone memorial wall tells us one true thing about each of the people on it. Those Benjamins and Justins, Ricardos and Samuels fought and died in the same war. Even if I can't say some of those names correctly, every single one of them is equally honorable and worthy.

3 *Kosic extends and deepens his theme of mispronunciation.*

4 *A reference to readings meets the critical requirements of Kosic's assignment and allows him to express his own ideas in contrast to others.*

Kosic 3

"Milos!"

Cody mispronounces my name again when he calls to point out an old guy wearing a soldier's uniform, standing in front of the memorial.

"Is he security or something?" I ask.

"No," answers Cody. "He must be looking for his old pal somewhere on the wall."

We are ready to go. The old guy remains there. In the heavy rain, he will continue searching no matter what his pal was called. It's not the name that matters. It's the person who stands behind it.

5 *An effective conclusion will often return to the opening and contain a memorable closing statement.*

Kosic 4

Works Cited

Muñoz, Manuel. "Leave Your Name at the Border." Convergences. Ed. Robert Atwan. 3rd ed. Boston: Bedford, 2009. 000–00.

Levitt, Steven D., and Stephen J. Dubner. "Trading Up: Where Do Baby Names Come From?" Convergences. Ed. Robert Atwan. 3rd ed. Boston: Bedford, 2009. 000–00.

Lin, Maya. "Between Art and Architecture." Convergences. Ed. Robert Atwan. 3rd ed. Boston: Bedford, 2009. 000–00.

6 *A works cited page provides a bibliography of sources the writer has drawn upon.*

1 An effective way to begin an essay is through the use of concrete language that establishes a specific setting and specific characters. Kosic not only situates himself and a friend at the Vietnam Veterans Memorial in Washington, D.C., but makes us feel the miserable weather conditions as well. The reader very quickly obtains a vivid picture of the scene. Note, too, that he doesn't open with a direct statement about his topic, what our names mean, but it is suggested by the memorial, which—as many of us know from countless images—is covered with the names of those who died in the Vietnam War.

2 Note the way Kosic introduces what will be the main topic of his essay. It flows smoothly from the specific dialogue. His friend Cody calls him "dude" to avoid using his real name, which Cody has difficulty pronouncing. From there, Kosic goes on to provide American readers with the origin and significance of the name "Milos."

3 Writers often use the body of the essay to develop its central concept. In this case, Kosic humorously describes how as a child he was unable to say his name correctly. In doing this, he lets readers know that his own childhood experience makes him sensitive to the difficulties of pronunciation. He can more readily identify with the mispronunciations he hears from Americans because he too was unable to pronounce the name "Milos" correctly.

4 Kosic meets the critical requirements of the assignment by integrating references to three readings that were part of the assignment. Note that this allows him to briefly express his own opposing ideas by bouncing them off two of the readings. He admits he isn't offended that his name is always mispronounced by Americans. He then questions a study showing that parents choose certain names for their children because they believe that these names will predict personal success.

5 In his conclusion, Kosic comes full circle by returning to the opening scene at the Vietnam memorial, reemphasizing the mispronunciation of his name, and making us aware of how significant the names on the wall are for old friends of the dead. He then closes with two short sentences that effectively summarize the essay's main point and echoes its title.

6 Kosic's MLA-style works cited page—and the parenthetical citations included in the body of the paper—provide readers with the sources he is responding to. He skillfully draws on these sources to support his main points about the significance of names and identity.

55

HOW TO USE THIS BOOK

Convergences **is a composition reader.** That means that it's a collection of material put together by an editor and a publisher to give you something to write about. Tradition has it that you, the student, will be more engaged with your own compositions when you read—or see—something that interests you. Also traditionally, composition readers usually have recognizable and familiar themes: people you know, places you've lived, groups you belong to. *Convergences* is built around some familiar and traditional themes, but when you read the introductions to the six chapters, you'll see that these themes are presented in a slightly different way. Part of how the book works is that it encourages you to see the layers of meaning in how we portray people, think of places, and tell stories.

Convergences **brings together readings from different media and genres.** Composition textbooks are traditionally composed of only one medium (and usually one genre): the essay. *Convergences* brings together powerful essays with texts from all kinds of media: movies, television, the web, advertisements, comics, music, and more, helping point out the connections between the writing you do in your college classes and the visual and verbal texts that surround us all.

Six clusters in each chapter group together a wide variety of texts, revealing the layers of our cultural conversations. Here's an example. A traditional composition reader might simply present a reading on immigration. In Chapter 5, in the "Us and Them: The New Immigration" cluster, a personal essay by Jhumpa Lahiri, "My Two Lives," is grouped with a poem by Alberto Ríos ("Lineas Fronterizas/Border Lines"); a piece of "op-art" by a Los Angeles graphic artist on a Chinese tradition that's fading in America; a comic strip that satirizes the U.S. government's ambivalence toward undocumented workers; and Emma Lazarus's famous poem "The New Colossus" ("Give me your tired, your poor . . ."), which is printed with an illustration that reflects the changing citizenry of the United States today.

Everything you read in *Convergences* is connected to something else. Chapter menus at the beginning of each of the six thematic units provide an at-a-glance table of its contents. Within each chapter are six clusters. These begin with cluster menus and shaded "toolbars" to help you easily navigate the contents. A caption for each text in a cluster gives you a bit of background information about where the piece came from and who created it. Surrounding the texts are the following:

- Pre-reading questions labeled "Consider before you read" to help you approach the text.

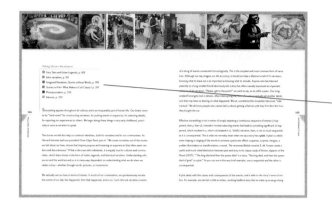

Chapter menus give you a bird's-eye
view of the unit's six interior clusters.

A toolbar at the top of the cluster introduction that
repeats in the running head helps you keep oriented.

Cluster menus offer a brief table of contents
of the six units within the chapter.

An introduction to each cluster explains
why the editor chose to put the pieces together.

57

A note for each text in a cluster gives you a bit of
background information about where the piece came
from and who created it.

"Consider before you read" questions help
you approach each text.

"Consider" questions in the margins help
you think critically as you read.

Two questions at the end of each reading help you **discuss** and **write** about that text.

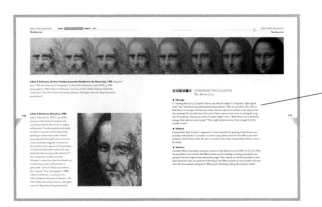

"Consider the cluster" questions on **message, method,** and **medium** ask you to use those three different critical lenses to consider the material as a group.

58

"Write" assignments at the end of each chapter invite you to compose your own texts about what you've read.

- Call-out questions in the margins labeled "Consider" to help you think critically about the text as you read.

- Post-reading "Discuss" and "Write" questions to help you brainstorm, exchange ideas, and write creative responses and essays about the work.

"Consider the cluster" questions at the end of each cluster ask you to think about message, method, and medium. They ask you to think about what the texts say, how they go about saying it, and what impact the medium has on a message.

"Write" questions appear at the end of each of the six units. These questions ask you to analyze, evaluate, compare, make a case, research, collaborate, create a memoir, or create a story and are labeled as such. These end-of-chapter questions give you the opportunity to work on many kinds of critical and creative assignments—written, visual, and multimedia.

At the end of the book, a glossary defines useful concepts for talking about traditional and visual rhetoric, marketing, or media. **Bold-faced terms** throughout the book highlight concepts that are particularly useful and that you'll find in the glossary.

COMMENT

"In schools and colleges, in these audio-visual days, doubt has been raised as to the future of reading — whether the printed word is on its last legs. One college president has remarked that in fifty years 'only five per cent of the people will be reading.' For this, of course, one must be prepared. But how prepared? To us it would seem that even if only one person out of a hundred and fifty million should continue as a reader, he would be the only one worth saving, the nucleus around which to found a university. We think this not impossible person, this Last Reader, might very well stand in the same relation to the community as the queen bee to the colony of bees, and that the others would quite properly dedicate themselves wholly to his welfare, serving special food and building special accommodations."

— E. B. White, circa 1940

1

Depicting Identities: the clusters

Any high school senior who's had a yearbook picture taken has encountered a common dilemma. The photographer or studio presents you with perhaps a dozen proofs, only one of which you are expected to select for the yearbook. How do you choose? Do you select the picture that makes you look most attractive, even if it's not a good likeness? Do you choose the one that most resembles you, not really caring about that pimple next to your nose? Or do you prefer a photograph that looks slightly unusual, one that makes you seem different from the way you imagine yourself to appear— maybe one that makes you look like someone else? And if you turn to friends or relatives for help in making the selection, what do you do when five different people prefer five different shots? When you finally settle on one photograph, what *reasons* would you give for your selection? What larger decision have you made about your self-image or your personal identity?

Most of us don't reflect so deeply on these matters and probably wouldn't fully articulate the reasons behind our selection of one particular photo over the rest ("I think this one just looks best" might be our answer if pressed). Yet the way we finally decide on a certain yearbook photograph offers some important insights into the complicated relationship between what we sometimes call our "real" or

"true" self and an artificial or fabricated image. Not only do these complicated relationships play a large role in our daily lives—we may, for example, see ourselves as constantly struggling to express an authentic personality instead of comfortably playing a conventional role—but they also exert an enormous influence in the world of art and literature, where authors and artists self-consciously explore the ways we depict our identity. The results of these creative explorations can then fold back into our actual lives—whether we are aware of the art or not—and may stimulate new modes of self-perception. In other words, we may come to see our struggle to establish an authentic self as simply another "role" we are playing.

Photographers refer to certain types of portraiture as **staged photography,** thus calling attention to the artificially constructed and theatrical nature of the image. This is not the same as when we pose for a portrait, which is also in many ways "staged"—with artificial lighting, plenty of cosmetic preparation, and sometimes even a scenic backdrop. In staged photography, however, the subject is deliberately playing a fictional role, and the photographer functions almost like a movie director. Think of it this way: suppose, instead of just having you sit in front of a camera and say "cheese" for your yearbook photo, the photographer posed you in a costume and setting that made you appear as though you were the lone survivor on a desert island. Your yearbook picture then would be an example of staged photography. We see this procedure in many photographs taken for book jackets or magazines, in which the subject—by means of costume, props, and pose—is made to appear a certain way: to look like a scholar, an outdoorsy type, a vamp, or a tough. In a later chapter, the writer Dorothy Allison describes such a photographic incident in her essay "What Did You Expect?" (see p. 588). Imagine a high school yearbook in which every senior photo was the result of a staged self-portrait—how would it alter the way you saw and understood your individual classmates? How would these photos

compare to the conventional pictures with their "cheesy" smiles? How many people do you know who use their yearbook photo for Facebook?

Although staged photographs may seem overly artificial and contrived, does that mean that cell phone and digital camera snapshots are more authentic and natural? Does our passport photograph tell the truth about us? When we see ourselves in a family snapshot, do we think, "That's really what I look like—that's me"? The snapshot, too, is an image, and its subjects, especially in many amateur photographs of family events, weddings, or trips, are very deliberately posed. "Stand over there," Dad says, "so I can get the Leaning Tower behind you." Thus, our yearbook photograph may be less posed than the snapshots of a family vacation. Even in crudely filmed home movies, as Judith Ortiz Cofer reminds us in her memoir "Silent Dancing" (see p. 68), the person filming tries to arrange and orchestrate a scene, tries to stage an activity that, looked at later, may seem awkwardly artificial. It is that amateur-like artificiality, however, that paradoxically makes home movies seem more "real" than a professional film that consciously uses sophisticated techniques to appear "natural."

However we depict ourselves and others—whether in painting or photography, in prose or poetry, on Facebook or YouTube—the medium we use plays a key role in shaping the message we send. On an everyday, practical level, we may disregard or overlook this process; the average person watching a movie or paging through a photo album is not paying close attention to the particular ways the person holding the camera has constructed whatever images she sees. For the most part, we look at pictures of people in the same way we look at everything else that surrounds us, and we therefore forget that the pictures are images and not the actual people they chemically or digitally depict. But for many

authors and artists, the medium is not invisible; rather, it's as significant—or even more so—than the subject itself.

This emphasis on artistry and technique can be seen in what is perhaps the most famous portrait ever painted: Leonardo da Vinci's *Mona Lisa*. As many critics have noted, Leonardo's method of blurring sharp outlines helps imbue the shadowy woman with a mystery that is enhanced by the painter's use of different perspectives for both the subject and her background. The mystery is further deepened by the possibility that what appears to some to be an actual woman and to others an imagined woman might in fact be no woman at all, but a self-portrait of Leonardo himself (see p. 145). Indeed, the *Mona Lisa* invites us to see that a portrait is not so much a straightforward pictorial representation of someone's appearance as it is a totally artful construct.

What artists do visually, writers perform verbally. Words, too, are a medium and are arranged and crafted in certain ways to achieve certain effects. In writing a memoir, a personal essay, or an autobiographical poem, the author is often keenly conscious of the way words and sentences not only reveal his or her life but also take on a life of their own. Our life story is not our life but a *story*, with all the shaping, selectivity, and distortions that the word conveys. A piece of writing may be wholly fictional yet so skillfully composed that it persuades us it is entirely true. And vice versa. A poem or photograph may seem on the surface to be staged or dispassionate, yet upon reflection and analysis it may disclose more sincere feeling than one that gushes over with sentimentality. In this chapter, we will closely examine a broad selection of depictions that in word and image challenge the way we customarily view ourselves and others. Some of the images may seem overly familiar and others unsettling, but all the selections will test the limits of such value-laden terms as "natural" versus "artificial," "real" versus "phony," and "spontaneous" versus "contrived."

COMMENT

"In writing these 'essays' (the Spanish word for essay, *ensayo*, suits my meaning better —it can mean 'a rehearsal,' an exercise or practice), I faced the possibility that the past is mainly a creation of the imagination also, although there are facts one can research and confirm."

— Judith Ortiz Cofer

HOME MOVIES

■ **Cluster menu: Home Movies**

Both photographs and home movies can stimulate our memories—sometimes, as is often the case in early childhood, even replacing or reconstructing what we know happened to us. Because so much of childhood occurs in a time when we think primarily in pictures, photographs and poetry are particularly effective media for conveying a time and place. In *Silent Dancing: A Partial Remembrance of a Puerto Rican Childhood* (1990), Judith Ortiz Cofer, a poet and memoirist, collects prose and poetry that play with photographs, home movies, and memories from her childhood, filling in real and imagined details of her bilingual, bicultural experiences in New Jersey and Puerto Rico.

Born in Puerto Rico in 1952, Judith Ortiz Cofer is the author of a number of award-winning books, many of which crisscross the boundaries of poetry, fiction, and nonfiction. In addition to *Silent Dancing*, she has written a novel, *The Line of the Sun* (1989); poetry collections, such as *Terms of Survival* (1987) and *Reaching the Mainland* (1986); another memoir, *Woman in Front of the Sun: On Becoming a Writer* (2000); *The Latin Deli: Prose and Poetry* (1993); *An Island Like You: Stories of the Barrio* (1995); and *The Year of Our Revolution: New and Selected Stories and Poems* (1998). Her two recent novels are *The Meaning of Consuelo* (2003) and *Call Me Maria* (2004). Cofer is a professor of English and creative writing at the University of Georgia.

67

Judith Ortiz Cofer, *Silent Dancing.* In "Silent Dancing," the title essay of her collection, Judith Ortiz Cofer revisits the Puerto Rican community of her New Jersey childhood by means of a five-minute silent home movie made by one of her relatives at a New Year's Eve party. Though clumsily shot, the film is in color—"the only complete scene in color I can recall from those years," the author says.

Judith Ortiz Cofer
SILENT DANCING

■ **Consider before you read.** *In this essay, Cofer explores how memory is intricately linked with visual images. How do pictures from Cofer's childhood interact with her memories? Do they help her recall things she has forgotten? Do they get distorted with time? How are the images preserved on the home movie different from the ones Cofer has kept in her mind through the years?*

We have a home movie of this party. Several times my mother and I have watched it together, and I have asked questions about the silent revelers coming in and out of focus. It is grainy and of short duration, but it's a great visual aid to my memory of life at that time. And it is in color—the only complete scene in color I can recall from those years.

We lived in Puerto Rico until my brother was born in 1954. Soon after, because of economic pressures on our growing family, my father joined the United States Navy. He was assigned to duty on a ship in Brooklyn Yard—a place of cement and steel that was to be his home base in the States until his retirement more than twenty years later. He left the Island first, alone, going to New York City and tracking down his uncle who lived with his family across the Hudson River in Paterson, New Jersey. There my father found a tiny apartment in a huge tenement that had once housed Jewish families but was just being taken over and transformed by Puerto Ricans, overflowing from New York City. In 1955 he sent for us. My mother was only twenty years old, I was not quite three, and my brother was a toddler when we arrived at *El Building*, as the place had been christened by its newest residents.

My memories of life in Paterson during those first few years are all in shades of gray. Maybe I was too young to absorb vivid colors and details, or to discriminate between the slate blue of the winter sky and the darker hues of the snow-bearing clouds, but that single color washes over the whole period. The building we lived in was gray, as were the streets, filled with slush the first few months of my life there. The coat my father had bought for me was similar in color and too big; it sat heavily on my thin frame.

I do remember the way the heater pipes banged and rattled, startling all of us out of sleep until we got so used to the sound that we automatically shut it out or raised our voices above the racket. The hiss from the valve punctuated my sleep (which has always been fitful) like a nonhuman presence in the room—a dragon sleeping at the entrance of my childhood. But the pipes were also a connection to all the other lives being lived around us. Having come from a house designed for a single family back in Puerto Rico—my mother's extended-family home—it was curious to know that strangers lived under our floor and above our heads, and that the heater pipe went through everyone's apartments. (My first spanking in Paterson came as a result of playing tunes on the pipes in my room to see if there would be an answer.) My mother was as new to this concept of beehive life as I was, but she had been given strict orders by my father to keep the doors locked, the noise down, ourselves to ourselves.

It seems that Father had learned some painful lessons about prejudice while searching for an apartment in Paterson. Not until years later did I hear how much resistance he had encountered with landlords who were panicking at the influx of Latinos into a neighborhood that had been Jewish for a couple of generations. It made no difference that it was the American phenomenon of ethnic turnover which was changing the urban core of Paterson, and that the human flood could not be held back with an accusing finger.

"You Cuban?" one man had asked my father, pointing at his name tag on the Navy uniform—even though my father had the fair skin and light-brown hair of his northern Spanish background, and the name Ortiz is as common in Puerto Rico as Johnson is in the United States.

"No," my father had answered, looking past the finger into his adversary's angry eyes. "I'm Puerto Rican."

"Same shit." And the door closed.

My father could have passed as European, but we couldn't. My brother and I both have our mother's black hair and olive skin, and so we lived in El Building and visited our great-uncle and his fair children on the next block. It was their private joke that they were the German branch of the family. Not many years later that area too would be mainly Puerto Rican. It was as if the heart of the city map were being gradually colored brown—*café con leche*[1] brown. Our color.

The movie opens with a sweep of the living room. It is "typical" immigrant Puerto Rican decor for the time: The sofa and chairs are square and hard-looking, upholstered in bright colors (blue and yellow in this instance), and covered with the transparent plastic that furniture salesmen then were so adept at convincing women to

69

---

[1] *café con leche:* Coffee with cream. In Puerto Rico it is sometimes prepared with boiled milk. [All notes are Cofer's.]

buy. The linoleum on the floor is light blue; if it had been subjected to spike heels (as it was in most places), there were dime-sized indentations all over it that cannot be seen in this movie. The room is full of people dressed up: dark suits for the men, red dresses for the women. When I have asked my mother why most of the women are in red that night, she has shrugged, "I don't remember. Just a coincidence." She doesn't have my obsession for assigning symbolism to everything.

The three women in red sitting on the couch are my mother, my eighteen-year-old cousin, and her brother's girlfriend. The novia *is just up from the Island, which is apparent in her body language. She sits up formally, her dress pulled over her knees. She is a pretty girl, but her posture makes her look insecure, lost in her full-skirted dress, which she has carefully tucked around her to make room for my gorgeous cousin, her future sister-in-law. My cousin has grown up in Paterson and is in her last year of high school. She doesn't have a trace of what Puerto Ricans call* la mancha *(literally, the stain: the mark of the new immigrant—something about the posture, the voice, or the humble demeanor that makes it obvious to everyone the person has just arrived on the mainland). My cousin is wearing a tight, sequined, cocktail dress. Her brown hair has been lightened with peroxide around the bangs, and she is holding a cigarette expertly between her fingers, bringing it up to her mouth in a sensuous arc of her arm as she talks animatedly. My mother, who has come up to sit between the two women, both only a few years younger than herself, is somewhere between the two poles they represent in our culture.*

■ **Consider.** *What are the two poles of Puerto Rican culture to which Cofer refers? How do you think her father would fit into the spectrum? Do the poles represent different qualities for men and women?*

70

It became my father's obsession to get out of the barrio, and thus we were never permitted to form bonds with the place or with the people who lived there. Yet El Building was a comfort to my mother, who never got over yearning for *la isla.* She felt surrounded by her language: The walls were thin, and voices speaking and arguing in Spanish could be heard all day. *Salsas* blasted out of radios, turned on early in the morning and left on for company. Women seemed to cook rice and beans perpetually—the strong aroma of boiling red kidney beans permeated the hallways.

Though Father preferred that we do our grocery shopping at the supermarket when he came home on weekend leaves, my mother insisted that she could cook only with products whose labels she could read. Consequently, during the week I accompanied her and my little brother to *La Bodega*—a hole-in-the-wall grocery store across the street from El Building. There we squeezed down three narrow aisles jammed with various products. Goya's and Libby's—those were the trademarks trusted by her Mamá, so my mother bought many cans of Goya beans, soups, and condiments, as well as little cans of Libby's fruit juices for us. And she also bought Colgate toothpaste and Palmolive soap. (The final *e* is pronounced in both these products in Spanish, so for many years I believed that they were manufactured on the Island. I remember my surprise at first hearing a commercial on television in which Colgate rhymed with "ate.") We always lingered at

La Bodega, for it was there that Mother breathed best, taking in the familiar aromas of the foods she knew from Mamá's kitchen. It was also there that she got to speak to the other women of El Building without violating outright Father's dictates against fraternizing with our neighbors.

Yet Father did his best to make our "assimilation" painless. I can still see him carrying a real Christmas tree up several flights of stairs to our apartment, leaving a trail of aromatic pine. He carried it formally, as if it were a flag in a parade. We were the only ones in El Building that I knew of who got presents on both Christmas day AND *Día de Reyes*, the day when the Three Kings brought gifts to Christ and to Hispanic children.

Our supreme luxury in El Building was having our own television set. It must have been a result of Father's guilt feelings over the isolation he had imposed on us, but we were among the first in the barrio to have one. My brother quickly became an avid watcher of Captain Kangaroo and Jungle Jim, while I loved all the series showing families. By the time I started first grade, I could have drawn a map of Middle America as exemplified by the lives of characters in *Father Knows Best*, *The Donna Reed Show*, *Leave It to Beaver*, *My Three Sons*, and (my favorite) *Bachelor Father*, where John Forsythe treated his adopted teenage daughter like a princess because he was rich and had a Chinese houseboy to do everything for him. In truth, compared to our neighbors in El Building, we were rich. My father's Navy check provided us with financial security and a standard of life that the factory workers envied. The only thing his money could not buy us was a place to live away from the barrio—his greatest wish, Mother's greatest fear.

In the home movie the men are shown next, sitting around a card table set up in one corner of the living room, playing dominoes. The clack of the ivory pieces was a familiar sound. I heard it in many houses on the Island and in many apartments in Paterson. In Leave It to Beaver, *the Cleavers played bridge in every other episode; in my childhood, the men started every social occasion with a hotly debated round of dominoes. The women would sit around and watch, but they never participated in the games.*

Here and there you can see a small child. Children were always brought to parties and, whenever they got sleepy, were put to bed in the host's bedroom. Babysitting was a concept unrecognized by the Puerto Rican women I knew: A responsible mother did not leave her children with any stranger. And in a culture where children are not considered intrusive, there was no need to leave the children at home. We went where our mother went.

Of my preschool years I have only impressions: the sharp bite of the wind in December as we walked with our parents toward the brightly lit stores downtown; how I felt like a stuffed doll in my heavy coat, boots, and mittens; how good it was to walk into the five-and-dime and sit at the counter drinking hot chocolate.

71

■ **Consider.** *Are there common themes to the few details Cofer remembers from her early days in New Jersey? What is the significance of these details?*

On Saturdays our whole family would walk downtown to shop at the big department stores on Broadway. Mother bought all our clothes at Penney's and Sears,
and she liked to buy her dresses at the women's specialty shops like Lerner's and
Diana's. At some point we'd go into Woolworth's and sit at the soda fountain to eat.

We never ran into other Latinos at these stores or when eating out, and it
became clear to me only years later that the women from El Building shopped
mainly in other places—stores owned by other Puerto Ricans or by Jewish mer-
chants who had philosophically accepted our presence in the city and decided to
make us their good customers, if not real neighbors and friends. These establishments were located not downtown but in the blocks around our street, and they
were referred to generically as *La Tienda, El Bazar, La Bodega, La Botánica.*
Everyone knew what was meant. These were the stores where your face did not
turn a clerk to stone, where your money was as green as anyone else's.

One New Year's Eve we were dressed up like child models in the Sears catalog: my brother in a miniature man's suit and bow tie, and I in black patent-leather
shoes and a frilly dress with several layers of crinoline underneath. My mother wore
a bright red dress that night, I remember, and spike heels; her long black hair hung
to her waist. Father, who usually wore his Navy uniform during his short visits
home, had put on a dark civilian suit for the occasion: We had been invited to his
uncle's house for a big celebration. Everyone was excited because my mother's brother
Hernan—a bachelor who could indulge himself with luxuries—had bought a home
movie camera, which he would be trying out that night.

Even the home movie cannot fill in the sensory details such a gathering left
imprinted in a child's brain. The thick sweetness of women's perfumes mixing
with the ever-present smells of food cooking in the kitchen: meat and plantain
pasteles, as well as the ubiquitous rice dish made special with pigeon peas—
gandules—and seasoned with precious *sofrito*[2] sent up from the Island by somebody's mother or smuggled in by a recent traveler. *Sofrito* was one of the items
that women hoarded, since it was hardly ever in stock at La Bodega. It was the
flavor of Puerto Rico.

The men drank Palo Viejo rum, and some of the younger ones got weepy. The
first time I saw a grown man cry was at a New Year's Eve party: He had been reminded of his mother by the smells in the kitchen. But what I remember most were the
boiled *pasteles*—plantain or yucca rectangles stuffed with corned beef or other meats,
olives, and many other savory ingredients, all wrapped in banana leaves. Everybody
had to fish one out with a fork. There was always a "trick" pastel—one without
stuffing—and whoever got that one was the "New Year's Fool."

There was also the music. Long-playing albums were treated like precious
china in these homes. Mexican recordings were popular, but the songs that brought
tears to my mother's eyes were sung by the melancholy Daniel Santos, whose life

---

[2] *sofrito:* A cooked condiment. A sauce composed of a mixture of fatback, ham, tomatoes, and many
Island spices and herbs. It is added to many typical Puerto Rican dishes for a distinctive flavor.

as a drug addict was the stuff of legend. Felipe Rodríguez was a particular favorite of couples, since he sang about faithless women and brokenhearted men. There is a snatch of one lyric that has stuck in my mind like a needle on a worn groove: *De piedra ha de ser mi cama, de piedra la cabezera . . . la mujer que a mi me quiera . . . ha de quererme de veras. Ay, Ay, Ay, corazón, porque no amas.*[3]. . . I must have heard it a thousand times since the idea of a bed made of stone, and its connection to love, first troubled me with its disturbing images.

The five-minute home movie ends with people dancing in a circle—the creative filmmaker must have set it up, so that all of them could file past him. It is both comical and sad to watch silent dancing. Since there is no justification for the absurd movements that music provides for some of us, people appear frantic, their faces embarrassingly intense. It's as if you were watching sex. Yet for years I've had dreams in the form of this home movie. In a recurring scene, familiar faces push themselves forward into my mind's eyes, plastering their features into distorted close-ups. And I'm asking them: "Who is she? Who is the old woman I don't recognize? Is she an aunt? Somebody's wife? Tell me who she is."

"See the beauty mark on her cheek as big as a hill on the lunar landscape of her face—well, that runs in the family. The women on your father's side of the family wrinkle early; it's the price they pay for that fair skin. The young girl with the green stain on her wedding dress is *La Novia*—just up from the Island. See, she lowers her eyes when she approaches the camera, as she's supposed to. Decent girls never look at you directly in the face. *Humilde*, humble, a girl should express humility in all her actions. She will make a good wife for your cousin. He should consider himself lucky to have met her only weeks after she arrived here. If he marries her quickly, she will make him a good Puerto Rican-style wife; but if he waits too long, she will be corrupted by the city—just like your cousin there."

"She means me. I do what I want. This is not some primitive island I live on. Do they expect me to wear a black *mantilla* on my head and go to mass every day? Not me. I'm an American woman, and I will do as I please. I can type faster than anyone in my senior class at Central High, and I'm going to be a secretary to a lawyer when I graduate. I can pass for an American girl anywhere—I've tried it. At least for Italian, anyway—I never speak Spanish in public. I hate these parties, but I wanted the dress. I look better than any of these *humildes* here. My life is going to be different. I have an American boyfriend. He is older and has a car. My parents don't know it, but I sneak out of the house

73

---

[3] *De piedra ha de ser . . . amas:* Lyrics from a popular romantic ballad (called a *bolero* in Puerto Rico). Freely translated: "My bed will be made of stone, of stone also my headrest (or pillow), the woman who (dares to) loves me, will have to love me for real. Ay, Ay, Ay, my heart, why can't you (let me) love. . . ."

late at night sometimes to be with him. If I marry him, even my name will be American. I hate rice and beans—that's what makes these women fat."

"Your *prima*[4] is pregnant by that man she's been sneaking around with. Would I lie to you? I'm your *Tía Política*,[5] your great-uncle's common-law wife—the one he abandoned on the Island to go marry your cousin's mother. I was not invited to this party, of course, but I came anyway. I came to tell you that story about your cousin that you've always wanted to hear. Do you remember the comment your mother made to a neighbor that has always haunted you? The only thing you heard was your cousin's name, and then you saw your mother pick up your doll from the couch and say: 'It was as big as this doll when they flushed it down the toilet.' This image has bothered you for years, hasn't it? You had nightmares about babies being flushed down the toilet, and you wondered why anyone would do such a horrible thing. You didn't dare ask your mother about it. She would only tell you that you had not heard her right, and yell at you for listening to adult conversations. But later, when you were old enough to know about abortions, you suspected.

"I am here to tell you that you were right. Your cousin was growing an *Americanito* in her belly when this movie was made. Soon after she put something long and pointy into her pretty self, thinking maybe she could get rid of the problem before breakfast and still make it to her first class at the high school. Well, *Niña*,[6] her screams could be heard downtown. Your aunt, her mamá, who had been a midwife on the Island, managed to pull the little thing out. Yes, they probably flushed it down the toilet. What else could they do with it—give it a Christian burial in a little white casket with blue bows and ribbons? Nobody wanted that baby—least of all the father, a teacher at her school with a house in West Paterson that he was filling with real children, and a wife who was a natural blond.

"Girl, the scandal sent your uncle back to the bottle. And guess where your cousin ended up? Irony of ironies. She was sent to a village in Puerto Rico to live with a relative on her mother's side: a place so far away from civilization that you have to ride a mule to reach it. A real change in scenery. She found a man there—women like that cannot live without male company—but believe me, the men in Puerto Rico know how to put a saddle on a woman like her. *La Gringa*,[7] they call her. Ha, ha, ha. *La Gringa* is what she always wanted to be. . . ."

The old woman's mouth becomes a cavernous black hole I fall into. And as I fall, I can feel the reverberations of her laughter. I hear the echoes of her last mocking

---

[4] *prima:* Female cousin.

[5] *Tía Política:* Aunt by marriage.

[6] *Niña:* Girl.

[7] *La Gringa:* Derogatory epithet used here to ridicule a Puerto Rican girl who wants to look like a blonde North American.

words: *La Gringa, La Gringa!* And the conga line keeps moving silently past me. There is no music in my dream for the dancers.

When Odysseus visits Hades to see the spirit of his mother, he makes an offering of sacrificial blood, but since all the souls crave an audience with the living, he has to listen to many of them before he can ask questions. I, too, have to hear the dead and the forgotten speak in my dream. Those who are still part of my life remain silent, going around and around in their dance. The others keep pressing their faces forward to say things about the past.

My father's uncle is last in line. He is dying of alcoholism, shrunken and shriveled like a monkey, his face a mass of wrinkles and broken arteries. As he comes closer I realize that in his features I can see my whole family. If you were to stretch that rubbery flesh, you could find my father's face, and deep within *that* face—my own. I don't want to look into those eyes ringed in purple. In a few years he will retreat into silence, and take a long, long time to die. *Move back, Tío*, I tell him. *I don't want to hear what you have to say. Give the dancers room to move. Soon it will be midnight. Who is the New Year's Fool this time?*

■ **Discuss.** *What does the adult narrator of this memoir understand that she couldn't as a child? Discuss the ways the mature consciousness can interpret her earlier sensory impressions.*

■ **Write.** *At the end of this selection, Cofer assumes the voices of several women attending the party. However, she never attempts to narrate what she herself was thinking at the time, giving us only the details most striking from a child's perspective. Using the details of both the party and Cofer's first experiences of New Jersey, write a paragraph or two in which you imagine what the young Cofer would say about the scene.*

75

Cover of *Silent Dancing: A Partial Remembrance of a Puerto Rican Childhood,* by Judith Ortiz Cofer. In the last essay of *Silent Dancing,* titled "The Last Word," Cofer describes a "face she's memorized: that of a very solemn two-year-old dressed in a fancy dress. . . . I am not smiling in any of these pictures." (© 1990 Arte Publico Press—University of Houston)

SILENT DANCING:

A Partial Remembrance
of a Puerto Rican
Childhood

JUDITH ORTIZ COFER

Judith Ortiz Cofer, *Lessons of the Past*. Cofer is best known for her poetry. "Lessons of the Past" describes a significant party of her childhood—like the one described in *Silent Dancing*. This one, however, is also the scene of the recurring argument with her mother described in her essay "The Last Word." Her mother says she did not fall in the fire; Cofer remembers that she did.

Judith Ortiz Cofer
LESSONS OF THE PAST

■ **Consider before you read.** *Why does Cofer dedicate this poem to her daughter? What parallels does the dedication draw between the writer's mother and her role as a mother to her own child? Or between herself as a girl and her daughter? What "lessons" does she want to pass on?*

FOR MY DAUGHTER

I was born the year my father learned to march in step
with other men, to hit bull's eyes, to pose for sepia photos
in dress uniform outside Panamanian nightspots—pictures
he would send home to his pregnant teenage bride inscribed:
To my best girl.

My birth made her a madonna, a husbandless young woman
with a legitimate child, envied by all the tired women
of the pueblo as she strolled my carriage down dirt roads,
both of us dressed in fine clothes bought with army checks.

        When he came home,
he bore gifts: silk pajamas from the orient for her; a pink
iron crib for me. People filled our house to welcome him.
He played Elvis loud and sang along in his new English.
She sat on his lap and laughed at everything.
They roasted a suckling pig out on the patio. Later,
no one could explain how I had climbed over the iron bars
and into the fire. Hands lifted me up quickly, but not before
the tongues had licked my curls.

        There is a picture of me
taken soon after: my hair clipped close to my head,
my eyes enormous—about to overflow with fear.

■ **Consider.** *In this poem, Cofer refers to a photograph taken of her when she was two years old. That photograph also appears on the cover of her memoir (opposite). If you studied the photograph without reading the poem, how might you describe the child's picture? How does Cofer's poetic reference to the photo affect your response to it?*

I look like a miniature of one of those women
in Paris after World War II, hair shorn,
being paraded down the streets in shame,
for having loved the enemy.

Consider. *What do you
think triggers her comparison
to the Parisian women after
World War II? Who were these
women? What similarities does
she suggest between herself
and those women? Is it only the
cropped hair?*

But then things changed,
and some nights he didn't come home. I remember
hearing her cry in the kitchen. I sat on the rocking chair
waiting for my cocoa, learning how to count, *uno, dos, tres,
cuatro, cinco,* on my toes. So that when he came in,
smelling strong and sweet as sugarcane syrup,
I could surprise my *Papasito*—
who liked his girls smart, who didn't like crybabies

with a new lesson, learned well.

■ **Discuss.** *How do the objects in the poem represent its characters—for example, the
father's dress uniform and the mother's silk pajamas? What do these items reveal about expectations for men and for women? How is the narrator involved in these expectations—both as a
person who has some of her own possessions and as an important "possession" of her parents?*

■ **Write.** *The reader's understanding of the two female characters in Cofer's poem—
mother and daughter—is complicated by references to other women—the French collaborators, with whom Cofer compares herself, and the Madonna, to whom her mother bears
some resemblance. In a short essay, discuss how these references characterize both mother
and daughter.*

CONSIDER THE CLUSTER
Home Movies

■ Message

In an essay, consider the emphasis Cofer places on the silence of the home movie. What role
does "silence" play in her essay? How frequently does she refer to the way things sound? What
connections does she establish between seeing and hearing? Between visuals and vocals?

■ Method

How does Cofer work the film into the organization of "Silent Dancing"? Why doesn't she
summarize the film in one place, say at the beginning, instead of referring to it at different
points in the essay? What is the effect of this method?

■ Medium

What story does the five-minute silent film tell? Does the film have a narrative movement at
all, or does Cofer invent one? Whose voices does she use in the extracted paragraphs? Why
does she introduce these voices?

OUR STUFF, OURSELVES

PERSONAL ESSAY | OBJECTS | SCREEN SHOT

■ **Cluster menu: Our Stuff, Ourselves**

Do the objects we own describe or define our personalities in any way? What picture can we paint of someone by just knowing what sort of car she drives or what brand of jeans he wears? Could you sneak into someone's room and form a reliable impression of that person by noting his or her possessions? Consumer researchers think that in many ways "we are what we own"; as a result, advertising agencies design **campaigns** that target certain products to certain types of personalities.

For his college thesis, John D. Freyer studied how consumer profiling works: "If you could collect information about how people consume goods and services, you could create a pretty good picture of their personality traits, and might even be able to predict the types of choices that they will make in the future." Later, as a graduate student, Freyer put some of his ideas into action by setting up a web site and selling all his material possessions on eBay. In "All My Life for Sale," he describes his spiritual journey into voluntary dispossession. At the same time, however, he supplies us with an amusing catalog of those possessions, with information about their origins, their histories, and their ultimate destinations. Freyer invites us, as we go through his inventory of what he sold at auction, to consider these varied, sometimes curious, but mostly mundane possessions as his own self-portrait. In that sense, they comprise—as Freyer apparently wishes us to see them—a portrait of the artist as a young man.

A graduate of Hamilton College with a degree in political science, John
Freyer was born in Syracuse, New York, in 1972. He has worked at nonprofit arts
foundations, in cinematography, and in graphic design. He received his MFA from
the School of Art and Art History at the University of Iowa in 2003 and is now a
lecturer in photography at the University of Iowa. In March 2007, Freyer sold the
fiction film rights to *All My Life for Sale* to Reason Pictures. He is currently at work
on a book tentatively titled *Second Hand Stories,* which chronicles his adventures
exploring the secondhand economy from coast to coast. Based on these stories,
he co-created with filmmaker Christopher Wilcha a television pilot that was broadcast on PBS. Freyer lives with his wife and three-year-old daughter (with another
on the way) in Iowa City.

John Freyer

ALL MY LIFE FOR SALE

80

■ **Consider before you read.** *What purpose does Freyer state for beginning to sell off
his possessions? How do his motivations evolve as the project continues? How does the
nature of the sale change as his understanding of its purpose changes?*

John Freyer, *All My Life for Sale.* In 2000, John Freyer made $6,000 auctioning off all his   ▶
stuff on eBay. An agent saw an item about his project and invited him to make it into a
book. The essay here serves as his introduction to the book and describes his sale and subsequent road trip to visit all his former possessions and their new owners. Freyer has
become a minor media celebrity and has inspired numerous similar projects. The essay
that follows is taken from Freyer's book *All My Life for Sale* (2002).

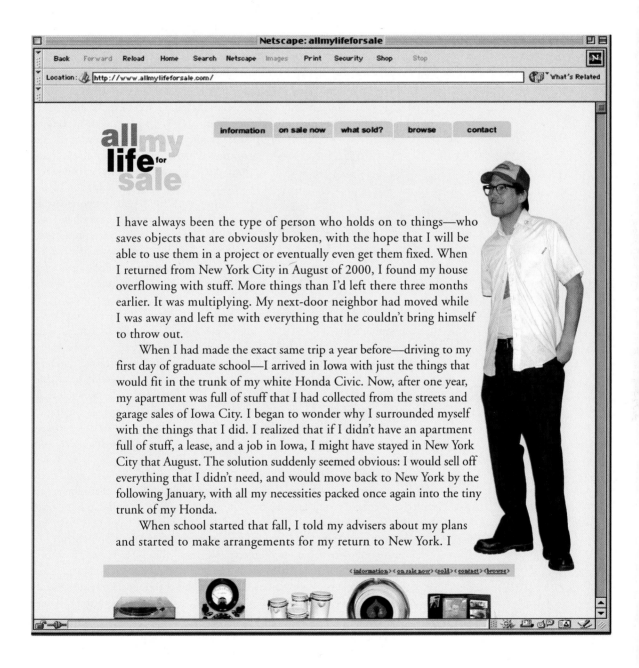

‹ **information** › ‹ **on sale now** › ‹ **sold** › ‹ **contact** › ‹ **browse** ›

I have always been the type of person who holds on to things—who saves objects that are obviously broken, with the hope that I will be able to use them in a project or eventually even get them fixed. When I returned from New York City in August of 2000, I found my house overflowing with stuff. More things than I'd left there three months earlier. It was multiplying. My next-door neighbor had moved while I was away and left me with everything that he couldn't bring himself to throw out.

When I had made the exact same trip a year before—driving to my first day of graduate school—I arrived in Iowa with just the things that would fit in the trunk of my white Honda Civic. Now, after one year, my apartment was full of stuff that I had collected from the streets and garage sales of Iowa City. I began to wonder why I surrounded myself with the things that I did. I realized that if I didn't have an apartment full of stuff, a lease, and a job in Iowa, I might have stayed in New York City that August. The solution suddenly seemed obvious: I would sell off everything that I didn't need, and would move back to New York by the following January, with all my necessities packed once again into the tiny trunk of my Honda.

When school started that fall, I told my advisers about my plans and started to make arrangements for my return to New York. I looked for another student to take over the classes that I was supposed to teach the following semester, talked to my landlord about ending the lease early, and decided that I would sell some of the stuff I no longer needed on the Internet auction site eBay. I owned a lot of things that people in Iowa wouldn't necessarily appreciate, since they could find much of what I planned to sell in their neighborhood thrift stores and even at their curbsides.

I listed a few items a week on eBay, and was amazed when they sold. I started to photograph the objects and write descriptions, and as I did that I couldn't help but think about where each object came from, and why I even had it in the first place. Many of my friends in New York were working for the booming online catalog industry, and spent their days writing copy for the products in their catalogs. This was the summer of 2000, and everyone I went to college with was making money hand over fist in the dot-com boom doing pretty basic Web design. Every week the news reported on the latest twenty-seven-year-old millionaires, art museums were forming for-profit online businesses, anything and everything was going dot-com.

I decided that I needed my own dot-com, that it would be interesting if I built an online catalog like the one my friends were building for Martha Stewart, but this one would have the lost and found objects that cluttered my Midwestern apartment. In early September, I sat down at my computer and started typing in catchy titles to a domain-registry service. Yardsale.com—not available. Garagesale.com—not available. Junkyard, junksale, housesale, lifesale, lifeforsale, allforsale, everythingsale—all not available. This was the era of people buying up domain names and selling them to corporations for millions of dollars. It seemed like every name was already registered. I eventually entered allmylifeforsale.com and the computer replied AVAILABLE.

Available. I registered it on the spot, thinking that someone else would get it if I didn't snap it up. Who was I kidding? Did I really think that there was someone else out there trying to come up with a domain name to build an online catalog that featured the random objects that occupied his life?

After the name was registered, I wasn't sure what I should do. My original plan was to sell off my unwanted objects and move what I had left to New York, but the domain name that I registered didn't really allow for such maneuvering. It didn't say some-of-my-unwanted-stuff-from-the-curb for sale, it emphatically said all. Having sold a few things on eBay, I started looking around my house, thinking about how long it would take for me to actually go through and auction every single thing I owned. I was overwhelmed, and my reasons for the sale in the first place were obscured by the daunting logistics of the task.

82

I knew I would need help if I was going to finish the sale by the end of December, so I invited everyone I knew—and even some total strangers—to my house in October for an inventory party. I handed everyone a clipboard and a handful of tags, and instructed them to tag things that they thought were "representative of my life in Iowa City." The party lasted into the early morning, and in the end more than six hundred items were tagged. This was exactly the structure that I needed. The inventory list included things that were found in boxes under my bed, items from my underwear drawer, things from my bathroom medicine cabinet—objects that I didn't even know I had. I now had a detailed list of possessions that was pretty representative of the "all" that the newly registered domain name specified.

I started to go through all of the items that were tagged—from my favorite shirts to the canned food in my cabinet. As I photographed each item, I reflected on the role that it played in my life and the stories that almost every object made me remember if I spent just a little bit of time with it.

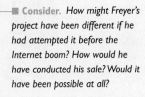

I was immersed in these objects' histories, and started to think about what would happen when I no longer owned them. As an undergraduate political science major, I wrote a thesis about the use of consumer profiling in business and government surveillance. Such profiling presumes that if you could collect information about how people consume goods and services, you could create a pretty good picture of their personality traits, and might even be able to predict the types of choices that they will make in the future.

The dot-com culture thrived on the idea that it could use the Internet to gather such information. All catalog-store business models included layer upon layer of customer-tracking technology. Some dot-coms were setting up businesses that operated at a considerable loss on the consumer-sales side, while selling consumer information to anyone who would buy it to make up the difference.

The histories contained in the objects that I owned could never be uncovered by the consumer profiles that were attached to me. What would happen to my customer profiles when I no longer owned these things? Would I soon have to forward my junk mail to the people who bought my objects on eBay?

In November, I started to sell items on eBay that I had simultaneously posted to the allmylifeforsale site. The first object I sold was my toaster. I sent it to Bill in Illinois. And almost immediately after I sent it, I wondered if Bill even cared about its history. I started to think about the history Bill would attach to my toaster—would it burn his toast, as it did mine? I also realized that the act of selling these objects would start to change my life in subtle ways. After I sold my toaster, I stopped eating toast.

83

■ **Consider.** *How might Freyer's project have been different if he had attempted it before the Internet boom? How would he have conducted his sale? Would it have been possible at all?*

It was also in November that I came to terms with the fact that there was no way I could finish selling everything I owned by the end of the year. I was able to list about ten items during the entire month of November; at that rate it would take me three years to get through all of the tagged items. So the project that grew out of my desire to leave Iowa was now keeping me there. The objects that prevented me from leaving were still doing so, but the other reasons for leaving soon became irrelevant.

The first items I sold ended up all over the country. The simple act of listing an item on eBay had the potential to distribute that item anywhere in the world. I wanted to know more about where all the things I was selling were going, so I started to include a request in the invoice that I sent to high bidders asking them to send me an update on the items they purchased. Some people withdrew from my auctions altogether, but as the sale went on, more and more people were interested in providing information. Over time, I started to receive photographs and stories from the various people who participated in the project, and I posted the updates on the allmylifeforsale site with pictures of the corresponding objects. A genealogy of objects emerged as the project continued, and people who visited the site could get a sense of the histories—old and new—that were attached to my former possessions.

As more people participated, a community seemed to form around allmylife-forsale. I was in almost daily contact with many of the high bidders, and was soon more interested in the people who bought things from me than I was in the objects I was selling. At about this time, I received an invitation to visit my salt shaker in Portland, Maine. I had never been to Maine, and thought about all the other places my stuff had gone that I had never seen, either.

So, halfway through the project, I sent out another message to all the high bidders saying that I was going to get in my car with whatever was left after the sale, and would like to visit all the people who had bought things from me. Within a week, I had received forty invitations to visit my former possessions. As the project continued, I started to include the prospect of my visit directly into the eBay listings, so the new owner would know in advance that their purchase might lead to a visit from me.

By the end, I had received more than one hundred invitations from all over the world. London, Melbourne, Tokyo, and New York—I didn't know how I would even go about it. On August 1, 2001, my apartment was completely empty; I had sold about six hundred items on eBay, another six hundred or so at a yard sale the week before, and I still had a few boxes of things left. I brought what I could to the local dump and put the remaining items into storage in various friends' basements.

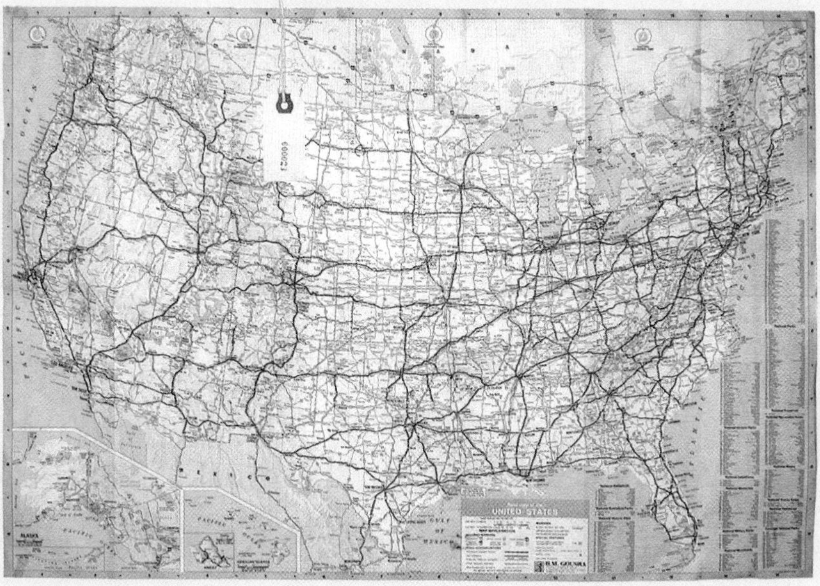

Tag # 000028
Map of USA
Auction ended: Jan-25-01
Cambridge, Massachusetts

85

I decided to start my trip in the Midwest and head east from there. The first visits seemed to go pretty well. I really liked the new owners of my things, and was happy to see that my objects were usually more prominently displayed and appreciated than they were when they were in my cluttered apartment. In the first leg of the trip, I tended to stay a few days in each place, trying to meet up with as many people as possible.

As I met more people, the awkwardness of meeting strangers started to wear off. I got comfortable staying in strangers' homes, meeting new people every day. Some might say too comfortable. By the end of the trip, I would help myself to food in the high bidder's refrigerator without a second thought. As I traveled, I posted daily updates on an online travelogue I created at temporama.com.

I was in the Northeast on September 11; in fact, I was in New York City. I had woken up at seven A.M. without an alarm at my friend Maya's house on Canal Street, and had decided to get an early start on my drive to Boston. At eight-forty-five I was sitting in traffic listening to WNYC somewhere just inside the Bronx on I-95. I listened to news radio during the entire four-hour drive to Boston, and by the time I arrived I was whipped up into the same panic that most of the country was in.

My last posting to Temporama was on September 10 from New York City, and I started to receive messages from random readers of Temporama—complete strangers—asking me if I was OK. Although I had been posting regularly to the travelogue, I guess I never really thought that people were reading what I wrote.

I suddenly realized that I wasn't alone on this journey, that many people were traveling along with me. I posted an update so that readers would know that I was OK, and then I tried to figure out what to do next.

I paused the trip for a few days, and eventually canceled my southern itinerary, heading back to Iowa to figure out whether I should continue. I contacted all the people who had invited me to visit and asked them if I was still invited under the current circumstances. Within a day or two, nearly everyone who had invited me to visit sent a new invitation.

I began my tour again, but the nature of my visits changed considerably as I continued. In the beginning, I would spend half my time trying to compose the right photograph of my former object. After September 11, I stopped caring so much about the objects that I was visiting and started caring more about the people who invited me. By the time I made it to Austin, Texas, I had been on the road for nearly three months and had slept on floors, couches, and lawns from coast to coast. The six thousand dollars that I'd made from selling nearly everything I owned had been spent on gas, car repairs, and heart-stopping food. After September 11, I always had a few hundred dollars with me in cash for emergency gas and lodging. While in Austin I started to spend that reserve, and I decided it was time to go home.

Although I hadn't made it to everyone who had invited me to visit, I knew that it was time to stop driving. That it was time to stop looking. I realized that

my sale had done far more than just provide me the means and the freedom to escape and start over. In fact, I no longer wanted to escape. I wanted to return to Iowa City and continue the life I'd started there. All too often in my life I had just picked up and left when things got difficult or overwhelming, and started over somewhere else. Upon returning to Iowa in November, I made a decision to finish my graduate study and to finally finish this project, which had gone on for more than a year. I had spent a year and a half contemplating the things that surrounded me, even after they were long gone. I no longer wanted to move to New York. I now knew that it was possible to engage the broader culture from somewhere besides a big city. After living out of the trunk of my car, location no longer seemed as relevant. I wanted a place to be grounded. I wanted to stop starting over.

COMMENT

"John Freyer personifies an American paradox. . . . He feels the need to collect, consume, and accumulate, and yet also desires a sense of urburdened freedom and the ability to travel at will."

— Will Helfrich, critic

D&D Auto Body Nylon Winter Jacket: Green nylon jacket with D&D AUTO BODY, UTICA NY in golden embroidery. Front snap closures and zip-down hood, yellow fuzz insulation, looks great. I purchased this jacket in Utica at the world's best Salvation Army. I once wore this jacket in an ice storm in Saratoga Springs, New York. The nylon was so slippery that I was able to slide down the entire length of Caroline Street on my stomach.

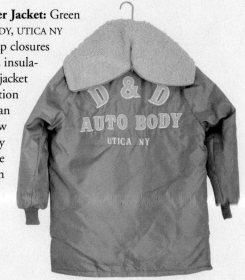

Tag # 000005
Final price: $15.77
Auction ended: Dec-24-00
Total bids: 15
Bellingham, Washington

Update: Ralph bought my only winter jacket in January of 2001. In one of the last e-mails that I received from him, he said that every time he watched the Weather Channel he felt a little guilty about buying my winter coat. That winter was one of the coldest on record in Iowa, with wind-chill factors averaging about twenty below zero for most of the month of January. Ralph was enrolled in auto-body-repair school last winter. I wonder if my jacket helped him pass his exams.

Jacket, Thesis, Fly-Fishing Patch, Bowling Shirt. Laid out as a catalog, each object in *All My Life for Sale* is displayed with the original description Freyer wrote about it on eBay, its final price, and an update telling us how it is now. The last thing to sell was the domain name, allmylifeforsale.com, which was bought by the University of Iowa, Museum of Art. These objects are taken from *All My Life for Sale*. (Copyright © 2002 by John D. Freyer. From *All My Life for Sale* by John D. Freyer. Reprinted by permission of Bloomsbury)

88

My Hamilton College Thesis: *Information Technologies and Their Role in Surveillance Societies.* This paper is a little out of date terminology-wise, but many of the predictions that I made in 1994 have been pretty right on. Back then I still called the Internet "the information superhighway," and most of my interactions with the Net came through the Gopher system and then Mosaic. The paper talks about how information technology is used to gather personal information in an effort to control people. I reviewed literature by Foucault and also looked at Jeremy Bentham's *Panopticon.* My current project, allmylifeforsale, is informed by my research into information technologies. Part of this project is to see what happens when all of the information collected about my spending patterns and the like is radically changed. If I no longer own the things that supposedly define the type of consumer that I am, will I still consume the same goods and services? Or should the telemarketers start to call the people who have bought my life? It's not a bad read if you can deal with the "information superhighway" language. I still have to thank Trey and Lanethea for proofreading this document.

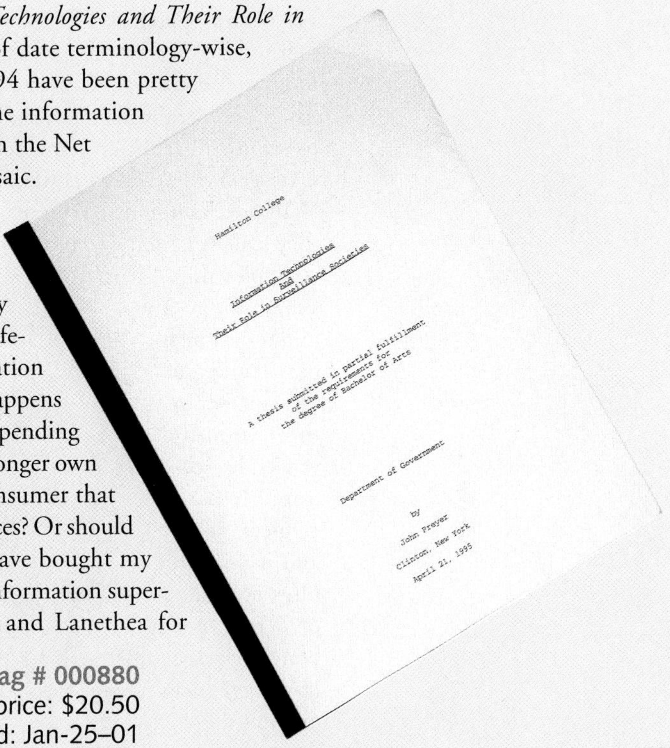

Tag # 000880
Final price: $20.50
Auction ended: Jan-25–01
Total bids: 14
New York, New York

Update: After I sold this on eBay I sent the auctions listing to my thesis adviser and to the president of Hamilton College. They both sent rather puzzled responses to my sale. I'm not sure they understood what I was up to, but neither did I at the time. The new owner, Skye, promised to read it. He must have, because I haven't heard from him since. Maybe he wrote the president of my college too, asking how they could have let me graduate.

Fly-Fishing Patch: When I was a kid my family used to spend a week each summer on the St. Lawrence River. Each year my father would try to entertain his four rambunctious boys by attempting to get them all to sit still long enough to fish. I never really liked to fish; it seemed a little pointless to me as a ten-year-old to stand still at the end of a dock and slowly reel in the line over and over and over again. I guess now I'd think it was meditative. My dad used to have his own "Bait of Champions." I'm not sure they will ever sell it in any championship bait shop, but you might be able to get it at your local market in the canned-vegetable section. He used canned corn, and it used to lure the smallest of mini-perch, bony rock bass, and if we were lucky a trout or two.

Tag # 000351
Final price: $13.50
Auction ended: Apr-27–01
Total bids: 15
Ridgefield, Washington

Update: I sent this to the same guy who bought my Spa City Rockers shirt. He said that even though he was disappointed with the shirt, he might hold on to the patch for a while before he throws it out.

90

Iranian Bowling Shirt: This is my most coveted bowling shirt. When I go bowling, I always bring my collection of bowling shirts, and this shirt is always the first to go. Only the closest of the close have ever worn this shirt. Trey found it for me in some thrift store in San Francisco, and it is from "New Show Pizza" in Tehran, Iran. I wonder if there is still a pizza joint in Tehran. I wore this shirt when I invented "The Butt Dance" at some Skidmore College art opening. The dance includes a slow hip gyration with your butt out to the right side a little for two beats and then to the left side for one beat. Something may tell you that I'm sort of a dork. . . .

Tag # 000244
Final price: $66.00
Auction ended: March-10–01
Total bids: 13
London, United Kingdom

Update: I talked to Trey today to see if he would read through the new text I have been working on for this book. He reminded me that about halfway through this project he really started to hate it. For a few months, talking to me was like having to read every page of my project twice: all my life, all the time. Also, as the project went on I started selling the things that I didn't really want to sell—the gifts that I received from friends and family, my cameras, and my books and catalogs. I guess I would hate a project where Trey sold off all the things that I ever gave him. I was wearing this shirt on the day that I went to the post office and received the English money order for the sixty-six-dollar bid.

■ **Discuss.** *Freyer admits at the beginning of this essay that he has pack-rat tendencies, and as readers we learn that his possessions, such as the Iranian bowling shirt, often have complicated histories even before they come into his hands. Would his project have worked if, instead of accumulating things from garage sales and thrift shops, he had bought them at retail stores? Would the stories of his objects have been less compelling? Would he have found a different "audience" for his site?*

■ **Write.** *If you had purchased something on Freyer's site, how do you think you would have responded to a request for a visit? Would you have invited him to your home, or would you have declined? In a few paragraphs, write a commentary on Freyer's project that would help explain your decision.*

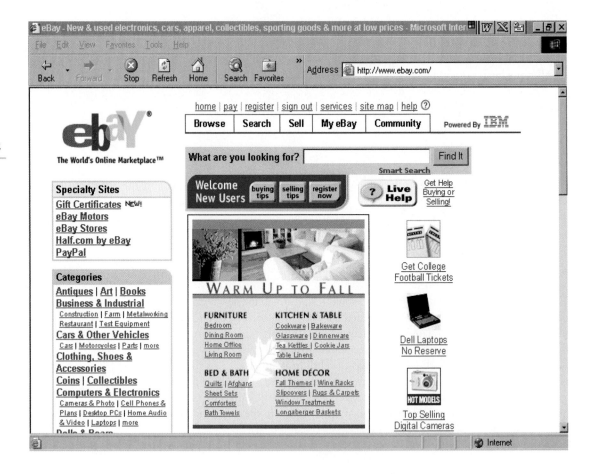

 CONSIDER THE CLUSTER
Our Stuff, Ourselves

■ **Message**

What would you say is the *meaning* of John Freyer's project? Economic? Spiritual? Artistic? Why does he call his project "all my life for sale" and not "all my things for sale"? What connections does he make between his life and his things? How did his undergraduate thesis provide him with the underlying concept for this project? What connections can you see between the point of his thesis (as he summarizes it in his essay) and the goal of his eBay project?

■ **Method**

The catalog format gives Freyer a methodology to follow: a clear picture of each object, with a description to the side and pertinent information prominently displayed. In an essay, closely examine Freyer's objects and his account of them and show how they provide you with a portrait of Freyer himself. In what ways do they project his identity and personality?

■ **Medium**

Why is eBay so important to Freyer's project? What does it enable him to do? What connections do you see between Freyer's project and a work of art? What connections does he suggest? Do you think that Freyer discovered his project as he proceeded to sell his stuff or that he began the project with the clear idea that it would become both a book and a kind of art exhibit? Why do you think allmylifeforsale.com was purchased by an art museum and not by a retailer?

93

◀ **eBay.** Since its start in 1995, eBay has become the most profitable site for web commerce. According to the site, "The eBay Community is made up of more than 100 million people around the world who buy and sell in the eBay marketplace. Users include individual buyers and sellers, small businesses, and even enterprises. From the buyer who shops on eBay for practical needs or for fun, to the seller who relies on eBay as a primary source of income, eBay becomes a part of members' lives." As John Freyer showed, people buy and sell almost everything on the site: collectibles, clothing, kitchen sinks. University of Iowa professor Kendrew McLeod even sold his soul in a four-ounce glass jar for $1,300. (These materials have been reproduced with the permission of eBay Inc. © 2008 eBay Inc. All Rights Reserved.)

YOU ARE WHAT YOU EAT

ESSAY | LISTS | 2 PHOTO ESSAYS | BRIEF ARGUMENT

■ **Cluster menu: You Are What You Eat**

94

To what extent is our personal identity linked to our food preferences and eat-ing habits? How literally should we take the old expression "You are what you eat"? That saying dates back to *The Physiology of Taste*, a famous book on food by the French culinary author Jean Anthelme Brillat-Savarin (1755–1826), who wrote: "Tell me what you eat, and I shall tell you what you are." The populariza-tion of the expression first appeared in a 1942 self-help book by Victor Lindlahr, *You Are What You Eat: How to Win and Keep Health with Diet*. That this belief has long persisted can be seen in the provocative twist given to it by a recent food expert, Amanda Hesser, who opens her essay "Shop Write" by saying: "If you are what you eat, then you are also what you buy to eat." She then proceeds to infer information about the identities of people based on their shopping lists.

Leigh Belanger, a reporter from the *Boston Globe,* also practices what she calls "food anthropology," as she tries to characterize people by using the con-tents of their refrigerators. "Our refrigerators tell us a lot about ourselves," Belanger claims. Try it yourself: study the photographs of eight open refrigerators on pages 100–103 and see if you can match the individual to the food.

Amanda Hesser, *Shop Write*. A 1993 graduate of Bentley College, Amanda Hesser (b. 1971) earned a culinary degree from a prestigious French cooking school in 1997. The author of *The Cook and the Gardener* (1999) and *Cooking for Mr. Latte* (2003), she is the food editor at *The New York Times Magazine* and writes regularly on food, wine, and entertainment. Hesser has said that her writing has tried "to capture that real-life slice of how we live and how we really eat, how we really cook, with all the flaws and sort of satisfaction bundled into one." "Shop Write" appeared in *The New York Times Magazine* on October 10, 2004. (Lists from Bill Keaggy/grocerylists.org)

Amanda Hesser
SHOP WRITE

■ **Consider before you read.** *Hesser uses the grocery lists collected on Bill Keaggy's site to make inferences about the individuals who wrote them and, more generally, about American culture. Do you find some of her claims more persuasive than others? Are the lists more revealing when studied separately or as a group?*

If you are what you eat, then you are also what you buy to eat. And mostly what people buy is scrawled onto a grocery list, those ethereal scraps of paper that record the shorthand of where we shop and how we feed ourselves. Most grocery lists end up in the garbage. But if you live in St. Louis, they might have a half-life you never imagined: as a cultural document, posted on the Internet.

For the past decade, Bill Keaggy, 33, the features photo editor at *The St. Louis Post-Dispatch,* has been collecting grocery lists and since 1999 has been posting them online at www.grocerylists.org. The collection, which now numbers more than 500 lists, is strangely addictive.

The lists elicit twofold curiosity—about the kind of meal the person was planning and the kind of person who would make such a meal. What was the shopper with vodka, lighters, milk and ice cream on his list planning to do with them? In what order would they be consumed? Was it a he or a she? Who had written "Tootie food, kitten chow, bird food stick, toaster scrambles, coffee drinks"? Some shoppers organize their lists by aisle; others start with dairy, go to cleaning supplies and then back to dairy before veering off to Home Depot. A few meticulous ones note the price of every item. One shopper had written in large letters on an envelope, simply, "Milk."

The thin lines of ink and pencil jutting and looping across crinkled and torn pieces of paper have a purely graphic beauty. One of life's most banal duties, viewed through the curatorial lens, can somehow seem pregnant with possibility. It can even appear poetic, as in the list that reads "meat, cigs, buns, treats."

95

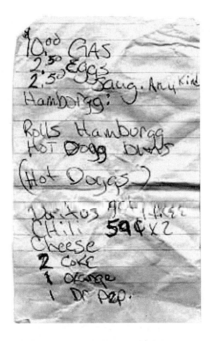

One thing Keaggy discovered is that Dan Quayle is not alone—few people can spell bananas and bagels, let alone potato.[1] One list calls for "suchi" and "strimp." "Some people pass judgment on the things they buy," Keaggy says. At the end of one list, the shopper wrote "Bud Light" and then "good beer." Another scribbled "good loaf of white bread." Some pass judgment on themselves, like the shopper who wrote "read, stay home or go somewhere, I act like my mom, go to Kentucky, underwear, lemon."

People send messages to one another, too. Buried in one list is this statement: "If you buy more rice, I'll punch you." And plenty of shoppers, like the one with both ice cream and diet pills on the list, reveal their vices.

Keaggy has always been a collector and recorder. When he was young, it was rocks and key chains. As a teenager, he published zines on freestyle biking and punk rock. These were just a warm-up. His collection of rocks in the shapes of shoes has been featured at the St. Louis Artists' Guild. And in addition to his grocery-list web site, he has an extensive personal web site, www.keaggy.com (the grocery lists can be found from here). At keaggy.com, there is a segment called "What's for Dinner?" Every time you click it, a new dining haiku appears. There is a sandwich web log, to which he adds photos of the sandwiches he eats every day during National Sandwich Month (August). A page called "mageirevo"

> ■ **Consider.** *Keaggy's collections and efforts at recording daily life are widely varied. Do they reveal any common concerns or interests on the part of their compiler? Like John Freyer's allmylifeforsale.com, Keaggy's collections have also reached audiences that might be surprising. Why do you think the St. Louis Artists' Guild was interested in his work?*

---

[1] *potato:* In 1992, Vice President Dan Quayle made headlines when he spelled *potato* wrong (he spelled it *potatoe*) while visiting a New Jersey sixth-grade classroom.—ED.

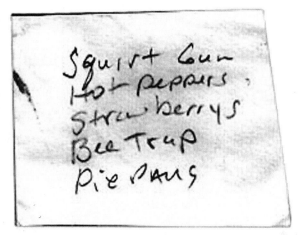

features "incredibly vague recipes," including one for "happy fun pork time," and a page called "found in the street" is dedicated to junk (not what he calls it) that he found when he biked to work from May 1 to May 31. And in "age: 30," Keaggy posts photos he took of himself every day of his thirty-first year, along with a brief description of what he was doing that day, which is almost as addictive as the grocery lists.

Keaggy finds most of his grocery lists at Schnucks, a regional chain with a branch down the street from his home. (Some lists have been sent in by a cashier at a grocery store in Iowa and someone in Tucson who once collected grocery lists.) Keaggy spots the lists in grocery carts, mostly, and sometimes in the checkout line or on shelves. "The funny thing is you never find them on the ground," he says. "On the best day, I'll find two or three, and on a bad day I'll find zero."

As a group, the lists are an enlightening barometer of eating and shopping trends, as well as of attitudes toward food. Almost none of them include fresh herbs, but cumin is surprisingly common. Evaporated milk is still popular, and feta is increasingly so. . . . Many shoppers are brand loyal: Swiffer, the disposable floor-mopping sheet, is doing a bang-up business in the heartland. And Parkay and Cool Whip are alive and well.

Except for one list, which includes everything from pigs in a blanket and "block cheese" to salmon and anchovy fillets, most lists fall into one of two categories. They seem to have been compiled either by foodies or by convenience junkies. This growing divide has been discussed in the food industry for nearly a decade, but no statistics have measured it. In these lists, however, the gap is as clear as day. A number of people simply write "food," as if it were like getting gas or picking up dry cleaning.

97

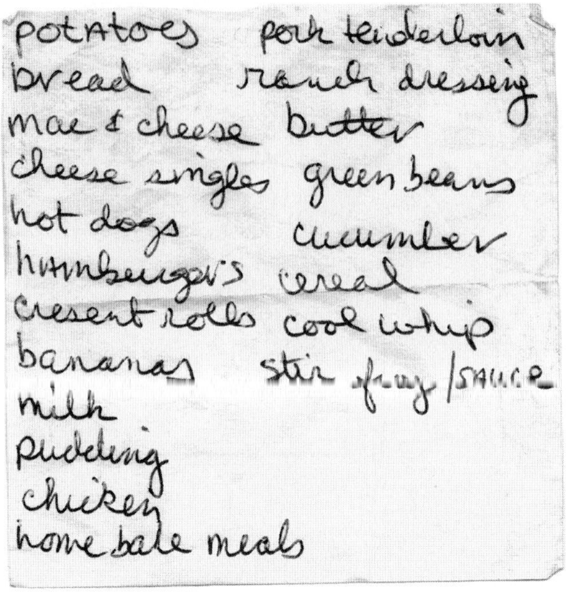

potatoes   pork tenderloin
bread   ranch dressing
mac & cheese butter
cheese singles green beans
hot dogs   cucumber
hamburgers cereal
cresent rolls cool whip
bananas   stir fry/sauce
milk
pudding
chicken
home bake meals

"You can see their lives from these lists even if you haven't been in their houses," Keaggy says.

Which bodes poorly for the individual who wrote: "Shell corn, bind holder, belt, knife, coolers, map, cellphone, hunting license, say good-bye to wife, kill deer, Mt. View Motel, kill deer."

■ **Discuss.** *Hesser discusses how grocery lists reveal trends in American culture. How would you expect these trends to develop in the next ten years? What items would you expect to see more often? What items do you think might disappear?*

■ **Write.** *Choose one of the lists reproduced here and write a short essay about the person who wrote it. What is the person like? What kind of day is he or she planning? Does the list represent everyday shopping? A special occasion? Is there anything on the list you have trouble fitting into your narrative?*

Leigh Belanger, *What's in Your Fridge?* Leigh Belanger is a Boston-based freelance journalist, a correspondent for *The Boston Globe*, and a member of the communications staff for the Chef's Collaborative and its online guide (chef2chef.net). A graduate of Evergreen State College in Olympia, Washington, Belanger is currently working toward her MA in food studies at Boston University. The following photo essay originally appeared in the Food section of *The Boston Globe* (February 28, 2007) with the original title "Refrigerators Are Packed with Clues about How We Live." Belanger argues: "Open any refrigerator and you can tell how its users live." To write the following piece, she investigated eight refrigerators in seven different households. "Call it food anthropology," she says. (Refrigerators A, C, D, E, and F by Erik Jacobs/Jacobs Photographic. Refrigerator B by Zara Tzanev.)

Leigh Belanger
WHAT'S IN YOUR FRIDGE?

99

■ **Consider before you read.** *Which items in these refrigerators are most revealing of their owners? Which are common enough that they don't seem to say much about the people who bought them? Does the model or the condition of the refrigerator itself tell you anything?*

Our refrigerators tell a lot about ourselves. Some are filled with the makings of a week's worth of meals; others hold only a yogurt and Fluffy's can of cat food. In some, the brands, amounts, and locations of milk and eggs never change. In others, you'll find little more than crusty ketchup, a loaf of bread, and a half-stick of butter.

Some people pack their lunches in advance and stack them in the fridge. Others shop and cook on a whim, filling their refrigerator with specialty foods and perishables. Kids' juices and snacks, a special brand of Latino soda, apples neatly lined up in rows, maybe even prescription drugs, camera film, or nail polish—all this could be in the fridge. The dynamic changes as life goes on: Households with children devote less space to beer; teens may claim space for vegetarian or low-fat items; empty nesters suddenly have space they never dreamed of once the kids are in college; pet foods claim their space, too.

We recently rummaged through a few refrigerators around Greater Boston to see what we could learn. You can take a look, too.

You Are What You Eat

■ **Quiz: Whose fridge is this?** *What do refrigerators—and the foods and beverages in them—hint at about their owners? About their owners' tastes? Lifestyles? Backgrounds? Try matching the profiles of these people with the refrigerators (shown on pp. 100–103) found in their kitchens.*

Profiles of refrigerator owners:

Robin Amer, Cambridge, MA. A public radio announcer, Amer has two roommates, and all cook and shop regularly for themselves and the household.

Sheila Fiekowsky, Waban, MA. A violinist for the BSO, she cooks most days for three adults, one teen, and a college child on breaks.

Sirlene Freitas, Revere, MA. This homemaker cooks daily for five adults and three children, ages 3 to 8, and stores food in not one, but two refrigerators.

Dante Funes, Boston, MA. A personal chef, he cooks daily for himself and his partner, even storing lunches for the next day.

Theresa Pieri, Waltham, MA. A senior at Bentley College, she and her roommate cook regularly and prefer low-fat meals.

Crystal Thompson, Jamaica Plain, MA. A financial consultant, she cooks nightly for herself, her husband, and their four children, ages 4 to 12.

100

Fridge A

Goya guava paste

Canned food, opened and unopened

Nine bottles of soda, including guarana

This fridge belongs to _____.

Fridge B

Sweet-potato, peanut-butter Thai curry sauce

Four varieties of nondairy milk, including organic chocolate almond

Six quarts of homemade vegetable soup

This fridge belongs to _____.

Fridge C

101

Egg Beaters, low-fat milk, low-fat mayonnaise, and low-fat sour cream

Empty plastic cup

Two whole chickens

This fridge belongs to _____.

You Are What You Eat

Fridge D

Open can of Fancy Feast

La Lechera

Plastic containers of beef stew, couscous salad, and tomato-fennel soup

This fridge belongs to _____.

Fridge E

Smucker's strawberry jelly

A plastic container of poached chicken in broth

In the crisper drawer, a bag of moldy mini pancakes and a bag of nail polishes

This fridge belongs to _____.

Fridge F

Fat-free cheese slices, fat-free Jell-O, and fat-free yogurt

A box of wine, Bud Lights, and Bailey's Irish Cream

A bottle of protein water

This fridge belongs to _____.

Answer Key

Fridge A. Sirlene Freitas, Revere, MA. Freitas's grandson likes to eat Goya guava paste from the can with sliced mozzarella. She keeps canned food, opened and unopened, in the fridge. It's a habit from her native Brazil. One shelf holds nine bottles of soda including the Brazilian guarana favored by the family.

Fridge B. Robin Amer, Cambridge, MA. Amer's fridge stores "some sweet-potato peanut-butter Thai curry sauce" she made. It also holds four varieties of nondairy milk, including organic chocolate almond.

Fridge C. Crystal Thompson, Jamaica Plain, MA. Thompson and her husband watch their cholesterol, so she buys Egg Beaters, low-fat milk, mayonnaise, and sour cream. An empty plastic cup was left on a shelf inside by their 6-year-old, who recently learned to help himself to items in the refrigerator. Two whole chickens on the bottom of the shelf will be stewed for Sunday supper.

Fridge D. Dante Funes, Boston, MA. Funes hates open cans in the fridge, but makes an exception for his cat's Fancy Feast. La Lechera is a sweetened and condensed milk that Funes puts in his coffee or uses to make a dessert called tres leches. On the second shelf is a stack of dishes Funes made for his partner to bring to work—beef stew, couscous salad, and tomato-fennel soup.

Fridge E. Sheila Fiekowsky, Waban, MA. Smucker's strawberry jelly is on the top shelf. "Always jelly," says Fiekowsky. "That's all they'll eat." The Tupperware container of poached chicken in broth (on the second right-hand shelf) is for Boccherini, the family's ailing 13-year-old Wheaton terrier. In the crisper drawer, Fiekowsky is horrified to find a bag of moldy mini pancakes she missed when cleaning. A bag of nail polishes is in there, too.

Fridge F. Theresa Pieri, Waltham, MA. Fat-free cheese slices, fat-free Jell-O, and fat-free yogurt. Pieri says she's eating more carefully. "Last semester I kind of ate whatever I wanted." There's some standard college booze—a box of wine, Bud Lights, Bailey's Irish Cream, also a bottle of "weird protein water." Pieri says, "It came with my cereal."

■ **Discuss.** *How many people were you able to correctly match with their refrigerators? For those that you missed, what contents might have been misleading?*

■ **Write.** *Without looking at your own refrigerator, write a few paragraphs about what its contents would say about you. Then open up the fridge and make a detailed list of what you see. Does the actual list match up to your subjective interpretation? Do you find any surprises?*

Lauren Greenfield, *The Food Court*. In these two photos, Lauren Greenfield documents the food courts around Los Angeles and the people who gather there. Greenfield grew up in Venice, California; her photographic documentary on coming of age in Los Angeles, *Fast Forward* (1997), was followed by a study of the different aspects of growing up female in America, *Girl Culture* (2002). Her photographs have appeared in many major magazines, including *Time, Newsweek, Vanity Fair, Life, and The New York Times Magazine.* These images first appeared in the January 2004 issue of *Los Angeles*. (© 2004 Lauren Greenfield)

■ **Consider before you read and view.** *Why do you think Greenfield chooses to photograph food courts instead of, for example, restaurants? How would you describe the food court as a public space? How are people expected to behave there?*

105

Lauren Greenfield, *Penny Wolfe and daughter Jessica, at the Manchu Wok at Santa Monica Place.*

Lauren Greenfield, *Hot Dog on a Stick employees Dominique King and Wendy Recinos at Baldwin Hills Crenshaw Plaza.*

■ **Discuss.** *Greenfield's subjects generally do not seem to notice her presence. Discuss how the candid nature of these photographs affects the way the viewer understands their subjects and their purpose. How would the images be different if the food court diners were looking into the camera?*

■ **Write.** *Compare Greenfield's photo of Penny and Jessica Wolfe with that of Dominique King and Wendy Recinos, the employees at Hot Dog on a Stick. Describe the tone of each photo and consider closely the way Greenfield portrays food and drink in these images. If we are what we eat (and drink), what do these photos say about us as a culture? About American food and identity? Also, what commentary does Greenfield convey about family relationships? About the lives (and work lives) of teens? About the mall as a center of American life? Be sure to draw on specific details from the images to support your argument.*

Michael Pollan, *We Are What We Eat*. Michael Pollan is the author of *The Omnivore's Dilemma: A Natural History of Four Meals* (2006, Penguin Press HC) on the ethics and ecology of eating and *The Botany of Desire: A Plant's Eye View of the World* (2001, Random House). Pollan is Knight Professor of Journalism at the University of California at Berkeley and a contributing writer for *The New York Times Magazine*. The following text is an edited excerpt from a speech he delivered in January 2005 at the Ecological Farming Conference in Asilomar, California.

Michael Pollan
WE ARE WHAT WE EAT

■ **Consider before you read.** *Pollan points out that the great majority of calories Americans consume come from the same source. What reasons does he give for this phenomenon? What potential problems does he identify?*

If you are what you eat, and especially if you eat industrial food, as 99 percent of Americans do, what you are is corn. During the last year I've been following a bushel of corn through the industrial food system. What I keep finding in case after case, if you follow the food back to the farm—if you follow the nutrients, if you follow the carbon—you end up in a corn field in Iowa, over and over and over again.

■ **Consider.** *What does Pollan mean by "industrial food"? If it is so common, where could you find alternatives?*

    Take a typical fast food meal. Corn is the sweetener in the soda. It's in the corn-fed beef Big Mac patty, and in the high-fructose syrup in the bun, and in the secret sauce. Slim Jims are full of corn syrup, dextrose, cornstarch, and a great many additives. The "four different fuels" in a Lunchables meal are all essentially corn-based. The chicken nugget—including feed for the chicken, fillers, binders, coating, and dipping sauce—is all corn. The french fries are made from potatoes, but odds are they're fried in corn oil, the source of 50 percent of their calories. Even the salads at McDonald's are full of high-fructose corn syrup and thickeners made from corn.

Corn is the keystone species of the industrial food system, along with its side-kick, soybeans, with which it shares a rotation on most of the farms in the Midwest. I'm really talking about cheap corn—overproduced, subsidized, industrial corn— the biggest legal cash crop in America. Eighty million acres—an area twice the size of New York State—is blanketed by a vast corn monoculture like a second great American lawn.

I believe very strongly that our overproduction of cheap grain in general, and corn in particular, has a lot to do with the fact that three-fifths of Americans are now overweight. The obesity crisis is complicated in some ways, but it's very simple in another way. Basically, Americans are on average eating 200 more calories a day than they were in the 1970s. If you do that and don't get correspondingly more exercise, you're going to get a lot fatter. Many demographers are predicting that this is the first generation of Americans whose life span may be shorter than their parents'. The reason for that is obesity, essentially, and diabetes specifically.

■ **Discuss.** *Are you surprised by the sameness underlying the apparent variety of foods from which Americans can choose? Discuss what might be causing this trend in the food industry. What are some possible solutions to the problem?*

■ **Write.** *What objections might be made to Pollan's analysis? For example, how would a corn farmer respond? Write a few paragraphs outlining arguments against Pollan's position. Then determine the grounds for these objections. Are they primarily economic, scientific, or cultural?*

 CONSIDER THE CLUSTER
You Are What You Eat

■ Message

In an essay, examine Brillat-Savarin's famous statement: "Tell me what you eat, and I shall tell you what you are." How do you interpret the remark? How would you apply it to someone—a friend, a parent, yourself? In your essay, take a close look at what you or someone you know eats for a day and decide if that evidence provides a reliable insight into your subject's identity.

■ Method

In logic and philosophy, the method of deducting one thing by means of examining another is usually called "making an inference." Both Amanda Hesser and Leigh Belanger make inferences about people based on their shopping lists and the contents of their refrigerators. In an in-class exercise, comment on the validity of these inferences. Do you think they are mainly humorous, or do you think they make sense? For example, if detectives discovered a shopping list dropped by the culprit at a crime scene, do you think they could form a reasonable depiction of the probable criminal?

■ Medium

Amanda Hesser notes that shopping lists can "have a purely graphic beauty" when "viewed through the curatorial lens." Consider what she is suggesting here about throwaway scraps of paper. In what ways do you think a shopping list can be considered a type of medium? Examine the lists reproduced in this chapter: What do they have in common? Do you think anyone would consciously create a shopping list intended as a work of art? What might such a work look like? How might someone "design" a shopping list?

WHAT'S IN A NAME?

110

"What's in a name?" asks Shakespeare's Juliet in one of literature's best-known passages: "That which we call a rose / By any other word would smell as sweet." But when it comes to our own personal names, why do so many of us consider them so vitally important? Why should it matter if our name is Britanny, Emily, Ellen, Grace, Ruth, Katrina, Irma, or Juliet? Wouldn't we be the same person in any case? Can our name affect who we are? Can it serve as a form of self-depiction?

These questions intrigued the authors of the best-selling *Freakonomics*, Steven D. Levitt and Stephen J. Dubner. In one chapter of that book, they examine the economic dynamics that cause certain first names to become extremely popular while leaving others sounding dull and unfashionable. Names may tell us more about our parent's aspirations than our own identities.

Whether fashionable or not, names can also be a source of cultural anxiety for those in this country who speak languages other than English and find their names consistently mispronounced or intentionally Americanized. This phenomenon is a common experience to Mexicans, as Manuel Muñoz writes in "Leave Your Name at the Border." "Ours," he says, "were names that stood as barriers to a complete embrace of an American identity, simply because their pronunciations required a slip into Spanish, the otherness that assimilation was supposed to erase. What to do with names like Amado, Lucio, or Élida? There are no English 'equivalents.'"

Perhaps no single American site displays the power of names more dramatically than the Vietnam Veterans Memorial in Washington, D.C. In "Between Art and Architecture," the monument's now-celebrated architect, Maya Lin, explains in her own words why individual names had to play such a central role in her design.

111

Greg Klee, *William, Bill, Billy.* Greg Klee is a designer and illustrator for *The Boston Globe.* This image appeared in the *Globe* on January 9, 2005, with an article on "onomastics," the study of proper nouns. (Reprinted by permission of *The Boston Globe*)

Manuel Muñoz, *Leave Your Name at the Border*. The author of two short-story collections, *Zigzagger* (2003) and *The Faith Healer of Olive Avenue* (2007), Manuel Muñoz has received a Constance Saltonstall Foundation Individual Artist's Grant in Fiction. His writing has been featured on National Public Radio's *Selected Shorts*. A native of Dinuba, California, Muñoz—who graduated from Harvard University and holds an MFA in creative writing from Cornell University—currently lives in New York City. His web site is manuel-munoz.com.

Manuel Muñoz

LEAVE YOUR NAME AT THE BORDER

■ **Consider before you read.** *In the past, how were immigrants' names altered when they came to America—either by the choice of the individual or by officials at places such as Ellis Island? How have these practices changed? Is the pressure still strong to have an "American-sounding" name?*

At the Fresno airport, as I made my way to the gate, I heard a name over the intercom. The way the name was pronounced by the gate agent made me want to see what she looked like. That is, I wanted to see whether she was Mexican. Around Fresno, identity politics rarely deepen into exacting terms, so to say "Mexican" means, essentially, "not white." The slivered self-identifications Chicano, Hispanic, Mexican-American, and Latino are not part of everyday life in the Valley. You're either Mexican or you're not. If someone wants to know if you were born in Mexico, they'll ask. Then you're From Over There—de allá. And leave it at that.

The gate agent, it turned out, was Mexican. Well-coiffed, in her 30s, she wore foundation that was several shades lighter than the rest of her skin. It was the kind of makeup job I've learned to silently identify at the mall when I'm with my mother, who will say nothing about it until we're back in the car. Then she'll stretch her neck like an ostrich and point to the darkness of her own skin, wondering aloud why women try to camouflage who they are.

I watched the Mexican gate agent busy herself at the counter, professional and studied. Once again, she picked up the microphone and, with authority, announced the name of the missing customer: "Eugenio Reyes, please come to the front desk."

You can probably guess how she said it. Her Anglicized pronunciation wouldn't be unusual in a place like California's Central Valley. I didn't have a Mexican name there either: I was an instruction guide.

When people ask me where I'm from, I say Fresno because I don't expect them to know little Dinuba. Fresno is a booming city of nearly 500,000 these days, with a diversity—white, Mexican, African-American, Armenian, Hmong, and Middle Eastern people are all well represented—that shouldn't surprise anyone. It's in the small towns like Dinuba that surround Fresno that the awareness of cultural difference is stripped down to the interactions between the only two groups that tend to live there: whites and Mexicans. When you hear a Mexican name spoken in these towns, regardless of the speaker's background, it's no wonder that there's an "English way of pronouncing it."

I was born in 1972, part of a generation that learned both English and Spanish. Many of my cousins and siblings are bilingual, serving as translators for those in the family whose English is barely functional. Others have no way of following the Spanish banter at family gatherings. You can tell who falls into which group: Estella, Eric, Delia, Dubina, Melanie.

It's intriguing to watch "American" names begin to dominate among my nieces and nephews and second cousins, as well as with the children of my hometown friends. I am not surprised to meet 5-year-old Brandon or Kaitlyn. Hardly anyone questions the incongruity of matching these names with last names like Trujillo or Zepeda. The English-only way of life partly explains the quiet erasure of cultural difference that assimilation has attempted to accomplish. A name like Kaitlyn Zepeda doesn't completely obscure her ethnicity, but the half-step of her name, as a gesture, is almost understandable.

Spanish was and still is viewed with suspicion: always the language of the vilified illegal immigrant, it segregated schoolchildren into English-only and bilingual programs; it defined you, above all else, as part of a lower class. Learning English, though, brought its own complications with identity. It was simultaneously the language of the white population and a path toward the richer, expansive identity of "American." But it took getting out of the Valley for me to understand that "white" and "American" were two very different things.

Something as simple as saying our names "in English" was our unwittingly complicit gesture of trying to blend in. Pronouncing Mexican names correctly was never encouraged. Names like Daniel, Olivia, and Marco slipped right into the mutability of the English language.

I remember a school ceremony at which the mathematics teacher, a white man, announced the names of Mexican students correctly and caused some confusion, if not embarrassment. Years later we recognized that he spoke in deference to our Spanish-speaking parents in the audience, caring teacher that he was.

■ Consider. *Why would the correct pronunciations embarrass the students?*

These were difficult names for a non-Spanish speaker: Araceli, Nadira, Luis (a beautiful name when you glide the *u* and the *i* as you're supposed to). We had been accustomed to having our birth names altered for convenience. Concepción was Connie. Ramón was Raymond. My cousin Esperanza was Hope—but her name was pronounced "Hopie" because any Spanish speaker would automatically pronounce the *e* at the end.

Ours, then, were names that stood as barriers to a complete embrace of an American identity, simply because their pronunciations required a slip into Spanish, the otherness that assimilation was supposed to erase. What to do with names like Amado, Lucio, or Élida? There are no English "equivalents," no answer when white teachers asked, "What does your name mean?" when what they really wanted to know was "What's the English one?" So what you heard was a name butchered beyond recognition, a pronunciation that pointed the finger at the Spanish language as the source of clunky sound and ugly rhythm.

My stepfather, from Ojos de Agua, Mexico, jokes when I ask him about the names of Mexicans born here. He deliberately stumbles over pronunciations, imitating our elders who have difficulty with Bradley and Madelyn. "Ashley Sánchez. ¿Tú crees?" He wonders aloud what has happened to the "nombres del rancho"—traditional Mexican names that are hardly given anymore to children born in the States: Heraclio, Madaleno, Otilia, Dominga.

My stepfather's experience with the Anglicization of his name—Antonio to Tony—ties into something bigger than learning English. For him, the erasure of his name was about deference and subservience. Becoming Tony gave him a measure of access as he struggled to learn English and get more fieldwork.

This isn't to say that my stepfather welcomed the change, only that he could not put up much resistance. Not changing put him at risk of being passed over for work. English was a world of power and decisions, of smooth, uninterrupted negotiation. There was no time to search for the right word while a shop clerk waited for him to come up with the English name of the correct part needed out in the field. Clear communication meant you could go unsupervised, or that you were even able to read instructions directly off a piece of paper. Every gesture made toward convincing an employer that English was on its way to being mastered had the potential to make a season of fieldwork profitable.

It's curious that many of us growing up in Dinuba adhered to the same rules. Although as children of farm workers we worked in the fields at an early age, we'd also had the opportunity to stay in one town long enough to finish school. Most of us had learned English early and splintered off into a dual existence of English at school, Spanish at home. But instead of recognizing the need for fluency in both languages, we turned it into a peculiar kind of battle. English was for public display. Spanish was for privacy—and privacy quickly turned to shame.

■ **Consider.** *What does Muñoz mean by "corrosive effect"?*

The corrosive effect of assimilation is the displacement of one culture over another, the inability to sustain more than one way of being. It isn't a code word

114

115

David Heatley, *Luis.* David Heatley is a comic book author, illustrator, designer, painter, sculptor, filmmaker, and musician. This illustration originally appeared with Manuel Muñoz's essay in *The New York Times* on August 1, 2007. For more on David Heatley, go to davidheatley.com. (Reprinted by permission of David Heatley)

for racial and ethnic acculturation only. It applies to needing and wanting to belong, of seeing from the outside and wondering how to get in and then, once inside, realizing there are always those still on the fringe.

When I went to college on the East Coast, I was confronted for the first time by people who said my name correctly without prompting; if they stumbled, there was a quick apology and an honest plea to help with the pronunciation. But introducing myself was painful: already shy, I avoided meeting people because I didn't want to say my name, felt burdened by my own history. I knew that my small-town upbringing and its limitations on Spanish would not have been tolerated by any of the students of color who had grown up in large cities, in places where the sheer force of their native languages made them dominant in their neighborhoods.

It didn't take long for me to assert the power of code switching in public, the transferring of words from one language to another, regardless of who might be listening. I was learning that the English language composed new meanings when its constrictions were ignored, crossed over, or crossed out. Language is all about manipulation, or not listening to the rules.

When I come back to Dinuba, I have a hard time hearing my name said incorrectly, but I have an even harder time beginning a conversation with others about why the pronunciation of our names matters. Leaving a small town requires an embrace of a larger point of view, but a town like Dinuba remains forever embedded in an either/or way of life. My stepfather still answers to Tony and, as the United States–born children grow older, their Anglicized names begin to signify who does and who does not "belong"—who was born here and who is de allá.

My name is Manuel. To this day, most people cannot say it correctly, the way it was intended to be said. But I can live with that because I love the alliteration of my full name. It wasn't the name my mother, Esmeralda, was going to give me. At the last minute, my father named me after an uncle I would never meet. My name was to have been Ricardo. Growing up in Dinuba, I'm certain I would have become Ricky or even Richard, and the journey toward the discovery of the English language's extraordinary power in even the most ordinary of circumstances would probably have gone unlearned.

I count on a collective sense of cultural loss to once again swing the names back to our native language. The Mexican gate agent announced Eugenio Reyes, but I never got a chance to see who appeared. I pictured an older man, cowboy hat in hand, but I made the assumption on his name alone, the clash of privileges I imagined between someone de allá and a Mexican woman with a good job in the United States. Would she speak to him in Spanish? Or would she raise her voice to him as if he were hard of hearing?

But who was I to imagine this man being from anywhere, based on his name alone? At a place of arrivals and departures, it sank into me that the currency of our names is a stroke of luck: because mine was not an easy name, it

Consider. *What is the significance for Muñoz of the correct pronunciation of names?*

116

Consider. *What is the author's purpose behind the anecdote about Eugenio Reyes and the woman gate agent?*

forced me to consider how language would rule me if I allowed it. Yet I discovered that only by leaving. My stepfather must live in the Valley, a place that does not allow that choice, every day. And Eugenio Reyes—I do not know if he was coming or going.

■ **Discuss.** *Is having two different pronunciations for a name like having two different names? Muñoz points out that this duality can sometimes separate your life into public and private realms. Discuss how having two ways of saying a name could affect people in school and beyond.*

■ **Write.** *What is lost when names pass out of use? Choose your own first name or that of someone in your family to write about. Is there any family heritage or tradition attached to it? If this name were no longer given to children, would those connections disappear? Are names less likely to bear this kind of significance now than they were a hundred years ago?*

117

Steven D. Levitt and Stephen J. Dubner are coauthors of *Freakonomics: A Rogue Economist Explores the Hidden Side of Everything* (2006, William Morrow), an international best seller (with 1.5 million copies sold in the United States alone); winner of the Quill Award for best business book, a Visionary Award from the National Council on Economic Education, and BookSense Book of the Year; and named as a Notable Book of 2005 by *The New York Times*. Levitt and Dubner currently write a monthly "Freakonomics" column for *The New York Times Magazine* and maintain freakonomics.com, a site that has been referred to as "the most readable economics blog in the universe." The following essay is an excerpt from *Freakonomics* that appeared on *Slate.com* on April 15, 2005.

Steven D. Levitt is a thirty-seven-year-old midwestern father of four who has been described as a self-effacing genius. An editor at *The Wall Street Journal* once said about Levitt: "If Indiana Jones were an economist, he'd be Steven Levitt." Levitt takes an intuitive approach to economics and uses data and measurement to make sense of the world.

Stephen J. Dubner has worked as an editor and writer for *New York Magazine* and *The New York Times Magazine* and as a writer for *The New Yorker*, *Time*, and *The Washington Post*. He has also been a PBS correspondent and is a contributor to ABC News. He is the author of *Confessions of a Hero-Worshiper* (2003, William Morrow), *Turbulent Souls: A Catholic Son's Return to His Jewish Family* (1998, William Morrow), and a forthcoming children's book, *The Boy with Two Belly Buttons*. Dubner lives in New York City.

Steven D. Levitt and Stephen J. Dubner

TRADING UP: WHERE DO BABY NAMES COME FROM?

Stephen J. Dubner

■ **Consider before you read.** *When parents name their children, what factors affect their decision? What hopes or expectations might their choice reveal? Where do they look to find names that will suit their vision of their children's future?*

The actual source of a name is usually obvious: There's the Bible, there's the huge cluster of traditional English and Germanic and Italian and French names, there are princess names and hippie names, nostalgic names and place names. Increasingly, there are brand names (Lexus, Armani, Bacardi, Timberland) and what might be called aspirational names. The California data show eight Harvards born during the 1990s (all of them black), 15 Yales (all white), and 18 Princetons (all black). There were no Doctors but three Lawyers (all black), nine Judges (eight of them white), three Senators (all white), and two Presidents (both black).

But how does a name migrate through the population, and why? Is it purely a matter of zeitgeist, or is there a more discernible pattern to these movements?

Consider the 10 most popular names given to white girls in California in 1980 and then in 2000. A single holdover: Sarah. So, where do these Emilys and Emmas and Laurens all come from? Where on earth did *Madison* come from? It's easy enough to see that new names become very popular very fast—but why?

Let's take a look at the top five girls' names and top five boys' names given during the 1990s among high-income white families and low-income white families, ranked in order of their relative rarity in the opposite category. Now compare the "high-end" and "low-end" girls' names with the most popular ones over-all from 1980 and 2000. Lauren and Madison, two of the most popular high-end names from the 1990s, made the overall top-10 list in 2000. Amber and Heather, meanwhile, two of the overall most popular names from 1980, are now among the low-end names.

There is a clear pattern at play: Once a name catches on among high-income, highly educated parents, it starts working its way down the socioeconomic ladder. Amber,

Steven D. Levitt

119

Heather, and Stephanie started out as high-end names. For every high-end baby given those names, however, another *five* lower-income girls received those names within 10 years.

Many people assume that naming trends are driven by celebrities. But how many Madonnas do you know? Or, considering all the Brittanys, Britneys, Brittanis, Brittanies, Brittneys, and Brittnis you encounter these days, you might think of Britney Spears; but she is in fact a symptom, not a cause, of the Brittany/ Britney/Brittani/Brittanie/Brittney/Brittni explosion—and hers is a name that began on the high end and has since fallen to the low. Most families don't shop for baby names in Hollywood. They look to the family just a few blocks over, the one with the bigger house and newer car. The kind of families that were the first to call their daughters Amber or Heather, and are now calling them Alexandra or Katherine. The kind of families that used to name their sons Justin or Brandon and are now calling them Alexander or Benjamin. Parents are reluctant to poach a name from someone too near—family members or close friends—but many parents, whether they realize it or not, like the sound of names that sound "successful."

Once a high-end name is adopted en masse, however, high-end parents begin to abandon it. Eventually, it will be considered so common that even lower-end parents may not want it, whereby it falls out of the rotation entirely. The lower-end parents, meanwhile, go looking for the next name that the upper-end parents have broken in.

So, the implication is clear: The parents of all those Alexandras and Katherines, Madisons and Rachels should not expect the cachet to last much longer. Those names are just now peaking and are already on their way to overexposure. Where, then, will the new high-end names come from? Considering the traditionally strong correlation between income and education, it probably makes sense to look at the most popular current names among parents with the most years of education. Here, drawn from a pair of databases that provide the years of parental education, is a sampling of such names. Some of them, as unlikely as it seems, may well become tomorrow's mainstream names. Before you scoff, ask yourself this: Do Aviva or Clementine seem any more ridiculous than Madison might have seemed 10 years ago?

Obviously, a variety of motives are at work when parents consider a name for their child. It would be an overstatement to suggest that all parents are looking—whether consciously or not—for a smart name or a high-end name. But they are all trying to signal *something* with a name, and an overwhelming number of parents are seemingly trying to signal their own expectations of how successful they hope their children will be. The name itself isn't likely to make a shred of difference. But the parents may feel better knowing that, from the very outset, they tried their best.

120

■ **Consider.** *Are Levitt and Dubner right in stating that a given name isn't likely to make much difference in one's success? Is it possible for a name to affect others' expectations?*

Most Popular Overall White Girl Names

__1980__	__2000__
1. Jennifer	1. Emily
2. Sarah	2. Hannah
3. Melissa	3. Madison
4. Jessica	4. Sarah
5. Christina	5. Samantha
6. Amanda	6. Lauren
7. Nicole	7. Ashley
8. Michelle	8. Emma
9. Heather	9. Taylor
10. Amber	10. Megan

Most Popular High-End White Girl Names in the 1990s

1. Alexandra
2. Lauren
3. Katherine
4. Madison
5. Rachel

Most Popular Low-End White Girl Names in the 1990s

1. Amber
2. Heather
3. Kayla
4. Stephanie
5. Alyssa

Most Popular High-End White Boy Names in the 1990s

1. Benjamin
2. Samuel
3. Jonathan
4. Alexander
5. Andrew

Most Popular Low-End White Boy Names in the 1990s

1. Cody
2. Brandon
3. Anthony
4. Justin
5. Robert

Most Popular Girls' Names of 2015?

Annika	Isabel
Ansley	Kate
Ava	Lara
Avery	Linden
Aviva	Maeve
Clementine	Marie-Claire
Eleanor	Maya
Ella	Philippa
Emma	Phoebe
Fiona	Quinn
Flannery	Sophie
Grace	Waverly

Most Popular Boys' Names of 2015?

Aidan	Jackson
Aldo	Johan
Anderson	Keyon
Ansel	Liam
Asher	Maximilian
Beckett	McGregor
Bennett	Oliver
Carter	Reagan
Cooper	Sander
Finnegan	Sumner
Harper	Will

■ **Discuss.** *Levitt and Dubner's analysis of names based on socioeconomic status reveals some interesting trends. What other types of analysis would you like to see to supplement this study? For example, would geography play a big role? Or the child's position in the birth order? Discuss what factors, in addition to socioeconomic status, you think would make the most impact on the popularity of names.*

■ **Write.** *Levitt and Dubner offer a compelling argument for changes in the popularity of names. However, in this excerpt they do not explain why a few names (such as Sarah) seem immune to these changes. In a short essay, discuss how some names escape the pattern the authors describe, and consider the reasons for the exception.*

National Geographic, *Top Baby Names by State, 2005.* Emily, the top name for girls born in the U.S. in 2005, and D'Brickashaw, the first name of a rookie for football's New York Jets, may seem widely dissimilar, but together they capture the zeitgeist. We're a nation of "lockstep individualists," notes Laura Watternberg, an author who tracks naming trends. "Everyone is determined to be different, but we all have the same taste," she says. These days, that taste leans toward names with vowels airing out the consonants rather than harder sounding appellations like Gertrude, an 1890s hit. The quest for distinctive names also means a reduced market share for even the hottest monikers. Nearly 4.5 percent of girls born in 1945 were Marys. In 2005, little Emilys took only 1.2 percent of the pool.—*Siobhan Roth* (Social Security Administration/National Geographic Image Collection)

122

COMMENT

"The name Katrina will soon join a list of nearly five dozen hurricane names that have been retired. When a hurricane does great harm to life or property, an affected country can request that its name be retired by the World Meteorological Organization. A retired name cannot be used again for at least 10 years to avoid confusion in legal actions and insurance claims. Last year, Charley, Frances, Ivan, and Jeanne were added to the list of retired Atlantic hurricane names. The only other year with four retired names was 1995. Hurricanes have been given names since 1950."

— *The New York Times*, "What Happens to Hurricane Names?"

Thursday, September 1, 2005

Top Baby Names 2005		
Jacob	**1**	Emily
Michael	**2**	Emma
Joshua	**3**	Madison
Matthew	**4**	Abigail
Ethan	**5**	Olivia
Andrew	**6**	Isabella
Daniel	**7**	Hannah
Anthony	**8**	Samantha
Christopher	**9**	Ava
Joseph	**10**	Ashley

Top Baby Names over the Decades		
Michael	**1995**	Jessica
Michael	**1985**	Jessica
Michael	**1975**	Jennifer
Michael	**1965**	Lisa
Michael	**1955**	Mary
James	**1945**	Mary
Robert	**1935**	Mary
Robert	**1925**	Mary
James	**1915**	Linda
John	**1905**	Mary

Maya Lin, *Between Art and Architecture*. With highly publicized antiwar rallies and massive organized protests, the Vietnam War created a cultural rift that can still be felt. Given the extreme positions maintained during the long course of the conflict, it would have been surprising if the drive afterward to construct a fitting memorial to the war had escaped controversy. What would this memorial memorialize? Victory or defeat? Courage, or disgrace? Maya Lin (b. 1959) was a senior at Yale when her design, the result of an architectural seminar, won the national competition for a Vietnam veterans memorial. She has subsequently designed the Civil Rights Memorial (1989) in Alabama; the Langston Hughes Library (1999) in Tennessee; and other projects. This essay is the fourth chapter of Maya Lin's book, *Boundaries* (2000). She writes that her book is "an extension of my art—and like my other works, it sits between two identities . . . a visual and verbal sketchbook, where image can be seen as text and text is sometimes used as image." We have reproduced the text of the essay here, with some of the images included.

Maya Lin
BETWEEN ART AND ARCHITECTURE

■ **Consider before you read.** *How does the inclusion of names in a work like Lin's change the nature of a monument? What is being memorialized in a more generalized monument? What is added or lost when the viewer is confronted with individual names?*

It's taken me years to be able to discuss the making of the Vietnam Veterans Memorial, partly because I needed to move past it and partly because I had forgotten the process of getting it built. I would not discuss the controversy surrounding its construction and it wasn't until I saw the documentary, *Maya Lin: A Strong Clear Vision,* that I was able to remember that time in my life. But I wrote the body of this essay just as the memorial was being completed— in the fall of 1982. Then I put it away . . . until now.

Todd Gipstein, Names on Vietnam Veterans Memorial. (© Todd Gipstein/Corbis)

I had studied earlier monuments and memorials while designing that memorial [a student project at Yale for a World War III memorial] and I continued this research for the design of the Vietnam memorial. As I did more research on monuments, I realized most carried larger, more general messages about a leader's victory or accomplishments rather than the lives lost. In fact, at the national level, individual lives were very seldom dealt with, until you arrived at the memorials for World War I. Many of these memorials included the names of those killed. Partly it was a practical need to list those whose bodies could not be identified—since dog tags as identification had not yet been adopted and, due to the nature of the warfare, many killed were not indentifiable—but I think as well the listing of names reflected a response by these designers to the horrors of World War I, to the immense loss of life.

The images of these monuments were extremely moving. They captured emotionally what I felt memorials should be: honest about the reality of war, about the loss of life in war, and about remembering those who served and especially those who died.

I made a conscious decision not to do any specific research on the Vietnam War and the political turmoil surrounding it. I felt that the politics had eclipsed the veterans, their service and their lives. I wanted to create a memorial that everyone would be able to respond to, regardless of whether one thought our country should or should not have participated in the war. The power of a name was very much with me at the time, partly because of the Memorial Rotunda at Yale. In Woolsey Hall, the walls are inscribed with the names of all the Yale alumni who have been killed in wars. I had never been able to resist touching the names cut into these marble walls, and no matter how busy or crowded the place is, a sense of quiet, a reverence, always surrounds those names. Throughout my freshman and sophomore years, the stonecutters were carving in by hand the names of those killed in the Vietnam War, and I think it left a lasting impression on me . . . the sense of the power of a name.

■ **Discuss.** *In this essay, Lin remembers her desire to touch the names carved into the Memorial Rotunda at Yale. Many people respond to her Vietnam memorial in the same way. Why do you think people want to physically touch the names? Does a name carry more significance than an ordinary word? How does this impulse to touch contribute to the power of Lin's memorial?*

■ **Write.** *Lin mentions the controversy that arose around the building of a Vietnam veterans memorial. Do some Internet research to find out different visions that people had for the site. Summarize the viewpoints you find. Then discuss how Lin's use of names satisfied or frustrated some of the demands of veterans, surviving family members, military officials, and others.*

 CONSIDER THE CLUSTER
What's in a Name?

■ **Message**

What point does Manuel Muñoz want to make by introducing and concluding his essay with a reference to the gate agent at the Fresno airport who was paging a missing customer? Why is this incident important to him? How does he connect it to his personal experience with naming? In an essay of your own, consider the importance of names and their proper pronunciation. Would you find it disrespectful if people mispronounced your own name? Why or why not? Do you get annoyed if people misspell your name or use a common nickname automatically that you don't use yourself?

■ **Method**

Suppose you could examine a computer list of every name that appears on the Vietnam Veterans Memorial. Most of the people named died in the 1960s and early 1970s. Do you think the most common names appearing on the memorial would reflect that era or be fairly similar to the popular names today? What method would you use to conduct your study? In what ways would it be similar to or different from the methods used by the authors of *Freakonomics*? As a brief in-class exercise, jot down a few things you think we could learn from such a study.

■ **Medium**

As an in-class assignment, make a list of all the various sources of popular names you can think of. In what ways do the movies, television, and the music industry contribute to the popularity of names? Which medium do you think plays the most significant role in popularizing names today? After reading Levitt and Dubner's "Trading Up: Where Do Baby Names Come From?" do you think the authors fail to pay sufficient attention to the media as a source of names?

FAMILY PHOTOS

ESSAY | 4 PHOTOS | ESSAY/INTERVIEW

128

"They are not your usual pictures of the children to send to the grandparents," the critic Janet Malcolm writes of the photographs in Sally Mann's collection *Immediate Family* (1992, Aperture). The "usual pictures" are a **genre** we all recognize: children in cute poses, darling outfits, stylized situations. Sally Mann's photographs of her young children are a bit different, Malcolm writes: "pictures to send to the Museum of Modern Art."

Immediate Family collects black-and-white pictures Mann took of her three children (Emmett, Jessie, and Virginia) over the course of several summers in Lexington, Virginia. These beautiful photographs have a languorous, sensual air, and they document childhood as almost wilderness territory. Some seem unstudied; some use artifice; some confront the direct gaze of the child. Most are taken outdoors as the children fish, sleep, swim, eat—sometimes clothed but often nude. The series has been the subject of much critical acclaim and controversy; some reviewers debate what statements, exactly, Mann is making about art, childhood, family, sexuality, life, and death. And some question Mann personally about her sense of parental responsibility. Mann—and her children, who are by now no longer children—have responded that while the subjects invoked by the photographs are *complicated,* there is nothing *wrong* in them, nor with Emmett, Jessie, and Virginia as a result of modeling for their mother.

Sally Mann began her career as a landscape photographer and has continued to excel in that genre. In 1988, she published *At Twelve: Portraits of Young Women* (Aperture). After *Immediate Family,* she published *Still Time* (1994, Aperture), again focusing on her children. She returned to her work on landscape photography, producing a series of haunting landscapes around her native Virginia titled *Mother Land: Recent Georgia and Virginia Landscapes* (1997, Edwynn Houk Gallery). Her most recent work includes *What Remains* (2003, Bulfinch), whose subject is mortality and death, and *Deep South* (2005, Bulfinch), a collection of landscapes.

129

Janet Malcolm, *The Family of Mann.* One of the nation's leading journalists, Janet Malcolm was born in Prague, Czechoslovakia, in 1934 and grew up in New York City. Her books cover a wide variety of topics, from psychoanalysis and true crime to photography and biography. She is the author of *Diana and Nikon: Essays on Photographs* (1980), in which "The Family of Mann" is included; *Psychoanalysis: The Impossible Profession* (1982); *The Journalist and the Murderer* (1990); *The Silent Woman: Sylvia Plath and Ted Hughes* (1994); and *In the Freud Archives* (1984). Her essays have been collected in *The Purloined Clinic: Selected Writings* (1993). Her most recent works include *The Crime of Sheila McGough* (1999) and *Reading Chekhov: A Critical Journey* (2001). Malcolm lives in New York with her husband, Gardner Botsford.

Janet Malcolm
THE FAMILY OF MANN

■ **Consider before you read.** *In the title of her essay, Malcolm puns on a phrase that suggests not just the photographer's real-life family but also the archetypal relations among human beings. What claims does she make in this essay about the relevance of Mann's photographs to the general condition of families and about the specific relationships between parents and children?*

The audacity and authority of Sally Mann's work are perhaps nowhere so immediately manifest as on the cover of her first collection of photographs, *At Twelve: Portraits of Young Women* (1988). The cover picture is a sort of double portrait: a girl stands in front of a clapboard house next to a chair on which a torn, oval photograph of another girl, from another time, has been propped. The girl in the old photograph wears a flounced dress and a bow in her hair, and has the stern, fixed, mildly sulky expression that nineteenth-century photographers regularly induced in young subjects; her hands are stiffly, self-protectively crossed over her stomach. The "actual" girl, in contrast, opens herself up to the photographer's scrutiny. Dressed in tight shorts and a T-shirt, she stands in an attitude of trusting relaxation, her legs parted, a hip outthrust, an arm extended to grip the chair holding the torn photograph. We do not see her expression—Mann has cropped the photograph at her chest and her knees—but we don't need to, because the body is so eloquent. Its transfixing feature—you could almost call it its "face"—is the girl's vulva, which plumply strains against the soft stretch fabric of the shorts, creating a radius of creases that impart a sculptural, almost monumental presence to this evocative, slightly embarrassing, slightly arousing sight of summer in America.

The photograph is radical, however, not because of the truth it renders about twelve-year-old-ness but because of the truth it renders about photography. As if anticipating the criticism that *Immediate Family*, her next book of photographs, was to attract—the charge that she exploits her young subjects—Mann offers an illustration of the medium's innate exploitativeness that is like an impatient manifesto. Of course the girl who posed for Mann in front of her house did not know—everything in the stance of her body tells us she did not—that Mann was taking a picture centering on her pudendum. We can almost see the girl's face squinting against the sun, arranging itself to levelly meet the camera's gaze, the gaze that has treacherously traveled elsewhere. The photograph both unrepentantly enacts and ruefully comments on the treachery. Mann knows, as the major photographers of our time know (the photographers whose company she joins with *Immediate Family*), that photography is a medium not of reassuring realism but of disturbing surrealism.

Sally Mann, *Jessie Bites*, 1985. From *Immediate Family*, by Sally Mann.
(Courtesy Sally Mann/Gagosian Gallery)

Family Photos

In *Immediate Family* Mann photographs her own three children, Emmett, Jessie, and Virginia, during warm weather over a period of seven years, in and around the family house in rural southwestern Virginia. The children wear bathing suits or light summer clothes or no clothes. The photographs are beautiful and strange, like a dream of childhood in summer. They are not your usual pictures of the children to send to the grandparents; they are pictures to send to the Museum of Modern Art. During John Szarkowski's tenure as director of the photography department at the Modern, he cultivated a kind of photography that Sally Mann brings to triumphant, sometimes transcendent, fruition. In *On Photography*, Susan Sontag compared the "sleekly calculated, complacently well-made, undialectical" productions of official Surrealism to photography's authentic, natural surrealism. Within photography, Szarkowski distinguished between the calculated, well-made, undialectical art photograph and the artless but vitally interesting snapshot, and he supported photographers who attempted the tour de force of the art snapshot. Of course, every photograph with any claim to interest is a tour de force—all the canonical works of photography retain some trace of the medium's underlying, life-giving, accident-proneness. But the Szarkowski photographers (William Eggleston, Lee Friedlander, Joel Meyerowitz, Garry Winogrand, Emmett Gowin, for example) put greater pressure on the snapshot side of the equation; their pictures are looser, messier, "uglier" than the results of the traditional mediation between the contingent and the premeditated. In Sally Mann's photographs the scale tips back toward the older "beautiful" photograph—without, however, any diminution of the appearance of photojournalistic chanciness and the sense of anxiety, disjunction, invasiveness, uncanniness by which the Szarkowski school is marked.

What mothers who photograph their children normally try to capture (or, as the case may be, create) are the moments when their children look happy and attractive, when their clothes aren't smeared with food, and they aren't clutching themselves. Mann, abnormally, takes pictures of her children looking sulky, angry, and dirty, displaying insect bites or bloody noses, and clutching themselves.

Reviewers of *Immediate Family* and of the exhibitions that preceded its publication harshly rebuked Mann for her un-motherliness and pitied the helpless, art-abused children. "At moments when any other mother would grab her child to hold and comfort, Mann must have reached instead for her camera," one reviewer wrote in a piece entitled "It may be art, but what about the kids," which concluded with the dictum, "Beauty does not validate exploitation. Motherhood should not give license to activities that are morally wrong. Nor should art." In the *TLS* [*Times Literary Supplement*], Julian Bell wrote, "I don't doubt that Sally Mann's children are doing better than most, but since she offers them for my inspection, I'll say that seems a rotten way to bring them up." Charles Hagen, a *New York Times* photography critic, offered no opinion of his own, but felt constrained to point out that "many people regard photographs of naked children as inherently exploitative and even pornographic, and will reject Ms. Mann's work on those grounds." He went on, "Other viewers will bristle at the sensual, emotionally drenched nature of Ms. Mann's vision of childhood, and will object

■ Consider. *What do the criticisms of Mann's work say about cultural ideas of motherhood? In provoking these comments, what expectations does she seem to be violating?*

132

Sally Mann, ***Blowing Bubbles,*** **1987.** From *Immediate Family*, by Sally Mann.
(Courtesy Sally Mann/Gagosian Gallery)

to her using children to act out the fantasies, some of them sexual, that are central to it."

One of the ways we make ourselves at home, so to speak, in the alien terrain of new art is to deny it its originality, to transform its disquieting strangeness into familiar forms to which we may effortlessly, almost blindly respond. To look at Sally Mann's photographs of her children as unfeeling or immoral is simply to be not looking at them, to be pushing away something complex and difficult (the vulnerability of children, the unhappiness of childhood, the tragic character of the parent-child relationship are among Mann's painful themes) and demanding a cliché in its place. With her summer photographs of Emmett, Jessie, and Virginia, Mann has given us a meditation on infant sorrow and parental rue that is as powerful and delicate as it is undeserving of the facile abuse that has been heaped on it.

"That seems a rotten way to bring them up." Is there a good—or even a good enough—way to bring them up? Mann asks this question in picture after picture. A photograph entitled *The Wet Bed* shows Virginia, the youngest child, at the age of two, lying in bed fast asleep on her back, her arms raised above her head as if they were cherub's wings, her torso stretched out in luxurious relaxation. She is naked; it is a hot night—a chenille bedspread lies in a heap at the foot of the mattress. Like Blake's[1] little girl lost, whose radiant innocence subdued beasts of prey as she slept in the wilderness, Mann's Virginia is the embodiment of invulnerable defenselessness: What harm can befall this beautiful, trusting child? But as we follow the photographer/mother's gaze and look down with her on the sleeping little girl, we feel her mother's fear. We take in the heavy darkness that frames the whiteness of the child's bed, out of which the image of the sleeping cherub emerges like a hallucinatory vision, and, above all, we are transfixed by the large pale stain that spreads from the child's body over the tautly fitted sheet. The stain is yet another insignia of Blakean innocence, another attribute of the time of life when nothing has yet happened to seriously disturb a child's blameless instinctuality. But the stain is also an augury of Blakean experience. It foretells the time when the child will have to be broken of its habit of trust in the world's benevolence. What Mann, in her introduction, calls "the predictable treacheries of the future" waft out of *The Wet Bed* as they do out of the book as a whole. All happy childhoods are alike: they are the skin that memory has grown over a wound. Children suffer, no matter how lovingly they are brought up. It is in the very nature of upbringing to cause suffering.

---

[1]The prolific English poet William Blake (1757–1827) is perhaps best known today for his *Songs of Innocence* (1789) and *Songs of Experience* (1794), two remarkable volumes of poetry that explore both the blissful and the bleak sides of childhood. A great illustrator and an early champion of sexual freedom, Blake published these works with intricately arranged hand-colored drawings and decorations that he intended to be viewed as an inseparable part of the text.—ED.

Sally Mann, *Emmett, Jessie, and Virginia,* 1990. From *Immediate Family,* by Sally Mann.
(Courtesy Sally Mann/Gagosian Gallery)

Sally Mann's project has been to document the anger, disappointment, shame, confusion, insecurity that in every child attach to the twenty-year-long crisis of growing up. She stalks and waits for, and sometimes stages, the moments that other parents and photographers may prefer not to see. That this anatomy of childhood's discontents is drawn in a paradisal southern summer landscape, and that the family in which the children are growing up is as enlightened, permissive, and affectionate as a family can be, only add to its power and authenticity.

With her pictures of her children's bloody noses, mean insect bites, cuts requiring stitches, faces and bodies smeared with mud and dirt and drips from ice cream, Mann offers striking metaphors for the fall from purity that is childhood's ineluctable trajectory. (We give it the euphemism "child development.") But where *Immediate Family* achieves its great ring of disturbing truth is in the "plot" that emerges from its pages the plot of how the three children have worked out their respective destinies within their family constellation, how they enact the roles that heredity, chance, and will have written for them in the bitter contest for the parents' love.

This plot is played out in every family, of course, with infinite variations and invariable pathos. In *Immediate Family,* Jessie appears as the tense, self-conscious, younger-sister-haunted older daughter; Emmett as the scowling, withholding, only son, warily stepping through the Oedipal minefield; Virginia as the baby, wearing her belatedness like a blanket against the chill of the others' precedence. The blows and stings of early child–parent and child–sibling relationships do not fade like insect bites and skin punctures but imprint themselves on us forever, determining who we are. Sally Mann's extraordinary contribution has been to give photographic expression to pathetic truths that have hitherto been the exclusive domain of psychologists and authors of great works of fiction. Photography's specificity gives the portrait of the Mann family its arresting, almost abashing intimacy. Its ambiguity—a photograph never says anything unequivocally, even when it most appears to be doing so—allows the family to escape with its secrets.

136

■ **Discuss.** *Does Malcolm overstate "the twenty-year-long crisis of growing up"? How much of her argument for Mann's photos depends on her view that suffering is inevitable in childhood?*

■ **Write.** *At the end of her essay, Malcolm describes the different roles the three children play in the drama of* Immediate Family. *Choose one of the Mann photos and write an analysis of how it represents these dynamics. How do the children's faces and postures reflect their personalities?*

Sally Mann, *Candy Cigarette***, 1989.** From *Immediate Family*, by Sally Mann.
(Courtesy Sally Mann/Gagosian Gallery)

Melissa Harris and Jessie Mann, *On Being Photographed.* Melissa Harris, the editor in chief at *Aperture* magazine, interviewed Jessie Mann for the winter 2001 edition of the magazine (no. 192). Harris explains: "Visiting Sally Mann and her family in August of last year [2000] I had the chance to spend time with Jessie—Sally and Larry Mann's middle child—who was preparing for her freshman year at college. I've known Jessie since she was nine years old, and it was wonderful to speak with her at this pivotal point in her life. Together, and with Sally's encouragement, we decided to do an interview about what it was like for Jessie to be photographed by her mother through the years. . . ." In the following piece, taken from the interview with Harris, Jessie Mann talks about her experience modeling for her mother.

Melissa Harris and Jessie Mann
ON BEING PHOTOGRAPHED

■ **Consider before you read.** *How does Jessie Mann respond to criticisms of her mother's work such as those mentioned in Janet Malcolm's essay? How does she interpret the photographs? Does she have concerns about* Immediate Family *that are different from those expressed by the critics?*

I think what's changed most in the way I feel about my mother's prints is that I don't look at them as pictures of *me* any longer. There's a point when you just have to look at them and appreciate what's meaningful about them as photographs rather than thinking, "Oh, that was the day we caught that really big fish." Because that's how other people see them. It's interesting now for me to look at their artistic significance. Maybe the pictures are more magical and mysterious and meaningful to me than they are to other people—although I've spoken to people who seem to pick up on the magic of that location and of our childhood, and seem to understand it as if they were there, because they can see it in the photographs. So it's interesting for me to see if I can feel what other people are getting from the prints.

When we were taking pictures, it created a relationship with Mom that's very different than other people's relationships—much more powerful. I just read

The Moor's Last Sigh by Salman Rushdie, in which the main character is painted by his mother through his whole life, and he talks about how this creates a completely different bond between mother and child. Because there already is a very powerful bond, then add to that the bond between artist and subject, and think about artists who study one subject for most of their lives, and the bond that they must have, the artistic bond. . . . On top of being our mother, she became a whole lot more. So that made our relationship stronger, but of course more complicated.

At some point, we realized this work was consequential, which I think was another side effect. Then later on, we became aware of the controversy the work was creating, and that made us question—well, what were her motives in taking the photographs? I don't mean anything sexual or negative—but we were hearing a lot of "bad mother" stuff, so it made us question her more than most children might question their mothers. So that added yet another layer of intensity to our relationship.

Up until recently Virginia, Emmett, and I haven't really discussed all of it very much. But now Emmett and I talk about it occasionally. We're at the point where questions have to be asked, as we begin to march out into the future, and we have to look back on our childhood. There's a reconciliation all children have with their parents once they get out of their teenage years. We're getting to it, but with a lot more issues to deal with: about the intensity and the conflict and the mother–child relationship when it's also artist–child. Maybe it was a harder childhood—or a more complicated one—than other children have.

But the other side of the coin is, we *enjoyed* being photographed. It gave us a sense of beauty. When you're around an artist all the time, you're always reminded of what's beautiful and what's special, and you can't forget it. Now, even though we are grown up—and Emmett and I are in college and living apart from her, and Ginna has begun boarding school—we still have that reminder. We got to travel, and meet a lot of great people, and had all this great exposure. So we have to factor those experiences into the moving-out on to our own things.

People don't usually recognize me now. I mean, very rarely. But the three of us have gained this strange status in society. It's different than child movie stars—we're sort of "art stars." But *child* art stars. No one really knows where we stand. But sometimes I'll meet people and they say, "Oh, I've just followed you; you're my favorite one of the kids." And I think, "*Favorite* one? . . ." It's very odd: the pictures are so significant to so many people that it can be very weird to me.

It's not something we can escape. The best analogy I have for it is the Glass family in the Salinger novels, and how each one of them handled growing out of that childhood celebrity and becoming their own people. Two of them went into the movie business, and one shot himself, and one seemed to drop off the face of the earth. They all had to deal with this child celebrity, childhood significance.

How do you parlay that into your future?

It's weird now when people say, "Well, now what are you going to do?" For so long, what we did was model—that's what we did. And now we have to choose

139

another career, at a time when most people are looking for their first career. We've had this great experience, we've met some of the great minds of our time, and we've *lived* with one of the great minds of our time [LAUGHS]—so how are we going to *use* that? Are we ever going to be able to live up to the significance of the experiences we've had, or live up to our mother?

Each of us is dealing with that pressure in a very different way. Emmett is completely daunted by it. He doesn't know what he wants, so he backs away from the whole thing: he's sometimes afraid to have any goals or any aspirations, doesn't want to get too involved or too intense. Mom is a very driven person, and really has little understanding of people who aren't that driven. Emmett has got to sort it out on his own. He and I are very close. Kind of like Franny and Zooey, we keep each other together. We help each other out. Nobody can understand what I'm going through like he can.

Ginna, on the other hand, was a lot younger than Emmett and me when those pictures were taken, so I think the experience for her was completely different. Her attitude right now is: "I want to have a normal life; I want to forget about this; I don't want to have to *use* it to my advantage; I don't want to either be living up to something or living down to something; I'm just going to be *living*." She's trying to go the middle road more than I've ever seen, trying to be "normal." And coming out of our family, that takes a lot of effort. . . . Ginna wants to be like everybody else, and these pictures have made that difficult. One of the things that Mom did best was always allow us to sort of *go* for it, to find out who we were, no matter what the cost. When I wanted to shave my head, she was there with the clippers. "Do it. Have fun. Explore yourself. I'm not going to tell you who you are." For me, that was a really great freedom, but I don't think Ginna responded to the whole situation like that.

I feel—because I've had all these experiences, and met all these people, and had conversations most other kids my age probably haven't had—that I have a *responsibility* to utilize these experiences in my future. Which is a lot to ask of myself. But not more than I can do. I'm not saying that I'm going to expect to be anything like my mother. I just want to do something that is meaningful, that has a significance outside just making a living. I think that's what I've been taught by all this.

I have a very clear-cut idea about what I want to do with my future, and I think in many ways that's like Mom: we both know exactly what we're going to do and how we're going to get there. I want to be an obstetrician/gynecologist. I think that comes from my feeling of needing to do something significant, outside of just surviving and providing. I think education about birth control and providing birth control and abortion for women is the best thing. . . . It's what our country needs most, because no doctors will become abortion doctors anymore. They're scared. I guess—like Mom's work, in a way—it's doing something that makes people uncomfortable but that needs to be done. She said something that no one wanted to hear, but it had to be said.

■ Consider. *Do Jessie Mann's characterizations of herself and her brother and sister as children seem to fit with Janet Malcolm's impressions of them as they appeared in the photographs? Now that they have grown up, how have their roles changed?*

140

There are so many levels to childhood that we as a society ignore, or don't accept. Rather than just saying it, she was able to capture it with photographs. It's easy to discount these things unless you can really see them in the kids' eyes, or see it in their actions.

I also think she brought out a certain sexuality in children that nobody wants to think about. Some people still have real problems with the pictures. . . . I'll make a friend, and eventually I'll say, "I wonder if I'm ever going to meet your parents?" And the person will answer, "Well, my Mom really opposes your mother's work, so you may not want to come over." I used to get all riled up about it. But now I understand—it's hard for people. I think if you have a certain background or beliefs those photographs could be upsetting or offensive. I don't agree with that point of view, but maybe there's something to their idea that that part of children shouldn't be played up. I can accept someone else's point of view about it. It's only when they start passing judgment about me as a person or my mother as a person that it gets to me.

All three of us are very defensive of Mom because of this, so it's hard to look back and wonder, "Well, what if the photos hadn't been there?" I know, no matter what, there would have been an amazing strain on my relationship with Mom. We're very similar—it's just the way we are made up. There was no way we were going to live together compatibly! But on some level, there's always the question: *Would things have been easier if it hadn't been for the photographs?* Yet at the same time, without them we wouldn't have had these extraordinary opportunities.

With Dad, the best analogy I can come up with is that Mom, Emmett, Virginia, and I—we're all drama queens, actors on a stage, doing our thing and putting on a performance. But Dad is the stage. Without him, we wouldn't have the emotional support we need to keep going. He's there to work between all these strong characters and keep everything together. He's a lawyer; he plays this very simple but absolutely essential role. He keeps us all sane. I can't imagine it's much fun for him. Well, keeping us on peaceful terms is probably good for him, too. He's really needed.

When Aperture published *Immediate Family*, Mom and Dad sat us down, and we had a family meeting. They asked, "Are you going to be okay with this?" Dad was a big part of making sure we *really* were okay; they sent us to a counselor to make sure we were okay with it. We were all pretty young, so I don't think anyone could have had any idea what it was really going to be like. But if I were back at that table today, making the decision, I'd still say, "Go ahead. Show them."

As a result of her upbringing, Mom's a little reserved. She isn't touchy-affectionate. She has a hard time letting us know how much she loves us. But I've also realized that each one of those photographs was her way of capturing, somehow—if not in a hug or a kiss or a comment—how much she cared about us, but obviously didn't have the ability to show us. Each one of those photographs is an affirmation of love. To me, it seems like she's overwhelmed with this feeling of love and she doesn't know what to do with it, so she photographs it.

141

I think that there's something similar going on with her landscapes. She won't admit to any religious or spiritual tendencies, and laughs at anyone who has them— "Oh, Jessie, you and your spiritual-growth thing again." But I've never seen anything so spiritual as those landscapes. It's her capturing—her understanding of God, her understanding of what life is about. Even though she'd never say it, she'd never tell anyone that's what she's photographing—and she'll probably disagree with me—it's *there*. Because she catches the *meaning* of the beauty around here.

■ **Discuss.** *In this interview, Mann mentions feeling a greater pressure to do something significant with her life after having been a subject of her mother's photographs. How does being in the public eye change expectations for the lives of the Mann children? Do you think expectations for an "art star" would be different from those for, say, a movie star?*

■ **Write.** *Write a short essay reflecting on how people would likely perceive you if they based their opinion on your childhood or teen photos. It might be helpful to look at some photos if they are available. Are your pictures more traditional than those of the Mann children? Does that make them a more accurate or a less accurate representation of your identity? Do any of the photos say more about the person taking them than about the subject?*

142

COMMENT

"There is absolutely one inarguable statement you can make about these pictures: they testify to a maternal passion that is not only natural but pretty close to universally experienced. Anyone who finds it 'dichotomous' that a mother should produce such saturatingly maternal images is beyond reasoning with."

—Sally Mann

CONSIDER THE CLUSTER
Family Photos

■ Message

After you read the interview with Jessie Mann and study the photograph, what do you think *Candy Cigarette* is attempting to "say"—if anything? What **caption** might you write for the photograph? For example, how does Sally Mann visually convey the issues of childhood and adulthood, innocence and experience, in this photograph of her daughter?

■ Method

As a photograph, *Candy Cigarette* seems to be both a casual snapshot and an artfully posed portrait. After closely examining the photograph, what elements would you say contribute to both effects? Which aspects of the photograph appear accidental or random? Which appear posed and artificial? Why would the photographer want to combine both kinds of photography—the snapshot and the studio portrait—within a single frame?

■ Medium

In the interview, Jessie Mann says that she and her siblings "*enjoyed* being photographed." How does having Jessie's own words on being the subject of such photography change the way you read *Candy Cigarette*? What kind of a portrait do Jessie's words paint of her mother?

143

THE *MONA LISA*

144

A superstar is a celebrity whose features we instantly recognize—today, usually because of continuous media coverage. Given today's standards, does Leonardo da Vinci's *Mona Lisa* qualify as a "superstar," as Joseph A. Harriss claims in "Seeking Mona Lisa"? Instantly recognized throughout the world, the portrait has been subjected to endless interpretation; yet much about the painting remains as enigmatic as the mysterious woman's famous smile. Who was the woman Leonardo painted? Was she the young wife of a Florentine official, as is commonly thought? What does her expression signify? And, perhaps most important, why has this particular portrait remained so universally appealing throughout so many centuries? Recent computer analysis suggests a remarkable possibility—that the mysterious Mona Lisa is no actual or imaginary woman but is instead none other than Leonardo da Vinci himself.

Though highly speculative, Lillian Feldman Schwartz's intriguing computer analysis may have been anticipated in 1919 by one of France's earliest modern artists, Marcel Duchamp. On one level, Duchamp was commenting on society's blind respect for artistic masterpieces; but on another level, was his masculinization of the *Mona Lisa* an indication that he, too, sensed a male presence behind the world's most famous smile?

The *Mona Lisa*. The Italian artist, architect, scientist, and inventor Leonardo da Vinci (1452–1519) painted the *Mona Lisa* five hundred years ago, between 1503 and 1506. Once completed, the painting remained in the artist's possession and was among his personal effects when he died in France. It thus became one of France's most treasured works of art and the leading attraction at the Louvre museum in Paris, where it has been on display since Leonardo's death in 1519. (Réunion des Musées Nationaux/Art Resource, NY)

Joseph A. Harriss, *Seeking Mona Lisa.* This informative essay covers the history of what the author calls "the most famous work in the entire 40,000-year history of the visual arts." Joseph A. Harriss is an American writer based in Paris, where he has lived for more than forty years. He has contributed to numerous magazines throughout his career but today writes mostly for *Smithsonian* magazine. This essay appeared in the May 1999 issue of *Smithsonian* magazine.

Joseph A. Harriss
SEEKING MONA LISA

■ **Consider before you read.** *Why is the* Mona Lisa *so incredibly popular? Does Harriss's history of the painting give you any ideas about why people are so devoted to it? Or why it shows up in so many contexts in popular culture?*

Going with the flow, I follow the body heat from the cavernous crypt beneath the Louvre's glass pyramid up past a dying Italian slave and a nude Greek warrior, a diminutive French general directing troops, and a carelessly draped lady with wings. On the second floor, in a room where you could comfortably play tennis, the background murmur grows to a clamor and the air, on this warm August day, is distinctly ripe. Harried tour leaders waving striped sticks or colorful scarves try to corral their polyglot charges. But most of them are busy jockeying and elbowing to get as close as they can to a bullet-proof, air-conditioned showcase for a glimpse of Leonardo da Vinci's 500-year-old portrait of a preternaturally poised Florentine lady.

Largely ignoring the room's other masterpieces of Italian classical painting, its splendid Tintorettos, Veroneses, and Titians, the throng aims high-performance cameras at the showcase and lets fly a fusillade of flashes, pinpoints of light bouncing back from its window. Many stand beside it to be photographed, as if they were in front of the Eiffel Tower. It all reminds me of when, as a young reporter, I occasionally had to cover chaotic, shoving, celebrity press conferences. Except here the superstar says nothing. She merely gazes back with a cool, appraising smile.

The *Mona Lisa* is the most famous work in the entire 40,000-year history of the visual arts. And if you don't agree with that, your argument is not with me but with the respected art historian Roy McMullen, who has studied the

■ *Consider. Given Harriss's description of the scene at the Louvre, what do you think he makes of the painting? Does he revere it? Does he think it is overrated?*

phenomenon extensively. "It provokes instant shocks of recognition on every continent from Asia to America," he observes, "reduces the Venus of Milo and the Sistine Chapel to the level of merely local marvels, sells as many postcards as a tropical resort, and stimulates as many amateur detectives as an unsolved international murder mystery." Like many celebrities, the *Mona Lisa* today is famous for being famous. Louvre officials estimate that most of the museum's first-time visitors come mainly to stare at this cross between a cultural archetype and an icon of kitsch.[1] Undoubtedly, the painting has become part of our collective subconscious. What they are looking for is the picture that has provoked—and been the object of—more crazy reactions, addled adulation, arcane analysis, gross imitations, scandalous takeoffs, and crass commercialization than any other work of art in history.

The painting's status as a world-class superstar was confirmed beyond any doubt when, in 1963, the French Minister of Culture, André Malraux—who called the painting "the most subtle homage that genius has ever rendered to a living face"—sent it to the United States and, a decade later, to Japan as a sort of itinerant ambassador of French culture, its Italian origins notwithstanding. On arriving in America in January 1963, in its own cabin aboard the SS *France*, the *Mona Lisa* was received more like a potentate than a painting. A tuxedoed President John F. Kennedy and an evening-gowned Jacqueline Kennedy formally welcomed it to Washington's National Gallery of Art, where the director, John Walker, hailed it as "the most famous single work of art ever to cross the ocean." White-gloved U.S. marines guarded the painting around the clock. Even though the museum was kept open evenings for the first time in its history, crowds waited for up to two hours to get a look at the famous face; one man asked a guard, in passing, what the grand building was used for when the *Mona Lisa* wasn't there. It was the same mob scene in February and March at New York's Metropolitan Museum of Art, with lines down Fifth Avenue for blocks in severe winter weather. In all, more than two million Americans ogled the *Mona Lisa*.

But Mona mania in America paled beside the frenzy in Japan, to the hand-wringing despair of some French aesthetes who complained that the work was being exhibited like Brigitte Bardot or a Folies Bergère *danseuse*. When the *Mona Lisa* arrived at Tokyo's National Museum in April 1974, visitors totaling 1.5 million thronged the building and were hustled past the painting for a ten-second look. A uniformed guard atop a podium directed the traffic. Outside, the hype approached

147

---

[1]A once derogatory term deriving from the German *kitschen* ("to throw together"), **kitsch** referred to art objects that were considered vulgar, inferior, tasteless, sentimental, or highly derivative—such as "collectible" figures of adorable little children, a maudlin portrait of a tearful clown, or paintings of cute kittens or puppies. Kitsch can be found anywhere but is especially plentiful in the souvenir shops of major cities. Wall calendars also commonly display kitsch. As some modern and contemporary artists began dissolving or outright dismissing the boundaries between "high" and "low" art, however, and as they self-consciously incorporated "kitschy" references into their work, the term has become less evaluative and more descriptive of a certain popular style.—ED.

148

◀ **Constantine Boym, *Mona Lisa Clock*, 1987.** The designer Constantine Boym (b. 1955) was born in Moscow, Russia, and studied architecture and design in Moscow and Milan, Italy. He is the author of *New Russian Design* (1992, Rizzoli) and lives in New York City's Lower East Side. Boym taught at the Parsons School of Design from 1988 to 2000 and founded his own studio in 1986 (Boym Partners Inc.), where he and his partners have designed furniture and everyday objects, including watches for Swatch and tableware for Alessi, as well as exhibition installations for a number of American museums. To create this *Mona Lisa* clock, Boym silk-screened an image of the painting on an 8 x 10 inch piece of aluminum. The clock is battery-operated, costs $25, and is available at Mxyplyzyk, a home decor shop in New York City. To see more of Boym's work, visit his web site: boym.com. (Courtesy of Boym Partners Inc.)

hysteria. Dozens of bars and nightclubs changed their names to Mona Lisa, one staging a Mona Lisa Nude Revue. A telephone number yielded a recording of the lady saying, in Italian, how happy she was to be in Japan. Japanese girls wore décolleté dark dresses with long sleeves, and parted their hair in the middle; some even resorted to plastic surgery in order to produce a more convincing Lisa Look.

The look that inspires such bizarre behavior is defined by the enigmatic, tight-lipped smile that has launched a thousand learned interpretations, lucid explanations—and loony analyses. Renowed art critic Bernard Berenson set the tone for serious appreciation when he proclaimed that Leonardo's subtle sfumato[2] technique of modeling light and shade reached its apex with the *Mona Lisa*. For centuries many an artist has tried to equal it as a sort of ultimate challenge, the Everest of oil painting. One, the French artist Luc Maspero, threw himself from the fourth-floor window of his Paris hotel in the mid-19th century, leaving a farewell note: "For years I have grappled desperately with her smile. I prefer to die."

Even when not inducing a death wish, the smile has often generated perplexity. Is it "more divine than human," as a 16th-century Italian writer had it, or "worldly, watchful and self-satisfied," according to British art historian Kenneth Clark? The 19th-century French Positivist thinker Hippolyte Taine seemed unable to make up his mind, variously called it "doubting, licentious, Epicurean, deliciously tender, ardent, sad," while novelist Lawrence Durrell puckishly dubbed it "the smile of a woman who has just eaten her husband." Feminist Camille Paglia went further: "What Mona Lisa is ultimately saying is that males are unnecessary," she opined. Salvador Dalí, ever provocative, even attributed the 1956 attack

149

---

[2] Many critics have observed that a large part of the Mona Lisa's enigmatic smile results from Leonardo's innovative use of a technique Italians termed *sfumato*, which noted art historian E. H. Gombrich describes as "the blurred outline and mellowed colors that allow one form to merge with another and always leave something to our imagination."—ED.

on the painting, when a young Bolivian threw a rock that put a small scar on the left elbow, to the smile. "Subconsciously in love with his mother, ravaged by the Oedipus complex," Dalí theorized, the young man was "stupefied to discover a portrait of his own mother, transfigured by the maximum female idealization. His own mother, here! And worse, his mother smiles ambiguously at him. . . . Attack is his one possible response to such a smile."

In our less poetic age, the trend has been more to physiological explanations for the smile. Was Mona Lisa, whoever she was, asthmatic? Simply a contented pregnant housewife? Some researchers have concluded that she probably smiled with her mouth closed because she was undergoing 16th-century-style mercury treatment for syphilis; the mercury would have turned her teeth an ugly black, and left her with a sorely inflamed mouth. A Danish doctor found that the model had congenital palsy affecting the left side of her face, backing up his theory by pointing out that she had the typically large hands of such patients. After due study, an orthopedic surgeon in Lyons, France, decided that Mona Lisa's semi-smile resulted from her being half-paralyzed either from birth or as the result of a stroke; one indication of this, he argued, was that her right hand looks relaxed but her left hand is strangely tense.

But more intriguing than why the model is smiling is the mystery of exactly *who* is doing the smiling. An early reference to a woman named Lisa comes from the 16th-century Italian art historian Giorgio Vasari—who himself never actually saw the painting. Writing around 1550, a good 40 years after the work was supposed to have been completed, Vasari says: "Leonardo undertook to paint for Francesco del Giocondo a portrait of Monna [a variation of *mona* or *madonna*, "lady"] Lisa his wife." Historians know that a Lisa Gherardini of Florence was married in 1495, at the age of 16, to Francesco di Bartolommeo di Zanobi del Giocondo, a 35-year-old Florentine official already twice a widower. But there's no evidence at all that del Giocondo commissioned the portrait from Leonardo, no sign he paid the artist, and, most important, no sign the painting was delivered to him, since Leonardo kept it with him until his death in Amboise, France, in 1519. Nor does Leonardo mention the project anywhere in his voluminous notebooks.

So art historians have had a field day trying to guess whose portrait it is. Some plump for Isabella d'Este, who knew Leonardo well in Milan and whose portrait he did in crayon, perhaps as a study for an oil painting. Others hold for Costanza d'Avalos, duchess of Francaville, who is mentioned in a contemporary poem as having been painted in mourning by Leonardo "under the lovely black veil." There's even speculation that a second portrait of Mona Lisa may have existed. That painting may have been commissioned by one Giuliano de' Medici— perhaps because he was so taken with the original portrait that he requested one

Andy Warhol, *Mona Lisa: 1963*. (© 2008 Andy Warhol ▶
Foundation for the Visual Arts/ARS, New York)

for himself. Evidence exists that he asked Leonardo to paint her, leading to the intriguing possibility that the artist did two *Mona Lisas*, one for her husband, Francesco, and one for Giuliano, who may have been her lover. Now there's something to smile secretly about.

Then there's the high-tech approach. Lillian Schwartz, a computer graphics consultant at the Lucent Technologies Bell Labs in New Jersey, has applied computer-based techniques to the mystery. After reversing Leonardo's self-portrait so the artist is facing to the left, then scaling the image and juxtaposing it with the *Mona Lisa* (whose subject also faces left) on the computer screen, Schwartz found that the noses, mouths, foreheads, cheekbones, eyes, and brows all line up. Conclusion: Leonardo started with an earlier portrait of a woman, then, finding himself without the sitter, used himself as the model—sans beard. She ties it all together with the knotted patterns, resembling basketwork, on the bodice of Mona Lisa's dress. Noting that Leonardo, like many Renaissance poets and artists, loved riddles and puns, she makes the connection between his name, Vinci, and *vinco*, the Italian word for the osier branches used in basketry. Voilà, the case is made. "That famous smile, so tantalizing for so many centuries, is the mirrored smile of da Vinci himself," she says confidently.

Not everyone is convinced. But the possibility of a pun lying at the heart of Leonardo's mystery painting is taken seriously at the Louvre. Giocondo, Lisa Gherardini's married name, means, in Italian, cheerful, merry, joyous, as does "jocund" in English. (A variant of the word supplies the French title for the painting, *La Joconde*.) Leonardo had already played with a sitter's name by incorporating a juniper bush in his portrait of Ginevra (similar to "juniper," *ginepro* in Italian) de' Benci that hangs in the National Gallery of Art. "He was punning on Mona Lisa's married name when he gave her a subtle smile in *La Joconde*," says Cécile Scailliérez, curator of 16th-century French and Italian painting at the Louvre. "He made it emblematic of her. What we really have here is an idea, more than a realistic portrait, the idea of a smile expressed in the form of a painting."

For at least the past 150 years, appreciation of the *Mona Lisa* has veered back and forth between awed Giocondolatry and burlesque Giocondoclasm. The overwrought school of heated, romantic interpretation might have begun, oddly enough, with the Marquis de Sade, who found Mona Lisa full of "seduction and devoted tenderness," and "the very essence of femininity," though given his tastes one wonders exactly what he meant. A bit later the great French historian Jules Michelet admitted, "This painting attracts me, calls me, invades me, absorbs me; I go to it in spite of myself, as the bird goes to the serpent."

The idea of Mona Lisa as femme fatale was launched. Walter Pater, leader of the 19th-century English Aestheticism movement and ardent advocate of art for art's sake, followed up turgidly. "She is older than the rocks among which she sits," he swooned; "like the vampire, she has been dead many times, and learned the secrets of the grave." Not only that; for him this exotic beauty expressed "the animalism of Greece, the lust of Rome, the mysticism of the middle age . . . the return of the Pagan world, the sins of the Borgias." Pater seemed badly in need of a cold shower, as was the French writer of the same period, Arsène Houssaye, who called her "treacherously and deliciously a woman, with six thousand years of experience, a virgin with an angelic brow who knows more than all the knowing rakes of Boccaccio."

Sigmund Freud, too, pulled out all the stops when trying to figure out the "beautiful Florentine lady." Neatly pigeonholding Leonardo as an obsessive neurotic in his book-length study *Leonardo da Vinci, A Study in Psychosexuality*, Freud decided that Mona Lisa's expression must have resembled the lost, mysterious smile of the artist's mother. As for Mona Lisa herself, he proclaimed her nothing less than "the most perfect representation of the contrasts dominating the love-life of the woman, namely reserve and seduction, most submissive tenderness and the indifferent craving, which confront the man as a strange and consuming sensuality." (On second thought, perhaps we had better not take the kids to the Louvre after all.)

Twentieth-century ideas on art became more down-to-earth—like, how much is it worth? King Francis I added the *Mona Lisa* to France's royal collections for 4,000 gold *écus*, or about $105,000. Today Louvre officials say that the *Mona Lisa's* monetary value is inestimable. In 1911, however, it was somewhere in between: the painting, though precious, was not yet such a superstar on the world art market that it couldn't be sold. That made it worth stealing.

The biggest art heist in history occurred that year, with Parisians waking up on August 23 to screaming headlines like the one in the daily *Excelsior*: "The Louvre's *Joconde* Stolen: When? How? Who?" The answers were a long time coming, as an army of French, German, Russian, Greek and Italian detectives went on a merry, futile chase for two years. Then, when the public was becoming resigned to the loss of the *Mona Lisa*, an Italian laborer named Vincenzo Perugia got tired of keeping the original in the false bottom of a trunk.

Perugia, who had worked in the museum, used his knowledge of it to lift the painting. He was put up to it by an Argentine con man named Eduardo de Valfierno, who had a skilled art forger knock off six copies. Valfierno then sold the copies to eager, if unscrupulous, collectors—five in North America, one in Brazil—who thought they were getting the real thing straight from the Louvre. The scam made him the equivalent today of $67 million. When Valfierno didn't claim the original—ironically, he didn't need it for the operation—Perugia naively offered it for sale to a Florence art dealer and was promptly pinched. The *Mona Lisa* returned to France on December 31, 1913, ensconced in a special compartment of the Milan-Paris express. Her retinue included an assortment of policemen, politicians, museum bureaucrats, and artists. Incredibly, the painting had suffered no physical damage.

The damage was to the blind veneration and respect in which the portrait had been held for centuries. Somehow the caper and its familiar, irreverent press coverage rubbed off some of the *Mona Lisa's* mystique. The age of Giocondoclasm had begun.

Even Bernard Berenson admitted a change of heart. "To my amazement," he wrote after the theft was announced, "I found myself saying softly: 'If only it were true!' And when the news was confirmed I heaved a sigh of relief. . . . She had

153

simply become an incubus, and I was glad to be rid of her." For this eminent con-noisseur of Western art, as surely for many others, all the bowing and scraping over the *Mona Lisa* had become a pain in the neck.

Suddenly the public couldn't get enough of jokey Giocondiana. One post-card showed a grinning, toothy Mona Lisa thumbing her nose at the public and saying, "I'm off to see my Vinci, thanks and good-bye, all you gawkers." Another postcard, after the return, showed her holding a baby with Perugia's picture in the background, as if she'd been on a romantic escapade.

With irreverence and reaction against "bourgeois" values the new order of the day, the painting that had been the image of perfect, inaccessible beauty became the ideal target for desperately modern iconoclastic artists, like the Dadaists, who were sick of the very idea of a masterpiece. Marcel Duchamp, unofficial leader of the Dada anti art movement, summed up the new zeitgeist[3] in 1919 with a few strokes of his brush. Taking a standard postcard reproduc-tion, he brushed in a pointy mustache and goatee on the sacred face, and added a naughty caption. Now his action looks like no more than a childish prank. But the uptight art establishment, raised on the likes of Pater and the traditions of academic painting, was shocked, *shocked.*

Today the *Mona Lisa* is in the paradoxical situation of being both the sym-bol of Art and the inspiration for kitsch. Artists vie to see who can do the most outrageous parody; advertising studios labor to come up with the funniest way to use the image to sell everything from aperitifs to airlines, golf clubs to strips that hold your nasal passages open. Collectors of Giocondiana have catalogued nearly 400 advertising uses of the image and counting, along with at least 61 products called Mona Lisa, made in 14 countries.

Want to mock Salvador Dalí's commercialism? Do a montage with his eyes and upraised mustache on Mona Lisa's face, then put his hands overflowing with money in place of hers. Touché! Want to make light of a weighty public figure, from Stalin to De Gaulle to Prince Charles? Caricature him as Mona Lisa. Funn*eee*! The portrait also has become the favorite of computer-age digitizers of images. In Paris, Jean-Pierre Yvaral has done more than 150 synthesized Mona Lisas com-posed of hundreds of geometric patterns that look abstract up close but become Herself from afar. Next big project: digital images of her on the tails of British Airways jetliners.

Though he's no high-flying art critic or historian, Jean Margat has his own answer to the painting's mythic hold on the imagination. A retired geologist, Margat, from his home near Orléans, France, presides over the Friends of Mona Lisa, a club of serious collectors of Giocondiana, of which Louvre director Pierre Rosenberg is a member, along with a woman in faraway Ann Arbor, Michigan.

---

[3]In German, *zeitgeist* literally means "the spirit of the time." Commonly used in literary and philo-sophical criticism, the term refers to the ideas that prevail in a particular period and place.—ED.

Marcel Duchamp, *L.H.O.O.Q.*, 1930.
Duchamp (1887–1968), who became a U.S.
citizen in 1954, was one of the first to use
ordinary objects as an inspiration for art, a
concept of "ready-mades." Duchamp used
bicycle tires, urinals, snow shovels, and other
common, "non-art" objects in work that ultimately influenced such later movements as
surrealism and pop art. Wanting to satirize
his era's overly reverential attitude toward
major works of art, Duchamp drew a conventional mustache and goatee on a roughly
5 x 8 inch print of the *Mona Lisa*. He then
added to his appropriation of Leonardo's
famous creation by giving his work a cryptic,
though crude, title. (© 2008 Artists Rights
Society (ARS), NewYork/ADAGP,
Paris/Succession Marcel Duchamp.
Photo by Cameraphoto Arte, Venice/Art
Resource, NY)

155

COMMENT

"The best-known satire on [the worship of high art] was Marcel Duchamp's
L.H.O.O.Q.: the moustache on the *Mona Lisa*, a gesture by now synonymous with
impish cultural irreverence. As is usual with Duchamp's puns, it works on several layers
at once. The coarse title—*L.H.O.O.Q.*, pronounced letter by letter in French, means:
'She's got a hot ass'—combines with the schoolboy graffito of the moustache and
goatee; but then a further level of anxiety reveals itself, since giving male attributes to
the most famous and highly fetishized female portrait ever painted is also a subtler joke
on Leonardo's own homosexuality (then a forbidden subject) and on Duchamp's own
interest in the confusion of sexual roles."

—Robert Hughes, from *The Shock of the New* (1991)

The *Mona Lisa*

It's almost elegant in its simplicity. If you have a hard time breathing, especially at night, Breathe Right strips hold your nasal passages open so you breathe easier. And for lots of people, that's something to smile about. Breathe Right strips. In cough and cold sections everywhere.

Breathe *Right*

Improves Breathing By Reducing Nasal Airflow Resistance

Drug-free *gently pulls open nasal passages*

10 Med/Lg

Don't Laugh. It Works.

Margat and other Friends get together once in a while for a convivial lunch in Paris where they discuss and compare their collections. Margat's takes up a good part of his two-story house and ranges from Mona Lisa T-shirts, posters, ballpoint pens, coffee mugs, drink coasters, condoms, panty hose, clocks, matchbooks, and thimbles bearing The Face, to truly rare—and expensive—items like a beaded curtain from Vietnam, a Persian rug, and a life-size Mona Lisa sculptured in two kinds of marble that he paid a pretty penny for in Switzerland. His latest enthusiasm is for a bit of kitsch created in Brooklyn and known as the Giggling Mona Lisa Pillow, which squeals with glee when squeezed in the middle. . . .

By [the year 2000] the painting may have its own special room at the Louvre, the better to admire it—and keep the crowd away from the other museumgoers—thanks to a $4.1 million grant from a Japanese television network. This biggest-ever act of cultural sponsorship in France leaves Louvre curators with mixed feelings. Already prisoners of the myth, they can't touch the *Mona Lisa* to clean it for fear of media and public outcry, although it's filthy and covered with thick yellowish varnish that would benefit from cleaning. "The new room will be an improvement," says a resigned Cécile Scailliérez, "but unfortunately it will make the *Mona Lisa* even more of a superstar by setting it apart." As for Jean Margat, the project leaves him cold. "Frankly I don't much like that painting," he says with a shrug. "To me it's not expressive and it doesn't look like a real person. But I guess it's timeless, *hélas.*"

■ **Discuss.** *Harriss's description of the crowds that came out in the United States and Japan to see the painting testifies to its fame. Can you think of other works of art or popular culture that have inspired such a frenzy? Do they have anything in common with the* Mona Lisa? *What do you think gives certain artists this power?*

■ **Write.** *Innumerable art critics have tried to describe Mona Lisa's smile. Write your own interpretation of her smile. You can use one of the arguments from Harriss's piece as a jumping-off point for your own writing, or you can go in a new direction. What do you think her expression means?*

◀ **Breathe Right®, *Mona Lisa* ad, "Something to Smile About," 1995.** As Joseph Harriss points out in his essay (p. 145), the *Mona Lisa* has inspired a number of kitschy parodies in advertising. Here *La Gioconda* sells Breathe Right nasal strips. According to Breathe Right's web site, the strips "gently open nasal passages so you can breathe through your nose and close your mouth, reducing snoring." As the text of the ad indicates, the strip is "almost elegant in its simplicity." The product, available in tan, clear, and mentholated varieties, is recommended to sufferers of nasal congestion caused by allergies, colds, or deviated septa. (Reproduced with the permission of GlaxoSmithKline)

Lillian F. Schwartz, *Da Vinci Timeline (Leonardo Morphed to the Mona Lisa)*, 1995. Adapted from "The Art Historian's Computer," in *Scientific American*, April 1995, p. 106. (Copyright © 1995 Lillian F. Schwartz. Courtesy of the Lillian Feldman Schwartz Collection, The Ohio State University Libraries. All rights reserved. Reproduced by permission)

158

Lillian F. Schwartz, *Mona/Leo*, 1988. Lillian Schwartz (b. 1927), one of the pioneers in the field of computer art, concludes that the *Mona Lisa* is really a self-portrait. Combining historical analysis with a computer-based study of the painting in conjunction with a sketch Leonardo did of himself while in his late sixties, Schwartz suggests an answer to the mystery of the appeal of this painting: "Could it be that both women and men find traits that are physically attractive?" This composite visually describes Schwartz's contention that the *Mona Lisa* is in fact Leonardo's self-portrait; it places the "surface" *Mona Lisa* next to the "second" face. (Copyright © 1988 Lillian F. Schwartz. Courtesy of the Lillian Feldman Schwartz Collection, The Ohio State University Libraries. All rights reserved. Reproduced by permission)

 CONSIDER THE CLUSTER
The *Mona Lisa*

■ **Message**

In "Seeking Mona Lisa," Joseph A. Harriss says that the subject's "enigmatic, tight-lipped smile" has "launched a thousand learned interpretations." Why do you think critics believe that there is a message in Mona Lisa's smile, that her expression contains some deep or hidden meaning? Do you think any of the critics Harriss quotes come close to solving the enigma? For example, what do you make of Camille Paglia's view: "What Mona Lisa is ultimately saying is that males are unnecessary"? How might someone derive that message from the woman's smile?

■ **Method**

Assume that Lillian Schwartz's argument is correct and that the painting of the *Mona Lisa* is actually a self-portrait of Leonardo. In a short essay, address how this fact affects your interpretation of the famous smile. Be sure to consider a few of the interpretations Harriss cites in his survey.

■ **Medium**

Consider Marcel Duchamp's notorious response to the *Mona Lisa* in his 1919 *L.H.O.O.Q.* Why do you think he drew what he did? What medium was he imitating in drawing a mustache and goatee? How else might he have altered the image? Also, why do you think he decided to draw these facial hair styles on a postcard of the *Mona Lisa*? Why not paint an exact imitation first and then draw the mustache and goatee? What point is Duchamp making about artistic media?

159

WRITE

1. **Analyze.** Compare the girls in the photographs by Sally Mann (*Candy Cigarette*, p. 135) and Weegee (*Mulberry Street Café*, p. 241). Do these two photographs have anything in common? Which photographer seems more interested in social context? Which photograph seems less "posed" or "staged"? Which do you think better expresses a young girl's personality? In your opinion, which photograph better expresses the photographer's artistic intentions? You needn't prefer one to the other; but weigh the respective merits of each photograph and describe in an essay the ways you think a talented photographer can capture in a moment (or in a "flash") someone's character or personality.

2. **Collaborate and research.** With the help of the Internet, you can search the 58,195 names that appear on the Vietnam Veterans Memorial. One useful site is http://thewall-usa.com/. For a collaborative research assignment your class should select thirty to forty male names you consider either common or popular (the lists provided by Levitt and Dubner will help). Then break into several small groups, each group working with a different list. Look up the names on your list and note how many with those names appear on the wall.

(For example, note how many men named Henry died in that conflict.) Afterwards, make your report and construct a list of ten to fifteen of the most common names on the wall. Were any names unusual? Do the names suggest anything about the backgrounds or identities of those who died? As an additional group assignment, research the names of those who have died in the war in Iraq and compare the two lists.

3. **Evaluate.** "But is it art?" That question often comes up as people respond to such works as Marcel Duchamp's *L.H.O.O.Q.* (p. 155) or John Freyer's allmylifeforsale.com (p. 80), a domain name purchased by a university art museum. In an essay, consider why many people question the artistic value of such works. What is it about these works that challenges or even contradicts a general sense of the nature of an agreed-upon work of art, such as Leonardo's *Mona Lisa*? Select either Duchamp's or Freyer's work and argue why you do or do not consider it a genuine work of art.

4. **Analyze.** In just about every culture, people's names have significance. What about your name? What is its significance to you, your family, and your community? Consider the "What's in a Name?"

cluster (p. 110) and write a brief critical essay about the issues—personal and cultural—surrounding naming. In your essay, be sure to address at least two texts in the cluster. For example, you might choose to respond to Manuel Muñoz's "Leave Your Name at the Border" (p. 112), which addresses the question: What happens to non-English names in an English-speaking culture? You might also respond to the analysis by Levitt and Dubner ("Trading Up: Where Do Baby Names Come From?" p. 118) about the economic and social dynamics behind naming. How do our names impact how we think of ourselves—and how others think of us? What do the lists of the most popular names in the United States in 2005 (p. 123) suggest about naming and about our collective attitudes toward names? Your essay should provide a solid critical analysis (what is the significance of naming?), draw from materials in the cluster (what do others have to say about naming?), and incorporate relevant personal experience and insights (how do I relate to this topic personally?).

5. **Research.** Who was Marcel Duchamp, and what role did he play in the development of modern art? Using reference sources, including the Internet, write a short profile of Duchamp. What impact did he have on the twentieth century? Why did he become an American citizen? After learning about Duchamp, explain how his ideas about art shape much of what we find in contemporary museums, such as Sally Mann's *Candy Cigarette* and John Freyer's domain name.

6. **Collaborate.** Imagine that, like John Freyer, you have decided to put "all of your life" up for sale. After reviewing Freyer's objects, select three items that you currently own and write a single-paragraph description of each one that would make it appealing to a buyer or an eBay auction. Do not identify yourself. Then submit your descriptions to your instructor, who will blindly exchange them with someone else's. After receiving the other person's descriptions, write a short essay in which you construct a profile of that individual based solely on the objects selected and their descriptions.

7. **Collaborate and evaluate.** The *Mona Lisa* raises a central question of art and literature: Can a work of art be applicable to all cultures? After dividing into groups, discuss whether a writer or an artist has an obligation to make his or her work universally relevant. You might consider whether all great works of art are automatically universal, even

despite the artist's intentions. Also, can a work be universal at all, or do we actually need to be part of a specific culture or language group to appreciate it? Think, too, about whether an advertisement can be universally persuasive. Then, still working as a group, identify works in this book (or from outside sources) that illustrate universality or its absence and evaluate them in a panel discussion.

8. **Create a memoir.** In a personal essay, consider the meals you ate as a child and throughout your early school years. Were you served generally wholesome food, or did most meals consist of convenience foods? Did you retain a preference for the food you ate as a child, or did you alter your eating habits as you grew older and became more independent? Did you form habits or preferences that have been hard to change? In your essay, try to focus on the particular foods you recall most vividly and how they became part of your life. You may also want to develop this topic as a graphic essay.

2

TELLING STORIES

Telling Stories: the clusters

Storytelling appears throughout all cultures and is an inseparable part of human life. Our brains seem to be "hard-wired" for constructing narratives, for putting events in sequences, for selecting details, for reporting our experiences to others. We begin doing these things in very early childhood, practically as soon as we learn to speak.

The stories we tell also help us construct identities, both for ourselves and for our communities. As Harvard historian and now president Drew Gilpin Faust puts it: "We create ourselves out of the stories we tell about our lives, stories that impose purpose and meaning on experiences that often seem random and discontinuous." If that is the case with individuals, it is equally true for cultures and communities, which share stories in the form of myths, legends, and historical narratives. Understanding who we are and the world around us is in many ways dependent on understanding what we do when we relate a story—whether through words, pictures, or movements.

We naturally see our lives in terms of stories. In much of our conversation, we spontaneously narrate the events of our day: this happened, then that happened, and so on. Such informal narrative consists

of a string of events connected chronologically. This is the simplest and most common form of narration. Although we may imagine our life as a story, it should not take a lifetime to tell it! In narration, knowing what to leave out is as important as knowing what to include. Anyone who has listened patiently to a long-winded friend laboriously tell a story has often casually expressed an important criticism of all narration: "Please, get to the point!" we want to say, as we stifle a yawn. Our long-winded friend gets lost in details, often interrupting the flow of events to include yet another detail, one that may have no bearing on what happened. Worse, sometimes the storyteller becomes "side-tracked." We all know people who cannot tell us about getting a flat tire until they first describe how they bought the car.

Effective storytelling is not a matter of simply repeating a continuous sequence of events (x happened, then y, then z); instead it involves selecting events that lead to something significant (x happened, which resulted in y, which culminated in z). Skillful narrative, then, is not so much sequential as it is *con*sequential. This is what we normally mean when we say a story has a **plot.** A plot is a deliberate shaping or staging of the events to achieve a particular effect: suspense, surprise, intrigue, a sudden illumination or transformation, a moral. The renowned British novelist E. M. Forster made a useful and much-cited distinction between plot and story in his classic study of fiction, *Aspects of the Novel* (1927): "'The king died and then the queen died' is a story. 'The king died, and then the queen died of grief' is a plot." As you can see in this very brief example, one is sequential and the other is consequential.

A plot deals with the causes and consequences of the events, and it adds to the story's level of artifice. For example, we can tell a child an artless, rambling bedtime story that we make up as we go along.

But if we want our story to have the impact of surprise or to make a moral point, we usually need to know our ending in advance. In a traditional narrative, plot follows an arc. Exposition gives us the information we need to understand what's going to happen (the back story): A mother and father and their two sons live in a sleepy small town in a neat little bungalow. Complication occurs when something happens to set up a major conflict. (In this hypothetical narrative, the complication happens when the father gets a new job and they're going to have to move.) Climax is the turning point in the story that occurs when the characters try to resolve the complication. (One of the little boys runs away from home.) And the resolution is the set of events that brings the story to its close. (The mother finds the little boy in his favorite place and helps him understand that moving will be okay.) It's rare for a plot to follow this traditional arc. Writers and filmmakers routinely rearrange the climax, or the resolution, for example—some movies start with the end, with the events that led up to it gradually revealed in a series of flashbacks. Playing with plot is a way to control our emotional response to a story and prepare us (or not prepare us!) for reversals or surprises. Plots—as we know from many films and detective stories—can be elaborately constructed.

Although narrative and story are commonly used interchangeably, we can best consider **narrative** as the overall construction of a story. As we know, the same story can be told in any number of ways. Deciding how to tell a story forms the basis of narrative art: Should we begin at the beginning or start at the end and proceed backward? Which events should we select, and how should they be arranged? Should we establish a strict time period or not worry about gaps in time? Should we report multiple

points of view or focus on a single perspective? Anyone who undertakes a screenplay, a novel, or a cartoon confronts these decisions, whether consciously or not. "All my films have a beginning, a middle, and an end," said the French director Jean-Luc Godard, "but not necessarily in that order." Actually, many psychological experiments have demonstrated that we don't necessarily remember things in chronological order. People who experience the same, seemingly spontaneous series of events (a series that is actually scripted and staged) will offer widely different reports of what happened, and in what order. Many so-called false memories are actually false sequences, which is why trial lawyers are always careful to compare one witness's recollection of a sequence of events with another's.

Narrative structure can be found everywhere: in jokes, lab reports, historical accounts, personal essays, songs and ballads, news coverage, comic books, movies, sitcoms, and ballets. Some television commercials are mininarratives lasting only a few seconds without dialogue or commentary. Even photographers find ways to work with sequential storytelling methods, as Nora Ephron dramatically demonstrates in her essay "The Boston Photographs." In most paintings and photographs, in which the depiction of time or movement is absent or minimal, we tend to recognize narrative spatially rather than temporally. In other words, we follow sight-lines instead of time-lines, and sight-lines are less coercive. That is not to say there is no story; only that we play an active role in constructing it. You'll find stories in this chapter that range from the carefully constructed to the utterly unscripted— but all speak to our desire to tell stories and know stories.

FAIRY TALES AND URBAN LEGENDS

One of the oldest forms of storytelling, and one common to all human societies, is the cautionary tale, a short narrative that has a distinct purpose: to warn people, often children, of potential dangers. The narrative usually takes the form: if x does y, then z will be the horrible outcome. In the typical cautionary tale, something is prohibited or forbidden, someone violates those conditions, and then that person suffers the consequences. Many **fairy tales** that we learn as children are essentially cautionary tales, designed to frighten us into proper and obedient behavior. One of the most enduring tales is "Little Red Riding Hood," a centuries-old folktale that exists in many different translations and narrative versions.

A modern form of the cautionary tale is the **urban legend**. Such narratives, which—unlike fairy tales—take place in a real contemporary world, are often exaggerated stories based in rumor that purport to be true. Not all urban legends are cautionary, but many of these stories come about because of prevalent fears within a society. For example, people are warned that hitchhikers are very likely to be homicidal maniacs or that a mosquito bite can cause AIDS. How many have heard grim stories of unwary travelers who went to a bar one night, were drugged, and woke the following morning in a bathtub filled with ice, only to discover that one of their kidneys has been surgically removed? One of the oldest urban legends dates back to the 1950s and is known by American folklorists as "The Hook." With the advances of the Internet, such preposterous stories now surface and spread more rapidly than ever before and find enormous numbers of believers willing to grant them credibility. On the other hand, the Internet also provides excellent refutations of such legends on such sites as Snopes.com and About.com.

Charles Perrault, *Little Red Riding Hood* (*Le Petit Chaperon Rouge*). The son of a wealthy Parisian family, a lawyer by training, a leading member of the Académie Française, and a court official, this French author and storyteller (1628–1703) is best known for the fairy tales he wrote and adapted from earlier folktales. Among his most famous works are "Le Petit Chaperon Rouge" (Little Red Riding Hood), "La Belle au Bois Dormant" (Sleeping Beauty), "Le Chat Botté" (Puss in Boots), "Barbe Bleue" (Bluebeard), and "Cendrillon" (Cinderella). Catherine Orenstein notes in her essay (p. 176) that Perrault composed "Little Red Riding Hood" (1697) for the amusement of the court of Versailles. The following is an 1889 translation by Andrew Lang (1844–1912), a Scottish author, critic, and collector of folktales and fairy tales. Included on page 177 is an illustration original to Perrault's 1697 text.

Charles Perrault

LITTLE RED RIDING HOOD (LE PETIT CHAPERON ROUGE)

■ **Consider before you read.** *How does Perrault's tale differ from the "Little Red Riding Hood" that you remember from childhood?*

■ Consider. *Why does the author emphasize how pretty the girl is?*

Once upon a time there lived in a certain village a little country girl, the prettiest creature who was ever seen. Her mother was excessively fond of her; and her grandmother doted on her still more. This good woman had a little red riding hood made for her. It suited the girl so extremely well that everybody called her Little Red Riding Hood.

One day her mother, having made some cakes, said to her, "Go, my dear, and see how your grandmother is doing, for I hear she has been very ill. Take her a cake, and this little pot of butter."

Little Red Riding Hood set out immediately to go to her grandmother, who lived in another village.

As she was going through the wood, she met with a wolf, who had a very great mind to eat her up, but he dared not, because of some woodcutters working nearby in the forest. He asked her where she was going. The poor child, who did not know that it was dangerous to stay and talk to a wolf, said to him, "I am going to see my grandmother and carry her a cake and a little pot of butter from my mother."

"Does she live far off?" said the wolf.

"Oh I say," answered Little Red Riding Hood; "it is beyond that mill you see there, at the first house in the village."

Charles Perrault. (The Art Archive/Musée du Château de Versailles/Gianni Dagli Orti)

"Well," said the wolf, "and I'll go and see her too. I'll go this way and go you that, and we shall see who will be there first."

The wolf ran as fast as he could, taking the shortest path, and the little girl took a roundabout way, entertaining herself by gathering nuts, running after butterflies, and gathering bouquets of little flowers. It was not long before the wolf arrived at the old woman's house. He knocked at the door: tap, tap.

"Who's there?"

"Your grandchild, Little Red Riding Hood," replied the wolf, counterfeiting her voice, "who has brought you a cake and a little pot of butter sent you by mother."

The good grandmother, who was in bed, because she was somewhat ill, cried out, "Pull the bobbin, and the latch will go up."

The wolf pulled the bobbin, and the door opened, and then he immediately fell upon the good woman and ate her up in a moment, for it had been more than three days since he had eaten. He then shut the door and got into the grandmother's bed, expecting Little Red Riding Hood, who came some time afterwards and knocked at the door: tap, tap.

"Who's there?"

Little Red Riding Hood, hearing the big voice of the wolf, was at first afraid; but believing her grandmother had a cold and was hoarse, answered, "It is your grandchild Little Red Riding Hood, who has brought you a cake and a little pot of butter mother sends you."

The wolf cried out to her, softening his voice as much as he could, "Pull the bobbin, and the latch will go up."

Little Red Riding Hood pulled the bobbin, and the door opened.

The wolf, seeing her come in, said to her, hiding himself under the bed-clothes, "Put the cake and the little pot of butter upon the stool, and come get into bed with me."

Little Red Riding Hood took off her clothes and got into bed. She was greatly amazed to see how her grandmother looked in her nightclothes, and said to her, "Grandmother, what big arms you have!"

"All the better to hug you with, my dear."

"Grandmother, what big legs you have!"

"All the better to run with, my child."

"Grandmother, what big ears you have!"

"All the better to hear with, my child."

"Grandmother, what big eyes you have!"

"All the better to see with, my child."

"Grandmother, what big teeth you have got!"

"All the better to eat you up with."

And, saying these words, this wicked wolf fell upon Little Red Riding Hood, and ate her all up.

Moral: Children, especially attractive, well bred young ladies, should never talk to strangers, for if they should do so, they may well provide dinner for a wolf. I say "wolf," but there are various kinds of wolves. There are also those who are charming, quiet, polite, unassuming, complacent, and sweet, who pursue young women at home and in the streets. And unfortunately, it is these gentle wolves who are the most dangerous ones of all.

■ **Discuss.** *In this story, the wolf has to impersonate two females: first the young girl, and then her grandmother. Could his plan have worked at all without this playacting? Does impersonation relate to the moral Perrault gives to the tale?*

■ **Write.** *Fairy tales as they are told in America almost always have happy endings. This French version of the story certainly does not. In a short essay, consider why fairy tales might be given happy endings. Do you know of other stories that acquire happier conclusions over time?*

Unknown author, *Little Red Riding Hood*. This 1908 version of "Little Red Riding Hood" was part of the Children's Red Book series published by Reilly & Britton (known later, in 1919, as Reilly & Lee).

Unknown author
LITTLE RED RIDING HOOD

■ **Consider before you read.** *At the beginning of this story, we are introduced to a character who didn't appear in the Perrault version: the forester. How does the addition of this character change the tale?*

Once upon a time there lived in a cottage on the edge of a wood a forester and his wife and little daughter. The little girl was a great pet with everybody. Whenever she went out she wore a red cloak with a hood to it, and the neighbors called her "Little Red Riding Hood." She made friends not only with people, but the birds and beasts, too, and she was not afraid of anything, not even the dark.

One day her mother said to her, "My child, take this pat of butter and bottle of blackberry wine to your grandmother. Do not stay too long, for I shall be worried."

Red Riding Hood was delighted to do her mother's errand, so she put on her scarlet cloak, kissed her mother good-bye, and started off to her grandmother's house. The way led through the woods, but Red Riding Hood was not the least bit afraid, and she went on as happy as a lark.

The birds kept her company and sang their sweetest songs. The squirrels ran up and down the tall trees and made her laugh at their funny antics; and now and then a rabbit would come across her path, and sometimes Red Riding Hood would run after the bunnies, but they always managed to get out of her way.

By and by she grew hungry, and sat down on a flat stone to eat the nice lunch her mother had put up for her, and oh, how good it tasted! It was very lonely in the woods, but Red Riding Hood thought only of the wild flowers, which were so beautiful, and she went out of the path to gather some violets, honeysuckle and sweet ferns, which made a very pretty nosegay, indeed. But, dear me! When she turned to go back to the path she could not find it, and she was scared, for she felt she was surely lost in the woods.

The birds knew that she was lost, and as she had been so good to them two of them flew down and called Red Riding Hood and led her out of the tangle of brushwood into the path again. While she sat resting for a few moments a wolf came up and spoke to her, which did not seem at all strange to Little Red Riding Hood, as wolves and fairies were quite common in those days.

173

"Good day," said the wolf; "where are you going by yourself, little girl?"

"I am going to my grandmother's," said Little Red Riding Hood.

"She ought to be proud of such a lovely granddaughter," said the wolf.

Pleased with this compliment Red Riding Hood let the wolf walk by her side, although the birds kept warning her that he was a wicked rogue.

"Where does your grandmother live?" asked the wolf in a sweet voice.

"Just outside the woods. You can see her cottage through the trees," said the little girl.

"Oh, yes," said the wolf, "I think I will call on the dear old lady just for the fun of the thing. Suppose you take the left path while I follow this one to the right, and we will have a little race to see which gets to the cottage first."

Of course the wolf knew he was sure to win the race, for he had chosen the shortest way, but Red Riding Hood suspected nothing. She was so young she did not know that wolves might seem to be mild as sheep, but still be wolves at heart. The wolf took the short road, and soon came to the grandmother's cottage. He rapped gently on the door, and the old lady, who was in bed, said:

"Is that you, darling? Pull the string and the latch will fly up," thinking it was Red Riding Hood, of course.

The wolf pulled the string and then opened the door and walked in.

"I am very glad you came, dear," said the grandmother, thinking her visitor was Red Riding Hood. "I am more poorly than usual, and it hurts me to turn my head. Take off your hat, dear, and come kiss me."

"That I will do at once!" said the wolf, and with glaring red eyes he sprang on the bed and ate her up. Then he got into the bed and put on granny's nightgown and cap and waited for Red Riding Hood to come.

At last the wolf heard a little rap at the door, and he called out, as the old lady had done:

"Is that you darling? Pull the string and the latch will fly up." His voice was harsh, but not unlike the grandmother's when she had a cold.

So Red Riding Hood pulled the string and went into the house, set her basket on the table and went up to the bedside.

She was scared at the change that she thought had come over her grandmother. What could be the matter with her to make her look like this? She must have some terrible disease.

"Why, Granny," she said, as soon as she could speak, "what big eyes you have got."

"The better to see you with, my child," said the wolf, imitating the grandmother's voice.

"O, Granny!" cried the child, "what a great long nose you have got."

"The better to smell with, my child."

"But, Granny, what great big ears you have got."

"The better to hear with, my child."

Red Riding Hood began to be more scared than she had ever been in her life, and her voice trembled when she said:

"O, Granny, what great—big—teeth—you've—got!"

"The better to eat you up!" said the wolf in his own voice, and he was just about putting his long sharp yellow fangs in poor Little Red Riding Hood, when the door was flung open and a number of men armed with axes rushed in and made him let go of his hold, and Red Riding Hood fainted in her father's arms. He was on his way home from work, with some other men, and was just in time to save his dear little daughter.

With one or two strokes of the axe the wolf's head was cut off, so that he would do no more harm in the world, and his body was tied to a pole and carried back in triumph by the foresters.

Friends from far and near came to see Little Red Riding Hood, and she had to tell over and over again just where she met the wolf, how he looked and what he said, until it seemed as if she never got out of the woods at all, not even in her dreams.

When the children were told the story it was always with this word of warning:

"When you are sent on an errand, go right along, and do it as quickly as you can. Do not stop to play on the road or to make friends with strangers, who may turn out to be wolves in sheep's clothes," and they promised to remember, and shuddered whenever they thought of what might have been the fate of dear Little Red Riding Hood.

■ **Discuss.** *Does this version of "Little Red Riding Hood" place more of the blame on the girl? What hints are there in the story that she is putting herself in danger? How much does the wolf gain from her pride?*

■ **Write.** *The author of this version makes a point to discuss Little Red Riding Hood's relationship with the animals of the forest. Why do you think the animals become so important in this story? Write an essay that addresses the question: What is the author trying to say about the girl's connection with nature and about how it reflects her character?*

Catherine Orenstein, *Dances with Wolves: Little Red Riding Hood's Long Walk in the Woods*. Catherine Orenstein's writing on culture and mythology has appeared in *The New York Times*, the *Washington Post*, *The San Francisco Examiner*, and *Ms. Magazine*. She has lectured at universities such as Harvard and Columbia and has appeared on television and on National Public Radio. In her 2002 book *Little Red Riding Hood Uncloaked: Sex, Morality, and the Evolution of a Fairy Tale* (Basic Books), she looks at the story over time— from the seventeenth century to the present—and considers our changing ideas about men and women and cultural attitudes toward sex and morality. The following essay was originally published in *Ms. Magazine* in 2004.

Catherine Orenstein

DANCES WITH WOLVES: LITTLE RED RIDING HOOD'S LONG WALK IN THE WOODS

■ **Consider before you read.** *What tools does Orenstein use to deconstruct the tale of Little Red Riding Hood? Notice how she introduces psychology, political history, and information about the production of books and about their audiences. Are there other methods you can identify?*

Mae West,[1] who mined the rich symbolic terrain of fairy tales, once famously quipped, "I used to be Snow White, but I drifted."

These days the social and sexual messages of fairy tales are no secret. Feminists in particular have long recognized that fairy tales socialize boys and especially girls, presenting them with lessons that must be absorbed to reach adulthood.

But what exactly are those lessons? We tend to think of fairy tales as timeless and universal, but in fact they express our collective truths even as those truths shift over time and place.

Take the story of Little Red Riding Hood, for example—a tale we all know well, though not as well as we think.

Once upon a time, "Little Red Riding Hood" was a seduction tale. An engraving accompanying the first published version of the story, in Paris in 1697, shows

---

[1]Mae West (1893–1980) was a celebrated and controversial actress known for her voluptuous figure and bawdy wit.

a girl in her déshabille, lying in bed beneath a wolf. According to the plot, she has just stripped out of her clothes, and a moment later the tale will end with her death in the beast's jaws—no salvation, no redemption. Any reader of the day would have immediately understood the message: In the French slang, when a girl lost her virginity it was said that *elle avoit vû le loup*—she'd seen the wolf.

Penned by Charles Perrault for aristocrats at the court of Versailles, "*Le petit chaperon rouge*" dramatized a contemporary sexual contradiction. It was the age of seduction, notorious for its boudoir histories and its royal courtesans, who rose to power through sexual liaisons and were often celebrated at court; those who made it to the King's bed might earn the title *maîtresse-en-titre*, official mistress.

Nonetheless, chastity was the feminine ideal, demanded by the prevailing institution of marriage—not the "fairy tale wedding" of modern fantasy, but the *mariage de raison*, orchestrated by parents for social or financial gain and often no more than a crass exchange of assets.

Hence the age of seduction was also an age of institutionalized chastity: Girls were raised in convents. By law a man could sequester daughters (or any female relatives) until marriage. Men and women alike could be disinherited, banished or even sentenced to death for the crime of *rapt*—meaning seduction, elopement or rape (among which the law made scant distinction). And young women were repeatedly warned of the dangers of unscrupulous suitors.

Perrault cloaked his heroine in red, the color of scandal and blood, suggesting the girl's sin and foreshadowing her fate. Her *chaperon*, or hood, also took on the tale's lesson, acquiring the meaning in English, which it already possessed in French, of one who guards girls, virtue. For good measure, Perrault added an explicit rhyming moral admonishing *demoiselles*—that is, young ladies of society—to remain chaste:

> Little girls, this seems to say,
> Never stop upon your way,
> Never trust a stranger-friend;
> No one knows how it will end.
> As you're pretty so be wise;
> Wolves may lurk in every guise.
> Handsome they may be, and kind.
> Gay, and charming—nevermind!
> Now, as then, 'tis simple truth—
> Sweetest tongue has sharpest tooth!

177

PETIT CHAPERON

ROUGE.

CONTE.

 L eſtoit une fois une petite fille de Vilage, la plus jolie qu'on eut ſçû voir;

Perrault's original illustration (1697).
(Bibliothèque Nationale de France, Réserve des Livres Rares)

Though Perrault's moral would eventually be eliminated from the fairy tale, his metaphor has survived to this day. Today we still use the term "wolf" to mean a man who chases women.

In the 19th century Red Riding Hood grew more discreet, and also acquired a man to safeguard her. A fatherly woodsman rescues Red from the beast's belly and gives her a second chance to walk the straight path through life in "Little Red Cap," published in 1812 by the German brothers Jacob and Wilhelm Grimm. This is the version of the tale that most people know today.

The Grimms did not faithfully preserve the lore of common folk, as they claimed in the preface to their first edition of *Children's and Household Tales.* Rather, they adapted the tale for a new children's audience, excising all erotic content along with Perrault's incriminating moral. Their revision suggested spiritual rather than sexual danger, and stressed the most important lesson of the day: obedience. That lesson easily found purchase in the social landscape of Victorian Europe.

A famous 1875 print by Walter Crane—appearing in a six-penny color "toy book" that made the story immensely popular in England, a hub of children's literature—shows the heroine cloaked in the garb and ideas of the Victorian working class. Women and children alike might be easily fooled by the wolf that Crane draws wearing a sheepskin—a Biblical reference to the Devil. Today the prudish Grimms' version of the fairy tale remains rife with suggestive details left over from Red Riding Hood's racier French past, yet modern readers remain remarkably and sometimes comically oblivious.

An 1867 illustration by Gustave Doré. (The Art Archive/John Meek)

In 1990, the storybook was banned in two California school districts because of an illustration showing Red's basket with a bottle of wine as well as fresh bread and butter. The story line of Red disrobing and climbing in bed with the wolf passed muster, but the *wine*, they said, might be seen as condoning the use of alcohol.

Not until the 20th century was the bowdlerized Red Riding Hood defrocked, so to speak, and redressed. Advertisements transformed the heroine, once a symbolic warning against the female libido, into an ode to Lust. Ripe young "Riding Hood Red" lipstick would "bring the wolves out," Max Factor promised, in a poster-sized ad appearing in *Vogue* in 1953. A 1962 advertisement in *The New Yorker* offered Red as a glamorous femme fatale, on her way to Grandma's in her "little Red Hertz."

And, "Without red, nothing doing," said a 1983 French advertisement for Johnnie Walker Red Label Scotch whisky, which showed a wolf bypassing a crestfallen girl clad in white. (Who wants to buy a drink for bleached goody-two-shoes?)

■ Consider. *Why do you think there are so many pop culture versions and interpretations of "Little Red Riding Hood"? Can you think of more recent commercials or television shows that parody the story?*

Storytellers from the women's movement and beyond also reclaimed the heroine from male-dominated literary tradition, recasting her as the physical or sexual aggressor and questioning the machismo of the wolf. In the 1984 movie *The Company of Wolves*, inspired by playwright Angela Carter, the heroine claims a libido equal to that of her lascivious stalker and becomes a wolf herself. In the Internet tale "Red Riding Hood Redux," the heroine unloads a 9mm Beretta into the wolf and, as tufts of wolf fur waft down, sends the hunter off to a self-help group, White Male Oppressors Anonymous.

The 1996 movie *Freeway* cast Reese Witherspoon as a tough runaway in a red leather jacket who is more than a match for the serial killer she meets while hitching her way to grandma's trailer park. And about that macho wolf? A 1989 "Far Side" cartoon by Gary Larson cast the beast on a psychiatrist's couch, in a floral nightgown. "It was supposed to be just a story about a little kid and a wolf," he says, "but off and on I've been dressing up as a grandmother ever since."

Modern fairy tales with strong heroines have abounded since the 1970s, when second-wave feminists such as Simone de Beauvoir, Andrea Dworkin and Susan Brownmiller pointed out how the classic fairy tales of Perrault and the brothers Grimm showcase passive, helpless, beauty-queen femininity. Such tales, they argued, made little girls long to become "glamorous victims."

Since then, men and women alike have rewritten many of the classic tales to reflect more modern ideas about women. But few outside the field of folklore know that some of our most popular stories have oral roots that are strikingly different from the literary tradition and feature heroines who are far from passive. Little Red Riding Hood is such a case.

Folklorists trace the origins of tales the same way paleontologists study the origins of species: by collecting, dating and comparing samples, noting common traits that suggest common ancestry, and attempting to construct a lineage. In the mid-20th century, scholars and collectors found a substantial body of stories from France. All were remarkably similar in plot and many shared an abundance of details, including cannibalism, defecation, a striptease, and a bedroom encounter with a beast.

They lacked, however, the usual fairy tale moral scolding the heroine. And most of them shared one more remarkable element: a clever heroine who escapes by her own wits. One memorable version of the story genre ends like this: Lying in bed with the villain—this time, a *bzou*, or werewolf—the heroine pretends she has to relieve herself. The bzou tells her to do it in the bed, but she refuses—"Oh no, that will smell bad!" she says in another variation—so the bzou ties a cord around the heroine's ankle and lets her out on the leash, tugging periodically to ensure she does not get away.

Once outside, however, the girl unknots the cord and ties it around a tree. With the bzou in belated pursuit, she escapes. Folklorists are now reasonably certain that this is how Little Red Riding Hood's adventure was told many years ago, around the fire or in the fields, long before she found her way to print.

What to make of this plot? Rather than the tales of female folly and punishment presented by Perrault and the brothers Grimm—and canonized by the popular psychologist Bruno Bettelheim as reflective of timeless, deep-rooted truths—this story contains many of the same elements that distinguish folk-tales and myths about male heroes.

Like most fairy tales, it follows a "rite of passage" structure, associated with coming of age (indeed, many fairy tales end in marriage, the symbolic recognition of adulthood). But rather than featuring a passive heroine who awaits rescue by a prince or woodcutter, this oral folktale features a heroine triumphant. It is not she but her adversary who is duped.

As is typical of tales about male heroes, the plot revolves around a test of self-reliance that some scholars call a "wisdom journey." Perhaps it should not be sur-prising that we don't often find such female characters in our classic literary fairy tales, which were penned by men in centuries when an unwed woman remained conceptually a child well into middle age.

But oral fairy tales were often *told* by women, to the repetitive rhythms of work, until spinning a yarn and telling a tale were one and the same. Spinning and sewing terms often appear in fairy tales—Rumplestiltskin spins straw into gold, Sleeping Beauty pricks her finger on a spindle, and in the oral ancestor of Red Riding Hood, the heroine meets her adversary at "the path of pins and needles."

Such terms, symbolic of women's work and skills, serve to remind us that these stories were once wives' tales—that is, stories told by women—before that term came to mean a lie. Should it be surprising that a woman storyteller would cast her heroine as more clever than her adversary? Or represent female maturity in different terms from male authors of history?

If these stories came only from one city or country, perhaps one would begin by searching for a particular explanation in that particular locale. But as it turns out, Red Riding Hood's empowered sisters have been found all around the globe—not only in France but throughout Europe and in lands as far away as China—which ought to make us broadly question our so-called timeless and universal stories about women, and our very notion of a heroine.

As Mae West knew, old stories can be reinvented. And heroines can always be reclaimed.

■ **Discuss.** *After discussing the ways Little Red Riding Hood has reappeared in the twentieth century, Orenstein turns from written and filmed versions of the story to older, oral histories. Why might stories retold within communities contain different elements than ones that are written down? Discuss why the more shocking aspects of the story ("cannibalism, defecation, a striptease, and a bedroom encounter with the beast") might be more acceptable in oral storytelling.*

■ **Write.** *Try writing your own escape narrative for Little Red Riding Hood. If her story can be understood as a "wisdom journey," how do you imagine her emerging victorious at the end?*

David Emery, *The Hook: An Urban Legend*. Freelance writer David Emery, a native of Oregon and a drummer with a degree in philosophy, enjoys sorting through the urban legends, hoaxes, and folklore of the Internet. On his web site (urbanlegends.about.com), Emery notes: "On this site we'll investigate, debunk, and, wherever possible, simply appreciate the strangest, scariest, funniest, most popular tall tales, rumors, and hoaxes people see fit to share, both online and off. I'm pleased to have you join me in what promises to be a constantly entertaining, ever-enlightening exploration of the folklife of the digital age." Here Emery records the urban legend known as "The Hook" and offers his own commentary on a story that, like other cautionary tales, just won't go away.

David Emery

THE HOOK: AN URBAN LEGEND

■ **Consider before you read.** *How do urban legends get started, and how do they spread? What function do you think they serve in society?*

A teenage boy drove his date to a dark and deserted Lovers' Lane for a make-out session. After turning on the radio for mood music, he leaned over and began kissing the girl.

A short while later, the music suddenly stopped and an announcer's voice came on, warning in an urgent tone that a convicted murderer had just escaped from the state insane asylum—which happened to be located not far from Lovers' Lane—and that anyone who noticed a strange man lurking about with a hook in place of his right hand should immediately report his whereabouts to the police.

The girl became frightened and asked to be taken home. The boy, feeling bold, locked all the doors instead and, assuring his date they would be safe, attempted to kiss her again. She became frantic and pushed him away, insisting that they leave. Relenting, the boy peevishly jerked the car into gear and spun its wheels as he pulled out of the parking space.

When they arrived at the girl's house she got out of the car, and, reaching to close the door, began to scream uncontrollably. The boy ran to her side to see what was wrong and there, dangling from the door handle, was a bloody hook.

COMMENTS ABOUT "THE HOOK"

Folks have been telling the "hook man" story since the 1950s, and indeed the implicit moral message—"Sex is naughty, and bad boys and girls will be punished!"—seems more appropriate to that simpler, more naive era. Just as this moral has come to be parodied in horror films (where formerly it was delivered with morbid solemnity), its "bygone" relevance has taken the teeth out of the cautionary tale over time.

Noting the improbable "tidiness" of the plot, Jan Harold Brunvand (see p. 183) has observed that "most tellers narrate the story nowadays more as a scary story than a believed legend." Small wonder. Given its exploitation by Hollywood in popular genre films like "Candyman" and "I Know What You Did Last Summer," most people under the age of 30 probably assume the story was invented by screenwriters.

Folklorists of a Freudian bent find meaningful sexual overtones in the imagery of the tale. The boy, who wants to get his "hooks" into the girl, is not only frustrated by her unwillingness but afraid of his own lustful impulses—a fear heightened by the stern "voice of conscience" emitting from the radio—and has to "pull out fast" before a deadly sin is committed. The tearing off of the madman's hook symbolizes castration. Proponents of this type of psychological interpretation find the sexual apprehensions of both boys and girls represented in the legend.

One of the earliest appearances of "The Hook" in print was in a "Dear Abby" column dated November 8, 1960:

DEAR ABBY: If you are interested in teenagers, you will print this story. I don't know whether it's true or not, but it doesn't matter because it served its purpose for me:

A fellow and his date pulled into their favorite "lovers' lane" to listen to the radio and do a little necking. The music was interrupted by an announcer who said there was an escaped convict in the area who had served time for rape and robbery. He was described as having a hook instead of a right hand. The couple became frightened and drove away. When the boy took his girl home, he went around to open the car door for her. Then he saw— a hook on the door handle! I don't think I will ever park to make out as long as I live. I hope this does the same for other kids.

182

■ **Consider.** *What does the letter writer's assertion about not knowing whether the story is true say about urban legends? Does it matter whether they are truth or fiction?*

■ **Discuss.** *Why are these stories labeled "urban" legends? What would be their counterpart? Rural legends? How are urban legends different from previous cautionary tales?*

■ **Write.** *Look up other urban legends online and choose one to use as the basis for a short essay. Using Emery's analysis of "The Hook" as a guide, identify and analyze the messages that underlie the story. What are listeners being cautioned against?*

Jan Harold Brunvand (writer) and DC Comics (artists), *The Hook.* The legendary house of DC Comics—founded in 1934, once known as Detective Comics, and now the world's biggest publisher of comics in English—decided to take folklorist Jan Harold Brunvand's urban legends and turn them into comics. This version of "The Hook" was published in *The Big Book of Urban Legends* (1994, Paradox Press), along with 199 other folktales that are divided into eight categories of legends: automobile, animal, horror, accidents, sex/scandal, crime, business/professional/governmental, and celebrity. Brunvand writes in his introduction: "Urban Legends (UL's, as I sometimes call them) are true stories that are too good to be true, and they are always said to happen to a Friend of a Friend (or FOAF). . . . There is a seemingly inexhaustible supply of these stories, and old legends are constantly being told, changed, retold, and then told again as new." However these stories are conveyed—as spoken word, as comics, or through the Internet—Brunvand observes, "they are tremendously popular, despite their low place on the cultural totem pole." (From *The Vanishing Hitchhiker: American Urban Legends and Their Meanings* by Jan Harold Brunvand. Copyright © 1981 by Jan Harold Brunvand. Used by permission of W. W. Norton & Company, Inc. "The Hook" artwork from *The Big Book of Urban Legends* © 1994 DC Comics. All Rights Reserved. Used with Permission.)

183

Jan Harold Brunvand and DC Comics
THE HOOK

■ **Consider.** *How does the artwork created by DC Comics represent the familiar story? How does the artist choose to depict the two characters, the location, and other elements?*

Fairy Tales and Urban Legends

184

◀ ■ Discuss. *The story is framed in this comic by panels featuring Sigmund Freud. Why does the comic foreground Freud in this way? Do the creators of the comic agree with the Freudian reading, or are they making fun of it?*

■ Write. *Choose one panel of the comic to analyze in writing. What is in the center of the frame, what is at the edges, and what is cut off? How does the artist use blank space or light and shading? Where is the text positioned? What effect do these choices have on the telling of the story?*

185

I'll Always Know What You Did Last Summer, **Sony Pictures Entertainment, 2006.** Based on a screenplay by Michael D. Weiss that was based on a novel by Lois Duncan, and directed by Sylvain White, this 1990s-style slasher film borrows heavily from the legend of "The Hook." The plot focuses on a group of four teens in Colorado who, one year after covering up a friend's accidental death, are stalked by a mysterious cloaked figure wielding a menacing, murderous (you guessed it) hook. As the movie trailer web site asks, "Can the friends survive and figure out the identity of their tormentor before they end up dead themselves?" (Sony Pictures/The Kobal Collection)

 CONSIDER THE CLUSTER
Fairy Tales and Urban Legends

■ Message

Note that both the Perrault and the Children's Red Book versions of "Little Red Riding Hood" contain explicit messages. In stories, such a message is commonly known as the *moral*—the valuable lesson we are meant to receive from a tale. What are the lessons conveyed by each version of this classic fairy tale, and how do they differ? Consider this question in class discussion: Would you know the message or moral of each tale if it hadn't been specifically stated at the conclusion?

■ Method

Compare Perrault's "Little Red Riding Hood" with the story of "The Hook." What similarities do you see between the two tales? In what ways do you think urban legends resemble fairy tales? What points of difference can you see? In a short essay, using the texts reprinted here or other tales you may prefer, discuss how fairy tales and urban legends are similar yet different.

■ Medium

Cautionary tales can be told in numerous ways. In fact, the oldest stories were passed on through oral traditions. Many TV commercials are cautionary tales: What dire consequences will befall you if you don't use this product or purchase that insurance? Consider different ways you might re-create "Little Red Riding Hood" in different media. What might the fairy tale look like if it were retranslated as a text message? As an in-class assignment, try imagining the opening part of the fairy tale in a different format.

MINI-NARRATIVES

The American novelist Ernest Hemingway reportedly claimed that the best story he ever wrote consisted of only six words: "For sale: baby shoes, never worn." Using this mini-narrative as a model, *Wired* magazine invited a number of noted writers from various popular genres to compose something similar. They also asked several prominent graphic designers to imagine how these tiny stories might appear in print. Some of the "concise masterpieces" they received are included in "Very Short Stories."

Mini-narratives can be located anywhere and take many forms: cartoons, TV commercials, newspaper headlines, spray-painted graffiti, greeting cards, text messages, and so on. *FOUND* magazine frequently features notes and messages that people find in various places. Some of these randomly found items convey stories that invite our attention, such as "Action! List!" "Stupid, Stupid, and Stupid," and "Science."

A major source of mini-narratives is the familiar comic strip. In "Family," we see one of America's leading cartoonists and graphic novelists, Chris Ware, at work distilling a complicated story into four panels for the Thanksgiving cover of *The New Yorker* magazine.

From *Wired* magazine, *Very Short Stories*, November 2006. Can you tell a science fiction story in just six words? *Wired* magazine challenged thirty-three writers to do just that, and it commissioned forty-five graphic designers to present them visually. Included here are six-word stories by the likes of William Shatner (aka Captain Kirk), Joss Whedon (creator of *Buffy the Vampire Slayer*), Stan Lee (co-creator of *Spider Man*, *X-Men*, and other Marvel superstars), Alan Moore (author of *Watchmen* and *"V" for Vendetta*), Kevin Smith (screenwriter, director of and actor in *Clerks*, *Law & Order*, and *Veronica Mars*), and a slew of sci-fi authors and comic book artists.

    The designers represented here are John Maeda (a computer scientist and MIT professor) and Stephen Doyle (of his own design studio, Doyle Partners, and formerly the associate art director for *Rolling Stone* and *Esquire*).

188

Wired Magazine
VERY SHORT STORIES

■ **Consider.** *What emotional responses do these very short stories produce in the reader? Curiosity, sympathy, fear? How do the writers convey these feelings so economically?*

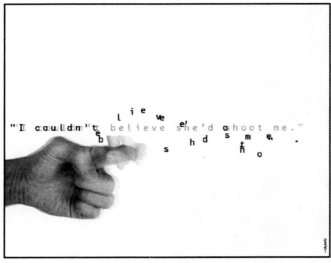

Designer: John Maeda.
(Reprinted by permission
of John Maeda)

"I couldn't believe she'd shoot me."
 —Howard Chaykin

Designer: John Maeda.
(Reprinted by permission
of John Maeda)

TIME MACHINE REACHES FUTURE!!! ...nobody there...
 —Harry Harrison

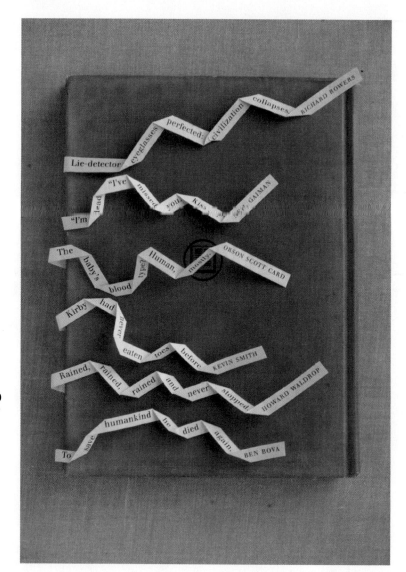

Designer: Stephen Doyle.
(Reprinted by permission of Doyle Partners)

190

■ **Discuss.** *With so few words to work with, the writers of these stories have to make everything count. Discuss how punctuation adds to the drama of these stories. Which ones would not work without their punctuation marks?*

■ **Write.** *How would you elaborate on these very short stories? Choose one of them and write a story that fills in the details of the plot.*

Found artifacts: FOUND magazine, *Action! List!* and *Stupid X 3*, and found ▶
photo: *SCIENCE*. Davy Rothart and Jason Bitner were inspired to create
FOUND magazine a few years ago on a snowy winter night in Chicago. As
Jason Bitner describes it at foundmagazine.com:

> "Davy went out to his car and found a note on his windshield—a note
> meant for someone else, a guy named Mario:

> > Mario,
> > I *&^%$#@ hate you. you [sic] said you had to work then whys [sic]
> > your car HERE at <u>HER</u> place??
> > You're a *&^%$#@ LIAR. I hate you I *&^%$#@ hate you.
> > > Amber
> > > PS: Page me later.

> We loved this note—its amazing mixture of anger and hopefulness—and
> so we shared it with as many folks as we could. Each friend we showed
> the Mario and Amber note seemed to have a few finds to show us in
> return. Clearly we weren't alone in our fascination with found stuff. . . .
> [W]e de-cided to start a magazine called *FOUND*, a showcase for all
> the strange, hilarious, and heartbreaking things people've picked up."

The following mini-narratives are two foundmagazine.com "Finds of the
Day" and "SCIENCE," a found Polaroid. (Covers reprinted by permission of
FOUND magazine)

191

Found artifacts

ACTION! LIST! AND STUPID X 3, AND FOUND PHOTO, SCIENCE

■ **Consider before you read.** *Are any of these found items meant to tell a story? Which
of their stories do you find most compelling?*

Action! List! FOUND **magazine "Find of the Day," June 3, 2006.**
The list below was found by Jane Pulliam in Tacoma, Washington, who writes: "I manage some apartments. One night the garbage was overflowing with a plastic bag full of Coke cans. When I opened the bag this 'Action List' was inside. Two things strike me as funny. The first is that getting a job is more important than getting off heroin. And second, besides a dozen empty Coke cans there were two empty half gallon jugs of chocolate milk. What happened to number nine?"

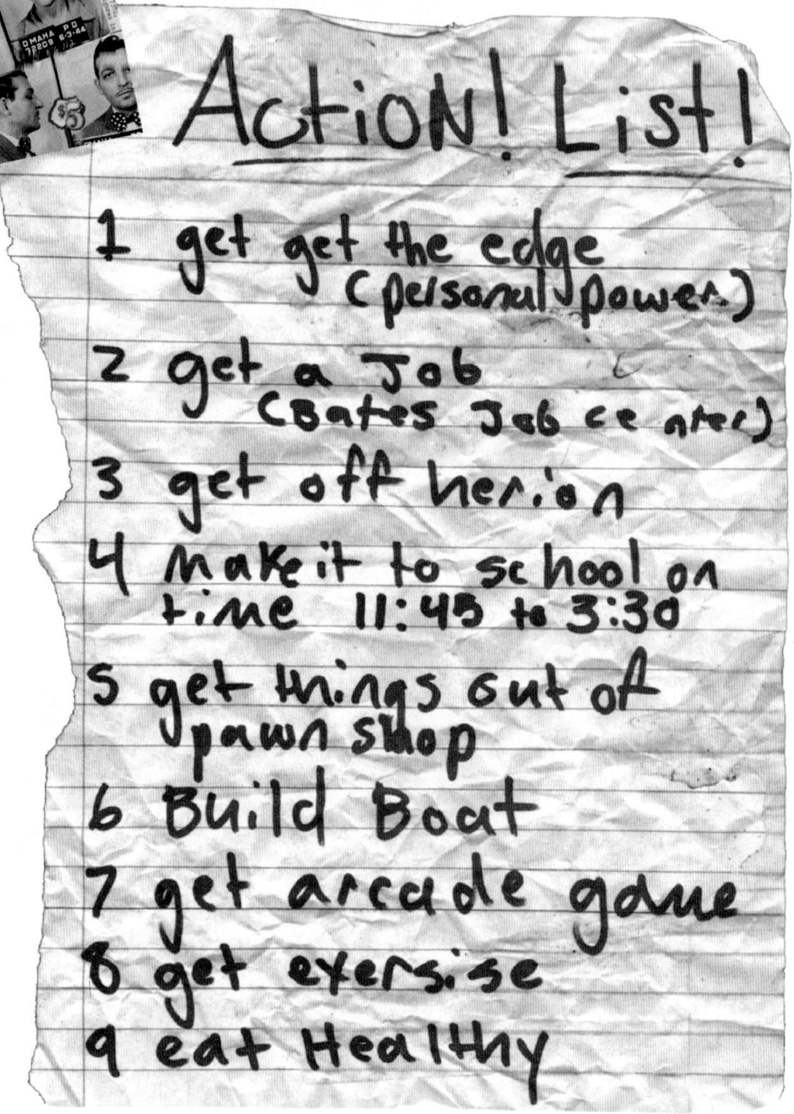

192

Action! List!

1 get get the edge
    (personal power)
2 get a Job
    (Bates Job center)
3 get off herion
4 make it to school on
    time 11:45 to 3:30
5 get things out of
    pawn shop
6 Build Boat
7 get arcade game
8 get exersise
9 eat Healthy

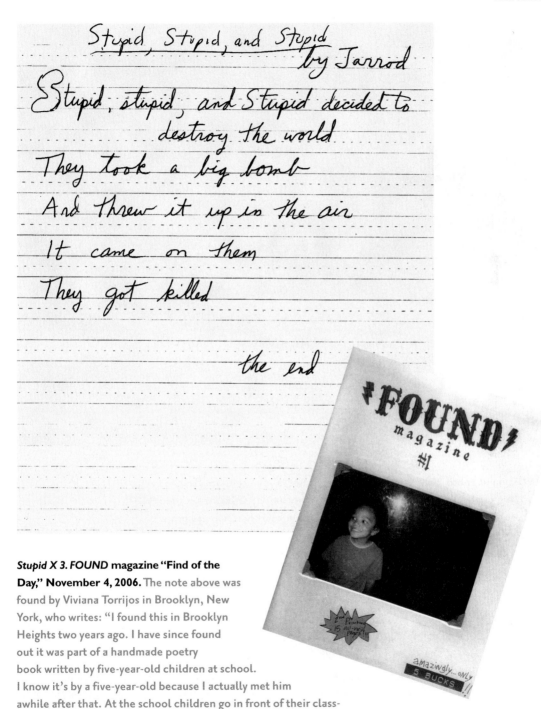

Stupid, Stupid, and Stupid
by Jarrod

Stupid, stupid, and Stupid decided to
destroy the world

They took a big bomb

And threw it up in the air

It came on them

They got killed

the end

193

***Stupid X 3. FOUND* magazine "Find of the Day," November 4, 2006.** The note above was found by Viviana Torrijos in Brooklyn, New York, who writes: "I found this in Brooklyn Heights two years ago. I have since found out it was part of a handmade poetry book written by five-year-old children at school. I know it's by a five-year-old because I actually met him awhile after that. At the school children go in front of their class-mates and say their own poetry out loud and the teacher writes it down. By the end of the month they have a 'book' for their parents."

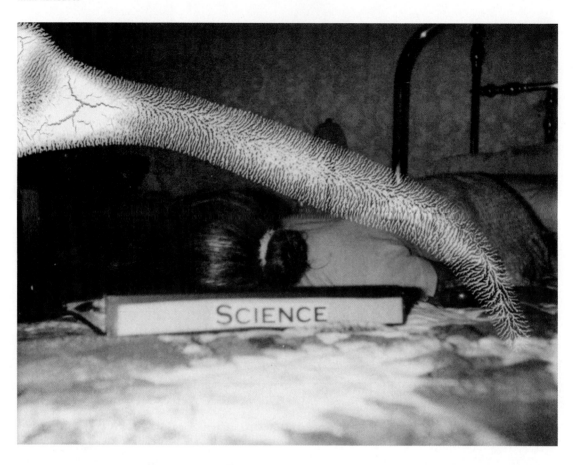

194

SCIENCE, found photo, 2007. In this Polaroid snapshot, a young girl has given in to the snooze-inducing quality of her homework and crashed out on her science notebook. But what's that mysterious and foliaceous form reaching over her? Biology project gone wrong? Plant friend (or foe)? A space alien desperate for class notes? Surely this is not just some weird chemical glitch. What stories does this picture tell you?

■ **Discuss.** *How much does the context in which the two "Finds of the Day" were discovered affect how we interpret their stories? Would finding them in different locations change the way we understand them?*

■ **Write.** *In his description of FOUND, Jason Bitner says that once he and Rothbart started showing their found object to people, they realized that others often had finds of their own. Why do you think we're so fascinated with found notes, pictures, and the like? In a short essay, discuss why you would pick up a find like the ones included here or why you would leave it.*

Chris Ware, *Family*, a *New Yorker* cover, 2006. Cartoonist and graphic novelist ▶ Chris Ware (b. 1967, Omaha, Nebraska) created this cover as part of a work in five parts on the theme of Thanksgiving for the November 27, 2006, issue of *The New Yorker*. The first four pieces in the issue were presented as *New Yorker* covers: *"Stuffing,"* featuring a man on a park bench feeding birds (note: this character also appears in panel 3 of *Family*); *Conversation*, a portrayal of two families, one in lively conversation and the other completely focused on a television screen; *Family*, the four-panel work included here; and *Main Course*, featuring the narrative of a pigeon and a chicken. The final part of the work is a comic strip, *Leftovers*. The covers are available at newyorker.com.

Because his work conveys tragedy and renders melancholy characters, Ware was once asked in an interview whether he is "pessimistic about human nature." He replied: "Not at all. I just try to be realistic, and optimism eventually seems to lead to one's heart being trounced, at least in my experience. I find it a very strangely solipsistic idea to believe that simply by being in jolly spirits all the time that 'everything's going to turn out okay.'" Ware is best known for his series called *The Acme Novelty Library* and his graphic novel *Jimmy Corrigan, the Smartest Kid on Earth*. He is currently at work on two graphic novels. (Chris Ware/*The New Yorker*, ©Condé Nast Publications)

195

Chris Ware
FAMILY, A *NEW YORKER* COVER

■ **Consider before you read and view.** *Which of the characters in this cartoon do you empathize with? How does the artwork direct your focus on the people in "Family"?*

THE NEW YORKER

THE CARTOON ISSUE

NOV. 27, 2006

Price $4.99

THE NEW YORKER

Nov. 27, 2006

"O.K., Mom and Dad, I'm going!
Happy #"$@"# Thanksgiving!"

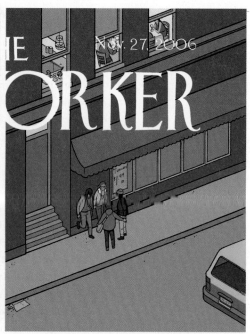

"I mean, I TOLD her not to use butter in the stuffing
because I wouldn't eat it … She has absolutely no respect for me
or my political beliefs!"

"No, seriously—you have to check that guy out! He is so EMO …
DUDE! YOU ARE SO EMO!"

"Well, at least we can be thankful there's no slavery anymore, right?
I mean, that, like, totally sucked."

◄ ■ **Discuss.** *Compare Ware's cartoon with the DC comic "The Hook" on page 184. How do the artists use space to create different moods?*

■ **Write.** *All of the captions in Ware's cartoon are the voice of the main character. Why do you think Ware makes this choice? Try writing the other side of the conversations—using the voices of the main character's parents and friends.*

CONSIDER THE CLUSTER
Mini-narratives

■ **Message**
How would you describe the central message of Chris Ware's "Family"? What do you think the four-panel comic strip is saying about family, holidays, and generational conflicts? How do you think the artist wants us to respond to the teenage girl, who is the only character in the selection who speaks? Imagine a fifth and concluding panel: What would be depicted, and what would you write as the caption?

■ **Method**
"Very Short Stories" shows two methods at work: a verbal composition that tells a story in six words and a visual composition that displays the mini-narrative. As an in-class exercise, show how you would visually display Ernest Hemingway's "For sale: baby shoes, never worn."

■ **Medium**
The Polaroid photograph "SCIENCE" was apparently flawed by a technical problem with the instant camera. How does this unintended visual glitch affect your reading of the picture? How did the medium in this case alter the message? What do you think the photographer originally wanted to capture? Write a mini-narrative based on this photo.

IMAGINED NARRATIVES: STORIES WITHOUT WORDS

| PAINTING | ESSAY | ANNOTATED PAINTING AND SKETCHES | ANALYTICAL ESSAY | 8 PHOTOS |

"If you could say it," the famous American artist Edward Hopper once argued, "there'd be no reason to paint." Yet Hopper's paintings—many of them now twentieth-century classics—tease us into constructing stories to accompany them, narratives that expand on images that seem fraught with unspoken emotions. In "A Close Reading," art critic Kathryn Shattuck attempts to uncover the buried story behind one of Hopper's most intriguing paintings, *Office at Night* (1940).

When it comes to photographs, however, are the stories we construct around them true or false, historical or fictional? We like to think that a photograph provides us with documentation that an event actually happened or offers us an accurate perception of reality, but how can we be certain of photographic validity? In his essay "Photographic Icons," Philip Gefter invites us to consider more carefully the stories behind some internationally admired photographs. Does it matter, for example, that the famous photo of Rosa Parks sitting in the front of a Montgomery, Alabama, bus was not taken on that momentous occasion but—as Parks reports—was deliberately posed a year after her refusal to give up her seat to a white man made civil rights history?

Berenice Abbott, *Edward Hopper in his studio*, 1948. "Edward Hopper didn't say very much," writes his biographer, Gail Levin. "In many ways he was a Victorian man, born in 1882, who lived most of his life in the twentieth century, and really never adjusted to a lot of the major societal and technological changes that took place. The changing role of women was very difficult for him. He expected women to behave like his mother had in the nineteenth century. He was afraid to fly on airplanes. He didn't like skyscrapers." (National Portrait Gallery, Smithsonian Institution/Art Resource, NY)

Born in Nyack, New York, Edward Hopper (1882–1967) studied painting at the New York School of Art under Robert Henri, among others; visited Europe as a young man; and settled in a top-floor Greenwich Village apartment in New York City. He once said that his aim in painting was "the most exact transcription possible of my most intimate impressions of nature. If this end is unattainable [then so is] perfection in any other ideal of painting."

He had no use for art that countered this ideal and considered much of the work of his contemporaries as merely decorative. "The man's the work," Hopper once said. "Something doesn't come out of nothing." His paintings convey a forlorn solitude, even when they portray more than one person. They also convey intimacy and even tension and possibility, as in *Office at Night*. But who's to say what (if anything) Hopper saw as the outcome of the scenario portrayed in the painting? He leaves it to us to imagine the narrative. As Kathryn Shattuck writes in the following essay, "So much is left unspoken" in the paintings of Edward Hopper.

Edward Hopper, *Office at Night*, 1940. "Hopper produced some of the most enduringly popular images in American art," writes a recent curator of the artist's work. "His quiet, yet riveting, pictures of people in their apartments, offices, and hotel rooms express both a sense of urban isolation and the bittersweet comfort of being alone." Scholars have written about his depression, his silence, his inability to express his emotions, and his conflicts with his wife. (Oil on canvas, 56.4 x 63.8 cm. Collection Walker Art Center, Minneapolis. Gift of the T. B. Walker Foundation, Gilbert M. Walker Fund, 1948.)

Kathryn Shattuck, *Edward Hopper's* **Office at Night:** *A Close Reading.* Kathryn Shattuck writes about arts and culture for *The New York Times.* The following annotated painting and sketches originally appeared in the Arts section of the *Times* on Sunday, July 9, 2006.

Kathryn Shattuck

EDWARD HOPPER'S *OFFICE AT NIGHT:* A CLOSE READING

■ **Consider before you read and view.** *How does Shattuck "read" this painting? Notice what she pays attention to: space, light, the positioning of the two characters' bodies. Could you apply her methods to other visual texts—an advertisement, for example, or a family snapshot?*

So much is left unspoken in the paintings of Edward Hopper: in the ache of barren expanses, behind the curtains of houses perhaps not quite vacant, and in the tension transmitted by his characters, who, even with others, were almost always alone.

"Hopper had no small talk," Lloyd Goodrich, a former director of the Whitney Museum of Art, wrote in a 1970 monograph. "He was famous for his monumental silences; but like the spaces in his pictures, they were not empty."

How, then, to interpret *Office at Night* (1940), on view at the Whitney as part of "Full House," its 75th-anniversary exhibition?

Does it depict a power struggle, a political comedy or the build-up to an office romp? Hopper preferred to leave the narratives to the viewer's imagination, said Carter Foster, the Whitney's curator of drawings.

Or, as Hopper put it, "If you could say it, there'd be no reason to paint."

In *Office at Night* a man in his 30's or 40's sits at a heavy desk in a sparsely furnished room, a voluptuous secretary standing with her hand in a file drawer nearby. Twisted in a provocative if physically strained position—both breasts and buttocks are visible—she could be looking at him. Or maybe she's wondering how her skin-tight dress will allow her to stoop down to pick up the paper dropped

■ *Consider. Could this quote from Hopper serve as a definition for art? Would you agree that art is a way of expressing what you can't normally say?*

on the floor, and if she does, what the outcome will be. A breeze enters an open window and rustles a blind as the man reads a document, apparently oblivious to the situation. Or is he?

"One gets the sense that Hopper was quite repressed," Mr. Foster said. "There's a lot of fantasy going on there. It's an exercise in voyeurism."

In a letter to the Walker Art Center, which owns the painting, Hopper said the work was "probably first suggested by many rides on the 'L' train in New York City after dark glimpses of office interiors that were so fleeting as to leave fresh and vivid impressions on my mind."

Hopper leaves those impressions blurred and layered. Is the relationship between the man and the woman emotional? Sexual? Or have they, like so many urbanites squashed into cramped quarters, simply become inured to each other?

At the time, the position of executive secretary was a relatively prestigious role for a woman, though inherently subservient. Still, this woman, with her fashionable attire, her makeup and her come-hither pose, could be the one with the power. Especially, as Mr. Foster and not a few other art historians have noted, if she does go for that paper.

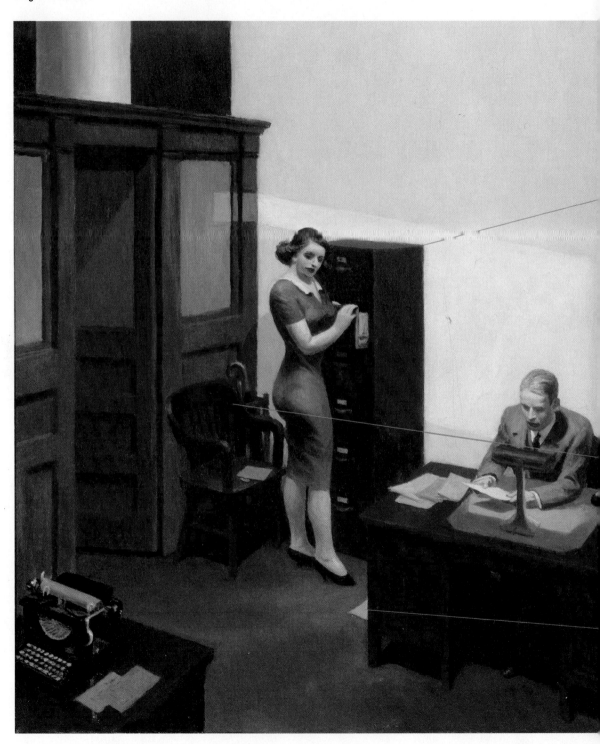

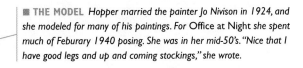

■ **THE MODEL** *Hopper married the painter Jo Nivison in 1924, and she modeled for many of his paintings. For* Office at Night *she spent much of Feburary 1940 posing. She was in her mid-50's. "Nice that I have good legs and up and coming stockings," she wrote.*

■ **A RUSTLING BLIND** *"For Hopper, wind often stood in for touch," Carter Foster of the Whitney said, citing some of Hopper's famous paintings of nudes, in which solitary women feel a breeze wafting by.*

■ **THE BACKGROUND** *A wooden chair and an umbrella handle echo the woman's curves. Hopper once indicated that this office had great meaning for him; perhaps it was his reference to* A Cotton Office in New Orleans *(1873) by Degas, which he admired.*

■ **THE PAPER** *Only in the final composition does Hopper drop a paper on the floor, injecting into the scene a tantailizing hint of dramatic—or comedic, you decide—possibility.*

206

ON THE FIRST DRAFTS OF EDWARD HOPPER'S *OFFICE AT NIGHT*

The Figures

Hopper went through six permutations in his studies. In the first, the secretary is alone and seen from the side. In the third, the man is added. Their placement was adjusted until Hopper had the interaction he wanted.

The Perspective

In early studies, the office is shown as if the viewer were standing inside it. Later, the perspective shifts: walls no longer meet at right angles, the ceiling disappears, and the floor tilts upward, so that one watches the scene from above.

Light Sources

Light comes from the desk lamp, the window and an unseen source from above. In this early study, Hopper had yet another window, through which the viewer is watching.

The Office

Studies show a painting on the wall behind the desk. This was removed, leaving a stark wall of shadow and light that enhances the distance, literal and figurative, between the characters.

■ **Discuss.** *Look at Hopper's sketch for this painting in which only the secretary is present. How does the introduction of a second figure add to the tension of the painting?*

■ **Write.** *The narrative behind this scene is ambiguous, partly because we don't know the two people's minds. Choose either the man at the desk or the secretary and write and account of his or her thoughts in the moment we are observing.*

Philip Gefter, *Photographic Icons: Fact, Fiction, or Metaphor?*   Philip Gefter, picture editor for *The New York Times* since 1999, has also held that position at *Aperture, Forbes, Fortune,* and *The San Francisco Examiner* Sunday magazine and is a founding member of the National Lesbian and Gay Journalists Association. In his role at the *Times,* Gefter assigns photographers, supervises picture editors, reviews more than a thousand pictures daily—and helps decide what images appear on page one of this preeminent newspaper each day. In the following essay, originally published in the winter 2006 issue of *Aperture,* Gefter writes, "Truth-telling is the promise of a photograph. . . . A photograph comes as close as we get to witnessing an authentic moment with our own eyes while not actually being there." But what is truth, even in "real" photos that have not been altered or digitally enhanced? Gefter invites us to reevaluate a collection of famous images and ask: What is real? Are photographs facts? Fiction? Something in between?

Philip Gefter

PHOTOGRAPHIC ICONS: FACT, FICTION, OR METAPHOR?

■ **Consider before you read.** *What is your threshold for truth in a photograph? How much posing, cropping, or altering is acceptable in a newspaper photograph? What about a photograph in a magazine? Or a museum?*

Truth-telling is the promise of a photograph—as if fact itself resides in the optical precision with which the medium reflects our native perception. A photograph comes as close as we get to witnessing an authentic moment with our own eyes while not actually being there. Think of all the famous pictures that serve as both documentation and verification of historic events: Mathew Brady's photographs of the Civil War; Lewis Hine's chronicle of industrial growth in America; the birth of the Civil Rights movement documented in a picture of Rosa Parks on a segregated city bus in Montgomery, Alabama. Aren't they proof of the facts in real time, moments in history brought to the present?

    Of course, just because a photograph reflects the world with perceptual accuracy doesn't mean it is proof of what spontaneously transpired. A photographic image might look like actual reality, but gradations of truth are measured in the circumstances that led up to the moment the picture was taken.

■ Consider. *Do you agree with Gefter's assessment that truth in photography is not black and white but a range of grays? Is this definition truer in photography than in other media?*

The viewer's expectation about a picture's veracity is largely determined by the context in which the image appears. A picture published in a newspaper is believed to be fact; an advertising image is understood to be fiction. If a newspaper image turns out to have been set up, then questions are raised about trust and authenticity. Still, somewhere between fact and fiction—or perhaps hovering slightly above either one—is the province of metaphor, where the truth is approximated in renderings of a more poetic or symbolic nature.

The impulse to define, perfect, or heighten reality is manifest in a roster of iconic photographs that have come to reside in the world as "truth." While Mathew Brady is known for his Civil War pictures, he rarely set foot on a battlefield. He couldn't bear the sight of dead bodies. In fact, most pictures of the battlefield attributed to Brady's studio were taken by his employees Alexander Gardner and Timothy O'Sullivan—both of whom were known to have moved bodies around for the purposes of composition and posterity.

In *Home of a Rebel Sharpshooter, Gettysburg* (1863), a picture by Gardner, the body of a dead soldier lies in perfect repose. His head is tilted in the direction of the camera, his hand on his belly, his rifle propped up vertically against the rocks. There would be no question that this is a scene the photographer happened upon, if it weren't for another picture by Gardner of the same soldier, this time his face turned away from the camera and his rifle lying on the ground.

In the Library of Congress catalog, the photograph *Dead Soldiers at Antietam* (1862) is listed twice, under the names of both Brady and Gardner. In the image, approximately two dozen dead soldiers lie in a very neat row across the field. Could they possibly have fallen in such tidy succession? Knowing what we do about Gardner's picture of the rebel soldier, the possibility lingers that he moved some of these bodies to create a better composition. Or it could be that other soldiers had lined the bodies up before digging a mass grave for burial. But whatever the circumstances that led to this picture, it is verifiable that the battle of Antietam took place on this field. We know that numbers of soldiers were killed. Evidence of the battle remains—the soldiers that died on that date, the battlefield on which they fought, the clothes they wore, and so on. Just how much of the subject matter does the photographer have to change before fact becomes fiction, or a photograph becomes metaphor?

"Mathew Brady used art to forge a relationship between photography and history, but when the memory of Brady the artist vanished, we came to accept his images as fact," Mary Panzer wrote in her 1997 book *Mathew Brady and the Image of History*. "Acknowledged or not, Brady's careful manipulation of his subjects continues to influence our perception, and still shapes the way in which we see his era, and the story of the nation."

Lewis Hine's 1920 photograph of a powerhouse mechanic symbolizes the work ethic that built America. The simplicity of the photograph long ago turned it into a powerful icon, all the more poignant because of its "authenticity." But in fact, Hine—who was interested in the human labor aspect of an increasingly mechanized world, and once claimed that "there is an urgent need for intelligent

209

Mathew Brady/Alexander Gardner, *Bodies of Confederate Dead Gathered for Burial*, Battle of Antietam, September, 1862. (Library of Congress)

interpretation of the world's workers"—posed this man in order to make the portrait. Does that information make the picture any less valid?

We see in the first shot that the worker's zipper is down. Isn't it a sad fact that the flaws in daily life should prevent reality from being the best version of how things really are? In our attempt to perfect reality, we aim for higher standards. A man with his zipper down is undignified, and so the famous icon, posed as he is, presents an idealized version of the American worker—dignity customized, but forever intact. Still, the mechanic did work in that powerhouse and his gesture is true enough to his labor. The reality of what the image depicts is indisputable, and whether Hine maintained a fidelity to what transpired in real time may or may not be relevant to its symbolic import.

Le Baiser de l'Hôtel de Ville (Kiss at the Hôtel de Ville, 1950) by Robert Doisneau, despite its overexposure on posters and postcards, has long served as an example of how photography can capture the spontaneity of life. What a breezy testament to the pleasure of romance! How lovely the couple is, how elegant their gesture and their clothing, how delightful this perspective from a café in Paris! It makes you believe in romantic love: you want to be there, as if you, too, would surely witness love blossoming all around you—or even find it yourself—while sitting at a café in the City of Light.

But despite the story this picture seems to tell—one of a photographer who just happened to look up from his Pernod as the enchanted lovers walked by—there was no serendipity whatsoever in the moment. Doisneau had seen the man and woman days earlier, near the school at which they were studying acting. He was on assignment for *Life* magazine, for a story on romance in Paris, and hired the couple as models for the shot. This information was not brought to light until the early 1990s, when lawsuits demanding compensation were filed by several people who claimed to be the models in the famous picture. Does the lack of authenticity diminish the photograph? It did for me, turning its promise of romance into a beautifully crafted lie.

Ruth Orkin was in Florence, Italy, in the early 1950s when she met Jinx Allen, whom she asked to be the subject of a picture Orkin wanted to submit to the *Herald Tribune. American Girl in Italy* was conceived inadvertently when Orkin noticed the Italian men on their Vespas ogling Ms. Allen as she walked down the street. Orkin asked her to walk down the street again, to be sure she had the shot. Does a second take alter the reality of the phenomenon? How do you parse the difference between Doisneau's staged picture and Orkin's re-creation?

Iwo Jima, Old Glory Goes Up on Mt. Suribachi was taken in 1945 by Joe Rosenthal, an Associated Press photographer. As documentation of a World War II victory, the picture immediately assumed symbolic significance—indeed, it won Rosenthal a Pulitzer Prize, and is one of the most enduring images of the twentieth century. For some time, it was considered a posed picture, but this was due to a misunderstanding. The famous image was the first of three pictures Rosenthal took of the flag being raised. For the last shot, he asked the soldiers to pose in front of the raised flag, thinking that the newspapers back home would expect a picture in which the soldiers' faces were visible. Later, asked if his picture of Iwo Jima was posed, he

212

Lewis Hine, an early variant of his *Powerhouse Mechanic*. (Courtesy of George Eastman House)

Lewis Hine, his final, iconic *Powerhouse Mechanic* **working on a steam pump, 1920.** (Courtesy of George Eastman House)

Ruth Orkin, *American Girl in Italy*, 1951. (Copyright Ruth Orkin 1952, 1980)

said yes—referring in his mind to that third frame, not the one that had been published. Still, that the moment captured in the well-known picture occurred just as we see it today surely confirms the truth-telling capability of photography.

The birth of the Civil Rights movement is often dated back to a moment in 1955 when Rosa Parks, a black woman, refused to give up her seat on a crowded city bus to a white man in Montgomery, Alabama. (While she was not the first black bus rider to refuse to give up her seat, her case became the one on which the legal challenge was based.) Many people assume that the famous picture of Parks sitting on a city bus is an actual record of that historic moment. But the picture was taken on December 21, 1956, a year after she refused to give up her seat, and a month after the U.S. Supreme Court ruled Montgomery's segregated bus system illegal. Before she died, Parks told Douglas Brinkley, her biographer, that she posed for the picture. A reporter and two photographers from *Look* magazine had seated her on the bus in front of a white man. Similar photo opportunities were arranged on the same day for other members of the Civil Rights community, including Martin Luther King. Here is a staged document that has

Joe Rosenthal, *Marines Raising American Flag on Iwo Jima,* **1945.** (AP Images,
Joe Rosenthal)

become a historic reference point, and a revealing parable about the relationship
of history to myth.

As a witness to events, the photojournalist sets out to chronicle what happens in
the world as it actually occurs. A cardinal rule of the profession is that the presence of the camera must not alter the situation being photographed. Four years
ago, Edward Keating, among the best staff photographers at the *New York Times,*
was fired because of questions raised about one picture he took that ended up in
the newspaper. This correction was published in the *Times* five days later:

> A picture in the early editions on September 20, 2002, showed a 6-year-
> old boy aiming a toy pistol alongside a sign reading "Arabian Foods"

United Press International, *Rosa Parks*, 1956. Rosa Parks sits in the front of a bus in Montgomery, Alabama. Parks was arrested on December 1, 1955, for refusing to give up her seat in the front of a bus in Montgomery. The man sitting behind Parks is Nicholas C. Chriss, a reporter for United Press International out of Atlanta. (Bettmann/Corbis)

outside a store in Lackawanna, N.Y., near Buffalo. The store was near the scene of two arrests in a raid described by the authorities as a pre-emptive strike against a cell of Al Qaeda, and the picture appeared with an article recounting the life stories of the detainees. The picture was not relevant to the article and should not have appeared.

The correction went on to say that photographers on the scene from other news organizations had reported that Keating asked the young boy to aim the toy pistol.

Edward Keating, *Boy with Pistol*, 2002. (Edward Keating/The New York Times)

Upon further inquiry and a full inspection of the images from the entire photo assignment, the "editors concluded, and Mr. Keating acknowledged, that the boy's gesture had not been spontaneous." Altering the reality of the situation is a violation of journalistic policy, and it turned Keating's image from fact to illustration—a potent editorial statement about the Arabic community at a highly sensitive moment.

Paradoxically, looking through the photography archives of the *New York Times*, one is struck by the numbers of prints in which one or more people have been airbrushed out of the picture. The technique has been used at times to highlight an individual relevant to a particular news story, or simply to sharpen a line for better reproduction on newsprint. Other pictures have red-pencil crop marks, with which the art director or picture editor isolated only that part of the image relevant to the news story. To be fair, these changes were made not for the sake of censorship, but rather as part of an editing process simply to filter out unwanted information—perhaps no more egregious than cutting down a subject's spoken quotation to its salient points.

In 1839, the invention of photography provided a revolutionary method of replicating reality in accurate visual terms. What a great tool for artists and painters to construct images with greater perceptual facility. The history of art is a continuum of constructed images that depict reality as it was truly, or else as it was imagined in ideal terms. Photography did not change that continuum; it only made the difference between perception and reality more difficult to determine.

■ **Discuss.** *Gefter writes that "truth-telling is the promise of a photograph." However, he writes, "just because a photograph reflects the world with perceptual accuracy doesn't mean it is proof of what spontaneously transpired." What, according to Gefter is "truth" (or "veracity") in photography? What determines this truth? To what extent does Gefter see the images included in his essay as "true"? Do you agree? Why or why not?*

■ **Write.** *Reread* The New York Times' *comments on Keating's "Boy with Pistol" and then write a letter to the editor, either supporting the* Times' *decision or defending the photograph.*

 CONSIDER THE CLUSTER
Imagined Narratives: Stories without Words

■ Message
What do you consider to be the main point of Philip Gefter's "Photographic Icons"? What are his examples intended to convey? Is Gefter saying that posed photographs are historically invalid? In a short essay, select one of the photographs Gefter discusses and make a case for its validity or invalidity.

■ Method
A museum curator says about *Office at Night* that "Hopper preferred to leave the narrative to the viewer's imagination." What makes someone think that there's a narrative at all? Consider Hopper's method of composition: What elements in the picture suggest a story behind the picture? What if you assumed that there is no story going on? What would you then find to say about the painting? Which possibility do you find more artistically satisfying: that the artist intends no story at all, or that the artist intends the viewer to make up a story?

■ Medium
Some photographers refer to themselves as "storytellers." Do you find this term to be an odd way to describe a photographer? In what ways can a photographer tell a story, considering that an individual photograph is extremely limited in its ability to depict narrative process, sequential movement, and the passage of time? In a short essay, consider carefully one of the photos in this chapter and explain how someone could find within it an unfolding story or narrative.

STORIES ON FILM: WHAT MAKES A CULT CLASSIC?

The definition of a cult film is understandably loose. For some, it could be a low-budget, minor movie that's fun because it's so bad, and for others it could be a well-regarded film that over the years has earned for itself a devoted following. A cult film therefore could be entertaining trash such as *The Rocky Horror Picture Show* (1975) or a cinematic masterpiece such as *Casablanca* (1942). Each of these films has its intensely loyal fans who can mouth every word spoken on the screen. Many cult classics are musicals or contain a strong musical component, which should not be surprising because songs are intended to be enjoyed over and over.

A good example of an enduring film that combines a powerful narrative with many memorable songs is *The Wizard of Oz* (1939). In "Out of Kansas," one of modern literature's most prominent writers, Salman Rushdie, with a notebook and a remote, closely studies the opening of this famous film as Dorothy and Toto are seen running down a country road. Rushdie is hoping to discover what makes *The Wizard of Oz* so magical.

Certain films not only attract a dedicated fan base but also become the topics of annual celebrations and conferences. For example, many college professors participate in a four-day academic celebration of the 1998 cult classic *The Big Lebowski*. In "How One Scene Can Say Everything," film critic Joe Morgenstern examines a powerful emotional episode in *Little Miss Sunshine*, the enormously popular independent film nominated for an Academy Award for Best Picture in 2007.

In his book *The Great Movies*, the noted film critic Roger Ebert collects his essays on his one hundred favorite films. One of these is *Star Wars*, a "space epic," he writes, that "has colonized our imaginations, and it is hard to stand back and see it simply as a motion picture, because it has so completely become part of our memories." One reason that *Star Wars* will endure artistically, says Ebert, is that it linked "state-of-the-art technology with a deceptively simple but really very powerful story." The director, George Lucas, worked with Joseph Campbell, the author of many books on myths, and was thus able to create a screenplay "that owes much to mankind's oldest stories."

Salman Rushdie, *Out of Kansas*. Salman Rushdie (b. 1947) is a British-Indian
novelist and essayist whose work includes *Midnight's Children* and *The Satanic
Verses*. The following essay is taken from a longer work titled *The Wizard of Oz*
(2004), part of the Film Classics series published by the British Film Institute.
Rushdie writes: "When I first saw *The Wizard of Oz*, it made a writer of me." He
argues that the driving force of the story is "the inadequacy of adults" and the
"weakness of grown-ups [that] forces children to take control of their own destinies." And, as the editors at the British Film Institute write, "Rushdie rejects the
conventional view that [the story's] fantasy of escape from reality ends with a
comforting return to home, sweet home."

Salman Rushdie

OUT OF KANSAS

221

■ Consider before you read.   *How do Rushdie's freeze-frames of* The Wizard of Oz
*help him analyze its meaning? What does he notice that viewers might miss when watching
the movie?*

The film begins. We are in the monochrome, "real" world of Kansas. A girl and
her dog run down a country lane. *She isn't coming yet, Toto. Did she hurt you?
She tried to, didn't she?* A real girl, a real dog, and the beginning, with the very
first line of dialogue, of real drama. Kansas, however, is not real, no more real
than Oz. Kansas is an oil painting. Dorothy and Toto have been running down
a short stretch of "road" in the MGM studios, and this shot has been matted
into a picture of emptiness. "Real" emptiness would probably not be empty
enough. It is as close as makes no difference to the universal grey of Frank Baum's
story, the void broken only by a couple of fences and the vertical lines of telegraph poles. If Oz is *nowhere*, then the studio setting of the Kansas scenes suggests that *so is Kansas*. This is necessary. A realistic depiction of the extreme
poverty of Dorothy Gale's circumstances would have created a burden, a heavi-
ness, that would have rendered impossible the imaginative leap into Storyland,
the soaring flight into Oz. The Grimms' fairy tales, it's true, were often brutally
realistic. In *The Fisherman and His Wife*, the eponymous couple live, until they

Metro-Goldwyn-Mayer, *The Wizard of Oz*, 1939. (Photofest)

meet the magic flounder, in what is tersely described as "a pisspot." But in many children's versions of the Grimms, the pisspot is bowdlerized into a "hovel" or some even gentler word. Hollywood's vision has always been of this soft-focus variety. Dorothy looks extremely well-fed, and she is not really, but *unreally*, poor.

She arrives at the farmyard and here (freezing the frame) we see the beginning of what will be a recurring visual motif. In the scene we have frozen, Dorothy and Toto are in the background, heading for a gate. To the left of the screen is a treetrunk, a vertical line echoing the telegraph poles of the scene before. Hanging from an approximately horizontal branch are a triangle and a circle (actually a rubber tyre). In midshot are further geometric elements: the parallel lines of the wooden fence, the bisecting diagonal wooden bar at the gate. Later, when we see the house, the theme of simple geometry is present once again; it is all right angles and triangles. The world of Kansas, that great void, is shaped into "home" by the use of simple, uncomplicated shapes; none of your citified complexity here.

▲ **Dorothy on the road in Kansas.**

Dorothy in the farmyard in Kansas. ▼

223

Throughout *The Wizard of Oz*, home and safety are represented by such geometrical simplicity, whereas danger and evil are invariably twisty, irregular and misshapen.

The tornado is just such an untrustworthy, sinuous, shifting shape. Random, unfixed, it wrecks the plain shapes of that no-frills life.

Curiously, the Kansas sequence invokes not only geometry but arithmetic, too: for when Dorothy bursts upon Auntie Em and Uncle Henry with her fears about Toto, like the chaotic force she is, what are they doing? Why do they shoo her away? "We're trying to count," they admonish her, as they take a census of eggs, counting their metaphorical chickens, their small hopes of income which the tornado will shortly blow away. So, with simple shapes and numbers, Dorothy's family erect their defences against the immense and maddening emptiness; and these defences are useless, of course.

Leaping ahead to Oz, it becomes obvious that this opposition between the geometric and the twisty is no accident. Look at the beginning of the Yellow Brick Road: it is a perfect spiral. Look again at Glinda's carriage, that perfect,

(Photofest)

(MGM/The Kobal Collection)

luminous sphere. Look at the regimented routines of the Munchkins as they greet
Dorothy and thank her for the death of the Wicked Witch of the East. Move on
to the Emerald City: see it in the distance, its straight lines soaring into the sky!
And now, by contrast, observe the Wicked Witch of the West: her crouching figure, her misshapen hat. How does she depart? In a puff of shapeless smoke. . . .
"Only bad witches are ugly," Glinda tells Dorothy, a remark of high Political
Incorrectness that emphasizes the film's animosity towards whatever is tangled,
claw-crooked, and weird. Woods are invariably frightening; the gnarled branches
of trees are capable of coming to life; and the one moment when the Yellow Brick
Road itself bewilders Dorothy is the moment when it ceases to be geometric (first
spiral, then rectilinear) and splits and forks every which way.

■ **Discuss.** *What is it about* The Wizard of Oz *that "made a writer" of Rushdie? Why
has it remained popular for so many decades? Does its longevity have anything to do with
the contrasts that Rushdie identifies in the movie?*

■ **Write.** *Choose another striking visual scene from* The Wizard of Oz. *It might help to
search for stills of the movie on the Internet. Write a brief analysis of the still using Rushdie's
opposition of simple geometric shapes with more complex ones. Does your image support his
thesis?*

Joe Morgenstern, Little Miss Sunshine: *How One Scene Can Say Everything.* Joe Morgenstern is the movie critic for *The Wall Street Journal* and one of only three film critics ever to win a Pulitzer Prize for Criticism (the award has also gone to Roger Ebert [see p. 229] of the *Chicago Sun-Times* and Stephen Hunter of *The Washington Post*). Morgenstern has written scripts for movies and television, including some episodes of *Law & Order.* In the essay that follows, Morgenstern deconstructs what he says are the best five minutes of *Little Miss Sunshine.* How can a family with a list of "flagrant failures" deal with a teen's anger, suffering, and "authentic tragedy," as Morgenstern writes, and begin to heal? What is the significance of the character Olive? And what is the importance of an independent, modestly funded film such as *Little Miss Sunshine* against the backdrop of "monster attractions with overhyped stars [that] peddle primitive promises"? This essay orginally appeared in *The Wall Street Journal* on February 17, 2007.

Joe Morgenstern

LITTLE MISS SUNSHINE: HOW ONE SCENE CAN SAY EVERYTHING

■ **Consider before you read.** *Think of one of your favorite movie scenes. As you read Morgenstern's analysis, compare this scene to your favorite. Do you like it for reasons similar to the ones he cites?*

We all have favorite scenes from classic films; the quirkiness and diversity of our choices can be astonishing. Lately, though, I've been struck by how many movie lovers share a fondness for the same part of the same recent picture. As soon as I bring up the subject of my favorite moment in *Little Miss Sunshine,* someone is sure to finish the sentence I've barely begun with, "The one where the son runs away from the van."

What makes that moment—actually a five-minute-long sequence—so memorable, or, in my view, enthralling? The question starts to answer itself when you take the time, as I've been doing, to study the sequence's substance on DVD. All of the ingredients that give the movie its special distinction can be found in the emotional and dramatic concentrate of what the DVD menu refers to as scene 16, "End of a Dream." Watch it on your own as a model of modern filmmaking, but read what I've written about it only if you've seen the film. There's no way to discuss such exceptional work without giving away crucial plot points, and my own point is to celebrate specifics, not to spoil pleasure.

The dream that ends has been dreamed by the touchingly tormented adolescent son, Dwayne, who wants to be a test pilot. He wants it so passionately that he has taken a vow of silence, inspired by his goofy reading of Nietzsche, until he gets into the Air Force Academy. We know he'll blurt out something sooner or later, so his silence is a blithely funny set-up in a film that's full of funny set-ups (the entire road trip is a set-up for Olive's performance at the climactic Little Miss Sunshine pageant) and unexpected payoffs.

Scene 16 begins as a welcome respite from the shock of the grandfather's death, followed by the hilarity of the encounter with a motorcycle cop who never notices the dead body in the back of the VW van. Inside the van, whose broken horn keeps bleating disconsolately, Olive whiles away the miles by giving her brother an eye test with a chart she found at the hospital. Then she gives him a color-blindness test, and suddenly the comedy turns dark. Dwayne can't see the green A inside the circle of red dots; he really is color-blind. That means, as his intermittently suicidal uncle Frank explains, he can never be a test pilot. At first Dwayne processes this slowly, but then the darkness explodes into full-blown horror as the boy goes berserk, beating on the seats and windows and, when the van stops, running from it down an embankment into a suburban field, where he finally breaks his silence with a heartbreaking cry of "F—! F—! F—!"

Within the space of a couple of minutes we've been whipsawed, though never manipulated, from a state of benign enjoyment through several intermediate zones, including anxiety, to a sense of authentic tragedy. That's remarkable enough, but the scene's central drama is yet to come. On the embankment's edge, Dwayne's father, mother, uncle and little sister stare down helplessly at the solitary boy, who has fallen to his hands and knees in an agonized crouch. His mother ventures toward him, tries to console him, but he'll have none of it—he lashes out furiously, reminding her of the family's flagrant failures. Following her retreat, Olive's father turns to his little girl and says, fairly hopelessly, "You want to try talking to him?" As she tiptoes down the slope, we wonder what this unworldly child can possibly say.

The answer is nothing, not a word. Olive puts one arm around Dwayne, rests her head against his shoulder and sits with him in healing silence.

It's a gorgeous resolution of a desperate situation. Until the color-blind test, Dwayne has been almost purely a comic character, no more dysfunctional in his monkish silence and punkish truculence than the rest of his screwed-up family—excluding Olive, of course, who's the film's radiant life force. His parents haven't taken the full measure of his chronic anger; to do so they'd have to hold themselves as well as their problem child to account. But the film takes Dwayne seriously from the start, even though we don't know, until scene 16, what the writer, Michael Arndt, and the directors, Jonathan Dayton and Valerie Faris, have in store for him.

The secret of the film's appeal is that it's neither a comedy with drama nor a drama with comedy, but a story that's open to its characters' behavior—where their feelings lead them is where the action goes. The secret of scene 16's power is that once the comedy takes a hairpin turn into tragedy, the only character who

■ **Consider.** *What is the definition of tragedy? Is tragedy in art different from tragedy in life?*

227

Big moment: Abigail Breslin and Paul Dano in *Little Miss Sunshine.* (Photofest)

intuits the depth of that tragedy finally gets to act on it. Olive doesn't draw on some mysterious wisdom. When her dad suggests that she try talking to Dwayne, she knows there's nothing to say. She's just a little kid who sees that her brother is suffering. But when she applies her comforting touch in that eloquent silence, the whole family, along with Dwayne, starts to heal.

Scene 16 is only one of 23, at least as the DVD divides the film—scenes that mix density with clarity, simplicity with complexity, in a modestly-budgeted enterprise that may well win an Oscar for Best Picture. If that should come to pass, it will be partly because this picture projects a bright ray of hope for the future of original films at a bleak, conformist time in the medium's history. While monster attractions with overhyped stars peddle primitive premises, belaboring one primal feeling at a time, *Little Miss Sunshine* ebbs and flows, dodges and feints, derives generous emotional dividends from fugitive feelings, and captures, without confining, the lovely firefly nature of life.

■ **Discuss.** *Morgenstern's admiration for* Little Miss Sunshine *seems to depend on its blending of comedy and tragedy. Why does he find this so compelling? Why is it relatively rare in movies?*

■ **Write.** *Try writing a monologue that Olive could deliver to her brother at the moment Morgenstern describes. Then consider how the scene would change if your monologue were inserted in place of Olive's "eloquent silence."*

Roger Ebert, Star Wars. The film critic Roger Ebert (b. 1942) writes a weekly review column for the *Chicago Sun-Times*, is syndicated in more than two hundred newspapers; has written books about film, including his *Great Movies* series, from which the following essay is drawn; is the host of an annual film festival; and is perhaps best known for *Siskel & Ebert*, a TV program that he hosted with Gene Siskel for twenty-three years. He now co-hosts a film review program with critic Richard Roeper called *Ebert & Roeper*. In his essay *"Star Wars,"* Ebert explores the film that in 1977 "combined a new generation of special effects with the high-energy action picture; it linked space opera and soap opera, fairy tales and legend, and packaged them as a wild visual ride." It began a time of "big-budget special effects blockbusters," writes Ebert, "a trend we are still living through." In addition to the impressive visual effects, *Star Wars* is just a good story. In order to write the screenplay for the film, George Lucas worked with Joseph Campbell, an expert in ancient and world myth. An excerpt from an interview with Campbell (included as a sidebar with the Ebert essay) gives a sense of what Lucas and Campbell were going for when they tapped into some very old stories to create something new. The following essay is repeated from Roger Ebert's book *The Great Movies* (2002).

Roger Ebert
STAR WARS

■ **Consider before you read.** *How does Ebert explain* Star Wars' *lasting popularity? What elements seem most important in guaranteeing its continued relevance?*

To see *Star Wars* again after twenty years is to revisit a place in the mind. George Lucas's space epic has colonized our imaginations, and it is hard to stand back and see it simply as a motion picture, because it has so completely become part of our memories. It's as goofy as a children's tale, as shallow as an old Saturday afternoon serial, as corny as Kansas in August—and a masterpiece. Those who analyze its philosophy do so, I imagine, with a smile in their minds. May the Force be with them.

Like *The Birth of a Nation* and *Citizen Kane, Star Wars* was a technical watershed that influenced many of the movies that came after. These films have little in common, except for the way they came along at a crucial moment in cinema

230

A scene from *Star Wars*—Darth Vader vs. Obi-Wan Kenobi.

(Lucas Film/20th Century Fox/The Kobal Collection)

history, when new methods were ripe for synthesis. *The Birth of a Nation* brought together the developing language of shots and editing. *Citizen Kane* married special effects, advanced sound, a new photographic style, and a freedom from linear storytelling. *Star Wars* combined a new generation of special effects with the high-energy action picture; it linked space opera and soap opera, fairy tales and legend, and packaged them as a wild visual ride.

    Star Wars effectively brought to an end the golden era of early-1970s personal filmmaking and focused the industry on big-budget special-effects blockbusters, blasting off a trend we are still living through. But you can't blame it for what it did; you can only observe how well it did it. In one way or another, all the big studios have been trying to make another *Star Wars* ever since (pictures like *Raiders of the Lost Ark, Jurassic Park, Independence Day*, and *The Matrix* are its heirs). It located Hollywood's center of gravity at the intellectual and emotional level of a bright teenager.

 Consider. *How do these films (such as* Raiders of the Lost Ark *and* Jurassic Park*) speak to a "bright teenager"? What does that phrase imply?*

It's possible, however, that as we grow older we retain, buried within, the tastes of our earlier selves. How else to explain how much fun *Star Wars* is, even for those who think they don't care for science fiction? It's a good-hearted film in every single frame, and shining through is the gift of a man who knew how to link state-of-the-art technology with a deceptively simple but really very powerful story. It was not by accident that George Lucas worked with Joseph Campbell, an expert on the world's basic myths, in fashioning a screenplay that owes much to mankind's oldest stories.

By now the ritual of classic film revival is well established: An older classic is brought out from the studio vaults, restored frame by frame, rereleased in the best

---

Joseph Campbell, *On the Mythology of* Star Wars. Joseph Campbell (1904–1987) was a professor of mythology, an author, and a scholar of comparative mythology and religion. George Lucas enlisted his help in creating the story for *Star Wars*. Campbell discusses his take on the story in the following excerpt from an interview with Bill Moyers that was aired on PBS and published in *The Power of Myth* in 1988.

BILL MOYERS: The first time I saw *Star Wars,* I thought, "This is a very old story in a very new costume." The story of the young man called to adventure, the hero going out facing the trials and ordeals, and coming back after his victory with a boon for the community—

JOSEPH CAMPBELL: Certainly [George] Lucas was using standard mythological figures. The old man as the adviser made me think of a Japanese sword master. I've known some of those people, and Ben Kenobi has a bit of their character.

BILL MOYERS: What does the sword master do?

JOSEPH CAMPBELL: He is total expert in swordsmanship. The Oriental cultivation of the martial arts goes beyond anything I've ever encountered in American gymnasiums. There is a psychological as well as a physiological technique that go together there. This character in *Star Wars* has that quality.

BILL MOYERS: There's something mythological, too, in that the hero is helped by a stranger who shows up and gives him some instrument—

JOSEPH CAMPBELL: He gives him not only a physical instrument but a psychological commitment and a psychological center. The commitment goes past your mere intention system. You are one with the event.

BILL MOYERS: My favorite scene was when they were in the garbage compactor, and the walls were closing in, and I thought, "That's like the belly of the whale that swallowed Jonah."

JOSEPH CAMPBELL: That's where they were, down in the belly of the whale.

BILL MOYERS: What's the mythological significance of the belly?

JOSEPH CAMPBELL: The belly is the dark place where digestion takes place and new energy is created. The story of Jonah in the whale is an example of a mythic theme that is practically universal, of the hero going into a fish's belly and ultimately coming out again, transformed.

theaters, and then relaunched on home video. With the 1997 "special edition" of the Star Wars trilogy, Lucas went one step beyond.

George Lucas in 1977, the year *Star Wars* was released.

(The Kobal Collection)

His special effects were so advanced in 1977 that they spun off an industry, including his own Industrial Light & Magic Co., the computer wizards who do many of today's best special effects. In 1997, Lucas put IL&M to work touching up the effects, including some that his limited 1977 budget left him unsatisfied with. Most of the changes are subtle; you'd need a side-by-side comparison to see that a new shot is a little better. There are about five minutes of new material, including a meeting between Han Solo and Jabba the Hut that was shot for the first version but not used. (We learn that Jabba is not immobile, but sloshes along in a kind of spongy undulation.) There's also an improved look to the city of Mos Eisley ("a wretched hive of scum and villainy," says Obi-Wan Kenobi). And the climactic battle scene against the Death Star has been rehabbed.

The improvements are well done, but they point up how well the effects were done to begin with: If the changes are not obvious, that's because *Star Wars* got the look of the film so right in the first place. The obvious comparison is with Kubrick's *2001: A Space Odyssey*, made ten years earlier, in 1967, which also holds up perfectly well today. (One difference is that Kubrick went for realism, trying to imagine how his future world would really look, while Lucas cheerfully plundered the past. Han Solo's Millennium Falcon has a gun turret with a hand-operated weapon that would have been at home on a World War II bomber, but too slow to hit anything at space velocities.)

Two Lucas inspirations started the story with a tease: He set the action not in the future but "long ago," and jumped into the middle of it with "Chapter 4: A New Hope." These seemingly innocent touches were actually rather powerful. They gave the saga the aura of an ancient tale and an ongoing one.

As if those two shocks were not enough for the movie's first moments, I learn from the critic Mark R. Leeper that this was one of the first films to pan the camera across a star field: "Space scenes had always been done with a fixed camera, and for a very good reason. It was more economical not to create a background of stars large enough to pan through." As the camera tilts up, a vast spaceship appears from the top of the screen and moves overhead, an effect reinforced by the surround sound. It is such a dramatic opening that it's no wonder Lucas paid a fine and resigned from the Directors Guild rather than obey its demand that he begin with conventional opening credits.

The film has simple, well-defined characters, beginning with the robots C-3PO (fastidious, a little effete) and R2-D2 (childlike, easily hurt). The evil Empire has all but triumphed in the galaxy, but rebel forces are preparing an assault on the Star Destroyer. Princess Leia (pert, sassy Carrie Fisher) has information pinpointing the Star's vulnerable point and feeds it into C-3PO's computer. When her ship is captured, the robots escape from the Star Destroyer and find themselves on Luke Skywalker's planet, where soon Luke (Mark Hamill as an idealistic youngster) meets the wise, old, mysterious Ben Kenobi (Alec Guinness) and they hire the freelance space jockey Han Solo (Harrison Ford, already laconic) to carry them to Leia's rescue.

Darth Vader threatens Princess Leia. Joseph Campbell wrote in *The Power of Myth*: "The monster masks that are put on people in *Star Wars* represent the real monster-force in the modern world. When the mask of Darth Vader is removed, you see an unformed man, one who has not developed as a human individual. He's a bureaucrat, living not in terms of himself, but in terms of an imposed system." (Lucas Film/20th Century Fox/The Kobal Collection)

The story is advanced with spectacularly effective art design, set decoration, and effects. Although the scene in the intergalactic bar is famous for its menagerie of alien drunks, there is another scene—when the two robots are thrown into a hold with other used droids—that equally fills the screen with fascinating throw-away details. And a scene in the Death Star's garbage bin (inhabited by a snake with a head curiously shaped like E.T.'s) is also well done.

Many of the planetscapes are startlingly beautiful and owe something to Chesley Bonestell's imaginary drawings of other worlds. The final assault on the Death Star, when the fighter rockets speed between parallel walls, is a nod in the direction of *2001*, with its light trip into another dimension: Kubrick showed, and Lucas learned, how to make the audience feel it is hurtling headlong through space.

Lucas fills his screen with loving touches. There are little alien rats hopping around the desert, and a chess game played with living creatures. Luke's weather-worn "Speeder" vehicle, which hovers over the sand, reminds me uncannily of a 1965 Mustang. And consider the details creating the presence, look, and sound of Darth Vader, whose fanged face mask, black cape, and hollow breathing are the setting for James Earl Jones's cold voice of doom.

Seeing the film the first time, I was swept away, and have remained swept ever since. Seeing this restored version, I tried to be more objective, and noted that the gun battles on board the spaceships go on a bit too long; it is remarkable that the Empire marksmen never hit anyone important; and the fighter raid on the enemy ship now plays like the computer games it predicted. I wonder, too, if Lucas could have come up with a more challenging philosophy behind the Force. As Kenobi explains it, it's basically just going with the flow. What if Lucas had pushed a little further, to include elements of nonviolence or ideas about inter-galactic conservation? (It's a great waste of resources to blow up star systems.)

The films that will live forever are the simplest-seeming ones. They have profound depths, but their surfaces are as clear to an audience as a beloved old story. The way I know this is because the stories that seem immortal—*The Odyssey, The Tale of Genji, Don Quixote, David Copperfield, Huckleberry Finn*—are all the same: a brave but flawed hero, a quest, colorful people and places, sidekicks, the discovery of life's underlying truths. If I were asked to say with certainty which movies will still be widely known a century or two from now, I would list *2001*, and *The Wizard of Oz*, and Keaton and Chaplin, and Astaire and Rogers, and probably *Casablanca* . . . and *Star Wars* for sure.

■ **Discuss.** *Ebert comments several times on how Star Wars mixes the old with the new, the familiar with the futuristic. How do you think that helps make the movie effective? What does Ebert like about it?*

■ **Write.** *Choose one of the more recent films Ebert mentions and analyze it using his essay as a model. Does the film you've chosen use some of the same methods of character-ization, plot structure, imagery, and the like?*

 CONSIDER THE CLUSTER
Stories on Film: What Makes a Cult Classic?

■ Message

Read Salman Rushdie's analysis of *The Wizard of Oz* carefully. Note the close attention he pays to shapes and imagery. In a short essay, explain how the shapes and images he perceives help reinforce the film's message. Do you agree with Rushdie about the effects of the visual elements? Can you come up with an alternate explanation, or add features you think he overlooks?

■ Method

Students often criticize instructors for "reading too much" into a text. In other words, the methods of interpretation used in critical analysis might be misapplied to something that is relatively simple or straightforward. For example, what do you think of Joe Morgenstern's critical analysis of one scene from *Little Miss Sunshine*? Or Joseph Campbell's interpretation of *Star Wars*? Do you find such responses overdone or pretentious? Or do you think such in-depth analysis adds to one's enjoyment of the movie?

■ Medium

When *The Wizard of Oz* was first released, people could see it—and thousands of other films—only by going to a movie theater. It wasn't until the 1950s that television began regularly featuring old films and not until the 1960s that most people could enjoy movies in color. Note that all the authors in this section refer to using tapes or DVDs. For an in-class assignment, write a brief account of how you think modern equipment has altered the way people now look at movies. Do you prefer watching a film in a movie theater or on your home screen? In what ways are the two experiences different?

PHOTOJOURNALISM

2 ANALYTICAL ESSAYS | 9 PHOTOS

Early photographers found themselves severely limited by their cumbersome equipment, and it wasn't until the development of smaller, handheld cameras that they could go beyond their studios and leave behind their clumsy tripods to adequately cover the daily flow of events. Photojournalism came of age in the 1930s, as big-city newspapers and popular photo magazines such as *Life* and *Look* capitalized on the public's appetite for photographs that offered news and entertainment primarily through imagery. Photographers were becoming reporters, and news stories often turned on a photo. Indeed, in effective photo-journalism, the picture tells the story without the need for caption or comment;

the photo does not simply illustrate or accompany the story. As equipment continued to improve and as the public's demand for sensational pictures grew, photographers not only covered stories but actually created them, as we saw in the death of Princess Diana. Her fatal and extensively reported car crash was (as many commentators have claimed) most probably caused by the motorcycle pursuit of celebrity photographers who went to great extremes to capture her every movement on film.

Although newspapers and magazines today could hardly exist without it, photojournalism as it is often practiced raises a number of ethical issues. How far should the camera be allowed to pry into someone's private life? Does the public really need to see pictures of death and mutilation? Should photojournalists be subjected to stricter professional standards? How far can sensational photographs be trusted to tell the full story? The collection of materials presented in the following pages takes a longitudinal look at sensationalism. It includes a few examples of photographs by Weegee (sometimes credited for being the father of **tabloid** photography), with an essay by Wendy Lesser. Another essay, "The Boston Photographs" by Nora Ephron, explores the impact that the now-famous photographs had when they were published in 1975. Finally, two photographs by Bronston Jones suggest an alternate way to handle sensational material in the wake of the terrorist attacks of September 11, 2001.

237

■ **Tabloid:** *A newspaper characterized by its small size, condensed stories, popular format, and emphasis on photography. The word often conveys a negative sense (as in "tabloid journalism") due to the way tabloids, or "tabs," have conventionally relied on sensationalism, gossip, celebrity features, and mass appeal.*

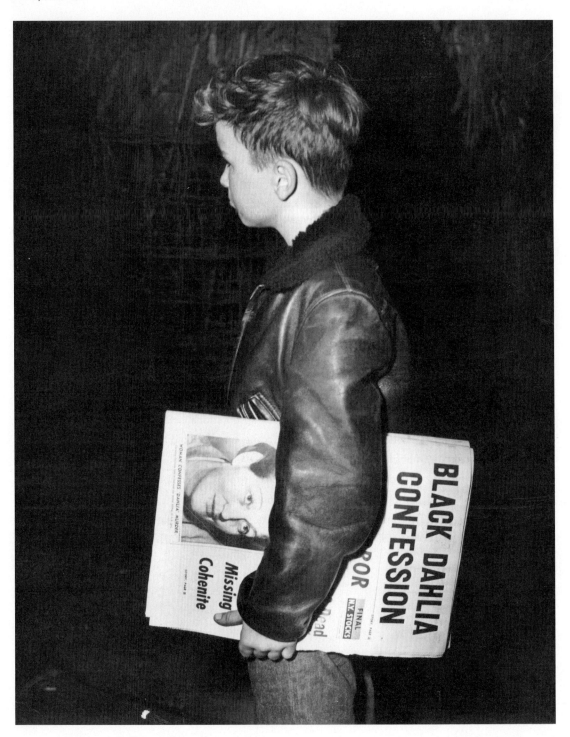

Wendy Lesser
WEEGEE

■ **Consider before you read/view.** *What does Lesser mean by the distinctions between inside and outside or interiority and exteriority?*

In Weegee's pictures, we are simultaneously inside and outside. We are given a scene that is spectacular, or stereotypical, or representative, or tabloid-cute; and we are also offered a sense of interiority, in the form of highly individual emotions rendered fleetingly and mysteriously. Weegee's best photos tell us two opposite things at once: that appearances are the only reality, and that the most important knowledge comes through imagining what lies behind appearances.

You can see this quite clearly in the photograph of the tabloid newsboy, which operates as both a sample of tabloid journalism and a commentary on it. Like the tabloids, this picture spells out its message in black and white: stark black letters against white paper, white paper against stark black background. Like the tabloids, it captures and exploits a very particular moment in time, a very particular sort of public event: a confession by a famous murderer (no doubt made famous by the tabloids themselves). But whereas the tabloid front page must show us a face to satisfy us—must let us know what the murderous woman actually looked like—Weegee's photo satisfies by hiding the newsboy's face. The boy, remaining anonymous, becomes both public and private, generic and particular.

And just as the newsboy faces at an oblique angle to us, Weegee's photo stands at an angle to the news it conveys. Looking at the photo, you have to tilt your head sideways to read the headlines and captions, so only one aspect of the double message can be taken in at once. If you can read the tabloid news, you can't "read" the boy, and vice versa.

◀ **Weegee, Newsboy.** (Weegee [Arthur Fellig]/International Center of Photography/Getty Images)

239

COMMENT

"Weegee was a hack—and that was the source of his power. He was raised on the Lower East Side where his father had a push-cart and doubled as the super in their cold-water tenement. He was, in the words of his friend Louis Stettner, 'a guttural ego-maniac,' and it shows in all his work."

— Daniel Wolff, *Threepenny Review* 56, Winter 1994

In another of its versions, this curious mixture of interiority and exteriority, private communication and public message, appears in the Mulberry Street café scene. The image is almost stereotypically Italian: the faces, the hand gestures, the high-waisted pants, the cups of espresso, the knicknacks and gewgaws on the glass-fronted shelves—not to mention all the Italian words, as if to spell it out: *This is Little Italy.* Ethnicity is of great interest to Weegee. (It's even there in the newsboy photo, in that bizarre word "Cohenite.") Ethnic identity is yet another form of inside versus outside, membership versus exclusion. It is also, for Weegee, an essential element of urban life. Ethnic definition—ethnic *self*-definition—is a sign of urbanity, or worldly-wiseness; at the same time, it marks the special provinciality of New York's neighborhoods.

But what makes this picture a Weegee is the little girl who stands on the far left side. She is the only female in the photo, and the only child. She is invisible to everyone else in the scene. (One man even walks right by her without noticing her presence.) She, on the other hand, sees everything. One arm akimbo, the other hand thoughtfully scratching her chin, her dark eyes so wide they are practically all whites, she also seems to be judging everything. Is this how all grown-up men live? Will Mulberry Street always be like this? Am I stuck here forever? *Yes* is the picture's answer. *Not exactly* is our response.

240

Weegee, *Mulberry Street Café*. One of the earliest photojournalists—and still among the most highly regarded—was Weegee (1899–1968). Born into a devout Jewish family in what is now Ukraine, Weegee (whose legal name was Arthur Fellig) immigrated to the United States as a child. He grew up in the slums of New York's Lower East Side, where as a teenager he learned how to take pictures in order to support himself. He was soon selling his striking flash photographs to various tabloids and earning a reputation for astonishing close-ups of an unraveling urban life. In the forward to *Naked City*, a collection of his photographs, Weegee's friend and editor wrote: "He will take his camera and ride off in search of new evidence that his city, even in her most drunken and disorderly and pathetic moments, is beautiful." (Weegee [Arthur Fellig]/International Center of Photography/Getty Images)

Weegee, *Dancing.*
(Weegee [Arthur Fellig]/International Center of Photography/ Getty Images)

A look of interiority on the face of a female subject also shapes the picture of the dancing woman and girl. Unlike the Caffe Bella Napoli photo, this picture has sprung loose from its setting. We don't know where we are, except that we are outside on the street somewhere, as the paving stones and stray newspapers suggest. In the background is a clot of black and white figures, some of whom are looking at the dancing couple, many of whom are not. The woman and the child are the only ones dancing, as far as we can see. They are, in that sense, making a public spectacle of themselves. But the expressions on their faces define the experience as a completely private one. For the girl, there is pleasure verging on delight. Is it delight at dancing, or at dancing with this woman? Is the woman her sister? Her mother? Her babysitter? A friend? We'll never know.

And for the woman there is also pleasure of a kind, but it is much more pensive. The richly reflective expression on her face is not exactly romantic melancholy, though it contains both sadness and longing. She is listening to a tune that no one else quite hears; she is looking at an empty space and seeing something. She almost seems to be reaching across the impassable gap between her moment in time and ours. The music that guided her steps has long since died, as has the man who took her photograph. But she keeps them alive for us.

■ **Discuss.** *In a literal sense, what a photograph captures is the surface of things. In what ways do the Weegee photographs suggest the "insides" of the people who are his subjects? How do we get to know them?*

■ **Write.** *Using Lesser's notions of inside and outside, write a short essay about the fourth Weegee photo,* Car Crash Upper Fifth Ave., July 13, 1941. *What do we have access to in this photograph? What are we shut out of?*

242

Weegee, *Car Crash Upper Fifth Ave., July 13, 1941.*
This on-the-spot photograph of two boys who just
wrecked a stolen car represents Weegee's uncanny
ability to capture a disturbing moment and do so
with an eye for detail and composition. (Weegee
[Arthur Fellig]/International Center of
Photography/Getty Images)

■ **Consider.** *Study this photograph. How has Weegee literally
shaped or framed the scene? What details inform you that an
accident has occurred? What is the effect of the injured boy's
reflection in the window vent? How does it contribute to
Weegee's overall composition? How does Weegee convey intimacy and vulnerability at the same time he is recording the
news of an accident?*

Nora Ephron, *The Boston Photographs.* Nora Ephron takes ethical questions head-on as she examines a dramatic sequence of photos showing a woman falling to her death from a fire escape during an attempted rescue from a burning apartment building. The daughter of two screenwriters, Ephron is now one of Hollywood's leading screenwriters (*When Harry Met Sally, Sleepless in Seattle*) and film directors (*Michael, You've Got Mail, and Lucky Numbers*). She began her career as a reporter and media critic for various New York papers and magazines. Ephron, who was born in 1941 and is a graduate of Wellesley College, has also published several collections of essays, including *Crazy Salad* (1975) and *Scribble, Scribble: Notes on the Media* (1978), from which "The Boston Photographs" is taken.

Nora Ephron

THE BOSTON PHOTOGRAPHS

■ **Consider before you read and view.** *Who is Ephron quoting at the beginning of her essay? Why does she begin with such a long quotation? What is its purpose in relation to the rest of the piece?*

244

"I made all kinds of pictures because I thought it would be a good rescue shot over the ladder . . . never dreamed it would be anything else. . . . I kept having to move around because of the light set. The sky was bright and they were in deep shadow. I was making pictures with a motor drive and he, the fire fighter, was reaching up and, I don't know, everything started falling. I followed the girl down taking pictures . . . I made three or four frames. I realized what was going on and I completely turned around, because I didn't want to see her hit."

You probably saw the photographs. In most newspapers, there were three of them. The first showed some people on a fire escape—a fireman, a woman and a child. The fireman had a nice strong jaw and looked very brave. The woman was holding the child. Smoke was pouring from the building behind them. A rescue ladder was approaching, just a few feet away, and the fireman had one arm around the woman and one arm reaching out toward the ladder. The second picture showed the fire escape slipping off the building. The child had fallen on the escape and seemed about to slide off the edge. The woman was grasping desperately at the legs of the fireman, who had managed to grab the ladder. The third picture showed the woman and child in midair, falling to the ground. Their arms and legs were outstretched, horribly distended. A potted plant was falling too. The caption said that the woman, Diana Bryant, nineteen, died in the fall. The child landed on the woman's body and lived.

The pictures were taken by Stanley Forman, thirty, of the *Boston Herald American.* He used a motor-driven Nikon F set at 1/250, f5.6-S. Because of the motor, the camera can click off three frames a second. More than four hundred newspapers in the United States alone carried the photographs; the tear sheets from overseas are still coming in. The *New York Times* ran them on the first page of its second section; a paper in south Georgia gave them nineteen columns; the *Chicago Tribune*, the *Washington Post* and the *Washington Star* filled almost half their front pages, the *Star* under a somewhat redundant headline that read: SENSATIONAL PHOTOS OF RESCUE ATTEMPT THAT FAILED.

The photographs are indeed sensational. They are pictures of death in action, of that split second when luck runs out, and it is impossible to look at them without feeling their extraordinary impact and remembering, in an almost subconscious way, the morbid fantasy of falling, falling off a building, falling to one's death. Beyond that, the pictures are classics, old-fashioned but perfect examples of photojournalism at its most spectacular. They're throwbacks, really, fire pictures, 1930s tabloid shots; at the same time they're technically superb and thoroughly modern—the sequence could not have been taken at all until the development of the motor-driven camera some sixteen years ago.

Most newspaper editors anticipate some reader reaction to photographs like Forman's; even so, the response around the country was enormous, and almost all of it was negative. I have read hundreds of the letters that were printed in letters-to-the-editor sections, and they repeat the same points. "Invading the privacy of death." "Cheap sensationalism." "I thought I was reading the *National Enquirer*." "Assigning the agony of a human being in terror of imminent death to the status of a side-show act." "A tawdry way to sell newspapers." The *Seattle Times* received sixty letters and calls; its managing editor even got a couple of them at home. A reader wrote the *Philadelphia Inquirer*: "*Jaws* and *Towering Inferno* are playing downtown; don't take business away from people who pay good money to advertise in your own paper." Another reader wrote the *Chicago Sun-Times*: "I shall try to hide my disappointment that Miss Bryant wasn't wearing a skirt when she fell to her death. You could have had some award-winning photographs of her underpants as her skirt billowed over her head, you voyeurs." Several newspaper editors wrote columns defending the pictures: Thomas Keevil of the *Costa Mesa*

245

Stanley Forman, *The Boston Photographs*, 1975. Photographer Stanley Forman won the Pulitzer Prize for Spot News Photography for these images, taken in Boston on July 22, 1975, and won a second in 1977 for a picture he took of a riot between whites and blacks over the integration of public schools in Boston. Forman was working for the *Boston Herald American* when he took these photographs, but more than four hundred newspapers across the country ran them the next day. (© Stanley J. Forman) ►

246

(California) *Daily Pilot* printed a ballot for readers to vote on whether they would have printed the pictures; Marshall L. Stone of Maine's *Bangor Daily News*, which refused to print the famous assassination picture of the Vietcong prisoner in Saigon, claimed that the Boston pictures showed the dangers of fire escapes and raised questions about slumlords. (The burning building was a five-story brick apartment house on Marlborough Street in the Back Bay section of Boston.)

For the last five years, the *Washington Post* has employed various journalists as ombudsmen, whose job is to monitor the paper on behalf of the public. The *Post*'s current ombudsman is Charles Seib, former managing editor of the *Washington Star*; the day the Boston photographs appeared, the paper received over seventy calls in protest. As Seib later wrote in a column about the pictures, it was "the largest reaction to a published item that I have experienced in eight months as the *Post*'s ombudsman. . . .

"In the *Post*'s newsroom, on the other hand, I found no doubts, no second thoughts . . . the question was not whether they should be printed but how they should be displayed. When I talked to editors . . . they used words like 'interesting' and 'riveting' and 'gripping' to describe them. The pictures told of something about life in the ghetto, they said (although the neighborhood where the tragedy occurred is not a ghetto, I am told). They dramatized the need to check on the safety of fire escapes. They dramatically conveyed something that had happened, and that is the business we're in. They were news. . . .

"Was publication of that [third] picture a bow to the same taste for the morbidly sensational that makes gold mines of disaster movies? Most papers will not print the picture of a dead body except in the most unusual circumstances. Does the fact that the final picture was taken a millisecond before the young woman died make a difference? Most papers will not print a picture of a bare female breast.

■ **Consider.** *What do these adjectives ("interesting," "riveting," "gripping") suggest about the editors' attitudes? Do they approach the pictures in a different way than their readers would?*

Is that a more inappropriate subject for display than the picture of a human being's last agonized instant of life?" Seib offered no answers to the questions he raised, but he went on to say that although as an editor he would probably have run the pictures, as a reader he was revolted by them.

In conclusion, Seib wrote: "Any editor who decided to print those pictures without giving at least a moment's thought to what purpose they served and what their effect was likely to be on the reader should ask another question: Have I become so preoccupied with manufacturing a product according to professional traditions and standards that I have forgotten about the consumer, the reader?"

It should be clear that the phone calls and letters and Seib's own reaction were occasioned by one factor alone: the death of the woman. Obviously, had she survived the fall, no one would have protested; the pictures would have had a completely different impact. Equally obviously, had the child died as well—or instead—Seib would undoubtedly have received ten times the phone calls he did. In each case, the pictures would have been exactly the same—only the captions, and thus the responses, would have been different.

But the questions Seib raises are worth discussing—though not exactly for the reasons he mentions. For it may be that the real lesson of the Boston photographs is not the danger that editors will be forgetful of reader reaction, but that they will continue to censor pictures of death precisely because of that reaction. The protests Seib fielded were really a variation on an old theme—and we saw plenty of it during the Nixon-Agnew years—the "Why doesn't the press print the good news?" argument. In this case, of course, the objections were all dressed up and cleverly disguised as righteous indignation about the privacy of death. This is a form of puritanism that is often justifiable; just as often it is merely puritanical.

Seib takes it for granted that the widespread though fairly recent newspaper policy against printing pictures of dead bodies is a sound one; I don't know that it makes any sense at all. I recognize that printing pictures of corpses raises all sorts of problems about taste and titillation and sensationalism; the fact is, however, that people die. Death happens to be one of life's main events. And it is irresponsible—and more than that, inaccurate—for newspapers to fail to show it, or to show it only when an astonishing set of photos comes in over the Associated Press wire. Most papers covering fatal automobile accidents will print pictures of mangled cars. But the significance of fatal automobile accidents is not that a great deal of steel is twisted but that people die. Why not show it? That's what accidents are about. Throughout the Vietnam war, editors were reluctant to print atrocity pictures. Why *not* print them? That's what that war was about. Murder victims are almost never photographed; they are granted their privacy. But their relatives are relentlessly pictured on their way in and out of hospitals and morgues and funerals.

I'm not advocating that newspapers print these things in order to teach their readers a lesson. The *Post* editors justified their printing of the Boston pictures with several arguments in that direction; every one of them is irrelevant. The pictures don't show anything about slum life; the incident could have happened anywhere, and it did. It is extremely unlikely that anyone who saw them rushed out and had his fire escape strengthened. And the pictures were not news—at least they were not national news. It is not news in Washington, or New York, or Los Angeles that a woman was killed in a Boston fire. The only newsworthy thing about the pictures is that they were taken. They deserve to be printed because they are great pictures, breathtaking pictures of something that happened. That they disturb readers is exactly as it should be: that's why photojournalism is often more powerful than written journalism.

■ **Discuss.** *Ephron points out that this sequence of pictures would not have been possible before the invention of the motor-driven camera. Discuss how advances in technology can sometimes present new ethical dilemmas. For example, what are the ethical guidelines for using camera phones? What rights does the photographer have to share or display pictures the subject didn't know were being taken?*

■ **Write.** *Ephron argues that the widespread agreement among newspaper editors not to publish pictures of dead bodies is "irresponsible—and more than that, inaccurate." Write a short essay either defending the publication of such pictures or discussing why the cultural taboo against showing dead bodies should be respected.*

249

Bronston Jones, *Missing* and *Contact Sheet*, **2001.** The ethical issues regarding photojournalism have most recently been explored as people debated what kinds of images were appropriate to show from the destruction of the World Trade Center on September 11, 2001. The photographs shown here, published as part of the September 11 Photo Project, represent a different way to document lives lost other than showing people jumping from the burning towers. Bronston Jones's photographs, taken in the days after the tragedy, are part of the traveling exhibit *Missing: Last Seen at the World Trade Center on September 11, 2001.* The image on page 251 is a contact sheet of 36 missing-person fliers; it would take 160 of these sheets to show the faces of all the missing and deceased. The *Missing* exhibit refocuses emphasis on the lives of those who were lost rather than on the destruction of the towers. As Jones puts it, "the people are real, the buildings are just real estate." (Copyright © 2001 Bronston Jones.)

MISSING

■■■■■■ CONSIDER THE CLUSTER
Photojournalism

■ **Message**

Nora Ephron devotes a good portion of her essay to examining the reasons various newspaper editors gave for publishing or not publishing Stanley Forman's photos. What is the central issue here? In your opinion, are the photos newsworthy or not? Certain editors claimed that publication of the photos was justified because they conveyed an important message; what is that message? Does Ephron accept that message? Do you think the photographer intended to convey that message? Many readers who saw the photos on front pages across the nation considered them voyeuristic. Would the photos have had the same impact if a caption had informed us that the woman had survived the fall?

■ **Method**

In many Weegee photographs, we see not only a subject or event but also an audience (sometimes an individual onlooker, often a crowd) that's witnessing it. In which of the four photographs does an audience play a significant role? Why do you think Weegee wants to build an audience into the picture? What effect do onlookers have on the emotional impact of the photographs? How does photographer Bronston Jones create emotional impact?

■ **Medium**

In her essay, Ephron praises Forman's photographs by calling them "perfect examples of photojournalism at its most spectacular. They're throwbacks, really, fire pictures, 1930s tabloid shots." Ephron is clearly placing Forman's work in the context of such tabloid photographers as Weegee. In an essay, compare Weegee's *Car Crash Upper Fifth Ave.* with Forman's photographs. What elements do they share? In what ways are they different? Do you agree with Ephron that these are the same type of photographs? In an essay, try to describe the major characteristics of classic tabloid photography.

MEMOIR

When we tell stories, very often we are constructing narratives of our own lives. Writers have been doing this for centuries in personal essays, and today the memoir is one of the most popular forms of literary expression. In the most persuasive and unforgettable personal essays and memoirs, the writer expands and enriches his or her life story to include other people and public events. The self is thus seen in a larger context and setting, which could include family members, friends, colleagues, and historical situations.

Of late, a new type of memoir has been receiving much attention—the graphic memoir. For decades, comics had been largely fictional, often focusing on bizarre characters and superheroes. But with the work of Robert Crumb, Art Spiegelman (see pp. 46–47), Lynda Barry (see p. 337), and Marjane Satrapi (see p. 448), graphic artists began exploring their own lives and backgrounds for material. Some of these works have become best sellers, beginning with Spiegelman's 1986 groundbreaking memoir, *Maus I: A Survivor's Tale*, and including most recently Alison Bechdel's 2006 autobiography, *Fun Home: A Family Tragicomic*. From that book's opening chapter, "Old Father, Old Artificer," we can see why Bechdel's graphic memoir has been compared to David Sedaris's family stories.

Alison Bechdel, *Old Father, Old Artificer,* **from** *Fun Home,* **2006.** Alison Bechdel (b. 1960) ▶
is a cartoonist known for her syndicated comic strip *Dykes to Watch Out For* (since 1983)
and the author of the recent best-selling graphic memoir *Fun Home: A Family Tragicomic.*
Bechdel, who has kept a journal since age ten, chronicles in *Fun Home* her childhood and
life with her father, an obsessive decorator, an English teacher, a funeral home director,
and a closeted gay man. *The New York Times Book Review* calls the memoir "the most
ingeniously compact, hyper-verbose example of autobiography to have been produced.
It is a pioneering work . . . so absorbing you feel you are living in [the artist's] world."
Bechdel takes her title from James Joyce's classic novel, *A Portrait of an Artist as a Young
Man*, which ends with a diary entry of the protagonist, Stephen Daedelus: "APRIL 27. Old
father, old artificer, stand me now and ever in good stead."

   What are her influences? "Autobiographical comics, I love them. I love them.
Watching everyone root through their psyche, it just delights me. Especially R. Crumb's
stuff." Bechdel is also a fan of *Mad* magazine and Edward Gorey and thinks of comics artist
Chris Ware (p. 195) as "some kind of insane genius." Of her creative process, Bechdel
says: "Writing and drawing are very separate processes for me. I'll have an idea about what
a panel will look like as I'm writing, but I often don't touch a pencil until the text is completely finished. . . . It's almost like I'm two different people, first the writer, and then the
sketcher and inker." Of writing a graphic book, Bechdel says: "You're intimately involved
with the whole book. You've caressed every surface of every page. If you write a regular
book, it's a one-dimensional construct, a line of text that flows endlessly. But here you
have to handle every page."

Alison Bechdel

OLD FATHER,
OLD ARTIFICER

■ **Consider before you read and view.** *How does Bechdel portray her family in the following memoir—and what is the tone of that portrayal? What is her relationship to her
father? Why does she call him the "old artificer"?*

NATIONAL BESTSELLER

"Brilliant . . . hilarious . . . a gripping story of filial sleuthery."
— *Time*

Houghton
Mifflin

Ne𝔴 York Times Bestseller

Los Angeles Times Bestseller

"Brilliant . . . hilarious." — *Time*

"If David Sedaris could draw, and if *Bleak House* had been a little funnier, you'd have ALISON BECHDEL's *Fun Home*." — Amy Bloom

Fun Home
A FAMILY TRAGICOMIC

ALISON BECHDEL

Houghton
Mifflin

CHAPTER 1

OLD FATHER, OLD ARTIFICER

LIKE MANY FATHERS, MINE COULD OCCASIONALLY BE PREVAILED ON FOR A SPOT OF "AIRPLANE."

AS HE LAUNCHED ME, MY FULL WEIGHT WOULD FALL ON THE PIVOT POINT BETWEEN HIS FEET AND MY STOMACH.

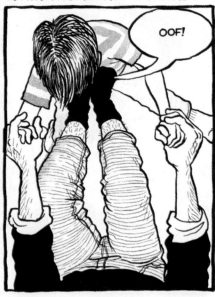

OOF!

IT WAS A DISCOMFORT WELL WORTH THE RARE PHYSICAL CONTACT, AND CERTAINLY WORTH THE MOMENT OF PERFECT BALANCE WHEN I SOARED ABOVE HIM.

IN THE CIRCUS, ACROBATICS WHERE ONE PERSON LIES ON THE FLOOR BALANCING ANOTHER ARE CALLED "ICARIAN GAMES."

257

CONSIDERING THE FATE OF ICARUS AFTER HE FLOUTED HIS FATHER'S ADVICE AND FLEW SO CLOSE TO THE SUN HIS WINGS MELTED, PERHAPS SOME DARK HUMOR IS INTENDED.

258

BUT BEFORE HE DID SO, HE MANAGED TO GET QUITE A LOT DONE.

HIS GREATEST ACHIEVEMENT, ARGUABLY, WAS HIS MONOMANIACAL RESTORATION OF OUR OLD HOUSE.

WHEN OTHER CHILDREN CALLED OUR HOUSE A MANSION, I WOULD DEMUR. I RESENTED THE IMPLICATION THAT MY FAMILY WAS RICH, OR UNUSUAL IN ANY WAY.

IN FACT, WE WERE UNUSUAL, THOUGH I WOULDN'T APPRECIATE EXACTLY HOW UNUSUAL UNTIL MUCH LATER. BUT WE WERE NOT RICH.

THE GILT CORNICES, THE MARBLE FIREPLACE, THE CRYSTAL CHANDELIERS, THE SHELVES OF CALF-BOUND BOOKS--THESE WERE NOT SO MUCH BOUGHT AS PRODUCED FROM THIN AIR BY MY FATHER'S REMARKABLE LEGERDEMAIN.

■ *Consider. What is the significance of the Victorian house? How does it function as a metaphor? Why does Bechdel choose to detail the house, furnishings, and repairs?*

259

MY FATHER COULD SPIN GARBAGE...   ...INTO GOLD.

HE COULD TRANSFIGURE A ROOM WITH THE SMALLEST OFFHAND FLOURISH.

HE COULD CONJURE AN ENTIRE, FINISHED PERIOD INTERIOR FROM A PAINT CHIP.

260

HE WAS AN ALCHEMIST OF APPEARANCE, A SAVANT OF SURFACE, A DAEDALUS OF DECOR.

FOR IF MY FATHER WAS ICARUS, HE WAS ALSO DAEDALUS--THAT SKILLFUL ARTIFICER, THAT MAD SCIENTIST WHO BUILT THE WINGS FOR HIS SON AND DESIGNED THE FAMOUS LABYRINTH...

THIS IS THE WALLPAPER FOR MY ROOM?

...AND WHO ANSWERED NOT TO THE LAWS OF SOCIETY, BUT TO THOSE OF HIS CRAFT.

BUT I **HATE** PINK! I **HATE** FLOWERS!

TOUGH TITTY.

HISTORICAL RESTORATION WASN'T HIS JOB.

(TWELFTH-GRADE ENGLISH)

ARCHI-TECTURAL DIGEST

IT WAS HIS PASSION. AND I MEAN PASSION IN EVERY SENSE OF THE WORD.

LIBIDINAL. MANIC. MARTYRED.

■ Consider. *How is Bechdel's father "martyred"?*

OUR GOTHIC REVIVAL HOUSE HAD BEEN BUILT DURING THE SMALL PENNSYLVANIA TOWN'S ONE BRIEF MOMENT OF WEALTH, FROM THE LUMBER INDUSTRY, IN 1867.

BUT LOCAL FORTUNES HAD DECLINED STEADILY FROM THAT POINT, AND WHEN MY PARENTS BOUGHT THE PLACE IN 1962, IT WAS A SHELL OF ITS FORMER SELF.

THE SHUTTERS AND SCROLLWORK WERE GONE. THE CLAPBOARDS HAD BEEN SHEATHED WITH SCABROUS SHINGLES.

THE BARE LIGHTBULBS REVEALED DINGY WARTIME WALLPAPER AND WOODWORK PAINTED PASTEL GREEN.

ALL THAT WAS LEFT OF THE HOUSE'S LUMBER-ERA GLORY WERE THE EXUBERANT FRONT PORCH SUPPORTS.

BUT OVER THE NEXT EIGHTEEN YEARS, MY FATHER WOULD RESTORE THE HOUSE TO ITS ORIGINAL CONDITION, AND THEN SOME.

HE WOULD PERFORM, AS DAEDALUS DID, DAZZLING DISPLAYS OF ARTFULNESS.

263

HE WOULD CULTIVATE THE BARREN YARD...

...INTO A LUSH, FLOWERING LANDSCAPE.

HE WOULD MANIPULATE FLAGSTONES THAT WEIGHED HALF A TON...

...AND THE THINNEST, QUIVERING LAYERS OF GOLD LEAF.

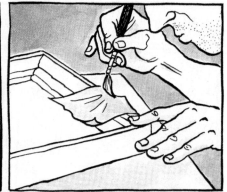

IT COULD HAVE BEEN A ROMANTIC STORY, LIKE IN *IT'S A WONDERFUL LIFE*, WHEN JIMMY STEWART AND DONNA REED FIX UP THAT BIG OLD HOUSE AND RAISE THEIR FAMILY THERE.

BUT IN THE MOVIE WHEN JIMMY STEWART COMES HOME ONE NIGHT AND STARTS YELLING AT EVERYONE...

...IT'S OUT OF THE ORDINARY.

DAEDALUS, TOO, WAS INDIFFERENT TO THE HUMAN COST OF HIS PROJECTS.

HE BLITHELY BETRAYED THE KING, FOR EXAMPLE, WHEN THE QUEEN ASKED HIM TO BUILD HER A COW DISGUISE SO SHE COULD SEDUCE THE WHITE BULL.

INDEED, THE RESULT OF THAT SCHEME--A
HALF-BULL, HALF-MAN MONSTER--INSPIRED
DAEDALUS'S GREATEST CREATION YET.

HE HID THE MINOTAUR IN THE LABYRINTH--
A MAZE OF PASSAGES AND ROOMS OPEN-
ING ENDLESSLY INTO ONE ANOTHER...

...AND FROM WHICH, AS STRAY YOUTHS AND
MAIDENS DISCOVERED TO THEIR PERIL...

...ESCAPE WAS IMPOSSIBLE.

THEN THERE ARE THOSE FAMOUS WINGS.
WAS DAEDALUS REALLY STRICKEN WITH
GRIEF WHEN ICARUS FELL INTO THE SEA?

OR JUST DISAPPOINTED BY THE DESIGN
FAILURE?

SOMETIMES, WHEN THINGS WERE GOING WELL, I THINK MY FATHER ACTUALLY ENJOYED HAVING A FAMILY.

AND OF COURSE, MY BROTHERS AND I WERE FREE LABOR. DAD CONSIDERED US EXTENSIONS OF HIS OWN BODY, LIKE PRECISION ROBOT ARMS.

OR AT LEAST, THE AIR OF AUTHENTICITY WE LENT TO HIS EXHIBIT. A SORT OF STILL LIFE WITH CHILDREN.

PUT HOT, SOAPY WATER IN THE SINK AND GET SOME CLEAN RAGS.

IN THIS REGARD, IT WAS LIKE BEING RAISED NOT BY JIMMY BUT BY MARTHA STEWART.

IN THEORY, HIS ARRANGEMENT WITH MY MOTHER WAS MORE COOPERATIVE.

IN PRACTICE, IT WAS NOT.

WHAT DO YOU THINK OF THIS GAS CHANDELIER?

BORDELLO.

AUCTION CATALOG

WE EACH RESISTED IN OUR OWN WAYS, BUT IN THE END WE WERE EQUALLY POWERLESS BEFORE MY FATHER'S CURATORIAL ONSLAUGHT.

MY BROTHERS AND I COULDN'T COMPETE WITH THE ASTRAL LAMPS AND GIRANDOLES AND HEPPLEWHITE SUITE CHAIRS. THEY WERE PERFECT.

268

I GREW TO RESENT THE WAY MY FATHER TREATED HIS FURNITURE LIKE CHILDREN, AND HIS CHILDREN LIKE FURNITURE.

MY OWN DECIDED PREFERENCE FOR THE UNADORNED AND PURELY FUNCTIONAL EMERGED EARLY.

I WAS SPARTAN TO MY FATHER'S ATHENIAN.   MODERN TO HIS VICTORIAN.

■ **Consider.** *What is the significance of Bechdel's comparisons of herself with her father?*

BUTCH TO HIS NELLY.   UTILITARIAN TO HIS AESTHETE.

269

I DEVELOPED A CONTEMPT FOR USE-LESS ORNAMENT. WHAT FUNCTION WAS SERVED BY THE SCROLLS, TASSELS, AND BRIC-A-BRAC THAT INFESTED OUR HOUSE?

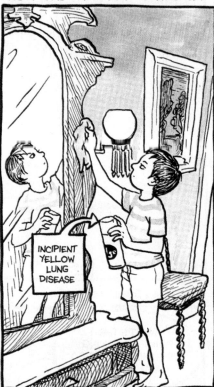

INCIPIENT YELLOW LUNG DISEASE

IF ANYTHING, THEY OBSCURED FUNCTION. THEY WERE EMBELLISHMENTS IN THE WORST SENSE.

PLING KLINK

THEY WERE LIES.

MY FATHER BEGAN TO SEEM MORALLY SUSPECT TO ME LONG BEFORE I KNEW THAT HE ACTUALLY HAD A DARK SECRET.

MOM SAYS HURRY UP.

"BRONZING STICK"

HE USED HIS SKILLFUL ARTIFICE NOT TO MAKE THINGS, BUT TO MAKE THINGS APPEAR TO BE WHAT THEY WERE NOT.

MASS WILL BE OVER BEFORE WE GET THERE.

THAT IS TO SAY, IMPECCABLE.

HE APPEARED TO BE AN IDEAL HUSBAND AND FATHER, FOR EXAMPLE.

IT'S TEMPTING TO SUGGEST, IN RETRO-SPECT, THAT OUR FAMILY WAS A SHAM.

THAT OUR HOUSE WAS NOT A REAL HOME AT ALL BUT THE SIMULACRUM OF ONE, A MUSEUM.

YET WE REALLY WERE A FAMILY, AND WE REALLY DID LIVE IN THOSE PERIOD ROOMS.

STILL, SOMETHING VITAL WAS MISSING.

AN ELASTICITY, A MARGIN FOR ERROR.

MOST PEOPLE, I IMAGINE, LEARN TO ACCEPT THAT THEY'RE NOT PERFECT.

BUT AN IDLE REMARK ABOUT MY FATHER'S TIE OVER BREAKFAST COULD SEND HIM INTO A TAILSPIN.

DON'T CHANGE IT! WE'RE LATE!

ALSO AN ENGLISH TEACHER

MY MOTHER ESTABLISHED A RULE.

NO COMMENTS ON HIS APPEARANCE. IS THAT UNDERSTOOD?

WHAT IF IT'S SOMETHING GOOD?

GOOD, BAD, IT DOESN'T MATTER.

IF WE COULDN'T CRITICIZE MY FATHER, SHOWING AFFECTION FOR HIM WAS AN EVEN DICIER VENTURE.

WE WERE NOT A PHYSICALLY EXPRESSIVE FAMILY, TO SAY THE LEAST. BUT ONCE I WAS UNACCOUNTABLY MOVED TO KISS MY FATHER GOOD NIGHT.

273

HAVING LITTLE PRACTICE WITH THE GESTURE, ALL I MANAGED WAS TO GRAB HIS HAND AND BUSS THE KNUCKLES LIGHTLY...

...AS IF HE WERE A BISHOP OR AN ELEGANT LADY, BEFORE RUSHING FROM THE ROOM IN EMBARRASSMENT.

■ **Consider.** *Why is Bechdel embarrassed when she kisses her father's hand?*

THIS EMBARRASSMENT ON MY PART WAS A TINY SCALE MODEL OF MY FATHER'S MORE FULLY DEVELOPED SELF-LOATHING.

HIS SHAME INHABITED OUR HOUSE AS PERVASIVELY AND INVISIBLY AS THE AROMATIC MUSK OF AGING MAHOGANY.

IN FACT, THE METICULOUS, PERIOD INTERIORS WERE EXPRESSLY DESIGNED TO CONCEAL IT.

MIRRORS, DISTRACTING BRONZES, MULTIPLE DOORWAYS. VISITORS OFTEN GOT LOST UPSTAIRS.

GRACIOUS, I ALMOST WALKED RIGHT INTO THIS!

MY MOTHER, MY BROTHERS, AND I KNEW OUR WAY AROUND WELL ENOUGH, BUT IT WAS IMPOSSIBLE TO TELL IF THE MINOTAUR LAY BEYOND THE NEXT CORNER.

AND THE CONSTANT TENSION WAS HEIGHT-ENED BY THE FACT THAT SOME ENCOUN-TERS COULD BE QUITE PLEASANT.

HIS BURSTS OF KINDNESS WERE AS INCAN-DESCENT AS HIS TANTRUMS WERE DARK.

275

ALTHOUGH I'M GOOD AT ENUMERATING MY FATHER'S FLAWS, IT'S HARD FOR ME TO SUSTAIN MUCH ANGER AT HIM.

I EXPECT THIS IS PARTLY BECAUSE HE'S DEAD, AND PARTLY BECAUSE THE BAR IS LOWER FOR FATHERS THAN FOR MOTHERS.

STOP SPLASHING!

IN MY EYES!

HOLD STILL, DAMMIT!

MY MOTHER MUST HAVE BATHED ME HUNDREDS OF TIMES. BUT IT'S MY FATHER RINSING ME OFF WITH THE PURPLE METAL CUP THAT I REMEMBER MOST CLEARLY.

THE SUFFUSION OF WARMTH AS THE HOT WATER SLUICED OVER ME...

...THE SUDDEN, UNBEARABLE COLD OF ITS ABSENCE.

WAS HE A GOOD FATHER? I WANT TO SAY, "AT LEAST HE STUCK AROUND." BUT OF COURSE, HE DIDN'T.

AGAIN!

276

IT'S TRUE THAT HE DIDN'T KILL HIMSELF UNTIL I WAS NEARLY TWENTY.

BUT HIS ABSENCE RESONATED RETRO-ACTIVELY, ECHOING BACK THROUGH ALL THE TIME I KNEW HIM.

MAYBE IT WAS THE CONVERSE OF THE WAY AMPUTEES FEEL PAIN IN A MISSING LIMB.

HE REALLY WAS THERE ALL THOSE YEARS, A FLESH-AND-BLOOD PRESENCE STEAMING OFF THE WALLPAPER, DIGGING UP THE DOGWOODS, POLISHING THE FINIALS...

277

...SMELLING OF SAWDUST AND SWEAT AND DESIGNER COLOGNE.

BUT I ACHED AS IF HE WERE ALREADY GONE.

◄ ■ **Discuss.** *What is the meaning of the word "artifice"? How does artifice function in Bechdel's family and in her memoir? Why is it so important to her father—and what specific situations make it evident to Bechdel as a child that he is concerned with artifice? What does she think of this? The title of Bechdel's book, from which this chapter is reprinted, is* Fun Home: A Family Tragicomic. *What does the title mean? And why does she name this section "Old Father, Old Artificer"?*

■ **Write.** *Consider the myth of Daedalus and Icarus (see pp. 279–81). In a brief essay, explain how—and why—Bechdel portrays her father in terms of this myth. Does she fit herself into the myth? If so, how? What is the effect of using this specific myth to help tell this story of herself, her father, and the rest of her family? How does it contribute to or detract from her memoir?*

Thomas Bulfinch, *Daedalus,* **1855.** Thomas Bulfinch (1796–1867) wrote in the introduction to his collection *Mythology*: "Without a knowledge of mythology much of the elegant literature of our own language cannot be understood and appreciated." The story of Daedalus—a mythical Greek inventor, skilled craftsman, and architect who created the legendary Labyrinth in which King Minos of Crete contains the beast called the Minotaur—is first recorded by the poet Homer in the eighth century B.C.E. When Daedalus falls out of favor with King Minos, he and his son Icarus attempt to escape by taking flight. Alison Bechdel refers to Daedalus, "that skillful artificer," and Icarus in "Old Father, Old Artificer," from *Fun Home* (on p. 258).

Thomas Bulfinch

DAEDALUS

■ **Consider before you read and view.** *Why does Daedalus decide to make wings for himself and his son Icarus? What is the "moral" to this story? Is it a cautionary tale for parents? For children? For both?*

Daedalus built the labyrinth for King Minos, but afterwards lost the favor of the king, and was shut up in a tower. He contrived to make his escape from his prison, but could not leave the island by sea, as the king kept strict watch on all the vessels, and permitted none to sail without being carefully searched. "Minos may control the land and sea," said Daedalus, "but not the regions of the air. I will try that way." So he set to work to fabricate wings for himself and his young son Icarus. He wrought feathers together, beginning with the smallest and adding larger, so as to form an increasing surface. The larger ones he secured with thread and the smaller with wax, and gave the whole a gentle curvature like the wings of a bird. Icarus, the boy, stood and lóoked on, sometimes running to gather up the feathers which the wind had blown away, and then handling the wax and working it over with his fingers, by his play impeding his father in his labors. When at last the work was done, the artist, waving his wings, found himself buoyed upwards and hung suspended, poising himself on the beaten air. He next equipped his son in the same manner, and taught him how to fly, as a bird tempts her young ones from the lofty nest into the air. When all was prepared for flight he said, "Icarus, my son, I charge you to keep at a moderate height, for if you fly too low the damp will clog your wings, and if too high the heat will melt them. Keep near me and you will be safe." While he gave him these instructions and fitted the wings to his shoulders, the face of the father was wet with tears, and his hands trembled. He kissed the boy, not knowing that it was for the last time. Then rising on his wings, he flew off, encouraging him to follow, and looked back from his own flight to see how his son managed his wings. As they flew the ploughman stopped his work

279

■ *Consider. Why does Daedalus bind the larger wings with thread and the smaller ones with wax?*

Jacob Peter Gowy, *The Fall of Icarus*. Among the best-known visual portrayals of the myth of Daedalus and Icarus are a painting by Pieter Bruegel the Elder (1558), a sketch by Peter Paul Rubens (1577–1640), and, shown here, a painting by Rubens' assistant Jacob Peter Gowy (active from 1632– ca. 1671) based on Rubens' work. Both the Rubens sketch and Gowy painting are based on the poet Ovid's version of the myth. However, while the poet suggests a bright, sunny sky as a backdrop to the tragedy, the artists chose to present a darkening sky and stormy sea. The final painting represents the most dramatic part of the story, conveying the vulnerability of human flesh and a sense of tragedy and loss as Icarus slips away from his father.

to gaze, and the shepherd leaned on his staff and watched them, astonished at the sight, and thinking they were gods who could thus cleve the air.

They passed Samos and Delos on the left and Lebynthos on the right, when the boy, exulting in his career, began to leave the guidance of his companion and soar upward as if to reach heaven. The nearness of the blazing sun softened the wax which held the feathers together, and they came off. He fluttered with his arms, but no featheres remained to hold the air. While his mouth uttered cries to his father it was submerged in the blue waters of the sea, which thenceforth was called by his name. His father cried, "Icarus, Icarus, where are you?" At last he saw the feathers floating on the water, and bitterly lamenting his own arts, he buried the body and called the land Icaria in memory of his child. Daedalus arrived safe in Sicily, where he built a temple to Apollo, and hung up his wings, an offering to the god.

■ **Discuss.** *What are the messages of the story of Daedalus and Icarus? Have you found references to this myth in other things you have read (aside from Bechdel's memoir)? If so, how was the story portrayed—and to what effect?*

■ **Write.** *What other father-son (or parent-child) myths or fairy tales are you familiar with? In an essay, compare and contrast another parent-child myth to the Daedalus and Icarus myth.*

 CONSIDER THE CLUSTER
Memoir

■ **Message**

Alison Bechdel introduces several classical myths into her childhood memoir. After reading the mythological account of Daedalus and Icarus, write a short essay in which you examine how that story helps enhance and deepen the meaning of her memoir.

■ **Method**

Alison Bechdel composes a segment of her autobiography in a medium that differs from typical autobiographies—hers takes the form of comics. Do you consider this medium an effective way to tell one's life story? Are there effects one can accomplish in a traditional prose memoir that can't be achieved in a graphic memoir, and vice versa? In an essay, discuss what you consider to be the advantages and disadvantages of each medium. You might consider how Bechdel's story would look if she wrote it without the use of illustration. Would it, for example, simply be the same text that appears in her graphic memoir?

■ **Medium**

Graphic writers employ different methods to compose their works. Some create images and texts at the same time, working panel by panel. For Bechdel, on the other hand, writing and drawing are two very separate processes (see her comments on p. 254)—that is, she writes first and draws and inks second. Do you see any evidence of her seperate processes in her finished work, "Old Father, Old Artificer"? Or, is her method invisible? Do you detect in Bechdel's work her sense of herself as "two different people, first the writer, and then the sketcher and inker"? Explain.

WRITE ■■■■■■

1. **Analyze.** Compare and contrast Weegee's *Car Crash Upper Fifth Ave., July 13, 1941* (p. 243) with Mary Ellen Mark's *The Damm Family in Their Car* (p. 518), or Mitch Epstein's Cocoa Beach Florida, 1983, or Jesse DeMartino's *Jason and Mike at the Cabin Near Huntsville, Texas, 1996* (p. 322). How does the car in each photo serve as an artistic "vehicle" for the photographer? How has each photographer used a car for compositional and framing purposes? In what ways in each photograph does the car contribute to a sense of intimacy? A sense of trouble? After reading Philip Gefter's essay (p. 208), which of the above photos do you think has the most artistic purpose behind it—that is, which photographer wants you to pay more attention to the craft of photography than to his or her subject? In an analytical essay that addresses some of these questions, make a case for the photograph you find most moving.

2. **Compare.** Compare Alison Bechdel's "Old Father, Old Artificer" (p. 254) with Dorothy Allison's "What Did You Expect?" (p. 588). What similarities can you find between the two selections? How does each writer connect family matters to storytelling? How does class consciousness enter each essay? In an essay, compare and contrast the ways each writer expresses a personal identity rooted in social and cultural values.

3. **Evaluate.** Review Alison Bechdel's graphic memoir (p. 254) in connection with Judith Ortiz Cofer's (p. 68) and Nicole Lamy's (p. 291). How does each individual rely on visual material? After reflecting on all three memoirs, write an essay in which you describe how you would go about incorporating visual material into your family history. What would your project be like? What material would you use, and how would it enhance your history? Would you combine text and image, use only text, or use only images?

4. **Evaluate.** Different movies appeal to different people; in fact, we can all name a movie that we've seen again and again—the teen movie or horror film or action adventure that we love to revisit. In a personal essay, write about the one film you most like to watch. Be sure ot focus on the effect it has on you as a film, as something you like to watch, and try to convey as best you can your *personal experience* of watching it.

5. **Create a story.** Everyone is familiar with urban legends such as "The Hook," several versions of which appear on pages 181–85. Using what you already

know and what you've learned in this chapter about urban legends, try to make up one of your own in a five-hundred-word narrative. Have fun, but be sure to make the details of your story sound so realistic and authentic that people will believe that it actually happened.

6. **Collaborate and analyze.** In small groups, identify the differences that occur when you narrate events in a story such as "Little Red Riding Hood" as opposed to those in a cartoon or a comic strip. In doing so, pay special attention to either Chris Ware's *Family*, (p. 196) or Marjane Satrapi's *At West Point* (p. 448). Then, each group should attempt to retell "Little Red Riding Hood" in a comic strip. Your drawn version does not need to look professional (although each group may have members who can draw better than others), but you should rough out the story and characters into frames. Try to restrict the cartoon to ten or fifteen frames. Afterward, the groups should compare their productions. How many different ways did the fairy tale get told? How did each group differ in the events and characters it included and excluded?

7. **Collaborate and make a case.** An interesting rule of art, especially contemporary art, is that every new piece of technology will in short time be put to artistic purposes. This process has been going on for some time, from 1960s artists who fashioned sculpture out of television sets, to a recent composer who programmed hundreds of cell phones to orchestrate a symphony, to a French writer who recently composed an entire novel using the slang, abbreviations, symbols, and made-up words that young people worldwide have adopted for cell phone text-messaging. After breaking into small groups, consider the rapid development as well as the convergence of electronic equipment and gadgets—all those new "hot items" at the consumer electronics shows. Select any recent example of one of these "toys" or "tools" and collaboratively draft up some ways you think an artist might reinvent it for aesthetic purposes.

8. **Make a case.** After rereading Nora Ephron's "The Boston Photographs" (p. 244) imagine that you are the chief editor of a newspaper and that the photographs in question have been submitted to you. Would you print them? Your staff is divided. You must make the decision. Write a two-paragraph memo to your staff that explains the reasons behind what you ultimately decide to do. Be sure to anticipate the criticism you will receive no matter how you decide.

WRITE

9. **Research.** Where do stories such as "Little Red Riding Hood" come from? Who made them up—and why? In a short research paper, provide a brief history of "Little Red Riding Hood" or another famous tale of your choosing. Be sure to identify the earliest source of the tale that you can find. Or, if you prefer, select an urban legend you have heard of and try to uncover the story of how it got started and became popular.

10. **Collaborate and analyze.** As an in-class exercise, study Edward Hopper's *Office at Night* (p. 201) and compose a two-paragraph story that you think verbally portrays what is happening visually. Afterward, compare your version with your classmates'. How many variations were produced? How many constructed similar stories?

SCIENCE

3

Shaping Spaces: the clusters

What do a billboard, a video game, an automobile, a basketball court, an airport, and a sidewalk have in common? They are all, in one sense or another, spaces — sites we can visit, inhabit, imagine, reconstruct, escape to, disappear in, fill up. Spaces can be as vast and open as a desert or as small and compact as a wren's nest, as simple as a blank sheet of paper or as complex as a Gothic cathedral. The word "space," of course, means different things to different people. To an astronaut, it can mean everything outside the earth's atmosphere; to a book designer, it may mean the absence of typographical clutter; to a magazine publisher, it represents what can profitably be sold to advertisers.

As cognitive scientists know, the concept of space is fundamental to human thought; the brain is wired for apprehending spatial forms and relations. These relationships, in fact, can be so powerful that people many years later will have forgotten everything about what went on in, say, sixth grade except where they sat. For some reason, spatial orientation exerts an enormous influence on memory. In "Life in Motion" (p. 291), Nicole Lamy alludes to Cicero, a rhetorician in ancient Rome who advised student orators to think of a sequence of places or rooms to help them memorize their speeches. Those of us who remember the assassinations of John F. Kennedy and Martin Luther King Jr.

(or perhaps more recently the World Trade Center and Pentagon attacks) can usually recall exactly where we were at the moment we heard the news.

By the time we reach adolescence, we all possess a fairly well-developed sense of physical space. We could not function or even survive without it — how could we possibly drive a car or even walk into a classroom? But the larger meanings of space — the ways we conceive of it — are easily overlooked, perhaps because we tend to focus on objects themselves and not on the spaces they inhabit, create, and often transform. For example, how many of us consider the interior of our cars a "sacred space," as the poet Stephen Dunn suggests in his poem "The Sacred" (p. 321)? Or, while shopping, how many of us pay close attention to the ways a mall is designed to encourage wandering and discourage a clear sense of destination? In developing spatial literacy, we need to retrain ourselves to observe not only objects but also the way they affect our sense of space or spatial location. Many modern artists now produce museum installations in order to educate the public's perceptual ability to see space not as something that's missing but as something that's always present in one form or another. Furthermore, whereas the average Internet user merely notices a colorful web site, a visually astute designer sees a medium that's helping dissolve the boundaries between private and public space.

Because we grow so habituated to spatial forms and perspectives, artists of all kinds — in painting, video, film, architecture, and so on — will deliberately try to challenge the customary ways we view the world around us. When an artist disrupts our conventional spatial orientation — for example, by complicating our mental categories of top/bottom, inside/outside, front/back, or surface/depth — the effect can be one of confusion and disorientation. Writers and artists like to call this effect "defamiliarization," to emphasize the way they have altered our perception of ordinary objects. Even when

a work appears to be as realistic as a straight-on photograph, we will probably find on closer inspection some elements of distortion, some degree of artistic contrivance that enables us to observe a scene or object in ways we probably wouldn't notice in actual life.

Look closely, for example, at Mitch Epstein's remarkable photograph *Cocoa Beach, Florida, 1983* (p. 323), and see how many lines of sight you can trace as your eye follows various angles and perspectives. As Epstein photographs it, the scene seems both familiar and unfamiliar. As part of the defamiliarization process, art also gives us extra eyes, so to speak, shifting us away from the normal frontal perspective that provides nearly all of our visual information. As Richard Estes, another contemporary artist who uses photographic techniques in his paintings, has said, "When you look at a scene or an object, you tend to scan it. Your eye travels around and over things. As your eyes move, the vanishing point moves; to have one vanishing point or perfect camera perspective is not realistic." Estes's comment helps us understand the counter-realism behind Epstein's colorfully realistic *Cocoa Beach* photograph. In its use of intersecting lines with different vanishing points and multiple surfaces crowded together, Epstein's photo — though of a real time and specific space — looks like nothing we've ever noticed before.

As the selections in this chapter (and others throughout the book) will show, reconceiving space is often a matter of dissolving or redrawing boundaries, multiplying or altering perspectives, rearranging or rotating coordinates. It's a matter of seeing and thinking outside the box, learning to perceive outside of our overly rationalistic visual habits. Just as poets and novelists do their thinking through imagery and metaphor, so do architects, sculptors, painters, photographers, film directors, and video artists think spatially as they work out creative problems by means of spatial formulations.

We confront spatial forms not only literally, as physical presences, but figuratively as well. When we read a novel, for example, we envision in a sort of nonphysical space the places and characters evoked by the novelist's language. Because so many writers emphasize narration and storytelling, we may overlook the fact that fiction also depends on nonlinear but linked visual elements that contribute significantly to the texture and meaning. Our subjective experience of reading is intensified as we translate the author's words into mental pictures of characters and scenes — visual details and features we will probably recall long after we've forgotten the story's bare chain of events.

The internalized space that we mentally construct when we read is not a real, physical space but rather is akin to the virtual space popularly known as "cyberspace," a term coined by a science fiction writer, William Gibson, in a 1981 short story. Gibson later expanded the concept in his award-winning novel *Neuromancer* (1984). Unlike the literal space that surrounds and situates us in the three-dimensional world, cyberspace is the abstract realm of electronic data and interactivity, where both vast distances and social boundaries can be instantly annihilated. Cyberspace is a rapidly expanding universe created by the convergence of computers, videos, and telecommunications networking technologies. Entered through our computer screens, cyberspace is the latest conceptualization of space, and its fusion of interdependent media continually and permanently reformats our modes of perception and communication as well as our ideas about what constitutes public space. As the final section of this chapter (Cyberspace) makes clear, a controversial issue today is whether cyberspace is (or soon will be) just as real as any concrete, physical space.

HOME

■ **Cluster menu: Home**

In *The Poetics of Space* (1958), the French philosopher Gaston Bachelard discusses how vividly our childhood memories are shaped by the houses we lived in. "All our lives we come back to them in daydreams," he claims. The images and essay in this section capture just how powerful the places we live can be — and how much emotion we invest in them.

In "Life in Motion" (2000), Nicole Lamy devises an interesting and imaginative autobiographical plan: she decides to revisit and photograph all the houses she lived in during her childhood. As she assembles this objective visual narrative, she subjectively reconstructs the scattered memories of a highly mobile childhood — she lived in twelve houses before she turned thirteen. "I wanted to gather the photos as charms against fallible memory," she writes, hoping that after binding them in an album she and her mother "could read our lives like straightforward narratives." The photographs by Bill Bamberger that follow, documenting the experiences of first-time, low-income home owners in the South, are narratives of a new sense of permanence rather than impermanence — but all focus on the four walls, roof, and front door of places people call home.

Nicole Lamy, *Life in Motion.* Nicole Lamy (b. 1967) has worked as managing editor of the *Boston Book Review* and of *Transition Magazine*, freelances as a book reviewer, and is currently living in Cambridge, Massachusetts, and working on a novel. When Lamy's essay was published in *The American Scholar* (Autumn 2000), it appeared with no photographs. She generously supplied us with the photos for this book.

Nicole Lamy
LIFE IN MOTION

■ **Consider before you read.** *Why does Lamy create this photographic project? What are her aims? Does she succeed? Why or why not?*

■ *Consider. Lamy's essay is divided into twelve numbered sections, corresponding to the twelve photographs. When the essay originally appeared, it contained no photos. In what ways do the pictures add to the essay? Do they depend on the essay as much as the essay depends on them? Explain.*

291

I

Three years ago I took pictures of all the houses I've lived in. The houses impress not in beauty but in number — twelve houses before I turned thirteen. For me the moves had always resisted coherent explanation — no military reassignments or evasion of the law. I wanted to gather the photos as charms against fallible memory, like the list of lost things I used to keep: a plastic purse filled with silver dollars, a mole-colored beret, strip of negatives from my brother's first day of kindergarten. I planned to bind the photos in an album and give them to my mother. Maybe then, I thought, we could read our lives like straightforward narratives. Wise readers know that all stories follow one of two paths: The Stranger Comes to Town or The Journey. My life in motion suggested both.

2

When idea turned to plan, I asked my father for a list of the addresses I couldn't remember. Instead, as I had hoped, he offered to drive me through Maine, New Hampshire, and Massachusetts himself. My father, too, took photographs, and I wanted to draw him into my life a little, remind him of the times during car trips when, as dusk deepened, he would switch on the light inside the car, without prompting, so that I could continue to read.

3

I photographed the houses and the apartments and the surprising number of duplexes (so often did we live in the left half of a house that I wonder if I've developed a right-hemisphere problem — I imagine the right side of my brain paler and more shriveled than its better half, as atrophied and bleached as an arm that has been in a cast all summer), though I never asked to be let inside. I remembered the flow of rooms in most houses and I could imagine walking through them in a sort of Ciceronian[1] memory system for childhood.

4

The photographs pretend no artistic merit. I centered most of the houses in my viewfinder as I stood on opposite sidewalks. Occasionally a branch or a piece of the neighboring house appears at the edge of the frame. Otherwise the book is a collection of residential mug shots. I wasn't accustomed to snapping pictures of whole buildings without people cluttering the frames, and as I focused before each shot I thought of the pictures my father had taken during his early twenties: ducks and snowdrifts and weathered cottages. Looking through my father's pictures, my mother would squint with mock earnestness at yet another image of a dilapidated barn and ask, "Where were we, behind the barn?"

5

At the first house — 125 Wood Street, a gray three-family at the edge of the campus where my father had been a sophomore — I toyed with perspective. I held my camera at my hip; I crouched by the mailboxes, trying to imagine a toddler's vantage point. No preschool impressions came flooding back; I gained nothing but stares from the neighbors. I thought of the family lore about the short time we lived on Wood Street. By 1972, the sixties still hadn't retreated from Lewiston, Maine. The perennial students who shared our building kept the house reeking pleasantly of weed, and our downstairs neighbor wandered up to our apartment now and again to shower, since her bathtub was occupied by her pet duck. Her thesis, my mother insisted, had something to do with roller skates, and she decorated her apartment with black lights and mini-marshmallows, dipped in fluorescent paint, which she stuck to branches that hung from her ceiling. At night, when the lights came on, visitors were treated to an electrifying set of unlikely constellations.

6

From Maine we moved south to New Hampshire. Rooting out the apartments in the freshly overdeveloped landscape of New Hampshire was a trickier prospect; some of the photos of these houses show unfamiliar additions, self-installed skylights. Some had new, paved-over driveways, others aluminum

---

[1] We have all experienced the powerful force that place exerts on our memory. Revisit an old apartment, house, neighborhood, or school, and specific memories will flash by in an instant, as one association leads to another. This mental phenomenon is so pervasive that in ancient Rome orators were trained to use spatial locations as an aid to memory. Cicero and others recommended that speakers construct in their imagination a spacious house or building and attach associations to particular locations within it so that as they mentally proceed through them in sequence, they will visually remind themselves of the separate points they plan to make. — ED.

siding. One apartment complex in southern New Hampshire remained intact, though the surrounding woods had been leveled to receive three new strip malls. When we wandered closer to the Massachusetts border, images reversed themselves and I found myself remembering the houses' odd absences: an oval of yellow grass showed where an above-ground pool had sat; a chimney stopped abruptly with no fireplace attached.

During each move, after the boxes had been unpacked, my father would turn their openings to the ground and use a pocketknife to cut windows and doors. The refrigerator boxes were best, skyscrapers with grass floors. In my cardboard house I would read cross-legged into the evening, ignoring my parents' invitations to take-out dinners in our new yard until my father lifted the box off me and walked away, bearing my cardboard home, leaving me blinking in the dusk.

7

Now when I leave my apartment for vacation, no matter how anticipated the trip, I experience numbing panic — will I ever see home again? I'm sympathetic to Rilke's Eurydice: What did she care about Orpheus and his willpower? Sure, she had her reasons: hell living had filled her with death and isolated her from human touch. No doubt she could have grown accustomed to the rocks and rivers of Hades. Who among us can get our mind around a move that drastic? From one side of the eternal duplex to the other. Each time I return home from vacation, rooms don't appear the same as I left them. Walls seem to meet floors at subtly altered angles. Careful inspection — heel-toe, heel-toe around each of the rooms — reveals no evidence of the perceived.

293

8

After my parents split, I kept most of my assorted five-year-old's treasures at the white three-family where I lived with my mother, watched over by a grim, disapproving landlady. My father's wall-to-wall-carpeted bachelor apartment always smelled faintly of hops; he and his two roommates all owned water beds and motorcycles. My personal inventory at my father's new home was limited to a Holly Hobbie nightgown, *The Little Princess*, and Milton Bradley's Sorry!, a game that requires players to apologize without sincerity after forcing their competitors to start again.

9

I found the postdivorce houses on my own. At one address, the brown-stained house I had known in early grade school wasn't there at all. Developers had knocked it down, then paved over the spot to provide parking for the neighboring convenience store and candy shop. On the winter afternoon when I visited, I snapped a photo of a stray shopping cart that had rolled away from the convenience store to the spot where the kitchen had been. The shot, of the lonely shopping cart illuminated by a hazy beam of light, has a Hallmark devotional-card quality. I have no sentimental feelings about the house, though. I even felt satisfaction when I saw the smoothly paved parking lot; it was as though I had willed the destruction

Nicole Lamy, *Life in Motion.* Lamy preserves her orginal photographs with old-fashioned photo corners in a handmade accordion book that, when flipped down, shows the houses in progression from first to last. She highlighted different details of the houses — details that stood out in her memory — with colored pencil. (Reprinted by permission of Nicole Lamy)

■ **Consider.** *Why do you think Lamy colored only parts of the photographs? What effect does it have?*

COMMENT

"This was really just a present like all kids make for their parents, just another version of a clay ashtray or a woven pot holder. It isn't meant to be art."

— Nicole Lamy

of the site of many childhood disappointments (new stepfather! mid-first-grade school switch! dog runs away from home!).

The edges of the photograph give more away. At the top of the frame I can spot a sliver of the foundation of the house that backed up to ours. My friend Annette lived there, an only child whose mother cut women's hair in the pink room adjacent to their dining room and whose father cured meat, hung in strips — dark and pale, meat and fat — in their cellar.

At the left edge of the frame, the tail of an *a* is visible, part of a glowing sign advertising "Gina — Psychic," the fortune-teller who set up shop next door.

10

In a decorative gesture, I planned to hand-color the photographs as if they were pre-Kodachrome portraits of children with blossom-pink cheeks and lips. Armed with the oils and pencils, however, I only touched up a piece of every home — a chimney, a storm door, a front gate. If stacked, they'd make a flip-book composite of a home.

Red shutters and verdant bushes decorate the house after the last fold in the book. There, the three of us — mother, sister, and new brother, aged three — began living alone together for the first time. The stepfather had come and gone, leaving the three of us to find balance in our uneasy triumvirate. Neighbors and shopkeepers looked at us, curious. I could tell that the age gaps perplexed them — too few years between a mother and daughter who chatted like girlfriends and too many between a sister and brother who looked almost like mother and son. Their confusion was compounded by my mother's youth and beauty and by the way at age thirteen I seemed to have passed directly to thirty-five.

The red-shuttered house was home the longest, and it is the only house my brother remembers. When I handed the coloring pencils over to him to spruce up the image of the old house, he colored the whole thing. He and my mother still live in that duplex, formerly the parish house for the Congregational church across the street. We haven't been the only ones comfortable there. Pets and pests flourish: a dog, rabbits, guinea pigs, escaped reptiles, moths and silverfish, hollow shells of worms in macaroni boxes, squirrels in the attic.

The parish house has walls that slant toward the middle and floor-boards that creak too frequently and too loudly to be creepy. During the first year, while discovering the rules and limits of our new family, we cleared the dining-room table each night after dinner and began to play.

The three of us played games from my mother's childhood — tiddledywinks, pick-up-sticks, PIT. And after my brother fell asleep, my mother and I drank tea and played Password, Boggle, and Scrabble, stopping only when the board was almost filled and our wooden racks held two or three impossible consonants. A few years ago, chasing a marble that had slipped through a wrought iron heating grate, my brother lifted the panel by one of its iron curls and found, caught in the black cloth, game pieces of all kinds: dice, tiddledywinks, cribbage pegs, smooth wooden squares with black letters — pieces we had barely missed from games we had continued to play.

11

When the photo project was complete, I felt a historian's satisfaction. I had gathered the proof of my life and given it a shape. To create the album I cut a long strip of black paper and folded and flipped it as if to cut paper dolls. I printed the images small and pasted them in the accordion book. Held from the top, the book tumbles open to reveal twelve homes logically connected.

My mother saw the book as evidence of a life hastily lived. When she unknotted the ribbon around the tidy package and allowed it to unfold, I watched her face seize up.

"Ha, ha," she pushed the sounds out with effort. "All my failures," she said as she held the book away from her in an exaggerated gesture. I had tried to piece a story out of a life that I saw as largely unplanned. For my mother, this life led by reaction had eventually settled into a kind of choice. I was ashamed I thought it was mine to figure out.

12

One night, a few weeks before I moved out of the parish-house duplex into my own apartment, I returned home and wheeled my bike around to the back of the house. Glancing up at the brightly lit windows, I was afforded an unusual glimpse of the daily theater of my family. From my spot in the yard I saw a woman in the kitchen chopping vegetables and talking on the phone, while a couple of rooms over, a gangly teenage boy sat in a chair by the television. Startled to be given a chance to see the house as a stranger might, I watched for a few moments and tried to imagine the lives of those inside.

■ **Consider.** *The photo album Lamy at last assembles turns out to have different meanings for mother and daughter. What are those two different meanings? Is one more "real" than the other?*

297

■ **Discuss.** *Discuss Lamy's tone in "Life in Motion." How does it change in different sections? How does it reveal her attitude toward the different houses she remembers?*

■ **Write.** *What would the homes of your childhood reveal about your life? Could you "imagine walking through them" the way Lamy can? Write a tour through one of your childhood homes, including as much detail as possible.*

Bill Bamberger, *Nancy (left) and Alejandra Camarillo, Plaza Florencia, San Antonio, Texas,* **2002.** For more than a decade, homes have provided the focus for the camera lens of Bill Bamberger, an award-winning photographer who has been documenting the experiences of first-time, low-income home owners in the South. Bamberger's photographs were featured at the National Building Museum in the winter of 2003–2004 in an exhibit entitled "Stories of Home." As the exhibit notes say, "Bamberger's hauntingly beautiful images remind us of the human side of architecture, illustrating how buildings — and homeownership — impact individuals, families, and communities." The sisters pictured here are first-generation Americans whose parents emigrated from Mexico. Here they stand on the front porch of their family home in a subdivision built by Habitat for Humanity of San Antonio. (© Bill Bamberger) ▶

Bill Bamberger
PHOTOS OF HOME

■ **Consider before you read/view.** *How does Bamberger's framing of the image guide the viewer's understanding? Sometimes he focuses on the home, taking a long view, and sometimes he looks close-up at the inhabitants. Why do you think he chooses to use different strategies for different subjects?*

298

COMMENT

"In these photographs, facial expressions speak volumes — and the range of emotions is vast. There is angst from heavy responsibility as well as a sense of tremendous satisfaction, pride, and accomplishment. There is apprehension of the unknown as well as enormous relief. There is self-esteem, self-worth, and validation, and there is the deep sadness that comes from saying goodbye and leaving familiar and comfortable surroundings. There is a sense of privacy, independence, security, and control over one's life. There is stability and continuity and family. There is longing and hope, and there is great joy."

— From the exhibition script for *Stories of Home*, National Building Museum

Bill Bamberger, *Christopher McDonald at home in Orchard Village, Chattanooga, Tennessee,* 1994. Orchard Village is a community of fifty-eight newly constructed homes occupied primarily by first-time home owners. (© Bill Bamberger)

◀ ■ **Discuss.** *What is the significance of Bamberger's choosing first-time home owners? How might these images be different if he had chosen people who had owned homes before?*

■ **Write.** *Reread the comment on facial expressions in Bamberger's photographs and then write your own analysis. Choose one of the photographs to focus on and consider the emotions you can read on the subject's face. What appears to be the emotional relationship between this person and his or her dwelling place?*

 CONSIDER THE CLUSTER
Home

■ **Message**

Bill Bamberger writes, "The meanings of 'home' and homeownership are interwoven with our dreams for the future and of the past." Nicole Lamy spends her essay trying to capture a sense of a childhood home when she lived in twelve different houses in twelve years. What does "home" mean to you? Is it a specific place? Does it represent the past — or the future? Is it people, an address, experiences, or something else?

■ **Method**

Lamy claims that the "photographs pretend no artistic merit." Why do you think she says this? How does she go about establishing this claim? Do you think Lamy would also claim that her essay pretends "no artistic merit"? What elements of deliberate artistry can you find in her essay? For example, are there extended threads of imagery? How does the reference to "lost things" in section I get picked up in other parts of the essay? How does Lamy use literary allusion?

■ **Medium**

The essay by Nicole Lamy and the photographs by Bill Bamberger are each "illustrated" in this text — the first by Lamy's accordion flip book, the second by quotations from photographer and subjects. How important do you think the pictures are to Lamy's essay? How important is the information about Bamberger's subjects to his photographs? Find a picture of the place *you* think of as home. Then write a description of it that conveys what it represents to you. Which medium — words or images — do you think better explores what "home" means?

THE BASKETBALL COURT

PERSONAL ESSAY | 6 PHOTOS | MAGAZINE COVER

As the words and images in this section demonstrate, a basketball court can be almost anywhere there are people with a passion for the game and a ball. When we talk about a sport — basketball, in this case — we're talking about a game that occurs in a circumscribed physical space; but sports space is serious for millions of people. It represents big business, big entertainment, and dreams, triumphs, disappointments, and egos that extend far beyond the lines drawn on a regulation court. For all the players represented here, whether pickup or professional, basketball occurs in a space bigger than a court.

Throughout his work, the renowned African American novelist John Edgar Wideman displays a remarkable sensitivity to place, always hoping to capture the exact physical surroundings that shape our lives. In "First Shot" (2001), he looks back on the day he first held a basketball and launched it toward a makeshift hoop that seemed "a mile high." Wideman, who later would become a major college player, doesn't remember at all whether the ball went in or not. But he will never forget the actual place where he took that first shot — and in his essay he takes us to the precise spot. Photographers Dana Lixenberg, Brad Richman, and Paul D'Amato all offer portraits of players in action — portraits that capture the place as well as the player.

John Edgar Wideman, *First Shot*. John Edgar Wideman (b. 1941) grew up in the 1940s and 1950s in Homewood, a black section of Pittsburgh, and he has written extensively of his childhood neighborhood in essays and fiction. He returned to it in *Hoop Roots* (2001), an autobiography that celebrates his love of basketball and the many ways the sport has permeated his memory and imagination. After the first shot described here, there were many more; Wideman graduated in 1963 from the University of Pennsylvania, where he received the university's creative writing award and starred on its basketball team, eventually becoming a member of the Philadelphia Big Five Basketball Hall of Fame. A Rhodes Scholar at Oxford in the mid-1960s and the recipient of a MacArthur fellowship and PEN/Faulkner award, Wideman has written many award-winning novels and collections of stories, including *A Glance Away* (1967), *Hurry Home* (1970), *The Lynchers* (1973), *Sent for You Yesterday* (1983), *Reuben* (1987), *Philadelphia Fire* (1990), *The Cattle Killing* (1996), *Two Cities* (1998), and *God's Gym* (2005). He is professor of Africana studies and English at Brown University. The following essay, which appears in *Hoop Roots* in a longer form, appeared in *The Boston Globe Magazine* (January 3, 1999).

John Edgar Wideman
FIRST SHOT

■ **Consider before you read.** *How might readers understand Wideman's title metaphorically? The essay dramatizes his first attempt to make a basketball shot, but what else is the young boy taking a "first shot" at?*

My grandmother's house, 7415, and everybody else's house on Finance faced the hillside crowned by railroad tracks. On my knees, just tall enough to see out, I'd press my chest against the back of the sofa under Grandma Freeda's front-room window and daydream away hours waiting for the next train's rumble to fill the house.

No matter how far forward you leaned over the couch's back, you couldn't see the place farther up, on the opposite side of Finance, the place I could lead you to today and show you where it all began, where I touched a basketball first time and launched my first shot. Since it couldn't be seen from the front window of my grandmother's house, that spot containing the only building on the track side of Finance was out of bounds. In those days, playing outdoors meant never going beyond the range of vision of the adult in charge, who shouldn't even need to step out of the house to keep an eye on you.

303

On a good day my mom, my grandmother, or one of my aunts might take me by the hand across Finance and let me roam the empty hillside. *Don't you try and cross the street till I come back over and get you. And don't you dare march yourself up close to those tracks.* Whoever escorted me repeated these commandments and a few others, usually ending with the rule *Better stay where I can see you or I'll snatch your narrow behind home, boy.*

Gradually I learned I could slip outside the frame of 7415's front window, just so I didn't stay away too long. The afternoon I fired my first shot at a hoop, I was testing, as I did daily in a hundred secret games, how much I could get away with.

From my perspective, a 6- or 7-year-old black boy on stolen time who seldom had much to do with white people, the guys up the street in a pool of sunshine launching shots at a crooked, netless hoop nailed to a wall seemed huge and old, but it's likely they were in their 20s and 30s, some probably teenagers. A few had stripped off their shirts; I remember pale flesh, hairy chests and armpits, lean rib cages, bony shoulders, long, lanky arms. They blend into the faces and bodies of guys I played with on mostly white teams in high school and college. For some reason one wears in my memory a full beard like the fair-haired Jesus on a calendar in Homewood AME Zion church. They didn't talk much as they took turns shooting, rebounding. Probably on a lunch break. Some lounged in the shade smoking, ignoring the hoops.

I don't remember anyone speaking to me when I stopped at the curb. And that was fine because it saved me having to figure out what to say back. Since I'd been taught at home to be polite to all grown-ups, especially polite, careful, and as close to silent as I could manage without

■ Consider. *"First Shot" is as much about a young boy testing the limits of his restrictions as it is about holding a basketball for the first time. What significance do you think the window at 7415 has for Wideman? What does it mean to him as a child? What has it come to represent from his adult perspective?*

304

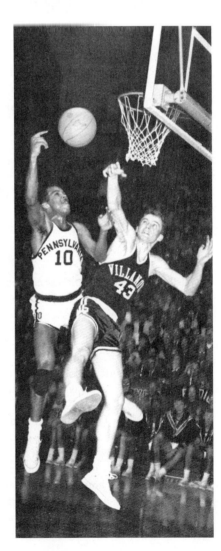

Wideman (in the number ten jersey) knows basketball. He was an All Ivy League player and team captain at the University of Pennsylvania in the early 1960s. (University of Pennsylvania Archives)

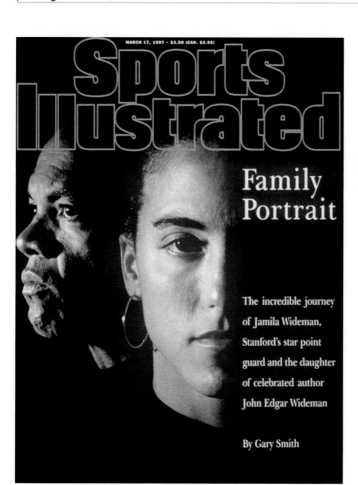

MARCH 17, 1997 • $3.50 (CAN. $3.95)

Sports Illustrated

Family Portrait

The incredible journey
of Jamila Wideman,
Stanford's star point
guard and the daughter
of celebrated author
John Edgar Wideman

By Gary Smith

Wideman's daughter Jamila (b. 1975) is also a gifted player. A left-handed point guard, Jamila excelled on the state-champion varsity team of Amherst High School (in Massachusetts); went on to Stanford University, where she was a four-year starter and team captain; and later played WNBA basketball. Jamila, who holds a law degree from New York University, has also established youth programs for basketball and literacy. Like her father, she wears jersey number ten. (Sports Illustrated/Time Inc.)

being impolite if the grown-up strangers happened to be white men, I was unsure if any appropriate form of address existed. Being unnoticed or ignored allowed me to observe them silently. I felt comfortably invisible, a ghost who risked sliding into view once or twice only long enough to keep the ball out of the street and guide it back into the ring of shooters.

I must have been standing there watching longer than I realized because finally one of them said something like, *That kid still there. C'mon, kid. Take a shot,* and either handed or passed me the ball. *Go on, try one, kid.*

I could say the ball felt enormous in my hands because it probably did. I could say I became suddenly shy, timid, and they had to coax me from the margin where I'd been silently watching. Say that once I stepped onto the smooth driveway in front of the hoop with the ball in my hands and the basket a mile high poking out from a board fastened to a beam in the brick wall, I could say how great it felt then to grip the ball for the first time, pat it so it rose off the asphalt back to my hands, then the thrill of lifting the ball, sighting over it at the hoop, organizing all my small weight under it to do what I'd watched the bigger, stronger white bodies do. No doubt all the above is true. I could also say the men laughed at the air ball I threw up or encouraged me and gave me more shots or that I heaved the ball high and straight and true so it banked off the board through the rim, *Two,* and everybody whooped and clapped. Could say any damned thing because I don't recall what happened, only that it happened, my first shot in that precise place, under the circumstances I'm relating, me AWOL from the 7415's front window, suddenly scared I'd lost track of time, shooting then hauling ass back down the track side of Finance because I'd probably been out of sight way too long. And the story grows, fact, fiction, and something in between, grows till I become who I am today, the story truer and less true as I invent it, as it invents me, but one thing's sure, the spot below the railroad tracks is still there and I've never forgotten my first shot.

■ Consider. *Why do you think Wideman raises the issue of truth and fiction in this final paragraph? Suppose he had recounted this incident in a short story instead of a memoir. Do you think he would have changed any details about his "first shot"? How do you think memoir is different from fiction based on personal experience? How much of this essay is composed of things Wideman admits he didn't see or can't exactly remember?*

■ **Discuss.** *Among the concerns of Wideman's essay are the binary distinctions of male/female and black/white. How do these oppositions shape the consciousness of the narrator as a young boy? How does he understand them as an adult?*

■ **Write.** *In a short essay, discuss Wideman's relationship to rules in this essay. How did he understand them when he was living on Finance Street? To what degree did he bend or break them?*

Dana Lixenberg, Brad Richman, and Paul D'Amato
BASKETBALL PHOTOS

■ **Consider before you view.** *You likely encounter basketball photographs most frequently in the sports pages of the newspaper. How do these photographs differ from journalistic photographs of basketball games? Are there any important similarities?*

Dana Lixenberg, *Tamika Catchings.* This photograph illustrated a profile of Catchings (b. 1979) that ran in the May 25, 2003, issue of *The New York Times Magazine,* portraying her as "the brightest hope" for the WNBA. It was taken by the celebrated Dutch photographer Dana Lixenberg, who has photographed homeless people, celebrities, and athletes with the same direct lens. Her work has been featured in most major magazines as well as in a collection of her portraits in *United States* (2001). Tamika Catchings is a star player for the Indiana Fever and was a member of the gold-medal-winning U.S. Women's Basketball Team at the 2004 Summer Olympic Games. In only four seasons, she became the fastest WNBA player to score 2,000 career points. Catchings is a five-time All-Star player and is president of the WNBA Player Association. (© Dana Lixenberg)

▶

307

COMMENT

"Catchings is the now and the future of the game. I've played and coached against the best players in the world, and no one has played like she does. In the best possible way, she plays like a guy."

— Nancy Lieberman, Olympic, collegiate, and professional basketball player; professional manager and coach; broadcaster; and the first woman to ever play in a men's professional league (USBL)

Brad Richman, *Silver Spring, Maryland, August 1993*. Brad Richman (b. 1971) spent nine years traveling across the country taking pictures of basketball courts, games, and players. A collection of these photographs, *America's Game*, from which these three photos are taken, has been exhibited at the Basketball Hall of Fame and has also appeared in *DoubleTake, Vibe, Fortune*, and *The Washington Post Magazine*. Richman, who grew up playing basketball and was known by friends on the court as the "White Shadow," gave up his dreams of the NBA, ending his basketball career in high school. At that time, he picked up a camera and began to take pictures. Richman recounts this shift: "I realized that 'shooting' basketball would be a wonderful way to unite two of my greatest passions. In 1992, I began to document the players and games at basketball courts in and around my hometown of Takoma Park, Maryland, a suburb of Washington, D.C." (© Brad Richman)

310

Brad Richman, *Portland, Maine, October 8, 2000*. Richman explains: "My travels have taken me to nearly forty states, and along the way I have visited and photographed at most of this country's legendary blacktops. But I have also discovered that the roots of the game generally take place in humbler settings — a backboard hanging over a garage door, a hoop nailed to the side of a barn, a milk-crate basket on an alley wall."

311

Brad Richman, *Washington, D.C., July 10, 1999.* "Basketball is a simple game —
all one needs is a ball and a hoop to play," writes Richman. "Yet I have discovered that this simple game can speak volumes about the American experience.
From inner-city New York to the fields of Indiana, through the Rocky Mountains
to the suburbs of Los Angeles, basketball offers the promise of the American
Dream. Unfortunately, the reality is one in a million make it to the professional
ranks. . . . Yet there is hope despite all those shattered dreams. Basketball teaches
the lessons of life — victory and defeat, joy and sorrow, teamwork and friendship —
and provides its own rewards, all in the spirit of a game."

Paul D'Amato, *Jump Shot,* **Chicago, 1993.** Paul D'Amato (b. 1956) has taught
at the Maine College of Art and Columbia College, Chicago, and is a contributor to *DoubleTake* magazine and *The New York Times Magazine,* among
other publications. This photograph is part of a larger collection called "Crazy
Rhythm: The Mexican Community on the South Side of Chicago." D'Amato
writes of these photographs that he "wanted to make pictures that were emotionally vivid and irrefutably real — that expressed the human drama of urban
living." (© Paul D'Amato)

■ **Discuss.** *Why does the New York Times photographer portray Tamika Catchings in
street clothes rather than in her uniform or gym clothes? As the only woman in this group
of photographs, how is her image different? Are there other factors that might account for
this difference?*

■ **Write.** *Think about what is included in each of these photographs besides the players
and the ball. Contrast the clutter of "Jump Shot/Tiro con salto" with the spareness of "Silver
Spring, Maryland." Write about how these settings contribute to different views of the game
of basketball.*

CONSIDER THE CLUSTER
The Basketball Court

■ Message

John Edgar Wideman can't remember what his first shot was like, but he can take us directly to the exact spot where it happened. Why do you think this is important to Wideman? What point is he making about memory and place? Why do you think he spends time describing the geography of his neighborhood? What do those details have to do with basketball?

■ Method

Look closely at the photographs by Paul D'Amato, Brad Richman, and Dana Lixenberg. Each is focusing on basketball — but each photograph frames the subject, and the court, differently. Use the concept of *framing* to identify the focus of each photograph. Does basketball represent something different in each, or is the court essentially the same?

■ Medium

Marketing campaigns surround professional athletics. The NBA, in particular, is renowned for marketing its talented players as superstar personalities. Using any ad featuring a star athlete, write an essay that considers how the medium of advertising uses individual talent to promote a specific product. What is being marketed — the person or the product? Or something else?

313

SACRED SPACES

314

A sacred place is a site that has a spiritual significance for a nation, a people, a community, or even an individual. Sacred places often inspire awe, mystery, and a reverential connection with a charismatic figure or with a key moment of history. Some sacred places are well known in major religions, such as the holy cities Mecca to Muslims and Bethlehem to Christians. Some public sites become sacred to a community because they were the scene of an enormous catastrophe, such as the site of the destroyed World Trade Center or the battlefield at Gettysburg, which Lincoln regarded as hallowed ground; or the scene of a great moral achievement, such as the site of Martin Luther King Jr.'s 1965 civil rights demonstration in Selma, Alabama.

One person's sacred space may be far different from another's — for example, one person may feel a sense of awe in visiting Elvis Presley's Graceland mansion in Memphis, Tennessee, while another may experience a similar emotion in visiting Emily Dickinson's house in Amherst, Massachusetts. But sacred places need not be public sites, as the materials gathered here show. They can be places we privately consider sacred — where we go for solace, serenity, transcendence, or perhaps sheer isolation from the world.

N. Scott Momaday, *The Way to Rainy Mountain*. N. Scott Momaday (b. 1934) brings together both the public and private dimensions of a sacred space: Rainy Mountain is a significant ancestral landmark for his people, the Kiowas, as well as the site near which his beloved grandmother is buried. On a visit to Rainy Mountain, which stands in the Oklahoma plains, Momaday reflects on the meaning of a place made sacred by both the habitation of his vanishing people and the enduring legacy of his deceased ancestors. Momaday was born in 1934 in Lawton, Oklahoma, and grew up on an Indian reservation. He has published widely in several media: poetry, prose, memoir, and history. Originally published in *The Reporter* in 1967, "The Way to Rainy Mountain" introduces Momaday's book of the same title, in which he explores the history and mythology of the Kiowa people.

"I am lucky," said N. Scott Momaday in a 2001 interview, "because I have a sense of my Indian heritage. That's very firmly fixed in my imagination and in my mind. I am more fortunate than most other people. When I published *The Way to Rainy Mountain*, someone said to me, 'You know, you're very lucky to know who you are, with respect to your grandparents, your great-grandparents, five generations back. . . . I don't know that about myself, or my people.' That came as a surprise to me . . . [to discover that so] few people know about their ancestry, even back a generation." When students tell Momaday that they don't know about their heritage, he says to them, "Well look, you've got an oral tradition. You've got a family oral tradition. . . . Tell me about your grandparents."

315

N. Scott Momaday
THE WAY TO RAINY MOUNTAIN

■ **Consider before you read.** *The English writer Aldous Huxley argued that essays were made up of a mixture of personal, factual, and universal material. Most essayists, he thought, tended toward one of the three categories or perhaps, if they were really good, two of them. How would you describe Momaday's essay in Huxley's terms?*

A single knoll rises out of the plain in Oklahoma, north and west of the Wichita Range. For my people, the Kiowas, it is an old landmark, and they gave it the name Rainy Mountain. The hardest weather in the world is there. Winter brings blizzards, hot tornadic winds arise in the spring, and in summer the prairie is an anvil's edge. The grass turns brittle and brown, and it cracks beneath your feet. There are green belts along the rivers and creeks, linear groves of hickory and pecan, willow and witch hazel. At a distance in July or August the steaming foliage seems almost to writhe in fire. Great green and yellow grasshoppers are everywhere in the tall grass, popping up like corn to sting the flesh, and tortoises crawl about on the red earth, going nowhere in the plenty of time. Loneliness is an aspect of the land. All things in the plain are isolate; there is no confusion of objects in the eye, but *one* hill or *one* tree or *one* man. To look upon that landscape in the early morning, with the sun at your back, is to lose the sense of proportion. Your imagination comes to life, and this, you think, is where Creation was begun.

I returned to Rainy Mountain in July. My grandmother had died in the spring, and I wanted to be at her grave. She had lived to be very old and at last infirm. Her only living daughter was with her when she died, and I was told that in death her face was that of a child.

I like to think of her as a child. When she was born, the Kiowas were living the last great moment of their history. For more than a hundred years they had controlled the open range from the Smoky Hill River to the Red, from the headwaters of the Canadian to the fork of the Arkansas and Cimarron. In alliance with the Comanches, they had ruled the whole of the southern Plains. War was their sacred business, and they were among the finest horsemen the world has ever known. But warfare for the Kiowas was preeminently a matter of disposition rather than of survival, and they never understood the grim, unrelenting advance of the U.S. Cavalry. When at last, divided and ill-provisioned, they were driven onto the Staked Plains in the cold rains of autumn, they fell into panic. In Palo Duro Canyon they abandoned their crucial stores to pillage and had nothing then but their lives. In order to save themselves, they surrendered to the soldiers at Fort Sill and were imprisoned in the old stone corral that now stands as a military museum. My grandmother was spared the humiliation of those high gray walls by eight or ten years, but she must have known from birth the affliction of defeat, the dark brooding of old warriors.

Her name was Aho, and she belonged to the last culture to evolve in North America. Her forebears came down from the high country in western Montana nearly three centuries ago. They were a mountain people, a mysterious tribe of hunters whose language has never been positively classified in any major group. In the late seventeenth century they began a long migration to the south and east. It was a journey toward the dawn, and it led to a golden age. Along the way the Kiowas were befriended by the Crows, who gave them the culture and religion of the Plains. They acquired horses, and their ancient nomadic spirit was suddenly free of the ground. They acquired Tai-me, the sacred Sun Dance doll, from that moment the object and symbol of their worship, and so shared in the divinity of the sun. Not least, they acquired the sense of destiny, therefore courage and pride. When they entered upon the southern Plains they had been transformed. No longer were they slaves to the simple necessity of survival; they were a lordly and dangerous society of fighters and thieves, hunters and priests of the sun. According to their origin myth, they entered the world through a hollow log. From one point of view, their migration was the fruit of an old prophecy, for indeed they emerged from a sunless world.

Although my grandmother lived out her long life in the shadow of Rainy Mountain, the immense landscape of the continental interior lay like memory in her

Joan Frederick, *Rainy Mountain, Kiowa Holy Place, Oklahoma.*
(© Joan Frederick)

blood. She could tell of the Crows, whom she had never seen, and of the Black Hills, where she had never been. I wanted to see in reality what she had seen more perfectly in the mind's eye, and traveled fifteen hundred miles to begin my pilgrimage.

Yellowstone, it seemed to me, was the top of the world, a region of deep lakes and dark timber, canyons and waterfalls. But, beautiful as it is, one might have the sense of confinement there. The skyline in all directions is close at hand, the high wall of the woods and deep cleavages of shade. There is a perfect freedom in the mountains, but it belongs to the eagle and the elk, the badger and the bear. The Kiowas reckoned their stature by the distance they could see, and they were bent and blind in the wilderness.

Descending eastward, the highland meadows are a stairway to the plain. In July the inland slope of the Rockies is luxuriant with flax and buckwheat, stonecrop and larkspur. The earth unfolds and the limit of the land recedes. Clusters of trees, and animals grazing far in the distance, cause the vision to reach away and wonder to build upon the mind. The sun follows a longer course in the day, and the sky is immense beyond all comparison. The great billowing clouds that sail upon it are shadows that move upon the grain like water, dividing light. Farther down, in the land of the Crows and Blackfeet, the plain is yellow. Sweet clover takes hold of the hills and bends upon itself to cover and seal the soil. There the Kiowas paused on their way; they had come to the place where they must change their lives. The sun is at home on the plains. Precisely there does it have the certain character of a god. When the Kiowas came to the land of the Crows, they could see the dark lees of the hills at dawn across the Bighorn River, the profusion of light on the grain shelves, the oldest deity ranging after the solstices. Not yet would they veer southward to the caldron of the land that lay below; they must wean their blood from the northern winter and hold the mountains a while longer in their view. They bore Tai-me in procession to the east.

A dark mist lay over the Black Hills, and the land was like iron. At the top of a ridge I caught sight of Devil's Tower upthrust against the gray sky as if in the birth of time the core of the earth had broken through its crust and the motion of the world was begun. There are things in nature that engender an awful quiet in the heart of man; Devil's Tower is one of them. Two centuries ago, because they could not do otherwise, the Kiowas made a legend at the base of the rock. My grandmother said:

> Eight children were there at play, seven sisters and their brother. Suddenly the boy was struck dumb; he trembled and began to run upon his hands and feet. His fingers became claws, and his body was covered with fur. Directly there was a bear where the boy had been. The sisters were terrified; they ran, and the bear after them. They came to the stump of a great tree, and the tree spoke to them. It bade them climb upon it, and as they did so it began to rise into the air. The bear came to kill them, but they were just beyond its reach. It reared against the tree and scored the bark all around with its claws. The seven sisters were borne into the sky, and they became the stars of the Big Dipper.

■ Consider. *How is this story about the Kiowas' "kinsmen in the night sky" representative of Momaday's essay as a whole? What does it reveal about the relationship of nature to mythology?*

From that moment, and so long as the legend lives, the Kiowas have kinsmen in the night sky. Whatever they were in the mountains, they could be no more. However tenuous their well-being, however much they had suffered and would suffer again, they had found a way out of the wilderness.

My grandmother had a reverence for the sun, a holy regard that now is all but gone out of mankind. There was a wariness in her, and an ancient awe. She was a Christian in her later years, but she had come a long way about, and she never forgot her birthright. As a child she had been to the Sun Dances; she had taken part in those annual rites, and by then she had learned the restoration of her people in the presence of Tai-me. She was about seven when the last Kiowa Sun Dance was held in 1887 on the Washita River above Rainy Mountain Creek. The buffalo were gone. In order to consummate the ancient sacrifice — to impale the head of a buffalo bull upon the medicine tree — a delegation of old men journeyed into Texas, there to beg and barter for an animal from the Goodnight herd. She was ten when the Kiowas came together for the last time as a living Sun Dance culture. They could find no buffalo; they had to hang an old hide from the sacred tree. Before the dance could begin, a company of soldiers rode out from Fort Sill under orders to disperse the tribe. Forbidden without cause the essential act of their faith, having seen the wild herds slaughtered and left to rot upon the ground, the Kiowas backed away forever from the medicine tree. That was July 20, 1890, at the great bend of the Washita. My grandmother was there. Without bitterness, and for as long as she lived, she bore a vision of deicide.

Now that I can have her only in memory, I see my grandmother in the several postures that were peculiar to her: standing at the wood stove on a winter morning and turning meat in a great iron skillet; sitting at the south window, bent above her beadwork, and afterwards, when her vision failed, looking down for a long time into the fold of her hands; going out upon a cane, very slowly as she did when the weight of age came upon her; praying. I remember her most often at prayer. She made long, rambling prayers out of suffering and hope, having seen many things. I was never sure that I had the right to hear, so exclusive were they of all mere custom and company. The last time I saw her she prayed standing by the side of her bed at night, naked to the waist, the light of a kerosene lamp moving upon her dark skin. Her long, black hair, always drawn and braided in the day, lay upon her shoulders and against her breasts like a shawl. I do not speak Kiowa, and I never understood her prayers, but there was something inherently sad in the sound, some merest hesitation upon the syllables of sorrow. She began in a high and descending pitch, exhausting her breath to silence; then again and again — and always the same intensity of effort, of something that is, and is not, like urgency in the human voice. Transported so in the dancing light among the shadows of her room, she seemed beyond the reach of time. But that was illusion; I think I knew then that I should not see her again.

Houses are like sentinels in the plain, old keepers of the weather watch. There, in a very little while, wood takes on the appearance of great age. All colors wear soon away in the wind and rain, and then the wood is burned gray and the grain appears and the nails turn red with rust. The windowpanes are black and opaque; you imagine there is nothing within, and indeed there are many ghosts, bones given up to the land. They stand here and there against the sky, and you approach them for a longer time than you expect. They belong in the distance; it is their domain.

Once there was a lot of sound in my grandmother's house, a lot of coming and going, feasting and talk. The summers there were full of excitement and reunion. The Kiowas are a summer people; they abide the cold and keep to themselves, but when the season turns and the land becomes warm and vital they cannot hold still; an old love of going returns upon them. The aged visitors who came to my grandmother's house when I was a child were made of lean and leather, and they bore themselves upright. They wore great black hats and bright ample shirts that shook in the wind. They rubbed fat upon their hair and wound their braids with strips of colored cloth. Some of them painted their faces and carried the scars of old and cherished enmities. They were an old council of warlords, come to remind and be reminded of who they were. Their wives and daughters served them well. The women might indulge themselves; gossip was at once the mark and compensation of their servitude. They made loud and elaborate talk among themselves, full of jest and gesture, fright and false alarm. They went abroad in fringed and flowered shawls, bright beadwork and German silver. They were at home in the kitchen, and they prepared meals that were banquets.

There were frequent prayer meetings, and great nocturnal feasts. When I was a child I played with my cousins outside, where the lamplight fell upon the ground and the singing of the old people rose up around us and carried away into the darkness. There were a lot of good things to eat, a lot of laughter and surprise.

319

And afterwards, when the quiet returned, I lay down with my grandmother and could hear the frogs away by the river and feel the motion of the air.

Now there is a funeral silence in the rooms, the endless wake of some final word. The walls have closed in upon my grandmother's house. When I returned to it in mourning, I saw for the first time in my life how small it was. It was late at night, and there was a white moon, nearly full. I sat for a long time on the stone steps by the kitchen door. From there I could see out across the land; I could see the long row of trees by the creek, the low light upon the rolling plains, and the stars of the Big Dipper. Once I looked at the moon and caught sight of a strange thing. A cricket had perched upon the handrail, only a few inches away from me. My line of vision was such that the creature filled the moon like a fossil. It had gone there, I thought, to live and die, for there, of all places, was its small definition made whole and eternal. A warm wind rose up and purled like the longing within me.

The next morning I awoke at dawn and went out on the dirt road to Rainy Mountain. It was already hot, and the grasshoppers began to fill the air. Still, it was early in the morning, and the birds sang out of the shadows. The long yellow grass on the mountain shone in the bright light, and a scissortail hied above the land. There, where it ought to be, at the end of a long and legendary way, was my grandmother's grave. Here and there on the dark stones were ancestral names. Looking back once, I saw the mountain and came away.

320

■ **Discuss.** *Take another look at the image of the cricket at the end of "The Way to Rainy Mountain." Why is it so striking to Momaday? How does he interpret it?*

■ **Write.** *Momaday describes both Rainy Mountain and his grandmother's house as enduring in a harsh natural world. Write an explication in which you compare the descriptions of these two places. In what ways does Momaday's language link them?*

Stephen Dunn, *The Sacred.* In this poem by Stephen Dunn (b. 1939), "The   ▶
Sacred," a teacher asks the students "if anyone had / a sacred place." After
the usual squirming that such a question triggers, there's an unexpected
answer. Is it possible that a *car* could be a sacred space? Not a religious site,
not a historical monument, not a favorite wilderness spot — but your own
car? Dunn's poem reminds us that once we begin to seriously consider the
full meaning of sacred places, we may discover more than we anticipated.
Stephen Dunn teaches creative writing at the Richard Stockton College of
New Jersey. He has received numerous awards for his poetry, including the
Pulitzer Prize for Poetry for *Different Hours* (2000).

Stephen Dunn
THE SACRED

■ **Consider before you read.** *How would you respond to the question asked in this poem? Why do you think it is a hard one to answer?*

After the teacher asked if anyone had
a sacred place
and the students fidgeted and shrank

in their chairs, the most serious of them all
said it was his car,
being in it alone, his tape deck playing

things he'd chosen, and others knew the truth
had been spoken
and began speaking about their rooms,

their hiding places, but the car kept coming up,
the car in motion,
music filling it, and sometimes one other person

who understood the bright altar of the dashboard
and how far away
a car could take you from the need

to speak, or to answer, the key
in having a key
and putting it in, and going.

321

■ **Discuss.** *In Dunn's poem, the word "sacred" has a broader meaning, but what words does he use that have a religious connotation? Discuss these word choices and how religion is related to Dunn's understanding of the sacred.*

■ **Write.** *What reasons does the poem give for why the car is considered sacred? In a short essay, elaborate on the phrases that suggest the car's significance for these students. Would you add anything to Dunn's explanation?*

322

Jesse DeMartino, *Jason and Mike at the Cabin Near Huntsville, Texas, 1996.*
What makes this spot sacred for these Texan skateboarders? This photograph
by Jesse DeMartino is part of a three-year project of photographing skateboarders. The exhibit, *Keep on Rolling: The Skateboarders of Houston*, was
shown at Rice University. DeMartino's work has been featured in *DoubleTake*,
Aperture, Shots, and *Creative Camera*. This photo was taken outside of the
small East Texas city of Huntsville in Walker County. Huntsville (population
35,000) grew out of a trading post set up in 1836. Today, the local prison
houses the state's execution chamber. (© Jesse DeMartino)

Mitch Epstein, *Cocoa Beach, Florida,* **1983.** Born in Holyoke, Massachusetts, in 1952, Mitch Epstein studied at the Rhode Island School of Design and Cooper Union in New York City. His widely published work appears in a number of international collections, including the Museum of Modern Art. His most recent book is *Work* (2007). Cocoa Beach on Florida's eastern coast, the location of this photograph, was first settled by Native Americans and then by a family of newly freed slaves after the Civil War. A devastating hurricane in 1885 dissuaded future settlers, and the land wasn't developed until an attorney purchased the property in 1920 and established the City of Cocoa Beach in 1925. Thanks to the space program at NASA's Kennedy Space Center and nearby Cape Canaveral, the city's population surged in the 1950s and 1960s. At one time (1924), high-speed car racing was welcomed on the beach, and, until the practice was banned in 1969, you could drive your car onto the beach and park right on the sand. (© 1983 Black River Productions, Ltd./Mitch Epstein. Courtesy of Sikkema Jenkins & Co., New York. Used with Permission. All rights reserved)

■■■■■■ CONSIDER THE CLUSTER
Sacred Spaces

■ Message

How would you summarize the meaning of Stephen Dunn's "The Sacred"? Why, for instance, do you think the setting is a classroom? When someone finally answers that his sacred place is his car, why do others know "the truth / had been spoken"? We often speak of knowing a meaning as "having the key" to something. How does that metaphor become literal in the last lines of the poem? What is the "key" to this poem?

■ Method

How does N. Scott Momaday in "The Way to Rainy Mountain" layer a sense of space with the act of storytelling? How is his writing stimulated by a link between the Kiowa landscape and ancestral legends and stories? What similarities do you see between the Kiowa tales he relates and his own method of composition?

■ Medium

Painters, writers, poets, philosophers, and others have explored the sacred for thousands of years — usually focusing on religious iconography or narratives from the Bible and other holy books. What is your sacred space, whether personal or public? What medium would you choose to show it to others (a photograph, a poem, a CD, or something else) — and why would that medium work best?

PUBLIC SPACE

ESSAY | 2 PHOTOS | BOOK COVER | PERSONAL ESSAY

■ **Cluster menu: Public Space**

If you've ever waited to catch a flight at an airport and spent time closely observing your environment, you were paying attention to "transit space" — those special areas of public space where we pause in our journeys from one place to another. In "Nowhere Man" (1997), the noted essayist and travel writer Pico Iyer defines himself as part of a modern group of "transit loungers" who "pass through countries as through revolving doors, resident aliens of the world, impermanent residents of nowhere." As the number of transit loungers has steadily increased, artists and architects have begun exploring — both critically and creatively — the special features of transit space, studying the ways it is designed and its emotional impact on travelers: Are airports designed, for example, to make travelers feel rested and comfortable, or do they instead engender feelings of stress and alienation?

Although in "Nowhere Man" Pico Iyer focuses on airport space, transit space can also be experienced in train and bus stations, elevators, subways, the lobbies of large hotels and corporations, gas stations, motels, parking lots, highway rest stops, and just about any other public space dedicated to the steady human process of coming and going.

Perhaps the most familiar form of transit space is the urban sidewalk, where many of us spend a good deal of time walking about or hanging out. Sidewalks become a world of their own, with complicated human movement and even more complicated forms of behavior as people jostle one another in crowds and make snap decisions on when to step aside and when not to. It is no surprise that city sidewalks have been prime locations for many sociological studies involving human behavior. An entire genre of photography, known as "street photography," has also concentrated on city sidewalks (see for example, the photographs of Wayne F. Miller on pp. 412–415, and Lauren Greenfield on p. 105) often with an emphasis on images of people clustering in groups or with a suggestion of anonymous violence. In recent literature, one of the most frequently read essays on how we maneuver the transit space of city streets "and sidewalks is Brent Staples's "Just Walk on By: A Black Man Ponders His Power to Alter Public Space." In this now classic short essay, Staples reflects on why he constantly takes precautions to make himself a less threatening figure in public space.

Pico Iyer, *Nowhere Man*. As the world becomes more globally connected and multicultural, "an entirely new breed of people," Pico Iyer notes, has come into existence; he includes himself as one of the new "transit loungers." Born in England to Indian parents in 1957, Iyer has been contributing essays regularly to *Time* magazine since 1982. His books include *Video Night in Katmandu* (1988), *The Lady and the Monk* (1991), *Falling Off the Map* (1993), *The Global Soul: Jet Lag, Shopping Malls, and the Search for Home* (2001), and *Sun After Dark* (2004). "Nowhere Man" first appeared in the May/June 1997 issue of the *Utne Reader*.

Pico Iyer
NOWHERE MAN

■ **Consider before you read.** *What aspects of modern society make the lifestyle Iyer describes possible? Since his parents' generation, what changes have occurred that allow him to live "nowhere"?*

By the time I was nine, I was already used to going to school by plane, to sleeping in airports, to shuttling back and forth, three times a year, between my home in California and my boarding school in England. While I was growing up, I was never within six thousand miles of the nearest relative — and came, therefore, to learn how to define relations in nonfamilial ways. From the time I was a teenager, I took it for granted that I could take my budget vacation (as I did) in Bolivia and Tibet, China and Morocco. It never seemed strange to me that a girlfriend might be half a world (or ten hours flying time) away, that my closest friends might be on the other side of a continent or sea. It was only recently that I realized that all these habits of mind and life would scarcely have been imaginable in my parents' youth, that the very facts and facilities that shape my world are all distinctly new developments, and mark me as a modern type.

It was only recently, in fact, that I realized that I am an example, perhaps, of an entirely new breed of people, a transcontinental tribe of wanderers that is multiplying as fast as international telephone lines and frequent flier programs. We are the transit loungers, forever heading to the departure gate. We buy our interests duty-free, we eat our food on plastic plates, we watch the world through borrowed headphones. We pass through countries as through revolving doors, resident aliens of the world, impermanent residents of nowhere. Nothing is strange to us, and nowhere is foreign. We are visitors even in our own homes.

The modern world seems increasingly made for people like me. I can plop myself down anywhere and find myself in the same relation of familiarity and strangeness: Lusaka is scarcely more strange to me than the England in which I was born, the America where I am registered as an "alien," and the almost unvisited India that people tell me is my home. All have Holiday Inns, direct-dial phones, CNN, and DHL. All have sushi, Thai restaurants, and Kentucky Fried Chicken.

This kind of life offers an unprecedented sense of freedom and mobility: Tied down nowhere, we can pick and choose among locations. Ours is the first generation that can go off to visit Tibet for a week, or meet Tibetans down the street; ours is the first generation to be able to go to Nigeria for a holiday — to find our

327

roots or to find that they are not there. At a superficial level, this new internationalism means that I can meet, in the Hilton coffee shop, an Indonesian businessman who is as conversant as I am with Magic Johnson and Madonna. At a deeper level, it means that I need never feel estranged. If all the world is alien to us, all the world is home.

And yet I sometimes think that this mobile way of life is as disquietingly novel as high-rises, or as the video monitors that are rewiring our consciousness. Even as we fret about the changes our progress wreaks in the air and on the airwaves, in forests and on streets, we hardly worry about the change it is working in ourselves, the new kind of soul that is being born out of a new kind of life. Yet this could be the most dangerous development of all, and the least examined.

For us in the transit lounge, disorientation is as alien as affiliation. We become professional observers, able to see the merits and deficiencies of anywhere, to balance our parents' viewpoints with their enemies' position. Yes, we say, of course it's terrible, but look at the situation from Saddam's point of view. I understand how you feel, but the Chinese had their own cultural reasons for Tiananmen Square. Fervor comes to seem to us the most foreign place of all.

Seasoned experts at dispassion, we are less good at involvement, or suspension of disbelief; at, in fact, the abolition of distance. We are masters of the aerial perspective, but touching down becomes more difficult. Unable to get stirred by the raising of a flag, we are sometimes unable to see how anyone could be stirred. I sometimes think that this is how Salman Rushdie, the great analyst of this condition, somehow became its victim. He had juggled homes for so long, so adroitly, that he forgot how the world looks to someone who is rooted — in country or in belief. He had chosen to live so far from affiliation that he could no longer see why people choose affiliation in the first place. Besides, being part of no society means one is accountable to no one, and need respect no laws outside one's own. If single-nation people can be fanatical as terrorists, we can end up ineffectual as peacekeepers.

We become, in fact, strangers to belief itself, unable to comprehend many of the rages and dogmas that animate (and unite) people. I could not begin to fathom why some Muslims would think of murder after hearing about *The Satanic Verses;* yet sometimes I force myself to recall that it is we, in our floating skepticism, who are the exceptions, that in China or Iran, in Korea or Peru, it is not so strange to give up one's life for a cause.

We end up, then, a little like nonaligned nations, confirming our reservations at every step. We tell ourselves, self-servingly, that nationalism breeds monsters, and choose to ignore the fact that internationalism breeds them too. Ours is the culpability not of the assassin, but of the bystander who takes a snapshot of the murder. Or, when the revolution catches fire, hops on the next plane out.

I wonder, sometimes, if this new kind of nonaffiliation may not be alien to something fundamental in the human state. Refugees at least harbor passionate feeling about the world they have left — and generally seek to return there. The exile at least is propelled by some kind of strong emotion away from the old country and toward the new; indifference is not an exile emotion. But what does the

328

■ Consider. *What do you make of this comparison? Why does Iyer introduce the idea of culpability at all — what is he guilty of? And in what sense is he equivalent to a bystander who snaps a picture of a murder victim? What does the snapshot represent in Iyer's equation? Why is it different from writing an essay?*

Sylvia Otte, *Airport Lounges.* Sylvia Otte's photography has appeared in *Audubon* magazine, *The Village Voice, The Washington Post Magazine,* and *Columbia College Today*. Otte also photographs jazz, classical, and hip-hop artists for recording labels, including Verve and Columbia. Her work is included in the book *In Praise of Women Photographers (and Photographers Who Just Happen to Be Women)* (1993, Time, Inc.). (left: Sylvia Otte/Punchstock; right: Sylvia Otte/Getty Images)

329

transit lounger feel? What are the issues that we would die for? What are the passions that we would live for?

Airports are among the only sites in public life where emotions are hugely sanctioned. We see people weep, shout, kiss in airports; we see them at the furthest edges of excitement and exhaustion. Airports are privileged spaces where we can see the primal states writ large — fear, recognition, hope. But there are some of us, perhaps, sitting at the departure gate, boarding passes in hand, who feel neither the pain of separation nor the exultation of wonder; who alight with the same emotions with which we embarked; who go down to the baggage carousel and watch our lives circling, circling, circling, waiting to be claimed.

■ **Consider.** *Analyze Iyer's final sentence. How does its imagery reinforce his language throughout the essay? What is the comparison in the final metaphor?*

■ **Discuss.** *What are the benefits of being a "transit lounger"? What problems does it bring? Discuss the extent to which Iyer thinks a more mobile life is a positive development.*

■ **Write.** *Do you agree with Iyer that feeling rootless might be "alien to something fundamental in the human state"? Write a response to "Nowhere Man," using your own experience to either support his conclusions or raise questions about them.*

Brent Staples, *Just Walk on By.*   Brent Staples (b. 1951) grew up in Chester, Pennsylvania, the eldest of nine children. He writes of his childhood — the poverty and responsibilities he faced at a young age — in his memoir, *Parallel Time: Growing Up in Black and White* (1994). Staples completed a college preparatory course before entering the Penn Morton School at Widener University at the encouragement of Professor Eugene Sparrow, the only black faculty member at Widener at the time (1969). Staples earned a degree in behavioral science and then, at the University of Chicago, earned a PhD in psychology. His real love, though, turned out to be journalism. In the early 1980s, he took a staff position at the *Chicago Sun-Times* and then moved on to *The New York Times,* where he is a member of the editorial board and a contributor to the commentary pages. Staples's work also appears in national magazines, including *Harper's, The New York Times Magazine*, and *Ms.*, in which "Just Walk on By" first appeared in 1986. In the following essay, Staples describes a nighttime walk he took through a Chicago neighborhood when he was in graduate school, as well as subsequent evening walks in New York City. (Reprinted by permission of HarperCollins Publishers)

330

Brent Staples

JUST WALK ON BY: A BLACK MAN PONDERS HIS POWER TO ALTER PUBLIC SPACE

■ **Consider before you read.** *Staples includes a lot of auditory detail to illustrate his nighttime walks. Why are sounds so important in this essay? As you read, make note of some examples of auditory description. How they contribute to Staples's themes?*

My first victim was a woman — white, well dressed, probably in her early twenties. I came upon her late one evening on a deserted street in Hyde Park, a relatively affluent neighborhood in an otherwise mean, impoverished section of Chicago. As I swung onto the avenue behind her, there seemed to be a discreet, uninflammatory distance between us. Not so. She cast back a worried glance. To her, the youngish black man — a broad six feet two inches with a beard and billowing hair, both hands shoved into the pockets of a bulky military jacket — seemed menacingly close. After a few more quick glimpses, she picked up her pace and was soon running in earnest. Within seconds she disappeared into a cross street.

> ■ *Consider. Why does Staples begin with the phrase "my first victim"? Where else in the essay does he use what he later refers to as "the language of fear" to talk about himself?*

That was more than a decade ago. I was twenty-two years old, a graduate student newly arrived at the University of Chicago. It was in the echo of that terrified woman's footfalls that I first began to know the unwieldy inheritance I'd come into — the ability to alter public space in ugly ways. It was clear that she thought herself the quarry of a mugger, a rapist, or worse. Suffering a bout of insomnia, however, I was stalking sleep, not defenseless wayfarers. As a softy who is scarcely able to take a knife to a raw chicken — let alone hold it to a person's throat — I was surprised, embarrassed, and dismayed all at once. Her flight made me feel like an accomplice in tyranny. It also made it clear that I was indistinguishable from the muggers who occasionally seeped into the area from the surrounding ghetto. That first encounter, and those that followed, signified that a vast, unnerving gulf lay between nighttime pedestrians — particularly women — and me. And I soon gathered that being perceived as dangerous is a hazard in itself. I only needed to turn a corner into a dicey situation, or crowd some frightened, armed person in a foyer somewhere, or make an errant move after being pulled over by a policeman. Where fear and weapons meet — and they often do in urban America — there is always the possibility of death.

In that first year, my first away from my hometown, I was to become thoroughly familiar with the language of fear. At dark, shadowy intersections in Chicago, I could cross in front of a car stopped at a traffic light and elicit the *thunk, thunk, thunk, thunk* of the driver — black, white, male, or female — hammering down the door locks. On less traveled streets after dark, I grew accustomed to but never comfortable with

331

people who crossed to the other side of the street rather than pass me. Then there were the standard unpleasantries with police, doormen, bouncers, cabdrivers, and others whose business it is to screen out troublesome individuals *before* there is any nastiness.

I moved to New York nearly two years ago and I have remained an avid night walker. In central Manhattan, the near-constant crowd cover minimizes tense one-on-one street encounters. Elsewhere — visiting friends in SoHo,[1] where sidewalks are narrow and tightly spaced buildings shut out the sky — things can get very taut indeed.

Black men have a firm place in New York mugging literature. Norman Podhoretz[2] in his famed (or infamous) 1963 essay, "My Negro Problem — And Ours," recalls growing up in terror of black males; they "were tougher than we were, more ruthless," he writes — and as an adult on the Upper West Side of Manhattan, he continues, he cannot constrain his nervousness when he meets black men on certain streets. Similarly, a decade later, the essayist and novelist Edward Hoagland extols a New York where once "Negro bitterness bore down mainly on other Negroes." Where some see mere panhandlers, Hoagland sees "a mugger who is clearly screwing up his nerve to do more than just *ask* for money." But Hoagland has "the New Yorker's quick-hunch posture for broken-field maneuvering," and the bad guy swerves away.

I often witness that "hunch posture," from women after dark on the warren-like streets of Brooklyn where I live. They seem to set their faces on neutral and, with their purse straps strung across their chests bandolier style, they forge ahead as though bracing themselves against being tackled. I understand, of course, that the danger they perceive is not a hallucination. Women are particularly vulnerable to street violence, and young black males are drastically overrepresented among the perpetrators of that violence. Yet these truths are no solace against the kind of alienation that comes of being ever the suspect, against being set apart, a fearsome entity with whom pedestrians avoid making eye contact.

It is not altogether clear to me how I reached the ripe old age of twenty-two without being conscious of the lethality nighttime pedestrians attributed to me. Perhaps it was because in Chester, Pennsylvania, the small, angry industrial town where I came of age in the 1960s, I was scarcely noticeable against a backdrop of gang warfare, street knifings, and murders. I grew up one of the good boys, had perhaps a half-dozen fistfights. In retrospect, my shyness of combat has clear sources.

Many things go into the making of a young thug. One of those things is the consummation of the male romance with the power to intimidate. An infant discovers that random flailings send the baby bottle flying out of the crib and crashing to the floor. Delighted, the joyful babe repeats those motions again and again, seeking to duplicate the feat. Just so, I recall the points at which some of my boyhood friends were finally seduced by the perception of themselves as tough guys. When a mark cowered and surrendered his money without resistance, myth and reality merged — and paid off. It is, after all, only manly to embrace the power

---

[1] Soho: A district of lower Manhattan known for its art galleries. — ED.
[2] Norman Podhoretz: A well-known literary critic and editor of *Commentary* magazine. — ED.

to frighten and intimidate. We, as men, are not supposed to give an inch of out lane on the highway; we are to seize the fighter's edge in work and in play and even in love; we are to be valiant in the face of hostile forces.

Unfortunately, poor and powerless young men seem to take all this nonsense literally. As a boy, I saw countless tough guys locked away; I have since buried several, too. They were babies, really — a teenage cousin, a brother of twenty-two, a childhood friend in his midtwenties — all gone down in episodes of bravado played out in the streets. I came to doubt the virtues of intimidation early on. I chose, perhaps even unconsciously, to remain a shadow — timid, but a survivor.

The fearsomeness mistakenly attributed to me in public places often has a perilous flavor. The most frightening of these confusions occurred in the late 1970s and early 1980s, when I worked as a journalist in Chicago. One day, rushing into the office of a magazine I was writing for with a deadline story in hand, I was mistaken for a burglar. The office manager called security and, with an ad hoc posse, pursued me through the labyrinthine halls, nearly to my editor' door. I had no way of proving who I was. I could only move briskly toward the company of someone who knew me.

Another time I was on assignment for a local paper and killing time before an interview. I entered a jewelry store on the city's affluent Near North Side. The proprietor excused herself and returned with an enormous red Doberman pinscher straining at the end of a leash. She stood, the dog extended toward me, silent to my questions, her eyes bulging nearly out of her head. I took a cursory look around, nodded, and bade her good night. Relatively speaking, however, I never fared as badly as another black male journalist. He went to nearby Waukegan, Illinois, a couple of summers ago to work on a story about a murderer who was born there. Mistaking the reporter for the killer, police hauled him from his car at gunpoint and but for his press credentials would probably have tried to book him. Such episodes are not uncommon. Black men trade tales like this all the time.

In "My Negro Problem — And Ours," Podhoretz writes that the hatred he feels for blacks makes itself known to him through a variety of avenues — one being his discomfort with that "special brand of paranoid touchiness" to which he says blacks are prone. No doubt he is speaking here of black men. In time, I learned to smother the rage I felt at so often being taken for a criminal. Not to do so would surely have led to madness — via that special "paranoid touchiness" that so annoyed Podhoretz at the time he wrote the essay.

I began to take precautions to make myself less threatening. I move about with care, particularly late in the evening. I give a wide berth to nervous people on subway platforms during the wee hours, particularly when I have exchanged business clothes for jeans. If I happen to be entering a building behind some people who appear skittish, I may walk by, letting them clear the lobby before I return, so as not to seem to be following them. I have been calm and extremely congenial on those rare occasions when I've been pulled over by the police.

And on late-evening constitutionals along streets less traveled by, I employ what has proved to be an excellent tension-reducing measure: I whistle melodies from Beethoven and Vivaldi and the more popular classical composers. Even steely New

333

Yorkers hunching toward nighttime destinations seem to relax, and occasionally they even join in the tune. Virtually everybody seems to sense that a mugger wouldn't be warbling bright, sunny selections from Vivaldi's *Four Seasons*. It is my equivalent of the cowbell that hikers wear when they know they are in bear country.

■ **Discuss.** *Discuss Brent Staples's "precautions" for his late-night walks. Are these ideal solutions to the problems he has described? How does the metaphor in the last sentence sum up Staples's position?*

■ **Write.** *Both Staples's "Just Walk on By" and John Edgar Wideman's "First Shot" (p. 303) focus on young men's changing conceptions of the world around them. In a short essay, compare Staples's and Wideman's understanding of masculinity. How does being male shape their ideas and their relationships with others?*

■■■■■■ CONSIDER THE CLUSTER
Public Space

■ **Message**

In what ways does the concept of "distance" inform both Iyer's and Staples's essays? Examine the meaning of "distance" in each essay and in a short paper discuss the differences and similarities. Which physical environment — the airport transit lounge or the city sidewalk — seems more "distancing"?

■ **Method**

Both Iyer's and Staples's selections can be considered personal reflective essays. What qualities of thought and attitude do you think characterize these essays? In a brief essay of your own, compare the two selections by demonstrating the similar methods of reflection that each writer uses.

■ **Medium**

Suppose you have been asked to transform these short reflective essays into half-minute YouTube films. As an in-class writing assignment, select one of the essays and describe — in either words, images, or both — how you would adapt it to video.

MENTAL SPACE:
THE HUMAN IMAGINATION

The language we use to describe our mental life is extremely dependent on spatial imagery. We speak of our "inner self," of feelings "deep inside," of a "voice within," and we frequently make a distinction between our "internal" and "external" identities. Yet what exactly is inside us — what are the images, thoughts, words, dreams, and experiences that make up our interior life? This age-old philosophical question is creatively explored by Lynda Barry in a recent graphic essay, "When Images Come to Us . . . Where Do They Come From?" Her essay, a closely linked series of collages (that is excerpted here) attempts to portray the lively jumble of thoughts and images that inhabit the interior spaces of our imaginations.

Are we stuck with the imaginations we were born with? Or can the human imagination be stimulated and expanded? In "Dream Machines," Will Wright, the famed creator of numerous video games, including *The Sims,* argues that games "actually amplify our powers of imagination." The newest generation of video games does so, Wright maintains, by inviting us to move creatively through what he calls "possibility space." Future games, he suggests, will allow us to expand our imaginations "in a totally new way" and will potentially "subsume almost all other forms of entertainment media."

Lynda Barry. Self-portrait. (Copyright Lynda Barry)

Interview: Elissa Schappell, From "A Conversation with Lynda Barry"

ELISSA SCHAPPELL: How does the graphic element dovetail with the narrative for you? Do you make the drawings first or second, or along with the story?

LYNDA BARRY: I make them at the same time. The exact same time. There isn't a plan beforehand. I very rarely pencil anything in or have a single idea before I start. There is something about just grinding the ink and moving the brush around that makes a comic strip come. I'm always surprised that it works this way, but it does.

ELISSA SCHAPPELL: How are your approaches to writing and making art different, if they are different?

LYNDA BARRY: The difference is scant because I use a brush to write fiction too. I can't write on a computer, not until I'm copying out the final draft do I put it on a computer. It's too easy to delete the thing that doesn't seem to fit — which often turns out to be the true story forming.

When I got stuck trying to write *Cruddy* on the computer I had an idea to try to write it with a small paintbrush on notebook paper. I was really at a point where I felt I had nothing to lose. What surprised me was how the story just started to form so much faster and so much more vividly than it had when I was just tapping my fingers around on a keyboard.

I got pretty excited about this brush-writing thing and wondered if anyone else had figured it out. Yeah, turns out about three thousand years ago in China they started to figure out this brush-and-ink-and-image thing. It's opened up an entire world to me, one that is much connected with Buddhism and Zen, by the way.

This discovery of the brush world has probably been the most important thing that's happened to me in my adult life.

— from *Tin House*, issue 29, "The Graphic Issue"

Lynda Barry, *When Images Come to Us . . . Where Do They Come From?* Lynda   ▶
Barry (b. 1956) is the creator of the syndicated comic strip *Ernie Pook's Comeek*
and the author of more than a dozen illustrated books that she classifies as
"autobifictionalography," or part fiction, part autobiography. Barry's characters
range from the "life-grooving" Marlys from *Down the Street* (1986) to herself in
One Hundred Demons (2002). Most of her work focuses on childhood and adolescent experience, and among her influences are Dr. Seuss, R. Crumb, Grimm's
fairy tales, *Ripley's Believe It Or Not!*, cave paintings, and religious art from
India. Barry's first comic strip was published in 1977 in the Evergreen State
College student newspaper, where friend and classmate Matt Groening (of *The
Simpsons* fame) served as co-editor. Barry, who previously made her home in a
suburb of Chicago, now lives in Footville, Wisconsin. The following work originally appeared in *Tin House*, issue 29, "The Graphic Issue," and appeared in her
work in progress, *What It Is*, published in early 2008 (by Drawn & Quarterly).
(Copyright Lynda Barry 2008, taken from *What It Is*, published by *Drawn &
Quarterly*)

Lynda Barry

WHEN IMAGES COME TO US . . . WHERE DO THEY COME FROM?

■ **Consider before you read/view.** *As you view these pages from Lynda Barry's graphic
essay, where is your eye drawn first? What jumps out at you immediately? What elements
take longer to absorb?*

337

◄   ■   **Discuss.** *The text in these collages comes in many different forms — printed in various sizes and fonts, handwritten by different people and using different tools. What is the effect of having so many different types of text? Do they represent different processes or different parts of the mind?*

■   **Write.** *Is there a narrative to Barry's arrangement of images? What story does this essay tell about the imagination? Write an analysis of how the sequence is important to "When Images Come to Us."*

Will Wright, Dream Machines, 2006   Considered one of the greatest game designers of all time, Will Wright (b. 1960) is the creator of *SimCity* (1989), *The Sims* (2000), and more than a dozen other video games, or "toys" as he fondly refers to them, including *Spore*, which is currently under development. He is also cofounder (with Jeff Braun) of Maxis, a game development company.

Born in Atlanta, Georgia, Wright attended a local Montessori school, which emphasized imagination, creativity, self-directed activity, and problem solving. He attributes his joy of play and invention to this early experience: "Montessori taught me the joy of discovery. . . . It showed you can become interested in pretty complex theories, like Pythagorean theory, say, by playing with blocks. It's all about learning on your terms, rather than a teacher explaining stuff to you. *SimCity* comes right out of Montessori — if you give people this model for building cities, they will abstract from it principles of urban design."

When Wright was nine years old, his father died of leukemia, and he and his mother moved to her hometown, Baton Rouge, Louisiana. Wright has said that from this point on his education went pretty much downhill — in his view, the conventional classroom with its eight hours of passive, repetitive tasks is more or less designed to produce factory workers. Despite this, Wright's interest in learning and creating continues. In the following essay, originally published in *Wired* magazine, Wright argues that games can offer us tools of imaginative self-expression — and that real learning takes place when people can imagine possibilities, create, and experience.

Will Wright
DREAM MACHINES

■   **Consider before you read.** *What do games teach us? According to Wright, what capacities does game playing develop? How do video games teach differently than games of the past? To what extent does the "space" of the video game foster creativity?*

The **human imagination** is an amazing thing. As children, we spend much of our time in imaginary worlds, substituting toys and make-believe for the real surroundings that we are just beginning to explore and understand. As we play, we learn. And as we grow, our play gets more complicated. We add rules and goals. The result is something we call games.

Now an entire generation has grown up with a different set of games than any before it — and it plays these games in different ways. Just watch a kid with a new videogame. The last thing they do is read the manual. Instead, they pick up the controller and start mashing buttons to see what happens. This isn't a random process; it's the essence of the scientific method. Through trial and error, players build a model of the underlying game based on empirical evidence collected through play. As the players refine this model, they begin to master the game world. It's a rapid cycle of hypothesis, experiment, and analysis. And it's a fundamentally different take on problem-solving than the linear, read-the-manual-first approach of their parents.

In an era of structured education and standardized testing, this generational difference might not yet be evident. But the gamers' mindset — the fact that they are learning in a totally new way — means they'll treat the world as a place for creation, not consumption. This is the true impact videogames will have on our culture.

Society, however, notices only the negative. Most people on the far side of the generational divide — elders — look at games and see a list of ills (they're violent, addictive, childish, worthless). Some of these labels may be deserved. But the positive aspects of gaming — creativity, community, self-esteem, problem-solving — are somehow less visible to nongamers.

I think part of this stems from the fact that watching someone play a game is a different experience than actually holding the controller and playing it yourself. Vastly different. Imagine that all you knew about movies was gleaned through observing the audience in a theater — but that you had never watched a film. You would conclude that movies induce lethargy and junk-food binges. That may be true, but you're missing the big picture.

So it's time to reconsider games, to recognize what's different about them and how they benefit — not denigrate — culture. Consider, for instance, their "possibility space": Games usually start at a well-defined state (the setup in chess, for instance) and end when a specific state is reached (the king is checkmated). Players navigate this possibility space by their choices and actions; every player's path is unique.

Games cultivate — and exploit — possibility space better than any other medium. In linear storytelling, we can only imagine the possibility space that surrounds the narrative: What if Luke had joined the Dark Side? What if Neo isn't the One? In interactive media, we can explore it.

Like the toys of our youth, modern videogames rely on the player's active involvement. We're invited to create and interact with elaborately simulated worlds, characters, and story lines. Games aren't just fantasy worlds to explore; they actually amplify our powers of imagination.

■ **Consider.** *How does "hypothesis, experiment, and analysis" sum up the scientific method? How does it work as an analogy for the way younger game players learn?*

341

Think of it this way: Most technologies can be seen as an enhancement of some part of our bodies (car/legs, house/skin, TV/senses). From the start, computers have been understood as an extension of the human brain; the first computers were referred to as mechanical brains and analytical engines. We saw their primary value as automated number crunchers that far exceeded our own meager abilities.

But the Internet has morphed what we used to think of as a fancy calculator into a fancy telephone with email, chat groups, IM, and blogs. It turns out that we don't use computers to enhance our math skills — we use them to expand our people skills.

The same transformation is happening in games. Early computer games were little toy worlds with primitive graphics and simple problems. It was up to the player's imagination to turn the tiny blobs on the screen into, say, people or tanks. As computer graphics advanced, game designers showed some Hollywood envy:

SimCity 4. Many video games attempt to create a sense of space, of "there." In *SimCity*, players manage a cityscape — they fight disasters, plan budgets, and govern hundreds of thousands of people. (© 2008 Electronic Arts Inc. All Rights Reserved. Used with Permission)

They added elaborate cutscenes, epic plots, and, of course, increasingly detailed graphics. They bought into the idea that world building and storytelling are best left to professionals, and they pushed out the player. But in their rapture over computer processing, games designers forgot that there's a second processor at work: the player's imagination.

Now, rather than go Hollywood, some game designers are deploying that second processor to break down the wall between producers and consumers. By moving away from the idea that media is something developed by the few (movie and TV studios, book publishers, game companies) and consumed in a one-size-fits-all form, we open up a world of possibilities. Instead of leaving player creativity at the door, we are inviting it back to help build, design, and populate our digital worlds.

More games now include features that let players invent some aspect of their virtual world, from characters to cars. And more games entice players to become creative partners in world building, letting them mod its overall look and feel. The online communities that form around these imaginative activities are some of the most vibrant on the Web. For these players, games are not just entertainment but a vehicle for self-expression.

Games have the potential to subsume almost all other forms of entertainment media. They can tell us stories, offer us music, give us challenges, allow us to communicate and interact with others, encourage us to make things, connect us to new communities, and let us play. Unlike most other forms of media, games are inherently malleable. Player mods are just the first step down this path.

Soon games will start to build simple models of us, the players. They will learn what we like to do, what we're good at, what interests and challenges us. They will observe us. They will record the decisions we make, consider how we solve problems, and evaluate how skilled we are in various circumstances. Over time, these games will become able to modify themselves to better "fit" each individual. They will adjust their difficulty on the fly, bring in new content, and create story lines. Much of this original material will be created by other players, and the system will move it to those it determines will enjoy it most.

Games are evolving to entertain, educate, and engage us individually. These personalized games will reflect who we are and what we enjoy, much as our choice of books and music does now. They will allow us to express ourselves, meet others, and create things that we can only dimly imagine. They will enable us to share and combine these creations, to build vast playgrounds. And more than ever, games will be a visible, external amplification of the human imagination.

343

■ **Discuss.** *At several points in his essay, Wright compares video games with Hollywood movies. Why does he make this comparison? Discuss how the two media differ.*

■ **Write.** *As part of the younger generation Wright describes, what is your experience of electronic games? Do you think that any of the criticisms mentioned are valid? Do you agree with Wright's ideas about their imaginative and educational possibilities? If you can, use a particular game you've played to illustrate your points.*

Mental Space

344

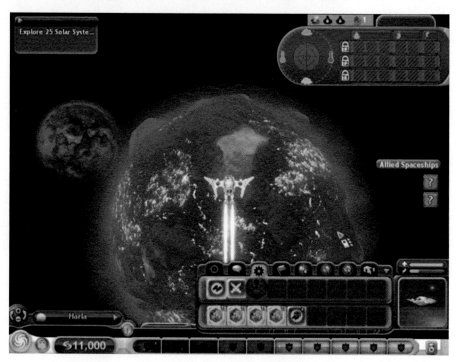

◄ **Will Wright, *Spore* game screens.** Will Wright connects video games with creativity and imagines them as "possibility spaces" for players. Co-created with Maxis (the publisher of *The Sims*), Wright's latest game, *Spore*, allows players to create and control the evolution of a species. It is divided into five main phases: tide pool; creature; tribal; civilization; and space. The player controls the creatures' development from simple organisms to intergalactic conquerors. Shown here are images from the "creature phase" and "space phase." (© 2008 Electronic Arts Inc. All Rights Reserved. Used with Permission)

CONSIDER THE CLUSTER
Mental Space: The Human Imagination

■ **Message**

In "Dream Machines," Will Wright takes a very positive view of games and the way they offer us "possibility space." But Wright doesn't define precisely what he means by "possibility space." In a response to Wright's essay, try to develop a definition of what Wright means by such a space. Do you agree with him that the "possibility space" offered by the latest video games will enhance human creativity to a greater extent than any other medium? Why or why not?

■ **Method**

Lynda Barry's drawings are often very busy, with images and writing arranged in what appears to be a haphazard manner. But after more careful examination, do you perceive a method behind her visual/verbal arrangements? Can you see an overall design or pattern to her work? In a short critical essay, select a single element of her drawings that you think helps describe the method of her composition.

■ **Medium**

In a speculative essay, use your imagination to predict the next stage of media evolution. Do you imagine, as does Will Wright, that the new evolving form will be games? If so, what will these games be like, and how will they be used? If not, what form will best enhance human creativity and imagination? Will literature, music, and art take on new dimensions? What technological changes will be necessary for the next stage of media evolution to occur?

345

CYBERSPACE

BILLBOARD | MAP | 2 PERSUASIVE ESSAYS | WEB SCREENS | SIDEBAR | ANALYTICAL ESSAY

Cluster menu: Cyberspace

Does cyberspace consist of real places such as San Francisco, Florida State University, and your local pizzeria? Or, as Jonathan G. S. Koppell argues in "No 'There' There," is it merely a figure of speech, a common way of talking with no basis in physical reality? When you visit an e-store and fill up your "shopping cart," you aren't literally in a store or actually wheeling a cart. Or are you? Some new media thinkers — and futurists — believe we are heading toward a "convergence" of cyberspace and the physical environment as new technology rapidly blurs the boundaries between the real and the virtual. In other words, we're heading toward the fictional world of William Gibson's 1984 science fiction classic, *Neuromancer*. As Gibson writes, "I coined the term 'cyberspace' in 1981 in one of my first science fiction stories and subsequently used it to describe something that people insist on seeing as a sort of literary forerunner of the Internet."

Yahoo! *A Nice Place to Stay on the Internet.* Although Google is the top-rated search engine (with about 50 percent of the market), Yahoo!, which ranks second (with roughly 25 percent of the market), claims to host "the world's most visited homepage." (© Vincent Soyez)

347

The question of just how real are the electronic places we visit on the Internet is becoming a controversial topic for artists, academics, and legal scholars, who see a number of issues — ranging from the legitimacy of art works to free speech — arising from our increasingly frequent travel into cyberspace. Some of that frequent travel has recently been to online virtual worlds, such as *Second Life*, where individuals can escape the confinements of real life and "meet anyone, go anywhere, and do anything in a realistic 3-D environment." Will *Second Life* and its successors transform our conventional notions of public space and human community? In "Living in a Virtual World," the editorial board of *The Week* explores some answers to these questions.

The Opte Project, *Mapping the Internet.* Created in 2003 by a young man named Barrett Lyon and other coders at the Opte Project (opte.org), this map represents a snapshot of the Internet. The project grew out of a conversation Lyon had with colleagues over lunch about an existing Internet-mapping project (see lumeta.com) that he felt he could improve on. "I can write a program that can map the entire net in a single day," Lyon said. With help, he did so and now shares his program code free of charge at opte.org. This map illustrates IP (Internet protocol) addresses as follows: red = Asia Pacifica; green = Europe, the Middle East, Central Asia, and Africa; blue = North America; yellow = Latin America and the Caribbean; white = unknown.

Jonathan G. S. Koppell, *No "There" There.* Jonathan Koppell teaches at the Yale School of Management and has published widely on public administration and politics. In this essay, he argues that cyberspace is really no place at all. This essay first appeared in the *Atlantic Monthly* in August 2000.

Jonathan G. S. Koppell
NO "THERE" THERE

■ **Consider before you read.** *Koppell's essay debunks the idea that the Internet is a brand-new space. What examples does he use to suggest that the Internet just raises new problems of kinds we have already seen? Do you agree with him? Why or why not?*

I'm a pretty Net-savvy guy. I read my morning newspaper online. I buy discount airline tickets online. I participate in animated sports banter online. I even manage my finances online (if transferring money to cover checks qualifies as "managing my finances"). Still, I have never been to the magical land called cyberspace.

Cyberspace isn't on any map, but I know that it must exist, because it is spoken of every day. People spend hours in *chat rooms.* They visit *web sites.* They travel through this electronic domain on an *information superhighway.* The language we use implies that cyberspace is a place as tangible as France or St. Louis or the coffee shop on the corner. But why, exactly, should we think of the Internet as a geographic location? I recently participated in a telephone conference call with people in several other states and countries. Were we all together in another "place"? I doubt that any of us thought so.

Many would say that it isn't just the act of communicating that makes cyberspace a place but the existence of a community consisting of broadly dispersed people. But that characteristic is not particularly distinctive. There are communities big and small that do not exist within any physical jurisdiction. Professional associations, alumni groups, and religious orders are among them. Members of such groups feel a kinship with other members with whom they have never interacted, in either the real or the virtual sense.

Some would respond, "Those people all had something in common before they forged connections across boundaries. But cyberspace communities were created online. There were no prior affinities to bring them together. That's unique." Is it? Ham radio operators have a global network of friends and acquaintances who came together solely through their use of that instrument. Do they exist in "hamspace"? And why is the manner in which people make first contact so significant? Do pen pals exist in "penpalspace"?

One reason that cyberspace is described as a place is to avoid downgrading it to the status of a mere medium, and perhaps especially to avoid comparisons with television. Those who would distinguish the Internet from television point out that Web denizens are not mere passive recipients of electronic signals. That may be (partly) true. But telephones and the postal system are also communications media that allow two-way communication. We don't regard them as places.

Thinking of the Internet as a place certainly makes it seem more intriguing. The idea of logging on and entering another space is suggestive in all sorts of ways. It raises issues of consciousness, allows us to think of ourselves as disembodied cybernauts, and sets us apart not just from our primitive ancestors but also from our recent ones. Not incidentally, representing the home computer and AOL membership as a gateway to another dimension helps to sell home computers and AOL memberships. The various web sites, IPOs, and dot-coms-of-the-day feed on the fervor surrounding our exploration of this strange new land. By morphing the Internet into a destination, cyberspace has become the Klondike of our age. (Curiously, Seattle is reaping the benefits this time around, too.)

Metaphors matter: they can help to shape our views and actions. Consider the widespread acceptance of the term "marketplace of ideas" as a metaphor for free speech. This representation emphasizes one's freedom to enter the arena of discourse, rather than one's ability to be heard. Thus, in the context of campaign-finance regulation, protection of free speech means that unlimited campaign expenditures are sacrosanct, but guaranteeing equal opportunities to reach the electorate is not a consideration. If, in contrast, we imagined not a marketplace but a classroom, enabling the quietest voice to be heard would be more important than protecting the rights of the loudest. Another example is the ill-fated "war on drugs." By conceiving of drugs as an enemy to be defeated in combat, we blind ourselves to many potential solutions. In the context of war the legalization of drugs amounts to capitulation to the enemy — even if it might address many of the problems, such as crime, disease, and chronic poverty, that were used to justify the war in the first place.

For its part, the cyberspace-as-place metaphor raises issues of logic and psychology that may ultimately impede wise management of the Internet. Lawrence Lessig, of Harvard Law School, argues in his book *Code and Other Laws of Cyberspace* (1999) that the government should not sit by while private code (software) writers define the nature of the Internet. Such a seemingly neutral stance, Lessig says, is not neutral but irresponsible. In the case of cyberspace, laissez-faire government simply defers decision-making authority to profit-seeking companies. Guided only by commercial interests, the development of the Internet is skewed to favor the corporation rather than the individual or society as a whole.

The problem, Lessig explains, is that legislatures and courts are reluctant to regulate the Internet. He lays out some compelling reasons why this is so, but he skips a crucial one. Because we think of the Internet as a place, the prospect of "going there" takes on an extra dimension. Legislatures are wary of bringing government to cyberspace — as if it somehow existed in some pure state beyond ordinary society. Judges are reluctant to bring law into this "new" arena, as if applying existing laws to Internet transactions would be tantamount to colonizing Antarctica or the moon. In the context of legal discussions, cyberspace is seen not as a potentially anarchic realm but as a virginal Eden; the introduction of law would not so much bring order as corrupt utopia. Republicans in Congress have vowed to "stand at the door to the Internet" to defend its sanctity. Their "E-Contract 2000" would, for example, prohibit sales taxes in cyberspace for at least five years — as if such a moratorium were needed to nurture the most dynamic sector of the economy. Many Democrats, equally eager to win favor in the industry, also support the concept of an online duty-free "zone."

As it happens, Lessig himself reinforces cyberspace-as-place thinking. He argues that the Internet user exists simultaneously in two "places," a physical location and cyberspace — thus making the application of law somewhat difficult. In reality, the problems created by Internet transactions simply involve making decisions about jurisdiction. Should a criminal computer user, for example, be subject to the laws of the state in which he resides, or to the laws of the state in which the victim resides? This can be a knotty question, but it is not a new problem — not a "cyberspace problem." Such determinations are made every day with respect to telephone and postal transactions. Are these problems more common because of the Internet? Yes. Do they involve more jurisdictions because of the Internet? Yes. But they do not involve their own jurisdiction, any more than matters initiated or conducted through the mails involve "postalspace."

That is not to say that the Internet will have no consequences for governance. The growth of the Internet may gradually shift the locus of authority upward, from local and state governments to the federal government or even international institutions, because as human interactions transcend political boundaries, only governments with broad jurisdictions will be able to monitor certain kinds of behavior and enforce certain kinds of laws. Law and government will adapt accordingly.

The cyberspace-as-place metaphor is probably here to stay. And it has its uses, as do the many other fanciful metaphors we use in everyday speech. But let's not be misled. The regulation of cyberspace — in areas from copyright to taxation to privacy — hardly represents the spoliation of a pristine and untamed land.

■ **Discuss.** *Koppell points out how much of the language we use to talk about the Internet is spatial. Why is this? What does society have invested in the idea of "cyberspace"? What is at stake?*

■ **Write.** *Koppell's essay appeared before the widespread popularity of social networking sites such as MySpace or Facebook. Write an analysis of how these sites do or do not function as separate spaces. How do you think Koppell would interpret them?*

Noah D. Zatz, *Sidewalks in Cyberspace.* The way widespread use of the Internet affects our democratic society is the subject of a highly influential essay that appeared in the *Harvard Journal of Law and Technology* (Fall 1998), in which Noah D. Zatz addresses a wide range of difficult issues stemming from the ways that cyberspace has altered our concepts of public forums, assembly, and free speech. Although the essay is too technical and lengthy to include in this text, the argument did require Zatz to add a section ("Mapping Physical and Electronic Space") that briefly and systematically clarifies what he considers to be the similarities and differences among the various kinds of space we currently inhabit. His concise classification of spatial concepts — such as distance, adjacency, and fixity — serves as a useful starting point for all subsequent discussion of the issue.

Noah D. Zatz

SIDEWALKS IN CYBERSPACE

352

■ **Consider before you read.** *How does cyberspace differ from "material" space? Note how Zatz divides his essay into three main areas in which cyberspace deviates from traditional notions of spatial relations.*

MAPPING PHYSICAL AND ELECTRONIC SPACE

Relationships among ordinary, physical places are primarily structured by relationships of distance and direction. Places occupy fixed locations in space, and although the significance of fixed relative location is substantially influenced by technological interventions and social practices,[1] geography matters nonetheless.[2] All other things being equal, places that are geographically close are causally intertwined more tightly than those far apart, though the extent to which this is true varies substantially with the nature of the causal mechanisms.[3]

In the material environment, spatial relationships are not symmetrical in all directions. A store should generally be far more concerned by garbage in front of its entrance than by the same garbage an equal distance above, below, or behind it.

---

[1] New York and Los Angeles may, in many senses, be closer to one another than to many points intermediate on the map.

[2] A store in downtown Manhattan would generally be wise to spend its money advertising in New York City rather than Buenos Aires, even if the people of Buenos Aires might be equally interested in its wares.

[3] For the purposes of the shared effects of a chemical spill, the Upper East Side and East Harlem will be tied to each other much more closely than either is to the Lower East Side, while changes in New York City policy toward abandoned buildings would yield a different ordering.

Perhaps more important, when moving a given distance *between* places, one always travels *through* other places.[4] Our efforts to move through space efficiently create bottlenecks, such as streets, sidewalks, and airport terminals, where people gather simply because they are on their way someplace else, and locations such as malls and business districts, where people congregate to take advantage of shared needs and low transportation costs. All of these bottlenecks are potential sites of blockade. Anything that enters a given place must pass through some other place adjacent to it. Any shopper who enters the store must pass by the picketer standing out front.

Cyberspace is different. Although within its bounds a discrete cyber-place may be substantially similar to analogous "real world" places, the relationships *among* cyber-places are vastly different. Three features are particularly salient: distance, adjacency, and fixity.

1. Distance

The most widely heralded spatial characteristic of cyberspace is its erasure of distance. Cyberspace, like many communication and transportation technologies before it, in significant ways eliminates and therefore equalizes distance. The distance between any two web sites, for instance, is just the entry of a new Uniform Resource Locator ("URL," for example, jolt.law.harvard.edu/), as is the distance between home and the airline ticket counter, library, or fashion boutique. This conclusion, however, is somewhat misleading because it assumes that one already knows where one is going. Nonetheless, cyber-distance is at least highly contingent and compressible. Although your first journey might require a long and winding road, a simple "bookmark" makes your second visit just a step across the street.

2. Adjacency

Except that there is no street to cross. The lack of direction and continuity in cyberspace means that there are no fixed spaces that lie between any other two, nor is the environment of one place affected much by any other. There are no neighbors in cyberspace and, therefore, no blockades, no loud noise bothering you from the disco next door, and no neighbor's tree dropping fruit on your side of the fence.

Of course, there *are* important and interesting relationships of adjacency on the web via hypertext links between sites. These relationships, however, are neither symmetrical nor exclusive, unlike in the material environment. That site A has a link to site B creates a limited spatial relationship between them, in the sense that visitors to A are more likely to travel to B than they would be in the absence of the link. In contrast to movement between neighboring plots of land, the ease of moving from A to B says nothing about the ease of moving from B to A. Moreover, since one can always go directly to B from any other point on the Web simply by entering its URL directly or by using a bookmark, there is no site through which one must pass in order to reach B.

■ **Consider.** *How do search engines function as "winding roads" or highways? Can you think of any other comparisons for the way search engines such as Google arrange or assist our experience of the Internet?*

353

---

[4] Driving from New York to Delaware is not simply a question of traversing a given distance, but of going through New Jersey.

3. Fixity

As is apparent from the preceding discussion, cyberspace is not simply a disordered set of places. There are important spatial relationships among sites, but they are of a different character than those among places in our material environment. Of particular import is the relative contingency of cyberspatial orderings. Relative to the physical environment, the spatial relationship between two places in cyberspace can easily shift based on how one arrives at a given place, or through the passage of time.

First, they are contingent upon one's course and means of travel. Not only is the relationship of adjacency asymmetrical, and thus contingent upon which of two sites one visits first, but the distance between two sites may be modified by a path through a third. Thus, site C may link to site A, while site D links to A and B. If one comes to A via C, the spatial relationship of A to B is different than if one comes to A via D, having passed an alternate path toward B. This sort of relationship is readily apparent in search engines — the closest thing cyberspace has to a highway system and whose function is to facilitate travel to other places. A search for "Corps" might place AmeriCorps and the Marine Corps in close proximity, while one could easily compose searches which would yield one but not the other.

Secondly, spatial relationships are highly subject to change over time. Whereas building a new road or airport, tearing down or building walls, or relocating the site of a store are time-consuming and costly affairs, adding or deleting links, changing keywords for search engines, bookmarking (or memorizing) an address, and moving a website to a new Internet Protocol ("IP") address are much less capital- and labor-intensive undertakings. When purchasing a parcel of land, "location is everything"; a substantial fraction of its price will reflect not the material characteristics of the place itself but its spatial relationships to other sites. Cyberspace, by contrast, disaggregates internal features of the place from its spatial characteristics.

While this feature renders the spatial ordering of cyberspace less reliable, it also leaves it more open to purposeful intervention. Although the spatial ordering of our physical landscape is a social construction in the sense that its particular form can be explained in terms of social processes of decision-making, the spatial ordering of cyberspace has far less permanence. Once built, a web site's *persistence* over time far more reflects a continuing social choice than the permanence of a bridge at a given site, despite subsequent regrets. Having built an information superhighway without sidewalks, we can still add them on without displacing either the roadway or the places abutting it.

■ **Discuss.** *Does Zatz's essay help support Jonathan Koppell's argument that cyberspace is not real space? To what extent does Zatz seem to believe in the spatiality of the Internet?*

■ **Write.** *Zatz points out that in the material world "location is everything" but that in cyberspace no site is inherently better than any other. How, then, do some sites get to be more lucrative, popular, or respected than others? In a short essay, analyze what creates value in Internet sites.*

Linden Lab, *Second Life*. According to the *SL* web site, "Second Life is a 3-D virtual world entirely built and owned by its Residents." Established in 2003 by Linden Lab, a software company in San Francisco, the world of *SL* is home to 9,490,843 Residents (and counting). You can sign up for *SL* as a user (or Resident, as you'll be known in *SL*) for free and create your own avatar (alter ego). You can accessorize your avatar, shop, go out clubbing, or buy property by using currency known as "Linden Dollars." (Second Life is a trademark of Linden Research, Inc. Certain materials have been reproduced with the permission on Linden Research, Inc. Copyright © 2001–2008 Linden Research, Inc. All Right Reserved)

COMMENT

"From the moment you enter *the World* you'll discover a vast digital continent, teeming with people, entertainment, experiences and opportunity. Once you've explored a bit, perhaps you'll find a perfect parcel of land to build your house or business.

- You'll also be surrounded by *the Creations* of your fellow Residents. Because Residents retain the rights to their digital creations, they can buy, sell and trade with other Residents.
- *The Marketplace* currently supports millions of US dollars in monthly transactions. This commerce is handled with the in-world unit-of-trade, the Linden Dollar, which can be converted to US dollars at several thriving online Linden Dollar exchanges.

Welcome to Second Life. We look forward to seeing you in-world."

—Secondlife.com

355

Linden Lab
SECOND LIFE

■ **Consider before you read/view.** *What do the following images suggest about the kind of activities offered in* Second Life (SL)? *How does* SL *differ from a traditional electronic game?*

WHAT IS SECOND LIFE?

The World

- **Create an Avatar**
- **Explore**
- **Meet People**
- **Own Virtual Land**
- **Have Fun**

The World

Create an Avatar

Explore

■ **Discuss.** *Second Life does not really have an end or a goal. Discuss how this differentiates it from other virtual worlds. Does it make* Second Life *more lifelike? Do you think it has more or less of what Will Wright calls "possibility space"?*

■ **Write.** *Analyze the name "Second Life." What does it suggest about the virtual world's relation to the "first life" of the physical world?*

Virtual World, Real Business

Linden Lab, the company that runs *Second Life,* is not yet profitable, but thousands of *Second Life* residents are. *Second Life* allows players to buy and sell what they create using "Linden dollars," online currency that can be exchanged on an open market for real-world money. *Second Life* banks, run either by Linden or independent entrepreneurs, get a commission for taking people's Linden dollars and transferring the equivalent in U.S. dollars into their PayPal accounts. Hot products include clothing, vehicles, and body parts. Every month, *Second Life*'s 250,000 active users spend $1.5 million in real money inside the game (the game itself is free to play). *Second Life*'s thriving economy has also attracted scores of companies, which pay a fee to build and maintain digital outposts. American Apparel runs a clothing store with re-creations of its hip outfits; Toyota and other automakers give away copies of their cars; Starwood Hotels rents virtual rooms. Beyond advertising to coveted tastemakers, the companies get valuable marketing data by observing how residents use their products. As a sign of how seriously *Second Life* is taken, Reuters has opened a full-time "in-game" news bureau (at Secondlife.reuters.com), which reports on the game's community. It covers both real-world news involving *Second Life* and "events" that take place only in cyberspace.

The Week **Editorial Board,** *Living in a Virtual World.* According to its editor in chief, *The Week: The Best of the U.S. and International Media* is "a witty, informative, important, and completely indispensable digest of the best reporting and writing from the U.S. and international press. In just 40 pages, it will bring you up to date on what's happening at home and abroad, and what the experts are saying about it. . . . [Our] editors scour hundreds of newspapers, magazines, and Web sites, searching for the most intriguing stories and the most thoughtful commentary — left, right, and everything in between." The following essay by the magazine's editorial board argues that the latest computer games are not really games, but "alternative realities in which players can battle monsters, have sex, and stage political rallies. What is life like inside these electronic fantasylands?"

The Week Editorial Board
LIVING IN A VIRTUAL WORLD

■ **Consider before you read.** *To what extent is Second Life "a forum for self-expression"? And what are the ethical questions raised by the game? For example, is it okay to use avatars to do things that you wouldn't do in real life? To do things that are illegal in real life?*

357

> *The latest computer games are not games in a conventional sense, but alternative realities in which players can battle monsters, have sex, and stage political rallies. What is life like inside these electronic fantasylands?*

WHAT ARE VIRTUAL WORLDS?

They are vast, often fantastical digital arenas, populated by the online personas of players who control their own characters while interacting with other players' characters. With ordinary computer games, an individual or a few friends play for a while and then turn the game off. But these "massively multiplayer online games" are experienced by thousands of people at once, and when a player logs off, the game keeps going. The most talked-about new game, *Second Life,* isn't even a game in any traditional sense. It has no prescribed goals and no way to "win" or "lose." Instead, players create their own characters, and anything can happen. During one recent week in *Second Life,* a virtual DJ spun records at a nightclub while a fat man in chaps pole-danced; improbably proportioned women in anti-Bush T-shirts staged an anti-war rally; and a gaggle of Elvis impersonators opened their own church.

HOW IS THIS ALL POSSIBLE?

Second Life lets users design their own avatars — online representations of themselves, which can be human, animal, or other. Its software also allows them to build anything they dream up. Some create private tropical villas, others public amusement parks. When "residents" meet online, they chat by typing words that appear on-screen, and enter commands to make their avatars move and gesture in ways that make them seem more like real people. Worldwide, some 15 million people spend at least part of their lives inside these 3-D virtual worlds. The most popular game, *World of Warcraft,* is a Tolkien-esque adventure in which players become elves or druids and team up to battle monsters and collect treasure. In a testament to the bonds people form online, when one player died recently in real life, his teammates held a virtual funeral. The solemn event on a snow-swept lakeshore moved some players to tears — until a rival clan descended on the mourners and slaughtered them.

WHY DO PEOPLE DO SUCH THINGS?

Many see environments such as *Second Life* as a forum for self-expression and exper-imentation. Musicians Suzanne Vega and Jay-Z have performed virtual concerts, using avatars that mimic them while they play live sets. Former Virginia Gov. Mark Warner held a town meeting. One American Indian man built a traditional village to educate people about his tribe. Edward Castronova, author of *Synthetic Worlds: The Business and Culture of Online Games,* believes virtual worlds can be used to experiment with social ideas. What if, say, Karl Marx had been able to test-drive his theories? Castronova wonders. He could have set up a world in which workers owned the virtual "means of production" and observed what ensued. But the most striking thing about the virtual world is the behavior it seems to unleash.

WHAT'S IT LIKE IN THERE?

It can get downright bizarre. Ordinary people indulge in activities they never would, or could, do in real life, from flying through space to dancing with total strangers. That's the tame stuff. Sex is commonplace, as is prostitution, and the virtual shenanigans can involve multiple partners, physically impossible bondage gear, and anthropomorphic animals. (*Second Life* is restricted to people over 18.) Critics have raised concerns about activities that would be illegal in the real world, such as the brothel that features rape fantasies, or people who indulge in sex acts using avatars that resemble children. But *Second Life* aficionados cherish the anything-goes ethic. "People have been playing Daddy and his little girl forever, as fantasy role-play in the bedroom," says a 35-year-old librarian who, as her 13-year-old avatar "Emily Semaphore," manages a *Second Life* club called Jailbait. Banning this in *Second Life,* she says, would be penalizing a "sexual thought crime."

ISN'T IT ALL FAIRLY HARMLESS?

Some psychologists worry that dangerous or perverted online personas could spill into the real world. Others have raised concerns about online addiction. Ohio psychologist Marty Traver says he's had several patients tell him that *World of Warcraft* was taking over their lives. "When clients started talking about gaming," Traver says, "I thought they meant gambling." Some people play their favorite interactive games for up to 40 hours a week, skipping meals and social engage-ments. In July, the first rehab clinic exclusively for online game addicts opened in Amsterdam. "They have troubles in school and have isolated themselves completely from the outside world," says clinic director Keith Bakker. Gamers respond that they spend less time playing than most Americans spend watching television, while experiencing more human interaction.

WHERE WILL THIS ALL LEAD?

It's anyone's guess, since it's such uncharted territory. But Mitch Kapor, CEO of Linden Lab, the company that created *Second Life,* believes the game, or something like it, has the potential to fundamentally change how humans interact. At a minimum, he says, it could be as revolutionary as the personal computer and the Internet. When people can meet anyone, go anywhere, and do anything in a realistic 3-D environment, he says, why would they continue to work and play on a two-dimensional computer desktop? "Spending part of your day in a virtual world will become commonplace," he says — and may even "accelerate the social evolution of humanity."

■ **Discuss.** *Do you agree with the Linden Lab CEO that spending time in a virtual world can "accelerate the social evolution of humanity"? Why or why not?*

■ **Write.** *Write a brief essay in which you address the following questions: What makes* Second Life *so popular among its users? What do users value about the* Second Life *environment? Alternately, you might want to consider the economic life within* Second Life*. For example, why would businesses invest in this virtual space? Why do users spend money there?*

 **CONSIDER THE CLUSTER**
Cyberspace

■ Message

What differences does Noah D. Zatz find between physical and electronic space? Do you think he considers the differences to be more critical than the similarities? Make a list of the key differences and similarities. Do you think Jonathan Koppell and Noah Zatz are basically in agreement about the "reality" of cyberspace? Can you detect any fundamental differences between their assessments of both spaces?

■ Method

Note that Zatz's classification system is largely abstract. How does he help you visualize the concepts of distance, adjacency, and fixity? Why do you think he titles this section of his essay "Mapping Physical and Electronic Space"? In what sense is he mapping — or is that, as Koppell might argue, itself only a metaphor?

■ Medium

"One reason that cyberspace is described as a place," says Koppell, "is to avoid downgrading it to the status of a mere medium." Is that what Koppell believes it is? If so, in what way would the Internet be a medium rather than a place? In what sense would thinking about cyberspace as a medium be a "downgrading"? In your opinion, is the Internet a medium like television? Or is it something much different? In an essay, discuss *Second Life* using the criteria described in Zatz's and Koppell's selections.

WRITE

1. **Create a memoir.** Using John Edgar Wideman's "First Shot" (p. 303) as a model, write a short autobiographical narrative that describes as accurately as possible the precise place where you did something for the first time. Choose an event, as Wideman does, that would come to have significance for you over time. For example, basketball came to be an extremely important part of his life.

2. **Analyze.** Will Wright considers the creativity of video games in terms of "possibility space." Do you think he would evaluate *Second life* in similar terms? In an essay, carefully consider the idea of what a "game" is. When is something a game, and when is it not? Is *Second Life* a video game in the same way as is Wright's *The Sims*? In your essay, consider whether games could evolve to such an extent that they would cease to be games.

3. **Compare and evaluate.** Both Nicole Lamy in "Life in Motion" (p. 291) and Judith Ortiz Cofer in "Silent Dancing" (p. 68) write personal essays in which they review their lives in relation to visual material — Lamy's photographs and Cofer's home movie. What similarities are there between the essays? In an essay of your own, discuss how visual material can be introduced in writing. Do you think

it always enhances the text? For example, should some stills from Cofer's home movie have been included with her essay? Remember, when Lamy's essay was first published, it did not feature the photographs. Which essayist is better at handling visual information? What standards would you use to make this evaluation? Consider, too, which writer is more influenced by visual media in constructing her essay.

4. **Collaborate and make a case.** Artists and travel writers are often accused of trying to make places more appealing or glamorous than they truly are — that is, of "romanticizing" them. Why do you think they do this? In a small group, find a selection in this chapter (or in the book as a whole) in which you think the author or artist has romanticized a place. Do you think N. Scott Momaday (p. 316) romanticizes the Kiowa landscapes? Does Bill Bamberger (p. 298) do the same in his photographs of first-time home owners?

5. **Evaluate and make a case.** Consider Mitch Epstein's "Cocoa Beach, Florida, 1983" (p. 323). How does your eye process that photograph? In an essay, discuss the photo. What information do you think Epstein wants it to convey? How is the picture angled and structured to best convey that

information? After studying the photograph detail by detail, describe any information you found that you did not process at first but rather sensed, perhaps subconsciously. Did you screen out some details when you initially looked at the photo? Try to articulate the process by which certain subconscious elements eventually became part of your conscious interpretation. This exercise could be applied also to Lynda Barry's graphic essay on imagination.

6. **Research and make a case.** The ad for Yahoo! (p. 347) plays on the idea that the Internet offers places to stay (like a hotel) where you meet new friends or romantic partners (who tell you that you look cute today). Using specific examples of sites that offer communities, write an essay about whether or not the Internet is "a nice place to stay." Do the groups that exist in chat rooms or other virtual communities indeed share a sense of place and connection? Or is the medium, as some people have claimed, always one of isolation, one where people actually interact less than they would without it?

7. **Create a space.** After reading the cluster introduction to "Sacred Spaces" (p. 314) and after considering the selections, try this thought experi-

ment: What do you think would be the *opposite* of a sacred space? In a short essay, try describing one such space. Alternately, you could sketch it out or represent it graphically through collage. Would it necessarily be a public site? Can you provide a concrete example? Can you find examples of such spaces in this chapter or elsewhere in the book?

8. **Research.** As explained at the start of this chapter, the word "cyberspace" was coined by novelist William Gibson, author of the 1984 science fiction novel *Neuromancer*. Locate a copy of the novel and read it; then, in a research paper, discuss the significance of that term to Gibson's novel. What particular meaning does it have in the novel? How is the word mainly used today? Has its meaning changed? Do you view cyberspace as a real place or an imaginary one? Explain, using screen shots from this book or the web to support your points.

9. **Evaluate.** Imagine that you are in film school and a group of your classmates has decided, after reading John Edgar Wideman's "First Shot" (p. 303), to make a short documentary of the event. How would you go about doing this? What details of the essay would you select to expand? Would

you eliminate anything? At what moment would you begin? How would you conclude? Would you introduce Wideman himself into the film? How many characters would you need? Would your film's general tone be realistic, gritty, or poetic? Would you shoot in color or black and white? What dialogue, if any, would you include? Form several small groups, and after breaking the essay down into approximately ten "shots," briefly describe in the outline form of a rough script or a storyboard what each shot would look like so that someone could visualize the sequence and imagery of your short film.

10. **Collaborate and compare.** Consider Pico Iyer's "Nowhere Man" (p. 327) and Brent Staples's "Just Walk on By" (p. 331) in relation to each other and to the excerpt to Noah D. Zatz's "Sidewalks in Cyberspace" (p. 352). After reading the essays, work in small groups to collaboratively construct a working definition of "public space." Try to articulate a brief definition — several sentences long — that will account for all the kinds of spaces that you agree belong to that category. For example, can the Internet be considered public space? Afterward, the groups can compare definitions and discuss their relative inclusiveness and effectiveness.

4

MAKING HISTORY

As Americans, we seem to toggle between two diametrically opposed attitudes toward history. On the one hand, we feel that history is — as the industrialist Henry Ford once said — "more or less bunk." This dismissive attitude encapsulated the sentiment of a young, pragmatic nation that believed in the unlimited promise of future progress and the futility of dwelling on the past. Today, educators and professional historians regularly complain about the average citizen's woeful lack of historical knowledge, often referring to it as a "national amnesia."

On the other hand, why is the History Channel one of the country's most successful cable TV stations? Founded in 1995 and running twenty-four hours a day, with almost all original programming, the channel reaches nearly eighty million households. Its managers believe that they have tapped into a phenomenal surge in historical interest, and the ratings prove it. Add to this the enormous popularity of historical films such as *Flags of Our Fathers, The Patriot, Gladiator,* and *The Passion of the Christ,* and it seems reasonable to conclude that, despite the concerns of educators, we have an almost obsessive interest in history, both our own and the world's.

Historians, however, may argue that public interest in historical programs and movies only proves their point: what Americans want is not genuine history but history packaged as popular entertainment. If you distort the facts, play fast and loose with accuracy, introduce box-office stars, and invent a romantic relationship to drive a story line, then the public might digest a few spoonfuls of history. But does anyone really believe that what actually occurred during the *Titanic*'s fateful cruise bears any resemblance to what happens in the film, with its fabricated love story and facile moralizing? The commercial pressure to entertain a large audience, many historians argue, inevitably leads to caricature and oversimplification. History then becomes just another commodity. In fact, the History Channel capitalizes on its popularity and familiar logo by selling a variety of merchandise, from videotapes to home furnishings.

Given that the past has vanished, how do we accurately recover it? How can we capture what it was like to live in another time? Films, photographs, and preserved or restored sites can offer some sense of the texture of the past — and some blockbusters budget astronomically for sets and costumes, trying to make us feel the physical presence of the past — but the problem with trying to encounter an authentic past is that history, even just yesterday's, can only be imagined. It cannot truly be relived because for that to occur, the past itself would need to become present, a condition that so far remains only within the realm of science fiction. This basic, insurmountable fact leads to a substantial amount of historical distortion, no matter what the medium. We see actors in films set in Elizabethan times displaying the cosmetically bright smiles of modern dentistry, while also speaking, gesturing, and behaving like contemporary Americans. We visit ancient sites wearing audio-tour headsets. We visit restored eighteenth-century villages equipped with wheelchair ramps and smoke detectors, and we find signs that no individual from that era could possibly make sense of: No Smoking, Restrooms, Ye Olde Gift Shoppe.

IN CONGRESS, JULY 4, 1776.

DECLARATION
BY THE REPRESENTATIVES OF THE
ITED STATES OF AMERICA,
IN GENERAL CONGRESS ASSEMBLED.

W   HEN in the Courfe of human Events, it becomes neceffary for one People to diffolve the Political Bands which have connected them with another, and to affume among the Powers of the Earth, the feparate and equal Station to which the Laws of Nature and of Nature's God entitle them, a decent Refpect to the Opinions of Mankind requires that they fhould declare the caufes which impel them to the Separation.
    We hold thefe Truths to be felf-evident, that all Men are created equal, that they are endowed by their Creator with certain unalienable Rights, that among thefe are Life, Liberty, and the Purfuit of Happinefs--That to fecure thefe Rights, Governments are inftituted among Men, deriving their juft Powers from the Confent of the Governed, that whenever any Form of Government becomes deftructive of thefe Ends, it is the Right of the People to alter or to abolifh it, and to inftitute new Government, laying its Foundation on fuch Principles, and organizing its Powers in fuch Form, as to them fhall feem moft likely to effect their Safety and Happinefs. Prudence, indeed, will dictate that Governments long eftablifhed fhould not be changed for light and tranfient Caufes; and accordingly all Experience hath fhewn, that Mankind are more difpofed to fuffer, while Evils are fufferable, than to right themfelves by abolifhing the Forms to which they are accuftomed. But when a long Train of Abufes and Ufurpations, purfuing invariably the fame Object, evinces a Defign to reduce them under abfolute Defpotifm, it is their Right, it is their Duty, to throw off fuch Government,

Because we are locked into our shared present, it is virtually impossible to know the past. This is true not only of our material re-creations of history but of our interpretive renditions as well. We read popular romances, some set in medieval or even ancient Europe, whose heroines are miraculously endowed with the insights and values of contemporary feminism. Some historians believe that this single-perspectivism is unavoidable, that objectivity is unattainable or possibly even politically sinister. For them, the chief task of history is to understand the present by learning how we arrived at where we are. Other historians believe that they have an obligation to suspend (or multiply) their own viewpoints and get as close as possible to the mind-set of another era. The great Dutch scholar Johan Huizinga wrote that historians must constantly put themselves "at a point in the past at which the known factors will seem to permit different outcomes." After all, those who fought at the battle of Gettysburg did not know how it would end.

To what extent is the history we see, hear, know, or read objective and reliable? And to what extent is it biased and fabricated? These are questions that every educated citizen asks at one time or another, whether watching a television documentary, enjoying a movie, reading a historical novel, visiting a museum, or touring a restored colonial town. How much should contemporary attitudes affect how history is portrayed? Should the protection of the natural environment stand in the way of preventing a restoration of a famous historical site? What part should multicultural sensitivities play in our reconstructions of history? That is, in the interests of truth and accuracy, should old enemies be depicted in the racist fashion they once were? Does "softening" the picture so as not to offend distort the record?

As more visual information becomes increasingly available and as new electronic technologies make factual data more accessible than ever before, the line between popular and academic history may grow even fuzzier. Over time, the movie versions of events, it seems, become as attached to those events as do any of the legitimate historical sources and documents; for some critics and historians, Vietnam films such as *The Deer Hunter*, *Apocalypse Now*, *Platoon*, or *Full Metal Jacket* are as much a part of our collective Vietnam experience as the My Lai massacre (see p. 440) or the evacuation of Saigon. The Internet has also opened historical "channels" that allow many people outside the customary academic or publishing hierarchies to put their own (or their community's) memories, stories, documents, and images on public record. Although this still leaves us with the obligation to sift the significant from the trivial or the factual from the fictive, it nevertheless advances the possibility of what socially minded historians have long been calling for: a less elitist history, a "history from below."

Whatever approach we take to history — whether we view it as an interpretation of the present, a reconstruction of the past, or a prophetic window into the future — it will continue to exert a powerful presence in our lives. We can now safely say that Henry Ford's famous dictum is self-refuting "bunk" — if it had been correct, it would not have been remembered. And we can also safely say that history's power can be the source of great understanding or great misery. Three months before he blew up the Alfred P. Murrah Federal Building in Oklahoma City in 1995, Timothy McVeigh — who viewed history as prophesy — wrote to the American Legion: "Does anyone even STUDY history anymore???"

COMPOSING AMERICA

■ **Cluster menu: Composing America**

The Library of Congress is a repository for many important documents that are
almost synonymous with the United States of America: the Declaration of
Independence, the Emancipation Proclamation, the Bill of Rights. We tend to
think of such official statements as polished manifestos created by a united government. Each of these documents, however, represents a composition: an argument or statement drafted first by one person, then revised by committee. This
cluster considers the history of the composition of two of America's most precious

historical documents, the Declaration of Independence and the Gettysburg Address. Anyone can view the Declaration at the National Archives in Washington, D.C. Yet many citizens who visit this iconic display are unaware that the impressive document in front of them is not the original Declaration, but rather the third, calligraphic, "official" version. Essays by Thomas Starr and James Munves reconstruct the history of this founding document and the implications and impact of the medium of its delivery — whether longhand, typography, or calligraphy. A PowerPoint presentation that converts another priceless document, the Gettysburg Address, into bulleted talking points invites us to consider our evolving ideas about effective composition and presentation.

369

Three Declarations. *From left to right:* draft, print, calligraphy. Jefferson's hand-corrected draft was rushed to printer John Dunlap, who typeset the broadside that was published throughout the colonies. Most Americans at the time who were politically informed and persuaded by the Declaration saw only the typeset text (the middle document). On the right is a facsimile of the calligraphic, "official" document that we know today as the iconic Declaration. (*draft*: Library of Congress, negative #LC-MSS 27748-i; *broadside*: Courtesy of The Massachusetts Historical Society; *calligraphy*: National Archives)

A Declaration by the Representatives of the UNITED STATES OF AMERICA, in General Congress assembled.

When in the course of human events it becomes necessary for one people to dissolve the political bands which have connected them with another, and to assume among the powers of the earth the separate and equal station to which the laws of nature & of nature's god entitle them, a decent respect to the opinions of mankind requires that they should declare the causes which impel them to the separation.

We hold these truths to be self-evident, that all men are created equal, that they are endowed by their creator with inherent & inalienable rights, that among these are life, liberty, & the pursuit of happiness; that to secure these rights, governments are instituted among men, deriving their just powers from the consent of the governed; that whenever any form of government becomes destructive of these ends, it is the right of the people to alter or to abolish it, & to institute new government, laying it's foundation on such principles & organising it's powers in such form, as to them shall seem most likely to effect their safety & happiness. prudence indeed will dictate that governments long established should not be changed for light & transient causes: and accordingly all experience hath shewn that mankind are more disposed to suffer while evils are sufferable, than to right themselves by abolishing the forms to which they are accustomed. but when a long train of abuses & usurpations [begun at a distinguished period & pursuing invariably the same object, evinces a design to subject them under absolute Despotism, it is their right, it is their duty, to throw off such government & to provide new guards for their future security. such has been the patient sufferance of these colonies; & such is now the necessity which constrains them to expunge their former systems of government. the history of the present king of Great Britain is a history of unremitting injuries and usurpations, among which appears no solitary fact to contradict the uniform tenor of the rest, all of which have in direct object the establishment of an absolute tyranny over these states. to prove this, let facts be submitted to a candid world, for the truth of which we pledge a faith yet unsullied by falsehood.

IN CONGRE

A DECLA

BY THE REPRESEN

UNITED STATE

IN GENERAL CON

WHEN in the Course of human Events, it becomes nece with another, and to assume among the Powers of the Nature's God entitle them, a decent Respect to the Opin to the Separation.

WE hold these Truths to be self-evident, that all unalienable Rights, that among these are Life, Liberty instituted among Men, deriving their just Powers from the Consent of the G Ends, it is the Right of the People to alter or to abolish it, and to institut its Powers in such Form, as to them shall seem most likely to effect their Safe tablished should not be changed for light and transient Causes; and according Evils are sufferable, than to right themselves by abolishing the Forms to which ing invariably the same Object, evinces a Design to reduce them under absolute and to provide new Guards for their future Security. Such has been the patien them to alter their former Systems of Government. The History of the pres having in direct Object the Establishment of an absolute Tyranny over these States.

HE has refused his Assent to Laws, the most wholesome and necessary for the

HE has forbidden his Governors to pass Laws of immediate and pressing Imp and when so suspended, he has utterly neglected to attend to them.

HE has refused to pass other Laws for the Accommodation of large Districts the Legislature, a Right inestimable to them, and formidable to Tyrants only.

HE has called together Legislative Bodies at Places unusual, uncomfortable, a fatiguing them into Compliance with his Measures.

HE has dissolved Representative Houses repeatedly, for opposing with manly

HE has refused for a long Time, after such Dissolutions, to cause others to be turned to the People at large for their exercise; the State remaining in the mean ti

HE has endeavoured to prevent the Population of these States; for that Purpose encourage their Migrations hither, and raising the Conditions of new Appropr

HE has obstructed the Administration of Justice, by refusing his Assent to Law

HE has made Judges dependent on his Will alone, for the Tenure of their Of

HE has erected a Multitude of new Offices, and sent hither Swarms of Officers

HE has kept among us, in Times of Peace, Standing Armies, without the co

HE has affected to render the Military independent of and superior to the Civil

HE has combined with others to subject us to a Jurisdiction foreign to our Con pretended Legislation:

FOR quartering large Bodies of Armed Troops among us:

FOR protecting them, by a mock Trial, from Punishment for any Murders wh

FOR cutting off our Trade with all Parts of the World:

FOR imposing Taxes on us without our Consent:

FOR depriving us, in many Cases, of the Benefits of Trial by Jury:

FOR transporting us beyond Seas to be tried for pretended Offences:

FOR abolishing the free System of English Laws in a neighbouring Province, as to render it at once an Example and fit Instrument for introducing the same ab

FOR taking away our Charters, abolishing our most valuable Laws, and alterin

FOR suspending our own Legislatures, and declaring themselves invested with

HE has abdicated Government here, by declaring us out of his Protection and

HE has plundered our Seas, ravaged our Coasts, burnt our Towns, and destro

HE is, at this Time, transporting large Armies of foreign Mercenaries to con cumstances of Cruelty and Perfidy, scarcely paralleled in the most barbarous Age

HE has constrained our fellow Citizens taken Captive on the high Seas to bear Brethren, or to fall themselves by their Hands.

HE has excited domestic Insurrections amongst us, and has endeavoured to brin known Rule of Warfare, is an undistinguished Destruction, of all Ages, Sexes and C

IN every stage of these Oppressions we have Petitioned for Redress in the most ed Injury. A Prince, whose Character is thus marked by every act which may de

NOR have we been wanting in Attentions to our British Brethren. We have w unwarrantable Jurisdiction over us. We have reminded them of the Circumstances Justice and Magnanimity, and we have conjured them by the Ties of our common Connections and Correspondence. They too have been deaf to the Voice of Justice denounces our Separation, and hold them, as we hold the rest of Mankind, Enem

WE, therefore, the Representatives of the UNITED STATES O pealing to the Supreme Judge of the World for the Rectitude of our Intentions, d lemnly Publish and Declare, That these United Colonies are, and of Right ought absolved from all Allegiance to the British Crown, and that all political Connecti solved; and that as FREE AND INDEPENDENT STATES, they Commerce, and to do all other Acts and Things which INDEPENDENT firm Reliance on the Protection of divine Providence, we mutually pledge to each o

Signed by ORDER and i.

JOHN H

ATTEST.
CHARLES THOMSON, SECRETARY.

PHILADELPHIA: PRIN

IN CONGRESS, JULY 4, 1776.

The unanimous Declaration of the thirteen united States of America.

S, JULY 4, 1776.

RATION

TIVES OF THE

OF AMERICA,

ESS ASSEMBLED.

e People to dissolve the Political Bands which have connected them
separate and equal Station to which the Laws of Nature and of
kind requires that they should declare the causes which impel them

reated equal, that they are endowed by their Creator with certain
ursuit of Happiness—That to secure these Rights, Governments are
t whenever any Form of Government becomes destructive of these
ernment, laying its Foundation on such Principles, and organizing
piness. Prudence, indeed, will dictate that Governments long es-
rience hath shewn, that Mankind are more disposed to suffer, while
ormed. But when a long Train of Abuses and Usurpations, pursuit is their Right, it is their Duty, to throw off such Government, while
of these Colonies; and such is now the Necessity which constrains
Great-Britain is a History of repeated Injuries and Usurpations, all
o this, let Facts be submitted to a candid World.

less suspended in their Operation till his Assent should be obtained;

unless those People would relinquish the Right of Representation in

rom the Depository of their public Records, for the sole Purpose of

is Invasions on the Rights of the People.

whereby the Legislative Powers, incapable of Annihilation, have re-

all the Dangers of Invasion from without, and Convulsions within.

the Laws for Naturalization of Foreigners; refusing to pass others

ishing Judiciary Powers.

e Amount and Payment of their Salaries.

r People, and eat out their Substance.

r Legislatures.

and unacknowledged by our Laws; giving his Assent to their Acts of

should commit on the Inhabitants of these States:

therein an arbitrary Government, and enlarging its Boundaries, so
nto these Colonies:
ntally the Forms of our Governments:
islate for us in all Cases whatsoever.
r against us.
es of our People.
Works of Death, Desolation, and Tyranny, already begun with cir-
ly unworthy the Head of a civilized Nation.
st their Country, to become the Executioners of their Friends and
nhabitants of our Frontiers, the merciless Indian Savages, whose

Terms: Our repeated Petitions have been answered only by repeat-
ant, is unfit to be the Ruler of a free People.
from Time to Time of Attempts by their Legislature to extend an
migration and Settlement here. We have appealed to their native
o disavow these Usurpations, which, would inevitably interrupt our
nsanguinity. We must, therefore, acquiesce in the Necessity, which
n Peace, Friends.

ERICA, in GENERAL CONGRESS, Assembled, ap-
Name, and by Authority of the good People of these Colonies, so-
REE AND INDEPENDENT STATES; that they are
them and the State of Great-Britain, is and ought to be totally dis-
Power to levy War, conclude Peace, contract Alliances, establish
s may of right do. And for the support of this Declaration, with
ives, our Fortunes, and our sacred Honor.

ALF of the CONGRESS,

NCOCK, PRESIDENT.

JOHN DUNLAP.

Thomas Starr, *The Real Declaration.* Thomas Starr, an associate professor of graphic design at Northeastern University, points out that the "official" handwritten document on display appeared some two months after a hastily printed version was distributed throughout the thirteen colonies. Why did the Continental Congress commission a calligraphic version in the first place? What does that decision say about democracy? (From *The Boston Globe,* June 29, 2003, p. D5)

Thomas Starr

THE REAL DECLARATION

■ **Consider before you read.** *How is Starr trying to change our thinking about the form of the Declaration of Independence? Why does it matter how the words that make up the Declaration look on the page?*

THIS WEEK, AS WE celebrate our country's independence, the Declaration of Independence itself is notably absent from the festivities. The National Archives[1] is closed while the document's display is being renovated. Does it matter that we are unable to see it?

At a time when the United States is attempting to spread democracy abroad, the Declaration's promise of "life, liberty, and the pursuit of happiness" seems more important than ever. We uphold the iconic calligraphy on parchment as the very document that expresses the principles on which our country is based. But in fact, that document expresses something quite different.

In early June 1776, Thomas Jefferson, Benjamin Franklin, John Adams, Robert R. Livingston, and Roger Sherman were appointed by the Continental Congress to collectively prepare a declaration on independence. Jefferson composed the text. It was revised by committee members before being presented to Congress on June 28. Although the vote for independence took place on July 2, the entire Congress then spent two days deleting a third of the text and making 39 additions and alterations. The text completed on July 4, like the government of the country it founded, was a collective effort.

The manuscript, which must have been so heavily edited as to be almost indecipherable, was sent that day to a typographer, not a calligrapher. John Dunlap, printer to Congress, took on what was surely the most important overnight printing job in history. The "Dunlap prints" were sent to the colonies, where they were often reset in type and republished locally. No holiday is more specific about its date than "the Fourth." What we commemorate that day is the first complete assembly of the Declaration's words, in type.

The work of declaring independence throughout the 13 colonies was the work of either a Dunlap print or one of its typographic descendants. Within two weeks the typographic text had already been republished in 24 newspapers, including two in Boston on July 18. That same day, at 1 P.M., the Declaration

■ **Consider.** *Why do we celebrate independence on the day of the printing of the Declaration and not on the day that it was signed? What does that suggest about the origins of the holiday or its purpose?*

372

---

[1]Note that the closing of the National Archives occurred in 2003; the Declaration of Independence is back on display.

was proclaimed from the balcony of what is now the Old State House, an event reenacted each July 4th at 10 A.M.

The calligraphic document was created only afterward; it was ordered on July 19 and not completed and signed until August 2. In 1776, Congress used calligraphy as a formalizing medium to add legitimacy to its most important papers, a tradition left over from monarchy. Publishing in type, however, was the medium of democracy. It is contradictory, then, that the symbol of our independence is the regal calligraphic document, rather than the humble, pluralistic Dunlap prints.

Calligraphy reveres the hand of the author by idealizing handwriting, which is not uniformly legible to readers. Typography idealizes and standardizes the letters of the alphabet, making them more accessible. Calligraphy implies a single author, and the product of the calligrapher is a singular document. Typography easily accommodates and assumes multiple authorship by merging many collaborators and edits into a seamless whole; type exists to produce multiple documents. Calligraphy is exclusive, elite, and vulnerable to loss or destruction; the calligraphic Declaration is now so faded that it is completely unreadable, more an image than a text. Typography is inherently plural and democratic. And because they are multiples, typeset texts are difficult to lose or destroy.

Collectivity is the essence of a democracy. The Declaration was collective in authorship, audience, and content. Its authors worked collaboratively and as representatives of others. Its audience comprised inhabitants of 13 distinct colonies distributed over a wide area. Its content fused readers into a union of equals. Its form of identical typographic prints perfectly reflected this. To underscore the role of typographic publication, Congress included it among its alterations to the Declaration: "We therefore . . . solemnly *publish* and declare . . . "

This July 4, as in 1776, all Americans are in equality with the Declaration. None of us will have access to the icon. But we all have equal access to the text. Through typography it remains ubiquitous, readily available to every American. We can find it in our homes in encyclopedias and almanacs. It is in libraries and bookstores. And, of course, it can be printed endlessly from the Web.

In January 1776, an ordinary citizen published a pamphlet that turned the tide of public sentiment in favor of independence. Thomas Paine's "Common Sense," which sold 100,000 copies that year alone — the equivalent of 9 million copies in contemporary America — paved the way for Congress to act that summer. Today, with technology on our desks that would be the envy of John Dunlap, we can all join in the collective debate that is democracy. We are all typographers and printers.

373

■ **Discuss.** *Starr enumerates the ways in which calligraphy is inferior to print. Can you think of any problems that come with typography? We assume that print is less personal to the author than handwriting, but does it have other drawbacks?*

■ **Write.** *Starr issues a challenge at the end of his essay. Write a response to his suggestion that "we can all join in the collective debate that is democracy." Do you agree with him that this debate is still closely tied to printing? How would you (or do you) use the medium of print for political purposes?*

James Munves, *Going to Press*. Thomas Jefferson began working on the first draft of the Declaration in June 1776. By the end of the month, he submitted it to a small committee (which included Benjamin Franklin and John Adams) for revision before it went to the entire Continental Congress, which made major changes. It was that manuscript — full of deletions, additions, and alterations — that went to the printer on July 4, 1776. In "Going to Press," James Munves provides a narrative history of the document's transformation from manuscript to print to calligraphy. Munves has written numerous historical narratives for young adults and older audiences; his most recent publication is *The Kent State Coverup* (2001). He has also written a novel, *Andes Rising* (1999). This chapter is reprinted from his book on the Declaration's composition, *Thomas Jefferson and the Declaration of Independence* (1978).

James Munves

GOING TO PRESS

■ **Consider before you read.** *Munves goes into great detail about the days immediately preceding and following the publication of the Declaration. Which of these details surprise you most? What parts of this very familiar story did you not know?*

There is no record of which of the five committee members went to the shop of John Dunlap to oversee the printing. Was it Jefferson, Adams, or that old printer and former employer of John Dunlap's uncle William, Benjamin Franklin? The printing was a rush job. As propaganda, the Declaration would be treated as a broadside (poster) printed on one side of a sheet of paper for display, with capital letters used to attract attention rather than in accordance with grammatical rules.

The rules of grammar in the eighteenth century were, in any case, not as firmly fixed as they are now. Nouns were capitalized haphazardly for emphasis. Jefferson went to the other extreme and used capital letters very sparingly — only at the beginnings of paragraphs and in the names of nations (Great Britain) or peoples (Indians). He used even fewer capital letters than we do today (leaving even *god* in lowercase). With all this, his style was closer to what came later than that of his contemporaries.

In setting the Declaration in type, Dunlap first of all put a new heading at the top:

IN CONGRESS, JULY 4, 1776.

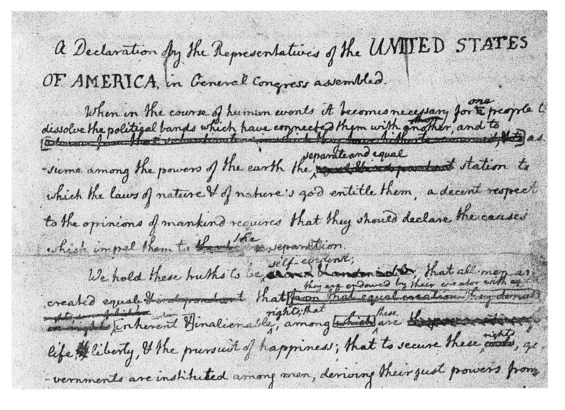

Draft Declaration of Independence (detail). Thomas Jefferson was assigned the job of drafting the Declaration by the Continental Congress. Here you see the numerous edits and additions — eighty-six in all — that were made by John Adams, Benjamin Franklin, and the other members of the committee. This is the document that was delivered to the printer for an overnight rush job. (Library of Congress, negative #LC-MSS 27748–i)

In the body of the Declaration, Dunlap capitalized the entire first word of each paragraph and the first letter of most of the nouns. He also got rid of the ampersands (&), spelling out *and* in all cases. . . .

Dunlap's apprentice dipped the leather roller into the greasy ink and squeaked it across the type. Paper was put into position, and the printer pulled the lever. The proof was examined, corrections were made, and the press run began, powered by the brawny arms of the apprentice.

The following morning a copy was glued into the Journal of Congress and others were dispatched to the states and to the troops in the field. The next day, Saturday, July 6, the Declaration appeared in a Philadelphia newspaper, the *Evening Post*.

IN CONGRESS, JULY 4, 1776.
A DECLARATION
BY THE REPRESENTATIVES OF THE
UNITED STATES OF AMERICA,
IN GENERAL CONGRESS ASSEMBLED.

WHEN in the Courſe of human Events, it becomes neceſſary for one People to diſſolve the Political Bands which have connected them with another, and to aſſume among the Powers of the Earth, the ſeparate and equal Station to which the Laws of Nature and of Nature's God entitle them, a decent Reſpect to the Opinions of Mankind requires that they ſhould declare the cauſes which impel them to the Separation.

We hold theſe Truths to be ſelf-evident, that all Men are created equal, that they are endowed by their Creator with certain unalienable Rights, that among theſe are Life, Liberty, and the Purſuit of Happineſs—That to ſecure theſe Rights, Governments are inſtituted among Men, deriving their juſt Powers from the Conſent of the Governed, that whenever any Form of Government becomes deſtructive of theſe Ends, it is the Right of the People to alter or to aboliſh it, and to inſtitute new Government, laying its Foundation on ſuch Principles, and organizing its Powers in ſuch Form, as to them ſhall ſeem moſt-likely to effect their Safety and Happineſs. Prudence, indeed, will dictate that Governments long eſtabliſhed ſhould not be changed for light and tranſient Cauſes; and accordingly all Experience hath ſhewn, that Mankind are more diſpoſed to ſuffer, while Evils are ſufferable, than to right themſelves by aboliſhing the Forms to which they are accuſtomed. But when a long Train of Abuſes and Uſurpations, purſuing invariably the ſame Object, evinces a Deſign to reduce them under abſolute Deſpotiſm, it is their Right, it is their Duty, to throw off ſuch Government, and to provide new Guards for their future Security. Such has been the patient Sufferance of theſe Colonies; and ſuch is now the Neceſſity which conſtrains them to alter their former Syſtems of Government. The Hiſtory of the preſent King of Great-Britain is a Hiſtory of repeated Injuries and Uſurpations, all having in direct Object the Eſtabliſhment of an abſolute Tyranny over theſe States. To prove this, let Facts be ſubmitted to a candid World.

HE has refuſed his Aſſent to Laws, the moſt wholeſome and neceſſary for the public Good.

Broadside Declaration of Independence (detail). John Dunlap, the printer, added the new heading at the top of the document: "In Congress, July 4, 1776." This is what we celebrate on Independence Day — the printing of the Declaration. John Hancock sent a copy of the initial printing to George Washington, who had it read to his assembled troops in New York on July 9. (Courtesy of The Massachusetts Historical Society)

There still had been no celebration. The members of Congress had little enough time for thoughts about their decision, let alone gaiety. They could think only of the fact of independence and its consequences. They made grim jokes about being hanged for treason. "Congress," a New Jersey delegate noted, might soon be "exalted on a high gallows."

On Monday, July 8, the *Pennsylvania Packet* announced, "This day, at twelve o'clock, the Declaration of Independence will be proclaimed at the State House." A small crowd of idlers, unemployed sailors, and a few others gathered around the platform in the State House yard to hear the Declaration read by Colonel John Nixon of the Philadelphia Committee of Safety. Bells were rung all day throughout the city. But the Liberty Bell, then in the State House steeple, probably was not rung. The rickety wooden steeple would have collapsed. The bell had been cast more than twenty years before, to celebrate the fiftieth anniversary of the Pennsylvania Assembly. Its strangely prophetic legend, *Proclaim liberty throughout the land and to the people thereof,* was taken from the Bible

(Leviticus 25, 10). The verse referred to the Hebrew custom of leaving the land idle every half-century.

That evening the Declaration was read again on the Commons, at the head of each battalion of Associators (Philadelphia militia), and there was more celebration. John Adams described the scene to his wife:

> Three cheers rended the welkin [sky]. The battalions paraded . . . and gave us the *feu de joie* [firing of guns in token of joy], notwithstanding the scarcity of powder.

The next evening the Declaration was heard by each brigade of the army in New York, arousing, in Washington's words, "hearty assent" and "warmest approbation." As news of the Declaration spread through the city, a crowd, uncowed by the British fleet — now 130 ships strong — in the harbor, overturned a gilded lead statue of King George III. It was later melted into bullets. Everywhere, in the days that followed, boisterous mobs tore down the symbols of royal authority, whether coats of arms on public buildings or scepters and crowns on the signboards of inns.

Jefferson remained annoyed at the way his Declaration had been edited. He spent many hours making copies of his version to send to Virginia friends to show them what Congress had done to the document. He sent copies to Richard Henry Lee; to the president of the Virginia convention, Edmund Pendleton; to his mentor George Wythe; to his neighbor, the Italian, Philip Mazzei; and probably to his old friend John Page. In some cases, he indicated Congress's changes right on the copies. To Richard Henry Lee, he sent a copy of his final draft along with the Dunlap broadside for comparison. "You will judge," he wrote Lee, "whether it is the better or worse for the Critics."

His friends, as writers' friends are wont to do, sympathized with him. Edmund Pendleton thought that the members of Congress had treated the Declaration just as badly as they had Jefferson's draft of the 1775 Declaration of Causes. They had, Pendleton said, changed it "much for the worse."

Lee wrote back that he wished

> sincerely, as well for the honor of Congress, as for that of the States, that the Manuscript had not been mangled as it is. It is wonderful, and passing pitiful, that the rage of change should be so unhappily applied.

Consolingly, he added that the piece was

> in its nature so good, that no Cookery can spoil the Dish for the palates of Freemen.

The cookery certainly spoiled the dish for the palate of Thomas Jefferson, who put his draft away and scarcely thought about the Declaration for many years. He did, however, along with a number of other members of Congress, sign an ornately hand-lettered (engrossed) copy on August 2, 1776.

377

378

Official Declaration of Independence (detail). Timothy Matlack, who was known for his skill at calligraphy, was given the job of recopying the print version for the "signers." He seems to have run out of room for the long title; he made *of the thirteen united* much smaller so that he could fit *States of America* on one line. (National Archives)

This copy, with the signatures of fifty-five signers, is enshrined in the National Archives in Washington. The engrossing was probably done by one of Secretary Thomson's assistants, Timothy Matlack. Matlack had been assigned the hand-lettering job on July 19, when Congress heard that New York had voted in favor of independence.

The new copy reflected New York's action in its title. The document could now boast that the states were unanimous:

The unanimous Declaration of the thirteen united States of America;

instead of, as before:

A DECLARATION By THE REPRESENTATIVES OF THE UNITED
STATES OF AMERICA, in GENERAL CONGRESS ASSEMBLED.

(In none of its official transformations has the document borne the title *Declaration of Independence*.)

In copying the Declaration, Matlack accidentally left out two letters of one word and also an entire word. He had to correct these omissions with carets and interlining:

> *en*
> He has dissolved Represtative Houses...
> ^

> *only*
> Our repeated petitions have been answeredby. . .
> ^

He also put an extra *t* in *Brittish,* eliminated all the paragraphing, and used capital letters in a completely haphazard fashion. Dunlap, in following broadside usage, had capitalized almost all the nouns. Matlack capitalized some and not others, following no sort of rule at all.

The signers of the Declaration, fearing hanging, kept their names secret. The engrossed, signed parchment copy was carefully hidden away by Charles Thomson. . . .

379

■ **Discuss.** *Munves pays close attention to what might seem like trivial aspects of the Declaration — capitalization, spacing, words omitted or misspelled. Why do you think these become important for Munves? What do they tell us about the document itself and about the culture that produced it?*

■ **Write.** *This essay contains several reminders of how dangerous it was for the Continental Congress to write the Declaration. As Munves points out, the signers "fear[ed] hanging." Why do you think Congress put these fears aside? How do they try to convince the general population that they are right? Reread the document, and then do a close reading of the language used to justify Congress's radical step.*

The Gettysburg Address — the "Nicolay Copy" and Transcript. Before delivering the Gettysburg Address on November 19, 1863, at the famous battlefield in Pennsylvania — a powerful speech that lasted only a couple of minutes — President Abraham Lincoln first drafted what he wanted to say. Shown here is one of the five known manuscripts. Lincoln gave one copy to each of his secretaries, John Nicolay (possibly the first draft) and John Hay (a later draft). Lincoln wrote the other three drafts well after November 19 for charitable purposes.

According to the Library of Congress, which houses the manuscripts, the Nicolay copy, shown here, is believed to be the earliest and is referred to as the "first draft." You can see that the first page of the Nicolay copy is written in ink on stationery from the Executive Mansion (as the White House was then known); the second page is written in pencil on a different type of paper. Scholars theorize that Lincoln began the draft in Washington, D.C., but revised it in Gettysburg on the day before the speech, rewriting the final passage, probably on paper from the home of Judge David Wills, where he was lodging.

Scholars believe that Lincoln created the Hay copy, also known as the "second draft," after the event, upon his return to Washington from Gettysburg. It differs significantly from the Nicolay copy and includes a number of hand edits. Scholars haven't fully explained this, but as the Library of Congress notes, the Nicolay and Hay documents are most closely associated with the final speech — and they are the ones that scholars continue to consult.

380

Abraham Lincoln, *The "Nicolay Copy" of the Gettysburg Address.* Shown ▶ here is the document believed to be Lincoln's first draft of his most famous speech. Notice that different stationery is used for pages one and two and that the second page is written in pencil. These differences suggest that he revised the ending significantly and perhaps worked on the text at different locations. (Library of Congress)

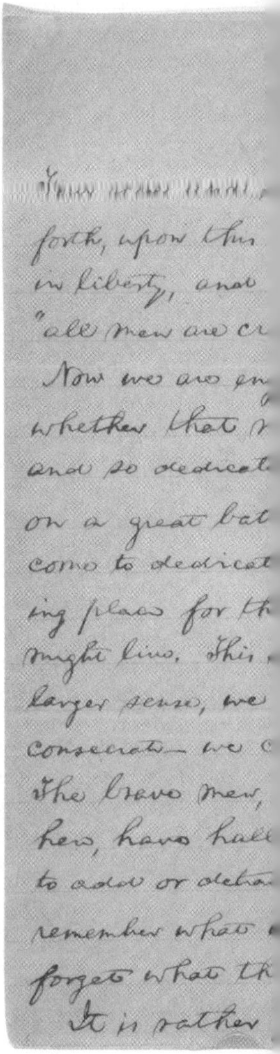

"Nicolay copy," page 1

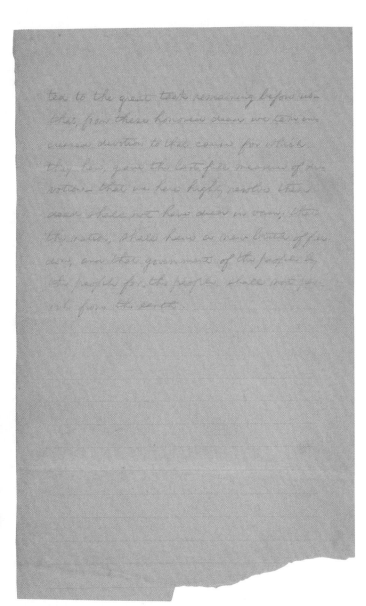

"Nicolay copy," page 2

Abraham Lincoln, *The "Nicolay Copy" of the Gettysburg Address*.
This is a transcript of the draft shown on page 381.

Four score and seven years ago our fathers brought forth, upon this continent, a new nation, conceived in liberty, and dedicated to the proposition that "all men are created equal"

Now we are engaged in a great civil war, testing whether that nation, or any nation so conceived, and so dedicated, can long endure. We are met on a great battle field of that war. We have come to dedicate a portion of it, as a final resting place for those who died here, that the nation might live. This we may, in all propriety do. But, in a larger sense, we can not dedicate — we can not consecrate — we can not hallow, this ground — The brave men, living and dead, who struggled here, have hallowed it, far above our poor power to add or detract. The world will little note, nor long remember what we say here; while it can never forget what they did here.

It is rather for us, the living, we here be dedicated to the great task remaining before us — that, from these honored dead we take increased devotion to that cause for which they here, gave the last full measure of devotion — that we here highly resolve these dead shall not have died in vain; that the nation, shall have a new birth of freedom, and that government of the people by the people for the people, shall not perish from the earth.

Mathew Brady, *Gettysburg, Pennsylvania*. This photo was taken on the occasion of Abraham Lincoln's famous address on November 19, 1863 — just four months after the Civil War's bloodiest battle was fought on these grounds. (National Archives photo no. NWDNS-III-B-0357)

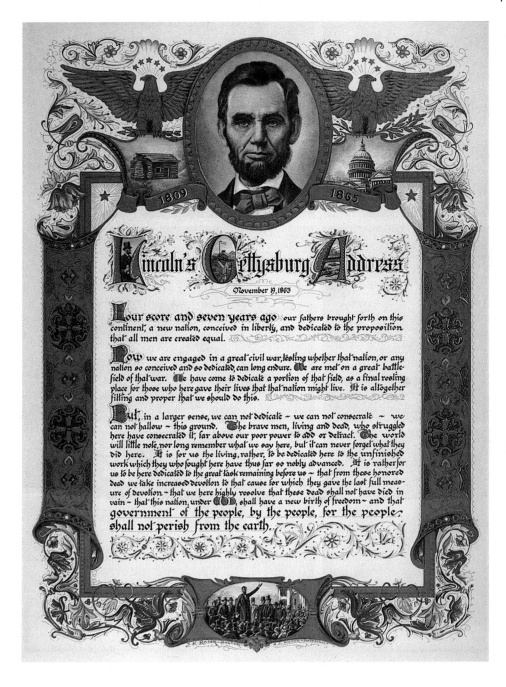

383

Abraham Lincoln, *The Gettysburg Address.* Calligraphy version. (Dr. Joseph N. Nathanson, *Abraham Lincoln Collection,* Rare Books and Special Collections Division, McGill University Library)

384

Gettysburg Cemetery Dedication

Abraham Lincoln

11/19/1863

Agenda

- Met on battlefield (great)
- Dedicate portion of field - fitting!
- Unfinished work (great tasks)

11/19/1863

Not on Agenda!

- Dedicate
- Consecrate
- Hallow
  (in narrow sense)
- Add or detract
- Note or remember what we say

11/19/1863

Review of Key Objectives & Critical Success Factors

- What makes nation unique
  - Conceived in Liberty
  - Men are equal
- Shared vision
  - New birth of freedom
  - Gov't of/for/by the people

11/19/1863

Organizational Overview

1
0.9
0.8
0.7
0.6
0.5
0.4
0.3
0.2
0.1
0
-87   Now
Years

New Nations

11/19/1863

Summary

- New nation
- Civil war
- Dedicate field
- Dedicated to unfinished work
- New birth of freedom
- Government not perish

11/19/1863

Peter Norvig, *A PowerPoint Presentation for the Gettysburg Address*. On these pages, you see two versions of the Gettysburg Address: the calligraphic text of the speech as read by Abraham Lincoln at Gettysburg, and a PowerPoint version created by using the AutoContent Wizard. Try putting the opening of the Declaration of Independence into PowerPoint or any other presentation program: What happens to the message as a result? (Peter Norvig)

CONSIDER THE CLUSTER
Composing America

■ **Message**

According to Thomas Starr, how do the typographic and calligraphic texts of the Declaration of Independence send different messages? Why do you think the National Archives displays the calligraphic text? Which text does Starr seem to prefer, and why? He considers only two texts; in your opinion, what message would be sent by the manuscript of the first draft, which retains all the committee and congressional revisions?

■ **Method**

James Munves tells the story of the Declaration as if he were there to see it, as a narrative. How effective is this method of recounting history? Which account do you find more compelling: Munves's narrative or Starr's more academic description? Why?

■ **Medium**

The draft and printed versions of the Declaration are similar in that they consist of words on paper (in contrast, the calligrapic text is on parchment). Can you think of other ways the document might be displayed today? For example, would putting the Declaration into electronic media alter its meaning in any way? If so, how?

PRESERVING THE PAST

■ **Cluster menu: Preserving the Past**

postcard	Helen Simpson, **"Lowell House," to Miss Ann Holliday,** October 20, 1944, p. 387
	It's 1944· What's it like in Cambridge, Massachusetts?
essay & scrapbook	Jessica Helfand, **What We Saved,** p. 389
	Mementos: How do photos, old concert tickets, and newspaper clippings tell the stories of our lives?

According to Jessica Helfand in her essay "What We Saved," the old-fashioned scrapbook is making a comeback: "Today," she writes, "'scrapbooking' is a peculiar craft phenomenon that has virtually exploded" in the years since 9/11. What can scrapbooks tell us about the past and the people who artfully kept these personal albums? On one level, we can obtain a vivid picture of the material world many decades ago — the clothes a young woman wore in the 1920s, the car she drove, and dances she attended. On another level, though, do such albums simply provide us with "fictions" and "stories" that we tend to invent but which never existed? To what extent can scrapbooks provide us with serious historical evidence and a glimpse into genuine autobiography? Are scrapbooks a kind of visual memoir or merely a hodgepodge of meaningless memorabilia? What, for example, can one conclude from such "scraps" of history as a postcard of Harvard University — accidentally preserved — from a midwestern woman visiting the Northeast in 1944 and writing back home about her trip?

LOWELL HOUSE. HARVARD UNIVERSITY. CAMBRIDGE. MASS.

387

Helen Simpson, *"Lowell House" Postcard to Miss Ann Holliday,* October 20, 1944.

This postcard, found in Cambridge, Massachusetts, in 2002, reads:

> 10/20/44
> Hello Ann
> First D.C., New York, Boston and Now Deah! old Cambridge just across the Charles
> River from Boston. You eat anywhere or go any place you wish in Boston absolutely
> no segregation along those lines. I am enjoying it. Ethel came to New York with me
> for a few days. The church I went to here is having a $10,000.00 Rally. I hope they get
> it. Regards to your parents.
> Helen Simpson

(Republican American)

Jessica Helfand, *What We Saved*. Jessica Helfand is a designer, writer, and
educator, as well as a partner at Winterhouse, a design studio in northwest-
ern Connecticut, where she works on projects in the areas of publishing and
editorial development, new media, and education. Her clients include a variety of journals, book publishers, universities, and museums. The company's
imprint, Winterhouse Editions, publishes literary works by authors such as
Paul Auster and Franz Kafka and books on design criticism. A former adjunct
professor at New York University, Helfand is Senior Critic at the Yale School
of Art. She has authored several books on design and culture, the most
recent of which is *Reinventing the Wheel* (2002, Princeton Architectural
Press). In the following essay, originally published in *Aperture: The Journal
of Fine Art Photography* (issue 183, Summer 2006), Helfand explores the
scrapbook — looking specifically at pictures and ephemera from the twentieth
century. Helfand raises the questions: What do the objects and photos we
save — and how we put these materials together — say about who we are?
What clues do our scrapbooks offer about us, about our lives and our cultural
moment, long after we're gone? (Images from "What We Saved: Pictures and
Ephemera in the Twentieth-Century Scrapbook" by Jessica Helfand,
Aperture magazine, Issue 183 [Summer 2006])

Jessica Helfand
WHAT WE SAVED

■ **Consider before you read.** *How does Helfand define a scrapbook? What does it include and not include? How is it significantly different from a photograph album?*

On Saturday May 25, 1918, Minnie Hazel Reed started a scrapbook. In it, she put anything that meant something to her: dance cards, a pressed flower, ticket stubs and party invitations, postcards, calling cards — and lots and lots of photographs. She kept poems and letters, documented her class trip to Washington, D.C., in the fall of 1919, and the proud celebration of her high-school graduation the following winter. There are clippings from the local paper, snapshots of her dearest friends and the inevitable, if indecipherable, annotations that accompany such subjective jottings.

To reconstruct the events of Minnie's life now, more than eighty-five years later, is to piece together a social history of an era long gone. But what emerges is not so much a serious chronology as a selective portrait of a particular time and place — of a young girl and her friends, of the clothes they wore, the cars they drove, and the dance cards that linked them, it only for an instant, in a state of romantic anticipation. That photographs play a central role in this book is only half the story; the other half lies in the memorabilia that circumscribes, and to a considerable extent amplifies, the story of a girl beginning her adult life.

Today, "scrapbooking" is a peculiar craft phenomenon that has virtually exploded in the five years since 9/11. (According to the Craft and Hobby Association, sales of scrapbooking supplies totaled $2.5 billion in 2003, and are headed steadily upward.) "Scrapping" (in contemporary parlance) is provoked by sentiment and propelled by sales of embellishments — brads, buttons, die-cuts, frames, grommets, hinges, labels, stickers, and a host of specialty papers that liberate the maker from the ponderous responsibility of certain visual choices. Whereas early twentieth-century scrapbooks were often characterized by the chance vestigial artifact, today's scrapbookers frequently opt for the prefabricated one. Such prescribed visual systems ensure handsome (if neutral) pages that serve to document, and ultimately to sanction, the memories that the earnest scrapbooker lovingly strives to preserve.

The notion of documenting one's life through the practice of keeping scrapbooks dates from the Renaissance, when the "commonplace book" originated. Here, readers wrote down textual passages of personal significance, including classical quotes, astrological predictions, personal anecdotes, and devotional texts. Such compilations were not only valuable to their owners, but over time would come to provide critical cues about the quality and range of intellectual life, showing us how information was both processed and prioritized.

389

■ **Consider.** *Why does Helfand use 9/11 as a marker? What does it imply about the reasons that people create scrapbooks?*

Toward the end of the eighteenth century, the English clergyman James Granger extended this notion with the introduction of a new kind of book that reconsidered scholarship in the context of more varied materials. "Grangerized" books were rebound and expanded with the addition of engravings, watercolors, manuscripts, documents, playbills, and other miscellaneous items. (Today, such volumes are more commonly known as "extra-illustrated books.") These books persisted through the following century, at a time when the preponderance of black-and-white printing — coupled with the advent of color lithography — made the acquisition of colored "scraps" something of a novelty. With the introduction of photography in general (and, at the turn of the twentieth century, the Brownie camera in particular), the notion of pairing found matter with personal snapshots came to allow for a new kind of graphic authorship, one that was easily

390

Scrapbook documenting one young man's life in the 1920s and '30s. The images provide a record of a train trip on the Gold Coast Limited and his time at Stanford University. (Collection Barbara Levine: photographed by Dana Davis)

tailored to the interests and budget of each member of the family. In 1873, Mark Twain, a lifelong scrapbook enthusiast, patented a "self-pasting" album that was an overnight success. By 1900, more than fifty different types of albums were available, and a new obsession was born.

While it has long been considered an activity favored by women, the compilation of scrapbooks was initially seen as a pastime that lent itself to any of a number of possibilities. The keeper of a scrapbook might choose to document home or school life, to chronicle sports statistics, or to create a hobbyist's record of birdwatching. Regardless of the theme, what mattered was the consideration with which materials were paired and sequenced, described and detailed, folded and pasted and carefully preserved. It is this perhaps more than anything else that characterizes the early twentieth-century scrapbook — a fascinating study in pictorial assemblage in which less is never more.

Ten years after Minnie began her album, a schoolgirl in Pittsburgh embarked on her own scrapbook journey. Dorothy Abraham kept valentines, paper napkins, and the plastic cellophane from a sweetheart's gift of chocolates. She saved ticket stubs from football games, school concerts, and something called "Stunt Day." She collected autographs, telegrams, invitations, and calling cards, and pasted in the portraits of each of her classmates and teachers. Included, too, are results from her driving test, a piece of school chalk, and a sample of her expert shorthand.

Ellen Donovan's memory book hails from Missouri and includes detailed descriptions of her outings ("Today we went Kodaking out on the lawn"), her numerous graduation gifts ("A cut glass bottle with Palmer's toilet water in it from Mrs. Brady"), and her extraordinary wardrobe: "The dress which I wore to the banquet was a party dress made very simply of light blue and silver changeable taffeta," she reports in the spring of 1922. "My shoes were white kid and I wore white silk hose, tulle around my shoulders and a wreath of silver leaves on my head." Ellen's girlfriends — with names like Sadie and Daisy, Olive and Pearl—penned their autographs with snippets of rhyming verse, while the boys signed their names with the formality characteristic of the aspiring American gentleman: "G. Cuthbertson," "L. H. Milligan," and an imperious-sounding "Meriwether L. Stuart."

Were Minnie or Dorothy or Ellen to have merely consigned their snapshots to a simple album, the records they kept would have been truthful but terse — for it is the act of chronicling through both image and artifact that produces such richly interwoven narratives of visual, cultural, and personal history. As author, editor, photographer, curator, and occasional protagonist, the scrapbooker engages in what today seems a comparatively basic exercise in graphic design. Combining pictures, words, and personal ephemera, these resulting works represent amateur yet stunningly authoritative examples of a particularly rich strain of visual autobiography.

Scholars have long studied the family photo album as a repository of social history, a folkloric time-capsule that reveals as much about its makers as its subjects. Photographs are, according to historian Marianne Hirsch, "the only material traces of an irrecoverable past," and therefore "derive their power and their important cultural role from their embeddedness in the fundamental rites of family life." The owner of the album may be the subject or the photographer (or both), and therein

391

Soldier's scrapbook, 1917–1933. This album was made by a young soldier who lived in Boone, Indiana, and was drafted in 1917, during World War I. He was later stationed in Paris. (Collection Barbara Levine: photographed by Dana Davis)

lies the book's peculiar charm — its unintended, ineffable clumsiness. Chronicling important events that the family deems worthy of posterity, such albums reveal a kind of episodic time in which snapshots represent isolated, often disconnected moments in a person's life. Such offerings are often the product of unskilled photographers whose efforts are prized more for their sincerity than for their quality.

Still, to produce a scrapbook, it is not enough merely to take pictures. One has to save them, classify them, and combine them with additional materials, committing to a series of decisions and subsequently *pasting them down* on the page. The pasting-in itself becomes a startling gesture of permanence — and while

photo corners permit the occasional migratory shift, the glued-down image is frequently anchored to a caption that virtually cements it in place.

Oddly, however, in spite of any presumed editorial clarity, a discovered scrapbook is something of a treasure precisely because its provenance — and its participants — remain so inevitably mysterious. Rarely tethered to any documented reality, such a book's anonymity is usually a foregone conclusion. But in truth, that mystery is somehow comforting, serving to protect the privacy of the album's silent protagonists. The British historian Val Williams has wisely observed that such albums, years later and in the hands of an anonymous viewer, become *fictions*: the sequences of images will be "read" in such a way as to construct stories, establish relationships, or find associations that, more likely than not, never existed. As evocative narrative, such books may prove compelling indeed, but as reliable evidence, the family album — like many a family — remains irrevocably flawed.

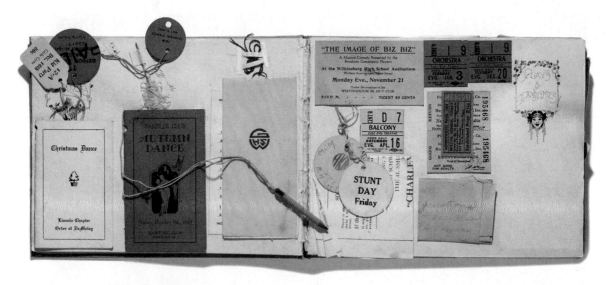

Dorothy Abraham's high-school scrapbook, Pittsburgh, 1928. Photographed by Jason Brownrigg.

394

Perhaps what is missing from the observations of so many historians is an appreciation of the emotional resonance of the book itself, a resonance made more palpable by the deliberate inclusion of personal memorabilia. Such records inevitably reveal more than mere photographic evidence, introducing sensory variables including touch, smell, and a kind of physicality that collectively produce further dimensions.

There is, for instance, the scrapbooker's handwriting: loopy, idiosyncratic, blotted into a blue-black pool of now-faded blotches — or equally revealing in its mechanical restraint, its structural integrity. There are the dog-eared pages; the compositional montages; the tiny pencil dangling from a silk thread, still sewn to its dance card from a long-forgotten sorority ball. There are the folded envelopes with their canceled stamps (do those addresses even still exist?), the torn invitations and makeshift silhouettes, all of them participants in this singular orchestration, a poignant choreographic swirl of frayed letters and fractured ribbons and a flurry of snapshots suspended in time.

I do not know what became of Ellen Donovan or Dorothy Abraham, or what led their scrapbooks to travel the itinerant route that brought them to my library. As for Minnie Reed, I do know this much: she went on to marry, to raise a family, and to live to the impressive age of 101. She did not share the scrapbook with me, her granddaughter, but left it to be discovered in a closet by a cousin of mine after Minnie died. We knew some, though by no means all, of this story of her early life: she had shared many of the photographs with us (proud, I now realize,

Minnie Reed's scrapbook, Philadelphia, 1918. Photographed by Jason Brownrigg.

395

that she had been so pretty and photogenic), but we knew nothing of the ancillary details. She went to Washington? She went to parties? There were men who danced with her besides Grandpop? Scrapbooks, it seems, derive their meaning (and their grace) from a long gestational cycle, one that demands patience and persistence, and perhaps as little rational intention as possible.

Paradoxical as it may seem, the scrapbook thrives on a curious blend of insider knowledge and outsider art. And it is in this tension — between personal sentiment and public space — that a true biographical odyssey emerges.

■ **Discuss.** *Discuss why Helfand waits until the end of her essay to reveal that Minnie is her grandmother. How does that choice change the emphasis of the essay? How would it have been different if she had revealed this relationship at the beginning?*

■ **Write.** *Helfand uses the language of travel to describe the creation of a scrapbook, calling it a "journey" or an "odyssey." Write an essay analyzing her use of the journey metaphor in describing the practice of scrapbooking. In what ways do the books she finds document their makers travels — either literal or figurative?*

 CONSIDER THE CLUSTER
Preserving the Past

■ Message

Postcards always leave room for a short message. Examine closely the message composed on the back of the postcard that shows one of Harvard's dorms, Lowell House. In a brief personal essay, consider the writer, the time, and the place, and discuss what you think this brief note means to you today.

■ Method

Helfand writes: "Regardless of the theme, what mattered [to scrapbookers of early twentieth century] was the consideration with which materials were paired and sequenced, described and detailed, folded and pasted and carefully preserved. It is this perhaps more than anything else that characterizes the early twentieth-century scrapbook — a fascinating study in pictorial assemblage in which less is never more." Keep this in mind as you look more closely at one or more of the scrapbook pages included here. What do the materials — and the specific ways they are presented — say about the person/people who created these pages? About their sense of themselves? About their creativity? Sense of fun? Connection to others and the larger society? About their particular moment in time?

■ Medium

Consider the different ways a "scrapbook" can be assembled in different media. As an in-class assignment, describe how you would put one together — what would you include and exclude? Can you imagine a "virtual scrapbook"? Can you picture a digital scrapbook that would be in part your visual memoir?

INDIAN GROUND

If it is virtually impossible to keep the present from influencing our view of the past, it is equally difficult to keep the past from crowding into the present. In his poem "The Texas Chainsaw Massacre," a double exposure of horrifying history and horror movie, Sherman Alexie brings together American popular culture and cultural history. In Colorado in 1864, a volunteer army of some 725 individuals led by Colonel John Chivington, a Methodist minister and prominent antislavery advocate, attacked a small village on the banks of Sand Creek. With authorization "to kill and destroy, as enemies of the country, wherever they may be found, all hostile Indians," they killed more than 125 Cheyenne and Arapaho Indians, most of them women, children, and elderly men. Alexie finds in the blood-drenched horror movie *The Texas Chainsaw Massacre* "the collected history/of America" as he moves from the film's butchery to "the killing grounds" of Sand Creek.

398

Bryanston Pictures, *The Texas Chainsaw Massacre,* **1973.** Alexie's poem takes its title from a now-classic horror movie, directed by Tobe Hooper, about an insane family of cannibals. Moving from drive-in feature to cult favorite, this film has been the subject of academic and pop culture acclaim (the film is on "top 100" lists, has been selected by the Museum of Modern Art for its permanent collection, and is routinely taught in film classes). The movie was remade and released in 2003. There are many theories that account for the American consumption of the horror movie, which really grew in the 1970s — the most common one being that we enjoy being frightened when we know that nothing can really hurt us. In short, some people want to experience *controlled* terror. (Photofest)

Sherman Alexie, *The Texas Chainsaw Massacre*. A Spokane/Coeur d'Alene Indian, Sherman Alexie (b. 1966) grew up on the Spokane Indian Reservation in Wellpinit, Washington. His career as a writer began almost immediately after his graduation from Washington State University in Pullman, where he majored in American studies. Since then, he has received many prestigious literary awards, including the Lila Wallace–Reader's Digest Writers' Award and the PEN/Hemingway Award, as well as several awards for screenplays. He wrote the screenplay for the films *Smoke Signals* (1998) and *The Business of Fancydancing* (2003). Alexie's most recent books include *Flight*, a novel (2007, Black Cat/Grove/Atlantic), and *Ten Little Indians*, a collection of short stories (2004, Grove/Atlantic). "The Texas Chainsaw Massacre" was published in the Summer 1992 issue of *The Kenyon Review*.

Sherman Alexie
THE TEXAS CHAINSAW
MASSACRE

399

■ **Consider before you read.** *How does Alexie manage to move between the plot of the movie and historical events? Are there moments in the poem that deliberately confuse the two?*

> What can you say about a movie so horrific even its title scares people away?
>
> — Stephen King

I
have seen it
and I like it: The blood,
the way like *Sand Creek*
even its name brings fear,
because I am an American
Indian and have learned
words are another kind of violence.

This vocabulary is genetic.
When Leatherface crushes the white boy's skull

with a sledgehammer, brings it down again and again
while the boy's arms and legs spasm and kick wildly
against real and imagined enemies, I remember

another killing floor

in the slaughter yard from earlier in the film,
all the cows with their stunned eyes and mouths
waiting for the sledgehammer with fear so strong
it becomes a smell that won't allow escape. I remember

the killing grounds

of Sand Creek
where 105 Southern Cheyenne and Arapaho women and children
and 28 men were slaughtered by 700 heavily armed soldiers,
led by Colonel Chivington and his Volunteers. *Volunteers.*

Violence has no metaphors; it does have reveille.

Believe me, there is nothing surprising
about a dead body. This late in the twentieth century
tears come easily and without sense:
taste and touch have been replaced
by the fear of reprisal. I have seen it

and like it: The butchery, its dark humor
that thin line "between art and exploitation,"
because I recognize the need to prove blood
against blood. I have been in places
where I understood *Tear his heart out
and eat it whole.* I have tasted rage
and bitterness like skin between my teeth.

I have been in love.

I first saw it in the reservation drive-in
and witnessed the collected history
of America roll and roll across the screen,
voices and dreams distorted by tin speakers.

400

■ **Consider.** *Horror is a genre that often borrows elements from comedy — witness the popularity of* Scream *and* Scary Movie, *both of which have combined the two. In these lines, Alexie refers to "its dark humor/that thin line 'between art and exploitation.'" What do you think he means by that? What do you think Alexie thinks about the horror movie as a genre? He equates* The Texas Chainsaw Massacre *to a real-life massacre, but does he really think they are on the same scale?*

Since then, I have been hungry
for all those things I haven't seen.

This country demands that particular sort of weakness:
we must devour everything on our plates
and ask for more. Our mouths hinge open.
Our teeth grow long and we gnaw them down
to prevent their growth into the brain. I have

seen it and like it: The blood,
the way like music
it makes us all larger
and more responsible
for our sins,
because I am an American
Indian and have learned

hunger becomes madness easily.

■ **Discuss.** *Why does Alexie say "I remember" about the events of Sand Creek, which occurred long before he was born? Discuss the properties of memory in this poem — how it works and why it is important.*

■ **Write.** *Alexie chooses to use the title of the movie as the title of his poem. Why do you think this particular title resonates for him? Write an exploratory essay, considering why other horror movie titles would not work in this context and why* The Texas Chainsaw Massacre *does.*

401

COMMENT

"I always tell people that the five primary influences in my life are my father, for his nontraditional Indian stories, my grandmother for her traditional Indian stories, Stephen King, John Steinbeck, and *The Brady Bunch*. That's who I am. I think a lot of Indian artists like to pretend that they're not influenced by pop culture or Western culture, but I am, and I'm happy to admit it. . . . It's a cultural currency."

— Sherman Alexie

Verlyn Klinkenborg, *Sand Creek*. This essay, with accompanying photographs, appeared as the first in a series "on forgotten places that stirred the American conscience" in the November/December 2000 issue of *Mother Jones.* Klinkenborg (b. 1952) is one of America's leading nonfiction writers; his work appears in many magazines, including *The New Republic, Harper's, Esquire, National Geographic, The New Yorker, Smithsonian, Audubon,* and *Mother Jones,* where he often contributes the text to photo-essays. Klinkenborg has been a member of *The New York Times* Editorial Board since 1997 and has taught literature and creative writing at schools such as Bennington College and Harvard University. A recipient of the Lila Wallace–Reader's Digest Writers' Award and a National Endowment for the Arts Fellowship, he is the author of *The Rural Life* (2003) and *Making Hay* (1997).

Verlyn Klinkenborg

SAND CREEK

402

■ **Consider before you read.** *What is Klinkenborg's purpose in writing this essay? What recent events prompted him to write it?*

In southeastern Colorado, about 130 miles from Pueblo, there is a small town called Chivington. Once, it had railroad shops and saloons and as many as 1,500 residents. There was even an East Chivington. But then the railroad shops moved away, taking the people with them, and all that remains of Chivington today is a Friends Church and the ruins of a brick schoolhouse, its roof caved in, its rafters collapsed upon each other like the ambitions of this civic corpse.

Chivington is named after a man who turned from the ministry to the military and made a reputation for himself fit only for a ghost town. The first time Colonel John M. Chivington came through the region he was at the head of some 725 men, members of the 3rd and 1st regiments of the Colorado Cavalry. It was early morning, well before daylight, and the date was November 29, 1864. He passed that way a second time two days later, on his way back southward to Fort Lyon and thence to Denver, where he received a hero's welcome. In the interval, Chivington and his men had ridden down at daybreak upon a village of 500 or 600 Cheyennes and Arapahos camped a few miles north of present-day Chivington on Sand Creek. There, the Colorado troops — most of them volunteers commissioned for a 100-day term of service — murdered between 125 and 160 Indians, mostly women, children, and the elderly. Black Kettle, the chief of one of the Cheyenne clans, had met with Chivington and other military leaders at Camp Weld in Denver in late September, and he believed that his village was at peace with the whites. At the sight of the troops riding toward him, Black Kettle raised a large American flag and a white flag on a lodge pole and stood holding it aloft. When the troops began firing, he fled.

The attack rolled northward from a sharp bend in Sand Creek, and when the shooting was over, Chivington's men returned to the Indian village to mutilate the bodies of the dead and burn their lodges and, almost incidentally, to murder a half-breed prisoner named Jack Smith. Nearly four years later, General William T. Sherman, passing through, stopped at Sand Creek to collect relics. One of his men later wrote, "We found many things, such as Indian baby skulls; many skulls of men and women; arrows, some perfect, many broken; spears, scalps, knives, cooking utensils, and many other things too numerous to mention. We laid over one day and collected nearly a wagon load."

Two of the Cheyennes killed at Sand Creek, War Bonnet and Standing in the Water, had visited Washington the year before and were photographed in the White House conservatory. They had been given a short course in geography and addressed by President Lincoln. "It is the object of this Government to be on terms of peace with you, and with all our red brethren," Lincoln said. "We make treaties with you, and will try to observe them; and if our children should some-times behave badly, and violate these treaties, it is against our wish."

Lincoln's words must be contrasted with those of a proclamation issued on August 11, 1864, by the territorial governor of Colorado, John Evans. Evans authorized "all citizens of Colorado, either individually, or in such parties as they may organize, to go in pursuit of all hostile Indians on the plains, scrupulously avoiding those who have responded to my call to rendezvous at the points indi-cated; also, to kill and destroy as enemies of the country, wherever they may be found, all such hostile Indians."

Almost 136 years to the day after that proclamation was issued and Colorado volunteers began to form the 100-day militia, I stood on a sand bluff overlook-ing the site of the Sand Creek massacre. It is now private property, but legisla-tion has been introduced in Congress by Senator Ben Nighthorse Campbell, who is a Northern Cheyenne, to create a Sand Creek Massacre National Historic Site here.

This is the kind of place, common in the rural West, where you might almost believe that nothing has changed since the event that made it memorable. There are a thousand — ten thousand — shallow washes like it on the high plains: a grassy flood zone, now thickly shaded with cottonwoods, the waters of Sand Creek nearly always in abeyance, except for pools here and there grown round with rushes where cattle stand flank-deep on hot days. Sand Creek flows to the southeast, but just below the massacre site it makes a long eastward bend before turning

Colonel John M. Chivington.
Chivington led the cavalry attack at
Sand Creek. (From the Denver
Public Library, Western History
Collection)

404

Cheyenne and Arapaho chiefs. This photo was taken after conversations about peace with U.S. military leaders in Denver. (From the Denver Public Library, Western History Collection)

south again. On a plain near the crook of that bend and to the north of it, Black Kettle's village had stood, one hundred and more buffalo-skin lodges, pony herds grazing on the high ground above the village. Now, in August, the shrill sound of grasshoppers rang out across the undulating flatland beyond Sand Creek. In November, they would have been silent.

It's always an illusion to believe that you can see the past unchanged. In the mid-1970s, a gas company ran a pipeline right through Sand Creek, just above the bend. The 1864 soil level is buried under some ten inches of new soil that has drifted in over the years. In 1887, a town called New Chicago lived for a grasshopper's lifetime just beyond the massacre site, sustained only by the hopes of a railroad coming through someday. Around 1910, local citizens formed the Chivington Canal Company and dug a canal that angles toward Brandon, a small town just east of Chivington. You can still see the line of the canal where it edges the massacre site. For several years, a farmer tried to raise a crop in the creek bend. New Chicago failed. The canal failed. The crop failed.

And over time, a clear sense of the location of Black Kettle's village had eroded as well. Relics of the kind that General Sherman found in abundance on the surface at Sand Creek had long since disappeared. An inconclusive archaeological study was conducted in 1997 by the state of Colorado. In 1999, the National Park Service — conducting an archaeological reconnaissance with local landowners and tribal representatives from the Northern and Southern Cheyennes and Northern and Southern Arapahos — rediscovered the village site, though there is still some dissent about its actual extent.

In 1950, local citizens placed a stone monument to the massacre on the sand bluff where I stood, a bluff that allows a view of much of the land that would be included in the Sand Creek Massacre historic site. The monument reads "Sand Creek Battle Ground Nov. 29 & 30. 1864," and it shows the head of a generic Indian in profile, looking almost like Liberty in her Indian headdress on the old copper cent, which could have been found in the pockets of Chivington's cavalry. People used to drive to this monument to park and drink and smoke dope and dump their trash and ferret out relics until Bill Dawson, the owner of much of the massacre site and the land that the monument sits upon, closed the access road, partly to stop an unruly traffic but also out of respect for the wishes of the Cheyennes and Arapahos, to whom this site is sacred.

I tried to imagine the running slaughter — it was never really a battle — that began in the slow light of late November, the pony herds cut off, the melee among the lodges, the sullen mutilation that began later that day and continued during the night and into the following day, the scalps flayed from the dead, the breasts cut from women and the scrotums from men to be used as tobacco bags, all attested

COMMENT

"So what are we to do with this recovered memory? The misplacement of the massacre site is easily corrected — but how to correct the massacre itself? It can't be done in any remedial sense; we can rewrite history, but not the past. The Sand Creek massacre happened; we can't take it back, however badly we might wish to."

— Larry Borowsky, historian

406

by witnesses who appeared before military and congressional investigations of Sand Creek in 1865. But the day I stood there, it was too peaceful a place to sustain such memories, and besides, those are memories that belong to the descendants of the people who camped there long ago. The night of November 29, 1864, wrote George Bent, a mixed-blood Cheyenne who survived the attack, "will never be forgotten as long as any of us who went through it are alive." It still lives, vividly, among the Cheyenne and Arapaho.

But before the running slaughter began, there had been a running argument, and that was much easier to imagine. Chivington did not ride down upon a peaceful village in hot blood. Nor did he attack peaceable Cheyennes in ignorance. He had just run for office and lost on a ticket that would have admitted Colorado to statehood. No sooner was the election over than Chivington began laying out his campaign against Black Kettle's village.

Political ambition and intractable moral ferocity drove Chivington, that and a panic caused by Confederate raids in southeastern Colorado and by the murder of the Hungate family — father, mother, and two young children — near Denver by four Arapahos. Two weeks after the Hungate murders, Governor Evans directed "all friendly Indians of the Plains" to separate themselves from hostile Indians and to rendezvous at assigned places of safety. It was precisely such a friendly village, camped in accordance with Evans' directive, that Chivington planned to attack.

He was forcefully confronted at every stage by men who opposed his plan because it meant betraying Black Kettle and the assurances of peace that had been made in council in late September. Though he rode with Chivington, Captain Silas Soule refused to take part in the killing, and he testified against Chivington during the military investigation of Sand Creek in early 1865, an act for which he was shot down on the streets of Denver by a Chivington supporter. The night before the massacre, Lieutenant Joseph Cramer told Chivington that the raid he was planning was murder and a violation of their word as officers and men. "Colonel Chivington's reply," Cramer wrote, "was, that he believed it to be right or honorable to use any means under God's heaven to kill Indians that would kill women and children, and 'damn any man that was in sympathy with the Indians.'" Again that evening Chivington was confronted by a group of officers and civilians, and again he damned their sympathy. Then he ordered his men to mount and ride northward through the night to Sand Creek.

Chivington had decided upon war and upon the deaths of the Cheyennes and Arapahos who favored peace. In the aftermath of Sand Creek, a man named J. W. Wright, outraged at Chivington's actions, neatly summed up the purpose of the massacre in an open letter. "An Indian war is on the country," he wrote. "Every effort has been made for two years to produce it." That war erupted on the Plains the following year. It took Chivington and Sand Creek to make it happen, to set in motion the machinery that would eventually kill Black Kettle, still seeking peace four years later, at Washita, in what is now Oklahoma. There, at dawn, George Armstrong Custer rode down upon Black Kettle's village again, employing Chivington's brutal tactics and his unswerving convictions.

407

Troops storming Sand Creek. When Chivington's men rode in, Black Kettle raised an American flag and a white flag as a sign of peace. (From the Denver Public Library, Western History Collection)

408

Brian Callahan, *Map of Sand Creek*. (Originally printed in *Mother Jones*)

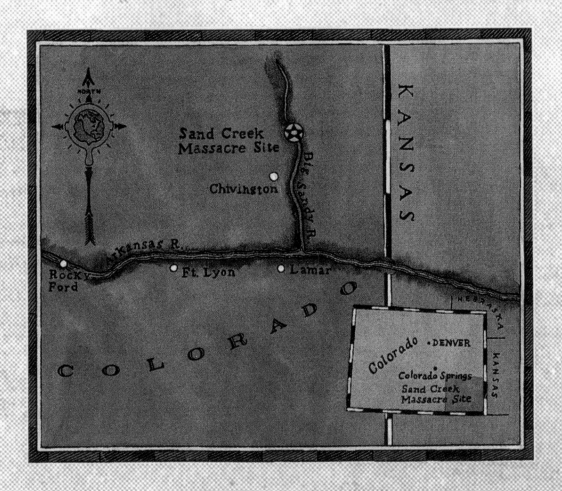

◀ ■ **Discuss.** *How did political motives lead to the massacre at Sand Creek? Discuss the reasons Klinkenborg gives for Chivington's attacks. To what extent was the village at Sand Creek just a convenient scapegoat?*

■ **Write.** *In writing this essay, Klinkenborg says that some parts of the story were easier to imagine than others. What is the place of imagination in history? Why does Klinkenborg hesitate to imagine "the running slaughter" itself? Write an essay about how imagination can enhance history and when it falls short.*

 CONSIDER THE CLUSTER
Indian Ground

■ **Message**

What connection does Sherman Alexie establish between *The Texas Chainsaw Massacre* and the massacre at Sand Creek? Why does the film evoke these historical memories? Alexie says several times that he has seen the movie and liked it—why? What appeals to him about it? Why do you think he repeats the phrase throughout? Do you think his poem is in favor of violence? Try putting the poem's final sentence into your own words.

■ **Method**

How much information do you need to read Alexie's poem? What does he expect you to know? What if you have never seen *The Texas Chainsaw Massacre* or know nothing about Sand Creek—can you still appreciate the poem? Explain how important the historical background is to your understanding. For example, did reading Klinkenborg's "Sand Creek" help you better understand Alexie's poem and position? Does the poem add anything to your reading of the essay?

■ **Medium**

Suppose you were creating a documentary film to commemorate the Sand Creek massacre. What elements from Klinkenborg's essay would you want to incorporate? How would you introduce visual information? What Native American artifacts would be important to your vision of the incident? Would you want to include Alexie's poem? Why or why not? What does a poem supply that a documentary film does not, and vice versa?

CHICAGO'S TENEMENTS

■ **Cluster menu: Chicago's Tenements**

One of the prime shaping forces of twentieth-century America was the Great Migration of the late 1930s and 1940s, when African Americans left their rural southern and heartland roots and settled in the northern cities. As thousands came to Chicago's South Side, they permanently altered the city's social and cultural atmosphere, an alteration that can be traced in the novels of Richard Wright, the prose and poetry of Gwendolyn Brooks, and the drama of Lorraine Hansberry, each of whom vividly brings us into impoverished neighborhoods with their crowded "kitchenette" apartments, storefront churches, beauty parlors, pool halls, nightclubs, and saloons. What these writers captured in words was also — around the same time — being permanently documented visually by Wayne F. Miller, a white photographer who decided to document the Great Migration as it affected his native Chicago. Miller's photographs have been praised as an important part of American urban history — but not "headline history." As critic Robert Stepto says of Miller's imagery, "This is news from the street presented in most of its variety."

Wayne F. Miller, *Two Girls Waiting outside a Tavern.*

◀ **Wayne F. Miller,** *Rabbits for Sale,* **1948.** Wayne F. Miller (b. 1918) served as a photographer in the U.S. Navy during World War II and in an illustrious career has worked for many magazines. He helped establish one of the world's major photography shows, *The Family of Man.* Robert Stepto writes that images like this one "record the fact that some migrants worked not in the industries but in the alleyways, selling ice and vegetables and peddling whatever they could from the backs of wagons." All photographs are reproduced from Miller's collected photographs in *Chicago's South Side: 1946–1948* (2000). (All photos © by Wayne F. Miller, courtesy of Wayne F. Miller/Magnum Photos, Inc.)

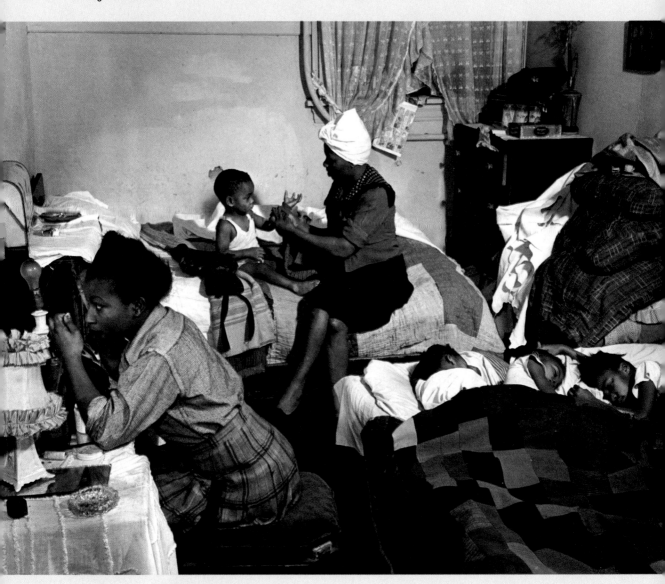

Wayne F. Miller, *One-Room Kitchenette* **(above) and** *Three Teenagers in Kitchenette Apartment* **(opposite).**
Kitchenettes often consisted of only one room, like that depicted in this photograph. In her novella
Maud Martha (1953), Gwendolyn Brooks describes a kitchenette that may have been more comfortable
than most: "Their home was on the third floor of a great gray stone building. The two rooms were small.
The bedroom was furnished with a bed and dresser, old-fashioned, but in fair condition, and a faded
occasional chair. In the kitchen were an oilcloth-covered table, two kitchen chairs, one folding chair, a
cabinet base, a brown wooden icebox, and a three-burner gas stove. . . . There was a bathroom at the end
of the hall, which they would have to share with four other families who lived on the floor."

Gwendolyn Brooks, *Kitchenette Building*, 1945. One of the nation's most prominent poets, Gwendolyn Brooks (1917–2000) grew up on Chicago's South Side,
the setting of the prize-winning collection *A Street in Bronzeville* (1945), which
included "Kitchenette Building." The volume garnered much literary attention
just about the time Wayne Miller began his photographic project, and Brooks's
verbal imagery of crammed apartments and segregated neighborhoods may have
stimulated Miller's visual interest in the South Side community.

Gwendolyn Brooks

KITCHENETTE BUILDING

■ **Consider before you read.** *Why doesn't Brooks specifically discuss the inhabitants of
the kitchenette? What parts of the poem give the reader a sense of what they are like, even
if Brooks does not tell us outright?*

We are things of dry hours and the involuntary plan.
Grayed in, and gray. "Dream" makes a giddy sound, not strong
Like "rent," "feeding a wife," "satisfying a man."

But could a dream send up through onion fumes
Its white and violet, fight with fried potatoes
And yesterday's garbage ripening in the hall,
Flutter, or sing an aria down these rooms

Even if we were willing to let it in,
Had time to warm it, keep it very clean,
Anticipate a message, let it begin?

We wonder. But not well! not for a minute!
Since Number Five is out of the bathroom now,
We think of lukewarm water, hope to get in it.

◀ ■ **Discuss.** *How do the literal features of the kitchenette compete with abstractions such as a dream? Where does Brooks paint the most vivid picture of the apartment? How does she imagine a dream would fit it?*

■ **Write.** *Why does Brooks describe the dream as something that must be warmed and kept "very clean"? How does she imagine it would fit into the lives of the people living in the kitchenette building? Write your thoughts about the kind of care a dream requires.*

COMMENT

"[I was convinced] that after the war, with a camera, I might be able to document the things that make this human race of ours a family. We may differ in race, color, language, wealth, and politics. But look at what we all have in common — dreams, laughter, tears, pride, the comfort of home, the hunger of love. If I could photograph these universal truths, I thought that might help us better understand the strangers on the other side of the world — and on the other side of town."

— Wayne F. Miller

417

Gordon Parks, *Speaking for the Past.* Gordon Parks (1912–2006) was an award-winning photographer, composer, and filmmaker; he was also the author of twelve books. Parks was born in segregated Fort Scott, Kansas, the youngest of fifteen children. Despite the poverty and racism of his childhood, he grew up with a sense of self-confidence largely because of the influence of his mother, who died when he was fifteen. "I had a mother who would not allow me to complain about not accomplishing something because I was black," Parks once said. "Her attitude was, 'If a white boy can do it, then you can do it, too — and do it better, or don't come home.' " Impressed by a photo essay on migrant workers that he saw in a magazine, Parks bought this first camera in 1938 and set out to photograph Chicago's South Side. He is best known for his famous photo essays for *Life* magazine. This essay is one of three that introduce Wayne F. Miller's *Chicago's South Side, 1946–1948.*

▶

Gordon Parks
SPEAKING FOR
THE PAST

■ **Consider before you read.** *How does Parks's acquaintance with the scenes presented in these photos as well as the photographer who took them affect his essay? How does he establish his closeness to both?*

I was born a black boy inside a black world. So, like moments rising out of my unfathomed past, many of Wayne Miller's images slice through me like a razor. And I'm left remembering hunks of my time being murdered away as I suffered blistering hot summers or ate the salt of equally cruel winters. For me those crowded kitchenettes, the loneliness of rented bedrooms, and the praying in leftover churches remain an ongoing memory. Here, far from the Kansas prairies where I was spawned, I just couldn't melt into the ghetto's tortuous ways — unlike so many others who, after a hard day's work, numbed the misery with booze and soothing music. "Hello blues. Blues, how do you do?"

New York's Harlem, Chicago's South Side — both cities of blackness crammed inside larger cities of whiteness — offered mostly hunger, frustration, and anger to their tenement dwellers. And those same tenements that imprisoned thousands are still there, refusing to crumble. I recall swarms of slow-moving people passing the chili shacks, rib joints, storefront churches, and funeral parlors — all with the same skin coloring but rarely speaking to one another. When you left your door you walked among strangers. Now there are a few new buildings going up to look smugly down at the old ones. Good music, laughter, and prayers are still in the air, but for many young blacks music, laughter, and prayers offer at most an uneasy peace.

At times I became disgruntled with this social imprisonment, even became angry with myself for not finding a way out. But eventually that anger grew tired of hanging out with me day and night, and little by little it left me alone. And for a long time I remained alone — still desperately searching for bread in the rubbish. That search was awful. I was constantly reaching for something denied me, or perhaps longing for something lost along the way.

Slowly the shadow of hope had spread its presence. Anger had fled — running as though it were escaping the violence festering inside me. Then gradually the light that avoided so many other hearts began falling on mine. But be free of doubt.

418

Wayne Miller shows us what I remember most — those garbaged alleys and wintry streets where snowflakes fell like tears, those numberless wooden firetraps called home, the homeless gathered around flaming trash cans to escape the hawk of winter, those crudely worded signs — COAL 50 cents, WOOD 25 cents — those old men reclining in forgotten chairs left at curbside for moving vans that never showed up. There where funerals had become a habit and hardship never seemed to be out of order.

How feeble the uncertainty! Wayne's camera appears to be inexhaustible as it goes from life to life — abruptly leaving one door to arrive at another. Then somewhere, perhaps a short distance away in a pool hall or restaurant, he finds brothers and sisters of the soul muddling through the grime and sipping Fox Head beer. Yet to some of their fortunate kinfolk that was a small thing. Having swum through the dust, they were now in tuxedos and ball gowns, dancing to the strains of Ellington's uptown music in a softly lit ballroom. "Hug me, sugar, and let the good times roll."

Where, one might ask, does Wayne Miller fit into this chaos that plagued my youth? A good question. Did he possess an insatiable curiosity that had to be fed, or was he perhaps treading the path of any competent photographic journalist? A close acquaintance with him for many years gives shape to my own answer. He was simply speaking for people who found it hard to speak for themselves. And that trait takes full measure of any journalist who is worth his salt. Once when a reporter wrapped that question around his neck, he answered unhesitatingly, and rather bluntly, "I am interested in expressing my subjects. I won't turn a nice guy into a son-of-a-bitch or a son-of-a-bitch into a nice guy. There are people who make pictures and people who take them. I take them. At times I have been so busy capturing what I was seeing that it was impossible to cry and work at the same time. Good images emerge from good dreaming. And, to me, dreaming is so important."

Wayne went to wherever his conscience called him, and his camera's eye baptized whatever confronted him. Earthbound and free of any shadowy miscellany, he made contact with the roots. And as no one can stop the waters flowing, neither can one eliminate his powerful images from our past. They will still be here with us, even if those tenements crumble in time, exhausted.

■ **Consider.** *What are the connotations of the word "baptized"? What is Parks saying about Miller's camera work?*

■ **Discuss.** *Parks uses several words with violent connotations in the opening of his essay. Which ones stand out to you? Why do you think he uses this language? What effect does it have on the reader? How does it set the tone for the rest of the piece?*

■ **Write.** *Write a response in which you explore the difference between making pictures and taking them. Why does Miller value the latter? Can you think of any photographers who prefer the former? What might be the benefits of "making" a picture?*

■■■■■■■ CONSIDER THE CLUSTER
Chicago's Tenements

■ **Message**

What idea does Wayne F. Miller portray in *Rabbits for Sale, 1948*? How does the photograph establish an urban environment? How does it convey the history of the migrant—the rural areas from which many of the new Chicagoans had recently come? What other connotations can you find in Miller's urban image? In what way can this picture be called a slice of history?

■ **Method**

Compare Wayne F. Miller's *One-Room Kitchenette* with Gwendolyn Brooks's well-known "Kitchenette Building." Remember that these two works were produced at nearly the same time. What visual and verbal images do they share? Gordon Parks quotes Miller as saying, "Good images emerge from good dreaming. And, to me, dreaming is so important." How does this comment help illuminate both photograph and poem? How is dreaming captured literally and figuratively?

■ **Medium**

Gordon Parks says in his essay that Miller was "simply speaking for people who found it hard to speak for themselves." How do photographs "speak"? What do you think Miller's *Three Teenagers in Kitchenette Apartment* is saying—both to those represented and to us as viewers?

RELIGION IN AMERICA:
THE SCOPES MONKEY TRIAL

In July 1925, one of the first skirmishes in what would be called America's "culture wars" took place in a boiling hot courtroom in the small town of Dayton, Tennessee. The news coverage was such that the trial has been considered one of the first "media circuses." Yet the defendant was no one of stature, and there was no sensational crime: John Scopes, an unimposing twenty-four-year-old schoolteacher, was in court facing the charge of having taught evolution in a biology classroom. The entire nation watched as two of its leading public figures — the agnostic trial attorney Clarence Darrow (1857–1938), one of the greatest defense lawyers in American history, and the populist elder statesman and spellbinding orator William Jennings Bryan (1860–1925) — clashed in acrimonious debate over the scientific evidence of Darwinian evolution versus the literal interpretation of the Bible.

In many ways, the trial (called the "monkey trial") was a staged event, with organizations such as the newly formed American Civil Liberties Union seeking the perfect defendant and the traditionalist Bryan using the arrest to make a case for "old-time religion." Before the trial, Bryan stated that "the contest between evolution and Christianity is a duel to the death. If evolution wins, Christianity goes." The trial lasted two weeks, with each side expressing its views on religious, scientific, and philosophical issues. The highlight of the trial occurred when the defense invited Bryan to take the stand as an "expert witness" on the Bible. Bryan mistakenly accepted this bold strategy and stepped into a barrage of questions that led to confused and contradictory statements. But the trial judge expunged Bryan's testimony from the court record, realizing that it was irrelevant to the specifies of the case. After all the oratorical fireworks, the jury decided in only a few minutes that Scopes was guilty; the state legislature had passed an act that prohibited the teaching of evolution, and Scopes had simply violated it. Several years later an appeals court reversed the decision, but, as Scopes had by then left teaching, there was never a retrial. Within a few days after the trial, William Jennings Bryan died of exhaustion. For many Tennesseans, as the statement by fundamentalist minister John Roach Straton (see p.433) demonstrates, the trial was not so much about the scientific merits of evolution but instead represented the invasion of a respectful and chivalric southern community by a materialistic and spiritually corrupt North. Some of the scars of the Civil War were still raw.

The trial, which has remained relevant for more than eighty years, made its way into American literature. The Scopes trial was transformed in 1955 into a popular American play by Jerome Lawrence and Robert E. Lee, *Inherit the Wind*. In 1960, the play was turned into a successful film of the same name, starring Spencer Tracy as Drummond (Darrow) and Frederic March as Brady (Bryan).

For a useful account of the famous trial, refer to Jeffrey P. Moran's *The Scopes Trial: A Brief History with Documents* (Bedford/St. Martin's 2002). For an early satire, refer to H. L. Mencken's classic essay "The Hills of Zion."

422

William Jennings Bryan and Clarence Darrow, from *The Scopes Monkey Trial Transcript*. When William Jennings Bryan unadvisedly agreed to take the stand as an expert, though hostile, witness, Clarence Darrow tried to trip him up on issues of scriptural credibility that had long been argued in debates between secularists and creationists. The following excerpts show Darrow using well-known biblical passages as he attempts to force Bryan into contradiction and incoherence.

William Jennings Bryan and Clarence Darrow

FROM THE SCOPES MONKEY TRIAL TRANSCRIPT

■ **Consider before you read.** *Why does Darrow choose these particular Bible passages when questioning Bryan? Do you see any similarities among them other than their unlikeliness?*

Darrow: Do you claim that everything in the Bible should be literally interpreted?

Bryan: I believe everything in the Bible should be accepted as it is given there; some of the Bible is given illustratively. For instance: "Ye are the salt of the earth." I would not insist that man was actually salt, or that he had flesh of salt, but it is used in the sense of salt as saving God's people.

· · ·

Darrow: But when you read that Jonah swallowed the whale — or that the whale swallowed Jonah — excuse me please — how do you literally interpret that?

Bryan: When I read that a big fish swallowed Jonah — it does not say whale.

Darrow: Doesn't it? Are you sure?

Bryan: That is my recollection of it. A big fish, and I believe it, and I believe in a God who can make a whale and can make a man and make both do what he pleases.

· · ·

Darrow: Now, you say, the big fish swallowed Jonah, and he there remained how long — three days — and then he spewed him upon the land. You believe that the big fish was made to swallow Jonah?

Bryan: I am not prepared to say that; the Bible merely says it was done.

Darrow: You don't know whether it was the ordinary run of fish, or made for that purpose?

423

John Scopes (above left). High school teacher and football coach John Scopes (1900–1970) said, "If you limit a teacher to only one side of anything, the whole country will eventually have only one thought. . . . I believe in teaching every aspect of every problem or theory." (Getty Images) *Clarence Darrow and William Jennings Bryan* (above right). An attorney and a leading member of the American Civil Liberties Union, Clarence Darrow defended John Scopes and the teaching of evolution at the famous Dayton, Tennessee, trial, arguing against William Jennings Bryan, the famous orator known as "the Great Commoner" for his belief in the goodness of the common man. Bryan, who opposed the teaching of evolution in public schools, aided the state prosecutor at the trial. (AP Photo)

Bryan:	You may guess; you evolutionists guess.
Darrow:	But when we do guess, we have a sense to guess right.
Bryan:	But do not do it often.
Darrow:	You are not prepared to say whether that fish was made especially to swallow a man or not?
Bryan:	The Bible doesn't say, so I am not prepared to say.
Darrow:	You don't know whether that was fixed up specially for the purpose?
Bryan:	No, the Bible doesn't say.
Darrow::	But do you believe he made them — that he made such a fish and that it was big enough to swallow Jonah?
Bryan:	Yes, sir. Let me add: One miracle is just as easy to believe as another.
Darrow:	It is for me.
Bryan:	It is for me.

Darrow:	Just as hard.
Bryan:	It is hard to believe for you, but easy for me. A miracle is a thing performed beyond what man can perform. When you get beyond what man can do, you get within the realm of miracles; and it is just as easy to believe the miracle of Jonah as any other miracle in the Bible.
Darrow:	Perfectly easy to believe that Jonah swallowed the whale?
Bryan:	If the Bible said so; the Bible doesn't make as extreme statements as evolutionists do.
Darrow:	That may be a question, Mr. Bryan, about some of those you have known.
Bryan:	The only thing is, you have a definition of fact that includes imagination.
Darrow:	And you have a definition that excludes everything but imagination, everything but imagination.
Stewart:	I object to that as argumentative.
Bryan:	You —
Darrow:	The witness must not argue with me, either.

. . .

Darrow:	Do you consider the story of Joshua and the sun a miracle?
Bryan:	I think it is.
Darrow:	Do you believe Joshua made the sun stand still?
Bryan:	I believe what the Bible says. I suppose you mean that the earth stood still?
Darrow:	I don't know. I am talking the Bible now.
Bryan:	I accept the Bible absolutely.
Darrow:	The Bible says Joshua commanded the sun to stand still for the purpose of lengthening the day, doesn't it, and you believe it?
Bryan:	I do.
Darrow:	Do you believe at that time the entire sun went around the earth?
Bryan:	No, I believe that the earth goes around the sun.
Darrow:	Do you believe that the men who wrote it thought that the day could be lengthened or that the sun could be stopped?
Bryan:	I don't know what they thought.
Darrow:	You don't know?
Bryan:	I think they wrote the fact without expressing their own thoughts.

. . .

Darrow:	Have you an opinion as to whether — whoever wrote the book, I believe it is, Joshua, the Book of Joshua, thought the sun went around the earth or not?
Bryan:	I believe that he was inspired.
Darrow:	Can you answer my question?
Bryan:	When you let me finish the statement.
Darrow:	It is a simple question but finish it.
Bryan:	You cannot measure the length of my answer by the length of your question.

Darrow: No, except that the answer be longer.
(Laughter in the courtyard.)

Bryan: I believe that the Bible is inspired, an inspired author. Whether one who wrote as he was directed to write understood the things he was writing about, I don't know.

Darrow: Whoever inspired it? Do you think whoever inspired it believed that the sun went around the earth?

Bryan: I believe it was inspired by the Almighty, and he may have used language that could be understood at that time —

Darrow: Was —

Bryan: (*cont.*): — instead of using language that could not be understood until Darrow was born.
(Laughter and applause in the courtyard.)

Darrow: So, it might not, it might have been subject to construction, might it not?

Bryan: It might have been used in language that could be understood then.

Darrow: That means it is subject to construction?

Bryan: That is your construction. I am answering your question.

Darrow: Is that correct?

Bryan: That is my answer to it.

Darrow: Can you answer?

Bryan: I might say, Isaiah spoke of God sitting upon the circle of the earth.

Darrow: I am not talking about Isaiah.

The Court: Let him illustrate, if he wants to.

Darrow: Is it your opinion that passage was subject to construction?

Bryan: Well, I think anybody can put his own construction upon it, but I do not mean that necessarily that is a correct construction. I have answered the question.

Darrow: Don't you believe that in order to lengthen the day it would have been construed that the earth stood still?

Bryan: I would not attempt to say what would have been necessary, but I know this, that I can take a glass of water that would fall to the ground without the strength of my hand and to the extent of the glass of water I can overcome the law of gravitation and lift it up. Whereas without my hand it would fall to the ground. If my puny hand can overcome the law of gravitation, the most universally understood, to that extent, I would not set power to the hand of Almighty God that made the universe.

Darrow: I read that years ago. Can you answer my question directly? If the day was lengthened by stopping either the earth or the sun, it must have been the earth?

Bryan: Well, I should say so.

Darrow: Yes? But it was language that was understood at that time, and we now know that the sun stood still as it was with the earth. We know also the sun does not stand still?

Bryan: Well, it is relatively so, as Mr. Einstein would say.

Anti-Evolution League. Outside the Dayton Courthouse, where the Scopes trial was conducted, evangelist T. T. Martin sold copies of his anti-evolution book, *Hell and the High School* (1923), in which he drew a connection between evolutionism and the "revolt of Youth" of the 1920s. (AP Photo)

Darrow: I ask you if it does stand still?

Bryan: You know as well as I know.

Darrow: Better. You have no doubt about it?

Bryan: No. And the earth moves around.

Darrow: Yes?

Bryan: But I think there is nothing improper if you will protect the Lord against your criticism.

Darrow: I suppose he needs it?

Bryan: He was using language at that time the people understood.

Darrow: And that you call "interpretation."

Bryan: No, sir; I would not call it interpretation.

Darrow: I say, you would call it interpretation at this time, to say it meant something then?

Bryan: You may use your own language to describe what I have to say, and I will use mine in answering.

Darrow: Now, Mr. Bryan, have you ever pondered what would have happened to the earth if it had stood still?

Bryan: No.

Darrow: You have not?

Bryan: No; the God I believe in could have taken care of that, Mr. Darrow.

Darrow: I see. Have you ever pondered what would naturally happen to the earth if it stood still suddenly?

Bryan: No.

Darrow: Don't you know it would have been converted into a molten mass of matter?

Bryan: You testify to that when you get on the stand, I will give you a chance.

Darrow: Don't you believe it?

Bryan: I would want to hear expert testimony on that.

Darrow: You have never investigated that subject?

Bryan: I don't think I have ever had the question asked.

Darrow: Or ever thought of it?

Bryan: I have been too busy on things that I thought were of more importance than that.

· · ·

Darrow: Do you believe that the first woman was Eve?

Bryan: Yes.

Darrow: Do you believe she was literally made out of Adam's rib?

Bryan: I do.

Darrow: Did you ever discover where Cain got his wife?

Bryan: No, sir; I leave the agnostics to hunt for her.

Darrow: You have never found out?

Bryan: I have never tried to find.

Darrow: You have never tried to find?

Bryan: No.

Darrow: The Bible says he got one, doesn't it? Were there other people on the earth at that time?

Bryan: I cannot say.

Darrow: You cannot say. Did that ever enter your consideration?

Bryan: Never bothered me.

Darrow: There were no others recorded, but Cain got a wife.

Bryan: That is what the Bible says.

Darrow: Where she came from you do not know. All right.

· · ·

■ **Discuss.** *It is clear from these sections of the transcript that at times the trial got well away from the particular teachings of one teacher, John Scopes. What does the transcript reveal about what is at stake in this trial beyond Scopes's career and his class's education? Discuss what larger questions brought this trial such intense national attention.*

■ **Write.** *Does either Darrow or Bryan come out as the clear winner in these exchanges? If you think so, use a close reading of the text to justify why you think one's logic is stronger than the other's. Or is this argument impossible to resolve?*

Jerome Lawrence and Robert E. Lee, from *Inherit the Wind.* Although Jerome Lawrence and Robert E. Lee fictionalized many of the trial participants and employed different names for all the characters, they nevertheless relied on some of the official transcripts. Compare this brief section of *Inherit the Wind,* when Darrow (here called Drummond) examines Bryan (here called Brady) on his knowledge of the Bible, with the actual dialogue recorded at the trial.

Jerome Lawrence and Robert E. Lee
FROM *INHERIT THE WIND*

■ **Consider before you read.** *How much do the authors of the play take directly out of the trial transcript? What do you notice about the parts they leave out or condense? What do they add to make the scene more dramatic?*

(Locates in court a copy of the Bible; without opening it, he scrutinizes the binding from several angles)

Drummond: Now let's get this straight. Let's get it clear. This *is* the book that you're an expert on?

(Brady is annoyed at Drummond's elementary attitude and condescension.)

Brady: That is correct.

Drummond: Now tell me. Do you feel that every word that's written in this book should be taken literally?

Brady: Everything in the Bible should be accepted, exactly as it is given there.

Drummond: *(Leafing through the Bible)* Now take this place where the whale swallows Jonah. Do you figure that actually happened?

Brady: The Bible does not say "a whale," it says "a big fish."

Drummond: Matter of fact, it says "a great fish" — but it's pretty much the same thing. What's your feeling about that?

Brady: I believe in a God who can make a whale and who can make a man and make both do what He pleases!

Voices: Amen, amen!

Drummond: *(Turning sharply to the clerk)* I want those "Amens" in the record! *(He wheels back to* Brady) I recollect a story about Joshua, making the sun stand still. Now as an expert, you tell me that's as true as the Jonah business. Right? (Brady *nods, blandly)* That's a pretty neat trick. You suppose Houdini could do it?

Brady: I do not question or scoff at the miracles of the Lord — as do ye of little faith.

429

■ **Consider.** *Why would Drummond want the "Amens" recorded? How does he think they support his case?*

430

Inherit the Wind. Christopher Plummer, left, as Henry Drummond, and Brian Dennehy, as Matthew Harrison Brady, in a 2007 revival of the 1955 play by Jerome Lawrence and Robert E. Lee at the Lyceum Theater in New York City. (Sara Krulwich/The New York Times/Redux)

Drummond:	Have you ever pondered just what would naturally happen to the earth if the sun stood still?
Brady:	You can testify to that if I get you on the stand. *(There is laughter.)*
Drummond:	If they say that the sun stood still, they must've had a notion that the sun moves around the earth. Think that's the way of things? Or don't you believe the earth moves around the sun?
Brady:	I have faith in the Bible!
Drummond:	You don't have much faith in the solar system.
Brady:	*(Doggedly)* The sun stopped.

Drummond:	Good. *(Level and direct)* Now if what you say factually happened — if Joshua halted the sun in the sky — that means the earth stopped spinning on its axis; continents toppled over each other, mountains flew out into space. And the earth, arrested in its orbit, shriveled to a cinder and crashed into the sun. *(Turning)* How come they missed *this* tidbit of news.?
Brady:	They missed it because it didn't happen.
Drummond:	It must've happened! According to natural law, or don't you believe in natural law, Colonel? Would you like to ban Copernicus from the classroom, along with Charles Darwin? Pass a law to wipe out all the scientific development since Joshua. Revelations — period!
Brady:	*(Calmly, as if instructing a child)* Natural law was born in the mind of the Heavenly Father. He can change it, cancel it, use it as He pleases. It constantly amazes me that you apostles of science, for all your supposed wisdom, fail to grasp this simple fact. *(Drummond flips a few pages in the Bible.)*
Drummond:	Listen to this: Genesis 4–16. "And Cain went out from the presence of the Lord, and dwelt in the land of Nod, on the East of Eden. And Cain *knew his wife!*" Where the hell did *she* come from?
Brady:	Who?
Drummond:	Mrs. Cain, Cain's wife. If, "In the beginning" there were only Adam and Eve, and Cain and Abel, where'd this extra woman spring from? Ever figure that out?
Brady:	*(Cool)* No, sir. I will leave the agnostics to hunt for her. *(Laughter.)*
Drummond:	Never bothered you?
Brady:	Never bothered me.
Drummond:	Never tried to find out?
Brady:	No.
Drummond:	Figure somebody pulled off another creation, over in the next county?
Brady:	The Bible satisfies me, it is enough.
Drummond:	It frightens me to imagine the state of learning in this world if everyone had your driving curiosity. *(Drummond is still probing for a weakness in Goliath's armor. He thumbs a few pages further in the Bible.)*

431

■ **Discuss.** Based on their questions and statements, discuss what kind of men Drummond and Brady are. Is one more likable than the other? Does either of the characters seem significantly different than in the trial transcript? Is the play directing your sympathies to one or the other, or are they neutral figures?

■ **Write.** In the actual trial, Clarence Darrow never took the stand. If he had, what kind of expertise would he have been called on to provide? Try drafting some questions that you think the character Brady would be likely to ask the Darrow character, Drummond.

The Reverend John Roach Straton, *The Most Sinister Movement in the United States*, December 26, 1925. A few months after the trial, a popular fundamentalist minister, John Roach Straton, heatedly argued against "the recent invasion of the sovereign state of Tennessee by a group of outside agnostics, atheists, Unitarian preachers, skeptical scientists, and political revolutionists."

The Reverend John Roach Straton

THE MOST SINISTER MOVEMENT IN THE UNITED STATES

■ **Consider before you read.** *Straton repeatedly uses words such as "aristocracy" and "sovereign." Why does he frame his argument in these terms? How does the language of politics reveal what issues Straton thinks are most important in the trial?*

The real issue at Dayton and everywhere today is: "Whether the religion of the Bible shall be ruled out of the schools and the religion of evolution, with its ruinous results — shall be ruled into the schools by law." The issue is whether the taxpayers — the mothers and fathers of the children — shall be made to support the false and materialistic religion, namely evolution, in the schools, while Christianity is ruled out, and thereby denied their children.

And with this goes the even deeper issue of whether the majority shall really have the right to rule in America, or whether we are to be ruled by an insignificant minority — an "aristocracy". . . of skeptical schoolmen and agnostics.

That is the exact issue in this country today. And that it is a very real and urgent issue is proved by the recent invasion of the sovereign state of Tennessee by a group of outside agnostics, atheists, Unitarian preachers, skeptical scientists, and political revolutionists. These uninvited men — including Clarence Darrow, the world's greatest unbeliever, and Dudley Malone, the world's greatest religious What-Is-It, — these and the other samples of our proposed "aristocracy" of would-be rulers, swarmed down to Dayton during the Scopes trial and brazenly tried to nullify the laws and overthrow the political and religious faiths of a great, enlightened, prosperous, and peaceful people.

And the only redeeming feature in all that unlovely parade of human vanity, arrogant self-sufficiency, religious unbelief, and anti-American defiance of majority rule was the courtesy, hospitality (even to unwelcome guests), forbearance, patience, and Christlike fortitude displayed by the noble judge, and the Christian prosecuting attorneys and people of Tennessee!

There was an element of profound natural irony in the entire situation. Darrow, Malone, and the other members of the Evolutionist Bund vicariously left their own communities and bravely sallied forth, like Don Quixote, to defeat the windmills and save other communities from themselves.

■ Consider. *Who is Don Quixote? Why does Straton compare Darrow to him?*

They left New York and Chicago, where real religion is being most neglected, where law, consequently, is most defied, where vice and crime are most rampant, and where the follies and ruinous immoralities of the rising generation — debauched already by religious modernism and a Godless materialistic science — smell to high heaven, and they went to save from itself a community where women are still honored, where men are still chivalric, where laws are still respected, where home life is still sweet, where the marriage vow is still sacred, and where man is still regarded, not as a descendant of the slime and beasts of the jungle, but as a child of God, with the wisdom and love of a divine Revelation in his hands, to guide him on life's rugged road, to give him the knowledge of a Savior from his sins, and to plant in his heart the hope of heaven to cheer him on his upward way!

And that is the sort of community which Darrow, Malone, and company left Chicago and New York to save!

Think of the illogic of it! and the nerve of it! and the colossal vanity of it!

Little wonder it is recorded in Holy Writ that "He that sitteth in the Heavens shall laugh" at the follies of men! And surely the very battlements of Heaven must have rocked with laughter at the spectacle of Clarence Darrow, Dudley Malone, and their company of cocksure evolutionists going down to save the South from itself!

It is all the other way around! The religious faith and the robust conservatism of the chivalric South and the sturdy West will have to save America from the sins and shams and shames that are now menacing her splendid life!

433

■ **Discuss.** *Straton uses the word "chivalric" twice to describe the South and calls the West "sturdy." Discuss the implications of these adjectives. What terms does Straton use to characterize the East?*

■ **Write.** *Why does Straton see irony in Darrow's coming to Tennessee? Write an essay about what Straton means and whether there really is **irony** in the situation.*

 CONSIDER THE CLUSTER
Religion in America: The Scopes Monkey Trial

■ **Message**

Consider the sentiments expressed by the Reverend John Roach Straton. What do you think of his argument? To what extent do you think his point of view depends on exaggeration?

■ **Method**

How would you describe Clarence Darrow's method of argument as he examines William Jennings Bryan? What main issue runs through his questioning? What is Darrow trying to get Bryan to admit? In an essay, discuss the techniques behind Darrow's examination and whether you think they are effective. Can you think of responses Bryan might have made that would better support his position?

■ **Medium**

In *Inherit the Wind,* the authors attempted to turn the Scopes trial into a Broadway play. In an essay, compare and contrast the excerpts from the actual trial with the way Lawrence and Lee have adapted it for dramatic purposes. What elements have they retained from the trial? How have they altered the actual dialogue? In your essay, explain why you think the playwrights made the changes they did. How has their chosen medium — the stage — affected the presentation of historical material?

434

EXPOSING WAR

PERSUASIVE ESSAY | PHOTOS | JOURNAL | TRANSCRIPT | AD | OP-ART/COMIC

■ **Cluster menu: Exposing War**

435

"Central to modern expectations, and modern ethical feeling," writes the renowned critic Susan Sontag, "is the conviction that war is an aberration, if an unstoppable one. That peace is the norm, if an unattainable one. This, of course, is not the way war has been regarded throughout history. War has been the norm and peace the exception." In our time, Sontag notes in her book *Regarding the Pain of Others* (2003), the public sees war largely through photographs and video clips. What do these images tell us about the reality of combat? What sense do we make of the harrowing pictures and atrocious images displayed in magazines and on our TV screens? Do we turn away from them, or do we — as Sontag suggests — let "the atrocious images haunt us"? For Sontag, the images "perform a vital function." They say: "This is what human beings are capable of doing — may volunteer to do, enthusiastically, self-righteously. Don't forget."

Although *Regarding the Pain of Others* covers a wide array of war images, from the Civil War through the war in Iraq, the book includes no photographs. In this chapter, we have included a few of the significant photographs Sontag mentions — Alexander Gardner's grim photograph of the battlefield at Gettysburg and Ronald L. Haeberle's astonishing photos of the My Lai massacre during the Vietnam War. Gardner's comments on his Gettysburg photo accompany the photograph, and the My Lai photos are supplemented by two documents from the subsequent military trial of the officer responsible for the massacre. Also included here is an advertisement that pertains to the argument Sontag makes in "Watching Suffering from a Distance," an excerpt from one of the final chapters of her book.

This cluster concludes with a visual essay by noted artist Marjane Satrapi that recounts a recent visit to the United States Military Academy at West Point, New York. What she experienced there bore little resemblance to what she anticipated.

Susan Sontag, *Watching Suffering from a Distance*. One of America's best-known and most admired writers, activists, and theorists, Susan Sontag was born in New York City in 1933; she grew up in Tucson, Arizona, and attended high school in Los Angeles. She received her BA from the College of the University of Chicago and did graduate work in philosophy, literature, and theology at Harvard University and Saint Anne's College, Oxford. Her publications include fiction, plays, screenplays, and eight important works of nonfiction, including *Against Interpretation* (1966), *On Photography* (1978), *Illness as Metaphor* (1979), *and Where the Stress Falls* (2001). Sontag also wrote on the photographs from the notorious Abu Ghraib prison in Iraq. She won numerous awards, including the National Book Award. The following essay is taken from chapter 8 of *Regarding the Pain of Others* (2003). In this book, Sontag explores war as we know it through images; along the way, she reconsiders some of the ideas she laid out in her highly influential book *On Photography*. Sontag died of leukemia in 2004.

Susan Sontag
WATCHING SUFFERING
FROM A DISTANCE

437

■ **Consider before you read.** *How does Sontag think images of human suffering affect viewers? Why should we look at them? Are there any circumstances when portraying suffering is unacceptable?*

To designate a hell is not, of course, to tell us anything about how to extract people from that hell, how to moderate hell's flames. Still, it seems a good in itself to acknowledge, to have enlarged, one's sense of how much suffering caused by human wickedness there is in the world we share with others. Someone who is perennially surprised that depravity exists, who continues to feel disillusioned (even incredulous) when confronted with evidence of what humans are capable of inflicting in the way of gruesome, hands-on cruelties upon other humans, has not reached moral or psychological adulthood.

No one after a certain age has the right to this kind of innocence, of superficiality, to this degree of ignorance, or amnesia.

There now exists a vast repository of images that make it harder to maintain this kind of moral defectiveness. Let the atrocious images haunt us. Even if they are only tokens, and cannot possibly encompass most of the reality to which they refer, they still perform a vital function. The images say: This is what human beings are capable of doing — may volunteer to do, enthusiastically, self-righteously. Don't forget.

This is not quite the same as asking people to remember a particularly monstrous bout of evil. ("Never forget.") Perhaps too much value is assigned to memory, not enough to thinking. Remembering *is* an ethical act, has ethical value in and of itself. Memory is, achingly, the only relation we can have with the dead. So the belief that remembering is an ethical act is deep in our natures as humans, who know we are going to die, and who mourn those who in the normal course of things die before us — grandparents, parents, teachers, and older friends. Heartlessness and amnesia seem to go together. But history gives contradictory signals about the value of remembering in the much longer span of a collective history. There is simply too much injustice in the world. And too much remembering (of ancient grievances: Serbs, Irish) embitters. To make peace is to forget. To reconcile, it is necessary that memory be faulty and limited.

If the goal is having some space in which to live one's own life, then it is desirable that the account of specific injustices dissolve into a more general understanding that human beings everywhere do terrible things to one another.

Parked in front of the little screens — television, computer, palmtop — we can surf to images and brief reports of disasters throughout the world. It seems as if there is a greater quantity of such news than before. This is probably an illusion. It's just that the spread of news is "everywhere." And some people's sufferings have a lot more intrinsic interest to an audience (given that suffering must be acknowledged as having an audience) than the sufferings of others. That news about war is now disseminated worldwide does not mean that the capacity to think about the suffering of people far away is significantly larger. In a modern life — a life in which there is a superfluity of things to which we are invited to pay attention — it seems normal to turn away from images that simply make us feel bad. Many more would be switching channels if the news media were to devote more time to the particulars of human suffering caused by war and other infamies. But it is probably not true that people are responding less.

That we are not totally transformed, that we can turn away, turn the page, switch the channel, does not impugn the ethical value of an assault by images. It is not a defect that we are not seared, that we do not suffer *enough,* when we see these images. Neither is the photograph supposed to repair our ignorance about the history and causes of the suffering it picks out and frames. Such images cannot be more than an invitation to pay attention, to reflect, to learn, to examine the rationalizations for mass suffering offered by established powers. Who caused what the picture shows? Who is responsible? Is it excusable? Was it inevitable? Is there some state of affairs which we have accepted up to now that ought to be challenged? All this, with the understanding that moral indignation, like compassion, cannot dictate a course of action.

The frustration of not being able to do anything about what the images show may be translated into an accusation of the indecency of regarding such images, or the indecencies of the way such images are disseminated — flanked, as they may well be, by advertising for emollients, pain relievers, and SUVs. If we could do something about what the images show, we might not care as much about these issues.

Images have been reproached for being a way of watching suffering at a distance, as if there were some other way of watching. But watching up close — without the mediation of an image — is still just watching.

Some of the reproaches made against images of atrocity are not different from characterizations of sight itself. Sight is effortless; sight requires spatial distance; sight can be turned off (we have lids on our eyes, we do not have doors on our ears). The very qualities that made the ancient Greek philosophers consider sight the most excellent, the noblest of the senses are now associated with a deficit.

It is felt that there is something morally wrong with the abstract of reality offered by photography; that one has no right to experience the suffering of others at a distance, denuded of its raw power; that we pay too high a human (or moral) price for those hitherto admired qualities of visions — the standing back from the aggressiveness of the world which frees us for observation and for elective attention. But this is only to describe the function of the mind itself.

There's nothing wrong with standing back and thinking. To paraphrase several sages: "Nobody can think and hit someone at the same time."

■ **Discuss.** *Discuss Sontag's assertion that "some people's sufferings have a lot more intrinsic interest to an audience." What might make some suffering more interesting to those viewing it? Are there ethical problems with these differences in interest?*

■ **Write.** *Do you agree with Sontag that a continual surprise at atrocity is a sign of "moral defectiveness"? Write a response in which you either explain why surprise is an immature reaction to images of suffering or give reasons why surprise is valid or even useful.*

439

COMMENT

"We were all part of it. I was like an accessory to the fact, if they want to call it murder. Every GI there was. . . . To me it was hard to rationalize, like, is that part of war? I mean, it may be the first time you see something like that, and what are you going to think. You don't know until you're there. You don't know until you experience it."

— Ronald L. Haeberle, combat photographer

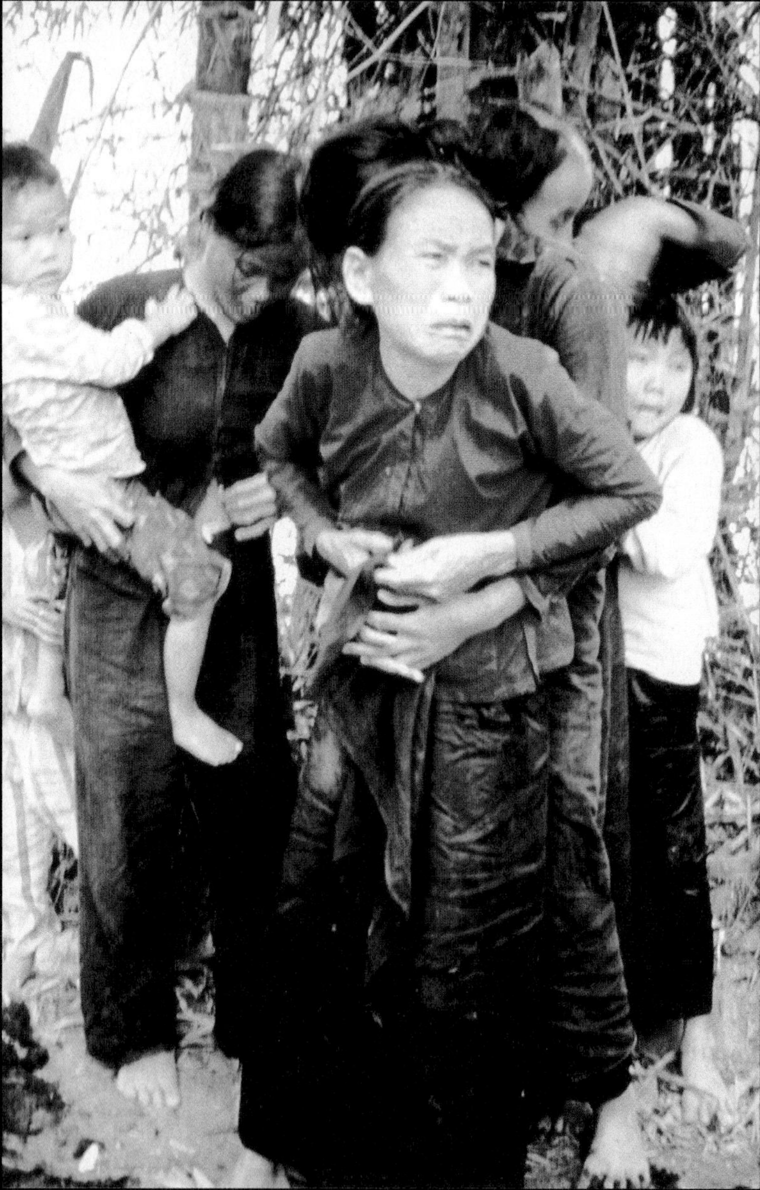

441

◀ **Ronald L. Haeberle,** *My Lai villagers before and after being shot by U.S. troops.*
Combat photography became part of military life in the mid-nineteenth century,
changing the nature of the public's relation to national conflicts. Photographs of
war satisfied public curiosity far more than sketches or words had previously, and
the military quickly learned that photographs could be incredibly useful in sway-
ing public opinion. During World War II, photographs were carefully released
and controlled — sometimes even staged — to satisfy the military's need to control its image and to celebrate American heroes in the field.

The Vietnam War, however, was as different for photographers as it was for the
soldiers in the field — photojournalists played an important role in exposing the
space between what the U.S. government wanted to claim and what was actually
happening. Haeberle, a combat photographer, accompanied Charlie Company to
My Lai and recorded the massacre on both his official black-and-white army camera and his personal color camera. When his personal photographs appeared in *Life*
magazine on December 5, 1969, they provoked international outrage and enormous media coverage. The pictures of the My Lai massacre are only one example —
albeit some of the most famous — of the images that sparked antiwar sentiments in
the United States. (Ronald L. Haeberle/Getty Images)

442

Thomas R. Partsch, *March 16–18, 1968.* Early in the morning of March 16, 1968, Captain ▶
Ernest Medina's Charlie Company attacked the small village of My Lai (the troops also
referred to it as "Pinkville"), expecting to encounter an enemy battalion. But Charlie
Company found no resistance and saw only civilians. For the next four hours, they killed
between four hundred and five hundred Vietnamese — mostly women, children, babies,
and the elderly. According to eyewitnesses, many women and girls were raped and then
brutally executed. Not all the soldiers participated; some refused to fire, and some tried
to stop what would become one of the most disgraceful episodes in U.S. military history.
The army tried to keep the incident secret, but there were too many leaks; in November
1969, the government launched an official investigation. Many Americans disbelieved the
rumors or excused them as an unfortunate part of warfare until they saw the shocking photographs released by *Life* magazine a month later. One of the men in Charlie Company
who kept a war journal was Thomas R. Partsch. During the subsequent military trial, the
relevant parts of his journal (March 16–March 18, 1968) were introduced as evidence.

Thomas R. Partsch
MARCH 16–18, 1968

■ **Consider before you read.** *What details of Partsch's account do you find most revealing? How does it differ from what an outsider might write about the war in Vietnam?*

<u>Mar 16 Sat.</u> got up at 5:30 left at 7:15 we had 9 choppers. 2 lifts first landed had mortar team with us. We started to move slowly through the village shooting everything in sight children men and women and animals. Some was sickening. There legs were shot off and they were still moving it was just hanging there. I think there bodies were made of rubber. I didn't fire a round yet and didn't kill anybody not even a chicken I couldn't. We are know suppose to push through 2 more it is about 10 A.M. and we are taken a rest before going in. We also got 2 weapons M1 and a carbine our final desti[na]tion is the Pinkville suppose to be cement bunkers we killed about 100 people after a while they said not to kill women and children. Stopped for chow about 1 P.M. we didn't do much after that. We are know setting up for the night 2 companies B and someone else we are set up in part of a village and rice patties had to dig foxhole area pretty level are mortars are out with us. Are serving hot chow tonite I looked in my pack for dry socks and found out they were stolen from the time we were out in the field the name of the villages are My Lai 4, 5, and 6. I am know pulling my guard for night. 1 1/2 hours I am with the 1st squad had pop and beer. Sky is a little cloudy but it is warm out.

 <u>Mar 17 Sun:</u> got up at 6:30 foggy out. We didn't go to Pinkville went to My Lai 2, 3, and 4 no one was there we burned as we pushed. We got 4 VC and a nurse. Had documents on them yesterday we took 14 VC. We pushed as far as the coast to the South China Sea there was a village along the coast also a lot of sailboats we stayed there for about an hour we went back about 2 kilometers to set up camp its in a graveyard actually we didn't pull guard but awake most of the night.

 <u>Mar 18 Mon:</u> moved back to another area 1 VC said he would take us to a tunnel he took us all over didn't find any after that we met with other platoons as we were going 2 guys hit mines there flack jackets saved them not hurt bad Trevino and Gonzalez . . . [T]here is a lot of fuss on what happened at the village a Gen was asking questions. There is going to be an investigation on Medina. We are not supposed to say anything. I didn't think it was right but we did it but we did it at least I can say I didn't kill anybody. I think I wanted to but in another way I didn't.

■ **Consider.** *What elements make Partsch's journal authentic? How do spelling and grammatical errors contribute? What details does he introduce that persuade you he is an actual participant and witness to the event? Why do you think he's keeping this journal? What does his attitude appear to be toward the massacre?*

443

■ **Discuss.** *Partsch mixes the events at My Lai with observations of the weather and discussion of mundane things such as socks and pop. How do these shifts affect you as a reader? What do they suggest about daily life in military service?*

■ **Write.** *What parts of this excerpt do you think the prosecutors in the military trial were most interested in? Write a list of what you would want to bring up in court and why you think it is important.*

William L. Calley Court-Martial Transcript, 1970. In this excerpt from his court-martial trial, Calley talks about his combat experiences before My Lai. After the investigation and trials, Lieutenant Calley, a platoon leader who claimed he acted under direct orders, was the only defendant found guilty of war crimes. In March 1971, he was sentenced to life imprisonment for multiple murders. He was pardoned and released in 1974.

William L. Calley
COURT-MARTIAL TRANSCRIPT

■ **Consider before you read.** *In this excerpt from his trial transcript, Lieutenant William L. Calley answers questions about some of the events that led up to the massacre. How does he try to explain his involvement? What does he say about his emotional state at the time?*

Q: Every time that the company would go, at least a company-sized unit, to try to get in that area and stay there, they encountered hostile fire, enemy fire, suffered casualties, and were driven out?

A: Yes, sir. [Calley was asked about an incident that occurred when he was returning to his company from in-country R and R. As he was waiting for a helicopter to take him to his men, he helped unload a chopper filled with casualties caused by a minefield.]

Q: What did you see and what did you do in connection with that helicopter when it landed back there and before you boarded up to go to meet your company?

A: The chopper was filled with gear, rifles, rucksacks. I think the most — the thing that really hit me hard was the heavy boots. There must have been six boots there with the feet still in them, brains all over the place, and everything was saturated with blood, rifles blown in half. I believe there was one arm on it and a piece of a man's face, half of a man's face was on the chopper with the gear.

Q: Did you later subsequently learn that those members that were emaciated in that manner were members of your company or your platoon?

A: I knew at the time they were.

Q: What was your feeling when you saw what you did see in the chopper and what you found out about your organization being involved in that kind of an operation?

A: I don't know if I can describe the feelings.

Q: At least try.

A: It's anger, hate, fear, generally sick to your stomach, hurt.

Q: Did it have any impact on your beliefs, your ideas, or what you might like to do in connection with somehow or other on into combat and accomplishing your mission? Am I making that too complicated for you?

A: I believe so.

Q: I'm trying to find out if it had any impact on your future actions as you were going to have to go in and if you did go in and reach the enemy on other occasions and if so, what was the impact?

A: I'm not really sure of what my actual feelings were at that time. I can't sit down and say I made any formal conclusions of what I would do when I met the enemy. I think there is an — that instilled a deeper sense of hatred for the enemy. I don't think I ever made up my mind or came to any conclusion as to what I'd do to the enemy.

Q: All right. Now did you have any remorse or grief or anything?

A: Yes, sir, I did.

Q: What was that?

A: The remorse for losing my men in the mine field. The remorse that those men ever had to go to Vietnam, the remorse of being in that situation where you are completely helpless. I think I felt mainly remorse because I wasn't there, although there was nothing I could do. There was a psychological factor of just not being there when everything is happening.

Q: Did you feel sorry that you weren't there with your troops?

A: Yes, sir.

445

■ **Discuss.** *Calley suggests that he felt remorse for not being there when the men from his company went into the minefield. Discuss why Calley focuses on this moment, when he wasn't even present. Are you surprised that he doesn't express any remorse for the mass killings in My Lai?*

■ **Write.** *Write an essay in which you compare Calley's verbal description of dismembered bodies with one of the photographs that Sontag mentions. Which has a greater impact on the listener or viewer? Is one more ethically justified than the other? How do words and images treat the subject of violence differently?*

COMMENT

"I think most Americans understood that the My Lai massacre was not representative of our people, of the war we were fighting, or of our men who were fighting it; but from the time it first became public the whole tragic episode was used by the media and the antiwar forces to chip away at our efforts to build public support for our Vietnam objectives and policies."

— Richard Nixon

446

Emina Uzicanin was just 5 years old. Her family was living on the outskirts of Sarajevo. On a sunny afternoon in May, Emina was playing in a field behind her Uncle's house. There, she spotted two little rabbits. As soon as she started toward them, the rabbits took off. So she began running. Five feet. Ten feet. That's when it happened. An ear-shattering explosion ripped through Emina's body — severing her left leg and leaving the rest of her badly scarred. Every 22 minutes another innocent civilian is killed or maimed by a land mine. Right now there are over 60 million unexploded land mines waiting just beneath the earth in nearly 70 countries. We need your help to rid the planet of land mines and to help its victims like Emina.

Physicians Against Land Mines
Member of the International Campaign to Ban Land Mines

www.banmines.org

◀ **The Center for International Rehabilitation (formerly known as Physicians against Land Mines),** *Emina's* **Story.** Although used primarily for military purposes, land mines exact a horrifying toll on civilian populations, primarily in developing nations. It is estimated that more than 80 percent of all land-mine victims are civilians. Of these, 30 to 40 percent are children under age fifteen. In 1999, 137 countries signed a treaty prohibiting the use, stockpiling, and production of land mines, but the United States, along with Russia and China, refused to sign. In 1996, Dr. William Kennedy Smith founded Physicians against Land Mines (PALM), which describes itself as a "nongovernmental organization whose mission is to end the death, dismemberment and disability caused by land mines." It sponsored public information initiatives, advocated reforms in international law, and ran numerous disability programs. PALM also educated the public through advertisements such as the one reprinted here, designed by advertising company Leo Burnett for use in magazines, in bus shelters, and inside buses and trains. Several magazines — including *Harper's, Atlantic Monthly, Bomb,* and *People* — have donated space for this ad campaign.

In 1998 PALM became the Chicago-based, not-for-profit organization 'Center for International Rehabilitation' (CIR) and initiated its Rehabilitation Engineering Research Center on Landmine Victim Assistance. Today the CIR conducts research, raises awareness, and promotes action to improve the quality and advancement of medical and rehabilitation services in remote and medically underserved areas. The CIR describes its work as "empowering individuals and communities across the globe to improve the lives of people with disabilities and expands treatment options, for those who otherwise would not have access to specialty care, through innovative engineering projects, capacity-building education programs, interactive online tools, and human rights advocacy." (Center for International Rehabilitation)

447

COMMENT

"Emina Uzicanin was just 5 years old. Her family was living on the outskirts of Sarajevo. On a sunny afternoon in May, Emina was playing in a field behind her Uncle's house. There, she spotted two little rabbits. As soon as she started toward them, the rabbits took off. So she began running. Five feet. Ten feet. That's when it happened. An ear-shattering explosion ripped through Emina's body — severing her left leg and leaving the rest of her badly scarred. Every 22 minutes another innocent civilian is killed or maimed by a land mine. Right now there are over 60 million unexploded land mines waiting just beneath the earth in nearly 70 countries. We need your help to rid the planet of land mines and to help its victims like Emina."

— "Emina's Story," from the Center for International Rehabilitation Web site (cirnetwork.org)

■ **Consider.** *What do you think the pronoun "its" refers to? Would you have expected the word "their" instead? Given the grammatical structure, what is Emina Uzicanin a victim of? How do you interpret the phrasing? Do you think the copywriter made a grammatical error?*

Marjane Satrapi

WHEN I WAS INVITED TO SPEAK AT WEST POINT

■ **Consider before you read/view.** *Satrapi composes her comic in a way that draws direct parallels between the imagined visit and the real one. What differences does this parallel structure highlight? When is it used for humor? When is it used to make serious points?*

◀ **Marjane Satrapi,** *When I Was Invited to Speak at West Point.* The internationally prominent artist and writer Marjane Satrapi was born in Iran in 1969. Her best-selling graphic memoir *Persepolis: The Story of a Childhood* (2003) was widely translated and named one of *Time* magazine's "Best Comix of the Year." *Persepolis* and *Perspolis 2: The Story of a Return* (2004) were the basis of a 2008 motion picture that enjoyed an Oscar nomination and a prize at the Cannes Film Festival. Satrapi's graphic commentaries (or "op-art") have appeared in newspapers worldwide, including *The New York Times,* where "When I Was Invited to Speak at West Point" was presented on May 28, 2005. (Reprinted by permission of Marjane Satrapi)

■ **Discuss.** *What assumptions about West Point inform Satrapi's ideas about what the visit will be like? Discuss perceptions of the military, especially military academies, and how Satrapi's experience complicates those perceptions.*

■ **Write.** *How does op-art as a genre compare with what you normally see in the op-ed page? Compare Satrapi's comic with a recent op-ed from* The New York Times. *Which do you find more engaging? More informative? Write an essay about the benefits and drawbacks of both media.*

 **CONSIDER THE CLUSTER**
Exposing War

449

■ **Message**
What do you think is the central message of Marjane Satrapi's graphic essay recounting her speech at West Point? What feature of the selection reinforces this message? As an in-class assignment, identify the main message but also explain what in your opinion complicates Satrapi's message. To what extent does she dramatize the complications?

■ **Method**
Sontag deliberately includes no photographs in her book. The editors of this book, however, made a decision to include a few of the pictures she refers to. Which method do you find most effective in this particular case: visually illustrating an argument, or choosing not to and having words speak for themselves? Explain your answer in a brief in-class essay.

■ **Medium**
Although Sontag focuses on photography as a medium for recording war and suffering, today we are more likely to see such images on television. What do you think is the strongest and most responsible medium for capturing the horror of war or the pain of others? Can you think of a moving picture that has lingered in your heart and mind as deeply as a still photograph? Or do words have a greater effect? In an essay, describe why you find one medium — whether photography, news footage, or text — more powerful than another.

WRITE ∎∎∎∎∎

1. **Analyze.** Note some of the similarities between the urban photographs of Weegee in Chapter 2 and those of Wayne F. Miller in this chapter. How would you describe the resemblance? What similarities can you find between, say, Weegee's "Mulberry Street Café" (p. 240) and Miller's "Two Girls Waiting outside a Tavern" (p. 413)? After examining Wendy Lesser's reading of Weegee's photos, write an essay in which you apply her analytical methods to one of Wayne Miller's pictures. How does the analysis contribute to your understanding of the photo's historical value?

2. **Research and collaborate.** Using the Internet, find out what you can about the Sand Creek massacre. Then, after reading the selection from Maya Lin on designing the Vietnam Veterans Memorial (p. 123), form several small groups to work independently on an appropriate design for a Sand Creek memorial. Be sure to touch on the relationship between the materials you would use and the site you would choose. Be sure also to anticipate criticisms you may receive from various interested parties. Afterward, form a panel in which a designated member of each group exhibits a rough sketch and provides a verbal description of the memorial's design.

3. **Compare and make a case.** In an essay, compare and contrast Susan Sontag's "Watching Suffering from a Distance" (p. 437) with Nora Ephron's "The Boston Photographs" (p. 243). In what ways are the essays similar? In what ways are the ethical issues similar? In your opinion, which writer deals with the ethical issues more effectively? Which set of photos do you find more disturbing? Why?

4. **Analyze and make a case.** Consider the Scopes trial in the context of the recent controversy between scientists and creationists. In an essay, discuss which issues and arguments that arose in the Scopes trial remain relevant today. Then consider how you think the issue has changed since 1925. For example, how have some of the terms now used in the debate changed? Can you picture a trial similar to the Scopes trial being aired on Court TV today? Would it attract the same degree of media attention? Who might be today's Darrows and Bryans?

5. **Evaluate.** After reviewing such selections as Jessica Helfand's "What We Saved" (p. 389) and Gordon Parks's "Speaking for the Past" (p. 418), consider in a reflective essay why preserving the past is important. Is there a logical or philosophical reason to do

450

MAKING HISTORY

so? Why do people save things, construct memorials, form collections, assemble scrapbooks, restore buildings and villages, reenact battles, and so on? Can you imagine a society in which no one cared to preserve the past or revist it?

6. **Collaborate and analyze.** Through the process of class discussion, collectively select a historical film (for example, *Malcolm X, Gandhi, The Patriot*) to watch as part of a class exercise. Watch it closely, especially noticing its use of historical details. Afterward, break into small groups and talk about the relation between the value of historical accuracy and the special demands of film. What aspects of the movie do you think were contrived or fabricated to serve the interests of entertainment — storytelling, emotional drama, and so on? What aspects do you think were handled accurately and truthfully? Did you think the movie was using an episode or character from the past mainly to reflect present-day values? Did you feel you had sufficient information beforehand to make these evaluations? In a paper, discuss how well the film you watched stacked up as history.

7. **Research and analyze.** A number of books and articles have been written about the My Lai massacre.

The investigation and trial captured the attention of the entire world. Using as much information as you can gather from library and Internet sources, write a research paper in which you describe how the facts of the incident leaked out. In your paper, explore the following questions, although you need not answer them all or in any particular order: What sequence of events immediately followed the massacre? Who talked and to whom? How did the army try to cover up the killings? How important were the eyewitness reports, and whose reports seemed most trustworthy? Did any Vietnamese testify? How important were the photographs in establishing the facts? Remember: the object is to narrate the step-by-step process of disclosure. Be sure to document your sources.

8. **Research.** Can the Internet provide the groundwork for a new social history in which people without credentials or influence tell their personal or communal stories? Can such sites become the foundation for what the historian Howard Zinn has called a "people's history" of the world? Can "virtual scrapbooks" serve serious historical purposes? In a paper that reflects your research of web sites and bulletin boards, identify those that now perform this historical function (or could possibly do

America's most bizarre and

so) and discuss how important these sites can be for future historians. You might take, for example, the Sand Creek massacre (p. 402): Can you find oral histories that give the perspectives of American Indians?

9. **Imagine and make a case.** Pretend that you have just won a national lottery to be the person to travel into the past in a time machine. The conditions: you can return to any moment you choose, but only for an hour, and although you will be invisible, you will retain your present consciousness. Write an essay about your imaginary voyage into the past. What moment did you select? How difficult was it to decide? Why did you finally choose that moment? Was there something you wanted to

know? What do you think you could tell the world when you returned?

10. **Research and analyze.** For a research project, read Gwendolyn Brooks's first volume of poetry, *A Street in Bronzeville* (1945), in conjunction with viewing whatever photographs of Chicago's South Side during that era you can find in the library or on the Internet. In a paper, discuss the ways in which the poet and the photographer converged toward the same subject matter. Do you think this convergence is accidental, or can you find reasons for the similarities? In your paper, make an attempt to show how these two different media can work toward similar artistic goals.

5

DIVIDING LINES

Dividing Lines: the clusters

Knowing who we are usually means knowing also who we are not. As individuals or in groups, we habitually define ourselves by our differences from others, drawing a line between "us" and "them." What are these powerful lines? Are they wholly imaginary, or do they have a concrete existence? To what extent do these lines shape personal identity and social behavior? How do they partition the world around us? Wherever you happen to be, if you pay close attention, you will notice dividing lines—both visible and invisible—everywhere. They include everything from the property boundaries of a suburban subdivision to the police barriers at a political demonstration, from a roommate's portion of a bookshelf to the variously priced seating sections of a stadium.

At certain points in our nation's history, religious differences—even relatively small ones between sects—led to widespread discrimination and violent conflict. The American Civil War was fought largely over the issue of slavery, which had been a constant source of regional and ideological tension since the nation's founding. In the 1960s, generational differences became heated, as counterculture leaders famously advised their followers not to trust anyone over the age of thirty, which meant essentially not to trust the authority of parents, political leaders, or teachers. In the 1990s, during the

Clinton presidency, both the Senate and the House were almost always divided according to strict party lines. The popular news media continue to present belligerent, polarized coverage of serious problems that—if you believe the commentators—have only two competing solutions, one liberal and the other conservative. The political terms "right" and "left" themselves originally referred to a sharp dividing line: conservative delegates to the French National Assembly, formed after the 1789 revolution, sat on the right side of the meeting hall, while radical delegates sat on the left.

The news media, which for the most part today frame the public issues, thrive on high drama and conflict: men versus women, black versus white, poor versus rich, gay versus straight, religious versus secular, blue-collar versus elite, human versus nonhuman. The model is invariably adversarial, as hard lines are drawn between opposing perspectives. Every story must have a conflict, and the more that conflict can be personalized—portrayed by individuals who instantly personify the various views—the better. Public discourse is reduced to extreme expression and accusation, as nuanced or moderate views find little air time. Complex or abstract stories are simplified by being physically embodied in a character who clearly stands for a position; thus, the news media find themselves every day rounding up the "usual suspects" for interviews and sound bites. This process has become so entrenched that it's difficult to tell when cultural, social, or political divisions are genuine and threatening or when they're fabricated or distorted by a news industry hungry for another juicy and profitable conflict.

Identifying serious divisions does, of course, play a major role in the maintenance of a just society. In the United States today, largely because of continuing legislation stemming from the Civil Rights Act of 1964, we are keen to detect unequal treatment based on "race, color, religion, sex, or national origin." We have also grown increasingly sensitive to the rights of the disadvantaged and disabled.

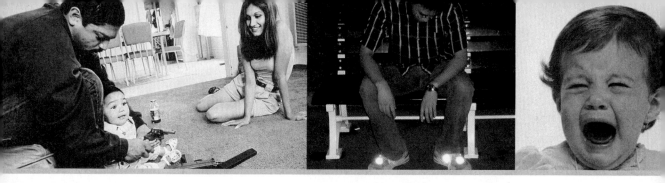

Much of what popularly goes under the name "multiculturalism" is a corrective response to the exclusionary practices of the past. Yet even as we strive to be inclusive and nondiscriminatory, the ideal of "diversity" depends on affirming differences. As citizens, we are asked to ignore differences but at the same time to recognize or even celebrate them. This seemingly contradictory state of mind often fuels contentious debates on race and gender matters or issues related to any victimized or marginalized group.

Many divisions have been intensified over the past several decades by what has become popularly known as "identity politics," a political position or perspective based on an individual's identification with a particular group, one typically based on gender, race, ethnicity, or sexual orientation. Since we all belong to multiple groups and have several allegiances, identity politics can lead to personal conflict, especially when we feel pressured to choose one allegiance over the rest. Within the earlier civil rights and antiwar movements, for example, young women frequently felt that they had to subordinate their feminist agenda in order to bolster the other efforts and that they had to endure the entrenched chauvinism of male leaders. What happens when the lines that divide one group from another are internalized within a single person? How do we decide whether ethnic heritage trumps gender or whether class matters more than race?

The convergence of multiculturalism and identity politics troubled many moderate-to-conservative political thinkers, who criticized the general movement for its simplistic relativism, archaic tribalism,

and naive anti-Americanism, which recognized marvelous human values everywhere on earth except at home. With political correctness added to the mix, even prominent liberals went on the offensive, criticizing the censorship and intimidation on college campuses that took the form of "speech codes." Although defenders of these codes believed they were contributing a much-needed sensitivity to minority perspectives and were helping curtail "hate speech," many others worried that writers, entertainers, artists, and even scholars were becoming increasingly controlled by the fear of offending one group or another.

The so-called culture wars were—and still are—vigorously fought on numerous fronts: in classrooms, press rooms, museums, and publishing houses. The broadcast media have found that they can turn the various culture wars into profitable entertainment by designing antagonistic talk shows, such as the enormously popular *O'Reilly Factor*, that regularly feature diametrically opposed political views. The success of these shows usually depends on one of the media's favorite conflicts: the hostility between the average citizen and the elite establishment. The conflict of "us" against "them" is, as we all know, one of life's persistent struggles, no matter who we are or what we believe. Urban gangs have little to do with establishments—elite or otherwise—yet their boundaries and turfs can be as violently disputed as those of hostile nations. Gang zones, however, are not official; they are not like the zoning laws that configure our towns and suburbs, where land use is strictly coded in order to benefit all who live and work within their limits. In this chapter, we will explore several kinds of dividing lines, large and small, hard and soft, public and private, with selections covering America's sexual, ethnic, political, and socioeconomic conflicts.

GENDER

■ Cluster menu: Gender

Throughout history and cultures, the differences between males and females have accounted for a seemingly endless amount of discussion, drama, and stereotyping. Although the subject is hardly new, we might think—judging from the continual stream of coverage it receives in the media—that the topic had only recently emerged as one of the central issues of our time. Nearly every day, on radio and TV shows, in magazine and newspaper features, and in comic strips and cartoons, we encounter some version of the popular notion that "men are from Mars and women are from Venus."

The idea that males and females seem to come from two different planets is counterbalanced today by the opposing notion that the differences between the sexes are socially and culturally constructed. This controversy cuts across many boundaries and disciplines—feminist studies, education, sports, the social and biological sciences, law and medicine, and so on. The material that follows explores just a few of the angles that writers and artists have taken when examining the issue of gender.

Roger Ressmeyer, *Crying Infants,* **1984.** Some experts claim that if we changed our patterns of childhood socialization and our expectations of what each sex is capable of, then we would discover that males and females are far more similar than we currently think. Others, however, claim that because sex is biologically determined, gender roles are more or less hardwired from infancy, if not earlier. (© Roger Ressmeyer/CORBIS)

ZITS   BY JERRY SCOTT AND JIM BORGMAN

Jerry Scott and Jim Borgman, *Zits* comic strip, *When Guys Hang Out.* Jerry Scott and Jim Borgman are cartoonists who work together on the award-winning comic strip *Zits* for the *Cincinnati Enquirer.* What do you think of the different communication styles that are portrayed here when "guys hang out" and when "girls hang out"? Do girls talk more than guys—and does it depend on the context? You might be surprised to learn that a recent study of college students conducted by the University of Arizona, the University of Texas, and Washington University, St. Louis, and reported on in *Science* magazine (July 2007) shows that both men and women speak about the same number of words each day (around sixteen thousand). (Zits © Zits Partnership, King Features Syndicate)

Penelope Scambly Schott, *Report on the Difference between Men and Women*. Although the literature surrounding the subject is vast, the writers of this text and the next have brilliantly managed to encapsulate their views in miniature. In Schott's mini-essay, we see a lifetime of marital experience distilled into a few paragraphs. Penelope Scambly Schott is a poet who also teaches college correspondence courses for adults. She is the author of a book-length historical poem, *Penelope: The Story of the Half-Scalped Woman* (1994) and of *The Pest Maiden: A Story of Lobotomy* (2004). Schott's latest book, *A is for Anne: Mistress Hutchinson Disturbs the Commonwealth* (2007), is a verse biography of Anne Hutchinson, who was expelled from Boston in 1638 by the Puritan fathers. Schott lives in Portland, Oregon.

Penelope Scambly Schott

REPORT ON THE DIFFERENCE BETWEEN MEN AND WOMEN

461

■ **Consider before you read.** *The "report" in the title suggests that this is a neutral, even scientific observation of the difference. How does the tone of Schott's essay support this title? Are there any moments when she diverges from pure reporting?*

After thirteen years and twenty-seven days of marriage, my husband turns to me and asks, "How come we never have lemonade?" He pauses. "That kind that comes frozen in a can?"

It's not like he's never been to the grocery store or I haven't asked him regularly if there's anything he'd like me to pick up, anything special he's in the mood for.

So on the twenty-eighth day of our fourteenth year of marriage, I go to the store and buy lemonade, that kind that comes frozen in the can. At the checkout, I push the frozen pale yellow cylinder onto the conveyor belt and look into the eyes of the middle-aged woman who is ringing up my groceries. Without preliminary, I announce, "After all the time we've been married, my husband just asked me yesterday, out of the blue, 'How come we never have lemonade?'"

■ *Consider. Why does Schott establish such a precise time frame in the beginning of her essay? What is the effect on the reader of this exactness?*

She looks back at me. The edges of her mouth flicker in and out. First the whole bottom of her face and then her shoulders begin to tremble. She convulses into giggling. Neither of us needs to say another word.

I go home, unbag, defrost the can, mix up his lemonade in a tall jar, shake it well, and put it in the refrigerator, front and center on the top shelf where even he can't miss it. When he comes in from work and starts browsing for something to drink, I say, "I bought lemonade today. It's right here in the front," and I point to it. He pours an enormous glass.

I wonder what else he secretly wants.

■ **Discuss.** *The subject of Schott's "Report" is a minor everyday event. Discuss why the last sentence suggests that this story about lemonade has larger implications.*

■ **Write.** *When Schott tells her story to the woman ringing her up at the grocery store, they seem to have a common understanding of what it means. How do you think they know this, even though neither one "needs to say another word"? Write a response in which you imagine the cashier's thoughts about Schott's revelation.*

462

> **Melanie Sumner, *Marriage*.** Melanie Sumner is a writer and reporter who has
> served in the Peace Corps, taught English in Senegal, and published a novel on
> growing up rich, female, and wild in the South, *The School of Beauty and Charm*
> (2001). Her work has been included in anthologies such as *Best of the South*,
> *New Stories from the South*, and *Living on the Edge: Fiction by Peace Corps
> Writers*. Sumner's mini–short story, like Schott's mini-essay, tells a great deal in
> a small space.

Melanie Sumner

MARRIAGE

■ **Consider before you read.** *How do the three voices we read in this story contrast with
one another? What do they suggest about the characters' personalities?*

"Every night," she told the marriage counselor, "he drinks a glass of milk. When
he's finished, he sets the empty glass on the kitchen counter and goes to bed. He
does not rinse it out. I have asked him and asked him. I've asked nicely, and I've
screamed. Why should I rinse his glass out for him every night? If I don't do it,
it's the first thing I see in the morning, this disgusting milk scum. I've even asked
him, 'Will you just put the glass in the sink?' But he won't."

The counselor looked at the husband, a balding, middle-aged man who sat
with his hands in his lap, a pleasant expression on his face.

"Did you hear what she was saying?" asked the counselor.

"Yes," said the man, nodding first at him, and then at his wife, to acknowledge everyone present.

A moment of silence passed. The counselor made a note on his pad, reminding
himself to pick up a gallon of milk after work. Then he made eye contact with the wife.

"There is something you need to understand," he said. "He will never, never
stop drinking that glass of milk before he goes to bed, and he will never rinse it
out. There is absolutely nothing you can do."

The woman looked surprised. Sometimes even after the divorce, she would
think about the counselor's words, marveling at his wisdom.

■ **Discuss.** *Do you agree with the woman that the counselor's remark displays great wisdom? Discuss why he strikes her as so wise. How profound is his advice?*

■ **Write.** *Why does the woman's complaint remind the counselor to buy milk? Write a
short essay about why Sumner includes that detail in the story. Does it give the reader any
insight into his character?*

■ Consider. *The photographer asks of this image, "Why presume the person behind you on the bus is some abstract stereotype you think they should be? At the time of this photo, these two were dating. Did you think that first?"*

464

Eric James, *School Bus.* This photograph was taken by a nineteen-year-old photographer and was published in *Look-Look*, a magazine for young writers, photographers, and artists. (© Look-Look Magazine/Eric James 2003)

Jan Morris, *Herstory*. Jan Morris (b. 1926), taking a broader view than Penelope Scambly Schott and Melanie Sumner, introduces us to significant gender differences and similarities. Born James Humphrey Morris, he felt from childhood that he should have been a girl—that he had simply been "wrongly equipped." Morris fathered five children before having a sex-change operation in 1972; he describes his transformation from James to Jan in the book *Conundrum*. A resident of Wales, United Kingdom, Jan Morris has worked as a military intelligence officer and a newspaper journalist and has authored books on British history and travel, as well as works of biography, memoir, and fiction. "Herstory" was published in 1999 in *Forbes ASAP*.

Jan Morris
HERSTORY

■ **Consider before you read.** *What assumptions about gender can you uncover in Morris's essay? How does she think people get a gender? Does gender have a purpose? If so, is that purpose social or biological?*

Twenty-seven years ago, almost on the cusp between the third and fourth quarters of the 20th century, I completed what was then simplistically called a change of sex. Nowadays it is more often euphemized as gender reassignment, and this shift of words is not simply semantic. It recognizes that across the civilized world, sex is no longer being seen as something absolute, and that the old immovable opposites of Male and Female may be converging after all.

When this happened to me—for I certainly did not ask for it, only obeyed an irresistible organic urge—it seemed to many people utterly astonishing, if not actually incredible. I was not the first person to undergo such a metamorphosis, but I suppose I seemed an unlikely candidate for it. I was a foreign correspondent and an established author, I had been a soldier, I was happily married with children, I was a staunch advocate of the stiff upper lip, grinning and bearing it, pulling myself together, and many another attitude popularly supposed to be particularly masculine. When it emerged that I had abandoned maleness and would, in the future, be known not as James but as Jan, some of my male acquaintances thought I must have gone off my head. Otherwise, why on earth would anybody rather be a woman than a man?

Gradually, though, it turned out that I was not crazy. I did not run away with
a property tycoon or appear topless in nightclubs. My family life remained happy
as ever, and I continued to write books. Now the quandary facing people was no
longer how best to humor me but how to deal with me as a woman rather than
as a man. And that is how it was that I first experienced for myself, in the world
of the 1970s, the great gulf that then still lay between the two halves of mankind.
The women's movement had long been stirring, but the great mass of people still
thought of male and female almost as separate species and treated them as differently as they would a dog and a cat.

Men, in those days, seem to me to have been much more courteous to women
(opening doors, taking hats off in elevators), but the dullards among them were
also much more condescending. They really did not take women very seriously.
I happened at that time to know rather a lot about oil politics in the Arab world
(I had been the Middle East correspondent for the *Times* of London), but I remember all too clearly with what patronizing contempt my opinions were dismissed
by men I met on airplanes. It just did not seem possible to them that a woman
could even be interested in, let alone conversant with, such grown-up, undomes-
tic matters, and the extraordinary thing was that men I had known for years now
instantly changed their personalities in my presence.

Women by and large were far less fazed. My change of life did not seem to
them so astonishing. They welcomed me as a recruit to the oppressed classes, and
they kindly helped me with the transition. Besides, I think some were attracted
by the very idea of a conjunction between male and female—for I did not try to
disguise the traits of temperament and intellect that remained with me from my
previous existence.

■ **Consider.** *Why might
women adjust more quickly to
Morris's "change of life"? How
does Morris account for their
sympathy?*

467

And in this they were, I think, far more responsive to the changing times
than most men were. For as the last decades of the century passed, that gap between
the sexes narrowed, and I began to be seen—to feel myself, too—not just as sym-
biotic but as symbolic, too. What was so unutterably bizarre, after all, in a sex
change? Which is the profounder entity: sex, which is a matter of hormones and
ovaries, or gender, which is spirit and taste, the form of talent, and the nature of
love? And anyway, are we not all an amalgam of male and female, in one degree
or another?

Of course, by then the historic rise of feminism was changing all the world's
attitudes. I could measure in male responses the tremendous shift of balance
between the sexes that was happening all around us—a redistribution of power
far greater and more fateful than any political revolution. No longer would male
mediocrities sweetly change the course of a conversation, if I ventured to insert a
thought about the possibilities of glasnost in the Soviet Union, or the historical
origins of Serbian intransigence. (And alas, perhaps only gentlemen of very uncertain age would remove their bowler hats when one entered the elevator.)

Slowly, tentatively, often reluctantly, the world was recognizing as nonsense
the antique inequality between the sexes, and the relationship between men and
women was achieving a new rationality. All revolutions are violent, and there was
certainly an element of brutal intolerance to this one. Often enough, standing in

the middle as I did, I felt myself sympathizing first with one party, then with another, as women rebelling against centuries of unfairness conflicted with men dazed by the collapse of so many inherited convictions. I could sympathize with women still scorned by damn fool bureaucrats and disgracefully underpaid; I felt sorry for men obliged to admit women into their cherished clubs, and willy-nilly to adapt their age-old conceptions. But I knew that such discomforts were only incidental to a vast beneficial rearrangement of humanity, not to be completed for another generation at least, and I felt a sort of undeserved pride to be standing as a living symbol of a great reconciliation.

For convergence, of course, is generally reconciliation. When you come up close, most things are not as bad as they looked from a distance, and men and women turn out to be not so different after all. Even physically, at the end of the 20th century, they are growing more alike: the women taller and stronger as they lead newer, freer lives, the men less macho as the organic need for brute force subsides.

Who would have thought, 50 years ago, that women would be playing soccer, let alone boxing? Or that men would habitually be sharing the housework—or for that matter, if we are to believe the hi-sci pundits (who are generally right), that they might one day be bearing babies? Who could have foreseen that the toughest politician in 1980s Europe would be female (Thatcher), and the most conciliatory in 1990s Africa, male (Mandela)?

Divinities of older times were sternly sexist, creating one sex first, elevating one above the other, obliging them to sit in separate parts of the temple. The deities of technology don't give a damn, and today's men and women bow down in perfect equality before the cybergods.

In the age of sperm banks and genetic engineering, nobody is much surprised by my life story. It is no big deal anyway: simply a matter, so the scientists say, of some birth anomaly of the brain. In another half century, I do not doubt, the convergence of the genders will have gone much further, and a good thing, too. By then I shall no longer be able to claim, even to myself, the status of a symbol. For one thing, switching between the sexes will be commonplace. For another, I shall be dead.

■ **Discuss.** *Does Morris's experience give her particular authority on the subject of gender? Discuss how her life gives her a unique perspective on the questions raised in this essay.*

■ **Write.** *What gains does Morris think the feminist movement has made? How does she expect gender perceptions to change in the future? Write a response in which you explain and assess Morris's claims of progress.*

 ## CONSIDER THE CLUSTER
Gender

■ Message

Explain what you think Jan Morris means when she writes that "the old immovable opposites of Male and Female may be converging after all." Could she mean that the two sexes are evolving biologically toward a new, third sex? Or that people can change their sex, as she has? Or that because of the feminist movement, women are becoming more like men and vice versa? Explain which of these summaries you think best conveys the message of Morris's essay, and why. Alternatively, do you think a different statement — or a combination of them all — works as a better summary of her viewpoint?

■ Method

What aspect of Melanie Sumner's method of writing in "Marriage" helps convey that her story is fictional? For example, if you rewrote the story in the first person — using the perspective of any one of the three characters — what information or details would you not be able to include? And if you turned Penelope Scambly Schott's essay into a story told in the third person, what information or details might you decide to include? How would the exclusion or inclusion of these elements affect your ability to produce an effective narrative?

■ Medium

Look carefully at Eric James's photograph of teenagers on a school bus. In what ways does the photograph visually convey the dividing lines of gender? Using Sumner's story or Schott's essay as a model, write a very short story or essay (no more than several paragraphs) in which you transform James's photograph into a brief prose narrative that dramatizes gender roles.

COLOR LINES

■ **Cluster menu: Color Lines**

In the introduction to his 1903 classic, *The Souls of Black Folk,* W. E. B. DuBois wrote presciently that "the problem of the Twentieth Century is the problem of the color line." He envisioned a century in which the races would be socially, culturally, and politically divided.

But will DuBois's prediction hold true for the twenty-first century? In "Race Over," the prominent African American sociologist Orlando Patterson tries to imagine America's racial future. He comes up with a national scenario, based largely on changing demographic patterns, that is both concise and controversial. "By the middle of the twenty-first century," Patterson predicts, "America will have problems aplenty. But no racial problem whatsoever."

Whether today's college generation will ever see such an uplifting future is highly debatable, but it has been noted by many commentators that, as the *New York Times* put it, "the under-25 members" of today's generation represent "the most racially diverse population in the nation's history." The growing attraction to young audiences of what some call "ethnic ambiguity" has not been lost on both the media and the marketing image-makers, who now feature stars, models, athletes, and artists whose ethnic heritages are not readily identifiable. One fashion magazine editor said recently: "We're seeing more of a desire for the exotic, left-of-center beauty that transcends race or class."

Orlando Patterson, *Race Over.* Orlando Patterson, a professor of sociology at Harvard University, specializes in the analysis of slavery in different societies and historical moments, from ancient Greece and Rome to the American South. As Patterson notes on his web page, he is interested in "the culture and practice of freedom; the comparative study of slavery and ethno-racial relations; the sociology of underdevelopment with special reference to the Caribbean; and the problems of gender and familial relations in the black societies of the Americas." He is especially concerned with the relationship between "cultural processes" and poverty. In addition to three novels, Patterson has published several scholarly works, most recently *Rituals of Blood: Consequences of Slavery in Two American Centuries* (1999). His essays have appeared in *The New York Times, Time, Newsweek, The New Republic,* and *The Washington Post.* In this essay, he explores the possibility of a time when race ceases to be a factor in systems of power. "Race Over" appeared in the January 10, 2000, issue of *The New Republic.*

Orlando Patterson
RACE OVER

471

■ **Consider before you read.** *In this essay, Patterson argues that in the near future, racial problems will not so much go away as be redirected. If race is no longer a defining factor in American life, what will replace it?*

One can quibble with W. E. B. DuBois's famous prediction for the twentieth century. This has been not simply the century of the color line but a century of Jim Crow and myriad other persecutions—many within color boundaries. But, if DuBois's epigraph was only half right, his modern-day disciples, who insist the color line will define the next 100 years as well, are altogether wrong. The racial divide that has plagued America since its founding is fading fast—made obsolete by migratory, sociological, and biotechnological developments that are already under way. By the middle of the twenty-first century, America will have problems aplenty. But no racial problem whatsoever.

For this we can thank four social patterns, each indigenous to a particular region of the country but which together will reshape the nation as a whole. The strongest and clearest might be called the California system. Cultural and somatic mixture will be its hallmark. A hybrid population, mainly Eurasian—but with a growing Latin element—will come to dominate the middle and upper classes and will grow exponentially, especially after the 2020s. Lower-class Caucasians, middle-class racial purists, and most African Americans, under pressure from an endless stream of unskilled Mexican workers, will move away. Those African Americans who remain will be rapidly absorbed into the emerging mixed population. The California system will come to dominate the American and Canadian Pacific Rim.

The second major pattern might be called the Caribbean-American system. Increasingly, the countries of the Caribbean basin will be socially and economically integrated with the United States. As their fragile and already declining economies collapse (most dramatically in post-Castro Cuba), they will swarm the mainland by legal and illegal means. Florida will be the metropolitan center of this system, although Caribbean colonies will sprout all over the Northeast. Caribbean peoples will bring their distinctive concept of race and color to America, one in which people marry lighter and "white" as they move up the social ladder. This system will differ from the California one in that the dominant element will be Afro-Latin rather than Eurasian. Since the Caribbean is much closer than Asia, this system will also create a distinctive social type: genuinely transnational and post-national communities in which people feel equally at home in their native and American locations. Increasingly, people will spend their childhoods and retirements in the Caribbean and their productive years in America. The Caribbean-American system will compete with the African American community not only in the lower reaches of the labor force but as the nation's major source of popular culture, especially in music and sports. But, despite these differences, the Caribbean-American system, like the California one, will render the "one drop" rule obsolete.

The third and most problematic system will be the one now emerging in the Northeast and urban Midwest. Here, the economic situation for all classes of African Americans and native-born Latinos is likely to deteriorate—with the ending of affirmative action, a shrinking public sector, and competition from skilled and unskilled (mainly Caribbean basin) immigrant labor. The rise of workfare without compensating provision for child care, combined with the growing pattern of paternal abandonment of children, will further undermine traditional family norms among African American, Latino, and, increasingly, the European American lower classes. Reversing the pattern that emerged after World War II, African Americans, Latinos, and the poorest Caucasians will move into the inner and secondary rings of what are now mainly European American middle-class suburbs. The middle classes will move to either gated exurbs or gentrified central cities—leaving a European American underclass that resembles other ethnic underclasses more and more.

But, although these developments will at first exacerbate racial conflict, they will ultimately transform racial frustrations into class ones. Indeed, for the first time in the nation's history, young, poor, and alienated Caucasians, African Americans, and Latinos will find common ground—based on social resentment and a common lumpen-proletarian,[1] hip-hop culture. Even as these young people

472   ■ **Consider.** *What is the "one drop" rule? How has it been applied in the past?*

---

[1]*lumpen-proletarian:* The word comes from the German and was used by Karl Marx to describe those living on the margins of society, such as the homeless, the permanently unemployed, etc.—ED.

periodically engage in murderous racial gang fights, intermarriage and miscegenation will escalate as the young poor of all races break away from present gender and racial taboos. In contrast to the California and Florida systems, the growing hybrid population in the Northeast and industrial Midwest will be lower-class, alienated, and out of control. But it will be hybrid nonetheless.

The exception will be in the Southeast, in what may be called the Atlanta pattern. African Americans and European Americans will cling to notions of racial purity and will remain highly (and voluntarily) segregated from each other. Affirmative action will be the bulwark of this system, the price the European American elite willingly pays for "racial" stability and the reassuring presence of a culturally familiar but socially distant African American group and a pliant working class. The old Confederacy will remain a place where everyone knows who is white and who is black and need reckon with no in-between. But, as opposed to the nineteenth and twentieth centuries, when the South defined the terms of racial engagement on which the entire nation interacted (more or less brutally), in the twenty-first century the Southern model will become an increasingly odd and decreasingly relevant anachronism.

For the decline of race as a factor in American life will result not only from immigration, which can perhaps be halted, but also from biotechnology. More and more in the coming decades, Americans will gain the means to genetically manipulate human appearance. The foundations of genetic engineering are already in place. Given the interest of the affluent population in male-pattern baldness, the restoration of hair loss after cancer treatment, and cancer-free tanning, science is likely to create dramatic new methods of changing hair texture and skin color. Indeed, last November, scientists at Columbia University transplanted scalp cells from one person to another. I don't expect many African Americans to choose straight-haired whiteness for themselves or their progeny, but many will opt for varying degrees of hybridity. In a world dominated by mass culture, many will embrace changes that enhance their individuality. Once dramatically manipulable by human action, "race" will lose its social significance, and the myth of racial purity will be laid to rest.

By the middle of the next century, the social virus of race will have gone the way of smallpox. The twenty-first century, relieved of the obscuring blinkers of race, will be a century of class and class consciousness, forcing the nation to finally take seriously its creed that all are created equal. It should be interesting.

■ **Discuss.** *Discuss the reasons Patterson gives for the new patterns he predicts. Are they primarily changes in the economic structure of America? In the culture? What role does technology play?*

■ **Write.** *Do you see any of the trends Patterson describes in your community? Single out a specific claim about how demographics will change and analyze it based on your own experience. Does your city or state seem to fit into any of the paradigms Patterson describes?*

473

Derek Jeter, 2007. New York Yankees player Derek Jeter is African American and Caucasian. He and the other celebrities pictured here are just a few of the individuals who represent the generation Ruth La Ferla refers to as "ethnically ambiguous," representatives of America's increasingly multiracial population.

Michael Loccisano/Getty Images

Jason Merritt/Getty Images

Jessica Alba, 2007. Actress Jessica Alba is French, Danish, Mexican Indian, and Spanish.

Jason Merritt/Getty Images

Vin Diesel, 2007. Actor Vin Diesel is half Irish and half undisclosed.

Frank Micelotta/Getty Images

Christina Aguilera, 2007. Singer Christina Aguilera is half Ecuadorean. She tweaks her looks often — sometimes blond, sometimes dark.

 CONSIDER THE CLUSTER
Color Lines

■ **Message**

To what forces does Orlando Patterson attribute the vast racial changes that he expects will occur in America within the next half century? Why do you think he gives no time in his essay to an analysis of legislative or judicial enactments? Do you suppose he thinks that further laws will not be necessary for the changes he envisions? According to Patterson, what will be the twenty-first century's equivalent of the color line?

■ **Method**

Patterson's case assumes a division of the United States into four geographic areas, each with unique characteristics. Two of these regions, however—the Northeast/industrial Midwest and the Southeast—present problems. Why do these regions not fit entirely into Patterson's demographic scenario? How does he acknowledge these exceptions and at the same time try to show that they support his argument? Do you think he succeeds?

■ **Medium**

Do you think the presence of celebrities you now see in the media suggests that Patterson is on to something? In what ways does the current marketing of mixed-ethnic personalities support Patterson's case? Do you think this media trend will continue well into the twenty-first century and help make race obsolete? What evidence do you see in the media today that the trend will or will not continue?

US AND THEM:
THE NEW IMMIGRATION

Although Americans like to think of the United States as a "melting pot," where people from all over the globe can be mixed together into a single identity, that ideal has occurred only sporadically over the nation's long and complex history of immigration. In recent years, fewer immigrants to the United States have come from Europe than in the past, and many more are coming from Asia and Latin America. For example, in 2004, more than one-third of all legal immigrants came from Mexico, India, and the Philippines. The new immigrants often see themselves as different from earlier "hyphenated" Americans. The Indian American novelist Jhumpa Lahiri notes in "My Two Lives" that unlike her Italian American or Irish American friends whose ethnic roots "had descended under-ground," her roots "were still tangled and green." Although proud of his Taiwanese roots, the graphic artist Nathan Huang sadly discovers in the autobiographical "A Red-Envelope Day" that the ethnic customs of immigrant families can be difficult to maintain on American soil.

Few boundary lines in recent years have been as contentious as that between the United States and Mexico. The immigration controversy between the two countries is the subject of daily news programs and talk shows, and constantly bombarded with often diametrically opposing views. In his poem "Líneas Fronterizas/Border Lines," Alberto Ríos steps back from the daily argumentation and takes a broader view of the border, seeing it as "what joins us, / Not what separates us." It is, however, a very long border and an exhausting task to seal it, as Ross MacDonald reminds us in his satirical comic strip "Borderline Loco!!"

Jhumpa Lahiri, *My Two Lives*. Jhumpa Lahiri (née Nilanjana Sudeshna) ▶ was born in 1967 in London, raised in Rhode Island, and educated at Barnard College and Boston University. Her first book, *Interpreter of Maladies* (1999), a collection of stories, won the 2000 Pulitzer Prize for Fiction, among several other awards. Her second book, *The Namesake,* a novel published in 2003, was made into a film in 2007. Lahiri, who currently lives in New York City, finds writing to be a personal challenge. "I've never written for anyone other than myself," she says. "No matter what people say or expect, at the end of the day, they're not the one in the room with me, writing." The following essay originally appeared in *Newsweek* on March 6, 2006.

Jhumpa Lahiri
MY TWO LIVES

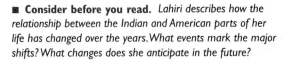

■ **Consider before you read.** *Lahiri describes how the relationship between the Indian and American parts of her life has changed over the years. What events mark the major shifts? What changes does she anticipate in the future?*

I have lived in the United States for almost 37 years and anticipate growing old in this country. Therefore, with the exception of my first two years in London, "Indian-American" has been a constant way to describe me. Less constant is my relationship to the term. When I was growing up in Rhode Island in the 1970s I felt neither Indian nor American. Like many immigrant offspring I felt intense pressure to be two things, loyal to the old world and fluent in the new, approved of on either side of the hyphen. Looking back, I see that this was generally the case. But my perception as a young girl was that I fell short at both ends, shuttling between two dimensions that had nothing to do with one another.

At home I followed the customs of my parents, speaking Bengali and eating rice and dal with my fingers. These ordinary facts seemed part of a secret, utterly alien way of life, and I took pains to hide them from my American friends. For my parents, home was not our house in Rhode Island but Calcutta, where they were raised. I was aware that the things they lived for—the Nazrul songs they listened to on the reel-to-reel, the family they missed, the clothes my mother wore that were not available in any store in any mall—were at once as precious and as worthless as an outmoded currency.

I also entered a world my parents had little knowledge or control of: school, books, music, television, things that seeped in and became a fundamental aspect of who I am. I spoke English without an accent, comprehending the language in a way my parents still do not. And yet there was evidence that I was not entirely American. In addition to my distinguishing name and looks, I did not attend Sunday school, did not know how to ice-skate, and disappeared to India for months at a time. Many of these friends proudly called themselves Irish-American or Italian-American. But they were several generations removed from the frequently humiliating process of immigration, so that the ethnic roots they claimed had descended underground whereas mine were still tangled and green. According to my parents I was not American, nor would I ever be no matter how hard I tried. I felt doomed by their pronouncement, misunderstood and gradually defiant. In spite of the first lessons of arithmetic, one plus one did not equal two but zero, my conflicting selves always canceling each other out.

When I first started writing I was not conscious that my subject was the Indian-American experience. What drew me to my craft was the desire to force the two worlds I occupied to mingle on the page as I was not brave enough, or

478

mature enough, to allow in life. My first book was published in 1999, and around then, on the cusp of a new century, the term "Indian-American" has become part of this country's vocabulary. I've heard it so often that these days, if asked about my background, I use the term myself, pleasantly surprised that I do not have to explain further. What a difference from my early life, when there was no such way to describe me, when the most I could do was to clumsily and ineffectually explain.

As I approach middle age, one plus one equals two, both in my work and in my daily existence. The traditions on either side of the hyphen dwell in me like siblings, still occasionally sparring, one outshining the other depending on the day. But like siblings they are intimately familiar with one another, forgiving and intertwined. When my husband and I were married five years ago in Calcutta we invited friends who had never been to India, and they came full of enthusiasm for a place I avoided talking about in my childhood, fearful of what people might say. Around non-Indian friends, I no longer feel compelled to hide the fact that I speak another language. I speak Bengali to my children, even though I lack the proficiency to teach them to read or write the language. As a child I sought perfection and so denied myself the claim to any identity. As an adult I accept that a bicultural upbringing is a rich but imperfect thing.

While I am American by virtue of the fact that I was raised in this country, I am Indian thanks to the efforts of two individuals. I feel Indian not because of the time I've spent in India or because of my genetic composition but rather because of my parents' steadfast presence in my life. They live three hours from my home; I speak to them daily and see them about once a month. Everything will change once they die. They will take certain things with them—conversations in another tongue, and perceptions about the difficulties of being foreign. Without them, the back-and-forth life my family leads, both literally and figuratively, will at last approach stillness. An anchor will drop, and a line of connection will be severed.

I have always believed that I lack the authority my parents bring to being Indian. But as long as they live they protect me from feeling like an impostor. Their passing will mark not only the loss of the people who created me but the loss of a singular way of life, a singular struggle. The immigrant's journey, no matter how ultimately rewarding, is founded on departure and deprivation, but it secures for the subsequent generation a sense of arrival and advantage. I can see a day coming when my American side, lacking the counterpoint India has until now maintained, begins to gain ascendancy and weight. It is in fiction that I will continue to interpret the term "Indian-American," calculating that shifting equation, whatever answers it may yield.

479

■ **Discuss.** *Why does Lahiri describe immigration as "humiliating"? How does the word reflect her experience or that of her parents?*

■ **Write.** *Write an explication of Lahiri's use of simile to describe her two lives. Why does she choose "siblings" as a comparison? What does the simile reveal about her complex heritage?*

Nathan Huang, *A Red-Envelope Day*. Nathan Huang is a Los Angeles–based car-toonist, artist, and illustrator whose work has appeared in such publications as *The New York Times*, *The Washington Post*, *The Los Angeles Times*, *The San Francisco Chronicle*, and *Esquire*. He has also done work for ESPN, Nike, and Fantagraphics Books, a publisher of comic books. Following is Huang's brief biography from his web site (nathanhuang.com): "Melancholic with a penchant for navel-gazing, Nathan spends most of his leisure time regretting past decisions and reliving the glory days. Tread lightly when approaching, as he is prone to sud-den bursts of weeping and self-loathing." The following op-art piece appeared on February 18, 2007, in *The New York Times* editorial pages.

Nathan Huang
A RED-ENVELOPE DAY

480

■ **Consider before you read/view.** *What is the significance of the red envelope to the young narrator? As a Chinese custom, how does it survive among immigrants to America?*

This is my family.

I know, it's a bit overwhelming.

One of the nice things about growing up in a large immigrant Taiwanese family is that it kept me from completely losing touch with my roots.

Because of them, I grew up with a lot of Chinese traditions, one of them being Chinese New Year.

There are many traditions associated with Chinese New Year.

Fireworks are used to scare off evil spirits, particularly a beast known as Nian. The lion dance serves much the same purpose.

Another important part of the holiday is food, which is often symbolic.

Dumplings symbolize prosperity because of their resemblance to ancient Chinese money.

Noodles represent longevity, so they should never be cut!

Fish is served because it sounds similar to the Chinese word for "plenty."

Cleaning the house before New Years is another custom, though one should never sweep on New Years Day. You could be sweeping out your good fortune!

The favorite custom among most children is the giving of the red envelope, or hong bao.

These red envelopes are decorated with gold symbols and given to children by older folk...

... AND THEY'RE FILLED WITH LUCKY MONEY!

My clearest childhood memory of Chinese New Year is from 3rd grade... the same year that a particularly annoying Chinese boy came to my school.

Being a rich, spoiled brat, he would boast endlessly about the money and gifts he received.

When Chinese New Year approached, I feared the oncoming show-off session...

Until I realized that my family was much larger than his. I would rub my red envelopes in his face.

Chinese New Year came...

...and went. I received nothing.

It turns out that the adults had gotten together secretly and agreed not to give red envelopes that year. Since we were such a large family, it was a matter of financial survival.

That, of course, meant...

Hey, check this out!

The First edition hologram cover for Pulverizer #1! Isn't it awesome?

Sigh.

I never received a red envelope after that.

end.

◀ ■ **Discuss.** *In his comic "A Red-Envelope Day," Huang uses multiple panel sizes to tell a story. Discuss why the artist varies size, especially when he is describing the New Year's traditions. How does this variation help him convey his message?*

■ **Write.** *For Huang, having a large family has both benefits and drawbacks. Write an analysis of how the young narrator feels about his big family. Do you think Huang feels differently now that he is an adult? What in the comic suggests his attitude?*

Alberto Ríos, *Líneas Fronterizas/Border Lines*. The award-winning poet and author Alberto Ríos (b. 1952) was raised in Nogales, Arizona, on the Mexico-Arizona border. The son of a Mexican father and an English mother, he grew up speaking Spanish and English, although at school he was punished for speaking Spanish. He writes that by the time he reached high school, he "could no longer speak Spanish" and had to relearn it. "In having to pay double and triple attention to language — first to forget, and then to relearn—I began to see earnestly how everything, every object, every idea, had at least two names." As a high school student, he was introduced to contemporary poetry and went on to study literature and psychology at the University of Arizona. Ríos is now a professor of English and creative writing at Arizona State University.

The poem "Líneas Fronterizas/Border Lines" was commissioned by the governor of Arizona in 2003 to honor the visit of Vicente Fox, who at the time was president of Mexico. Ríos read both the Spanish and English versions to a crowd of three thousand in Phoenix on November 4, 2003, but it wasn't published until the Spring 2007 issue of the *Virginia Quarterly Review*.

Alberto Ríos
LÍNEAS FRONTERIZAS/BORDER LINES

■ **Consider before you read.** *How does Ríos's epigram add to your understanding of the poem? What kind of stance does it suggest about border disputes?*

Líneas Fronterizas

Un peso cargado por dos
No pesa más que la mitad.

El mundo en un mapa parece el dibujo de una
    vaca
En la carnicería, todas esas líneas mostrando
Dónde cortar.

Ese dibujo de la vaca es también un
    rompecabezas,
Mostrando cómo caben muy bien juntas
Todas las piezas extrañas.

La manera en que miramos el dibujo
Nos hace ver la diferencia.

Parecemos vivir en un mundo de mapas:
Pero en verdad vivimos en un mundo hecho
No de papel ni de tinta sino de gente.
Esas líneas son nuestras vidas. Juntos,

Demos vuelta al mapa hasta que veamos
    claramente:
La frontera es lo que nos une,
No lo que nos separa.

Border Lines

A weight carried by two
Weighs only half as much.

The world on a map looks like the drawing
    of a cow
In a butcher's shop, all those lines showing
Where to cut.

That drawing of the cow is also a jigsaw
    puzzle,
Showing just as much how very well
All the strange parts fit together.

Which way we look at the drawing
Makes all the difference.

We seem to live in a world of maps:
But in truth we live in a world made
Not of paper and ink but of people.
Those lines are our lives. Together,

Let us turn the map until we see clearly:
The border is what joins us,
Not what separates us.

483

■ **Discuss.** *Discuss Ríos's assertion that "we live in a world made / Not of paper and ink but of people." What difference does this perception make when it comes to borders?*

■ **Write.** *What do the two comparisons Ríos finds for the map—a butcher's drawing and a jigaw puzzle—suggest about borders? Write an essay in which you examine these two examples of figurative speech. In what ways do they reinforce or contradict each other?*

Ross MacDonald, *Borderline Loco!!* The following *Dead-Eye Comic* by Ross MacDonald originally appeared near the Alberto Ríos poems (see p. 483) in the Spring 2007 issue of the *Virginia Quarterly Review.* MacDonald, an illustrator, comics artist, animator, children's book author, and set designer, has had his work appear in publications such as *The New Yorker, Vanity Fair,* and *Newsweek.* He has designed a postage stamp, developed a parody for *Saturday Night Live,* worked on movies including *Seabiscuit,* and lectured on design history. MacDonald's artist's statement (at ross-macdonald.com) emphasizes the importance of a driving idea in using words and images. "Any scribbler can draw a perfect rendition of a kitten, but thinking up the concept of a kitten hanging precariously onto a clothesline with its front paws, with the caption 'hang in there, baby'—that, my friends, is the genius of illustration."

Ross MacDonald's
Dead-Eye Comics
BORDERLINE LOCO!!

484

■ **Consider before you read/view.** *MacDonald's comic lampoons the symbolic figure of Uncle Sam. What do you know about Uncle Sam's history? What does his image mean to you today? Do you see other examples of American iconography in this comic?*

■ **Discuss.** *Discuss the turn in the final panel of the comic. How does it complete the humorous portrait of Uncle Sam? What message about border policy does it convey?*

■ **Write.** *How does the comic dramatize the difficulty of sealing the border between the United States and Mexico? Write an analysis of the visual techniques (use of space, motion lines and the like) that MacDonald uses to highlight the problem.*

Emma Lazarus, *The New Colossus*. The New York City–born poet Emma Lazarus (1849–1887) wrote this sonnet in 1883. Engraved on a bronze plaque in the base of the Statue of Liberty (in 1903), Lazarus's poem once reflected what many Americans felt was the government's welcoming attitude toward immigrants in the familiar lines: "Give me your tired, your poor, / Your huddled masses yearning to breathe free." Today, the political climate has shifted and is marked by conservative attitudes of many involved in the debate around immigration. Specifically, under the presidency of George W. Bush, the federal government adopted stricter policies toward immigration, including increased border patrols, more detention centers for "illegal aliens," and the deportation of temporary workers whose work authorizations have expired (see whitehouse.gov/infocus/immigration).

Emma Lazarus

THE NEW COLOSSUS

■ **Consider before you read.** *The Colossus of Rhodes was a huge statue of a Greek god constructed on the Greek island of Rhodes in the third century B.C. As the tallest statue of its time it became known as one of the Seven Wonders of the Ancient World. It was destroyed by an earthquake some fifty years after its construction. In her now famous sonnet, how does Emma Lazarus compare America's Statue of Liberty to the ancient colossus? What qualities does the new colossus embody?*

Not like the brazen giant of Greek fame,
With conquering limbs astride from land to land;
Here at our sea-washed, sunset fates shall stand
A mighty woman with a torch, whose flame
Is the imprisoned lightning, and her name
Mother of Exiles. From her beacon-hand
Glows world-wide welcome; her mild eyes command
The air-bridged harbor that twin cities frame.
"Keep, ancient lands, your storied pomp!" cries she
With silent lips. "Give me your tired, your poor,
Your huddled masses yearning to breathe free,
The wretched refuse of your teeming shore.
Send these, the homeless, tempest-tost to me,
I lift my lamp beside the golden door!"

■ **Discuss.** *The words spoken by "the new colossus," which appear on the Statue of Liberty's tablet, are by far the most famous part of Lazarus's poem. How does seeing those words in the context of the rest of the poem change the way you understand them?*

■ **Write.** *Why does part of this particular poem appear on the Statue of Liberty? Is its primary audience immigrants entering the country or people who already live here? Write an essay in which you consider the reasons this poem was chosen.*

Paul Vitello and Tamara Shopsin, *The Uncitizens*. The image below, by *New York Times* artist Tamara Shopsin, appeared in that paper (on March 26, 2006) with an essay by Paul Vitello titled "The Uncitizens: Kiss Me, I'm Illegal." In his essay, Vitello covers the various terms used today to describe immigrants. He writes: "There is an almost magical power in naming. . . . To give a person, an act, or a group its name is to define it, assert a measure of control over how it is perceived." So what should we call people from other countries who have come to live in the United States? Vitello writes: "Murky self-described patriot groups call them 'terrorists.' On combative talk radio shows the term is 'illegal aliens.' Advocates for immigrants prefer the Emma Lazarus–evoking 'economic refugees.'" The most common term is "illegal immigrants," although as Vitello points out, grammatically speaking, the adjective "illegal," when used correctly, modifies only actions and things—not people. [President George W. Bush preferred "undocumented immigrants."] As Vitello writes, "[T]here may be no neutral language possible in the immigration debate—any more than there is in other emotionally-charged human interactions."

Illustration © Tamara Shopsin

487

Paul Vitello and Tamara Shopsin
THE UNCITIZENS

■ **Consider before you read/view.** *What are the connotations of each of the terms Shopsin includes on her Statue of Liberty? Do any seem more positive than the others? Which seems most derogatory?*

◀ ■ **Discuss.** *Why does Shopsin use the image of the Statue of Liberty to make a point about politics and language? What does the Statue of Liberty represent as an American icon? What is the relationship between what the Statue of Liberty means and the phrases Shopsin has inscribed on her drawing of it?*

■ **Write.** *Political arguments often hinge on the terminology used. Can you think of another political issue in which naming is important? Write an essay that lists the different terms that come into play and analyze their meanings.*

 CONSIDER THE CLUSTER
Us and Them: The New Immigration

■ **Message**

As an in-class assignment, summarize what you think is the message of Ross MacDonald's "Borderline Loco!!" Try to do so in one or two sentences. Can you do the same with Nathan Huang's "A Red-Envelope Day"?

■ **Method**

How does Alberto Ríos propose that we solve the problem of borders? In an essay, describe Ríos's visual method in "Líneas Fronterizas/Border Lines." How does he persuade us to view borders in a new way? Can you explain why he chooses the images he does?

■ **Medium**

Note that in "My Two Lives" Jhumpa Lahiri suggests that she came to writing as a way "to force the two worlds [she] occupied to mingle on the page" because she was not able to do so in life. Write a short personal essay that allows you to interpret or explore something about your background or identity that you might not be able to do in real life. How does the act of writing encourage self-discovery? Or can you imagine a different medium that you would rely on for this purpose?

WHO WANTS DIVERSITY?

3 PHOTOS | PERSUASIVE ESSAY | AD

The word "diversity" has become, like the word "community," one of those terms with a plus-sign hovering over it: the word automatically suggests something that everyone is supposed to value. It is a key term in the media, in education, and in politics; in fact, many corporations have established departments in "diversity training."

Yet is diversity really what Americans want, or is it a fashionable concept that people merely say they want? If it is truly desired, then why, asks David Brooks in "People like Us," are Americans so undiverse in so many ways? Does the idea of diversity go against the grain of human nature? As Brooks claims: "what I have seen all around the country is people making strenuous efforts to group themselves with people who are basically like themselves"—and the photographs from *America 24/7,* reproduced here, document a few of those groups. An advertisement for the Council on American Islamic Relations shows an alternate view of diversity in America.

490

Dennis McDonald, *Berkeley, New Jersey.* This photograph and the   ▶
two that follow on pages 492 and 494 are taken from a best-selling
and comprehensive photographic project, *America 24/7* (2003),
the "largest collaborative photography project in history."
Thousands of amateur and professional photographers were
invited to go out during the week of May 12–18, 2003, and "show
the world what it means to be American." The resulting collection
captures a highly diverse nation. But as these photos show, our
melting pot is also a country in which people tend naturally to
form groups and share space on the basis of self-selection, social
distinctions, and cultural affinity. (© Dennis McDonald)

492

Kurt Wilson, *St. Ignatius, Montana.* "The Amish usually marry within their own communities, which tends to reduce the pool of surnames. Heidi Miller, Hannah Miller, Naomah Miller, and Emily Miller (holding cat) are actually from three separate families. Their solid-colored dresses and white caps are designed to encourage humility and separateness from the outside world." (© Kurt Wilson)

David Brooks, *People like Us*. In this essay, David Brooks examines the difference between what people *say* about diversity and what they *do*. Brooks has been a journalist and cultural commentator for more than twenty years, since his graduation from the University of Chicago in 1983. He worked first as a police reporter and then at *The Wall Street Journal*, where he was variously the book review editor, movie critic, and op-ed editor. For the last thirteen years, he has been the editor of *The Weekly Standard*, a contributing editor at *Newsweek* and *The Atlantic Monthly*, and a commentator on NPR and *The NewsHour with Jim Lehrer*. He is now a columnist with *The New York Times*. He is also the editor of *Backward and Upward: The New Conservative Writing* (1996) and the author of *Bobos in Paradise: The New Upper Class and How They Got There* (2001) and *On Paradise Drive: How We Live Now (and Always Have) in the Future Tense* (2004). "People like Us" first appeared in the September 2003 issue of *The Atlantic Monthly*.

David Brooks
PEOPLE LIKE US

■ **Consider before you read.** *What does Brooks think are the benefits to grouping with people like ourselves? What problems arise when we are too efficient at creating like-minded communities and institutions?*

493

Maybe it's time to admit the obvious. We don't really care about diversity all that much in America, even though we talk about it a great deal. Maybe somewhere in this country there is a truly diverse neighborhood in which a black Pentecostal minister lives next to a white anti-globalization activist, who lives next to an Asian short-order cook, who lives next to a professional golfer, who lives next to a post-modern-literature professor and a cardiovascular surgeon. But I have never been to or heard of that neighborhood. Instead, what I have seen all around the country is people making strenuous efforts to group themselves with people who are basically like themselves.

Human beings are capable of drawing amazingly subtle social distinctions and then shaping their lives around them. In the Washington, D.C., area Democratic lawyers tend to live in suburban Maryland, and Republican lawyers tend to live in suburban Virginia. If you asked a Democratic lawyer to move from her $750,000 house in Bethesda, Maryland, to a $750,000 house in Great Falls, Virginia, she'd look at you as if you had just asked her to buy a pickup truck with a gun rack and to shove chewing tobacco in her kid's mouth. In Manhattan the owner of a $3 million SoHo loft would feel out of place moving into a $3 million Fifth Avenue apartment. A West Hollywood interior decorator would feel

Who Wants Diversity?

dislocated if you asked him to move to Orange County. In Georgia a barista from Athens would probably not fit in serving coffee in Americus.

It is a common complaint that every place is starting to look the same. But in the information age, the late writer James Chapin once told me, every place becomes more like itself. People are less often tied down to factories and mills, and they can search for places to live on the basis of cultural affinity. Once they find a town in which people share their values, they flock there, and reinforce whatever was distinctive about the town in the first place. Once Boulder, Colorado, became known as congenial to politically progressive mountain bikers, half the politically progressive mountain bikers in the country (it seems) moved there; they made the place so culturally pure that it has become practically a parody of itself.

But people love it. Make no mistake—we are increasing our happiness by segmenting off so rigorously. We are finding places where we are comfortable and where we feel we can flourish. But the choices we make toward that end lead to the very opposite of diversity. The United States might be a diverse nation when considered as a whole, but block by block and institution by institution it is a relatively homogeneous nation.

When we use the word "diversity" today we usually mean racial integration. But even here our good intentions seem to have run into the brick wall of human nature. Over the past generation reformers have tried heroically, and in many cases successfully, to end housing discrimination. But recent patterns aren't encouraging: according to an analysis of the 2000 census data, the 1990s saw only a slight increase in the racial integration of neighborhoods in the United States. The number of middle-class and upper-middle-class African American families is rising,

Gary Fandel, *West Des Moines, Iowa*.
(© Gary Fandel)

494

but for whatever reasons—racism, psychological comfort—these families tend to congregate in predominantly black neighborhoods.

In fact, evidence suggests that some neighborhoods become more segregated over time. New suburbs in Arizona and Nevada, for example, start out reasonably well integrated. These neighborhoods don't yet have reputations, so people choose their houses for other, mostly economic reasons. But as neighborhoods age, they develop personalities (that's where the Asians live, and that's where the Hispanics live), and segmentation occurs. It could be that in a few years the new suburbs in the Southwest will be nearly as segregated as the established ones in the Northeast and the Midwest.

Even though race and ethnicity run deep in American society, we should in theory be able to find areas that are at least culturally diverse. But here, too, people show few signs of being truly interested in building diverse communities. If you run a retail company and you're thinking of opening new stores, you can choose among dozens of consulting firms that are quite effective at locating your potential customers. They can do this because people with similar tastes and preferences tend to congregate by ZIP code.

The most famous of these precision marketing firms is Claritas, which breaks down the U.S. population into sixty-two psycho-demographic clusters, based on such factors as how much money people make, what they like to read and watch, and what products they have bought in the past. For example, the "suburban sprawl" cluster is composed of young families making about $41,000 a year and living in fast-growing places such as Burnsville, Minnesota, and Bensalem, Pennsylvania. These people are almost twice as likely as other Americans to have three-way calling. They are two and a half times as likely to buy Light n' Lively Kid Yogurt. Members of the "towns & gowns" cluster are recent college graduates in places such as Berkeley, California, and Gainesville, Florida. They are big consumers of DoveBars and *Saturday Night Live.* They tend to drive small foreign cars and to read *Rolling Stone* and *Scientific American.*

Looking through the market research, one can sometimes be amazed by how efficiently people cluster—and by how predictable we all are. If you wanted to sell imported wine, obviously you would have to find places where rich people live. But did you know that the sixteen counties with the greatest proportion of imported-wine drinkers are all in the same three metropolitan areas (New York, San Francisco, and Washington, D.C.)? If you tried to open a motor-home dealership in Montgomery County, Pennsylvania, you'd probably go broke, because people in this ring of the Philadelphia suburbs think RVs are kind of uncool. But if you traveled just a short way north, to Monroe County, Pennsylvania, you would find yourself in the fifth motor-home-friendliest county in America.

Geography is not the only way we find ourselves divided from people unlike us. Some of us watch Fox News, while others listen to NPR. Some like David Letterman, and others—typically in less urban neighborhoods—like Jay Leno. Some go to charismatic churches; some go to mainstream churches. Americans tend more and more often to marry people with education levels similar to their own, and to befriend people with backgrounds similar to their own.

My favorite illustration of this latter pattern comes from the first, noncontroversial chapter of *The Bell Curve.* Think of your twelve closest friends, Richard J. Herrnstein and Charles Murray write. If you had chosen them randomly from the American population, the odds that half of your twelve closest friends would be college graduates would be six in a thousand. The odds that half of the twelve would have advanced degrees would be less than one in a million. Have any of your twelve closest friends graduated from Harvard, Stanford, Yale, Princeton, Caltech, MIT, Duke, Dartmouth, Cornell, Columbia, Chicago, or Brown? If you chose your friends randomly from the American population, the odds against your having four or more friends from those schools would be more than a billion to one.

Many of us live in absurdly unlikely groupings, because we have organized our lives that way.

It's striking that the institutions that talk the most about diversity often practice it the least. For example, no group of people sings the diversity anthem more frequently and fervently than administrators at just such elite universities. But elite universities are amazingly undiverse in their values, politics, and mores. Professors in particular are drawn from a rather narrow segment of the population. If faculties reflected the general population, 32 percent of professors would be registered Democrats and 31 percent would be registered Republicans. Forty percent would be evangelical Christians. But a recent study of several universities by the conservative Center for the Study of Popular Culture and the American Enterprise Institute found that roughly 90 percent of those professors in the arts and sciences who had registered with a political party had registered Democratic. Fifty-seven professors at Brown were found on the voter-registration rolls. Of those, fifty-four were Democrats. Of the forty-two professors in the English, history, sociology, and political-science departments, all were Democrats. The results at Harvard, Penn State, Maryland, and the University of California at Santa Barbara were similar to the results at Brown.

What we are looking at here is human nature. People want to be around others who are roughly like themselves. That's called community. It probably would be psychologically difficult for most Brown professors to share an office with someone who was pro-life, a member of the National Rifle Association, or an evangelical Christian. It's likely that hiring committees would subtly—even unconsciously—screen out any such people they encountered. Republicans and evangelical Christians have sensed that they are not welcome at places like Brown, so they don't even consider working there. In fact, any registered Republican who contemplates a career in academia these days is both a hero and a fool. So, in a semi-self-selective pattern, brainy people with generally liberal social mores flow to academia, and brainy people with generally conservative mores flow elsewhere.

■ **Consider.** *How persuasive do you find Brooks' claim (mentioned several times) that diversity goes against "human nature"? What evidence does he use to support this claim? How persuasive do you find his evidence?*

497

The dream of diversity is like the dream of equality. Both are based on ideals we celebrate even as we undermine them daily. (How many times have you seen someone renounce a high-paying job or pull his child from an elite college on the grounds that these things are bad for equality?) On the one hand, the situation is appalling. It is appalling that Americans know so little about one another. It is appalling that many of us are so narrow-minded that we can't tolerate a few

WE'RE ALL AMERICANS...

BUT, WHICH ONE OF US IS A MUSLIM?

We all are...we're American Muslims. It's impossible to make general assumptions about Muslims because we represent more than one billion people from a vast range of races, nationalities and cultures – from the South Pacific to the Horn of Africa. Only about 18 percent of Muslims live in the Arabic-speaking world. The largest Muslim community is in Indonesia. Substantial parts of Asia and most of Africa have Muslim majority populations, while significant minorities are to be found in the countries of the former Soviet Union, China, North and South America, and Europe.

American Muslims are an equally diverse group of people. We're immigrants from across the globe who came here seeking freedom and opportunity. We're the children of immigrant parents, and descendants of Africans who have called America home for generations. We're converts of varied nationalities and ethnic backgrounds. We're doctors, lawyers, teachers, politicians, civil rights activists, mothers, fathers, students... making our homes and raising our families in communities across America.

What we all have in common is a shared faith and a shared commitment to our nation's safety and prosperity. We're Americans and we're Muslims.

WE'RE AMERICAN MUSLIMS

Number one of fifty-two in the *Islam in America* series.
To learn more about the series, visit www.americanmuslims.info

CAIR
COUNCIL ON AMERICAN-ISLAMIC RELATIONS

people with ideas significantly different from our own. It's appalling that evangelical Christians are practically absent from entire professions, such as academia, the media, and filmmaking. It's appalling that people should be content to cut themselves off from everyone unlike themselves.

The segmentation of society means that often we don't even have arguments across the political divide. Within their little validating communities, liberals and conservatives circulate half-truths about the supposed awfulness of the other side. These distortions are believed because it feels good to believe them.

On the other hand, there are limits to how diverse any community can or should be. I've come to think that it is not useful to try to hammer diversity into every neighborhood and institution in the United States. Sure, Augusta National should probably admit women, and university sociology departments should probably hire a conservative or two. It would be nice if all neighborhoods had a good mixture of ethnicities. But human nature being what it is, most places and institutions are going to remain culturally homogeneous.

It's probably better to think about diverse lives, not diverse institutions. Human beings, if they are to live well, will have to move through a series of institutions and environments, which may be individually homogeneous but, taken together, will offer diverse experiences. It might also be a good idea to make national service a rite of passage for young people in this country: it would take them out of their narrow neighborhood segment and thrust them in with people unlike themselves. Finally, it's probably important for adults to get out of their own familiar circles. If you live in a coastal, socially liberal neighborhood, maybe you should take out a subscription to *The Door,* the evangelical humor magazine; or maybe you should visit Branson, Missouri. Maybe you should stop in at a megachurch. Sure, it would be superficial familiarity, but it beats the iron curtains that now separate the nation's various cultural zones.

Look around at your daily life. Are you really in touch with the broad diversity of American life? Do you care?

■ **Discuss.** *Does Brooks propose any solutions to our lack of diversity? Do you think his ideas would work? Discuss how you think Americans could make good on their intentions for diversity.*

■ **Write.** *Write a response to the final questions in "People like Us." After reading Brooks's essay, are you convinced that diversity is decreasing? If so, are you concerned about that trend?*

◀ **CAIR,** *We're All Americans.* This advertisement was the first of fifty-two in the Islam in America series created by the Council on American-Islamic Relations after September 11, 2001. The ad makes a different argument about diversity than Brooks's essay does; the ad stresses that "people like us" is a larger category than just one particular religion. (Courtesy of the Council on American-Islamic Relations)

■■■■■■ CONSIDER THE CLUSTER
Who Wants Diversity?

■ Message

What is David Brooks saying about "diversity" in his essay? Does he define the word precisely? What do you think his position is? Is he opposed to the ideal of diversity, or would he prefer that Americans actually become more diversified than they are? As an in-class writing assignment, explain his position as accurately as you can in a single paragraph.

■ Method

Each of the texts uses examples—some verbal, some visual—of specific people or kinds of people to make its points about how we are alike or different. Evaluate the examples offered by each text for their effectiveness. Which method do you find most persuasive?

■ Medium

The photographs, advertisement, and essay in this section all make claims about diversity in America. To what degree do you think our commitment to diversity grows from our history as a melting pot? In what medium would you portray your own philosophy about diversity—in a photograph, a movie, an essay, a cartoon, or something else? Imagine that you're trying to reach as many people as possible. Then outline or sketch out how you would convey this complicated idea in the most direct, persuasive way possible.

500

TURF WAR

ANALYTICAL ESSAY   4 PHOTOS

One of the most intense group identities a young person can develop is with a gang, especially in cities where a gang offers both protection and an escape from anonymity. In the 1940s and 1950s, street gangs were commonly white and were drawn around neighborhood lines. Authorities regarded them as training camps for "juvenile delinquency" and a subsequent life of crime. By the 1960s, urban gangs were growing increasingly divided along racial and ethnic lines, a social phenomenon depicted in the popular musical and film *West Side Story.* By the 1980s, gangs had grown more violent; members were equipped with high-powered weapons and were increasingly connected with drug trafficking. More recently, gangs have been responsible for generating an explosion in popular culture—their clothing and gestures can be seen, and their music and slang heard, in every sub-urban shopping mall in the United States. In "Gangstas," the noted National Public Radio commentator Richard Rodriguez uses the photographs of Joseph Rodriguez to take a close though unromanticized view of Latino gang life in Los Angeles in the early 1990s.

Richard Rodriguez, *Gangstas.* Richard Rodriguez was born in San Francisco in
1944 into a working-class Mexican American family. He graduated from
Stanford University in 1967 and received an MA from Columbia University
two years later. A prize-winning reporter and essayist for *The NewsHour with
Jim Lehrer,* an editor at Pacific News Service, and a contributing editor for
Harper's Magazine, U.S. News & World Report, and the Opinion section of
the Sunday *Los Angeles Times,* Rodriguez has published widely in magazines
and newspapers. He is the author of a well-known memoir, *The Hunger of
Memory: The Education of Richard Rodriguez* (1982); a collection of essays,
Days of Obligation: An Argument with My Mexican Father (1992); and
Brown: The Last Discovery of America (2002), a discussion about the
"browning" of America that completes Rodriguez's "trilogy on American
public life." "Gangstas" first appeared in a special issue of *Mother Jones* on
the subject of guns in January/February 1994.

Richard Rodriguez

502

GANGSTAS

■ **Consider before you read.** *What is the tone of Rodriguez's essay? His feelings about
gang life are more complex than simply negative or disapproving. Do you see any contradictions in his attitudes? How would you describe his multiple emotional responses to the photographs by Joseph Rodriguez? How does he feel about his own life in comparison?*

Oh, how I hate their stupid sign language, occult and crooked palmings, finger-
Chinese. I hate their Puritan black. Their fat heads shaved like Roundheads in
the age of Cromwell—the penitentiary look—not Cavalier. I hate their singlets. I
hate their tattoos, sentimental prick-roses. I hate their jargon. I hate their ban-
dannas. I hate rap.

Anyway, there I was at my sissy gym the other day—read the *Wall Street
Journal,* lose a few pounds on the StairMaster—and what do you think accompanied me through the canyons of Wall Street, but insidious black, male, heterosex-
ual rap. There it was—the music of thump—blasting through the blond pagan
house of abs and pecs.

I hate the rhymed-dictate. Rap dictates not thought but rhyme, encourages
rhythmic sloganing and jingle—monotony posing as song, attitude posing as
thought.

503

Joseph Rodriguez, *Chivo*. Boyle Heights, 1993. On Joseph Rodriguez's web site, he tells us that this photo was taken "the morning after a rival gang tried to shoot Chivo for the fourth time. Chivo teaches his daughter how to hold a .32-caliber pistol while her mother looks on." The winner of a 1993 Mother Jones International Fund for Documentary Photography award, Joseph Rodriguez has had his photography published in many magazines. His books include *East Side Stories: Gang Life in East L.A.* (1996), from which all the photographs shown here are taken. (All photos courtesy of Joseph Rodriguez/Black Star)

Is there a more complicated love affair going on in America? We know for a fact, those of us who read the *Wall Street Journal,* that white middle-class children buy more rap than black children. We don't know why. Or we say we don't.

Forget the sociological abstraction! The other day, I was looking through some snapshots of my niece and nephew that my sister had left on the drainboard. Snow. Tent. Skis. Birthday party. Clowns. Balloons. And then this: the nine-year-old boy and the six-year-old girl are posing in the backyard of their suburban house as gangstas. The boy with a bandanna on his head, a mustache and goatee painted on. The girl with a T-shirt and dangling earrings. They were both signing with their fingers. They had dead eyes.

My initial reaction was amusement at their charade. Even pride. They got it so right. MTV, I guess. But to what reality are my niece and nephew drawn?

We adults do most heartily deplore what is happening in the "inner city." Those of us who live elsewhere are shocked by the mayhem—little pops and flares in the night and answering sirens, far away. We deplore all of it. And when something hideous happens, which it does, in the morning paper or on the news, then we mutter something, a thought—not a thought—a blank bubble, like an unmarked van, passes through our consciousness and its freight is obscene loathing we dare not enunciate: ANIMALS. SCUM.

The commercial on the eleven o'clock news is a rap for cola, with black children in black, mouthing a mindless jingle which celebrates the elixir. And the eleven o'clock news, which leads with an "Animals on the Loose" story, ends with five minutes of contract mayhem—pro football and ice hockey fights and baseball teams in Baltimore or basketball players in Boston duking it out before cheering fans.

I went to a fancy benefit for some Mexican American charity. The entertainment, alternating with the sentimental mariachis, included several famous comics and actors doing "street stuff"—Edward James Olmos, for example, did his famous pachuco bit, the slouch, hands in his pocket, the head cocked back, the legs far out in front. HEY MANNNNN, WHA'S HAPPENIIIIING? The standard black jargon with an East L.A. whine. Like, "no steenkin' badges, mannnnn."

What I like best about Joe Rodriguez's photographs is that they are devoid of middle-class *nostalgie de la boue*.[1] Still, part of the turn-on of these photos is that we can stare without fear of being killed. None of us should stare at such faces in real life.

They get on the bus in their Raiders jackets, their ears plugged with huge brainstorms of rap—that's what they hear; we hear a tiny, metallic tish, tish, tish leaking from their earphones—they board the city bus in groups, talk loud, for they are giants, pirates . . .

It would be a smart idea not to look at them—no, I mean it—these are children, but they are children with machetes and guns and no point of ref-france, so betta show me def-france, or you are outta breff, once I blow your brains to hell.

Keep your eyes to yourself. Read your paperback. Read your magazine. Do not make eye contact. They are children so wary of any "dis" they might "smoke" you for staring.

Stare instead at Joe Rodriguez's photos, the Mexican American chapter of youthful offenders. Examine their four-block piece of L.A. Look at the neat houses of some of them, not exactly lead-peeling, stinkin' tenements in Spanish Harlem. East L.A. is not Spanish Harlem. And L.A., like Miami, has a better climate for

---

■ **Consider.** *Rodriguez describes both the gang tattoos and the mariachi band as "sentimental." What does he mean when he uses this word? What is the appeal of these very different forms of expression?*

504

[1] *nostalgie de la boue:* French, "yearning for slime."—ED.

Joseph Rodriguez, *Members of Florencia 13 gang outside school.* South Central, 1992.

child murder than New York or Chicago. On a sweetly scented January night one can hang out, throw rocks at buses or at the cars on the freeway.

Some of these children are good-looking, some not. (They seem, in either case, unaware of the difference.) They look more American than Mexican to my eye, with an American irony on their faces, especially the child-women who look like they are made up for *Elektra*.[2]

Clearly, Joe Rodriguez has put in his time with these children. What his camera does not explain is why they look so dead to conscience. Mother Church

---

[2]***Elektra:*** Richard Strauss's opera based on Sophocles' tragedy *Elektra*. The combination of tragedy and opera would, in most productions, mean heavy, masklike makeup for the performers.—Ed.

had always told us that the "age of reason" begins around the age of seven, well before hormones sprout domes. Is it that they know we are watching? Gangsta life reduces to an attitude, a pose. These children appear prisoners of street theater, even when they are in the family kitchen. Only one, the child staring into the Los Angeles night sky, has an expression to which a caption of "wonder" might fit.

As actors, they seem only to exist in the plural. Dress the same. Spell identically with their fingers. They shave each other's heads and watch each other's backs. The gang regards the greatest sinner to be the member who wants out.

These children of East L.A. puzzle us for being so intensely communal. We Americans honor the idea of the youthful rebel. We have taken our meaning from the notion of adolescent rebellion. (James Dean rebels against the mad British

Joseph Rodriguez, *Mike Estrada holds a photo of his father who is in prison.* Boyle Heights, 1993.

king.) Huck Finn is the nineteenth century's romantic hero, free of the school-marm, free of his drunk pappy, free as a runaway slave on a raft.

If within the neighborhood the lost-boy brotherhood is the only society going, outside—in the city of adults—the child appears solitary, defiant. It is in this defiance the child is most interesting to the city. The rapster becomes Huck Finn. The stance, the dress, the music of this outsider exercise erotic appeal.

In the fall 1993 issue of *Esquire Gentleman,* a magazine of no distinction or exception, there is an article by Mark Leyner called "Gangsta Allure." ("What becomes a man most? Evil, of course. Smug, sinister dudes get all the hot action. Here's how to look like a real Reservoir Dog.") In Paris recently, at a show of Jean Colonna's "outlaw chic," the models fired blank cartridges at the photographers at the foot of the runway.

Bang! The theatrical turns real and then we of the audience are horrified. *Look, my God, look, the baby in his tiny coffin, draped with gauze.*

MONSTERS! ANIMALS!

On the other side of the fascination with the rebel is this high moral distancing. Consign the gangsta to subhumanity. But when this child falls, he leaks blood. They are not monsters, after all.

If, as God's silence to Job suggests, there is something inexplicable about evil—either the evil the night commits against us or the evil we inflict on each other—there is also less mystery to the cruelty in East Los Angeles than we otherwise pretend.

Is it so inexplicable that a child never embraced might be seduced by the cult of power? An Oakland cop says to me: "Have you ever been in a physical fight? It may be the only moment in your life when you can control the outcome."

These photographs do not tell us about crack mothers or schools that don't work or pappy dead or in prison. Documentary without a hint of narrative comes dangerously close to the vision Diane Arbus[3] saw in her madness. Children appear grotesques. Spawn of some hideous neighborhood (not ours) without trees or sun or air. A land of roaches and rats and unnatural mothers.

No man is an island entire of itself. Didn't we learn that in high school? There is no possibility of a healthy suburb radiant from a corrupt inner city. The children of East L.A. live in the same city as Madonna and Tom Bradley and Harvard-educated screenwriters who use coke for inspiration to sell a believably tarnished vision of the world to the children of the crack mother in Compton. In this Los Angeles an Austrian muscle man becomes kin to the Kennedys and a movie mogul who kills with dead eyes.

And look: there is always a TV in the houses of East L.A. And it's always on. In the suburbs we use TV to watch the mayhem of the inner city. But on the TV

507

---

[3]Diane Arbus (1923–1971), American photographer, now famous for her gritty pictures of urban alienation and the socially marginalized.—ED.

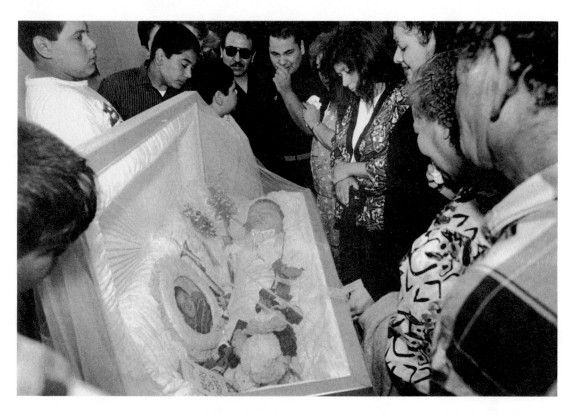

508

Joseph Rodriguez, *Funeral of two-and-a-half-year-old Thomas Regalado III.* East Los Angeles, 1992.

COMMENT

"One picture ran today in the *New York Times*: the two and a half year old in the coffin at the funeral. I was really depressed. I can't understand why one must always show violence or famine to be recognized as an accomplished photojournalist."

— Joseph Rodriguez

in the inner city, they watch us. The bejeweled pimp in his gold BMW parodies the Beverly Hills matron on Rodeo Drive. The baby with the gun in his chubby fist is spiritual heir to John Wayne and his feminist cowgirl wife Annie Oakley, and to the country that was settled with guns in the cowboy movies, and in truth.

The political left used to speak of "community" when Americans were more interested in the separation of the rich from the poor. But lately the left has gotten involved with the self-actualization movement, a most American movement for being so centered on the individual. Now the talk is all about my right to do my own thing with my own body and it's nobody's business if I do. The right responds with a nostalgic creak about "family values," as though this country was ever a place of family values, and not a country where healthy families prepared their children to leave home.

We are people who believe in the first-person singular pronoun—which is our strength. But our weakness is that we don't comprehend our lives in common, the ways we create one another in the American city. As Americans we have always feared the city; with Huck we have always wanted to escape. Thus do we look at the faces of East L.A.: we consign the children to some remote kingdom of THEM.

Thirty years ago, I grew up listening to the black Protestant hymns of the civil rights movement. In the 1960s, black America was perceived by most Americans as the moral authority of this nation. Today we are to believe that the inner city is so bereft of moral life that children must be taken out of town—taken where? To moral Walnut Creek? Moral Evanston?

Even black intellectuals and smart filmmakers propose that what is needed is to get the children out of the city. It is a romantic notion that has survived into our century. Transport street children, get them away from concrete and broken glass and piss smell, expose them to a redemptive green world. This notion credits to trees powers that we used to assign to the soul. And it assumes that what is needed to heal the children of East L.A. is something leafy rather than the human touch.

We do not believe in souls. We believe in pecs and abs. We do not believe in the city. We believe in nightmares and monsters. Finally, these photographs do not embarrass us, though they should. Looking at these faces, we never guess why we use the music of violence to build up our skinny arms.

509

■ **Discuss.** *Throughout "Gangstas," Rodriguez repeatedly refers to the gang members as children. Discuss his insistence on this word. What point is he trying to make? Does the fact that these are children make them less guilty? Does it make their crimes more frightening?*

■ **Write.** *Having read "Gangstas," choose one of Joseph Rodriguez's photographs and write a close reading of it. How does it comment on gang violence and the humanity of its participants? Does it support Richard Rodriguez's assertions about the gangster lifestyle, or does it complicate them?*

COMMENT

"This is the view of the barrio we need — human and complex, the
black and white as well as the grey. Through our media we usually
only receive a fragment of the neighborhood, a slice of narrative. . . .
The media's sensationalism easily divides barrio and suburb into 'us'
and 'them.' We need the rest of the story to be told, as in these photographs. Then it won't be so easy to deny that the barrio kids are
'our' children too."

— Ruben Martinez, from the introduction to
Joseph Rodriguez's *East Side Stories*

 CONSIDER THE CLUSTER
Turf War

■ **Message**

Richard Rodriguez says that he is puzzled by the "communal" aspects of the gangs. What does
he mean by this? In his essay, what does he oppose to the communal? After reading his essay,
which do you think he regards as most important: the individual or the community?

■ **Method**

Richard Rodriguez praises Joseph Rodriguez's photographs for lacking "middle-class *nostalgie
de la boue*" (French, "yearning for slime"), meaning that they don't romanticize their subject.
Do you agree with him? Do you find in the photographs a different attitude toward the gang
members than you find in the essay? In your opinion, who portrays the gangs better: the essayist or the photographer?

■ **Medium**

Richard Rodriguez admits right from the start of his essay that he hates the gang subculture.
What does he especially hate about it? What features does he seem to dislike most of all?
How do the photographs capture these features? Do the photos support the text and vice
versa? Explain your assessment of how they work together.

ON THE MARGINS

■ **Cluster menu: on the Margins**

Homelessness has been a national problem for well over a century, repeatedly offering visible proof that not every American participates in the American Dream. The situation grows worse in periods of recession and low employment, when many workers and families who already live on the edge lose their basic means of support and find themselves on the street. A major concern throughout the Great Depression of the 1930s and again in the late 1980s during Ronald Reagan's second term, the issue has returned once more to the forefront since the collapse of the 1990s economy and the subsequent loss of many jobs. Although the homeless population also consists of the mentally ill and substance abusers—along with those who are inveterate drifters—it nevertheless always climbs when the job market dwindles and social services are curtailed. The materials that follow document the lives of just a few of those people who live outside of a world many of us take for granted—a world where you have a comfortable place to go at the end of the day.

COMMENT

"Whence this army of homeless boys? is a question often asked. The answer is supplied by the procession of mothers that go out and in at Police Headquarters the year round, inquiring for missing boys, often not until they have been gone for weeks and months, and then sometimes rather as a matter of decent form than from any real interest in the lad's fate. The stereotyped promise of the clerks who fail to find his name on the books among the arrests, that he 'will come back when he gets hungry,' does not always come true. More likely he went away because he was hungry. Some are orphans, actually or in effect, thrown upon the world when their parents were 'sent up' to the island or to Sing Sing, and somehow overlooked by the 'Society,' which thenceforth became the enemy to be shunned until growth and dirt and the hardships of the street, that make them old early, offer some hope of successfully floating the lie that they are 'sixteen.' A drunken father explains the matter in other cases, as in that of John and Willie, aged ten and eight, picked up by the police. They 'didn't live nowhere,' never went to school, could neither read nor write. Their twelve-year-old sister kept house for the father, who turned the boys out to beg, or steal, or starve. Grinding poverty and hard work beyond the years of the lad; blows and curses for breakfast, dinner, and supper; all these are recruiting agents for the homeless army. Sickness in the house, too many mouths to feed."

—Jacob Riis, from *How the Other Half Lives* (1890)

513

◀ **Jacob Riis, *Homeless Boys, New York City,* c. 1890.** "Half the world knows not how the other half lives," wrote the great English poet George Herbert, whose memorable phrase was borrowed by photographer/social reformer Jacob Riis for his classic exposé of the New York slums. Skilled in both print and photojournalism, Riis published *How the Other Half Lives* (from which this posed photo was taken) in 1890, and over the course of several editions it quickly became a model of how photography could reveal to the public what the public would perhaps rather not see. Throughout the twentieth century, photographers such as Lewis Hines, Dorothea Lange, Walker Evans, and, into the present, Mary Ellen Mark, followed in Riis's tradition of documentary photography, offering penetrating visual records of lives on the margins of society—the poor, the homeless, the addicted, the abandoned, the desperately ill. (Copyright Museum of the City of New York; part of the Jacob A. Riis Collection [image 121])

Lars Eighner, *On Dumpster Diving.* Lars Eighner (b. 1948) lost his job as a mental-hospital attendant in Texas and found himself trying to survive on the street. He not only survived but went on to write what is now a classic essay on the subject of homelessness. In "On Dumpster Diving," an essay that has retained its relevance for almost two decades, Eighner, without self-pity and with sly wit, describes the fine art of scavenging for survival. His account is full of practical advice: "By far the best way to go through a Dumpster is to lower yourself into it. Most of the good stuff tends to settle at the bottom because it is usually weightier than the rubbish." Eighner now supports himself by writing essays and short stories; he is the author of *Travels with Lizbeth* (1994), a memoir of his homeless years wandering with his dog. "On Dumpster Diving" first appeared in the Fall 1991 issue of *Threepenny Review.*

Lars Eighner

ON DUMPSTER DIVING

■ **Consider before you read.** *What common assumptions about "scavenging" does Eighner confront in his essay? How does he challenge these assumptions? Are there any he affirms as true? What surprises you most about his careful assessment of Dumpster diving?*

Long before I began Dumpster diving I was impressed with Dumpsters, enough so that I wrote the Merriam-Webster research service to discover what I could about the word "Dumpster." I learned from them that "Dumpster" is a proprietary word belonging to the Dempsey Dumpster company.

Since then I have dutifully capitalized the word although it was lower-cased in almost all of the citations Merriam-Webster photocopied for me. Dempsey's word is too apt. I have never heard these things called anything but Dumpsters. I do not know anyone who knows the generic name for these objects. From time to time, however, I hear a wino or hobo give some corrupted credit to the original and call them Dipsy Dumpsters.

I began Dumpster diving about a year before I became homeless.

I prefer the term "scavenging" and use the word "scrounging" when I mean to be obscure. I have heard people, evidently meaning to be polite, using the word "foraging," but I prefer to reserve that word for gathering nuts and berries and such which I do also according to the season and the opportunity. "Dumpster diving" seems to me to be a little too cute and, in my case, inaccurate because I lack the athletic ability to lower myself into the Dumpsters as the true divers do, much to their increased profit.

I like the frankness of the word "scavenging," which I can hardly think of without picturing a big black snail on an aquarium wall. I live from the refuse of others. I am a scavenger. I think it a sound and honorable niche, although if I could I would naturally prefer to live the comfortable consumer life, perhaps—and only perhaps—as a slightly less wasteful consumer owing to what I have learned as a scavenger.

While my dog Lizbeth and I were still living in the house on Avenue B in Austin, as my savings ran out, I put almost all my sporadic income into rent. The necessities of daily life I began to extract from Dumpsters. Yes, we ate from Dumpsters. Except for jeans, all my clothes came from Dumpsters. Boom boxes, candles, bedding, toilet paper, medicine, books, a typewriter, a virgin male love doll, change sometimes amounting to many dollars: I acquired many things from the Dumpsters.

I have learned much as a scavenger. I mean to put some of what I have learned down here, beginning with the practical art of Dumpster diving and proceeding to the abstract.

What is safe to eat?

After all, the finding of objects is becoming something of an urban art. Even respectable employed people will sometimes find something tempting sticking out of a Dumpster or standing beside one. Quite a number of people, not all of them of the bohemian type, are willing to brag that they found this or that piece in the trash. But eating from Dumpsters is the thing that separates the dilettanti from the professionals.

Eating safely from the Dumpsters involves three principles: using the senses and common sense to evaluate the condition of the found materials, knowing the Dumpsters of a given area and checking them regularly, and seeking always to answer the question "Why was this discarded?"

Perhaps everyone who has a kitchen and a regular supply of groceries has, at one time or another, made a sandwich and eaten half of it before discovering mold on the bread or got a mouthful of milk before realizing the milk had turned. Nothing of the sort is likely to happen to a Dumpster diver because he is constantly reminded that most food is discarded for a reason. Yet a lot of perfectly good food can be found in Dumpsters.

Canned goods, for example, turn up fairly often in the Dumpsters I frequent. All except the most phobic people would be willing to eat from a can even if it came from a Dumpster. Canned goods are among the safest of foods to be found in Dumpsters, but are not utterly foolproof.

Although very rare with modern canning methods, botulism is a possibility. Most other forms of food poisoning seldom do lasting harm to a healthy person. But botulism is almost certainly fatal and often the first symptom is death. Except for carbonated beverages, all canned goods should contain a slight vacuum and suck air when first punctured. Bulging, rusty, dented cans and cans that spew when punctured should be avoided, especially when the contents are not very acidic or syrupy.

515

Heat can break down the botulin, but this requires much more cooking than most people do to canned goods. To the extent that botulism occurs at all, of course, it can occur in cans on pantry shelves as well as in cans from Dumpsters. Need I say that home-canned goods found in Dumpsters are simply too risky to be recommended.

From time to time one of my companions, aware of the source of my provisions, will ask, "Do you think these crackers are really safe to eat?" For some reason it is most often the crackers they ask about.

This question always makes me angry. Of course I would not offer my companion anything I had doubts about. But more than that I wonder why he cannot evaluate the condition of the crackers for himself. I have no special knowledge and I have been wrong before. Since he knows where the food comes from, it seems to me he ought to assume some of the responsibility for deciding what he will put in his mouth.

For myself I have few qualms about dry foods such as crackers, cookies, cereal, chips, and pasta if they are free of visible contaminates and still dry and crisp. Most often such things are found in the original packaging, which is not so much a positive sign as it is the absence of a negative one.

Raw fruits and vegetables with intact skins seem perfectly safe to me, excluding of course the obviously rotten. Many are discarded for minor imperfections which can be pared away. Leafy vegetables, grapes, cauliflower, broccoli, and similar things may be contaminated by liquids and may be impractical to wash.

Candy, especially hard candy, is usually safe if it has not drawn ants. Chocolate is often discarded only because it has become discolored as the cocoa butter de-emulsified. Candying after all is one method of food preservation because pathogens do not like very sugary substances.

All of these foods might be found in any Dumpster and can be evaluated with some confidence largely on the basis of appearance. Beyond these are foods which cannot be correctly evaluated without additional information.

I began scavenging by pulling pizzas out of the Dumpster behind a pizza delivery shop. In general prepared food requires caution, but in this case I knew when the shop closed and went to the Dumpster as soon as the last of the help left.

Such shops often get prank orders, called "bogus." Because help seldom stays long at these places pizzas are often made with the wrong topping, refused on delivery for being cold, or baked incorrectly. The products to be discarded are boxed up because inventory is kept by counting boxes: a boxed pizza can be written off; an unboxed pizza does not exist.

I never placed a bogus order to increase the supply of pizzas and I believe no one else was scavenging in this Dumpster. But the people in the shop became suspicious and began to retain their garbage in the shop overnight.

While it lasted I had a steady supply of fresh, sometimes warm pizza. Because I knew the Dumpster I knew the source of the pizza, and because I visited the Dumpster regularly I knew what was fresh and what was yesterday's.

516

The area I frequent is inhabited by many affluent college students. I am not here by chance; the Dumpsters in this area are very rich. Students throw out many good things, including food. In particular they tend to throw everything out when they move at the end of a semester, before and after breaks, and around midterm when many of them despair of college. So I find it advantageous to keep an eye on the academic calendar.

The students throw food away around the breaks because they do not know whether it has spoiled or will spoil before they return. A typical discard is a half jar of peanut butter. In fact nonorganic peanut butter does not require refrigeration and is unlikely to spoil in any reasonable time. The student does not know that, and since it is Daddy's money, the student decides not to take a chance.

Opened containers require caution and some attention to the question "Why was this discarded?" But in the case of discards from student apartments, the answer may be that the item was discarded through carelessness, ignorance, or wastefulness. This can sometimes be deduced when the item is found with many others, including some that are obviously perfectly good.

Some students, and others, approach defrosting a freezer by chucking out the whole lot. Not only do the circumstances of such a find tell the story, but also the mass of frozen goods stays cold for a long time and items may be found still frozen or freshly thawed.

Yogurt, cheese, and sour cream are items that are often thrown out while they are still good. Occasionally I find a cheese with a spot of mold, which of course I just pare off, and because it is obvious why such a cheese was discarded, I treat it with less suspicion than an apparently perfect cheese found in similar circumstances. Yogurt is often discarded, still sealed, only because the expiration date on the carton had passed. This is one of my favorite finds because yogurt will keep for several days, even in warm weather.

Students throw out canned goods and staples at the end of semesters and when they give up college at midterm. Drugs, pornography, spirits, and the like are often discarded when parents are expected—Dad's day, for example. And spirits also turn up after big party weekends, presumably discarded by the newly reformed. Wine and spirits, of course, keep perfectly well even once opened.

My test for carbonated soft drinks is whether they still fizz vigorously. Many juices or other beverages are too acid or too syrupy to cause much concern provided they are not visibly contaminated. Liquids, however, require some care.

One hot day I found a large jug of Pat O'Brien's Hurricane mix. The jug had been opened, but it was still ice cold. I drank three large glasses before it became apparent to me that someone had added the rum to the mix, and not a little rum. I never tasted the rum and by the time I began to feel the effects I had already ingested a very large quantity of the beverage. Some divers would have considered this a boon, but being suddenly and thoroughly intoxicated in a public place in the early afternoon is not my idea of a good time.

I have heard of people maliciously contaminating discarded food and even handouts, but mostly I have heard of this from people with vivid imaginations

517

■ **Consider.** *Look carefully at this photograph. What details make you feel this is a family on the edge? How would you describe the expressions of the various family members? What do you consider to be the photograph's focal point? How has Mark set up the image to reinforce the family's separateness from mainstream society? What compositional role does the automobile play in the photograph?*

◀ **Mary Ellen Mark, *The Damm Family in Their Car, Los Angeles, California*, 1987.** Mary Ellen Mark (b. 1940) is one of the most recognized photographers to document lives along the margins—a recent survey by *American Photo* magazine ranked her as the most influential woman photographer of all time. In 1987 and again in 1994, Mark followed a North Hollywood, California, homeless family—Dean, Linda, Chrissy, and Jesse Damm—who lived in their car in North Hollywood at the time this photograph was taken. As a documentary photographer, Mark does not simply shoot and run but gets very close to her subjects, their families, and their communities: "I'm just interested in people on the edges. I feel an affinity for people who haven't had the best breaks in society. . . . What I want to do more than anything is acknowledge their existence." Mark says of photography: I am always trying to discover which photographs work, why they work, what is necessary to include in a photograph, and what you can leave out. Often the strongest images are those that exclude elements and leave more to the imagination." (Copyright © Mary Ellen Mark)

who have had no experience with the Dumpsters themselves. Just before the pizza shop stopped discarding its garbage at night, jalapeños began showing up on most of the discarded pizzas. If indeed this was meant to discourage me it was a wasted effort because I am native Texan.

For myself, I avoid game, poultry, pork, and egg-based foods whether I find them raw or cooked. I seldom have the means to cook what I find, but when I do I avail myself of plentiful supplies of beef which is often in very good condition. I suppose fish becomes disagreeable before it becomes dangerous. The dog is happy to have any such thing that is past its prime and, in fact, does not recognize fish as food until it is quite strong.

Home leftovers, as opposed to surpluses from restaurants, are very often bad. Evidently, especially among students, there is a common type of personality that carefully wraps up even the smallest leftover and shoves it into the back of the refrigerator for six months or so before discarding it. Characteristic of this type are the reused jars and margarine tubs which house the remains.

I avoid ethnic foods I am unfamiliar with. If I do not know what it is supposed to look like when it is good, I cannot be certain I will be able to tell if it is bad.

No matter how careful I am I still get dysentery at least once a month, oftener in warm weather. I do not want to paint too romantic a picture. Dumpster diving has serious drawbacks as a way of life.

I learned to scavenge gradually, on my own. Since then I have initiated several companions into the trade. I have learned that there is a predictable series of stages a person goes through in learning to scavenge.

At first the new scavenger is filled with disgust and self-loathing. He is ashamed of being seen and may lurk around, trying to duck behind things, or he may try to dive at night.

(In fact, most people instinctively look away from a scavenger. By skulking around, the novice calls attention to himself and arouses suspicion. Diving at night is ineffective and needlessly messy.)

Every grain of rice seems to be a maggot. Everything seems to stink. He can wipe the egg yolk off the found can, but he cannot erase the stigma of eating garbage out of his mind.

That stage passes with experience. The scavenger finds a pair of running shoes that fit and look and smell brand new. He finds a pocket calculator in perfect working order. He finds pristine ice cream, still frozen, more than he can eat or keep. He begins to understand: people do throw away perfectly good stuff, a lot of perfectly good stuff.

At this stage, Dumpster shyness begins to dissipate. The diver, after all, has the last laugh. He is finding all manner of good things which are his for the taking. Those who disparage his profession are the fools, not he.

He may begin to hang onto some perfectly good things for which he has neither a use nor a market. Then he begins to take note of the things which are not perfectly good but are nearly so. He mates a Walkman with broken earphones and one that is missing a battery cover. He picks up things which he can repair.

At this stage he may become lost and never recover. Dumpsters are full of things of some potential value to someone and also of things which never have much intrinsic value but are interesting. All the Dumpster divers I have known come to the point of trying to acquire everything they touch. Why not take it, they reason, since it is all free.

This is, of course, hopeless. Most divers come to realize that they must restrict themselves to items of relatively immediate utility. But in some cases the diver simply cannot control himself. I have met several of these pack-rat types. Their ideas of the values of various pieces of junk verge on the psychotic. Every bit of glass may be a diamond, they think, and all that glistens, gold.

I tend to gain weight when I am scavenging. Partly this is because I always find far more pizza and doughnuts than water-packed tuna, nonfat yogurt, and fresh vegetables. Also I have not developed much faith in the reliability of Dumpsters as a food source, although it has been proven to me many times. I tend to eat as if I have no idea where my next meal is coming from. But mostly I just hate to see food go to waste and so I eat much more than I should. Something like this drives the obsession to collect junk.

As for collecting objects, I usually restrict myself to collecting one kind of small object at a time, such as pocket calculators, sunglasses, or campaign buttons. To live on the street I must anticipate my needs to a certain extent: I must pick up and save warm bedding I find in August because it will not be found in Dumpsters in November. But even if I had a home with extensive storage space I could not save everything that might be valuable in some contingency.

Mary Ellen Mark, *Chrissy Damm and Adam Johnson, Liano, California,* **1994.** In an interview that appeared in the Winter 1997 issue of *Aperture,* Mary Ellen Mark says of this image: "When I was photographing the Damm family, I would just spend all day. This is Chrissy with her boyfriend, Adam. This is in the house where they were squatting; they were no longer living in a car, but rather a shack without water or electricity. I just hung out with the kids. They were in love. . . . I think Jesse likes us. With Chrissy, it's a little harder to tell. She is more complex. Everything is hidden with her." (Copyright © Mary Ellen Mark)

I have proprietary feelings about my Dumpsters. As I have suggested, it is no accident that I scavenge from Dumpsters where good finds are common. But my limited experience with Dumpsters in other areas suggests to me that it is the population of competitors rather than the affluence of the dumpers that most affects the feasibility of survival by scavenging. The large number of competitors is what puts me off the idea of trying to scavenge in places like Los Angeles.

Curiously, I do not mind my direct competition, other scavengers, so much as I hate the can scroungers.

People scrounge cans because they have to have a little cash. I have tried scrounging cans with an able-bodied companion. Afoot a can scrounger simply cannot make more than a few dollars a day. One can extract the necessities of life from the Dumpsters directly with far less effort than would be required to accumulate the equivalent value in cans.

Can scroungers, then, are people who *must* have small amounts of cash. These are drug addicts and winos, mostly the latter because the amounts of cash are so small.

Spirits and drugs do, like all other commodities, turn up in Dumpsters and the scavenger will from time to time have a half bottle of a rather good wine with his dinner. But the wino cannot survive on these occasional finds; he must have his daily dose to stave off the DTs. All the cans he can carry will buy about three bottles of Wild Irish Rose.

I do not begrudge them the cans, but can scroungers tend to tear up the Dumpsters, mixing the contents and littering the area. They become so specialized that they can see only cans. They earn my contempt by passing up change, canned goods, and readily hockable items.

There are precious few courtesies among scavengers. But it is a common practice to set aside surplus items: pairs of shoes, clothing, canned goods, and such. A true scavenger hates to see good stuff go to waste and what he cannot use he leaves in good condition in plain sight.

Can scroungers lay waste to everything in their path and will stir one of a pair of good shoes to the bottom of a Dumpster, to be lost or ruined in the muck. Can scroungers will even go through individual garbage cans, something I have never seen a scavenger do.

Individual garbage cans are set out on the public easement only on garbage days. On other days going through them requires trespassing close to a dwelling. Going through individual garbage cans without scattering litter is almost impossible. Litter is likely to reduce the public's tolerance of scavenging. Individual garbage cans are simply not as productive as Dumpsters; people in houses and duplexes do not move as often and for some reason do not tend to discard as much useful material. Moreover, the time required to go through one garbage can that serves one household is not much less than the time required to go through a Dumpster that contains the refuse of twenty apartments.

But my strongest reservation about going through individual garbage cans is that this seems to me a very personal kind of invasion to which I would object if

I were a householder. Although many things in Dumpsters are obviously meant never to come to light, a Dumpster is somehow less personal.

I avoid trying to draw conclusions about the people who dump in the Dumpsters I frequent. I think it would be unethical to do so, although I know many people will find the idea of scavenger ethics too funny for words.

Dumpsters contain bank statements, bills, correspondence, and other documents, just as anyone might expect. But there are also less obvious sources of information. Pill bottles, for example. The labels on pill bottles contain the name of the patient, the name of the doctor, and the name of the drug. AIDS drugs and antipsychotic medicines, to name but two groups, are specific and are seldom prescribed for any other disorders. The plastic compacts for birth control pills usually have complete label information.

Despite all of this sensitive information, I have had only one apartment resident object to my going through the Dumpster. In that case it turned out the resident was a university athlete who was taking bets and who was afraid I would turn up his wager slips.

Occasionally a find tells a story. I once found a small paper bag containing some unused condoms, several partial tubes of flavored sexual lubricant, a partially used compact of birth control pills, and the torn pieces of a picture of a young man. Clearly she was through with him and planning to give up sex altogether.

Dumpster things are often sad—abandoned teddy bears, shredded wedding books, despaired-of sales kits. I find many pets lying in state in Dumpsters. Although I hope to get off the streets so that Lizbeth can have a long and comfortable old age, I know this hope is not very realistic. So I suppose when her time comes she too will go into a Dumpster. I will have no better place for her. And after all, for most of her life her livelihood has come from the Dumpster. When she finds something I think is safe that has been spilled from the Dumpster I let her have it. She already knows the route around the best Dumpsters. I like to think that if she survives me she will have a chance of evading the dog catcher and of finding her sustenance on the route.

Silly vanities also come to rest in the Dumpsters. I am a rather accomplished needleworker. I get a lot of materials from the Dumpsters. Evidently sorority girls, hoping to impress someone, perhaps themselves, with their mastery of a womanly art, buy a lot of embroider-by-number kits, work a few stitches horribly, and eventually discard the whole mess. I pull out their stitches, turn the canvas over, and work an original design. Do not think I refrain from chuckling as I make original gifts from these kits.

I find diaries and journals. I have often thought of compiling a book of literary found objects. And perhaps I will one day. But what I find is hopelessly commonplace and bad without being, even unconsciously, camp. College students also discard their papers. I am horrified to discover the kind of paper which now merits an A in an undergraduate course. I am grateful, however, for the number of good books and magazines the students throw out.

523

In the area I know best I have never discovered vermin in the Dumpsters, but there are two kinds of kitty surprise. One is alley cats which I meet as they leap, claws first, out of Dumpsters. This is especially thrilling when I have Lizbeth in tow. The other kind of kitty surprise is a plastic garbage bag filled with some ponderous, amorphous mass. This always proves to be used cat litter.

City bees harvest doughnut glaze and this makes the Dumpster at the doughnut shop more interesting. My faith in the instinctive wisdom of animals is always shaken whenever I see Lizbeth attempt to catch a bee in her mouth, which she does whenever bees are present. Evidently some birds find Dumpsters profitable, for birdie surprise is almost as common as kitty surprise of the first kind. In hunting season all kinds of small game turn up in Dumpsters, some of it, sadly, not entirely dead. Curiously, summer and winter, maggots are uncommon.

The worst of the living and near-living hazards of the Dumpsters are the fire ants. The food that they claim is not much of a loss, but they are vicious and aggressive. It is very easy to brush against some surface of the Dumpster and pick up half a dozen or more fire ants, usually in some sensitive area such as the underarm. One advantage of bringing Lizbeth along as I make Dumpster rounds is that, for obvious reasons, she is very alert to ground-based fire ants. When Lizbeth recognizes the signs of fire ant infestation around our feet she does the Dance of the Zillion Fire Ants. I have learned not to ignore this warning from Lizbeth, whether I perceive the tiny ants or not, but to remove ourselves at Lizbeth's first pas de bourrée.[1] All the more so because the ants are the worst in the months I wear flip-flops, if I have them.

(Perhaps someone will misunderstand the above. Lizbeth does the Dance of the Zillion Fire Ants when she recognizes more fire ants than she cares to eat, not when she is being bitten. Since I have learned to react promptly, she does not get bitten at all. It is the isolated patrol of fire ants that falls in Lizbeth's range that deserves pity. Lizbeth finds them quite tasty.)

By far the best way to go through a Dumpster is to lower yourself into it. Most of the good stuff tends to settle at the bottom because it is usually weightier than the rubbish. My more athletic companions have often demonstrated to me that they can extract much good material from a Dumpster I have already been over.

To those psychologically or physically unprepared to enter a Dumpster, I recommend a stout stick, preferably with some barb or hook at one end. The hook can be used to grab plastic garbage bags. When I find canned goods or other objects loose at the bottom of a Dumpster I usually can roll them into a small bag that I can then hoist up. Much Dumpster diving is a matter of experience for which nothing will do except practice.

Dumpster diving is outdoor work, often surprisingly pleasant. It is not entirely predictable; things of interest turn up every day and some days there are finds of great value. I am always very pleased when I can turn up exactly the thing I most wanted to find. Yet in spite of the element of change, scavenging more than most other pursuits tends to yield returns in some proportion to the effort and intelli-

---

[1] *pas de bourrée:* A transitional ballet step.

gence brought to bear. It is very sweet to turn up a few dollars in change from a Dumpster that has just been gone over by a wino.

The land is now covered with cities. The cities are full of Dumpsters. I think of scavenging as a modern form of self-reliance. In any event, after ten years of government service, where everything is geared to the lowest common denominator, I find work that rewards initiative and effort refreshing. Certainly I would be happy to have a sinecure again, but I am not heartbroken not to have one anymore.

I find from the experience of scavenging two rather deep lessons. The first is to take what I can use and let the rest go by. I have come to think that there is no value in the abstract. A thing I cannot use or make useful, perhaps by trading, has no value however fine or rare it may be. I mean useful in a broad sense—so, for example, some art I would think useful and valuable, but other art might be otherwise for me.

I was shocked to realize that some things are not worth acquiring, but now I think it is so. Some material things are white elephants that eat up the possessor's substance.

The second lesson is of the transience of material being. This has not quite converted me to a dualist, but it has made some headway in that direction. I do not suppose that ideas are immortal, but certainly mental things are longer-lived than other material things.

Once I was the sort of person who invests material objects with sentimental value. Now I no longer have those things, but I have the sentiments yet.

Many times in my travels I have lost everything but the clothes I was wearing and Lizbeth. The things I find in Dumpsters, the love letters and ragdolls of so many lives, remind me of this lesson. Now I hardly pick up a thing without envisioning the time I will cast it away. This I think is a healthy state of mind. Almost everything I have now has already been cast out at least once, proving that what I own is valueless to someone.

Anyway, I find my desire to grab for the gaudy bauble has been largely sated. I think this is an attitude I share with the very wealthy—we both know there is plenty more where what we have came from. Between us are the rat-race millions who have confounded their selves with the objects they grasp and who nightly scavenge the cable channels looking for they know not what.

I am sorry for them.

■ **Discuss.** *What do the things that Eighner finds discarded say about their individual owners or about societies? Can you expand on his discussion? What preoccupations or neuroses do they reveal? Choose a specific example or two from the essay and write an analysis of what the items meant to their owners and why they ended up in the trash.*

■ **Write.** *In this essay, Eighner moves from practical considerations to larger philosophical lessons he has learned. How does he manage to make these rhetorical shifts in his writing? Why do you think he structures the piece the way he does? Write an essay in which you pick out a few turning points in "On Dumpster Diving" and discuss why they are important to Eighner's argument.*

Margaret Morton, *Mr. Lee*. Morton has gathered photographs and oral histories in *Fragile Dwelling* (New York: *Aperture*, 2000), a collection that documents the inventive ways in which homeless people create places and communities. This text accompanies several photographs of Mr. Lee, two of which are reproduced here.

Margaret Morton

MR. LEE

■ **Consider before you read.** *What resources—both physical and psychological—does Mr. Lee put into building his home? What is necessary for the structure, and what is there for ornament or for some other purpose?*

At the crest of the Hill, just before it narrows to a ravine and plummets toward Forsyth Street, stands the curious home of Mr. Lee, an immigrant from Guangdong Province in China, who found his way to the encampment in 1989. He brought few possessions but soon astonished his neighbors by constructing a house without pounding a nail or sawing a board. It is bound together with knots. Bright yellow plastic straps wrap his soft rounded hut, binding old mattresses and bedsprings into walls. The exterior is festooned with red bakery ribbons, paper lanterns, and castoff calendars that celebrate the Chinese New Year. Oranges, symbols of prosperity, have hardened in the bitter cold and hang from the straps like ornaments.

Every morning, Mr. Lee quietly draws Chinese characters on flat sheets of cardboard and lashes them to the outside of his hut: CONGRATULATIONS TO MR. LEE FOR HAVING A BIG COMPANY, HE HAS HUNDREDS OF THOUSANDS OF WORKERS, EACH WORKER GETS PAID $500 A DAY, PROSPERITY TO MR. LEE, MR. LEE THE GREAT INVENTOR. He does not write about the job he once held as a restaurant worker in Queens, or about his last apartment, a walk-up on Mott Street.

At dawn, when Mr. Lee leaves the Hill, he places a stone against his door and secures it with elaborate knots. He slowly wanders the streets of Chinatown with two burlap rice sacks slung over his shoulder, pausing to collect bits of cloth and cord left by morning delivery trucks. In the early evening he returns and, with great ceremony, ties his new treasures to the exterior of his hut. Mr. Lee sometimes binds these objects in such a way that they take on new forms and identities. The majestic cluster of fruit perched atop his roof is in fact a teddy bear, which he found on the street and skillfully transformed.

■ *Consider. What do these signs mean to Mr. Lee? Why does he turn these imagined scenarios into headlines visible to people who might pass his hut?*

◀ **Margaret Morton,** *Mr. Lee's House, the Hill.* The photograph of Mr. Lee's house is included in Margaret Morton's book *Fragile Dwelling* (2000), a collection of photographs documenting the various ways New York City's homeless people have constructed their own housing. As her publisher says: "To Morton, these assemblages of crates, scrap wood, broken furniture, and other debris of the modern city are not an eyesore to be quickly dismissed and then forgotten. They are in fact, as she shows us, homes—laboriously and ingeniously built, little by little, piece by piece." Morton spent ten years on this project, taking photographs and recording oral histories. A professor of art at The Cooper Union for the Advancement of Science and Art, Morton, who received her MFA degree from Yale, has published several other books, including *The Tunnel and Transitory Gardens* (1995). Her photographs have been widely exhibited and featured in numerous magazines in the United States and abroad.

Margaret Morton,
Mr. Lee, Chinatown.
(© Margaret Morton)

528

■ Consider. *What connection does the photographer establish between Mr. Lee and his house? In your judgment, how do the photographs of Mr. Lee and of his house reinforce the connection Morton makes in her verbal description?*

Much like his house, Mr. Lee is soft and round and held together by knots. Bits of wire twisted through buttonholes fasten his multiple layers of second-hand clothing.

■ **Discuss.** *How do you think Mr. Lee would fit into Lars Eighner's taxonomy of scavengers, scroungers, and collectors? Discuss the similarities and differences between the things the two men acquire and the uses to which they put those things.*

■ **Write.** *In Morton's description of both Mr. Lee and his house, knots take on a symbolic resonance. What does it say about Mr. Lee that he builds a house "without pounding a nail or sawing a board" but purely by tying things together? Write an analysis of how knots function both literally and figuratively to make up Mr. Lee's home.*

 CONSIDER THE CLUSTER
On the Margins

■ **Message**

What lessons does Lars Eighner learn from his experience in the art of Dumpster diving? How do these lead to ethical principles? Are these principles applicable to everyone, even the affluent? What do you think Eighner means when he writes: "I think of scavenging as a modern form of self-reliance"?

■ **Method**

What characterizes Mr. Lee's method of construction? Where does he find his supplies? How does his method help reveal something about his personal and ethnic identity? How does Margaret Morton's brief "oral history" help you make sense out of Mr. Lee's distinctive style? Can you find any similarities between Mr. Lee's methods and Lars Eighner's craft? In what ways do they both demonstrate "self-reliance"?

■ **Medium**

In her afterword to *American Odyssey*, Mary Ellen Mark writes: "Photographs can be enigmatic. They sometimes work because of what is included in the frame, and sometimes because of what is not." This is a principle that can be applied to all works of art, regardless of the medium: we need to observe what the artist has included as well as what he or she has left out. Can you apply Mark's principle to all of the photographs depicting homeless people in this section? After noting what's included—details, postures, expressions, backgrounds, and so on—identify elements you think the photographers omitted. Why do you think those particular elements were omitted?

529

WRITE ■■■■■■

1. **Collaborate and make a case.** Suppose you want to turn Lars Eighner's "On Dumpster Diving" (p. 514) into a documentary film. After rereading the essay carefully, break into small groups. Each group will design a plan for how the essay would be filmed. What details of Eighner's essay would you include? Which ones would you exclude? How would your film convey his ideas? What would be your lead idea? At a panel session, someone representing each group should discuss his or her group's plan.

2. **Evaluate.** Richard Rodriguez organizes his essay around his response to a photo essay by Joseph Rodriguez (p. 503) in which the photographer tries to document both the personal and criminal aspects of gang members' lives. Other photographers in this book attempt similar projects: for example, Mary Ellen Mark and Margaret Morton turn their lenses on the homeless in an attempt to make visible a side of society that remains invisible to many. Using Rodriguez's, Mark's, or Morton's pictures as a starting place, write an essay that begins with your response to the photographs themselves and ends with a larger statement about how you respond to the issues they invoke. Do the photographs make it clear how the photographer wants us to respond? Does the desire of the recorder make a difference, or does the record speak for itself? Explain.

3. **Analyze and make a case.** In most written arguments, the writer will employ two sets of terms—one set of words intended to be taken positively that support or reinforce the writer's position, and an other set of words intended to have negative meanings. The terms, often left undefined, are not necessarily used as a dictionary would define them. Go through the essays by David Brooks, Orlando Patterson, Jan Morris, and Jhumpa Lahiri, identifying some key terms that you think each author intends to be taken as positive or negative. Then choose a term you think plays a significant role in the argument but should be taken in a different sense from what the author intended. In an essay, discuss how the author uses this term and why you disagree with this usage.

4. **Make a case.** David Brooks ends "People like Us" (p. 493) by saying: "Look around at your daily life. Are you really in touch with the broad diversity of American life? Do you care?" In a short personal essay, craft a response to both questions. Are you personally in contact with diverse groups of people and opinions, or are you usually surrounded by people whose appearance and ideas pretty much resemble your own? Then consider the second question: Does it matter to you at all? Don't forget to explain why it does or doesn't matter.

When Guys Hang (

DUDE

5. **Research.** A critic has coined the term "auto-graphics" to describe the new graphic memoir. For a research assignment, read Gillian Whitlock's article "Autographics: The Seeing 'I' of the Comics" (in *Modern Fiction Studies*, 52/4, Winter 2006) and use it as a way to assess Alison Bechdel's "Old Father, Old Artificer" (p. 254), Marjane Satrapi's "When I Was Invited To Speak At West Point" (p. 448), and Nathan Huang's "A Red-Envelope Day" (p. 480). In your paper, discuss Whitlock's claim that the form of autographics provides us with "new ways of thinking in life narrative across cultures."

6. **Collaborate and make a case.** Practice the art of disputation. Break into small groups. Using Orlando Patterson's "Race Over" (p. 471) as the central issue, prepare a list of points that challenges Patterson's argument that race will no longer be a major concern by the middle of the twenty-first century. The list of points should dispute Patterson's demographic forecast; his discussion of mixed ethnicity; his examples, statistics, and any other elements of his case that can be called into question. Appoint a speaker for the group who will summarize to the class all the available arguments against Patterson's claim. After listening to all the points, the class as a whole should judge which ones present the strongest case against Patterson's argument.

7. **Collaborate and create.** Both Melanie Sumner's "Marriage" (p. 462) and Penelope Scambly Schott's "Report on the Difference between Men and Women" (p. 461) suggest gender stereotypes that are often found in cartoons. After breaking into a collaborative group, select either one of these texts, identify the stereotypes, and try transforming the story or essay into a cartoon. The cartoon need not be professionally rendered but should effectively translate the author's mini narrative into picture and text. Afterward, groups should compare their productions.

8. **Imagine and create a memoir.** Consider Margaret Morton's "Mr. Lee's House, the Hill" (p. 527) in conjunction with her photograph of Mr. Lee and the oral history she composed about him. Then consider Mr. Lee's house in conjunction with the cluster titled Home (see p. 290) in Chapter 3, Shaping Spaces. Using Nicole Lamy's memoir as a model, compose a brief personal essay in the voice of Mr. Lee in which he describes his house and what it means to him.

9. **Create a personal essay.** Using Jhumpa Lahiri's "My Two Lives" (p. 477) as a model, write a short personal essay in which you describe a situation that has forced you to be part of two

worlds, to live two lives, whether in terms of cultural differences, class background, or another type of dividing line. Try to describe clearly your encounters with both worlds and whether you feel you have succeeded in bridging the gap between the two.

10. **Analyze.** How do photographers capture gender differences? How do they express the dividing lines that often exist between men and women? Select about five photographs in this book (or feel free to use material from outside) and consider how the photographers were conscious of gender differences. What common features can you detect? Are men and women (or boys and girls) presented differently? Are they positioned differently? After studying your sample photographs, write an essay in which you analyze at least three ways that men and women tend to be portrayed in photographs according to gender roles. (In preparation, you might review Lauren Greenfield's photo, "Sara, 19," in the section about photographs that appears in the Introduction on pp. 32–33.)

6

PACKAGING CULTURE

Does she...or doesn't she?

Packaging Culture: the clusters

In one of the most remarkable convergences of our time, shopping has now become so closely linked to our entire culture that it is difficult to see where one's social experiences end and one's consumerism begins. We live in a packaging culture; mass consumption has permeated every nook and cranny of American life. As the architect Sze Tsung Leong puts it: "Not only is shopping melting into everything, but everything is melting into shopping." Although consumer culture became a marked characteristic of the second half of the twentieth century, the rapid rise of an all-pervasive commercialism is being felt more powerfully now than ever before.

Critics have recently begun to study shopping as a key social and cultural phenomenon. A few years ago, *The New York Times* introduced in its weekly magazine a popular section called Consumed, which puts an intellectual spin on the daily experience of buying products. Recent studies of shopping include Sharon Zukin's *Point of Purchase: How Shopping Changed American Culture,* Lizabeth Cohen's *A Consumer's Republic: The Politics of Mass Consumption in Postwar America,* Paco Underhill's *Why We Buy: The Science of Shopping,* and, more recently, James Twitchell's *Branded Nation* and Carlos Broto's *New Shopping Malls.* One of the landmark texts in the development of

serious study of the subject is the lavishly illustrated *Harvard Design School Guide to Shopping.* Continually updated, the book examines how "shopping has infiltrated, colonized, and even replaced almost every aspect of urban life." As the text points out, perhaps "the beginning of the twenty-first century will be remembered as the point where the urban could no longer be understood without shopping."

We constantly witness how the consumer environment has wrapped itself around our lives, blurring distinctions between product and package, marketable item and marketing image, contents and container. On television over the past few years, we have grown accustomed to a new version of the old commercial, the "infomercial." This clever approach imitates a conventional talk-show format (often with a studio audience), but in reality it is a long, drawn-out sales pitch. In similar fashion, newspapers now regularly publish "advertorials," ads for products, institutions, or causes roughly disguised as serious editorials. Moreover, glossy magazines have for so long been jam-packed with advertising that just a few years ago publishers decided to go all the way and simply produce subscription and newsstand magazines wholly devoted to products with no independent editorial content: catalogs disguised as magazines. An example is *Lucky,* which bills itself as "the magazine about shopping." *The New York Times* reported that *Lucky* "may be the first consumer magazine in the United States to use advertising motifs to design every page of editorial content. Articles, in the traditional sense, are nowhere to be found."

Indeed, marketing has fused with all kinds of media. When popular films incorporate consumer products into their story lines or background imagery, the technique is called "product placement." For example, when an actor in a film buys a Pepsi or wears a Patagonia vest or sends a package via

FedEx, the visibly identified product or company benefits not only from the wide exposure but also from its association with the movie star. In addition, the contrived promotion (which an agency has usually paid for) looks natural; it does not resemble an advertisement. Video games have also introduced product placement. One of the most effective examples of product placement can be seen almost everywhere: brand-name clothing. Instead of being paid by corporations for displaying their products, consumers pay the corporations for the privilege of publicly advertising their brand names and logos, such as Nike, Old Navy, and Tommy Hilfiger. In this way, our own bodies become walking billboards—yet another advertising medium.

Like all other media, the Internet has become a productive channel of consumerism, as shopping joins e-mail as one of the most popular online activities. With their multiple links and pop-up ads, web sites are designed to attract potential shoppers. E-stores have borrowed heavily from the vocabulary of brick-and-mortar retail outlets, and consumers can cruise virtual aisles while filling up their shopping carts or adding to their wish lists. Although many people are happy to avoid the hassles of on-site shopping, some express disappointment that a medium with such far-reaching cultural potential as the Internet has essentially been transformed into a gigantic shopping mall. As the computer guru and software engineer Ellen Ullman wrote: "It's enormously sad to see the Internet being turned into the world-wide infomercial. The scariest part is the way web site owners speak unabashedly about blurring the lines between editorial content and advertising, eagerly looking forward to the web as a giant product-placement opportunity."

As the boundaries dissolve between shopping and all other activities, how do we separate commercialism and consumerism from everything else? Can valid distinctions still be made? When we view a beautiful landscape, do we instead perceive valuable "real estate"? Do we look solely for "brand name" prestige when we "shop" for a college? Is patriotism so closely tied to shopping today that, as Ian Frazier put it, "Money and the economy have gotten so tangled up in our politics that we forget we're citizens of our government, not its consumers"? Do we support a politician on the basis of ideas and ideals, or mainly because of a charismatic image created by political consultants? Is the best part of a trip to a famous art museum our visit to the museum store? When we enhance our bodies at the gym, are we really doing it for health purposes or to become a more desirable "commodity"? When does self-esteem turn into self-promotion? To what degree does our self-identity depend on brand images, consumer satisfaction, and how closely we conform to a marketer's profile?

This chapter will examine the many ways consumer culture shapes our attitudes, values, and expectations. It explores how advertising penetrates all media, sometimes directly but at other times disguised as noncommercial messages. The selections and activities in this chapter examine the phenomenon of "social marketing" and explore how those committed to noncommercial causes and public advocacy nevertheless rely on traditional strategies of product advertising, thus further blurring the line between the exchange of ideas and the consumption of ideas. You will be asked to consider how the way something is packaged—whether a product, a person, or an opinion—affects the way we perceive and relate to it. And throughout the chapter, you will be invited to unpack some packages and see what's really inside.

HOW TO MAKE AN AD

Most of the advertising we read in magazines, hear on the radio, and see on television is written by copywriters—men and women who have a unique verbal talent, especially for catchy phrases and witty expressions. One of the ways copywriters may become famous is by creating memorable slogans. A **slogan** is a catchy phrase or sentence that is closely linked to the product, used repetitively throughout the ad, and perhaps even continued throughout a series of ads. A famous slogan used for many years to sell Listerine mouthwash has entered the language: "Always a bridesmaid, never a bride." Another was AT&T's "Reach out and touch someone." In this cluster, you can read about the creation of one of advertising's most well-known slogans, "Does she . . . or doesn't she?" These slogans differ from certain other well-known slogans in that they do not name a brand. Slogans that do—such as "This Bud's for you"—are technically termed "nameonics" because they simultaneously reinforce the brand name. A type of slogan that's set to music and sung on radio and television is a **jingle**. A jingle usually consists of a simple rhymed verse set to an easy tune. As everyone knows, jingles have a way of stubbornly sticking in our minds.

Because advertising can combine so many elements—words, visuals, voice, music, drama, stage settings, and so on—an advertising agency's copywriting team usually works in tandem with graphic artists, designers, music producers, and filmmakers, all led by an art director, who in turn may report to the marketing chief of the corporation that has hired the agency. As we learn to examine and evaluate advertising, we need to remain aware that advertising in any fashion is a wholly collaborative enterprise, involving the skills of numerous people. We must also be attentive to the type of advertising under consideration: Is it a print ad intended for newspapers or magazines (see "How to Create Your Own Print Ad" on p. 540), a television commercial, a radio spot, a billboard, a direct-mail item, a web-page pop-up? All these commercial texts have their own special means of delivering their messages.

Some advertising campaigns can make a large impact on the culture. For example, the popular "cavemen" commercials created for the automobile insurance company, GEICO, quickly became so much a part of popular culture that they were transformed into a full-blown, though short-lived, situation comedy. The process clearly shows how easily the boundaries between advertising and entertainment can be dissolved.

539

Adbusters, *How to Create Your Own Print Ad*. The nonprofit organization Adbusters educates people about the dangers of advertising—but it does so by "using the master's tools," that is, by employing the same techniques of advertising that are used in the service of selling material goods. These instructions are a fascinating look into the way advertising companies think about the texts they create. (Image courtesy of www.adbusters.org)

Adbusters

HOW TO CREATE YOUR OWN PRINT AD

■ **Consider before you read.** *What does Adbusters' step-by-step account of the process of creating an ad say about their ethos? Why would they share this knowledge? Why wouldn't the advertising industry write a similar analysis?*

1. Decide on your communications objective
2. Decide on your target audience
3. Decide on your format
4. Develop your concept
5. The visual
6. The headline
7. The copy
8. Some mistakes to avoid

I. DECIDE ON YOUR COMMUNICATIONS OBJECTIVE

The communications objective is the essence of your message. If you want to tell people not to eat rutabagas because it's cruel, then that's your communications objective. A word of caution: though perhaps the most important of your eight steps, this is also the one that beginners tend to neglect. A precise and well-defined objective is crucial to a good ad. If your objective isn't right on, then everything that follows will be off as well.

■ *Consider. Who is the target audience for these instructions? Given the way they're written, what can you tell about the readers that Adbusters wants to reach?*

2. DECIDE ON YOUR TARGET AUDIENCE

Who is your message intended for? If you're speaking to kids, then your language and arguments will have to be understandable to kids. On the other hand, if you're speaking to high income earners (for example, if you're writing an ad to dissuade people from wearing fur coats), then your language will have to be more sophisticated. So define who your target audience is, because that will decide how your message is conveyed.

3. DECIDE ON YOUR FORMAT

Is it going to be a poster, a half-page magazine ad, or a tiny box in the corner of a newspaper? Make this decision based on the target audience you're trying to reach, and the amount of money you can afford to spend. If you're talking to kids, a poster in one high school will not only cost less, it will actually reach more of your target audience than a full-page ad in the biggest paper in town. When it comes to deciding on the size of your ad, the larger the ad, the more expensive it will be to produce and run. Don't let that discourage you. You can do a lot with a small ad so long as it's strong, clear, and properly targeted.

4. DEVELOP YOUR CONCEPT

The concept is the underlying creative idea that drives your message. Even in a big ad campaign, the concept will typically remain the same from one ad to another, and from one medium to another. Only the execution of that concept will change. So by developing a concept that is effective and powerful, you open the door to a number of very compelling ads. So take your time developing a concept that's strong.

Typically, an ad is made up of a photograph or a drawing (the "visual"), a headline, and writing (the "copy"). Whether you think of your visual or your headline first makes little difference. However, here are a few guidelines worth following.

5. THE VISUAL

Though you don't absolutely require a visual, it will help draw attention to your ad. Research indicates that 70% of people will only look at the visual in an ad, whereas only 30% will read the headline. So if you use a visual, then you're already talking to twice as many people as you otherwise might. Another suggestion is to use photographs instead of illustrations whenever possible. People tend to relate to realistic photographs more easily than unrealistic ones. But whether you choose a photograph or an illustration, the most important criterion is that the image be the most interesting one possible and at least half your ad whenever possible.

The Visual
Noticed by 70%

HEADLINE HEADLINE HEADLINE
HEADLINE HEADLINE HEADLINE

Headline
Read by 30%

SUBHEAD

Body Copy
Read by 5%

Sub Captions
Read by 15%

SUBHEAD

Signature
Read by 10%

6. THE HEADLINE

The most important thing to remember here is that your headline must be short, snappy and must touch the people that read it. Your headline must affect the reader emotionally, either by making them laugh, making them angry, making them curious or making them think. If you can't think of a headline that does one of these four things, then keep thinking. Here's a little tip that might help: try to find an insight

541

or inner truth to the message that you're trying to convey, something that readers will easily relate to and be touched by. Taking the rutabagas example once again, it might be tempting to write a headline like: "Stop Exploiting These Migrant Workers." However, with a little thought, a more underlying truth might be revealed—that migrant workers are as human as we are, and that our actions do hurt them. From that inner truth, you might arrive at the headline: "Do unto others as you would have them do unto you." Of course, the headline doesn't have to be biblical, though that in itself will add meaning and power for many people. Finally, whenever possible, avoid a headline longer than fifteen words. People just don't read as much as they used to.

7. THE COPY

Here's where you make the case. If you have compelling arguments, make them. If you have persuasive facts, state them. But don't overwhelm with information. Two strong arguments will make more of an impression than a dozen weaker ones. Finally, be clear, be precise, and be honest. Any hint of deception will instantly detract from your entire message. Position your copy beneath the headline, laid out in two blocks two or three inches in length. Only about 5% of people will read your copy, whereas 30% will read your headline. By positioning your copy near your heading, you create a visual continuity which will draw more people to the information you want to convey. Use a serif typeface for your copy whenever possible. Those little lines and swiggles on the letters make the reading easier and more pleasing to the eye.

Subheads

If you have lots of copy, break it up with interesting subheads, as we've done in the graphic [on the previous page]. This will make your ad more inviting, more organized, and easier to read.

The Signature

This is where the name of the organization belongs, along with the address and phone number. If you don't have an organization, then think of a name that will help reinforce the message you're trying to convey. Perhaps "Citizens for Fairness to Migrant Rutabaga Pickers" would work for the example we've been using. This isn't dishonest. Your organization doesn't have to be incorporated or registered for it to be real.

8. SOME MISTAKES TO AVOID

The single most common mistake is visual clutter. Less is always better than more. So if you're not certain whether something is worth including, then leave it out. If your ad is chaotic, people will simply turn the page, and your message will never be read. The second most common mistake is to have an ad that's unclear or not easily understood (haven't you ever looked at an ad and wondered what it was for?). The best way to safeguard against this is to do some rough sketches of your

542

■ **Consider.** *Pick any print ad from a magazine or other source. Go through the categories listed here. Does the ad make "mistakes"? Does it have all the elements that are recommended here: a communications objective, an argument, subheads, a signature? Who is the target audience? What format is the ad in? What is the concept?*

visual with the headline and show it around. If people aren't clear about your message, then it's probably because your message is unclear. And however tempting, don't argue with them or assume that they're wrong and that your ad is fine. You'll be in for an unpleasant surprise. Proofread your ad, then give it to others to proofread, then proofread it yet again. Typographical errors diminish your credibility and have an uncanny habit of creeping into ads when you least expect it.

■ **Discuss.** *Discuss how Adbusters uses research to support its instructions for making an ad. What useful information does research provide to Adbusters? Can you think of other data that research might be able to fill in that would help advertisers make their work more effective?*

■ **Write.** *Choose another medium (for example, TV sitcoms, sport radio shows, billboards) and break it down into its elements the way Adbusters does for the print ad. Write a list that would guide someone through creating a new addition to the genre.*

James B. Twitchell, How to Advertise a Dangerous Product. In this essay, advertising expert and historian James B. Twitchell (b. 1943) examines the origins of the Miss Clairol campaign and explains the thinking behind Shirley Polykoff's verbal and visual strategy, one that artfully transmitted a different message to men than it did to women. A professor of English and advertising at the University of Florida, Twitchell has written extensively on advertising and material culture. He contributes regularly to *Creativity* magazine and has written three book-length studies of advertising, *Adcult USA: The Triumph of Advertising in American Culture* (1997), *Lead Us into Temptation: The Triumph of American Materialism* (1999), and *Twenty Ads That Shook the World: The Century's Most Groundbreaking Advertising and How It Changed Us All* (2001). Twitchell's most recent books are *Living It Up: Our Love Affair with Luxury* (2002), *Branded Nation: The Marketing of Megachurch, College Inc., and Museumworld* (2004), and *Where Men Hide* (2006), a book on male spaces on which he collaborated with photographer Ken Ross, and *Shopping for God: How Christianity Went from In Your Heart to In Your Face* (2007). The following essay on advertising is from *Twenty Ads That Shook the World*.

James B. Twitchell

HOW TO ADVERTISE A DANGEROUS PRODUCT

■ **Consider before you read.** *What is "dangerous" about hair color? What potential threats does it pose, both commercially and socially? How does the advertising deliberately address these threats?*

Two types of products are difficult to advertise: the very common and the very radical. Common products, called "parity products," need contrived distinctions to set them apart. You announce them as "New and Improved, Bigger and Better." But singular products need the illusion of acceptability. They have to appear as if they were *not* new and big, but old and small.

So, in the 1950s, new objects like television sets were designed to look like furniture so that they would look "at home" in your living room. Meanwhile, accepted objects like automobiles were growing massive tail fins to make them seem bigger and better, new and improved.

Although hair coloring is now very common (about half of all American women between the ages of thirteen and seventy color their hair, and about one in eight American males between thirteen and seventy does the same), such was certainly not the case generations ago. The only women who regularly dyed their hair were actresses like Jean Harlow, and "fast women," most especially prostitutes. The only man who dyed his hair was Gorgeous George, the professional wrestler. He was also the only man to use perfume.

In the twentieth century, prostitutes have had a central role in developing cosmetics. For them, sexiness is an occupational necessity, and hence anything that makes them look young, flushed, and fertile is quickly assimilated. Creating a full-lipped, big-eyed, and rosy-cheeked image is the basis of the lipstick, eye shadow, mascara, and rouge industries. While fashion may come *down* from the couturiers, face paint comes *up* from the street. Yesterday's painted woman is today's fashion plate.

In the 1950s, just as Betty Friedan was sitting down to write *The Feminine Mystique,* there were three things a lady should not do. She should not smoke in public, she should not wear long pants (unless under an overcoat), and she should not color her hair. Better she should pull out each gray strand by its root than risk association with those who bleached or, worse, dyed their hair.

This was the cultural context into which Lawrence M. Gelb, a chemical broker and enthusiastic entrepreneur, presented his product to Foote, Cone & Belding. Gelb had purchased the rights to a French hair-coloring process called Clairol. The process was unique in that unlike other available hair-coloring products, which coated the hair, Clairol actually penetrated the hair shaft, producing softer, more natural tones. Moreover, it contained a foamy shampoo base and mild oils that cleaned and conditioned the hair.

545

When the product was first introduced during World War II, the application process took five different steps and lasted a few hours. The users were urban and wealthy. In 1950, after seven years of research and development, Gelb once again took the beauty industry by storm. He introduced the new Miss Clairol Hair Color Bath, a single-step hair-coloring process.

This product, unlike any hair color previously available, lightened, darkened, or changed a woman's natural hair color by coloring and shampooing hair in one simple step that took only twenty minutes. Color results were more natural than anything you could find at the corner beauty parlor. It was hard to believe. Miss Clairol was so technologically advanced that demonstrations had to be done onstage at the International Beauty Show, using buckets of water, to prove to the industry that it was not a hoax. This breakthrough was almost too revolutionary to sell.

COMMENT

"The question 'Does she or doesn't she?' wasn't just about how no one could ever really know what you were doing. It was about how no one could ever really know who you were. It really meant not 'Does she?' but 'Is she?' It really meant 'Is she a contented homemaker or a feminist, a Jew or a Gentile—or isn't she?' "

— Alix Frick, advertising executive and
Shirley Polykoff's daughter

In fact, within six months of Miss Clairol's introduction, the number of women who visited the salon for permanent hair-coloring services increased by more than 500 percent! The women still didn't think they could do it themselves. And *Good Housekeeping* magazine rejected hair-color advertising because they too didn't believe the product would work. The magazine waited for three years before finally reversing its decision, accepting the ads, and awarding Miss Clairol's new product the "Good Housekeeping Seal of Approval."

FC&B passed the "Yes you *can* do it at home" assignment to Shirley Polykoff, a zesty and genial first-generation American in her late twenties. She was, as she herself was the first to admit, a little unsophisticated, but her colleagues thought she understood how women would respond to abrupt change. Polykoff understood emotion, all right, and she also knew that you could be outrageous if you did it in the right context. You can be very naughty if you are first perceived as being nice. Or, in her words, "Think it out square, say it with flair." And it is just this reconciliation of opposites that informs her most famous ad.

She knew this almost from the start. On July 9, 1955, Polykoff wrote to the head art director that she had three campaigns for Miss Clairol Hair Color Bath. The first shows the same model in each ad, but with slightly different hair color. The second exhorts "Tear up those baby pictures! You're a redhead now," and plays on the American desire to refashion the self by rewriting history. These two ideas were, as she says, "knock-downs" en route to what she really wanted. In her autobiography, appropriately titled *Does She . . . Or Doesn't She?: And How She Did It*, Polykoff explains the third execution, the one that will work:

#3. Now here's the one I really want. If I can get it sold to the client. Listen to this: *"Does she . . . or doesn't she?"* (No, I'm not kidding. Didn't you ever hear of the arresting question?) Followed by: *"Only her mother knows for sure!"* or *"So natural, only her mother knows for sure!"*

I may not do the mother part, though as far as I'm concerned mother is the ultimate authority. However, if Clairol goes retail, they may have a problem of offending beauty salons, where they are presently doing all of their business. So I may change the word "mother" to "hairdresser." This could be awfully good business—turning the hairdresser into a color expert. Besides, it reinforces the claim of naturalness, and not so incidentally, glamorizes the salon.

The psychology is obvious. I know from myself. If anyone admires my hair, I'd rather die than admit I dye. And since I feel so strongly that the average woman is me, this great stress on naturalness is important [Polykoff 1975, 28–29].[1]

While her headline is naughty, the picture is nice and natural. Exactly what "Does She . . . Or Doesn't She" do? To men the answer was clearly sexual, but to

■ **Consider.** *In her memo, Shirley Polykoff worries that she might not be able to sell her client on "Does she . . . or doesn't she?" as a hook for the campaign. What obstacle do you think she anticipates? Where do you think the phrase comes from? Do you think Polykoff made it up?*

■ **Consider.** *Twitchell discusses the ad's ambiguity. What makes the headline ambiguous? In what sense is the ambiguity intentional? From the advertiser's perspective, what positive effects will the ambiguity produce? How might it help sales? Besides the headline, what other ambiguities does Twitchell find in the ad?*

546

---

[1]Shirley Polykoff, *Does She . . . Or Doesn't She?: And How She Did It* (Garden City, N.Y.: Doubleday, 1975).

women it certainly was not. The male editors of *Life* magazine balked about running this headline until they did a survey and found out women were not filling in the ellipsis the way they were.

Women, as Polykoff knew, were finding different meaning because they were actually looking at the model and her child. For them the picture was not presexual but postsexual, not inviting male attention but expressing satisfaction with the result. Miss Clairol is a mother, not a love interest.

If that is so, then the product must be misnamed: it should be *Mrs.* Clairol. Remember, this was the mid-1950s, when illegitimacy was a powerful taboo. Out-of-wedlock children were still called bastards, not love children. This ad was far more dangerous than anything Benetton or Calvin Klein has ever imagined.

The naughty/nice conundrum was further intensified *and* diffused by some of the ads featuring a wedding ring on the model's left hand. Although FC&B experimented with models purporting to be secretaries, schoolteachers, and the like, the motif of mother and child was always constant.

So what was the answer to what she does or doesn't do? To women, what she did had to do with visiting the hairdresser. Of course, men couldn't understand. This was the world before unisex hair care. Men still went to barber shops. This was the same pre-feminist generation in which the solitary headline "Modess . . . because" worked magic selling female sanitary products. The ellipsis masked a knowing implication that excluded men. That was part of its attraction. Women know, men don't. This you-just-don't-get-it motif was to become a central marketing strategy as the women's movement was aided *and* exploited by Madison Avenue nichemeisters.

Polykoff had to be ambiguous for another reason. As she notes in her memo, Clairol did not want to be obvious about what they were doing to their primary customer—the beauty shop. Remember that the initial product entailed five different steps performed by the hairdresser, and lasted hours. Many women were still using hairdressers for something they could now do by themselves. It did not take a detective to see that the company was trying to run around the beauty shop and sell to the end-user. So the ad again has it both ways. The hairdresser is invoked as the expert—only he knows *for sure*—but the process of coloring your hair can be done without his expensive assistance.

547

■ **Discuss.** Does Twitchell's claim that "[y]ou can be very naughty if you are first perceived as being nice" still have relevance to advertising? Can you think of any contemporary examples that play with this dichotomy? If so, are you surprised that this method still works on consumers?

■ **Write.** Twitchell places the "Does she . . . or doesn't she?" ad in its social political context. Write an essay in which you analyze the significance of the ad's date to its message. In what ways does the ad reinforce the values of the 1950s? How does it gesture toward the changes of the late 1960s and early 1970s?

Shirley Polykoff and Miss Clairol, *Does She . . . or Doesn't She?* Advertising often hinges on ▶
ambiguity—we tend to look twice at an ad that can be read in more than one way, or that
has a "surprise" hidden within it. Advertisements also often promote products that promise
us a key into a way of life that we would otherwise not have access to. In the 1950s, people
generally kept quiet about what they did to enhance their appearance—for example,
"respectable" women would never admit to coloring their hair. Today, when even major
league baseball players flamboyantly dye their hair, it may seem peculiar to think that such
behavior was once secretive. When an advertising firm decided to market hair coloring to
women back in the mid-1950s, the biggest problem was how to persuade women that it was
acceptable. The problem was creatively handled by one of the first women to make a name
in copywriting.

Shirley Polykoff (1908–1998) designed the "Does she . . . or doesn't she?" campaign,
which became one of the most famous and successful in advertising history. Polykoff was
born into a Jewish immigrant family from Russia and wrote that as a child, "I remember reading magazine advertisements with special attention. They seemed to be a window opening
into a wondering world—the world of mainstream America—that I avidly wanted to be a part
of." She details her immigrant background and advertising career in an entertaining autobiography, appropriately titled *Does She . . . Or Doesn't She? And How She Did It* (1975).
The "Does she . . . or doesn't she?" campaign ran for almost twenty years (1956–1972), during which time the number of American women coloring their hair increased from 7 percent
to more than 40 percent. (From *Good Housekeeping*, August 1963)

548

Shirley Polykoff and Miss Clairol
DOES SHE . . . OR DOESN'T SHE?

■ **Consider before you read/view.** *What qualities does the ad emphasize—both in the
photograph and in the text? What image of the Clairol woman is it trying to present? How
much does this image have to do with hair?*

■ **Consider.** *Advertisements are a careful combination of words and
image. Consider the ad's image. Why do you think Polykoff wanted to focus
on mothers? How does the ad's copy reinforce the image? Because the product is called "Miss Clairol," why do you think Polykoff didn't feature younger,
single women? Why might that strategy not work? Why do you think she
intentionally omitted the presence of a husband? Find a contemporary Clairol
print ad and analyze the relationship between copy and image. How has the
message changed from the "Does she . . . or doesn't she?" campaign?*

Does she...or doesn't she?®

Hair color so natural only her hairdresser knows for sure!™

Are mothers getting younger or do they just look that way! She, for one, has the fresh, wholesome quality, the bright, shining hair that just naturally keeps a woman looking prettier, younger — as though she's found the secret of making time stand still. In a way she has. It's with Miss Clairol, the most beautiful, most effective way to cover gray and to revitalize or brighten fading color.

Keeps hair in wonderful condition — so soft, so lively — because Miss Clairol carries the fresh color deep into the hair shaft to shine outward, just the way natural color does. That's why hairdressers everywhere recommend Miss Clairol and more women use it than all other haircolorings. So quick and easy. Try it yourself. Today.

Even close up, her hair looks natural. Miss Clairol keeps it shiny, bouncy. Completely covers gray with the younger, brighter lasting color no other kind of haircoloring can promise — and live up to!

MISS CLAIROL *HAIR COLOR BATH is a trademark of Clairol Inc. ©Clairol Inc. 1963*

549

◄ ■ **Discuss.** *What do the promises of the ad reveal about women's concerns? Discuss what fears or worries the creators of the ad are playing on.*

■ **Write.** *Write a visual analysis of the "Does she ... or doesn't she?" ad. What choices have the ad's creators made about how to position the two models, how to crop the photograph, and where to place the text? How do all of these visual elements help accomplish what Polykoff wanted to accomplish with the ad?*

GEICO
SO EASY A CAVEMAN CAN DO IT

GEICO, "But Can They Survive Your Prejudice?" The Government Employees Insurance Company—GEICO—is an American auto insurance company well-known for its imaginative, slightly off-beat advertising campaigns. The "So Easy a Caveman Can Do It" ad series, which began running in 2004, is the creation of The Martin Agency. To view some of the TV spots, go to the advertising section at martinagency.com. To check out the cavemen's metro-fabulous apartment and impressive dance moves, go to cavemanscrib.com.

Shown here is actor Jeff Phillips as the GEICO caveman, an educated and urbane Neanderthal, who is deeply and repeatedly offended by GEICO's slogan "So Easy A Caveman Can Do It." This ad, a send-up of political correctness and parody of pieces created by organizations such as the American Civil Liberties Union (for examples go to aclu.org/multimedia), is aimed at fighting stereotypes about cavemen. (GEICO 2008).

■ **Consider before you read/view.** *What accounts for the success of the GEICO caveman ad campaign?*

OUTLASTED DINOSAURS AND THE ICE AGE, BUT CAN THEY SURVIVE YOUR PREJUDICE?

Sadly, negative stereotypes and characterizations of Cavemen continue to persist. You've seen them, portrayals of Cavemen as inarticulate and dim-witted. Cartoons showing Cavemen wearing animal skins and carrying thick wooden clubs. That was over 300,000 years ago! We are the fathers of modern-day tools and weaponry and still you depict us carrying sticks!

Recently, GEICO Auto Insurance has been running a series of print and TV ads that completely perpetuate a negative stereotype — that Cavemen are unsophisticated simpletons, that we have inferior intelligence. The slogan for their website, geico.com, is "So easy a caveman can do it." This could not be more insensitive or offensive.

We hope you'll join us in our fight for respect. Cavemen are smart, thoughtful, intelligent, cognitive, ambitious, social beings. We may not look like you, but we are just like you.

UP WITH CAVEMEN

Cavemen are people too.™

GEICO's marketing vice president, Ted Ward, explained in an interview with *Esquire* magazine (March 20, 2007) why the company chose a caveman to sell their insurance.

> Here you have this Neanderthal from hundreds of thousands of years ago, in today's world. We liked the visual juxtaposition of current technology and cave people coming together.

The Martin Agency's Joe Lawson, the main writer for the campaign, explains:

> Everyone likes humor, and we use dialogue-driven humor [in this series], whereas most commercials or sitcoms are over the top or slapstick. People are leaning toward more subtle, character-driven dialogue. It's why shows like *The Office* and single camera comedies, like *Extras*, do well.

Lawson points out the social commentary that he intended.

> The cavemen on a very subtle level are reflecting and commenting on something that's going on in culture, yes. The ad campaign acknowledges the world we live in, and ours is a very politically correct country. People seem to feel victimized in some way no matter who they are, and that's reflected in the ad.

Lawson knew the ads were a hit when they began to be referenced in the popular media and to show up on YouTube.

> Advertising is not a science, nor is it an art. It's an abyss. You learn all you can, you use every tool you have, but in the end, if you're doing what you're supposed to do, you're going where no one's gone before. After the second round of commercials came out, we knew we had something. The press and blogosphere were definitely taking notice.

■ **Discuss.** *As mentioned by Joe Lawson at The Martin Agency, the GEICO ads appear on YouTube. Usually, advertisers pay for time slots in which to pitch their products to viewers. In this case, individuals posted the ads online so that they could watch them multiple times beyond the company's original placing. What does this say about the status of advertising in the twenty-first century? Does YouTube only benefit advertisers? Or does it take away their control of the message?*

■ **Write.** *Write an analysis of how GEICO's "But Can They Survive Your Prejudice?" works as a parody. What expectations do readers have of the types of ads on which this piece is modeled? What issues do such ads usually address? How does this piece connect with ad man Joe Lawson's ideas about social commentary and political correctness? What do you think of the GEICO parody, and why?*

■■■■■■ CONSIDER THE CLUSTER
How to Make an Ad

■ Message

In "How to Create Your Own Print Ad," we learn that "[t]he communications objective is the essence of your message." After reading the descriptions of both the Miss Clairol ad and the commercial for GEICO auto insurance, how would you describe in one sentence their communications objectives?

■ Method

In an essay, compare Adbusters' advice on how to write a print ad with a classic example of such an ad, Miss Clairol's "Does she . . . or doesn't she?" In what ways does the Miss Clairol ad appear to conform to Adbusters' advice on text, layout, target audience, and so on? Can you find aspects of the ad that seem to violate Adbusters' rules?

■ Medium

Consider the descriptions of the creative processes that went into the print ad for Miss Clairol and the GEICO ad. How did a consideration of the medium that would deliver each ad affect the creative processes? Try reversing the advertising assignment: How could the Miss Clairol ad be transformed into a TV commercial and the GEICO commercial into a print ad? As an in-class writing assignment, brainstorm some ways these changes of medium could be achieved.

A NEW ETHICS OF CONSUMPTION

| 2 PERSUASIVE ESSAYS | SPOOF AD | POSTER | AD POSTER | GRAPH & CHART | ▶ |

555

When Marilyn Monroe sang "Diamonds Are a Girl's Best Friend" in the 1953 hit film *Gentlemen Prefer Blondes,* the song was applauded as one of the greatest show tunes ever. Today, the performance might provoke a heated political protest, as more and more people have begun to deplore the ethics of the diamond industry and—angered by the popular movie *Blood Diamond*—have boycotted certain sources of the expensive gem.

Diamonds are among the latest items of consumption that have fueled protests and rallied many to launch a serious global discussion about a new ethics of consumption. To what extent are we aiding horrendous labor practices or damaging the environment when we purchase cheap knockoffs of luxury handbags or buy an enormous gas-guzzling SUV? What are the ethical consequences, asks the prominent environmental writer Bill McKibben in "SkyMall: Pie in the Sky," of buying so many useless and expensive items? The "essential secret of American consumer life," he says, is that "we've officially run out not only of things that we need, but even of things that we might plausibly desire." As the counter-marketing organization Adbusters advertises, should we all support a "Buy Nothing Day"?

Consider, for example, one of the most common items that can be seen practically everywhere we look—on college campuses; in the streets; in cafeterias; in parks; in dorm rooms, fitness centers, airport lounges, stadiums, and arenas; in malls and museums—the plastic water bottle. Is it contradictory behavior for someone to worry about the environment and developing-world issues while carrying around with them everywhere they go plastic bottles of expensive water? An opinion in this cluster essay examines this growing concern of consumer ethics. As one scientist says: "More than 90 percent of the environmental impacts from a plastic bottle happen before the consumer opens it."

Bill McKibben, SkyMall: Pie in the Sky. Bill McKibben is an author, professor, and environmentalist. He grew up in Lexington, Massachusetts, and attended Harvard, where he was president of the college newspaper, *The Crimson*. He is currently a scholar-in-residence at Middlebury College and lives in Vermont and the Adirondacks with his wife, author Sue Halpern, and daughter. A former staff writer for *The New Yorker*, McKibben is a frequent contributor to *The New York Times*, *The Atlantic Monthly*, *Harper's*, *Mother Jones*, *Granta*, *Rolling Stone*, *Outside*, *Orion*, and *Grist Magazine*, where he also serves as a board member. McKibben writes about environmental and ethical issues, including global warming, alternative energy, human genetic engineering, overpopulation, and consumerism. He is the author of eight books, the first being *The End of Nature* (1989), one of the first books on climate change written for a popular audience; his most recent is *Deep Economy: The Wealth of Communities and the Durable Future* (2007), in which he critiques the "growth economy" and argues for "local-scale enterprise." The following essay was originally published in the March/April 2006 issue of *Orion* and was titled "Pie in the Sky: Solutions to Problems You Never Knew You Had." In it, McKibben argues that "we've officially run out not only of things that we need, but even of things that we might plausibly desire." (For more on Bill McKibben, see billmckibben.com.)

Bill McKibben
SKYMALL: PIE IN THE SKY

■ **Consider before you read.** *What makes the SkyMall catalog different from other catalogs or the offerings in other stores? Who does McKibben think buys from it? Would the SkyMall work as a physical store?*

Question: should anyone who requires a "revolutionary new laser technology system" in order to figure out if they're parking in the right spot inside their own garage really be allowed behind the wheel in the first place? Compared with the other tasks of a driver—making right-hand turns, making left-hand turns, deciphering the red-amber-green vernacular of a stoplight—safely positioning your auto within the confines of your own garage seems like a fairly straightforward task, the kind of thing that might not require a laser. But you'd be surprised how useful lasers can be. The Hairmax Laser Comb, for instance, used only fifteen minutes a day, three times a week, results in noticeably thicker locks and tresses. And not just lasers. Ions are also surprisingly useful—confusingly, negative ions. A lamp made of salt crystal mined from the Himalayas emits them, aiding you in the fight against "dust mites" and also "depression."

If there's any piece of writing that defines our culture, I submit it's the SkyMall catalogue, available in the seat-back pocket of every airplane in North America.

To browse its pages is to understand the essential secret of American consumer life: we've officially run out not only of things that we need, but even of things that we might plausibly desire. But we in the airline traveling class still have a few problems to solve in our lives. Judging from the joys on offer, our particular worries at the moment might be categorized as follows:

I'm overworked and overtired. In which case, I need a $4,000 massaging recliner with voice control, synthetic leather ("softer, more plush than leather"), and thirty-three airbags—a machine that "pampers your body and soothes your soul." And if perchance I drift off to sleep, "the peaceful progression wake-up clock" will rouse me with infinite care. "Thirty minutes before wake-up time, the light glows softly, brightening over the next half hour, while faint aromatherapy scents release into the air. Fifteen minutes before wake up, the clock generates one of six soft nature sounds." In case that isn't quite enough, I might want to back it up with the "sensory assault alarm clock," whose large, wired vibrating pad placed under the mattress shakes you awake in time to turn off the clock before it emits a ninety-five-decibel alarm and starts flashing a strobe light.

I have an immense supply of trousers, and hence require the closet organizer trouser rack to keep twenty pairs of slacks neatly hung and readily accessible. The five-eighths-inch-diameter birch dowels "reduce creasing of even fine fabrics," and "nylon washers between the dowels ensure smooth swing motion."

I distrust my neighbors and my government, and so would benefit from a giant-capacity mailbox that holds up to two weeks of mail (catalogues, presumably). "Don't bother a neighbor to get your mail, and don't tell the post office you'll be away."

I am extremely, extremely clean. I'm therefore thankful that my toothbrush has been ultravioletly cleansed overnight to remove the "millions of germs" that would otherwise accumulate, and my room is protected against "airborne bacteria, viruses, and germs" by a Germ Guardian machine, "proven by a Harvard researcher," which "takes ultraviolet C energy and multiplies its germ-killing power in our exclusive Intensifier Chamber." Also, I have another very similar-looking machine "now with exclusive Ozoneguard" in case any ozone is nearby. And a soap dispenser with infrared sensor technology for my shower, a "no-touch approach that dramatically reduces the chance of spreading germs."

I have way too many watches, and therefore might benefit from a $300 case that will shake them all with "intermittent timers and directional controls" to mimic the action of a human wrist and hence keep them fully wound at all times.

I have plugged in so many things that the planet has warmed considerably, reducing the chances that my children will experience a natural winter. So I have purchased a "weatherproof light projection box that rests on your front lawn and transforms the entire facade of your house into an illuminated snowscape. The box creates the illusion of gently falling snow flurries by directing a bright white beam onto a rotating mirrorball." Flake size and fall rate are, pleasingly, adjustable. I have opted also to purchase an "exclusive heavy duty vinyl snow castle" that will "set up almost anywhere in just minutes with the included electric pump." A real snow castle would, SkyMall notes, "take hours to build and require lots of snow," but this version "encourages children to use their imaginations while having fun."

I have an enormous number of remote controls, and hence need caddies to store them, small "buddy lights" to illuminate them, and locator devices to find them when I have mislaid them.

I may be devolving. Though for eons my ancestors have grilled meat over flames, I am no longer very clear on the concept and so would like a digital barbecue fork that I can stick into my burger or steak and receive a readout indicating whether it is currently rare, medium, or well done. Also, it would help a lot to have all the lights already strung on my artificial Christmas tree, and the difficult task of marinating would be much easier if I had a $199.95 marinating machine. Frankly, I've lately found grilled cheese sandwiches more trouble than I want, but with my dishwasher-safe Toastabag I can simply place a slice of cheese between two slices of bread and pop it in my toaster. (Depressing the toaster lever still requires my thoughtful attention, as does chewing the resulting treat.)

There are a few problems SkyMall can't solve (the lack of community that comes when you live in a giant stuff-filled house marooned on its half-acre lot, the lack of security that comes when your country is spending its money on remote-control golf balls instead of, say, healthcare and retirement savings). And there's always the vexing question of what the people who are making these items think about the people who will buy them. (I was in a shower curtain factory in rural China last year where the very nice people sewing the curtains told another visitor that they'd never actually encountered a shower curtain outside the factory. If that's true for a shower curtain, one wonders what their fellow workers make of the traveling wine trolley, the pop-up hot dog cooker, the hand-held paper shredder with wood-grain plastic handle.)

But this kind of talk sounds tired, clichéd, left over from the '60s. Everyone knows that the most important thing we can do is grow the economy. When you buy the Designated Driver, a faux golf club that you store in your bag to dispense forty-eight ounces of cold beverages, then you grow the economy. No doubt about it. Also, the Vintage Express Aging Accelerator that ages your bottle of wine ten years in ten seconds by surrounding it with "extremely powerful Neodymium magnets to replicate the Earth's magnetic field." Only a real jerk or a Christian or something would point out that there might possibly be items in this world that it would make more sense to spend our money on. (Insecticide-impregnated bednets to stop the spread of malaria run about five dollars. If only they came in self-erecting pastel versions that would also rouse you out of bed with gentle nature sounds.)

559

■ **Consider.** *In the last paragraph, McKibben anticipates some possible responses to his article. How does he think his detractors would label him? What do these labels suggest about his position in American culture?*

■ **Discuss.** *McKibben obviously thinks that the products offered in the SkyMall catalog are ridiculous, but he also has more serious problems with them. Discuss the implications McKibben draws from the unnecessary goods in the catalog. What is their cultural significance?*

■ **Write.** *McKibben's paragraph headings humorously identify the kinds of consumers to whom SkyMall is targeted. Using another catalog, write your own set of headings for the people who might buy its products. What are they looking for?*

Kasper Hauser
SKYMAUL

■ **Consider before you read/view.** *Does Kasper Hauser have the same opinion of SkyMall as Bill McKibben? How does their parody present a graphic critique of the catalog? On what points would they agree with McKibben's verbal critique?*

Kasper Hauser, *SkyMaul*. Kasper Hauser is a four-man comedy troupe that has been described by *Time Out New York* as "one of the few comedy teams which has rightfully earned the description 'Pythonesque'; bouncing from one bizarre idea to another (a restaurant in which every item involves a pony's head), the foursome's show combines a hyperactive imagination with an inspired sense of lunacy." They have co-written and starred in two films and have appeared in comedy clubs around the world and also on Comedy Central. SkyMaul is Kasper Hauser's spoof on SkyMall, the über-consumeristic in-flight catalog that Bill McKibben lampoons (on p. 577). For more Kasper Hauser spoofs and information, see kasperhauser.com. (Cover design on p. 561 by Vince Bohner. Cover photos: adultery, pepper spray, and Sky Monkeys by Mario Parnell; ring from stock.xchng; Llamacycle from iStockphoto .com, designed by Spero Nicholas)

■ **Discuss.** *What is the purpose of the quote from Dave Barry? Discuss who Dave Barry is and why Kasper Hauser takes him as their authority. How are viewers supposed to take the recommendation?*

■ **Write.** *Using the quotes from SkyMall in McKibben's essay as a model, write catalog text for one of the products on the cover of SkyMaul. Your description can be a parody in the spirit of Kasper Hauser's, but it should also consider the way catalogs attempt to sell products to readers.*

Adbusters
BUY NOTHING DAY

Amnesty International, France
WHAT PRICE FOR THOSE DIAMONDS?

■ *Consider before you read/view. What are the different purposes of—and different audiences for—these two posters? What elements of each stand out most on first viewing? In which is the text most striking? Which emphasizes image? How do these differences affect their impact on you?*

562

Adbusters, Buy Nothing Day. *Adbusters* is a not-for-profit activist magazine whose articles and visuals often parody marketing and other types of media. According to adbusters.org, *Adbusters* is "an ecological magazine dedicated to examining the relationship between human beings and their physical and mental environment. We want a world in which the economy and ecology resonate in balance. We try to coax people from spectator to participant in this quest. We want folks to get mad about corporate disinformation, injustices in the global economy, and any industry that pollutes our physical or mental commons." Buy Nothing Day is an annual event founded by the Canadian artist Ted Dave and promoted by *Adbusters* magazine. It is an international day of protest against consumerism during which participants do not purchase anything for twenty-four hours. In the United States, Buy Nothing Day is held on the day after Thanksgiving, one of the busiest shopping days of the year. (Photo-illustration by Josh Max Rubinstein 2006)

ONCE UPON A
TIME
HOMOSAPIENS WERE AT
PEACE
WITH THE PLANET
EARTH
THEN WE BECAME
CONSUMERS
AND NOW WE ARE AT
WAR
WITH EVERYTHING

563

Amnesty International, France, *What Price for Those Diamonds?* The release of the 2006 movie *Blood Diamond*, which portrays how diamond companies in the 1990s ignored atrocities committed by rebels in Sierra Leone who sold diamonds to buy arms—as well as the advertising counterattack by the diamond industry (see, for example, diamondfacts.org)—have led many to ask questions about the origins of the diamond, a gem that has long been the iconic symbol of love and commitment. According to international rights groups like Amnesty and Global Witness, "dirty" or "conflict" diamonds still reach the market. These groups say there is no real way to tell whether a diamond is "clean" or whether it has helped fund crimes against humanity. See Global Witness's site blooddiamondaction.org (Courtesy Amnesty International)

■ Discuss. *Discuss the imagery each poster uses. What sentiments are the leaf and tree appealing to in the Adbusters poster? How does the Amnesty poster use and subvert the traditional imagery used by the diamond industry? What is the group trying to reveal about the appeal of diamonds?*

■ Write. *The Buy Nothing Day and Amnesty International posters not only challenge consumerism but also suggest a larger critique of society. Write an essay about the implications of the "Once upon a Time" poster or the "What price for those diamonds" poster. How do they comment on contemporary political issues?*

Tom Standage, *Our Thirst for Bottled Water.* Born in London, Tom Standage is business and technology editor for *The Economist* and has covered science and technol-ogy for *The Guardian, The Daily Telegraph, Wired,* and *Prospect.* He is the author of *A History of the World in Six Glasses* (2005), about signature beverages throughout history; *The Mechanical Turk* (2002), about an eighteenth-century chess-playing machine; *The Neptune File* (2000), a narrative of "the pioneers of planet hunting"; and *The Victorian Internet* (1999), "the remark-able story of the telegraph." At his web site, Standage writes: "There's nothing I enjoy writing about more than the history of science and technology. I try to indulge my love of history as often as possible, but it's quite tricky if you work, as I do, for a weekly news magazine. One solution is to write books. Another is to find a way to link modern developments to historical ones. So I do both." Standage says of innovations: "Simply put, I think the right attitude to new tech-nologies is to regard them with historically-informed skepticism." The following essay, which Standage refers to as his "diatribe against bottled water," originally appeared in *The Guardian* on August 5, 2005.

Tom Standage

OUR THIRST FOR BOTTLED WATER

■ **Consider before you read.** *What common ideas about bottled water have contributed to its popularity? How does Standage challenge those ideas? Are you surprised by any of the facts he includes in his argument?*

Can you tell the difference between bottled water and tap water? Last summer, I held a blind tasting with some friends to find out. We put London tap water up against nine bottled waters and did our best to identify the interloper. The varia-tion in taste was wide. Some waters tasted silky smooth; others had a chemical tang. Yet the water from the tap did not stand out at all: only one of us correctly identified it.

And yet we buy bottled water anyway, in enormous quantities. Each person in Britain now drinks an average of 33 litres per year, and consumption has doubled in the past five years, according to the latest figures from market researcher Mintel.[1] This year, we will spend £1.7bn on around 2bn litres of the stuff. Globally, bottled water is now a £25bn industry, and its consumption is growing faster than that of any other drink.[2] Why has it become so popular?

It cannot be the taste, given that most people cannot tell the difference. Indeed, much bottled water is derived from municipal water supplies, though it is sometimes filtered, or has additional minerals added to it. Its greater "purity" is an illusion. In one study, published in the *Archives of Family Medicine*, researchers found that a quarter of the samples of bottled water tested had significantly higher levels of bacteria than tap water in Cleveland. The scientists concluded that "use of bottled water on the assumption of purity can be misguided." Nor is there any health or nutritional benefit. Another study by the University of Geneva found that bottled water was no better from a nutritional point of view than tap water.

Fashion and convenience have much to do with water's popularity: the practice of carrying a small water bottle around was pioneered by supermodels, and a bottle of water is more portable when you are out and about on a hot day. But why not refill the bottle in your bag from the tap?

Of course, that is not an option for many people in the developing world. And that is why I find the enthusiasm for bottled water not simply illogical or peculiar, but distasteful. For those of us in the developed world, safe water is abundant, yet we decadently choose to shun the tap water under our noses, and drink bottled water instead. Our choice of water has become a lifestyle option. For many people in developing countries, however, access to water remains a matter of life or death.

More than 2.6 billion people, more than 40% of the world's population, lack basic sanitation, and more than 1 billion people lack reliable access to safe drinking water. The World Health Organisation estimates that 80% of all illness in the world is due to waterborne diseases, which kill around 5 million people a year.

Meeting the UN's goal of reducing by half the number of people without access to clean water and sanitation by 2015 would cost £6.2bn a year beyond current spending on water projects, says the International Water Management Institute. This is less than a quarter of global annual spending on bottled water. I have no objections to people drinking bottled water in the developing world; it is often the only safe supply. But for those of us in the developed world, it is time for a rethink.

How about a tax on bottled water, with the proceeds being used to fund water projects? The problem is that it is very difficult to ring-fence tax revenues in this

565

---

[1]One litre equals a little more than one U.S. quart.—ED.
[2]As this book goes to press, one British Pound equals 1.73 U.S. dollars.—ED.

way, and it would then be up to governments to decide which water projects to support. What about "ethical" water, such as the new Ethos Water just launched by Starbucks, where a small donation from every bottle sold goes to water charities? I applaud the sentiment, but the donation is tiny, and it does not address the heavy environmental costs associated with bottled water, which is shipped at vast expense from one part of the world to another, is then kept refrigerated before sale, and causes huge numbers of plastic bottles to go into landfill.

I have concluded that the logical response is to stop spending money on bottled water altogether, and to give the money directly to water charities, such as Water Aid, instead. If you can, try filtering the water, either using a jug-based or tap-based filter. It will soon pay for itself, given that bottled water costs between 250 and 10,000 times as much as tap water. So give your tap water another try. You may conclude, as I have, that bottled water has an unacceptably bitter taste.

■ **Discuss.** *Standage makes a few exceptions to his argument against bottled water. In what cases does he think bottled water is acceptable or even necessary? Would you add anything to his list of exceptions?*

■ **Write.** *"Our Thirst for Bottled Water" lists several reasons why bottled water is "distasteful." Write an essay in which you analyze these reasons. Which reasons do you think Standage sees as most compelling? Which do you find most important?*

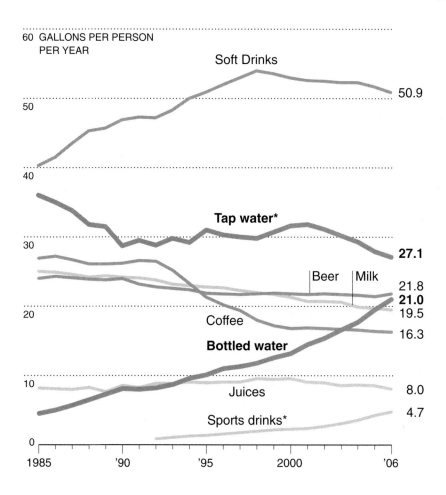

The *New York Times, Lots of Bottles.* (From Bill Marsh, "A Battle Between the
Bottle and the Faucet," *The New York Times,* July 15, 2007)

567

■■■■■■ CONSIDER THE CLUSTER
A New Ethics of Consumption

■ Message

After reading the selection by Bill McKibben, draft an in-class essay in which you discuss how McKibben might define a consumer's ethical responsibilities. What is he saying about the limits of consumerism? In your draft, try to state one brief principle of consumer ethics that you take away from his essay. Can you apply that principle to the arguments against bottled water?

■ Method

Look carefully at Adbusters' Buy Nothing Day poster. In a short critical essay, discuss the ways Adbusters uses the verbal and graphic methods of traditional consumer advertising to promote an opposition to consumption. In your essay, try to identify at least three ways that their poster resembles a typical ad for a product you would find in a magazine. Explain why you do or do not consider this method effective.

■ Medium

Suppose you decided to start an environmentalist movement at your college to discourage the use of bottled water. As an in-class writing assignment, briefly say how you would go about this and what you think the most effective medium—a print letter to the paper, a poster, a public demonstration—would be to promote your message. Be creative: consider a concrete campaign to get your message across.

THE MALL

There are many places where Americans can shop—supermarkets, convenience stores or neighborhood stores, car dealerships, downtown shopping centers, flea markets, online retail shops, and specialized discount chains such as Home Depot, Toys"R"Us, or Sports Authority (these are known as destination stores because consumers make special trips to shop there). But when the average consumer or the cultural critic thinks about shopping, only one place captures the imagination: the suburban shopping mall.

For many years, people shopped in the "downtown" shopping district of their city, where they could find several competing department stores. But with the enormous demographic shift from the city to the suburbs in the 1950s, and as families became increasingly dependent on automobiles, retailers quickly sensed that the decades-old downtown shopping district was doomed. In 1956, a Jewish immigrant from Austria who had barely escaped the Nazis, Victor Gruen (1903–1980), made the first step toward changing the landscape of America by designing the nation's first entirely enclosed, climate-controlled shopping mall in Edina, Minnesota. In doing so, Gruen not only permanently altered Americans' ideas of public space but also revolutionized traditional patterns of shopping. The following materials—an essay by Matt Snyders, mixed media by artist Barbara Kruger, and an assortment of comments and photographs—explore what the mall has come to mean in American life, both as a place and as a philosophy.

COMMENT

"Not only is shopping melting into everything, but everything is melting into shopping. Shopping is the medium
by which the market has solidified its grip on our spaces,
buildings, cities, activities, and lives. It is the material outcome of the degree to which the market economy has shaped
our surroundings, and ultimately ourselves."

— architect Sze Tsung Leong, from ". . . And Then There Was Shopping,"
in the *Harvard Design School Guide to Shopping*

570

Barbara Kruger, *I shop therefore I am.*   One of the main features of contemporary art is the way it has absorbed commercial media for its own
aesthetic and political purposes. A leader in this movement is Barbara
Kruger (b. 1945), who mixes text and image in a mesmerizing fashion that
resembles the slogans and graphics of mass persuasion, yet with surprising twists and juxtapositions. Kruger has playfully adopted the famous
statement made by the French philosopher René Descartes (1596–1650),
"I think, therefore I am," and placed her revised statement of being on a
card that has the exact dimensions of a credit card. (Barbara Kruger,
"Untitled" [I shop therefore I am]. 111" X 113", photographic
silkscreen/vinyl, 1987. Courtesy Mary Boone Gallery, New York)

COMMENT

"Direct address has motored my work from the very beginning. I like it because it cuts through the grease. It's a really economic and forthright approach to the viewer. It's everywhere and people are used to it. They look at each other when they talk (most of the time). They watch TV. Talking heads and pronouns rule, in the best and worst sense of the word. I'm interested in how identities are constructed, how stereotypes are formed, how narratives sort of congeal and become history."

— Barbara Kruger

Matt Snyders, *The Full MoA (Mall of America).* Matt Snyders is a journalist based in Minneapolis who writes for *City Pages.* For the following essay, Snyders spent an entire week at the Mall of America in the Twin Cities (Minneapolis and St. Paul, Minnesota) during operating hours, from 10:00 a.m. to 9:30 p.m. Early in his week at MoA, Snyders wrote, "I won't go insane. There's too much fun to be had in this place." Find out why the MoA needs no heating and how long it takes to trek its 4.2 million square feet. Hear about Snyder's encounters with sharks and shopaholics; his first manicure and oxygen therapy session; his attempt to get a night's rest; and his darkest moments, including his expulsion from a themed restaurant. Snyders's essay was published in *City Pages* on November 28, 2007, along with sixteen photos, some shown here, by photojournalist Nick Vlcek. (See citypages.com.)

Matt Snyders

THE FULL MoA (MALL OF AMERICA)

■ Consider before you read. *Snyders writes that "[i]n many ways, the MoA is a distilla-tion of America itself." Keep this in mind as you read the following essay. What does Snyders mean by this? Do you agree?*

For many Twin Cities residents, the Mall of America means one thing: Your out-of-town friends are visiting and want to see the cities' most obvious landmark.

Our much-maligned mega-mall represents a highly evolved, if slightly mutated, specimen of a genus that sprung into being more than 80 years ago. The first modern shopping centers began sprouting up in America in the 1920s when car-owning shoppers began fleeing crowded and dirty city centers. The rise of suburbia expe-dited malls' popularity. During the '80s, super-malls came into vogue, as exem-plified by the West Edmonton Mall in Canada, opened in 1981—to this day, it is the only mall in North America to best the MoA in total area. Eleven years later, our own colossus of consumerism opened its doors on the consecrated grounds of the old Met Stadium.

It's true that Southdale Center in Edina, opened in 1956, holds the distinc-tion of being the world's first climate-controlled enclosed shopping mall. And yes, Eden Prairie Center is where Kevin Smith filmed *Mallrats.* But the Mall of America, despite now being "only" the 14th-largest mall in the world in terms of total

The Mall of America, Bloomington. ▶
(Mark Erickson/Getty Images)

leaseable area, is the one Twin Cities shopping precinct that manages to pull double duty as a tourist destination.

In many ways, the MoA is a distillation of America itself. Many of our nation's idiosyncrasies—both good and bad—can be observed the moment you step inside its hallowed halls: our preoccupation with jaw-gaping enormity, our irrepressible capitalist spirit, our cultural diversity, our insistence on wearing shorts even in mid-November.

But how to go about wrapping your head around a monolith that employs more than 11,000 workers, including clerks, security guards, tour guides, and ride operators? That spans 4.2 million square feet? That rakes in almost $2 billion a year from visitors? That, according to an awesomely arbitrary stat rundown on its web site, can fit seven Yankee Stadiums into it?

One way is to eat, breathe, drink, and sleep in the place for seven days, inhabiting it during all open hours, 10:00 a.m. to 9:30 p.m. Which is exactly what I did. I realized going in that boredom would be my greatest adversary. These misgivings were compounded by the guidelines I was determined to follow:

- I was not to leave the building for any amount of time during open hours.
- I was to at least step foot in every one of the mall's 520-plus stores.
- I was required to sleep a minimum of one night in the mall. Somehow.
- No outside food, water, or alcohol. Everything consumed must be purchased onsite.
- No iPod or other distractions allowed.
- No poking fun at the mall's Santa Clauses.
- Not even the one that kind of looks like a pedophile.

DAY ONE

As I stepped inside, finding respite from the bitter morning cold, I took solace in the fact that at least my new home would be climate-controlled. I was excited to discover from mall officials that there's no need to heat the building. The skylights above the sprawling amusement park in the mall's core provide warmth via the greenhouse effect. In addition, the body heat emitted from the teeming hordes of shoppers—typically 100,000 or so per day—keep the temp at a balmy 70 degrees even on cloudy days.

The latter is not a pleasurable tidbit for the queasy to ponder. It's one thing knowing that warmth is due to UV rays trapped inside the building. It's quite another to realize the coziness you're enjoying comes courtesy of carbon dioxide emitted from the toxic pores of the garlic-reeking yeti standing in front of you in line at Sbarro.

I pushed these thoughts aside and found my way to the Rainforest Café, an artifice of a restaurant chockfull of faux foliage, plaster rocks, and sadness. The plastic barstools are shaped and painted to resemble the torso or legs of assorted tigers, zebras, and giraffes. I sat atop what appeared to be a decapitated mountain gorilla and tried to gather my strength for the week ahead.

The bartender struck up a conversation. I asked about the types of people that most often come through. According to mall officials, about 40 percent of visitors are tourists, mostly from Canada, England, Japan, Germany, and Scandinavia. The bartender confirmed a relative paucity of locals.

"They do their shopping at Southdale and whatnot," he said. "Just too hectic here, I guess. Spend too much time in here and you'll go insane."

I thought about the bartender's words as I walked out of the dank restaurant and into the bright mall corridor.

No, I thought. *Not me. I won't go insane. There's too much fun to be had in this place.*

Thus began my hurried meet-and-greets through a sizeable cross section of the mall's first-floor retailers. I started on the west side, a.k.a. The West Market, beginning at Nordstrom and making my way south toward Macy's.

"What can you tell me about this place?" I asked two clerks at Solstice, an uppity sunglasses retailer.

"Well," said Renae, a petite Laotian girl, exchanging a confused glance with her co-worker. "We've had a few celebrities come through here. Sydney Rice came in here and bought a $300 pair of Marc Jacobs. Brooke Hogan was here. But she didn't buy anything, 'cause she got mobbed by her fans."

" 'Fans?' "

"And Hinder came through once," she continued. "Their bassist, Joseph Garvey, bought a pair of Gucci."

At 5:00 p.m., I shambled up to the food court for supper. Every clerk had been exceedingly helpful and candid. One, an affable kiosk worker from Ethiopia, told me that the Mall of America is home to a gaggle of pteranodons. (I should note that she had a thick accent and there's a chance I misunderstood her.)

By 8:30, I was still going strong. My feet hurt a bit (I had probably walked three or so miles), but I had met some great people and figured that, if anything, the week would fly by too fast. When closing time arrived at 9:30 p.m., I was almost sorry to leave.

"Screw it, I'm jumping."
(© 2007 Nick Vlcek)

575

DAY TWO

The morning started with a trip to Bebe's Sport, a store specializing in high-end fitness clothes for women. The store's manager introduced me to Ashley, the Mall of America's most notorious shopaholic.

"You're not going to believe how much this woman shops," the manager told me. "All the clerks in a lot of stores know her. You should follow her around and watch her shop."

With big, frosted hair framing a heavily made-up and fake-baked face, Ashley resembled a slender, über-hip Stepford wife. And while she was unwilling to disclose her age, I had it pinned at 41, give or take three years.

She agreed to let me tag along with her and her 13-year-old daughter–slash–shopping protégé, Julia, on the condition that I (1) not use their real names, (2) not divulge what her boyfriend does for a living (suffice it to say he's a "very successful businessman"), and (3) stay on the lookout for "any big sales."

"Okay," I said as the elevator whisked the three of us to the third floor. "Deal. If you don't mind me asking, though, what do you do for a living?"

"I'm a stay-at-home mom," she said. "But I'm not home often. I'd say I come here about six days a week—hey, let's go to Nordstrom Rack!"

For those not in the know, Nordstrom Rack is the clearance offshoot of Nordstrom, arguably the MoA's highest-end retailer. In essence, it's the dilapidated crack house to Nordstrom's posh coke pad. And Ashley was itchin' for a fix.

"So how much would you say you spend a week shopping?" I asked as she sifted ferociously through a clearance rack of children's clothes.

"Huh?" she asked distractedly. "Oh God, I suppose three grand. No! More like two. Hey! What do you think of this shirt, Julia? Isn't it cute?!" Ashley whirled around and showed me a blue-pinstriped shirt. "This was regularly $24.50, but it's on sale for $12.90! Isn't that amazing?"

"Sure," I said. "But what's even more amazing is that you spend $104,000 a year shopping!"

She stopped abruptly and glared at me. "You shouldn't have told me that," she said. "That makes it sound soooo much worse! $104,000! God, my boyfriend would have a heart attack if he knew I spent that much!"

Well, I thought, *she's obviously exaggerating her spending habits to make an impression. No one could spend that much a year.* I threw out a test question: "How many pairs of shoes do you own?"

"Ha! A few hundred, at least. Which is insane because I have pairs I haven't even *worn.* Some are still *in the box!*"

"Is all of this . . ." I paused and searched for a delicate way of putting it. "Do you find all this satisfying?"

"To be honest," she said matter-of-factly, "no." She turned thoughtful. "It's kind of like an addiction. It really is! Sure, it satisfies, but only for a little while, so then I go shopping again. It keeps going and going. And I have *the worst* buyer's remorse. Look at these!" She held up a pair of glitter-sprinkled Pumas she had picked out for Julia. "Aren't they cute?"

DAY THREE

I started the day by wolfing down a near-lethal dose of crustaceans at Bubba Gump Shrimp Co., then went to Nail Trix, Inc. to get a manicure. And a pedicure. Yes: full treatment.

I've never had a manicure or pedicure before, nor do I plan on having either one again. But this assignment obligated me to partake

576

Wolfing down lo mein.
(© 2007 Nick Vlcek)

in as many mall services as physically and financially possible, and I'd just as soon get the more embarrassing ones out of the way pronto.

Gentlemen, let me tell you something about manicures and pedicures you might not know: They're awesome. Hear me out. Disregarding the mangled cuticles, the irritatingly weird sensation of having your toenails filed, and the embarrassment of being mocked by a trio of Goth kids through the store window, it's really not that bad. For $50, you sit in black pleather chair with your feet in a tub of warm water. Two Vietnamese women proceed to simultaneously clip your fingernails and wash your rotting feet. As they do

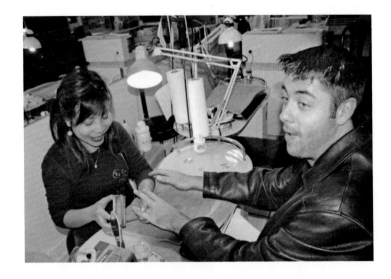

A manicure. Why not? Remember, you can't spell "manicure" without "man." (© 2007 Nick Vlcek)

this, they chatter in Vietnamese, stopping occasionally to giggle. That is because they are making fun of you. They will then file down and polish your nails with the kind of strange drills and equipment rarely seen outside a dentist's office. While they do this, they will continue to make fun of you. But not to worry: At the end of the experience, they put lotion on your feet, hands, and arms and massage it in, leaving you feeling refreshed. Emasculated and humiliated, but refreshed.

I emerged from the salon whistling—that's how good I felt—but it wasn't long before my playful little ditty was drowned out by a much more declarative beat. The music could only mean one thing: Abercrombie & Fitch was lurking just around the corner.

DMX Music, Inc.—an Austin, Texas–based company that packages music for retail stores—has a term for the clubby, piercing melodies I was hearing: "Foreground music." For years, the firm has provided Abercrombie & Fitch with tunes, or, as they put it, "proprietary technology and systems that deliver the desired experience." Think of it as a hipper, more obnoxious version of Muzak. I thought DMX's motto was, "Where my dogs at?" but according to the web site it's: "To some people engineering consumer behavior is weird science, to us it's an art."

The high-decibel music does a damn good job of killing one's ability to think. Never in the history of human folly have two people debated international trade policy within 25 feet of an Abercrombie & Fitch. To check out the effect for myself, I took a step inside and recorded my thought process in my notebook. Here's what I wrote: OOMCHA, OOMCHA, OOMCHA, BA-DA-DA, OOMCHA, OOMCHA, OOMCHA, BA-DA-DA, SHOP! (WHAT?) BUY! (WHO?) BA-DA-DA, YELLOWCARD RULEZ. (This goes on and on for many pages.)

577

DAY FOUR

I spent the better part of today occupying the Amusement Park Formerly Known as Camp Snoopy (the moniker was abandoned in 2006 due to a dispute between the mall and United Media, the owner of the Peanuts brand). There I partook of the disorienting madness of the Mighty Axe, the centrifugal vertigo of the Timberland Twister, and the sheepish "God-I-hope-no-one-I-know-sees-me-riding-this-fucking-thing" rapture of the Tree Swing. Unfortunately, Paul Bunyan's Log Chute was out of commission because of a logjam that left one poor sap with a massive headache.

During the afternoon, I worked my way along the mall's south side, a.k.a. South Avenue, toward the east side, a.k.a. East Broadway. I figured it was time to check out Underwater Adventures, which at 1.2 million gallons is the world's largest underground aquarium. Although I was disappointed to learn the place lacked an aviary (no pteranodons), I did get to hang out with Sharky, the aquarium's toothy mascot.

John Sullwold, a lanky, good-natured "PR specialist" for the aquarium, introduced me to the two guys who portray Sharky, the coupon-dispensing mascot. Sullwold asked me not to use the names of Sharky's alter egos, so as not to sully the mascot's mystique. "Just go with Sharky #1 and Sharky #2," he advised.

Sharkys #1 and #2 sat in the break room at opposite ends of the table. Sharky #2 thoughtfully ate his roast beef sandwich. Sharky #1 sat to my left and did most of the talking.

"I'm usually very laid-back and shy," Sharky #1 said. "And I have a bit of a stuttering problem. When I'm Sharky, I'm a totally different person. I can be wild and animated and run around just being a huge dork."

"So how is that different from your day-to-day life?" quipped Sharky #2, taking a sip from his Arby's cup.

"Ha, ha," replied Sharky #1 sarcastically.

"What's the worst thing about being Sharky?" I asked.

The Sharkys turned, and silently consulted one another. "It can be physically grinding, especially when you're working off-site in the summer heat," offered Sharky #2.

"One time, some punk kid tackled me from behind," added Sharky #1.

"We get that kind of shit a lot," confirmed Sharky #2.

578

Beholding a majestic beast. (© 2007 Nick Vlcek)

"I guess when people see mascots, they forget that an actual person is inside," mused Sharky #1. "Or something."

With that, I left the Sharkys and decided to sample the mall's various relaxation services. This was hump day, so I figured I'd get myself physically replenished. Unfortunately, MinneNapolis—the store that rented mall-weary customers private sleeping quarters for 70 cents a minute—closed last year, so a powernap was out of the question. Aqua Massage seemed like a reasonable substitute.

I crawled inside the coffin-like enclosure and lay on my stomach. Eight bucks got me ten minutes, during which powerful water jets blasted incessantly against the thin, waterproof tarp protecting my back. It's a bit like being in a car wash.

Next up: Oxynate, an oxygen bar–slash–massage parlor, complete with painted cumulonimbus clouds adorning sky-blue walls. The store's lone employee, Cynthia—a rotund black woman with a penchant for calling customers "Sugar"—led me to the back of the store, where an array of plush chairs lined the wall.

"All right, Sugar, you're going to sit in this chair with this in your nose," Cynthia said, handing me a tube with two tiny spines to be placed up my nostrils. "This will give you 95 percent oxygen. You can choose a different scent if you'd like."

The tube led to a bong-like water tank divided into three segments, each labeled a different scent: Ocean Mist, Tropical Watermelon, or Original. I went with Original. Cynthia left me alone to relax.

But I couldn't. Maybe it was because of the six coffees sloshing around in my belly, but I found the massage chair fiercely uncomfortable. Blunt machinery relentlessly prodded and kneaded my back, neck, legs, and hindquarters. I briefly considered crying out for help, but decided to try to fight through it, transcend the pain, find nirvana.

Nirvana felt like being pummeled to death with a sack of grapefruit.

After my 15 minutes were up, Cynthia led me to the bar near the front of the store. Time for Phase Two of Operation Chillax.

I sat at the bar, again huffing sweet-smelling oxygen. Cynthia offered me a water and a highly concentrated caffeine drink, both included with the $20 fee. She proceeded to whip out an ominous-looking device with dozens of flimsy metal tentacles extending from a battery-pack core. It was a scalp-massager, and it felt good.

"You know, I had an 84-year-old woman come in here one time," Cynthia said. "When I showed her this, she asked me, 'Can I use it *anywhere?*'" Cynthia laughed heartily. "Lord, I hope I'm still that frisky when I'm that age!"

I laughed nervously, paid the bill, and got the hell out of there.

DAY FIVE

Last night, I managed to get the "spend one night at the mall" requirement out of the way when the good people at Underwater Adventures let me "sleep with the sharks." I lay on a mat under the 100-or-so-foot glass tunnel and watched the sand tiger and nurse sharks swim lazily overhead. A massive birthday party—some 40 kids ages 6 to 10—slept down there as well. The little bastards jibber-jabbered like caffeinated gibbons all night long. Which is understandable, I suppose. But sound travels well through that glass corridor and, consequently, I got less than two hours

579

of shut-eye. At 4:34 a.m., I grew quite convinced it wouldn't be long before Bloomington police escorted me out of the mall on 40 counts of murder.

As for today's events. . . .

I'm well aware that there are few things creepier than an unkempt, unshaven dude brooding alone at Hooters. But that was me today for about an hour.

Desperate to mend my ailing self-respect, I eventually left my table and sauntered up to the bar and asked if there was anybody—waitresses, cooks, regulars, anybody—who'd make for an interesting interview. Which is how I met Christina Sanders, the deadliest waitress ever to don orange hot pants.

Hyperbole? Probably, but let's roll with it.

With two tours of duty in Iraq under her belt, Sanders, 23, spoke and acted in the detached, world-weary fashion you'd associate less with a Hooters girl and more with . . . . well, more with a person who's seen two tours of duty as a combat engineer in Iraq.

"If you're a woman in the Marines, you're considered either a dyke, a slut, or a bitch," she explained as she poured a beer behind the bar. "I decided I'd play the part of the bitch. It's the only way to get respect."

"Did you see much combat, or . . . ?" I trailed off, realizing the absurdity of trying to discuss war stories with Eddie Money's "Two Tickets to Paradise" blasting in the background. "It's cool if you'd rather not talk about it."

"No, I'm fine talking about it," she said.

"Was it scary?" *Stupid question!* "I mean, what was the most frightening thing that happened when you were there?"

"Hmmm . . . a roadside bomb hit our Humvee once. I shit my pants. I didn't realize it until we got back."

"Realize what?"

She flashed an embarrassed smile. "That I shit my pants."

"No!"

"Yes."

"I'm sorry," I said. "I don't mean to laugh; it's not funny. I'm just surprised that you'd be so upfront about . . . that." She shrugged nonchalantly and took off to attend to another customer.

I didn't know it then, but that hour spent at Hooters would be among my last sane moments in the Mall of America.

DAY SIX

The lack of slumber and the monotony of my days were beginning to erode my morale. Everything—the bright lights, the distant drone of the shoppers' jabbering, the smell of plastic rebellion wafting from Hot Topic—meshed together and enveloped me in a hollow, dreamlike stupor. Paralyzing boredom.

I lay on a bench, my coat shielding my eyes from the unforgiving fluorescents. The thought of crawling over to a bar and just getting rip-roaring, unapologetically shitty entered my mind, but I brushed it aside. Can't drink on the job. That would be foolhardy. Maybe I'd go to a movie and try to take a nap—

Wait. Why *not* get unapologetically shitty? It was wholly irresponsible, sure, but maybe—just maybe—it would give me my second wind. Yes. It was settled.

Having successfully rationalized the idea to myself, I ambled over to Kokomo's Island Café, a Caribbean-themed restaurant/bar featuring a garish tropical decor.

I hunkered down on a barstool and chatted up the bartenders: Kristen, a bubbly blonde; Brittany, her brunette duplicate; and Jason, a wiry little guy with a quick laugh. I was a bit lonely, so I chided the trio into drinking with me. They were hesitant at first, but eventually caved.

They served up an array of shots with peculiar names such as "Mr. Little John's" (Bailey's and Rumpleminz), "Bart Simpson Purple Squishy Pants" (Absolut

Benchwarmer.
(© 2007 Nick Vlcek)

Peach, Absolut Mandarin, grape Pucker, and margarita mix), and "Tequila" (tequila). The next two hours unfolded in a blur. I remember at one point asking Jason who the hell was paying for all the booze. "Don't worry," he winked. "We'll give you the writer hook-up. That's how we roll around here. You treat us right, we'll treat you right." Which, in my current headspace, I thought was just fantastic. Journalistically unethical and physically unhealthy, but utterly fantastic.

A few regulars came in and we all whooped it up. For reasons I can't recall, someone brought up the topic of the smoking ban.

Alcohol mixed with sleep deprivation mixed with the restlessness of being cooped up for six days does strange things to a person's inhibitions. It doesn't just lower them; it grinds them into the floor and leaves a three-foot deep crater of neurotic rage. It was time to take what I drunkenly assumed to be a principled stand. I demanded a cigarette from Brittany.

"I thought you don't smoke," she said.

"Just give me a cigarette."

Cigarette in hand, I stumbled over to each patron, one after the other, and asked if they minded if I smoked. "Yeah, go ahead," some said. Others were more into the spectacle and shouted variants of "Do it!" Once I got everyone's blessing, I stood in the middle of the floor and held the cigarette to my nose. "Do it, already!" the crowd roared.

I lit the cigarette to the inebriated cheers of a few onlookers. I was soon raving.

"People say this law is about smokers' rights versus nonsmokers' rights, but that's not what this is about!" I bellowed. "It's a matter of principle. It's a matter of property rights!"

An uncomfortable silence descended. You could almost hear the record scratch. "It should be *the owner's* call whether he wants smoking or not! Not ours. Not the city or state government's. Even if our intent is good, what kind of

581

arrogance makes us think we have the right to someone else's property?" I took an exaggerated drag from the cigarette.

A few people clapped, probably because they figured I'd shut up if they showed me approval. Unfortunately, I didn't.

"There's a lot of this shit going on right now. Saying we should give up liberty for security. Saying we should give up property rights for health reasons. It's all bullshit. Can't you see? You can't be truly free when you're constantly trying to control everyone else."

"Sir?" It was the manager, Nick, standing beside me.

"Just wait. I'm not finished—"

"Sir, I'm going to have to ask you to put that out."

"Sure. I—"

"Come with me."

"What?"

He pulled me aside. "I'm going to have to ask you to leave," he said. "I don't want to see you in here for the rest of the week."

I told him, okay, you're just doing your job, here, have the rest of my beer, don't worry, I'm not sick or anything.

Begging for forgiveness from the manager of Kokomo's Island Café. To no avail.
(© 2007 Nick Vlcek)

DAY SEVEN

Last day. Feeling haggard. Embarrassed. Vaguely nauseated. Hungover.

I spent this morning meandering through the amusement park and listening to the screams emanating from the roller coasters. They no longer sounded like gleeful yelps of fun—more like horrified shrieks of the damned.

Any one of these screams could be from a victim warding off a mugger, or fending off a gaggle of pteranodons, and no one would bat an eye, let alone call for help. Not here. Not in a place where blood-curdling screeches are more commonplace than laughter.

At noonish, I left that hellish echo chamber and wandered through the myriad kiosks dotting the corridors, trying not to make eye contact with the gregarious workers who accosted me.

"Sir, do you have a moment?"

"Sir, come try this! It's nice!"

"Sir, are you okay? You don't look so good."

Many had accents. As I would find out later, kiosk workers disproportionately hail from Israel and Russia.

"Their work ethic compared to Americans is not even close," says Ryan Carroll, the 24-year-old owner of two Green Tea kiosks. "They'll come here for three or four months, work their asses off, go back to their country, and they're set for life."

The booths generally cost $50,000 a year to rent, and proprietors hawk everything from Confederate flag belt buckles to perfumed lotions to T-shirts that say things like, "I'll give up beer right after I give up breathing." In a way, the setup's a throwback to old market squares, only with worse puns. (The two worst offenders both sell purses: Sacks in the Cities and Sacks Appeal.)

I tried to talk to three Israeli chaps working at a booth called Natural Beauty, but they seemed suspicious. They must have thought I was doing some kind of investigative hit piece on their booth, because one of them took me aside and said, "Do not write anything bad about us. The owner is very powerful in the Israeli mafia and he will kill you if you do."

By the time afternoon rolled in, I was too exhausted to walk any farther. At 2:13 p.m., I lay on a bench near the entrance of Macy's and counted the seconds going by:

2:21: A woman sitting on the other side of the bench says to her friend, "I'm not racist, but I hate Mexicans."

3:23: I see Sharky entertaining a cluster of children outside a Caribou Coffee.

4:30: I discover a $3,300 pen at Paradise Pen Company.

4:50: I take 18th place in a race simulation at the NASCAR Silicon Motor Speedway Racing Center.

5:57: I observe a large woman mercilessly beating her child in Legoland.

7:12: I sit on a bench in the amusement park, casually emitting high-pitched, tortured screams.

7:15: An Alan Thicke clone tells me, "Stop that nonsense."

583

8:00: I drag myself to Caribou Coffee and start scribbling paranoid jeremi-ads in my notebook.

9:30: I exit the north doors and mosey through the busily emptying parking lot to my car. I feel worn-out and ill. But free.

MATT SNYDERS'S EXPENSE REPORT

Day One

- McDonald's breakfast platter, orange juice: $7.09
- Thai Kitchen: $7.43
- Teavana, Mate Vana tea: $2.13
- Aquafina water: $1.48
- Tiger Sushi: $14.44

Day Two

- Arby's: $8.92
- Movie ticket, American Gangster (matinee): $6
- Caribou Coffee, coffee: $2.03
- Asian Chao: $9.04

Day Three

- Bubba Gump Shrimp Co., Shrimper's Heaven platter: $24.32
- Pedicure/manicure, Nail Trix, Inc.: $50
- Cold Stone, chocolate ice cream cone: $3.80

Day Four

- Park at MoA Unlimited Ride Wristband Voucher: $24.95

- KFC Express, sandwich meal: $7.21
- Underwater Adventures tour: $8.50
- Aqua Massage, 10 minutes: $8
- Caribou Coffee, 6 coffees: $12.18
- Oxynate, oxygen/massage: $21.33

Day Five

- Starbucks in Barnes & Noble, coffee: $1.89
- Hooters, fish sandwich, one beer: $20.09
- Stadium Sports Grill, hamburger: $10.80

Day Six

- Long John Silver's platter: $9.96
- Caribou Coffee, 3 coffees: $6.09
- Sbarro, pepperoni slice, drink: $6.21
- Kokomo's Island Café: $58.02

Day Seven

- Famous Dave's, ribs: $12.05
- NASCAR Silicon Motor Speedway Racing Center, one race: $9.87
- Cousins Sub: $8.08

TOTAL: $404.16

584

■ **Discuss.** *What does the Mall of America (the fourteenth-largest mall in the world) reflect and illustrate about American life, ideals, and obsessions? Who are the people who shop there? The people who work there? Discuss which of Snyders's discoveries and observations most surprised you, and why. Which of the people he encounters impress you most, and why. Also, discuss Snyders's tone. How effective is it in conveying what he has to say about the MoA?*

■ **Write.** *Write a response to the case Snyders makes about the Mall of America. What assumptions does he hold about the MoA? About people in general? By the end of his week at the MoA, to what extent have his assumptions changed? What arguments or main points does Snyders make about his observations of people and behavior at the MoA? Address one or two specifically, and why you agree or disagree with his perspective. Alternately, track Snyders's own behavior. How does he behave by the end of the week, and why?*

COMMENT

"I am called a retail anthropologist. . . . I've spent my adult life studying people while they shop. I watch how they move through stores and other commercial environments — restaurants, banks, fast-food joints, movie theaters, car dealerships, post offices, concert halls, malls. In fact, you can observe a lot of a community's life in its mall. . . . The retail arena is the best place I know to learn what people wear and eat and how they interact with their parents, friends, lovers, and kids. . . . By studying the shopping mall and what goes on there, we can learn quite a bit about ourselves from a variety of perspectives: economic, aesthetic, geographic, spiritual, emotional, psychological, sartorial. Just step inside."

— Paco Underhill, founder of a behavioral market research firm, from "Inside the Machine"

CONSIDER THE CLUSTER
The Mall

■ Message
As the architect Sze Tsung Leong notes, "Not only is shopping melting into everything, but everything is melting into shopping." In what ways does Matt Snyders's essay reinforce that observation? In a short essay, examine this text and describe the kinds of experiences the author finds that demonstrate this two-way melting process.

■ Method
Consider Paco Underhill's comment on "retail anthropology." What do you think a retail anthropologist studies? What methods does he or she employ to study shopping patterns and behavior? What academic disciplines would be most useful for someone who undertakes such studies? Would a retail anthropologist look at shopping malls differently than Matt Snyders does? As an in-class writing assignment, explain why or why not.

■ Medium
Sze Tsung Leong calls shopping a "medium". Do you agree? What do you think he means? Consider the various media you are familiar with. In an essay that draws on Snyders's essay—the contents of this cluster—discuss whether you think shopping could correctly be called a medium.

585

CELEBRITY

■ Cluster menu: Celebrity

586

What makes a celebrity? As the historian Daniel J. Boorstin wryly puts it, celebrities are people known for their "well-knownness." That is, to become a celebrity, your attainments or accomplishments matter less than the extent of media coverage you receive—being well known in itself will suffice to turn any-one into a celebrity. An obscure young White House intern with very few personal achievements can by virtue of a scandal become more universally known than, say, the president of Harvard University or 95 percent of the U.S. Senate. This is largely because mass media coverage generates more mass media coverage until it becomes nearly impossible to escape the blitz of stories, interviews, photo-graphs, video clips, talk-show gossip, and editorials. It was this instant celebrity that artist Andy Warhol meant when he said, "[I]n the future, everyone will be world famous for 15 minutes" (for more about this concept, see Josh Tyrangiel's

"Andy Was Right" on p. 595). Still, instant celebrities such as Monica Lewinsky are rare compared to the more common celebrities—movie stars, recording artists, and athletes—spawned by the various entertainment industries and supported by a wide network of publicity channels, from magazines such as *In Style* or *People* to TV shows such as *Larry King Live* or *The Tonight Show with Jay Leno*.

Writers, too, can become celebrities, a phenomenon Dorothy Allison examines in an autobiographical essay, "What Did You Expect?" Allison describes the surprise with which she is greeted as she goes on her book tours, the moment of recognition when a desk clerk realizes the woman before her is a Famous Author. The materials gathered here—a personal essay, an analytical essay, photographs, book and magazine covers, and film and video stills—all play a part in the celebrity package.

Celebrity also can reach a more transcendent level where the personality achieves a mythic significance. Often—but not always—such celebrity is reserved for those who die young or in mid-career (Elvis Presley; John Lennon; Marilyn Monroe; John F. Kennedy; Diana, princess of Wales); living mythic celebrities include Michael Jackson and Muhammad Ali. At this level, the celebrity becomes an **icon**. Originally a term that referred to the image of a holy person, "icon" derives from the ancient Greek *eikon,* meaning a likeness or image. The word, however, has grown into a key term of popular culture studies, referring to personalities such as those above who have achieved a superabundance of fame and are so universally known that their names never need appear with their photos for identification.

But is the rapid rise of web video creating a new kind of celebrity? In "On YouTube, Everyone's an Anti-Star," Evan Lushing explores the quality of "anti-charisma" that now characterizes the "movie stars" of new video entertainment.

587

Dorothy Allison, *What Did You Expect?* Dorothy Allison (b. 1949) describes herself as "a feminist, a working-class storyteller, a Southern expatriate, a sometime poet, and a happily born-again Californian" (dorothyallison.net). As a writer, Allison's subject matter includes her experience growing up poor, white, and lesbian in South Carolina. Born to a fifteen-year-old unwed mother and abused by her stepfather, Allison transcended her circumstances by being the first in her family to finish high school and going on to attend college and earn a master's degree. She is a member of the Fellowship of Southern Writers and the winner of the 2007 Robert Penn Warren Award for Fiction. Her first story collection, *Trash* (1988), won two Lambda Literary Awards and the American Library Association Prize for Lesbian and Gay Writing. In 1992, her (largely autobiographical) novel won her mainstream recognition; *Bastard Out of Carolina* was translated into more than a dozen languages and went on to be made into a movie for Showtime, directed by Angelica Huston. Allison has also published a collection of essays, *Skin: Talking about Sex, Class, and Literature* (1994); a memoir, *Two or Three Things I Know for Sure* (1995); and a best-selling novel, *Cavedweller* (1998). Allison, who tours frequently to lecture and read her work, was a writer-in-residence in the spring of 2008 at Emory University in Atlanta. She is currently at work on a novel titled *She Who* and lives in northern California with her partner and son.

In "What Did You Expect?" Allison writes on the topic of being photographed for a magazine; refusing to be pictured "sprinkled with powdered sugar," the author settles for a more realistic image. The essay was first published in *Allure* magazine in April 1998.

588

Dorothy Allison
WHAT DID YOU EXPECT?

■ *Consider before you read. How do expectations shape the way people relate to Allison? How much are these expectations shaped by the content of her work? Or by generic ideas about what writers are like?*

The photographer is a professional; her pictures appear in major magazines. She has two assistants, five cameras, and a no-nonsense attitude toward the people she sets out to capture. She calls half a dozen times, and during each conversation presents more ideas for how she wants to shoot me. Sprinkle with powdered sugar— that is her favorite. I don't think so, I keep telling her. But every time she calls, she brings ir up again. "I read some of your stuff, all that food and southern cooking," she tells me. "Really, it would be cool, just a knockout."

"It would be a cliché," I tell her. "Let's just do a regular picture, an everyday picture of a woman writer who doesn't like to have her picture taken at all."

"Do I look like the kind of woman who should be dipped in powdered sugar?" I ask Alix when I get off the phone.

"Absolutely," she says, laughing, and then flashes the smile that is one of the reasons we have lived together for almost ten years.

"You'd look funny, Mama." Our son, Wolf Michael, is right behind Alix. At five years old, he likes the idea of sugar, but he can tell from my expression I am not enthused.

"Well, it's not going to happen, angel-boy."

What was she thinking, this photographer who wanted to sprinkle me with sugar? Who did she think I was? Was she planning some rude joke I only barely comprehended?

Whenever I have to deal with interviewers or photographers, I find myself wondering the same thing. Do they know who I am? Do they know what my work is truly about? I imagine the editor who sends them out, the one who tells them, "A southerner, she writes about rednecks, about child abuse and incest, battered mothers and gospel music. Supposed to be a lesbian with a child. Has a novel coming out. See if you can get her to do something interesting."

It's that word "interesting" that makes me nervous. They all seem to have it in their eyes. Say something interesting. Do something different, something redneck or lesbian. What is it you imagine that to be? I want to ask. And always, *Who do you think I am?*

A few year ago I went to Charleston, South Carolina, on behalf of the Last Great Places project for the Nature Conservancy. I had promised to write about the marshes that my family had visited when I was a girl, but by the time I arrived I was, as usual, exhausted and worried about what I could possibly say about birds and rice plantations. I took a taxi from the airport to the inn where I was supposed to stay, getting there near ten o'clock—too late, I knew, for dinner or talking to the man who was to drive me out to the coast the next day. I'll eat some crackers and go right to bed, I promised myself as I staggered up to the checkout desk. The man behind the polished mahogany desk frowned at me. "I'm afraid we have no vacancies," he told me sternly.

"I have a reservation," I told him. I pulled out my confirmation number on a page that had been faxed from the inn two weeks before.

He read the letter closely but kept looking over at me, his eyes moving down from my wrinkled jacket to my black tennis shoes. I travel a lot and have learned the hard way to wear what's comfortable. For this trip I hadn't even brought my usual dress-up outfit. I was, after all, going to be tromping through muddy marshes, not reading at a bookstore or talking to college students.

"Hmm," he said, frowning. "Let me check on this." He stepped into an alcove off to one side and picked up a phone.

589

I looked around. It was a very nice inn. The mahogany desk matched the breakfront by the staircase. Cut flowers were on every table. The carpet was deep and pale russet, nothing like the industrial carpet I see in most hotels. I felt my shoulders hunch and my neck pull tight. You don't belong here, I thought, and looked again at the man whispering into the phone. When he walked back to where I stood, he looked even more uncomfortable than I felt.

"You're Ms. Allison, the writer?" He looked at my suitcase as if there would be some label on it that would prove I wasn't Ms. Allison at all.

I looked down at my comfortable shoes and loose rayon trousers, the carryon suitcase with its broken zippers, the satchel beside it with my notebook and emergency supplies of raw peanuts and vitamins. I wondered what kind of writer usually stayed at this inn, maybe the kind who dressed better and freshened their makeup before getting off the plane, maybe the kind who checked their luggage and traveled with their husbands, or even the kind who had matching luggage and a little computer in a snazzy leather bag. Was I really a writer, someone who had a reservation, who was here to do a piece of work and deserved a comfortable bed and a quiet room—or a fraud, a runaway from a trailer park who would steal the hotel towels and peel the shelf liner out of the drawers in the breakfront when no one was watching?

"I am," I told the man. "Is there a problem, or do you have my room?"

He gave me my key, but he did it reluctantly, and for the three days I was there he watched me closely every time I crossed the lobby. I imagined that when I left, he would count the towels and check the drawers to see if the shelf liner remained.

"I thought you were blond," the escorts say when they come to meet me at the airport. "I thought you'd be taller." "Older." "Younger." They hold out my book and look from the picture on the back cover to me. "You're much prettier than your picture," they say sometimes. Some say the picture doesn't look like me at all, though it does. There's my squint, my lips pressed together, my wide cheekbones and tired eyes. I look like my picture but not the picture they expect. Sometimes when I see them looking from me to the picture in their hands, I check myself out in the closest reflective surface. I am always the same, sometimes a little heavier or thinner, but always the same stooped, stubborn shoulders, ready grin, and ragged hair—my mama's replica, only in nicer clothes and better shoes.

Dorothy Allison, 1958. This photograph of a nine-year-old Allison is taken from her memoir, *Two or Three Things I Know for Sure* (1995). (Copyright © Dorothy Allison. Reprinted by permission of The Frances Goldin Literary Agency)

590

For years I've been telling friends that the only place you really see working-class women is in pictures taken at disasters. Car wrecks and mining disasters, that's where you find women who look like me. It's kind of a joke, though it is not funny, and it's not entirely accurate. We're the stars of the tabloid talk shows, and we're typically seen covering our faces or sitting slumped in despair while our husbands, boyfriends, brothers, or cousins are hauled away in handcuffs on *Cops.* The first time I saw that television show, I sat through the whole thing with my mouth hanging open, unable to look away and barely able to stand what I was seeing. Family, community, memory, and my people—vividly rendered on videotape and in simple human anguish. Whenever I meet an escort in an airport, I remember how I felt watching *Cops,* the shame and the outrage. Do they recognize how much I look like those pitiful white girls leaning against the patrol cars? Is that what they see when they come to meet me, the assistant professors who teach my books, the graduate students who want to write their own novels and hope to learn how by making notes on what I say? Is that why they sometimes hesitate and check my picture again? *Are you the writer?* they ask.

COMMENT

"I did not want to be who the world wanted to make me. . . . I wanted to go to college, not become another waitress or factory worker or laundry person or counter-help woman like all the other women I knew. Everywhere I looked I saw a world that held people like me in contempt—even without the added detail of me being a lesbian."

— Dorothy Allison

This is what I look like, I tell myself when people hesitate at meeting me. This is who I am. This is what a 48-year-old woman looks like when she comes from my family but hasn't worked in a factory all her life, has mostly worked at desk jobs, hasn't given birth to children or had cancer yet, and sees a dentist fairly regularly. I know exactly how much I resemble my mother, and where the difference lies.

I have my mama's hips, full and lush, and her mouth, too often clamped stubbornly tight. I have the same shadows under my eyes she had and her square strong chin, but it is when I smile or laugh that I look most like her. I have trained myself not to drop my eyes, but even when I manage not to do it, I often find myself smiling crooked—an uncertain apologetic smile that is all about feeling uncomfortable with being looked at too closely. My mother would cover her mouth when she smiled, an effort to shield her stained teeth. Years ago I discovered that my version of that was to drop my hair across my eyes as if by doing that I could look out but the world could not see me clearly. I could be safe and hidden, as safe and protected as a woman covering her smile with her hand, or a girl looking away so no one can see her eyes. Not safe at all, not protected, merely pretending to be so.

My mother worked as a waitress or a cook from the time she was a girl till just before she died. My earliest memories are of her sitting at the kitchen table with her little mirror and makeup bag, her short blond hair put up in pin curls, her fingers smoothing foundation over her cheeks. She would pluck her eyebrows into delicate arched lines and carefully fill in the shadows under her eyes with thick makeup. Only when her mask was in place would she release her hair and comb it into shape. Then she would smile at me and my sisters in her mirror.

591

Book cover, *Bastard Out of Carolina*.
The novel was published in 1992, hailed by critics and rave reviews, and nominated for a National Book Award. The narrator is a twelve-year-old girl, "Bone" Boatwright, who shares many of Allison's own experiences: illegitimacy, poverty, and rape. Book covers are marketing tools—the representation of the girl here tries to suggest the issues of class and sexuality and also to sell the book as a certain kind of literary fiction. (From *Bastard Out of Carolina* by Dorothy Allison, copyright © 1992 by Dorothy Allison. Used by permission of Dutton, a division of Penguin Group [USA] Inc. Photo © Elizabeth DeRamus)

"Ready for the world," my mother would announce, then flatten her lips together to even out her lipstick. "Ready for anything."

What my mama wore seemed to me like war paint—armor and shield and statement of intent. Don't mess with me, my mama's sculpted eyebrows seemed to warn. I'm ready for you, her dark eyeliner announced.

My sisters adopted the family armor easily, developing the ability to apply mascara while talking on the phone or blush while pulling curlers out of their hair. I never did. I brushed my hair straight back and scrubbed my face, wore my hair long and loose, and declared my independence by refusing to sleep with my hair in curlers. Now and then I would use some black eyeliner or dab my lips with a tangerine lip gloss but with no real enthusiasm. I was going to be different. I wasn't going to be anything like what was expected of me.

■ Consider. *What does it mean to refuse to be what people expect of you? By the end of the essay, do you think Allison refuses to conform to expectations?*

Like all the other girls I met in college, I adopted the uniform of blue jeans and T-shirts. I believed myself a new creature, a woman who would never wear a girdle or get up early to put on her makeup before going out into the world. The kind of girl who worried about makeup and split ends and the shape of her butt could never be serious. I wanted to be serious. I wanted to be a revolutionary. I wanted to remake the world. Women who were working at remaking the world were supposed to move through the world as men did, disdainful of foolish obsessions like weight or hairstyle or the size of one's breasts. My ideal of the revolutionary feminist was a fantasy creature—a mixture of Wonder Woman, Joan of Arc, and the drawing of a samurai woman I found in a sketchbook. My ideal might not be beautiful, but she wouldn't care. I wouldn't care either—no matter if I did. I would act like I didn't care what I looked like, what people thought of me. If I acted like that long enough, I believed, sooner or later it would be so. I would get past my embarrassment, my self-conscious smiles and hangdog expressions.

Film still, *Bastard Out of Carolina.* Starring Jennifer Jason Leigh as Anney, the mother, the movie version of the book was directed by Anjelica Huston and funded by Ted Turner. Turner decided it was too graphic to be shown on his TNT network, however, and it was subsequently picked up by Showtime. The book itself has been banned from classrooms and school libraries for its graphic nature. The character of Bone is played by actress Jenna Malone, shown here. (Photofest)

I would look like one of the women who carried banners in parades in big cities, with their eyes trained on the horizon and their faces shining with pride and determination. A woman who could do the necessary and do it without worrying about what people thought, that was what I aimed to make myself.

I have failed of course. I still worry about what people think. That is why I have so much trouble standing still for the camera's lens or choosing what to wear before walking across a stage or even biting my lips before answering the questions put to me by reporters. Who I think I should be and who I am are still not quite the same, though I try to behave as if that is not so. I show up wherever I can with my mother's smile but without the makeup she so carefully applied, with my straightforward fictions of working-class families and the brutal difficulty of achieving anything like redemption. My persona is as much a conscious rejection of my mother's armored features as it is an attempt not to cater to the prejudices and assumptions of a culture that seems not to want to look at women like me. It is not seamless, merely stubborn.

I was finally photographed in a Laundromat leaning on a washing machine with a basket propped on one hip. Why am I doing this? I kept wondering. But I had turned down so many of the photographer's requests, this one seemed almost reasonable. I kept laughing at myself and grinning weakly at the women who were actually doing their laundry.

The photographer sighed as she packed up her equipment. "I sure wish you'd let me sprinkle you with powdered sugar," she mumbled one more time.

I pushed my hair back off my face and shifted my aching hips. "Maybe next time," I told her. And then I gave her one of my mother's smiles, strong and stubborn, a smile that, to anyone who knows me, clearly said, No one is ever going to get a picture of me like that.

■ **Discuss.** *What does Allison think that her personal appearance says about her background? Discuss the features she shares with her mother and how she differs from her mother and other women in her family. What social or psychological similarities underlie the physical ones?*

■ **Write.** *For people in the spotlight, the ability to control one's image is an important from of power. Write an essay in which you consider the power dynamics of Allison's relationship with her photographer. Why is it so important to the photographer to get Allison to pose the way she wants? And why is Allison so adamant in her refusal?*

Josh Tyrangiel
ANDY WAS RIGHT

■ **Consider before you read.** *What does Tyrangiel see as the important technology changes since Andy Warhol made his famous pronouncement about everyone's fifteen minutes of fame? How have these new technologies changed the way we view celebrity? Do you agree that they fulfill Warhol's prediction?*

Nostradamus looked into the future and saw plagues, earthquakes, wars, floods, and droughts. In the prediction game, this is known as covering your ass. In 1968 Andy Warhol was more precise. He squinted ahead and declared that "in the future, everyone will be world famous for 15 minutes." Warhol nailed it. Not only has his prophecy eclipsed his fame, but as a cultural observation, 15 minutes has had its 15 minutes.

We forget that it took a man at the nexus of art and self-promotion to figure out that as cameras shrank and screens multiplied, the barriers to fame would someday be eradicated. Call it Warhol's Theorem. Anyone who has uploaded a video to YouTube or posted a MySpace profile might be considered a child of Warhol—except that Warhol's vision of fame was very different from how he actually lived. "Oh, he was impossible," says Dr. Robert B. Millman, a psychiatrist and Warhol acquaintance who, not coincidentally, invented the term acquired situational narcissism. "When you were with him, you'd feel as if he didn't have the slightest interest in knowing you. All he wanted to know was what you thought of him—or *that* you thought of him."

From the son of an immigrant Czech coal miner in Pittsburgh, Pa., to the bleached dandy at the center of Studio 54's human carnival, Warhol willed himself into a celebrated object of others' imaginings—a blank slate on which culture

Celebrity

Andy Warhol, *Self-Portrait.*

(© The Andy Warhol
Foundation for the Visual
Arts/CORBIS)

596

writers, semioticians, and hipsters projected themselves. It's not an accident that
the Velvet Underground recorded *I'll Be Your Mirror* while he was their manager,
or that his most famous self-portrait is of him putting his finger to his lips. As the
art critic Harold Rosenberg put it, He was "the figure of the artist as nobody,
though a nobody with a resounding signature."

There's something admirable and uniquely American in the act of self-
creation—but it helps if you actually create something. In a conceptual artist, cul-
tivating emptiness falls within the acceptable bounds of shtick. (Even Warhol's
originals were reproductions.) But Warhol also put his blankness behind a series
of conspicuous velvet ropes, turning a democratic notion—we're all stars, or at
least we all could be—into something slightly toxic.

YouTube and MySpace and all the other Web 2.0 tools out there haven't eliminated exclusivity or narcissism. You've still got to think you're pretty damned interesting to post a video of yourself talking to a computer screen in your bedroom.
But they have changed the way the fame game is played. A blank slate is not enough.
To get fame—in the form of page views, comments, and friend tags—you have to
put yourself out there in a way that allows others to relate. "[YouTube] is narcissistic to the extent that you're thinking about yourself," says Millman. "But to get

ahead, you need some empathy. It's weird, but it's a lot better to be famous this way than to covet the fame of others by reading *Us* magazine."

If Warhol were living in the Web 2.0 era, it would be interesting to see if he would use the medium as a chance to reveal something about himself or to obfuscate even more effectively. He'd probably do both—as lonelyboy15. But YouTube is Pop art in a form far closer to Warhol's original, uncorrupted vision than he could ever have imagined. And 15 minutes has been replaced by a new prophecy: "On the Web, everyone is famous to 15 people." Appropriately enough, many people share authorship of that one.

■ **Discuss.** What does Tyrangiel mean when he says that "15 minutes has had its 15 minutes"? Discuss what has replaced Warhol's concept of fame. Does Tyrangiel see this change as a positive one?

■ **Write.** Choose a portrait photo of Warhol (either the one on p. 596 or one you find on the Internet) and write an analysis of how it represents him. How does Warhol try to shape his celebrity? What kind of persona does he present for the camera?

Time
PERSON OF THE YEAR: YOU

Time cover, Person of the Year: You. Each year, *Time* magazine features an issue and cover devoted to a celebrity or notable public figure of the caliber of, for example, Princess Diana. However, the first 2007 issue of *Time* named you as person of the year. Instead of a glossy photo of a celebrity, the cover features a mirrored surface on a computer screen. Hold the magazine up to your face, and there you are—person of the year. (Note: Josh Tyrangiel's essay comparing Andy Warhol and Generation Web 2.0 also appears in this issue of *Time*. See p. 595.)

Evan Lushing, *On YouTube, Everyone's an Anti-Star.* The following biography was provided by Evan Lushing: "Evan grew up in South Orange, New Jersey, that great suburban cauldron of creativity (see Zach Braff, Lauryn Hill, et al.), and spent his childhood in Jerseyan idyll—capture the flag with the neighborhood kids, pool parties, and Nintendo. Notably, he was an early adopter of the Internet; a regular user in the early '90s of among other portals Prodigy, AOL, and the short-lived Sierra Online Network. He left his childhood Valhalla at the age of 16 for the distant Northern Lands of the Phillips Exeter Academy, where he was schooled in Latin and the SATs. Thereupon, he matriculated a little further south to Harvard College, where he spent two years studying mathematics, and the next two years being castigated for writing 'math-y' jokes for the *Harvard Lampoon*. In the meantime, he's studied a few semesters at the Harvard Law School, lived among artists in China, and created funny web videos for cold hard cash. Most recently, he's the co-author (with Greg Atwan) of the upcoming *The Facebook Book*, a satire of a Web 2.0 phenomenon even more important than YouTube."

Evan Lushing
ON YOUTUBE, EVERYONE'S
AN ANTI-STAR

599

■ Consider before you read. *As a new medium, what new criteria does YouTube establish for gaining a wide audience? What aspects of traditional stardom are useless or even detrimental if you want to achieve YouTube fame?*

YouTube, like the Internet itself, offers the promise of instant and arguably unearned fame. In the early days of the site, which marked the beginning of web video as a widespread medium, many of the most-viewed videos featured adolescents lip-synching to popular songs. The single most watched video (with a viewing audience of Super Bowl magnitude) is of a middle-aged man dancing to a catalog of popular songs. Conan O'Brien joked during his hosting stint at the 2006 Emmy awards that instead of watching television, America was on YouTube watching cats sit on toilets. While this observation was not as far from the truth as you might think, it shouldn't be taken as a commentary on the anti-intellectualism of our culture. Indeed, when a medium is in its infancy, the familiar and the mundane will dominate it. Think back to the early period of film and the corner-store Kinetoscope,[1] when a sneeze, a kiss, or a galloping horse fascinated an audience.

Now that some of the novelty has worn off, it is by no means easy to become popular on YouTube. The challenge to do so is straightforward: What is the most entertaining thing that you can squeeze into a quarter of a minute on a 4 by 3 inch low-resolution box? Though many web videos last upwards of two minutes, they invariably hook the viewer in the first fifteen seconds. They have to; the price of having a world-wide audience is world-wide competition. Your audience's attention span is reduced to its quantum minimum. Such are the brutalities and banalities of the YouTube marketplace. If you want your fifteen nanoseconds of fame, you'd better deliver the digital equivalent of a sucker punch.

To understand web-video fame, it is helpful to understand what it is not.

On a movie screen, the stars are literally larger than life. Their impact is analogous to that of the huge statues of the Gods in a Roman temple. They are as inaccessible as portraits in a museum.

On television, the stars inhabit your living room and become your friends. Nonetheless, they're more popular, better looking, and wealthier than you. That's why they're on television.

On the web, the stars could be your friends in real life. They could in fact be you. It seems wrong to even use the word "star" to describe someone who becomes famous because of a web video. Without a barrier to entry, there can be no mystique. We need some other term. A star is always the brightest object in the room; an anti-star, on the other hand, is always the least bright. Indeed, an anti-star makes the other people shinier in comparison. This is what YouTube produces: anti-stars. Whether or not they are truly "recognized-on-the-street-corner" famous, anti-stars have no mystique. Even if they have managed to become well-known, however briefly, on the Internet, they are not celebrated, and are thus not celebrities.

This is why traditional media approaches have failed on the Internet. Except for music videos and clips from shows with heavy college-age demographics like *The Daily Show*, the popular stuff on YouTube is invariably amateurish. Casting someone good-looking or cool in your video doesn't work because charisma doesn't translate at low resolution. Anti-charisma, however, does. Anti-charisma is not quite the same as being uncharismatic; it is just being familiar and approachable and very much *not* larger than life. If charisma is the quality that makes you an effective leader, anti-charisma is what makes you an effective sidekick. If a star is famous for being famous, an anti-star is famous only to the extent that s/he entertains you.

Proof of this phenomenon can be found by examining four classics (such as they are) of the web-video medium. These are four early popular favorites that everyone who's watched the growth of YouTube over the past few years still remembers.

1. "Star Wars Kid"—a teenager simulates a light-saber battle in his garage, without a light-saber

■ **Consider.** *How does Lushing's revision of the Andy Warhol quote differ from Tyrangiel's? Which one is more descriptive of Internet stardom?*

600

---

[1] *Kinetoscope* (see caption on p. 603)

2. "The History of Dance"—a middle-aged man dances to a medley of popular tunes on an otherwise bare stage
3. "Numa Numa Guy"—a jowly man enthusiastically lip-synchs to a techno dance song
4. "Pachelbel Guitar Hero"—a young teenager flawlessly plays an arrangement of Pachelbel's famous canon on an electric guitar

These four videos have a lot in common. They all feature males, alone, in one setting, doing something that does not involve talking. Three of the four feature a musical soundtrack, and the fourth (arguably) involves dancing. None have high production values, but all are well made. All hold your attention without the use of narrative or special effects or obvious conflict. All work with some element from popular culture. But most critically, they all riff on the themes of anti-charisma and anti-stardom.

"Star Wars Kid's" popularity rests on a central irony, namely, that many people who watched the video shared the hapless kid's enthusiasm for the sci-fi epic. A tubby student at the heart of his awkward years acts out a fantasy, which to even harbor (let alone act out on camera) is gut-bustingly embarrassing. On the other hand, it's a very relatable fantasy. If you want to be a super-hero, act like one. The tension of the video lies in the unanswered question of why he wanted to commit his rhapsody to tape. Did he in fact plan on digitally rendering the pale-green glow of the light-saber in post-production, as the web community did for him in any case? Or was he just curious to see if his moves were any good? The video did not make its creator more popular, though it did make him Internet famous.

"The History of Dance," on the other hand, produces the equal but opposite effect. Its balding, middle-aged, goofy-dad star is post-embarrassment. This is the secret to the video's Super Bowl ratings charm. Imagine your embarrassment if your own dad were to gesticulate in public to music and rework the scene into his triumph. It's not that the dad star is suddenly good (although he's definitely not bad); it's that he's infinitely self-assured and the audience is loving it. After your first viewing, the effect wears off, but you still have to admit, "Wow, that man must have been *fearless* to pull off a stunt like that."

"The History of Dance" guy from YouTube.
(Courtesy Judson Laipply)

601

"Numa Numa Guy" might be proud to see what became of his contribution. More likely, he would be unable to understand the root of the excitement. "I merely sang my favorite song in front of a camera, just being myself," he would reply; "it is pretty boring." His humiliation being less severe than Star Wars Kid (who sued his classmates for releasing the video), Numa Numa Guy asserts that emotional reactions depend upon the individual. Of course we all adopt fashions and do things that we later look back on and cringe. Who are we to judge?

"Pachelbel Guitar Hero" plays his gig flawlessly, and then turns off the camera. He shows no emotion. At no point, does he "rock out" in any sense of the term. But you're in awe of him as a technical master, the way you might feel about a monk who sat in a tree for a decade. A week later you read about him in *The New York Times* and are pleased to learn he seems well-adjusted. Nevertheless, so little of his face is seen in the video (it's focused on the fret-board and shadowed by a baseball cap) that he remains an exceptional busker[2] rather than an actual rock star. If you're anonymous, you can't have groupies.

The question remains whether web video can produce an old-fashioned star of the "name-in-bright-lights" variety. Considering that the average youngster spends more time on the net than watching television, the implications of this question are enormous. Will we return to a pre-celebrity era, where entertainers occupy the same niche as skilled craftsmen? Or will streaming HD[3] replace grainy web-video before we find out?

The Kinetoscope. The Kinetoscope was an early motion-picture device developed by Thomas Edison and William Dickson between 1888 and 1892. The forerunner to the motion-picture film projector, the Kinetoscope was encased in a cabinet in which strips of film bearing image sequences were conveyed rapidly between a lens and a lightbulb. At the top of the cabinet, a peephole allowed the viewer to catch momentary glimpses of the images. The Kinetoscope was first unveiled in 1893 at the World's Columbian Exposition in Chicago; by 1894, a "Kinetoscope parlor" with ten machines featuring ten short films (such as a man sneezing, a horse running, and a couple kissing) opened in New York City.

Shown here are (1) exterior and interior views of the Kinetoscope and (2) a still from one of Edison's earliest films, *Kinetoscopic Record of a Sneeze* (1893), starring a man named Fred Ott. (Library of Congress Motion Picture, Broadcasting and Recorded Sound Division, Washington, D.C.)

---

[2]***busker:*** British slang meaning "street performer."—ED.
[3]***HD:*** refers to high definition; HD video is available for television and, as the author suggests, will soon be available on computers.—ED.

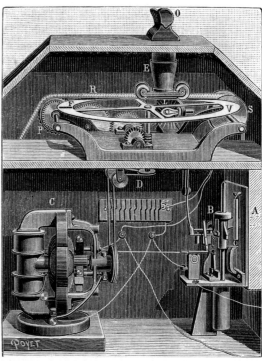

The Kinetoscope. (Mary Evans Picture Library/The Image Works)

Fred Ott, the star of Edison's short movie *Kinetoscopic Record of a Sneeze.* (Photofest)

◀ ■ **Discuss.** *Discuss Lushing's notion of "anti-charisma." Why does it translate well to the web? Can you think of any celebrities from movies or television who exhibit this quality?*

■ **Write.** *Go to YouTube and browse through some of the most watched videos. Do they support Lushing's analysis of the early days of YouTube and the kind of content that is suited to it? If not, how have the videos changed? Write a response to his essay, discussing whether the common features he identifies still apply. You might also look at one of the "classics" he mentions for comparison.*

 CONSIDER THE CLUSTER
Celebrity

■ **Message**

What do you think Andy Warhol meant by his 1968 comment that "in the future, everyone will be world famous for 15 minutes"? In an in-class writing assignment, express in a paragraph your sense of Warhol's famous statement. Why do you think it became famous? Do you take it literally? What is he saying about celebrity?

■ **Method**

Dorothy Allison resists the way a photographer wants to portray her. What is it about the photographer's methods that disturbs Allison? Why is she even uncomfortable posing for the photo she finally consents to do? In an essay, discuss why the issue of class is so important to Allison's dilemma of being photographed and what method of representing class would be most appropriate, in your opinion. If you were the photographer assigned for the task, how would you proceed?

■ **Medium**

How is YouTube or other examples of new media shaping our culture of celebrity? Do you agree with Evan Lushing's assessment that a new kind of celebrity is now being created by these new media? Consider this topic in an essay in which you examine how recent forms of self-expression such as YouTube, Facebook, and MySpace alter the public's conception of who and what a celebrity really is. Will they enable anyone to turn himself or herself into a celebrity? Will they diminish the power and allure of actual supercelebrities, such as athletes, singers, and film stars? Using Lushing's opinions as a starting point, address these questions— or others like them—in your response to the topic.

604

THE BODY

In his defense of slavery, the ancient Greek philosopher Aristotle argued that one reason some men are intended to be slaves is that "it is the intention of nature to make the bodies of slaves and free men different from each other." Slaves have "robust," muscular bodies that enable them to carry out heavy physical labor, unlike the bodies of Athenian citizens, who are useless for "such servile labors, but fit for civil life." Aristotle's stereotype prevailed in the Western world for centuries, long after the institution of slavery ended, as people assumed a muscular male body belonged mainly to farmers, blacksmiths, and common laborers. The muscular body became so identified with labor and the working classes that not having one could signify a superior social standing.

605

A similar phenomenon occurred with respect to suntans. A tanned individual was presumably someone who had to work outdoors in the hot sunshine. Thus, a deeply tanned body was generally considered unappealing and a sign of inferior social status. A thin body with a fair complexion (as can be seen in many eighteenth- and nineteenth-century portraits) indicated a higher social standing and suggested what was then valued as "gentility." Good looks, therefore, were not inseparable from socioeconomic factors. The American poet Walt Whitman—"the Poet of Democracy"—was one of the first individuals to praise manual labor, sunbathing, and robust bodies; throughout his work, he celebrated the physical attributes of his fellow working-class Americans.

The materials that follow include—along with several images—an essay by the well-known culture critic Camille Paglia that examines the motivation to resculpt our bodies and faces as well as a research paper by Eric Tyrone McLeod on the social evolution of the ideal male body.

Camille Paglia, *The Pitfalls of Plastic Surgery.* Camille Paglia (b. 1947), author, feminist, social critic, and agitator, is University Professor of Humanities and Media Studies at the University of the Arts in Philadelphia. Through her "militantly interdisciplinary" approach to writing, in which she incorporates theories from media, literature, history, and biology, Paglia hopes to renew creativity in the arts. She believes that "for committed writers in any genre (including nonfiction), writing is an approach to the world, a way of life." She is a contributing editor at *Interview* magazine and a former columnist for *Salon.com*, where many of her essays on the arts, culture, and politics have been published. Her books include *Sexual Personae: Art and Decadence from Nefertiti to Emily Dickinson* (1990), *Sex, Art, and American Culture* (1992); and *Vamps and Tramps: New Essays* (1994). Her most recent book is *Break, Blow, Burn: Camille Paglia Reads Forty-three of the World's Best Poems* (2005), and she is currently at work on an essay collection to be published by Vintage Books.

   In the following essay, originally published in *Harper's Bazaar* (May 1, 2005), Paglia argues that plastic surgeons, with their limited idea of beauty, will "continue to homogenize women." Plastic surgery, she asserts, is a major force in American life: "nothing . . . will stop the drive . . . toward beauty and the shimmering illusion of perfection."

606

Camille Paglia

THE PITFALLS OF PLASTIC SURGERY

■ **Consider before you read.** *What are Paglia's objections or reservations about plastic surgery? How are they different from the most common critiques of the practice? What are these critiques, as Paglia summarizes them?*

Plastic surgery is living sculpture: a triumph of modern medicine. As a revision of nature, cosmetic surgery symbolizes the conquest of biology by human free will. With new faces and bodies, people have become their own works of art.

   Once largely confined to the entertainment and fashion industries, plastic surgery has become routine in the corporate workplace in the U.S., even for men.

A refreshed, youthful look is now considered essential for job retention and advancement in high-profile careers. As cosmetic surgery has become more widespread and affordable, it has virtually become a civil right, an equal-opportunity privilege once enjoyed primarily by a moneyed elite who could fly to Brazil for a discreet nip and tuck.

The questions raised about plastic surgery often have a moralistic hue. Is cosmetic surgery a wasteful frivolity, an exercise in narcissism? Does the pressure for alteration of face and body fall more heavily on women because of endemic sexism? And are coercive racist stereotypes at work in the trend among black women to thin their noses or among Asian women to "Westernize" their eyes?

All these ethical issues deserve serious attention. But nothing. I submit, will stop the drive of the human species toward beauty and the shimmering illusion of perfection. It is one of our deepest and finest instincts. From prehistory on, tribal peoples flattened their skulls, pierced their noses, elongated their necks, stretched their earlobes, and scarred or tattooed their entire bodies to achieve the most admired look. Mutilation is in the eye of the beholder.

Though cosmetic surgery is undoubtedly an unstoppable movement, we may still ask whether its current application can be improved. I have not had surgery and have no plans to do so, on the theory that women intellectuals, at least, should perhaps try to hold out. (On the other hand, one doesn't want to scare the horses!) Over the past 15 years, I have become increasingly uneasy about ruling styles of plastic surgery in the U.S. What norms are being imposed on adult or aging women?

I would suggest that the current models upon which many American surgeons are basing their reworking of the female face and body are far too parochial. The eye can be retrained over time, and so we have come to accept a diminished and even demeaning view of woman as ingenue, a perky figure of ingratiating girliness. Neither sex bomb nor dominatrix, she is a cutesy sex kitten without claws.

In the great era of the Hollywood studio system, from the 1920s to the early '60s, pioneering makeup techniques achieved what plastic surgery does now to remold the appearance of both male and female stars. For example, the mature Lana Turner of *Imitation of Life* or *Peyton Place* was made to look like a superglamorous and ravishingly sensual version of a woman of Turner's own age. The problem today is that Hollywood expects middle-aged female actors to look 20 or even 30 years younger than they are. The ideal has become the bouncy Barbie doll or simpering nymphet, not a sophisticared woman of the world. Women's faces are erased, blanked out as in a cartoon. In Europe, in constrast, older women are still considered sexy: Women are granted the dignity of accumulated experience. The European woman has a reserve or mystique because of her assumed mastery of the esoteric arts of love.

Why this cultural discrepancy? Many of the founders of Hollywood, from studio moguls to directors, screenwriters, makeup artists, and composers, were European émigrés whose social background ranged from peasant to professional. European models of beauty are based on classical precedents: on luminous Greek

607

sculpture, with its mathematical symmetry and proportion, or on Old Master oil paintings, with their magnificent portraiture of elegant aristocrats and hypnotic femmes fatales. As an upstart popular form with trashy roots in nickelodeons and penny arcades, Hollywood movies strove to elevate their prestige by invoking a noble past. The studios presented their stable of stars as a Greek pantheon of resurrected divinities, sex symbols with an unattainable grandeur.

But Hollywood's grounding in great art has vanished. In this blockbuster era of computerized special effects and slam-bang action-adventure films, few producers and directors root their genre in the ancestry of the fine arts. On the contrary, they are more likely to be inspired by snarky television sitcoms or holographic video games, with their fantasy cast of overmuscled heroes and pneumatic vixens. The profound influence of video games can be seen in the redefining of today's ultimate female body type, inspired by Amazonian superheroines like Lara Croft: large breasts with a flat midriff and lean hips, a hormonally anomalous profile that few women can attain without surgical intervention and liposuction.

Maximizing one's attractiveness and desirability is a justifiable aim in any society, except for the most puritanical. But it is worrisome that the American standard of female sexual allure may be regressing. In the post-1960s culture of easy divorce on demand, middle-aged women have found themselves competing with nubile women in their 20s, who are being scooped up as trophy second wives by ambitious men having a midlife crisis. Cosmetic surgery seems to level the playing field. But at what cost?

Good surgery discovers and reveals personality; bad surgery obscures or distorts it. The facial mask should not be frozen or robotic. We still don't know what neurological risks there may be in long-term use of nonsurgical Botox, a toxin injected subcutaneously to paralyze facial muscles and smooth out furrows and wrinkles. What is clear, however, is that unskilled practitioners are sometimes administering Botox in excessive amounts, so that even major celebrities in their late 30s and 40s can be seen at public events with frighteningly waxen, mummified foreheads. Actors who overuse Botox are forfeiting the mobile expressiveness necessary to portray character. We will probably never again see "great faces" among accomplished older women—the kind of severe, imperious, craggy look of formidable visionaries like Diana Vreeland or Lillian Hellman.

The urgent problem is that today's cosmetic surgeons are drawing from too limited a repertoire of images. Plastic surgery is an art form: Therefore, surgeons need training in art as well as medicine. Without a broader visual vocabulary, too many surgeons will continue to homogenize women, divesting them of authority and reducing them to a generic cookie-cutter sameness. And without a gift for psychology, surgeons cannot intuit and reinforce a woman's unique personality.

For cosmetic surgery to maintain or regain subtlety and nuance, surgeons should meditate on great painting and sculpture. And women themselves must draw the line against seeking and perpetuating an artificial juvenility that obliterates their own cultural value.

◀ ■ Discuss. *Discuss Paglia's assertion that there is good surgery and bad surgery. What separates them? Do you agree with the distinction she makes?*

■ Write. *What is Paglia's purpose in this essay? Write an essay focusing on what other ideas she is responding to and what new solutions she proposes. Does her answer to the problems of plastic surgery seem like an effective one?*

Charles Atlas
FAME INSTEAD OF SHAME

■ Consider before you read/view. *What is the Charles Atlas ad selling besides Atlas's "Dynamic Tension" method? What does it promise to men?* ▶

■ Discuss. *Before-and-after pictures are a staple of advertisements for dieting or exercise programs. The Charles Atlas ad, however, uses not two contrasting images, but seven panels of a comic to convey a narrative progression. Discuss the ad's storytelling method. Do you think it is more effective than a simple before-and-after picture? Or does the latter have more of an impact?*

■ Write. *Consider the ad as personal testimony. Why does the text refer to Atlas's personal experience? What is the importance of including his photograph and his signature? Why does he insist that the reader "[a]ddress [him] personally" when requesting more information? Write an essay about the use of first-person perspective in this advertisement.*

Eric Tyrone McLeod, *Selling Out: Consumer Culture and Commodification of the Male Body.* In this carefully researched essay, McLeod explores the ways in which the ideals of masculinity changed considerably in the twentieth century, especially in its last decades, as male musculature took on significance it never had before. McLeod surveys the social evolution of the "ideal" body, the growth of bodybuilding, the present glorification of enormous muscles, and "what it means to be a 'man' in the consumerist mentality." This essay first appeared in *Post Road* (November 6, 2003). McLeod recently graduated from Arizona State University's Barrett Honors College with a degree in exercise science. He also holds a degree in Russian from Arizona State University.

Eric Tyrone McLeod

SELLING OUT: CONSUMER CULTURE AND COMMODIFICATION OF THE MALE BODY

611

■ **Consider before you read.** *Why did the female body become commodified before the male body did? What reasons does McLeod give for why men are catching up to women in terms of their preoccupation with physical perfection?*

The human body, particularly within the last half of the 20th century, has been transformed into something to buy, something to work on as a supreme testament to one's self-worth. The result of a cultural preoccupation with the body is the rise of a self-obsessed public—once seen as predominantly female, now certainly male as well—fearful of any indication of aging or physical flaw. The body, female and more recently male, is one of the primary means for marketers to move product; within consumer culture the body "is proclaimed as a vehicle of pleasure: it's desirable and desiring" (Featherstone). D. Kirk puts it this way: "Media representations of bodies are, in a sense, re-constructing bodies by repackaging the associations between bodies and values that people make in their everyday lives." The bodies that represent the values marketed as desirable are clearly difficult for the vast majority of the population to achieve—or, if achieved, to maintain. And even if the "ideal" body is attained, there is nothing stopping the industry from changing that ideal to maintain discontent. Scholar Susan Bordo maintains in her 1999 book *The Male Body:* "ideals of beauty can be endlessly tinkered with . . . remaining continually elusive, requiring constant new purchases, new kinds of work on the body." Because contentment is anathema to a consumer culture, it is against the best interests of the culture to have a satisfied and content consumer base.

Varda Burstyn, in his book *The Rites of Men,* articulates that the key to selling "lies in activating a series of sometimes irrational associations geared to stimulate the emotions that drive people to buy, notably desire and anxiety." If the market depends on the permanent dissatisfaction of its customers, how is that condition fostered in the public? Mike Featherstone sees certain themes, "infinitely revisable, infinitely combinable," that "recur within advertising and consumer culture imagery: youth, beauty, energy, fitness, movement, freedom, romance, exotica, luxury, enjoyment, fun." The buyer is led to believe that life is improved via commodity in ways unrelated to functional purpose. Promoting anxiety about appearance, then, generates desire for transfiguration: "Body image industries make money off your bodily insecurities, and they're not going to make a profit by telling you that you look fine already."

Americans largely believe a significant measure of their worth as individuals is determined by their ability if not to actually *perform* as athletic and/or sexual dynamos, then at least to *look* as if they could. The effect that the body-as-commodity mindset has had upon women has been studied for some time now, but only in the past ten to twenty years has attention been paid to the effect of these same messages on men. Marketers have come to realize that men can be made to feel just as insecure about their physical appearance as women have been for decades. Economically, the growing parity of women has meant the erosion of one of the primary means American men cling to in defining masculinity: a role as primary breadwinner. "The development of capitalism after World War II saw a continued erosion of traditional means of male expression and identity due to . . . women's continued movement into public life," writes critic Michael Messner. As a result, women have increased freedom to be discriminating in their romantic and sexual choices, and corporations have been quick to jump on the insecurities these changes have engendered in men, aiming to instill preconceived notions of idealized male beauty and sexual performance. The early 20th-century ideal of the genteel, morally upstanding male has given way to a more aggressive, competitive ideal: the notion of the "hypermasculine" male. Varda Burstyn defines this as a cultural "shift in emphasis from 'character' to 'sex appeal.'"

Before World War II, American men were largely unexposed to any uniform notion of personal worth through attainment of a physical ideal. What defined masculinity was *internal* character; external appearance had little to do with perceptions of worth in men. Health of the male population was associated with spirituality and high morals, often linked to a sense of nationalistic pride via the efforts of President Theodore Roosevelt in his attempt to link physical fitness with national security. Roosevelt imagined that the physical robustness of American men was a key factor in repelling national threats. The rising fear of increased immigration at that time led to the depiction of foreign peoples as scrawny, malnourished, and sickly. In contrast, a corpulent (white) man was seen as a success, someone that had the financial means to provide for himself and his family many times over.

By the 1920s, with the rise in popularity of the flapper's androgynous look, the perception of health had virtually reversed itself: now immigrants were depicted as being fat and slovenly, gluttonous invaders capable of taking over the country. The early years of the 20th century also witnessed the beginnings of a national obsession with sport at the collegiate level. The meaning and importance of organized sport transcended mere physical activity and began to take on an importance connected to national pride: "Empire and nation became identified with team sports," Toby Miller asserts of the era. By the end of the 1940s, Hollywood and public sports had helped to set the stage for the revision of the masculine ideal. All that was missing was an efficient means to transmit this new ideal to an ever-growing population; with the advent of television in the 1950s, this was swiftly rectified.

The rise of consumer culture in America began in earnest shortly after World War II: once the industrial might of the country was transformed from military to domestic concerns. The rise of factory farming and scientifically engineered agriculture meant that the United States was blessed with a surplus of food, and innovations in labor-saving technology ensured that Americans would be exerting less physical effort to ensure themselves a piece of the "good life." In the 1950s the very idea of *physical* labor (and, by extension, physical exertion of any sort) carried a negative class connotation; if you worked with your hands, you had not advanced in the pursuit of the American Dream. Yet as early as 1953, *Time* magazine announced that the U.S. was becoming a nation of "fatties"; physical health was still largely a non-issue for the American population at this time. According to the magazine's calculations, half the women and a quarter of the men in America were overweight. For the diet industry in America—still in its infancy—the focus was primarily on women. A woman's worth was determined by how close she came to achieving the socially constructed notion of the *female* American dream: Susan Bordo sees that "women, for their part, were expected not only to provide a comfortable, well-ordered home for men to return to but to offer beauty, fantasy, and charm for a man to 'escape' to and restore himself with after the grim grind of the working day." The health, too, of men was also considered the responsibility of their wives, since wives maintained the household. A middle-class man told by his doctor to lose a little weight by "cutting back" subsequently shifted the burden of responsibility onto his wife, who might encourage him to leave something behind on his dinner plate—or to skip his evening cocktail. Diets for men revolved around the vilification of carbohydrates (a trend currently in revival) with the sole exception of alcohol ("Drinking Man's Diet" plans, allowing generous alcohol intake, were introduced in the 1950s).

President Dwight Eisenhower initiated campaigns to "fight the flab" in the name of patriotic opposition to communism; physical fitness once again became tied to national security and pride when studies showed children of Eastern European and Asian nations were in better health than their American counterparts. Yet exercise prescriptions and programs in the 1950s were concerned with seeing results with as little exertion as possible. Devices were invented to shake, roll, jiggle, and shock one's body loose of unwanted fat. As early as 1951 machines

613

were invented to electrically stimulate muscles to tone and shape (we have seen the return of these devices on the market, promising a "hardbody" with little to no effort). In this period, too, American life began to shift in the mid-century to a culture increasingly based on the cultivation of self-esteem. The necessities of life had been secured by a majority of Americans; manufacturers began to look for ways to create desire and perceived need for luxury items. The end of the 1950s witnessed the beginnings of unchecked consumerism and the rise of its relationship to self-importance and the concept of self-development.

By the 1960s, not only had television become a primary influence in American social life, but the patriarchal status quo faced its greatest challenge to date with the social upheavals of the age. While the seismic shifts in the cultural paradigm are too great to discuss here, it is important to note the result of this atmosphere on perceptions of masculinity within the social structure. Taking stock of their political and social situation as never before, women judged it lacking. The American male's ironclad role as provider began to show cracks in its foundation, and certainly one important factor influencing the crisis of masculinity was "the increasing involvement of women in traditionally male-dominated social arenas" (White and Gillett). The birth control pill was introduced to the public in May 1960, and the patriarchal structure received a jolt. More than a few male scholars began to worry that women would become lascivious, seeking out mates and partners based not on ability to provide economic security, but to explore "carnal fulfillment." Pressure was on men to perform sexually. With the arrival of women's liberation came the suggestion, and more often the understandable demand, that men had a role to play in the sexual satisfaction of their partners. Men were required not only to be fertile providers for their mates but also to be skilled and attractive while doing it. As Burstyn points out, "The *Playboy* man became the ideal representative of 1960s capitalism and its world political order. For such men, the sexual practices of the 'new virility' and the consumer-pornographic culture could deliver on two important levels: they valorized 'uninvolved' sexual exchange, and . . . provided symbolic confirmation of men's difference from and superiority to women."

But for the physical fitness of the American population, the dominant theme remained the link between national security and pride with the health of the common man. As a way of fighting the ever-present threat of communism, President Kennedy, like Eisenhower before him, promoted nationwide fitness programs in the schools. These programs often consisted of little more than group calisthenics performed half-heartedly, but the impetus for the collective health of the population was there: a new context for fitness was emerging. The 1960s produced a profound sense of anxiety: the American military fiasco in Vietnam left men with little sense of what was reliable in society, and government officials lost public credibility and trust. As a result, individuals began to look more within themselves for a sense of stability and purpose. "Attention to the self offered refuge from a world that was becoming darkly unpredictable," as Lynne Luciano puts it. America had seen a decline in its prestige and influence on a global scale, and economic stagnation further eroded any sense of security and direction within the nation. With this shift came increasing importance placed on the image men

■ **Consider.** *What are some of the "seismic shifts" in American society that McLeod is referring to? In what ways were the 1960s a cultural turning point?*

614

presented to the world as a marker of their worth. In targeting men, the fitness and diet industries no longer played to the idea of "health" so much as to the ideal of *transforming* one's physical self as a medium of expressing oneself to others. Physical appearance and the image one presented to the world were now the focus of the newly instituted cult of youth and self-expression.

The 1970s, then, widely valorized the acquisition and preservation of a youthful, sexy body; for men, the emphasis was on a gradually increasing ideal of muscularity. This emphasis on physical appeal manifested in the nation's growing number of health clubs, which began to replace singles bars as opportunities to meet the opposite sex. As Sam Fussell puts it in "Bodybuilder Americanus": "Yesterday's muscle pits [are] today's fern bars". And in the continuing decline or outright absence of spirituality in their lives, many men began to look towards physical development and exertion as a means towards spiritual fulfillment. This was a particularly strong sentiment of the "jogging boom" of the 1970s. The concept of the long-distance runner as pseudo-ascetic, coupled with the activity's chemical euphoria (brought on by the infamous "endorphin-high"), presented running as much a spiritual quest as a means of keeping the cardiopulmonary system in good working order. Men lagged behind women in consumption of beauty products, diet aids, and exercise equipment, but the gap was closing.

As Lynne Luciano sees it, "washboard stomachs and bulging pectorals [are] the 1980s version of the 1950s house or a new station wagon." Toby Miller, author of *Sportsex,* claims that in the 1980s, "The traditional ways of understanding consumers—race and class—were supplanted by categories of self-display." Wages and salaries for the working class declined in the 1980s, heightening public anxiety and increasing the need for men to discover a means of self-identity and expression other than their earning power. This means lay in the presentation of the physical self. Health became of secondary importance in the 1980s; it was OK if you felt ill or depressed, according to the popular Billy Crystal character on *Saturday Night Live,* so long as you "looked mahvelooos." The embarrassment over national fiascoes like the Vietnam War and the Iran hostage crisis, coupled with the shrinking role of men as sole provider in the average household, meant society began to look increasingly in directions other than economics and politics for signifiers of masculinity. One signifier was muscle. The body became a predominant symbol of male power and strength after decades of seismic cultural changes in traditional views of masculinity. The book *Sport and Postmodern Times* glosses the shift the following way: "The Reagan administration capitalized on the logic of will by redeploying an amplified individualism and will that located America's decline and uncertain status of bodies and historical movements that it marked through the lack of will: the social and countercultural movements of the 1960s and the feminized Carter administration" (Rail).

Hollywood accelerated this shift with the promotion of action-adventure movies portraying actors such as Arnold Schwarzenegger, Sylvester Stallone, and Jean-Claude Van Damme. "United States national popular culture became saturated with images of hard, addicted, cyborg bodies," as Cheryl Cole puts it in *Sport and Postmodern Times.* As little as ten years prior, weight lifters were seen as

615

unusual: a subculture that exercised but with seemingly little athletic purpose for it. Weight lifting now took on new status in the eyes of the "common man"; by the mid-80s it was the physical activity in which most middle class men engaged. Associated with the growing obsession with muscularity was a hysteric fear of fat. A 1987 study showed that among MBA graduates, workers could expect to lose $1,000 a year in annual salary for every excess pound they carried. Being out of shape became firmly entrenched in the national psyche as a major character flaw. In the workforce it was no longer sufficient to be qualified for a job, one had to look qualified for it. A study by Kathleen Martin et al. observing the effects of exercise on image impression found that people tended to regard a subject who exercised as "A harder worker, more confident, [having] more self-control than both . . . nonexercising and control targets." Being overweight branded one lazy and out of control; being thin was a sign of ambition and vitality. "Major corporations frequently require executives to tailor their body shapes to the company ethos," Miller points out. Older men seeking new opportunities in an era of middle management downsizing began to turn to plastic surgeons in record numbers for facelifts and other elective procedures. Bordo quotes a cosmetic surgeon: "'A youthful look,' as one says, 'gives the appearance of a more dynamic, charging individual who will go out and get the business.'" Burstyn sees that the 1980s, a time of remasculinization and remilitarization after the defeat of Vietnam and the stagnant economy of the 1970s, represent "a vast proliferation of men's cultural genres as well as an expansion in the world of sport."

By the 1990s millions of Americans participated in some form of weight training, which by and large had nothing to do with health and fitness and everything to do with improving self-image. Muscularity took on an importance for American men on an unprecedented scale, pushed along by corporations anxious to capitalize on men's insecurities over failing to measure up to a media-driven ideal. The effects are clear even in toy making, where action figures such as G.I. Joe went through a remarkable transformation. In its original incarnation, had the G.I. Joe doll been 5'10" tall (the male average), his dimensions would have included a 32-inch waist, a 44-inch chest, and 12-inch biceps (an attainable physique for adult males). But as one study observes, "earlier Joes are shamed by the . . . figure introduced in 1991. His waist had shrunk to 29 inches, and his biceps are up to $16\frac{1}{2}$ inches—approaching the limits of what a lean man might be able to achieve without steroids" (Pope et al.). Where children had been receiving messages as to the impossible standards of desirable female body types through Barbie dolls in the past, they were now receiving equivalent messages about male bodies.

Although the 1990s saw a slight decline in the portrayal of heavily muscled actors in leading roles, the emphasis on muscles and leanness still clearly exists today, and we are currently subject to public admiration and criticisms of our physical selves like never before; fat continues its leading role as the "Great Satan" of the American psyche. In *Seven* (1995) actor Kevin Spacey portrayed a chilling serial killer whose victims embodied the seven deadly sins of the Catholic Church. For the sin of gluttony, he forced a morbidly obese man to eat until he burst. The killer describes the victim to police as "an obese man, a disgusting man, a man you would point out to your friends so you could join together in mocking him, a man who if you saw him while you were eating, *you wouldn't be able to finish your meal.*" Spacey went on to portray a character in the film *American Beauty* whose mid-life crisis compels him to seek exercise advice from his neighbors in order to "look better naked." Bordo, an academic feminist, comments that the male torso has become the most utilized body part, male or female, to sell commodities:

> Feminists might like to imagine that Madison Avenue heard our pleas for sexual equality and finally gave us "men as sex objects." But what's really happened is that women have been the beneficiaries of what might be described as a triumph of pure consumerism—and with it, a burgeoning male fitness and beauty culture—over homophobia and the taboos against male vanity, male "femininity," and erotic display of the male body that have gone along with it.

As more and more images of male bodies are made available by popular culture for public consumption, we need to interrogate what it means to be a "man" in the consumerist mentality. The male body is often depicted in film and advertising as heavily muscled, hairless, and oiled, more a machine than organic entity. The projected power of masculinity is the primary goal, often through actual or metaphoric display of the phallus as a "yardstick" of masculinity. Our culture "encourages men to think of themselves as their penises," Bordo says; it still "conflates sexuality with something we call 'potency.'" Taking their cue from a project that tracked the bodily dimensions of *Playboy* centerfolds over the years to show they were getting steadily thinner, Pope et al. applied the same scrutiny to the male centerfolds in *Playgirl*. What they observed is consistent with the depiction of ideal males in most other arenas of popular culture: "The average *Playgirl* centerfold man has shed about 12 pounds of fat, while putting on approximately 27 pounds of muscle over the last twenty five years."

The cultural obsession with muscularity is also a preoccupation with size, and this even includes the size of commodities males consume. Witness the rise of the macho cigar culture (as though one phallus on the male weren't enough); the entertainment industry's continued focus on lean, muscled actors paired with large-breasted women; and the design and production of ever-bigger sport utility vehicles (SUVs) that can barely keep up with consumer demand. Men's magazines, too, have exploded in their diversity and proliferation over the last ten years. *Men's Health* magazine alone jumped in circulation from 250,000 in 1990 to 1.5 million in 1997. These publications mirror their counterparts marketed to women in that they offer diet and exercise tips, along with articles offering sexual advice. Headlines of the June 2001 issue scream such promises as "Pack on Muscle!" "Drop those last 10 pounds!" "Instant Sex—Touch Her Right Here" "Your Perfect Sex Partner—Find Her on p. 125!" Interestingly enough, when one turns to the latter article it actually concerns trying to find one's perfect spouse—but it is the sexual aspect of marriage that is the article's focus.

To correct bodily flaws and stave off future degeneration, Americans throw a staggering amount of money at the fitness and beauty industries. The authors of

617

The Adonis Complex, Pope et al., state that in 1999 Americans spent $4 billion on gym memberships and home exercise equipment. In addition, "men received 690,361 cosmetic procedures, including 217,083 hair transplantations or restorations, 65,861 chemical peels, 54,106 liposuctions, and 28,289 treatments to remove varicose veins" (Pope et al.). This total does not include face lifts, rhinoplasty, pectoral and calf implants, and penis augmentations. The authors go on to cite a study conducted in 1997 by Euromonitor that estimated American men spent $3.5 billion annually on men's toiletries, and estimate that billions more are spent yearly on supplements, protein products, and herbal extracts. Pope et al. note that "male body-image industries—purveyors of food supplements, diet ads, fitness programs, hair-growth remedies, and countless other products—now prey increasingly on men's worries, just as analogous industries have preyed for decades on the appearance-related concerns of women."

In the current role that sports plays in America we can see the deleterious effects of hypermasculine ideals. Over the course of a century sport has become something more than a popular pastime; it is akin to a religious experience. Baron Pierre de Coubertin, founder of the modern Olympic games, wrote in 1929 that the Olympics were to be revived and modernized under the concept that "modern athletics is a religion, a cult, an impassioned soaring" (Burstyn). "In industrial society," Burstyn notes, "sport has overtaken many of the previous functions of an established patriarchal church and organized religion: the moral instruction of children, the ritual differentiation of men and women, the worship by both of a common divinity forged in the masculine model." Hence NBA all-star Charles Barkley's infamous statement in the early nineties that "I am not a role model" is nothing short of heresy.

"Sport and its associations have become the great cultural unifiers of the nineteenth and twentieth centuries," affirms Burstyn; yet still, "sport is a religion of domination and aggression constructed around a male godhead." Sports provide an anchor for traditional concepts of masculinity in a world where these concepts constantly undergo challenge and change by the prevailing zeitgeist. Within the realm of sport, men have a refuge free from the encroaching equality of women, a space where they can compete, display aggression, and engage in zero-sum competition that produces clear winners and losers. Burstyn writes, "In a gender arrangement of compulsory heterosexuality such as the one that has prevailed in capitalist societies, surplus masculinity is produced through a creation of a feminine-phobic, overcompensating masculinity that tends to domination and violence." Nowhere in society is this more evident than in professional sports.

African American professional athletes suffer the dual burden of providing a male ideal to the general public, as well as an example of the black male to a white public. Michael Jordan was transformed from a black athlete to the white public's notion of a model African American, characterized by his unthreatening demeanor and decided reluctance to comment on anything remotely political. "Michael Jordan . . . exemplified the healthy body, the athletic body . . . the body distanced from the threatening black masculinity inscribed on that other predominant inner-city figure—the addict" (Rail). As a result Jordan has achieved nearly messianic stature in the white media, crossing racial lines as the epitome of grace and

618

genteel mannerism off the basketball court (but still driven by hypermasculine notions *on* the court). In contrast, athlete O.J. Simpson represents the black pariah, having betrayed the trust and adoration of the white public, which collectively feels he got away with the murder of his wife Nicole Brown Simpson in 1995. Mike Tyson is the representation of masculinity (and in particular the African American male) gone horribly wrong; aggression lashing out uncontrollably through rape/violence against women, biting off the ear of Evander Holyfield during a match, and other psychotic outbursts both verbal and physical. "Commercial discourse has also tended to . . . heighten reactionary ideas about black men. It has done so primarily by exploiting the hypersexuality and violence embedded in the racist cultural legacy" (Burstyn). For many whites, Simpson and Tyson reaffirm their darkest fears about the black male. As Bordo points out, "When a white boy acts like a thug, he proves he's not a sissy to the other white boys in his group; when a black boy engages in the same behavior, the same white boys may regard it as proof that he's a jungle brute after all."

With professional sports as the vanguard of masculine ideals, the use of drugs and other potentially hazardous methods to attain the perfect body in the general populace is assured. "The public health problem of steroid use would be minor if the victims were only a few professional athletes and actors. But millions of boys and men have looked to these men as role models, and have longed to have bodies like theirs" (Pope et al.). Yet resistance training, or weight lifting, represents perhaps the most universal means men employ in attempting to realize the hypermasculine ideal. Former bodybuilder–turned–social critic Sam Fussell notes "steroids or not, a natural bodybuilder is an oxymoron. Bodybuilding is to flesh what origami is to paper." Bodybuilding has its own lifestyle and code, but unlike most subcultures, it also strives to align itself with traditional cultural values. The leaders of the bodybuilding industries have done their utmost—with varying degrees of success—to integrate bodybuilding into mainstream culture. "They strive to gain respect by projecting a persona of wholesomeness. . . . Three values are heavily projected to the public via the leading publications: health, heterosexuality, and rugged individualism" (Yiannakis et al.). Accompanying the enhanced body image bodybuilders acquire through larger muscles is pride in the implication that they have extraordinary discipline: while anyone can accumulate material goods, striving for and attaining an almost freakish level of muscularity requires not only physical *effort* but a strong work ethic.

The desire to modify the body in such a drastic way is indicative of the changing ideals of masculinity in society. The recent explosion of interest in bodybuilding is related to the growing threat to male privilege represented by female gain in social arenas like the workplace and/or family: "The resurgent cultural ideal of the muscular body in contemporary culture and the increased popularity of body-work practices are symptomatic of a trend in our culture seeking to reestablish an ideology of gender difference in the face of emancipatory forces" (White and Gillett). Once seen as deviant and somehow sexually suspect by the general populace, body-building has become a legitimate means of self-transformation in a 21st-century consumer culture. As one critic puts it: "Body-building, then, *stands to gain cultural*

619

acceptance by being what was previously most reprehensible, that is, self-indulgent, narcissistic, excessive, and sexually exotic" (Yiannakis et al., italics mine).

In and of itself bodybuilding provides little by way of genuine societal power to its devotees: bodybuilder Fussell argues that muscle symbolically replaces the financial or political power he lost, or never had: "the reconstructed, pumped-up male body promises control, control over your every muscle fiber, control over your immediate environment." Further, "it's materialism incarnate, *with muscles replacing money as numerical gradations, as incremental units of self-worth.* It's as American as conspicuous consumption, with status the goal, envy the motivation" (Fussell, italics mine). With strength and power over self and others the only legitimate social currency, the net effect of the bodybuilding culture is a reaffirmation of the dangerous hypermasculine ideal. Strength, aggression, and size are reinforced as societal markers of positive masculinity, and traditional gender roles are glorified. Fussell sees bodybuilding producing "the romantic idealization of . . . natural man, untrammeled by thought, by knowledge of good and evil, by, in fact, knowledge. Intellect is held to be effete, essentially feminine and suspect."

Obsessive bodybuilding—as with other factors like steroid use, and extreme dieting—can also contribute to body image disorders in males: "The emergence of 'megarexia,' a condition in which male bodybuilders obsessively perceive themselves as too fat or too thin regardless of how muscular they become, is highly conducive to the rationalization of steroid abuse" (White and Gillett). As men are convinced of the need to adhere to a media-driven ideal in order to feel successful, they become prey to the same false promises that the diet industries have made to women. Bordo mentions that, despite the reigning cultural perception that by and large only women are affected by eating disorders, by 1999 *one million men had been diagnosed with an eating disorder* (compared to eight million women). Male reluctance to admit to having a "female disease" means that men are reluctant to seek treatment.

Liposuction is now performed on almost as many men as women to get rid of stubborn fat. A particular form of liposuction is now practiced which sucks the fat from around the abdominal wall, thereby producing the coveted "six-pack" abdominal definition. Chin reshaping (which may involve reshaping the existing bone structure or inserting a plastic implant) can deliver "lantern jaw" looks. Pectoral and calf implants can increase the size of those body parts resistant to training. Penile augmentation (which involves severing ligaments holding the penis to the abdominal wall—so that it hangs lower and appears longer—and the injection of fat into the shaft of the penis) promises that no man need be ashamed of his "endowments." Cosmetic surgery has experienced a surge in male patients only in the last thirty years or so, and procedures aimed at men are now as diverse as procedures for women (for instance, hair transplantation/restoration usually involves scalp grafts, hair plugs, or even a bizarre set of titanium anchors screwed into the skull into which to snap hairpieces).

Psychology Today ran a poll in 1997 that found that 43% of men surveyed were unsatisfied with their overall appearance. Of these, 63% did not like their abdomens, 52% their weight, 45% their overall muscle tone. 17% of the men polled would subtract three years from their life if it meant they could achieve their ideal body. Bordo emphasizes the dilemma women have faced in attempting to emulate media notions of beauty: "We try to accomplish the impossible, and often get into trouble. Illusions set the standard for real women, and they spawn special disorders and addictions: in trying to become as fat-free and pore-less as the ads, the fleshy body is pushed to achieve the impossible." The recent emphasis on male beauty ideals has ensured that men are no longer relatively immune to the sting of this paradox. Bordo notes further that "I never dreamed 'equality' would move in the direction of men worrying more about their looks rather than women worrying less." Socially conditioned to possess a natural reluctance to discuss emotions and anxiety, the majority of mainstream American men are without significant support for their bodily insecurities. "And so this 'feeling and talking taboo' adds insult to injury: to a degree unprecedented in history, men are being made to feel more and more inadequate about how they look—while simultaneously being prohibited from talking about it or even admitting it to themselves" (Pope et al.). But as Varda Burstyn sees it, if we can reclaim "physical culture *from* corporate culture, we can balance 'masculine' with 'feminine' in our culture and within ourselves."

Bibliography

Bordo, Susan. *The Male Body: A New Look at Men in Public and in Private.* New York: Farrar, Straus, and Giroux, 1999.

Burstyn, Varda. *The Rites of Men: Manhood, Politics, and the Culture of Sport.* Toronto: University of Toronto Press, 1999.

Featherstone, Mike, ed. *The Body: Social Process and Cultural Theory.* London: Sage Publications, 1991.

Fussell, Sam. "Bodybuilder Americanus." *Michigan Quarterly Review,* 32(4), 1993.

Loland, N. W. "Some Contradictions and Tensions in Elite Sportsmen's Attitudes Towards Their Bodies." *International Review for the Sociology of Sport,* 34/3, 1999.

Luciano, Lynne. *Looking Good: Male Body Image in Modern America.* New York: Hill & Wang, 2001.

Messner, Michael A. "Sports and Male Domination: The Female Athlete as Contested Ideological Terrain." *Sociology of Sport Journal,* 5, 1988.

Messner, Michael A., and Don F. Sabo. *Sex, Violence, and Power in Sport: Rethinking Masculinity.* Freedom, CA: Crossing Press, 1994.

Miller, Toby. *Sportsex.* Philadelphia: Temple University Press, 2001.

Pope, Harrison G., K. A. Phillips, and R. Olivardia. *The Adonis Complex: The Secret Crisis of Male Body Obsession.* New York: The Free Press, 2000.

Rail, Genevieve, ed. *Sport and Postmodern Times.* New York: State University of New York Press, 1998.

Rowe, David. "Accommodating Bodies: Celebrity, Sexuality, and 'Tragic Magic.'" *Journal of Sport and Social Issues,* February, 1994.

Sharp, M., and D. Collins. "Exploring the 'Inevitability' of the Relationship Between Anabolic Steroid Use and Aggression in Human Males." *Journal of Sport & Exercise Psychology,* 20, 1998.

White, P. G., and J. Gillett. "Reading the Muscular Body: A Critical Decoding of Advertisements in *Flex* Magazine." *Sociology of Sport Journal,* 11, 1994.

Yiannakis, Andrew, and Merril J. Melnick, eds. *Contemporary Issues in Sociology of Sport.* Champaign, IL: Human Kinetics, 2001.

◄ ■ **Discuss.** *Discuss the different meanings McLeod attaches to different exercise trends. For example, why did running take on a "spiritual" significance in the 1970s? In what way does bodybuilding play into American ideas about individualism? Can you think of any current exercise trends that reveal something about our culture?*

■ **Write.** *Write an essay in which you look at the Charles Atlas "Fame Instead of Shame" ad in light of McLeod's paragraphs about masculinity in the 1940s and shortly after World War II. How does the ad fit into McLeod's narrative about changing male body image? Does the ad provide support to his argument?*

 CONSIDER THE CLUSTER
The Body

■ **Message**

What is Camille Paglia saying about plastic surgery? Is she opposed to it? In a three-paragraph essay, try to summarize Paglia's position in your opening paragraph and then use the next two to support or refute her position by introducing additional reasons of your own.

■ **Method**

McLeod's essay depends heavily on his research of the topic. Do you think he could have written his essay without reference to other published sources of information? Suppose he had simply visited gyms and weight rooms to make observations and take notes: Would he have arrived at similar conclusions? What if he had based his essay strictly on personal experiences? Look at McLeod's research method more closely. Which studies does he seem to refer to most often? Can you find information in the essay for which the author doesn't give a source? As a short in-class assignment, provide some examples of these and explain why you think they don't require sources.

■ **Medium**

Using McLeod's essay as your source of information, write an essay in which you consider how the human body—both male and female—once it becomes a commodity, can also become subject to all other forms of packaging and marketing. Can muscles be thought of as packaging? Can displaying the body be considered a form of marketing? What is the merchandise, and what is being marketed? Explain some of the media implications of bodily commodification.

SELLING COOL

623

Is it cool to smoke? If so, which is more cool—a Camel No. 9 or a Marlboro? Is it cool to own the latest gadget from Apple? Is it cool to sport a gold tooth? Which burger is cooler: a MacDonald's or a White Castle? Are tattoos still cool? Is it cool to receive a perfect score on the SATs or to graduate *summa cum laude*? A central question of modern social life and certainly contemporary consumption is, How does anyone know what's cool and what isn't? Who decides? If everyone smoked, would it be cool to smoke?

Advertising agencies and marketing firms, of course, have learned since the days of the 1960s counterculture that cool sells. Their only problem is to catch the perfect wave, to be sure they are promoting a Nike jersey and not a Nehru jacket. As Malcolm Gladwell describes in "The Coolhunt," teams of experts ("coolhunters") are employed throughout corporate America to find ways of identifying people or products as cool and then capitalizing on that identification. The cooler something is, the more people will want to possess it, to become identified with it. For marketing purposes, cool is—as the former CEO of Coca-Cola has suggested — "the convergence of content and commerce."

As Apple learned long ago, the concept of cool works especially well when anti-establishment images or attitudes can be made to serve the corporate establishment. This is one reason why what becomes cool can start from underground or marginalized groups, or "outcasts," as Denis Wilson describes them in "A Look under the Hoodie." In today's commercial market, shopping for certain brands is supposed to make one feel subversive. Adbusters, an anti-consumption organization, has designed ads and products (see p. 628) to counter this tendency of capitalism to turn what opposes it into a profitable advantage. Adbusters' aim is to help subvert global capitalism by making our resistance to shopping and certain products even cooler.

Malcolm Gladwell, *The Coolhunt*. Malcolm Gladwell (b. 1963) is the best-selling author of *The Tipping Point: How Little Things Can Make a Big Difference* (2002) and *Blink: The Power of Thinking without Thinking* (2005). Gladwell was born in England, grew up in Ontario, studied history at the University of Toronto's Trinity College, and now lives in New York City. He has worked as a reporter for *The Washington Post* and has been a staff writer for *The New Yorker* since 1996. Gladwell is the winner of a National Magazine Award and in 2005 was named one of *Time* magazine's "100 Most Influential People." In his interviews, he explains the focus of his writing: "I like looking at things that we take for granted. . . . I'm not interested in the exotic." This selection, excerpted from an article in *The New Yorker* (March 17, 1997), lays the groundwork for the premise of his book *The Tipping Point*. In "The Coolhunt," Gladwell asks: Who decides what's cool?

Malcolm Gladwell
THE COOLHUNT

625

■ **Consider before you read.** *What does Gladwell learn from the coolhunters about the nature of coolness? What qualifies these particular people to go out and find cool? Why is determining what's cool an increasingly important task for marketers?*

Baysie Wightman met DeeDee Gordon, appropriately enough, on a coolhunt. Baysie was a big shot for Converse, and DeeDee, who was barely twenty-one, was running a very cool boutique called Placid Planet, on Newbury Street in Boston. Baysie came in with a camera crew—one she often used when she was coolhunting—and said, "I've been watching your store, I've seen you, I've heard you know what's up," because it was Baysie's job at Converse to find people who knew what was up and she thought DeeDee was one of those people. DeeDee says that she responded with reserve— that "I was like, 'Whatever'"—but Baysie said that if DeeDee ever wanted to come and work at Converse she should just call, and nine months later DeeDee called. This was about the time the cool kids had decided they didn't want the hundred-and-twenty-five-dollar basketball sneaker with seventeen different kinds of high-technology materials and colors and air-cushioned heels anymore. They wanted simplicity and authenticity, and Baysie picked up on that. She brought back the Converse One Star, which was a vulcanized, suède, low-top classic old-school sneaker from the nineteen-seventies, and, sure enough, the One Star quickly became the signature shoe of the retro era. Remember what Kurt Cobain was wearing in the famous picture of him lying dead on the ground after committing suicide? Black Converse One Stars. DeeDee's big score was calling the sandal craze. She had been out in Los Angeles and had kept seeing the white teen-age girls dressing up like cholos, Mexican gangsters, in tight white tank tops known as "wife beaters," with a bra strap hanging out, and long shorts and tube socks and shower sandals. DeeDee recalls, "I'm like, 'I'm telling you, Baysie, this is going to hit. There are just too many people wearing it. We have to make a shower sandal.'" So Baysie, DeeDee, and a designer came up with the idea of making a retro sneaker-sandal, cutting the back off the One Star and putting a thick outsole on it. It was huge, and, amazingly, it's still huge.

Today, Baysie works for Reebok as general-merchandise manager—part of the team trying to return Reebok to the position it enjoyed in the mid-nineteen-eighties as the country's hottest sneaker company. DeeDee works for an advertising agency in Del Mar called Lambesis, where she puts out a quarterly tip sheet called the L Report on what the cool kids in major American cities are thinking and doing and buying. Baysie and DeeDee are best friends. They talk on the phone all the time. They get together whenever Baysie is in L.A. (DeeDee: "It's, like, how many times can you drive past O. J. Simpson's house?"), and between them they can talk for hours about the art of the coolhunt. They're the Lewis and Clark of cool.

■ Consider. What does Gladwell's assertion about Baysie and DeeDee being "the Lewis and Clark of Cool" imply? What parallels is he trying to draw between the two pairs of people?

What they have is what everybody seems to want these days, which is a window on the world of the street. Once, when fashion trends were set by the big couture houses—when cool was trickle-down—that wasn't important. But sometime in the past few decades things got turned over, and fashion became trickle-up. It's now about chase and flight—designers and retailers and the mass consumer giving chase to the elusive prey of street cool—and the rise of coolhunting as a profession shows how serious the chase has become. The sneakers of Nike and Reebok used to come out yearly. Now a new style comes out every season. Apparel designers used to have an eighteen-month lead time between concept and sale. Now they're reducing that to a year, or even six months, in order to react faster to new ideas from the street. The paradox, of course, is that the better coolhunters become at bringing the mainstream close to the cutting edge, the more elusive the cutting edge becomes. This is the first rule of the cool: The quicker the chase, the quicker the flight. The act of discovering what's cool is what causes cool to move on, which explains the triumphant circularity of coolhunting: because we have coolhunters like DeeDee and Baysie, cool changes more quickly, and because cool changes more quickly, we need coolhunters like DeeDee and Baysie.

I used to think that if I talked to Baysie and DeeDee long enough I could write a coolhunting manual, an encyclopedia of cool. But then I realized that the manual would have so many footnotes and caveats that it would be unreadable. Coolhunting is not about the articulation of a coherent philosophy of cool. It's just a collection of spontaneous observations and predictions that differ from one moment to the next and from one coolhunter to the next. Ask a coolhunter where the baggy-jeans look came from, for example, and you might get any number of answers: urban black kids mimicking the jailhouse look, skateboarders looking for room to move, snowboarders trying not to look like skiers, or, alternatively, all three at once, in some grand concordance.

If you want to understand how trends work, and why coolhunters like Baysie and DeeDee have become so important, a good place to start is with what's known as diffusion research, which is the study of how ideas and innovations spread. Diffusion researchers do things like spending five years studying the adoption of irrigation techniques in a Colombian mountain village, or developing complex matrices to map the spread of new math in the Pittsburgh school system. What they do may seem like a far cry from, say, how the Tommy Hilfiger thing spread from Harlem to every suburban mall in the country, but it really isn't: both are about how new ideas spread from one person to the next.

One of the most famous diffusion studies is Bruce Ryan and Neal Gross's analysis of the spread of hybrid seed corn in Greene County, Iowa, in the nineteen-thirties. The new seed corn was introduced there in about 1928, and it was superior in every respect to the seed that had been used by farmers for decades. But it wasn't adopted all at once. Of two hundred and fifty-nine farmers studied by Ryan and Gross, only a handful had started planting the new seed by 1933. In 1934, sixteen took the plunge. In 1935, twenty-one more followed; the next year, there were thirty-six, and the year after that a whopping sixty-one. The succeeding figures were then forty-six, thirty-six, fourteen, and three, until, by 1941, all but two of the two hundred and fifty-nine farmers studied were using the new seed. In the language of diffusion research, the handful of farmers who started trying hybrid seed corn at the very beginning of the thirties were the "innovators," the adventurous ones. The slightly larger group that followed them was the "early adopters." They were the opinion leaders in the community, the respected, thoughtful people who watched and analyzed what those wild innovators were doing and then did it themselves. Then came the big bulge of farmers in 1936, 1937, and 1938—the "early majority" and the "late majority," which is to say the deliberate and the skeptical masses, who would never try anything until the most respected farmers had tried it. Only after they had been converted did the "laggards," the most traditional of all, follow suit. The critical thing about this sequence is that it is almost entirely interpersonal. According to Ryan and Gross, only the innovators relied to any great extent on radio advertising and farm journals and seed salesmen in making their decision to switch to the hybrid. Everyone else made his decision overwhelmingly because of the example and the opinions of his neighbors and peers.

Isn't this just how fashion works?

The key to coolhunting is to look for cool people first and cool things later, and not the other way around. Since cool things are always changing, you can't look for them, because the very fact they are cool means you have no idea what

627

628

to look for. What you would be doing is thinking back on what was cool before and extrapolating, which is about as useful as presuming that because the Dow rose ten points yesterday it will rise another ten points today. Cool people, on the other hand, are a constant.

When I was in California, I met Salvador Barbier, who had been described to me by a coolhunter as "the Michael Jordan of skateboarding." He was tall and lean and languid, with a cowboy's insouciance, and we drove through the streets of Long Beach at fifteen miles an hour in a white late-model Ford Mustang, a car he had bought as a kind of ironic status gesture ("It would look good if I had a Polo jacket or maybe Nautica," he said) to go with his '62 Econoline van and his '64 T-bird. Sal told me that he and his friends, who are all in their mid-twenties, recently took to dressing up as if they were in eighth grade again and gathering together—having a "rally"—on old BMX bicycles in front of their local 7-Eleven. "I'd wear muscle shirts, like Def Leppard or Foghat or some old heavy-metal band, and tight, tight tapered Levi's, and Vans on my feet—big, like, checkered Vans or striped Vans or camouflage Vans—and then wristbands and gloves with the fingers cut off. It was total eighties fashion. You had to look like that to participate in the rally. We had those denim jackets with patches on the back and combs that hung out the back pocket. We went without I.D.s, because we'd have to have someone else buy us beers." At this point, Sal laughed. He was driving really slowly and staring straight ahead and talking in a low drawl—the coolhunter's dream. "We'd ride to this bar and I'd have to carry my bike inside, because we have really expensive bikes, and when we got inside people would freak out. They'd say, 'Omigod,' and I was asking them if they wanted to go for a ride on the handlebars. They were like, 'What is wrong with you? My boyfriend used to dress like that in the eighth grade!' And I was like, 'He was probably a lot cooler then, too.'"

This is just the kind of person DeeDee wants. "I'm looking for somebody who is an individual, who has definitely set himself apart from everybody else, who doesn't look like his peers. I've run into trendsetters who look completely Joe Regular Guy. I can see Joe Regular Guy at a club listening to some totally hardcore band playing, and I say to myself 'Omigod, what's that guy doing here?' and that totally intrigues me, and I have to walk up to him and say, 'Hey, you're really into this band. What's up?' You know what I mean? I look at everything. If I see Joe Regular Guy sitting in a coffee shop and everyone around him has blue hair, I'm going to gravitate toward him, because, hey, what's Joe Regular Guy doing in a coffee shop with people with blue hair?"

629

◀ ***Adbusters, Think Globally Before You Decide It's So Cool.*** This spoof ad is one of an ongoing series in which *Adbusters* uses the techniques of advertising to target what it sees as particularly egregious corporate offenders from the fashion, tobacco, alcohol, and food industries. Here Adbusters asks readers to reconsider what's "cool". (Image courtesy of www.adbusters.org)

We were sitting outside the Fred Segal store in West Hollywood. I was wearing a very conservative white Brooks Brothers button-down and a pair of Levi's, and DeeDee looked first at my shirt and then my pants and dissolved into laughter: "I mean, I might even go up to you in a cool place."

Picking the right person is harder than it sounds, though. Piney Kahn, who works for DeeDee, says, "There are a lot of people in the gray area. You've got these kids who dress ultra funky and have their own style. Then you realize they're just running after their friends." The trick is not just to be able to tell who is different but to be able to tell when that difference represents something truly cool. It's a gut thing. You have to somehow just know. DeeDee hired Piney because Piney clearly knows: she is twenty-four and used to work with the Beastie Boys and has the formidable self-possession of someone who is not only cool herself but whose parents were cool. "I mean," she says, "they named me after a tree."

Piney and DeeDee said that they once tried to hire someone as a coolhunter who was not, himself, cool, and it was a disaster.

"You can give them the boundaries," Piney explained. "You can say that if people shop at Banana Republic and listen to Alanis Morissette they're probably not trendsetters. But then they might go out and assume that everyone who does that is not a trendsetter, and not look at the other things."

"I mean, I myself might go into Banana Republic and buy a T-shirt," DeeDee chimed in.

Their non-cool coolhunter just didn't have that certain instinct, that sense that told him when it was O.K. to deviate from the manual. Because he wasn't cool, he didn't know cool, and that's the essence of the third rule of cool: you have to be one to know one. That's why Baysie is still on top of this business at forty-one. "It's easier for me to tell you what kid is cool than to tell you what things are cool," she says. But that's all she needs to know. In this sense, the third rule of cool fits perfectly into the second: the second rule says that cool cannot be manufactured, only observed, and the third says that it can only be observed by those who are themselves cool. And, of course, the first rule says that it cannot accurately be observed at all, because the act of discovering cool causes cool to take flight, so if you add all three together they describe a closed loop, the hermeneutic circle of coolhunting, a phenomenon whereby not only can the uncool not see cool but cool cannot even be adequately described to them. Baysie says that she can see a coat on one of her friends and think it's not cool but then see the same coat on DeeDee and think that it is cool. It is not possible to be cool, in other words, unless you are—in some larger sense—already cool, and so the phenomenon that the uncool cannot see and cannot have described to them is also something that they cannot ever attain, because if they did it would no longer be cool. Coolhunting represents the ascendancy, in the marketplace, of high school.

Once, I was visiting DeeDee at her house in Laurel Canyon when one of her L Report assistants, Jonas Vail, walked in. He'd just come back from Niketown on Wilshire Boulevard, where he'd bought seven hundred dollars' worth of the latest sneakers to go with the three hundred dollars' worth of skateboard shoes he'd bought earlier in the afternoon. Jonas is tall and expressionless, with a pea-coat, dark jeans, and short-cropped black hair. "Jonas is good," DeeDee says. "He works with me on everything. That guy knows more pop culture. You know: What was the name of the store Mrs. Garrett owned on *The Facts of Life*? He knows all the names of the extras from eighties sitcoms. I can't believe someone like him exists. He's fucking unbelievable. Jonas can spot a cool person a mile away."

Jonas takes the boxes of shoes and starts unpacking them on the couch next to DeeDee. He picks up a pair of the new Nike ACG hiking boots, and says, "All the Japanese in Niketown were really into these." He hands the shoes to DeeDee.

"Of course they were!" she says. "The Japanese are all into the tech-looking shit. Look how exaggerated it is, how bulbous." DeeDee has very ambivalent feelings about Nike, because she thinks its marketing has got out of hand. When she was in the New York Niketown with a girlfriend recently, she says, she started getting light-headed and freaked out. "It's cult, cult, cult. It was like, 'Hello, are we all drinking the Kool-Aid here?'" But this shoe she loves. It's Dr. Jay's in the Bronx all over again. DeeDee turns the shoe around and around in the air, tapping the big clear-blue plastic bubble on the side—the visible Air-Sole unit—with one finger. "It's so fucking rad. It looks like a platypus!" In front of me, there is a pair of Nike's new shoes for the basketball player Jason Kidd.

I pick it up. "This looks . . . cool," I venture uncertainly.

DeeDee is on the couch, where she's surrounded by shoeboxes and sneakers and white tissue paper, and she looks up reprovingly because, of course, I don't get it. I can't get it. "Beyooond cool, Maalcolm. Beyooond cool."

■ **Consider.** *Why is DeeDee impressed by Jonas's knowledge of pop culture trivia? How is this cultural knowledge related to the coolhunt?*

631

■ **Discuss.** *Why does Gladwell give up on the idea of producing "an encyclopedia of cool" (p. 626)? Discuss whether he is right that such an account of coolness would be impossible. If you agree, what is it about cool that makes it so hard to quantify?*

■ **Write.** *Choose a recent fashion trend in your school or among your friends and write an analysis of it using the categories established by diffusion research (p. 627). Did this trend follow the pattern beginning with innovators and eventually trickling down to laggards? By the time the laggards caught on, had the innovators already moved on? Does your experience confirm the research?*

Denis Wilson, *A Look under the Hoodie*. Denis Wilson is a freelance journalist in Philadelphia. In the following essay, which originally appeared in the op-ed section of *The New York Times* (December 23, 2006), Wilson traces the origin and history of the hooded sweatshirt and explains how it "became the mark of an outcast," even exuding "sinister appeal." "The hoodie," he argues, "manages to balance somewhere between defiance and comfort."

Denis Wilson

A LOOK UNDER THE HOODIE

■ **Consider before you read.** *How are current associations with the hoodie related to its history? In what ways has the meaning of the garment changed? Who is most likely to wear a hoodie now?*

Thirty years ago, Rocky Balboa made his first triumphant ascent of the steps of the Philadelphia Museum of Art, a scene cemented in the American cinematic consciousness. Simultaneously a workingman's hero, a street thug, and a striving athlete, Rocky came to embody the underdog, and his bare-bones workout gear reflected his origins in a tough Italian neighborhood in Philadelphia.

While jogging through the predawn landscape, he protected himself from the winter cold with sweatpants, a knit cap, and a well-worn gray hooded sweatshirt. And as Rocky pulled himself out of anonymity, he brought with him what would become a mainstay of American fashion: the hoodie.

Today, this humble garment is worn by everyone from infants to grandparents. Yet it still signifies outcast status—so much that it has been banned by some schools and nightclubs. But this is not Rocky's fault.

The hooded sweatshirt began, in the 1930s, as a practical piece of clothing. Champion created the first ones for laborers in the frozen warehouses of upstate New York. (It is appropriate that—in both the original *Rocky* and in *Rocky Balboa*—the boxer dons a gray hoodie, steps into a meat locker, and batters a bloody carcass.)

Eventually, hooded sweatshirts were produced for football and track athletes, who would lend theirs to their girlfriends, and eventually the hoodie was everyday wear.

In the mid- to late 1970s, just as the Italian Stallion was becoming a hometown hero, hip-hop culture was developing on the streets of New York City. The hooded sweatshirt fit its unruly, us-against-the-world profile just as well as it fit

Sylvester Stallone in *Rocky*. (Revolution/MGM/The Kobal Collection/John Bramley)

Rocky's. But hip-hop trendsetters used the hoodie also to cloak and isolate themselves, and lent it a sinister appeal.

The sweatshirt hood can work much like a cobra hood, put up to intimidate others. But even more important is its ability to create a shroud of anonymity. This came in handy for at least two types of people operating in hip-hop's urban breeding ground: graffiti writers and so-called stick-up kids, or muggers. Wearing a hoodie meant you were keeping a low profile, and perhaps up to something illegal.

Other subcultures adopted the hoodie, too—skaters, snowboarders, and hardcore punk music fans—and so signified their status as outcasts.

By the late 1990s, hip-hop's rising popularity inspired clothing makers like Tommy Hilfiger and Ralph Lauren, and even high-fashion designers like Gucci and Versace, to start making hooded sweatshirts.

Motherwear, a clothing company that caters to breastfeeding mothers, now offers a hoodie with two side flaps, perhaps reflecting the jacket's utter domestication.

Mos Def, actor and hip-hop superstar. (© Jerome Albertini/CORBIS)

And so the hoodie manages to balance somewhere between defiance and comfort. But that reflects its roots. Rocky Balboa is beloved as much for his average-Joe, big-lug appeal as for his bone crushing and face pounding. And sometimes a hoodie is just soft and warm.

■ Discuss. *Discuss the hoodie's connection with "keeping a low profile." Can you elaborate on what Wilson says about how it went from having outlaw connotations to being popular for "everyone from infants to grandparents"?*

■ Write. *Taking Wilson's essay as your model, research and write a cultural history of another iconic article of clothing (for example, blue jeans or the leather jacket). What can you find out about its origins and whom it was originally designed for? How has its appeal changed over time?*

When commercial enterprises assume for their own use the concepts, styles, or items that have authentically appeared in various subcultures or local communities, the process is usually called "co-optation." In this way, the fashion industry co-opts a particular urban *"look"* that started in the streets and turns it into a commercial brand. One of the leading studies of this phenomenon is Thomas Frank's *The Conquest of Cool: Business Culture, Counterculture, and the Rise of Hip Consumerism* (1997). In this provocative and comprehensive account of how advertising and marketing profitably co-opted the subversive movements of the 1960s, Frank offers a complex view of the way that American counterculture and commercialism feed off each other. What follows is a short excerpt from the book's first chapter, "Of Commerce and Counterculture".

635

Thomas Frank
THE CONQUEST OF COOL

■ **Consider before you read.** *What ideas about coolness does Frank challenge in this excerpt? How, in his opinion, is our thinking about coolness wrong?*

Apart from certain obvious exceptions at either end of the spectrum of commodification (represented, say, by the MC-5 at one end and the Monkees at the other) it was and remains difficult to distinguish precisely between authentic counterculture and fake: by almost every account, the counterculture, as a mass movement distinct from the bohemias that preceded it, was triggered at least as much by developments in mass culture (particularly the arrival of The Beatles in 1964) as changes at the grass roots. Its heroes were rock stars and rebel celebrities, millionaire performers and employees of the culture industry; its greatest moments occurred on television, on the radio, at rock concerts, and in movies. From a distance of thirty years, its language and music seem anything but the authentic populist culture they yearned so desperately to be: from contrived cursing to saintly communalism to the embarrassingly faked Woody Guthrie accents of Bob Dylan and to the astoundingly pretentious works of groups like Iron Butterfly and The Doors, the relics of the counterculture reek of affectation and phoniness, the leisure-dreams of white suburban children like those who made up so much of the Grateful Dead's audience throughout the 1970s and 1980s. . . .

It is more than a little odd that, in this age of nuance and negotiated readings, we lack a serious history of co-optation, one that understands corporate thought as something other than a cartoon. Co-optation remains something we vilify almost automatically; the historical particulars which permit or discourage co-optation— or even the obvious fact that some things are co-opted while others are not—are simply not addressed. Regardless of whether the co-opters deserve our vilification or not, the process by which they make rebel subcultures their own is clearly an important element of contemporary life. And while the ways in which business anticipated and reacted to the youth culture of the 1960s may not reveal much about the individual experiences of countercultural participants, examining their maneuvers closely does allow a more critical perspective on the phenomenon of co-optation, as well as on the value of certain strategies of cultural confrontation, and, ultimately, on the historical meaning of the counterculture.

■ Discuss. *What does it mean to co-opt something? What would be involved in the "history of co-optation" that Frank calls for? What would it help us understand?*

■ Write. *The examples of counterculture that Frank gives are all from the 1960s. What current ideas or means of expression are countercultural? Write an essay considering recent trends in light of Frank's assertions about co-optation. Do they confirm his idea that even apparently rebellious artists are inextricably linked with the corporate world? Does any true counterculture exist?*

 CONSIDER THE CLUSTER
Selling Cool

■ **Message**

In an essay, respond to Malcolm Gladwell's "The Coolhunt" by describing an object you own that you consider cool. Apply what Gladwell calls the "first rule of the cool" to your subject in an attempt to explain as best you can what makes it truly cool.

■ **Method**

Can something that's generally considered "uncool" be made to seem cool? As an in-class assignment, imagine you work for an ad agency and have been asked to design an ad that makes a product hardly anyone considers cool into something that is. First think of the product and then think of the method you would use to accomplish this assignment.

■ **Medium**

Denis Wilson claims that the first *Rocky* movie helped make the hooded sweatshirt a fashion trend. In an essay, consider something you first noticed in the media—movies, TV, MTV, and so on—and describe how and why it appealed to you. How much of the appeal was due to the item itself? How much was due to the celebrity who used or wore it? Conclude your essay by considering whether movies or TV can make something cool in itself or whether they depend on its being discovered first in real life.

WRITE ▪▪▪▪▪▪

1. **Collaborate and make a case.** Break into several groups and, using *Adbusters*' "How to Create Your Own Print Ad" (p. 540) as a guide, create a rough draft of a print ad either for a product you invent or for something familiar that you seldom see advertised—perhaps your college or a local hangout. Afterward, groups should compare their creations and discuss what advertising elements and strategies seem most and least effective.

2. **Collaborate and make a case.** After reading Eric Tyrone McLeod's essay on the commodification of the body (p. 611), break into small groups and discuss how both men and women can be adversely affected by striving for media ideals of physical perfection. Then imagine your group has formed an organization against such media ideals that could inform the public about resisting extreme alterations to the human body. Create a name for your organization (check the entry on abbreviation in the glossary) and then, after studying some of the examples of opinion ads, prepare a rough draft of an advertisement that promotes your cause. Try to think of a catchy headline; also be sure to offer in the body of your ad's copy some reasons why attempting to achieve certain physical ideas could actually be harmful.

3. **Create.** Write a sci-fi essay. Architects, city planners, and retailing experts are beginning to see a decline in the popularity of the giant shopping mall, but at present no one has a vision of what might replace it. Using your imagination, write a short essay that visualizes the next new shopping experience. Describe what the new architecture would look like and—on the basis of your own shopping experiences—what improvements the mall replacement would offer to consumers.

4. **Create a memoir.** After reading Bill McKibben's "SkyMall: Pie in the Sky" (p. 557), write a short personal essay describing the most frivolous or useless thing you've ever bought. What motivated you to buy it? What reasons did you give for buying it? Were there good reasons not to buy it? Do you still own it? Do you enjoy it, or are you embarrassed by it? In your essay, describe the item carefully and explain why you found it appealing.

5. **Collaborate and analyze.** As mentioned in the book's Introduction, the eminent literary critic Raymond Williams once observed that the biggest problem with advertising is not, as most people imagine, that it promotes a materialistic view of the world (p. 35). The problem, he argued, is that

advertising is not materialistic enough. After breaking into small groups, discuss what you think Williams meant by this apparently paradoxical comment. Then each group should collect from various sources (this book included) examples of product ads—for automobiles, appliances, food, electronic gadgets, and so on—that support his opinion. After surveying the ads, each group should select a single print ad that best exemplifies Williams's point about lack of materialism. One person from each group should then present this example to the entire class and point out how and why the particular ad fails to be sufficiently materialistic. A key question to ask is, What is being sold?

6. **Research and analyze.** Write a pop culture research paper. Quite a few movies have featured shopping malls in a significant role. Using your own memory and resource tools at your school's library or on the Internet, compile a list of films that have featured malls. Use this list as the basis of a research essay on the way the film industry has depicted the shopping mall. Can you find some of the earliest examples? Can you detect changes in the way malls have been presented over time? How do films generally portray malls? This research paper can either be constructed as a

historical overview or focus on one film in which the mall is of special significance. Either way, your paper must cite sources and criticism.

7. **Make a case.** The architect Sze Tsung Leong maintains that shopping is a medium (p. 571). If this is the case, what isn't a medium? Of course, this is a difficult question. But do your best thinking. In a short reflective essay, consider the general concept of a medium (see also the book's Introduction, p. 10) and make a case for either position: (a) No human experience can exist outside of or separate from some kind of medium, or (b) human beings can and do have unmediated experiences.

8. **Collaborate and compare.** As a media scholar has said, when people talk of cool, they often compile a list of what's cool and what isn't. Try this as a class exercise. On the chalkboard, make two columns— "Cool" and "Uncool"—and fill them in by taking suggestions from everyone. See how many agree or disagree with the suggestions. You may want to add another column of "Semicool" to list suggestions in case there is strongly divided opinion. What does your final list say about how easy or difficult it is to distinguish between what is cool and what isn't?

YOU'RE RUNNING
BECAUSE YOU WANT THAT RAISE,
TO BE ALL YOU CAN BE.
BUT IT'S NOT EASY
WHEN YOU
WORK
SIXTY HOURS A WEEK
MAKING SNEAKERS IN AN
INDONESIAN FACTORY
AND YOUR FRIENDS
DISAPPEAR

9. **Make a case.** As an artist, Barbara Kruger (p. 570) chooses unusual canvases for delivering her message: billboards, buses, magazines, plaques, bus stops. Does her work fit your definition of art? In an essay, discuss how Kruger's work relies on familiar types of advertising and yet is not in itself advertising. What does she borrow from the advertising world, and how does she transform it? You may want to use the Internet and reference library to learn more about Kruger's life and art.

GLOSSARY

abbreviation: The shortening of a word or phrase, usually for convenience, efficiency, or memorability. Nicknames are a common form of abbreviation (Bob for Robert, Sue for Susan). Many shortenings become standard or common words in themselves (phone = telephone, abs = abdominal muscles). In communications, two important forms of abbreviation are **initialisms** and **acronyms.** Initialisms consist of the first or key letters of words and the letters are pronounced individually: ACLU (American Civil Liberties Union), WNBA (Woman's National Basketball Association), UFO (unidentified flying object). Initialisms have become popular in e-mail and in live chat rooms, where commonly used phrases are often abbreviated: BRB (be right back), GTG (got to go). Although many people refer to such abbreviation as acronyms, that word technically applies only to abbreviation that are pronounced as words or that form new words: AIDS (acquired immune deficiency syndrome) and RAM (random-access memory) are examples of the former; laser (*l*ight *a*mplification by *s*timulated *e*mission of *r*adiation) is an example of the latter. Since acronyms can be rhetorically effective, many organizations adopt them to reinforce their message: NOW (National Organization for Women), MADD (Mothers Against Drunk Driving).

abstract art: Art that focuses on form, structure, and patterns of color (rather than concrete images) to evoke broad or general ideas and emotions. Abstract art often lacks a recognizable subject, which allows for different perceptions and opinions.

acceptance: Positive reception or response from an audience. In constructing arguments, writers usually estimate the degree of acceptance their message is likely to have from a particular audience. In rhetoric, delivering a message to an audience that already accepts your position is often called preaching to the converted. Thus, if you are advocating an antiregulation policy for firearms, it is far easier to address your message to the National Rifle Association than to a pro–gun control group. In consumer behavior theory, acceptance measures the reception of a message by an individual. Advertisers hope for optimum acceptance through the use of positive imagery. "You deserve a break today" was a popular McDonald's advertising slogan designed to put the consumer in an accepting mood.

action: In narrative, the leading events. The action of a story or essay might be a small part of the whole piece. In advertising, the word "action" refers to the process of moving individuals to think of a product or service in a favorable light and to behave accordingly.

advertisement: A public announcement that promotes a product, service, business, or event to increase awareness and sales. Advertisements are present in nearly every form of media and are powerful means of communication. Advertisements in broadcast media are known as commercials. Advertisers in print media buy space, whereas those in broadcast media buy time.

advertising photography: The use of photographs to promote and sell products. Advertising photographs are powerful because they increase memorability.

advertorial: A combination of advertisement and editorial designed to promote an interest or opinion. Advertisements created by special interest groups that lobby for legislative change often take the form of advertorials.

advocacy advertisement: An advertisement that aims to raise consciousness, gather support, or speak in favor of a specific social cause. Among these types of advertisements are public service announcements and political ads. Advocacy advertising is also sometimes referred to as "cause marketing."

aerial photography: Photographs taken from the sky, sometimes using infrared film, at a great distance from the subject. This method of photography is useful in landscape photography, archaeological surveys, military reconnaissance, or any other area that deals with a large distant subject.

allegory: Artistic work in which elements (characters, places, images, etc.) are understood to represent something else, often spiritual, moral, or political. George Orwell's novel *Animal Farm* is an allegory in which farm animals represent humans in a workers' rebellion. The book gives a symbolic depiction of problems with government, caste, and injustice in society.

alliteration: Repetition of consonant sounds, generally at the beginning of words but also at key or successive syllables. Alliteration is widespread in poetry (Shakespeare: "When to the sessions of sweet silent thought / I summon up remembrance of things past") and in prose that strives for impact (Tom Paine: "These are the times that try men's souls"). Advertising copy frequently makes use of alliteration, especially when the desire is to create a memorable or catchy slogan.

ambiguity: The condition that exists when a term or statement can be interpreted in several different ways, leaving the audience unsure as to which meaning is correct. Quite common in ordinary communication, ambiguity is often the unintentional result of a semantic or grammatical error. In literary works, authors sometimes intentionally use ambiguous expressions to create multiple meanings or uncertainty. Deliberate ambiguity is also frequently found in advertisements.

analogy: A comparison made between two similar subjects to clarify a meaning. Analogies are used in speech, writing, and art to give an example or show how two or more things are alike. An analogy can be drawn between children fighting on a playground and countries going to war.

architecture: The art and science of designing and constructing buildings. The word "architecture" can also denote the structure of something created; the framework or structural makeup of a piece of writing or a web page can be considered its architecture.

argument: The use of logical reasoning to support a particular point of view. Also, a form of discourse that attempts to convince an audience that a specific claim or proposition is true wholly because a supporting body of logically related statements is also true.

audience: A group of people who will see, hear, or otherwise experience a performance, a work of art, or any other form of written or verbal communication. Since everyone perceives information differently, audience is a major consideration in rhetoric and writing. An author can make a piece of work more effective by keeping in mind the particular group being addressed. An audience can be a literal group attending a performance or an anonymous widespread group reading or watching broadcasts. Martin Luther King Jr.'s "I Have a Dream" speech had a literal audience (those who attended the speech), an implied audience (the American people), and an anonymous cumulative audience (any person that has since heard or read the speech).

blog: Short for "weblog," blog refers to a page with hyperlinks to other pages, often with short bits of accompanying text telling surfers about where the links are going.

campaigns: In marketing and advertising, the strategies that companies implement in television, radio, and print media to attract consumers to buy their products.

caption: Written information accompanying an image that explains to the viewer what he or she is looking at.

cartography: The science or process of making maps.

causation: The act of making something occur or the process of bringing something into being. Causation presupposes the belief that every action or state of being is the result of a previous action. In media or art, causation refers to that which evokes a reaction from an audience. In writing, it is a key element of explanation and plot development.

classification: The categorization of items in groups according to type. Classification is a procedure for identifying and organizing the parts of a subject.

cliché: Once a word or phrase enters the common vernacular as a widely accepted way of describing something, it becomes a cliché. Drab and unimaginative, clichés are the work of a lazy mind. They weaken the overall quality of a speech or text. Examples include a critic referring to a new movie as a "tour-de-force," or a poet writing a line such as "his eyes were as blue as the ocean."

collage: A picture made by adhering various images or objects onto a surface. A collage can consist of bits of paper, pieces of cloth, photographs, and other various objects randomly or purposefully arranged.

color: Reflected light that is perceived by human beings as variations of the primary shades — red, blue, yellow. Color is used to meet or break a convention in art, or to evoke an emotion. In advertising, color is often used to attract and keep the consumer's attention. In writing, the word "color" is used to describe the use of elaborate detail; vivid descriptions are said to "add color" or make a scene more visual for the reader.

comic: Words and drawing arranged sequentially to tell a story or joke. Comic strips syndicated in newspapers and comic books are two of the most familiar genres, though recently writers / illustrators have merged the comic book with serious fiction to produce the graphic novel, one of the best-known being Art Spiegelman's *Maus*.

comparison: A search for similarities between two or more subjects drawn from the same class or general category. Comparing two subjects is often an effective way to construct an argument or provide an opinion.

composition: A term that can be applied to many types of expression, including writing, music, art, architecture, photography, film, design, typography, and advertising. Composition essentially refers to the way something is made or made up (the word means literally putting together), particularly the way in which its parts are arranged and how they relate to the whole.

computer art: Pictures created or altered using digital technology. Each dot of light on the computer screen is called a pixel (from "picture" + "element"). The combination of pixels in a sequence creates a visible image. Computer artists can alter the order of pixels to enhance or even change the image.

content: The meaning or message behind a work of art. Every photograph, painting, novel, essay, or movie usually has a theme or idea that it tries to convey to its audience. The content of a painting that shows an African American man standing beside chains might be the idea of slavery, while the content of a particular news report might be the presidential election.

context: Context can be understood in two distinct ways: Most immediately, the term refers to whatever surrounds a word, image, passage, or text — where the text was taken from. Knowing the immediate context of an excerpt (a magazine or a Web site or an article about slavery, what the text before and after said, etc.) helps explain its full meaning. In a larger sense, context can refer to the historical, social, or economic moment from which a text emerged.

contrast: A process that highlights the differences between two or more subjects. Showing differences often magnifies the pros and cons of like subjects.

contrivance: An artificial device that makes an object or event appear clever and spontaneous, though it is actually planned and affected. "Contrived" carries a negative connotation, suggesting that the subject aspires to be genuine but ultimately appears unrealistic or unconvincing to the audience.

convergence: Diverse things coming together at a single point from different directions.

cyberspace: A term coined by novelist William Gibson in 1984 to describe the invisible networking system of computers and digitized data throughout the world. The word "cyberspace" is often used to describe the Internet and virtual reality.

definition: The meaning of a word (as in a dictionary or a glossary). As a rhetorical term, definition refers to the practice of exploring the full meaning of a concept in an extended essay. Definition also pertains to other media: in visual areas such as photography or television, it denotes an image's degree of clarity. In recordings, definition relates to the sharpness of the sound.

demographics: Statistical information about the consumer population, including size and growth, based on factors such as age, sex, occupation, and family size. Advertisers often determine their target market on demographic information. (See also *target market*.)

description: A verbal or visual account or representation of a person, place, object, or state of mind. Detailed description can often make information clearer or more manageable for an audience. Objective description is primarily factual and excludes mention of the writer or artist's personal evaluation or response. Subjective description includes attention to both the subject described and the writer or artist's response to it.

digital imaging: The conversion of an analog photograph to a digital image through the use of a computer scanner.

digital photography: The process of creating or altering photographs through the use of digital technology and computer graphics. (See *digital imaging*.)

documentary photography: The use of photographs to record information. Documentary photography can inform the viewer, conjure an emotional response, or convey a socially conscious message through the use of visual stimuli. Judicial photography, medical photography, photojournalism, biographic photography, scientific photography, war photography, and travel photography are some examples.

draft: A drawing or sketch, usually of a preliminary nature; also a preliminary version of any kind of writing. A finished work is usually preceded by several drafts.

emphasis: A means of ascribing more importance to an issue by way of drawing special attention to its message.

feminism: A term that is generally used to refer to the belief in securing women's rights and privileges equal to those of men for employment. It is also specifically used to refer to a political movement and organization that actively seeks such rights, especially active in the 1970s.

format: The physical dimensions or components of something. In photography, the dimensions of photographic film, traditionally measured in millimeters or inches. The photographer chooses a specific film format for aesthetic reasons, depending on the type of photos he or she wishes to take. In book publishing, the format of a textbook would refer to all the components that make up that book—the different colors used, the margins, the arrangement of pictures and written text.

frame: The limit of what is recorded in a painting, photograph, or image at a given time. In photography, this refers to the size and extent of an image on a negative. In film and video, the frame is the area covered by the camera and is what we see on the screen. Framing is especially important in photography in that the photographer can usually choose how to frame the picture so that certain images are included and others excluded. Framing is applied to many different kinds of expression: one frames an argument by putting it a certain way or constructing specific limits.

genre: Any of the categories existing within each creative discipline that allow for the organization of specific forms or methods of expression. Magical-realism, fantasy, and romance are three examples of genres found in fiction.

hyperbole: Exaggerated expression used for emphasis or persuasion. Hyperbole makes up a large portion of everyday speech, where words like "terrific," "great," or "super," are commonly used, along with extreme expressions: "I'm starving" instead of "I'm hungry." When deliberately used in advertising or publicity purposes to promote excitement, such exaggerations are popularly known as "hype." Movie ads will try to stimulate public interest through superlatives conveniently supplied by reviewers: "The most breathtakingly gorgeous film of the year."

hypermedia: Multiple forms of media (text, graphics, etc.) processed through computer applications. Hypermedia is concerned with not only relaying information but also reminding users of the medium itself.

hypothesis: An unproved theory that is tentatively accepted as true in order to provide a basis for further investigation or argument. In an essay we often first state our idea about a subject as a hypothesis, which we then examine, develop, support, and restate it as a conclusion.

illustration: In writing, a process in which authors select examples to represent, clarify, and support ideas, statements, and principles. Also the visual elements used to clarify or supplement a text, such as the illustrations in a dictionary or encyclopedia.

informative essay: An essay whose purpose is to educate readers on a given topic using research, facts, and a logical structure.

installation: The arrangement of a work (or works) of art in a gallery or exhibition. The art is placed or hung in a specific order so the audience will most likely view each piece according to the artist's wishes.

irony: A kind of antithesis created through the use of words that suggest the opposite of their literal meaning or through a situation in which the results do not match the intentions or expectations. Countries going to war in the hope of obtaining peace is an example of irony. In written expression, irony often depends on understanding the context and inferring the tone of voice.

jingle: A catchy, easily recognizable piece of music associated with a product or service, played during a television or radio advertisement. A mnemonic device, the jingle is successful when it persuades a consumer to purchase the advertised product or service.

kitsch: A defining fashion, media, or product design from a particular era whose cultural value is renewed after a period of obsolescence. Kitsch tends to connote items of dubious sophistication and includes arcana as diverse as shag carpeting, busts of Lenin, and reruns of *The A-Team.*

media: Technically, the plural of **medium**. In common use, though, refers to various means of mass communication such as newspapers, television, and radio.

medium: A means of conveying ideas or information. Includes all forms of mass communication (television, radio, newspaper) as well as personal and interactive forms of communication (audio and video recordings, the Internet, letters, and e-mail).

memoir: Personal writing reflecting on a person's contributions to the world. Autobiographical yet different from autobiography, the memoir documents life as remembered by the author.

message: A term that refers to *what* a text is saying. A message can be a discrete unit of communication, a condensed moral or organizing concept, or a strong signal or gesture that delivers a clear idea.

metaphor: A verbal or visual image used to represent or symbolize something else. Metaphors are often used in literature to expose the reader to a theme or idea without being obvious or overbearing. In Mary Shelley's *Frankenstein,* the monster is viewed by many as a metaphor for the rebels of the French Revolution: both monster and rebels became too powerful to control, even by their creators.

method: A term that refers to *how* a text is put together—generated, expressed, structured, and put to purpose.

modernism: A style of art that rejects the artistic styles and restrictions of the past. Because artistic expression changes with time, it is difficult to describe the modernist style at any given point. However, modernists usually have a radical new attitude about both past and present that affects their entire concept of art.

montage: A work of art that consists of overlapping images or themes, often borrowed or appropriated from other works. In film, a montage is a display of overlapping visual images, often fading in and out of focus and set to music. Writers can achieve a montage effect by describing in detail a number of different images at once, giving the reader a layered mental picture.

mundane: Ordinary, commonplace. In literature, many writers use mundane aspects of life to project a larger concept. Arthur Miller's play *Death of a Salesman,* whose main character is the "everyman" Willy Loman, deals with the difficulties of family relationships and failure to live up to expectations.

narration: A way of telling what happened by linking a succession of events together into a meaningful sequence. In writing, narration refers to the main voice, which often speaks directly to the reader.

narrative art: Art that represents a story or events taking place. Many paintings depict scenes in progress and thus allow the viewer to infer what has happened or is about to happen. (See also **narration**.)

opinion essay: A composition in which the author advances his or her personal beliefs in a persuasive and well-reasoned manner with the intention of convincing readers of the expressed opinion's importance or veracity.

parallelism: The arrangement of words, phrases, sentences, paragraphs, and sections of a composition so that similar elements are given equal emphasis or form. Parallelism is a basic principle in both grammar and rhetoric.

parody: A deliberate imitation, usually for comic or satirical purposes, of any written, artistic, or musical work or expression. For example, the Beatles routinely parodied other musical styles. A successful parody depends on the audience's understanding that the imitation is done purposefully—thus much parody is exaggerated so that the point is unmistakable.

pattern: A series of images or pieces of information that, when considered as a whole, conveys a certain message or agenda. The emergence of patterns in literature and visual arts contributes to the formation of different styles and genres.

personal essay: A composition that focuses on the author's individual experience.

perspective: A particular way of seeing, literally or figuratively. An individual's perspective is affected by his or her personal history and experiences, character, mood, circumstances, and any other qualities that makes a person unique. In fiction, perspective is synonymous with ***point of view***.

photo-essay: A magazine item that combines text and photography. The photographs provide a visual reference and add clarity to the text.

photojournalism: Photographic images that accompany text dealing with news coverage. The photographs give the audience a visual reference of what is occurring and often relay as much information about the story as the written article does.

photo-realism: A painting style in which the artist imitates the precision and objective qualities of a photograph. Computer photo-realism is the process of making digital images that resemble photographs.

plot: The closely linked sequence of events in a story. In literature, plot refers to the things that "happen" in the story.

point of view: The vantage point from which a piece of writing is presented. In expository prose, the author's point of view might be compared to a light illuminating an object: the strength, color, and position of that light not only determine what aspect of the object we see but also affect what kind of response we have to it.

Polaroid: A camera that passes exposed film between rollers that release chemicals needed for development. With this apparatus, photos can be shot and developed automatically, within minutes. (The word is also applied to the resulting photograph: "a Polaroid picture.")

pop art: Contemporary art that appeals to a wide (popular) audience. Andy Warhol is perhaps the most famous pop artist. His unusual artworks, such as paintings of Campbell soup cans and sculptures of Brillo cartons, made him internationally known.

portraiture: The making of a painting or photograph of a person's face or body. Portraiture focuses on the human form, with particular attention to physical detail. Leonardo DaVinci's *Mona Lisa* is a famous portrait.

postmodernism: An artistic and literary movement that resists the concrete images of modernism. In fiction, postmodern writers often create unusual effects through the use of disjointed and nonlinear plots, bizarre characters, and metafiction (writing about writing). Postmodernist painters tend to paint unrecognizable subjects to elicit emotion from the viewer and call attention to the artwork itself rather than to create a definitive picture. Where the modernist impulse grew out of seeing works (paintings or poems) as isolated objects or texts, much of postmodernism depends on viewing a work in an expanded or unexpected context; for example, the museum space itself will become an element of the exhibited work. Postmodernist artists often blur traditional boundaries between high and low culture, different media, or art and commerce. Despite an enormous amount of attention, the term has received no fully successful definition: some influential critics believe the movement is over, while others think it never existed in the first place.

premise: A statement given as the basis of an argument. Etymologically meaning "to place before," premises are the assumptions from which deductive reasoning proceeds.

propaganda art: Art publicized by a government or other organization to promote a policy, idea, doctrine, or cause.

public art: Art produced for and by the community.

purpose: The overall goal or aim of a work, the effect it hopes to achieve, the agenda or cause it promotes, or the response it expects to receive from an audience.

representation: A depiction of a person, place, thing, or idea. Representational art contains a recognizable subject and a clear objective.

résumé: A document that summarizes for prospective employers the skills, job objectives, and past experience of an individual. A résumé can also refer to a summary of events.

rhetoric: The art of effective or persuasive expression. Rhetorical methods have been taught since antiquity and still remain a central ingredient of most writing courses. The term has recently been expanded to include elements of visual persuasion as well.

search engine: A term that refers to a program that searches web documents for specified keywords and returns a list of documents where the keywords are found. Search engines like Google, Alta Vista, and Yahoo! also offer services like chat rooms and other functions that will keep users coming back to their site.

self-portrait: A visual image or verbal description in which the artist and subject are the same. Many artists photograph, paint, and write about themselves to gain perspective on or insight into their own identity.

sensationalism: An emphasis on the most lurid and shocking aspects of a subject. Many gossip magazines sensationalize the lives of celebrities in order to attract an audience.

sequence: The arrangement of images, objects, or words in a series.

simile: An explicit comparison of two things normally not considered alike, usually brought together by the word "like" or "as." Thoreau compared grass to a ribbon: "The grass-blade, like a long green ribbon, streams from the sod into the summer." Dickens drew a simile between a character and a cannon: "He seemed a kind of cannon loaded to the muzzle with facts, and prepared to blow them clean out of the regions of childhood at one discharge."

slogan: A phrase, often copyrighted, that attempts to encapsulate an organization's defining principle in a manner that is both memorable and efficient. For instance, think of Nike's simple, effective "Just Do It."

staged photography: Photographs in which the subject plays a fictional role with a specific costume and pose. Most staged photographs are used for advertisements — a picture of people sunbathing on a beach could advertise a summer resort.

story: A fictional or nonfictional representation of an experience or series of events.

surreal: Having strange and irrational qualities. In surrealist art, the artist strives to render a dreamlike rather than a concrete effect. Writing, movies, and television can also have a surreal effect when tone, plot, and character do not conform to the audience's expectations. The term is commonly used to suggest real experiences that seem unreal; many eyewitnesses of the September 11, 2001, World Trade Center attacks repeatedly said in interviews that the experience seemed "surreal."

syllogism: A formal deductive argument composed of a major premise (All human beings are mortal), a minor premise (Joe is a human being), and a conclusion (Therefore, Joe is mortal).

tabloid: A popular, small-format newspaper or magazine with an emphasis on sensationalism and gossip. Tabloids often give personal information about celebrities, recount bizarre occurrences, and display unusual or sometimes even altered photographs.

target market: A group of consumers for whom a company creates a product or to whom it advertises a product. The target market is the group identified as most likely to buy a specific product.

war photography: Photographic coverage of a war or other conflict. Many war photos are considered art and are on display in museums and galleries. Often dramatic and emotional, war photography gives the viewer a sense of the destructive nature of war.

Acknowledgments

Text Credits

Sherman Alexie. "The Texas Chainsaw Massacre." First published in *The Kenyon Review New Series* 14.3 (Summer 1992). Copyright © 1992 by Sherman Alexie. Reprinted by permission of the author.

Dorothy Allison. "What Did You Expect?" Copyright © 1998 by Dorothy Allison. Originally published in *Allure* (April 1998). Reprinted by permission.

Leigh Belanger. "What's in Your Fridge?" originally published as "Refrigerators are packed with clues about how we live," *Boston Globe,* February 28, 2007. Copyright © 2007. Used by permission of the *Boston Globe.*

David Brooks. "People Like Us," *The Atlantic Monthly* (September 2003). Copyright © 2003 by David Brooks. Used by permission of the author.

Gwendolyn Brooks. "Kitchenette Building" from *A Street in Bronzeville* by Gwendolyn Brooks. Copyright © 1945 by Gwendolyn Brooks. Reprinted by consent of Brooks Permissions.

Joseph Campbell. "On the Mythology of *Star Wars*" from *The Power of Myth* by Joseph Campbell and Bill Moyers. Copyright © 1988 by Apostrophe S Productions, Inc., and Bill Moyers and Alfred Van der Marck Editions, Inc., for itself and the estate of Joseph Campbell. Used by permission of Doubleday, a division of Random House, Inc.

Judith Ortiz Cofer. "Silent Dancing" and "Lessons of the Past" from *Silent Dancing: A Partial Remembrance of a Puerto Rican Childhood* by Judith Ortiz Cofer (Houston: Arte Público Press–University of Houston, 1990).

Stephen Dunn. "The Sacred" from *Between Angels* by Stephen Dunn. Copyright © 1989 by Stephen Dunn. Used by permission of W. W. Norton & Company, Inc.

Roger Ebert. "Star Wars" from *The Great Movies* by Roger Ebert. Copyright © 2002 by Roger Ebert. Used by permission of Broadway Books, a division of Random House, Inc.

Lars Eighner. "On Dumpster Diving" from *Travels with Lizbeth* by Lars Eighner. Copyright © 1993 by Lars Eighner. Reprinted by permission of St. Martin's Press, LLC.

David Emery. "The Hook." © 2007 by David Emery (http://urbanlegends.about.com/od/horrors/a/the_hook.htm). Used with permission of About, Inc., which can be found online at www.about.com. All rights reserved.

Nora Ephron. "The Boston Photographs" from *Scribble, Scribble: Notes on the Media* by Nora Ephron (Alfred A. Knopf, 1978). Copyright © 1978 by Nora Ephron. Reprinted by permission of International Creative Management, Inc.

Thomas Frank. "The Conquest of Cool" from *The Conquest of Cool* by Thomas Frank. Copyright © 1997 by the University of Chicago. Used by permission of the University of Chicago Press.

Philip Gefter. "Photographic Icons: Fact, Fiction, or Metaphor?" *Aperture* magazine, Issue 185 (Winter 2006). Copyright © 2006. For more information or to order the book, please visit www.aperture.org. Aperture is a not-for-profit public foundation dedicated to promoting photography as a unique form of artistic expression.

Malcolm Gladwell. "The Coolhunt," *The New Yorker,* March 17, 1997. Copyright © 1997 by Malcolm Gladwell. Reprinted by permission of the author.

Stephen Jay Gould. "A Time of Gifts," *New York Times,* September 26, 2001. Reprinted by permission of Rhonda Roland Shearer.

David Guterson. "Enclosed. Encyclopedic. Endured: One Week at the Mall of America." Copyright © 1993 by David Guterson. Originally appeared in

Harper's Magazine (Vol. 287, August 1993). Reprinted by permission of Georges Borchardt, Inc., on behalf of the author.

Melissa Harris and Jessie Mann. "Jessie Mann on Being Photographed," based on an interview with Melissa Harris, "*Jessie at Eighteen:* Daughter, Model, Muse: Jessie Mann on Being Photographed," *Aperture* magazine, Issue 162 (Winter 2001). Copyright © 2001. For more information or to order the book, please visit www.aperture.org. Aperture is a not-for-profit public foundation dedicated to promoting photography as a unique form of artistic expression.

Joseph A. Harriss. "Seeking Mona Lisa," *Smithsonian Magazine* (May 1999). Copyright © by Joseph Harriss. Reprinted by permission of the author.

Jessica Helfand, "What We Saved: Pictures and Ephemera in the Twentieth-Century Scrapbook," *Aperture* magazine, Issue 183 (Summer 2006). Copyright © 2006. For more information or to order the book, please visit www.aperture.org. Aperture is a not-for-profit public foundation dedicated to promoting photography as a unique form of artistic expression.

Amanda Hesser. "Shop Write," *New York Times Magazine,* October 24, 2004. Copyright © 2004 by the *New York Times.* All rights reserved. Used by permission and protected by the copyright laws of the United States. The printing, copying, redistribution, or retransmission of this material without express written permission is prohibited.

"How to Create Your Own Print Ad," *Adbusters.* Courtesy www.adbusters.org.

Pico Iyer. "Nowhere Man," *Utne Reader,* May/June 1997. Copyright © 1997 by Pico Iyer. Reprinted by permission of the author.

Verlyn Klinkenborg. "Sand Creek," *Mother Jones,* November/December 2000. Copyright © 2000 Foundation for National Progress. Reprinted by permission of *Mother Jones.*

Jonathan G. S. Koppell. "No 'There' There," *The Atlantic Monthly,* August 2000. Copyright © 2000 by Jonathan G. S. Koppell. Reprinted by permission of the author.

Milos Kosic. "It's Not the Name that Matters." Reprinted courtesy of Milos Kosic.

Jhumpa Lahiri. "My Two Lives" from *Newsweek,* March 6, 2006. © 2006 Newsweek, Inc. All rights reserved. Used by permission and protected by the copyright laws of the United States. The printing, copying, redistribution, or retransmission of this material without express written permission is prohibited.

Nicole Lamy. "Life in Motion" from *The American Scholar* 69.4 (Autumn 2000). Copyright © 2000 by Nicole Lamy. Reprinted by permission of the author and the publisher.

Jerome Lawrence and Robert Edwin Lee. Excerpt from *Inherit the Wind.* Copyright as an unpublished work 1951 by Jerome Lawrence and Robert Edwin Lee. Copyright © 1955 and renewed 1983 by Jerome Lawrence and Robert Edwin Lee. Used by permission of Random House, Inc.

Wendy Lesser. "Weegee" from *Threepenny Review* 56 (Winter 1994). Copyright © 1994. Reprinted by permission of Wendy Lesser and *Threepenny Review.*

Steven D. Levitt and Stephen J. Dubner. "Trading Up: Where Do Baby Names Come From?" Excerpted from *Freakonomics* by Steven D. Levitt and Stephen J. Dubner. Copyright © 2005 by Steven D. Levitt and Stephen J. Dubner. Reprinted by permission of HarperCollins Publishers.

Maya Lin. "Between Art & Architecture" from *Boundaries* by Maya Lin. Copyright © 2000 by Maya Lin Studio, Inc. Abridged and used with the permission of Simon & Schuster Adult Publishing Group.

"Living in a Virtual World," *The Week: The Best of the U.S. and International Media* 7.297 (Feb. 16, 2007). Copyright © 2007. Reprinted by permisson.

Evan Lushing. "On YouTube Everyone's an Anti-Star." Reprinted courtesy of Evan Lushing.

Janet Malcolm. "The Family of Mann" from *Diana & Nikon: Essays on Photography* by Janet Malcolm. Copyright © 1997 by Janet Malcolm. Reprinted by permission of the author.

Bill McKibben. "Small Change: Pie in the Sky," *Orion Magazine,* March/April 2006, pp. 14–15. Copyright © 2006 by Bill McKibben. Reprinted by permission of the author.

Eric Tyrone McLeod. "Selling Out: Consumer Culture and the Commodification of the Human Body." Copyright © 2003 by Eric T. McLeod. Originally published in *Post Road,* November 6, 2003. Reprinted by permission of the author.

N. Scott Momaday. "The Way to Rainy Mountain" from *The Way to Rainy Mountain.* Copyright © 2001 by N. Scott Momaday. Reprinted by permission of the University of New Mexico Press.

Joe Morgenstern. "*Little Miss Sunshine:* How One Scene Can Say Everything," originally published as "How

Melanie Sumner. "Marriage." Copyright © 2003 by Melanie Sumner. Originally appeared in *Harper's* (October 2003). Reprinted by permission of Georges Borchardt, Inc., on behalf of the author.

James B. Twitchell. "How to Advertise a Dangerous Product" from *Twenty Ads That Shook the World* by James B. Twitchell. Copyright © 2000 by James B. Twitchell. Used by permission of Crown Publishers, a division of Random House, Inc.

Josh Tyrangiel. "Andy Was Right," *Time,* December 25, 2006–January 1, 2007. Copyright TIME, Inc. Reprinted by permission. TIME is a registered trademark of TIME, Inc. All rights reserved.

Paco Underhill. Excerpt from *Call of the Mall: The Geography of Shopping.* Originally appeared as part of "Inside the Machine" in the *Wilson Quarterly* (Winter 2004). Adapted with the permission of Simon & Schuster Adult Publishing Group. Copyright © 2004 by YOBOW, Inc.

"What's in a Name?" *National Geographic* (January 2007). Copyright © 2007. Siobhan Roth/National Geographic Image Collection. Used by permission.

John Edgar Wideman. Excerpt from "First Shot," from *Hoop Roots* by John Edgar Wideman. Copyright © 2001 by John Edgar Wideman. Reprinted by permission of Houghton Mifflin Harcourt Publishing Company. All rights reserved.

Denis Wilson. "A Look Under the Hoodie," *New York Times,* December 23, 2006. Copyright © 2006 by the *New York Times.* All rights reserved. Used by permission and protected by the copyright laws of the United States. The printing, copying, redistribution, or retransmission of this material without express written permission is prohibited.

Will Wright. "Dream Machines," *Wired* 14.04 (April 2006). Originally published in *Wired.* Copyright © 2006 by Will Wright. Used by permission of the author.

Noah D. Zatz. "Mapping Physical and Electronic Space" from "Sidewalks in Cyberspace," *Harvard Journal of Law & Technology* 12.1 (Fall 1998). Copyright © 1988 by Noah D. Zatz. Reprinted by permission of the publisher.

Additional Art Credits

Sherman Alexie author photograph. By permission of Ulf Andersen/Getty Images.

Dorothy Allison author photograph. By permission of Leon Borensztein/Getty Images.

Charles Atlas advertisement. "Charles Atlas®", "*How Joe's Body Brought Him Fame Instead of Shame,*" copyright © 2008, under license from Charles Atlas, Ltd. PO Box "D," Madison Square Station, New York, NY 10159. (www.CharlesAtlas.com)

Lynda Barry portrait. Copyright Lynda Barry

Alison Bechdel author photograph. By permission of Greg Martin.

David Brooks author photograph. By permission of Alex Wong/Getty Images.

Gwendolyn Brooks author photograph. © Bettmann/Corbis.

Jan Harold Brunvand and DC Comics: *The Hook.* Artwork from *The Big Book of Urban Legends* © 1994 DC Comics. All Rights Reserved. Used with Permission.

Judith Ortiz Cofer author photograph. By permission of Peter Frey, University of Georgia.

Stephen J. Dubner author photograph. By permission of Michael Benabib.

Roger Ebert author photograph. By permission of AP Images/Charles Rex Arbogast.

Thomas Frank author photograph. By permission of Susan Biddle/ *The Washington Post.*

Philip Gefter author photograph. By permission of Tony Cenicola/ *The New York Times*/Redux.

Malcolm Gladwell author photograph. By permission of Brooke Williams.

Jessica Helfand author photograph. By permission of *The Republican American.*

Edward Hopper, 1882–1967. Study [A] for *Office at Night* (1940). Conte crayon on paper, sheet 8 ½ × 11 in. (21.6 × 27.9 cm). Whitney Museum of American Art, New York; Josephine N. Hopper Bequest, 70.169. © Heirs of Josephine N. Hopper, licensed by the Whitney Museum of American Art.

Edward Hopper, 1882–1967. Study [B] for *Office at Night* (1940). Conte crayon on paper, sheet 8 7/16 × 10 15/16 in. (21.4 × 27.8 cm). Whitney Museum of American Art, New York; Josephine N. Hopper Bequest, 70.168. © Heirs of Josephine N. Hopper, licensed by the Whitney Museum of American Art.

Nathan Huang author photograph. By permission of Nathan Huang.

Kasper Hauser group author photograph. Photos by Lisa Keating; Design by James Reichmuth.

Pico Iyer author photograph. Mark Richards.

Milos Kosic author photograph. Courtesy of Milos Kosic.

Jhumpa Lahiri author photograph. By permission of Evan Agostini/Getty Images.

Steven D. Levitt author photograph. By permission of AP Images/Charles Rex Arbogast.

Maya Lin author photograph. By permission of AP Images/Scott Applewhite.

Evan Lushing author photograph. Courtesy of Evan Lushing.

Joe Morgenstern author photograph. By permission of AP Images/Dow Jones.

Jan Morris author photograph. By permission of David Hurn/Magnum Photos

Manuel Muñoz author photograph. Copyright ©2007 by Helena Maria Viramontes. Reprinted by permission of Stuart Bernstein Representation for Artists, New York. All rights reserved.

Catherine Orenstein author photograph. By permission of Jerry Bauer.

Rosa Parks documentary photograph. ©Douglas Kirkland/Corbis.

Orlando Patterson author photograph. By permission of Kris Knibbe/Harvard News Office.

Charles Perrault author photograph. By permission of The Art Archive/Musée du Château de Versailles/Gianni Dagli Orti.

Charles Perrault, from *Histoires ou Contes du Temps Passé,* "Le Petit Chaperon Rouge" (Little Red Riding Hood) of 1697, an illustration by an unknown artist. By permission of the Bibliothèque Nationale de France, Réserve des Livres Rares.

Michael Pollan author photograph. By permission of Suzanne De Chillo/ *The New York Times*/Redux.

Alberto Ríos author photograph. By permission of Miriam Berkley.

Richard Rodriguez author photograph. ©Roger Ressmeyer/Corbis.

Salman Rushdie author photograph. By permission of Jerry Bauer.

Susan Sontag author photograph. ©Sophie Bassouls/Corbis Sygma.

Tom Standage author photograph. By permission of Judah Passow.

James Twitchell author photograph. Courtesy James B. Twitchell.

Josh Tyrangiel author photograph. By permission of Jay Colton/Getty Images.

Camille Paglia. ©Misa Martin/Reuters/Corbis.

Students, need help with your writing?

Visit the Re:Writing Web site

bedfordstmartins.com/rewriting

Re:Writing is a comprehensive Web site designed to help you with the most common writing concerns. You'll find advice from experts, models you can rely on, and exercises that will tell you right away how you're doing. And it's all free and available any hour of the day. You can find help for the following situations at the specific areas of **bedfordstmartins .com/rewriting** listed below.

Need help with grammar problems? **Exercise Central**

Stuck somewhere in the research process? (Maybe at the beginning?) **The Bedford Research Room**

Wondering whether a Web site is good enough to use in your paper? **Evaluating Online Sources Tutorial**

Having trouble figuring out how to cite a source? **Research and Documentation Online**

Need help creating the Works Cited page for your research paper? **The Bedford Bibliographer**

Confused about plagiarism? **Avoiding Plagiarism Tutorial**

Want to get more out of your word processor? **Using Your Word Processor**

Trying to improve the look of your paper? **Designing Documents with a Word Processor**

Need to create slides for a presentation? **Preparing Presentation Slides**

Interested in creating a Web site? **Mike Markel's Web Design Tutorial**